THE JOURNALS OF LEWIS & CLARK

Meriwether Lewis

THE
JOURNALS
OF THE EXPEDITION

UNDER THE COMMAND OF

Capt.ˢ LEWIS and CLARK

to the *sources* of the MISSOURI, thence *across*

the ROCKY MOUNTAINS and down

the river COLUMBIA to the PACIFIC Ocean,

performed during the YEARS 1804–5–6

by ORDER of the Government of the United States.

EDITED BY

NICHOLAS BIDDLE

with an introduction by JOHN BAKELESS

AND ILLUSTRATED WITH WATER COLORS AND DRAWINGS
BY CARL BODMER AND OTHER CONTEMPORARY ARTISTS

VOLUME ONE

THE HERITAGE PRESS

New York

RELEASED

34589

*The special contents of this edition are copyright © 1962
by The George Macy Companies, Inc.*

INTRODUCTION
by John Bakeless

The dream of sending an expedition across North America to explore the vast western areas still unknown to white men—and, at the same time, to find a practical commercial land route to the Pacific—had haunted Thomas Jefferson for some twenty or thirty years before he became President in 1801. And though Mr. Jefferson himself, in all his life, had never traveled westward more than fifty miles beyond his beloved plantation, Monticello, in Albemarle County, Virginia, he had already tried repeatedly to find the right man who would make the great dream a reality. Five times he had tried to get an expedition started and five times he had failed.

Like most human motives, Mr. Jefferson's were mixed; but, varied though his reasons were for desiring a western exploring expedition, all of them were wholly disinterested. Mr. Jefferson was moved mainly by that purely scientific curiosity that marked his whole life. Thoughts of the vast stretch of unknown North America were always with him. He wondered what was there. He wondered about the Indians—their arts, their life, their languages. He wondered about living animals and plants, and was equally interested in fossils, especially the mammoth or mastodon tusks and skeletons that were being discovered, notably at Big Bone Lick, in Kentucky. Indians told him that some of the great beasts were still alive. Rumors of the Great Salt Lake or the salt deserts of the West reached him in rather vague and distorted forms, some of the rumors turning them into a mountain of salt. (Skeptics, who liked to jeer at Mr. Jefferson's scientific interests, suggested there was probably an American eagle, carved in rock salt, sitting on top of it!)

As a responsible statesman, Mr. Jefferson had other reasons for being concerned about the Great West. In the first place, he knew that these vast areas must one day be of enormous economic importance to the United

States. The fur trade, which had long been immensely profitable, was at the moment largely in the hands of the British, including French Canadians, coming overland from Canada. Trade with the eastern Indians had always been profitable for Americans. If a route up the Missouri River to the Rockies could be opened up, the profits would be greater still. Here, too, the expanding population to be expected in the future could find room for homes, farms, great cities.

Mr. Jefferson was equally concerned with what the West could contribute to the American political future, a consideration which to him, as a statesman, was paramount. Though no one could yet imagine the enormous future strength of the American states, it was obvious that there must be an enormous expansion. Even before the Revolution, settlers were pushing west beyond the Blue Ridge. George Rogers Clark's frontier victories during the Revolution carried the flag north of the Ohio River and westward to the Mississippi. Later, after Napoleon's empire gathered strength and it was evident that he would reclaim Louisiana from Spain, control of the West became a matter of American national survival.

If Napoleon reclaimed Louisiana from Spain, the militaristic French Empire would be a dangerous neighbor along the whole Mississippi frontier and could, at any time, cut off the trade of the western states at New Orleans. Along the Gulf Coast, the French would also wedge the Americans in. To the North, in Canada, were the British, whose navy could at any time blockade the Atlantic Coast. Expand westward to the Pacific and none of this would matter. Otherwise, the infant American republic would be all but strangled.

It was essential to know what was in the West before America could possess it. Exploration of the Great West would satisfy Mr. Jefferson's long-standing curiosity. It would also make his country a secure and powerful nation.

When Mr. Jefferson began to concern himself with these matters, only one small party of white men (with one Negro) had ever crossed the Continent. Cabeza de Vaca and a few survivors of the Narváez expedition had made their way from Florida to Mexico in 1535–1536, along a route somewhere north of the Gulf Coast. In 1793, after Mr. Jefferson had failed in his five futile efforts to send explorers across the Continent, the Canadian, Alexander MacKenzie, became the second traveler to reach the Pacific overland.

Mr. Jefferson had made his first attempt at an expedition in 1783. The Revolution was still not officially over—that is, no final treaty of peace had yet been signed—but it was perfectly clear that the United States was independent and that hostilities would never be resumed. He had become alarmed by a rumor that the British were planning to send an expedition from the Mississippi across "Louisiana" (which meant all non-Spanish territory between the great river and the Rockies) and also across California (an area which, however ill-defined, certainly included a large slice of the Pacific Coast). Although this was said to be merely scientific exploration, Mr. Jefferson strongly suspected that, having just lost thirteen colonies, the British were now looking for new ones in the West. He feared they had "thoughts of colonising into that quarter."

It was time for him to make his first attempt to organize a western expedition. On December 4, 1783, he wrote General George Rogers Clark (whose much younger brother William was, years later, to join Meriwether Lewis in the Lewis and Clark expedition). General Clark had demonstrated his skill as a wilderness leader by driving the British out of the "Ohio country," the great stretch of land from Pennsylvania to the Mississippi.

Would the general, who had conquered what was then thought of as "the Northwest," like to lead a transcontinental exploring party into a new and greater Northwest? The general declined; and Mr. Jefferson, who had very dim hopes of being able to raise the money anyhow, gave up that part of his plan, but not the great plan itself. Mr. Jefferson was a very determined man.

Three years later, when American Minister to France, he met John Ledyard, an adventurous Connecticut Yankee who had once been a British marine. Jefferson tried twice to send this kindred spirit to the Pacific Coast. The first scheme was for Ledyard to cross Europe, Asia, and the Pacific and thence—alone—traverse the Rockies and the unknown Plains. When Catherine the Great refused Ledyard a Russian passport across Siberia, the daring Yankee took passage abroad a British ship, which was stopped by British customs officers. Still undiscouraged, Ledyard returned to St. Petersburg and secured a passport while the Empress was out of town. This time he journeyed far across Siberia before the Russian police caught up with him, and Ledyard decided to return to America. According to the second plan he was to start westward from Kentucky; but he went to Egypt before returning, and died there.

When in 1792 the distinguished French botanist, André Michaux, proposed to cross the Continent, Mr. Jefferson and President Washington both contributed to his expenses; but Michaux turned out to be a French secret agent—and one more scheme for exploration failed. Meriwether Lewis, then a mere boy, whose family's plantation was only a few miles from Monticello, volunteered for Michaux's expedition; but Mr. Jefferson, who knew the family well (in fact, he bought some particularly fine, home-cured hams from Lewis's mother), refused to consider him because he was too young.

When, however, Mr. Jefferson, as President, at last had the power to give definite orders for a transcontinental expedition, he remembered his youthful neighbor. Lewis had, in the meantime, become a Regular Army officer and risen to the rank of Captain. Mr. Jefferson had lost track of him, though he knew, vaguely, he was somewhere in the army and rather thought he was still a lieutenant. But when a President wants to know an army officer's whereabouts, the wheels of official Washington turn swiftly. Captain Lewis, then on duty as a paymaster, returned to Pittsburgh, after a wilderness journey from Detroit, on March 5, 1801. He found waiting for him a letter from the President.

Mr. Jefferson offered his young friend a job as his secretary. That, at least, is what the letter seemed to say—openly. But President Jefferson, veteran that he was of both politics and diplomacy, was skilled in saying things between the lines. In this case, the letter had to go through the War Department and President Jefferson was not giving any secrets away—not yet. His phrasing was a little obscure—obscure, that is, to every one but

Captain Meriwether Lewis. It was not hard for that astute young man to read between the lines.

Meriwether Lewis was probably worse fitted than any man in North America to be a secretary to anybody. For one thing, his grammar was dubious. Besides, he had never learned to spell and he never would— Lewis must have known that. On the other hand, he was, as the President later said, the one best man to lead an expedition across North America— he must have known that, too. When he remembered his effort to go with Michaux nine years before, when he thought of the President's lifelong interest in the Great West, and when he read the letter carefully, there was no doubt at all what the great man really meant to say, though no one but Lewis could ever have guessed.

Mentioning his recent "appointment" to the Presidency, Mr. Jefferson explained he wanted a secretary who could "contribute to the mass of information which it is interesting for the administration to acquire." What information did the President of the United States need from a young infantry captain? "Your knowledge of the Western country," explained the President—and this "for public as well as private purposes." He also mentioned the army's "relations." At the moment the United States army had no relations at all, except with Indians. Western country? Indians? Both public and private purposes? Captain Lewis knew well enough what private purposes Mr. Jefferson had always had with regard to exploring the Western country and dealing with the Indians in it. Now that he was President Jefferson, they were public purposes.

To Lewis (but not to most other readers) the letter said in effect: "Now I'm President and I'm giving the orders. I have always wanted to send out a western expedition. You have always wanted to go on one. Become my nominal secretary. Help me plan the expedition. Then lead it!"

Captain Lewis settled his accounts as paymaster of the First Infantry as fast as he could and, on March 22, 1801, plunged into the Pennsylvania forests with three horses—for himself, his baggage, and official papers—on his way to Washington.

For the next two years or more, Lewis lived in the White House, usually alone with the now widowed President. It is a pity there is no record of the long talks that must have gone on, as the two men, in the lonely mansion, planned for the expedition they both had dreamed about for years. Congress was persuaded without difficulty to make a small appropriation. It cost almost nothing to explore half a continent, because so many of the men were soldiers, who would have been drawing pay anyhow, whether they were drilling and drinking in dull garrisons, or struggling desperately up the wide Missouri and across the Rockies. Lewis was eventually sent to Philadelphia for supplies and some hasty scientific training.

Both President Jefferson and his secretary at first anticipated that the expedition would have secured Spanish permission to pass through Louisiana to the Rockies. President Jefferson hoped the Spanish government would grant this for what he called a "literary" group, by which odd phrase he meant explorers engaged merely in scientific (i.e., "literary") inquiry. It was probably a vain hope, considering the habitual Spanish suspicion of Americans on or beyond the Mississippi, and the speed with which the Spanish government in Mexico arrested Zebulon M. Pike when he strayed into Spanish territory a few years later.

It was clear that Lewis would need another officer. The journey would be long, hard, and dangerous. Lewis himself might die, be killed, or be incapacitated by wounds or illness. It might become necessary—as in fact turned out to be the case repeatedly—to divide the expedition. In that case a competent officer ought to command each section.

The President told Captain Lewis to choose the man he wanted. The captain's thoughts turned to two men. One was his old friend and former company commander, William Clark. The other was a brother officer in Lewis's own regiment, Captain Moses Hook. Clark, his first choice, had left the Regulars some years earlier and was now living at his father's plantation near Louisville, mainly engaged with the business affairs of General George Rogers Clark. When Lewis's letter came, the younger brother took it to the elder. Neither one can have been much surprised that Mr. Jefferson's mind still dwelt upon his favorite scheme. George Rogers Clark, remembering (and perhaps regretting) his refusal of a similar suggestion some twenty years earlier, urged young William Clark to join Lewis. Clark accepted, and at once began enrolling sturdy young men, as Lewis had requested.

Captain Moses Hook, Lewis's second choice, knew Lewis wanted him as a companion if he could not get Clark. When Clark promptly accepted, Hook's hopes vanished; but with complete magnanimity, he continued to assist the preparations for the expedition in every possible way.

The success of the Lewis and Clark expedition was remarkable. It crossed the Continent from the Mississippi to the Oregon-Washington coast, exploring, mapping, collecting, and recording—as ordered. It brought back the first maps of the Missouri River—Rocky Mountain—Columbia River country, together with large and important linguistic, botanical, zoological, geographical, and commercial collections and reports. It opened the way immediately for a huge and profitable fur trade. It opened the way for the settlers who followed the fur trade and thus for the gradual Americanization of the Great West. It did this at the trivial cost of a few thousand dollars. It carried a baby with it from North Dakota to Oregon and safely back. From North Dakota to Oregon and back to St. Louis, the expedition had no disciplinary troubles whatever.

The "Corps of Discovery," as the explorers liked to call their company, was an "all-American" organization, composed of white men, one Negro, one full-blooded Indian, one half-breed.

The Lewis and Clark expedition did not make America; but without the Lewis and Clark expedition, the modern United States of America would never have existed in its present form.

The success of this daring enterprise was wholly due to the thoroughness with which plans were prepared—diligent collection of military intelligence, detailed logistics, and critical selection of personnel—and, later, to the brilliant leadership and ideal discipline of the two captains, both of them experienced Army officers, long accustomed to handling men and to the rough, dangerous life of the frontier.

Thanks largely to Mr. Jefferson's years of interest in western exploration, almost all of the scanty information about it was in the hands of the two leaders before they set off. They were aware from the beginning that the critical moment would come with the arrival at the foothills of the Rockies, when they would have to leave their boats, find Indians, counsel with them, and thus procure the horses without which the expedition could never get itself and its essential baggage across the high passes of the Rockies.

To make sure they would be able to explain their purposes to the Indians, Lewis and Clark secured the services of the veteran plainsman, George Drouilliard (or Drewyer, to use the highly personal spelling of the Journals). Having spent his life among them, Drouilliard understood the sign language, in which the Plains tribes could communicate with each other readily, no matter how mutually unintelligible their speech might be.

Although this language of pure gesture was a linguistic marvel, it had inevitable limitations. Consequently, when the two captains discovered the famous Shoshone squaw, Sacagawea, living with her worthless French-Canadian husband, Toussaint Charbonneau, among the Indians in North Dakota, they promptly employed Charbonneau, who brought with him Sacagawea, one of his two wives, and her baby. While Charbonneau was the most useless member of the Lewis and Clark expedition, Sacagawea made up for all his shortcomings, and also for the inconvenience of taking a newborn baby along.

Despite a naif popular impression—one that was perpetuated as late as 1961 by no less a person than President John F. Kennedy—Sacagawea did not "guide Lewis and Clark across the continent." So long as they were on the Missouri and Columbia Rivers they needed no guides. All they had to do was follow the streams. When they did need a guide at the Fork of Maria's River and the Missouri, to show them which of the two big rivers was the real Missouri, Sacagawea knew no more about the country than the explorers soon learned for themselves, with a little reconnoissance. Like most Indians, she knew her own tribal territory and, otherwise, nothing about geography. When near the Shoshone country, she made a few useful suggestions; but, even then she could tell little.

Nevertheless, it was Sacagawea who saved the expedition, in its moment of crisis at the foot of the Rockies. There was only a little time left to cross before snow blocked the high passes. Horses the explorers had to have at once. They could get them only from Indians. Yet they had journeyed hundreds of miles from their 1804–1805 winter quarters, without seeing a single Indian. At almost the last moment, the expedition had the good fortune to fall in with the very band from which Sacagawea had been kidnapped some years before and of which her brother now was chief. There was now no real need of Drouilliard's sign language, though it frequently proved useful. Through Sacagawea the travelers could readily converse with the Shoshones; friendly relations were easily maintained. The white men were able to purchase pack horses and, with them, to cross to the Pacific side of the mountains.

The presence of a squaw and papoose was, to some degree, a protection to the expedition. Suspicious Indian tribes, doubtful whether these well-armed strangers might not be a war party, were at once reassured when they saw a woman and her child. Even so, Nez Percé tradition avers that their warriors at first planned to massacre them all, but were dissuaded by one of their own squaws, who, when her life was in danger, had once been saved by friendly white trappers.

(Perhaps it is well to say here that the mystery of Sacagawea's death is solved at last. She *was* the Shoshone squaw, wife of Charbonneau, "a good and the best Woman in the fort," who died of a "putrid fever" at Manuel Lisa's fort on the upper Missouri, December 12, 1820, as recorded in the diary of the trader, John Luttig. But Charbonneau had had at least two Shoshone wives and possibly a good many more. It was therefore long believed possible that the woman who died in 1820 was not the heroine of the Lewis and Clark expedition, and that the real Sacagawea was an old squaw who called herself by the same or a similar name and who died at Wind River, Wyoming, in 1884. If she had, in fact, been the "real Sacagawea," this would have made her well over ninety; but some Indians do live to great ages and there was nothing impossible in this woman's claim to have been with Lewis and Clark. There is now known, however, a notebook belonging to Clark in his last years. In this he had entered the names of members of the expedition, with notes on their whereabouts. After Sacagawea's name he notes her death. The note is not dated, but since Clark himself died in 1838, the old squaw who died in Wyoming in 1884 cannot have been the Sacagawea of the expedition.)

Lewis and Clark knew, before they started, that their men would have to live off the land. In good game country, where the hunters were successful, the expedition ate, every day, four deer, or one elk and a deer, or one buffalo, depending on the potluck of the hunters, who habitually followed the expedition's boats closely enough to bring their kill to the Missouri's banks.

The captains took the utmost care to ensure an adequate supply of ammunition. Gunpowder was sealed in waterproof kegs, so that it could not possibly get wet. The kegs themselves were made of lead, so that each could be melted down into bullets when empty. In the event powder might possibly fail, Lewis took along a powerful air gun, which needed no powder. Adequate supplies, mapping and other scientific equipment, as well as Indian presents and tobacco, were carried, together with tools enough to build forts, cabins, canoes, and, on one occasion, wagons. The medicine supply, in spite of accidental losses, was always sufficient both for the white men and for numerous delighted Indian patients.

There were really only two logistical errors. No one had realized how much more valuable, in the eyes of Pacific Indians, were blue beads—"chief beads"—than any others. And Lewis, used to the bark canoes of eastern Indians, had not realized that on the Plains there would be neither bark nor proper animal skins to cover the metal framework of the collapsible boat he had himself designed.

In selecting their enlisted personnel, the two leaders had been careful to take only hardy and healthy young men, discarding mere adventurers. They had not, however, always been able to get properly disciplined soldiers. The problem thus created they met by a series of courts-martial in the first months of the expedition in 1804. Having thus discovered possible trouble-makers at the start, they sent all doubtful men home in the spring of 1805, with the returning boat of their civilian French *engagés*—

rivermen who had agreed to go only the first "leg" of the journey. After that, it is noteworthy that there were no courts-martial and no disciplinary troubles through all the worst hardship and dangers of the next two years. The choice of Sacagawea was, of course, a triumph of personnel work.

The expedition maintained proper guards and reconnoissance afloat and ashore, and the two officers took pains to see that arms were always in order. As a result, there was only one Indian attack, which was promptly beaten off, without casualties among the explorers. The expedition lost only one man, who died of what was probably appendicitis—for which, in those days, operation was impossible.

Most of all, the expedition succeeded because its leaders were Meriwether Lewis and William Clark. Since the days when Roman consuls tried to control armed forces jointly, it had been notorious that divided command leads to disaster. Captain Lewis and "Captain" Clark, however, contrived to exercise joint command with entire success. It was an achievement very nearly unique in military history—all the more remarkable because President Jefferson had certainly meant Lewis to command, with Clark as his subordinate. Lewis, however, had promised Clark they would be equals. The situation was not helped when the War Department insisted on commissioning Clark (who as a first lieutenant had been Ensign Meriwether Lewis's company commander) as a second lieutenant. With any individuals save these firm friends, the situation might have been disastrous. The two privately arranged that Clark should be "Captain on an Expedition for North Western Discovery," while Lewis remained (what he really was), "Captain, 1st Infantry." The enlisted men never guessed. When, on their return, Congress tried to grant Lewis more land than Clark, he firmly resisted and, to the end, the two friends were equal.

Very little news of the Lewis and Clark expedition reached President Jefferson after the boat returned from North Dakota in the spring of 1805. Trickling from tribe to tribe across hundreds of miles of empty prairie, in the incomprehensible aboriginal way, a rumor reached him in January, 1806, that the explorers had secured horses and entered the Rocky Mountain passes. By July, 1806, it was known in North Dakota Indian villages that they had reached the Pacific; but the expedition itself arrived safely in St. Louis in September, 1806, before the report had reached the white settlements. A few days earlier, the surprised explorers had learned from a Missouri River trader that they had long since been "given out" as lost, and that only President Jefferson still had hope of their safe return.

The two captains began writing letters and preliminary reports as soon as they reached St. Louis; but it was years before their extensive journals saw print. After some time in the East, they returned to St. Louis, Lewis as governor of Louisiana and Clark as brigadier commanding the Missouri militia. In 1807, Lewis issued two prospectuses for their proposed book, began arrangements for illustrations, and tried to find a professional writer who would come to St. Louis as his literary assistant. Lewis had made little progress in this effort when, in September, 1809, stopping in Tennessee en route to Washington, he was murdered or—according to the story believed by Jefferson—committed suicide.

Clark, after bringing the manuscripts of the journals together, persuaded Nicholas Biddle to edit them. Biddle was a young magazine editor, who later abandoned publishing to become president of the Bank of the United States. The two spent several days together at the home of Clark's father-in-law in Virginia, after which Biddle took the papers to Philadelphia and Clark went back to St. Louis. He sent George Shannon, youngest and best-educated member of the expedition, to assist Biddle, while Shannon himself pursued his Philadelphia law studies.

In addition to the journals of the two officers, Biddle used the journals kept by two of the sergeants. One of these, since it is described as having "already been published," was the one kept by Patrick Gass. It is to be feared that Biddle used only the printed version, which a local parson had zealously expurgated and rewritten, in rolling literary periods, very nearly ruining what had originally been one of the liveliest and saltiest narratives ever written. ("Paddy" was, for instance, very explicit about the amours of the expedition with the Indian girls—not even the parson could quite disguise everything.) The other document was certainly the journal of Sergeant John Ordway, which Clark had bought and given to Biddle.

Though Biddle did practically all of the editing, he could not quite finish the book or see it through press, since he was elected to the Pennsylvania State Senate. A Philadelphia newspaperman, Paul Allen, "received and prepared it for the press," according to Biddle. Allen signed the preface because Biddle "did not think it right to take from him the credit of his own exertion and care," though in fact, Allen had merely "put the finishing hand to the volumes."

In view of the distance and slow communication with St. Louis, William Clark never saw the manuscript before publication. Even when the *History of the Expedition* appeared in print in 1814, no one remembered to send him a copy, and two years later Clark, in St. Louis, was still struggling to find one. The publishers had failed, and neither they nor Clark profited by the book though it subsequently went through many editions both here and abroad. It appears, however, that Clark was satisfied with the Biddle-Allen version, which gives the essentials of the original journals (themselves very prolix and repetitious) and provides a swiftly flowing and accurate narrative—an absolutely unique picture of primitive North America and an unequaled story of high adventure.

Elbowroom Farm, Great Hill
Seymour, Connecticut

LETTER of THOMAS JEFFERSON
relating to Captain MERIWETHER LEWIS

Monticello, August 18, 1813

SIR

In compliance with the request conveyed in your letter of May 25, I have endeavoured to obtain, from the relations and friends of the late governor Lewis, information of such incidents of his life as might be not unacceptable to those who may read the narrative of his western discoveries. The ordinary occurrences of a private life, and those also while acting in a subordinate sphere in the army, in a time of peace, are not deemed sufficiently interesting to occupy the public attention; but a general account of his parentage, with such smaller incidents as marked his early character are briefly noted; and to these are added, as being peculiarly within my own knowledge, whatever related to the public mission, of which an account is now to be published. The result of my inquiries and recollections shall now be offered, to be enlarged or abridged as you may think best; or otherwise to be used with the materials you may have collected from other sources.

Meriwether Lewis, late governor of Louisiana, was born on the 18th of August, 1774, near the town of Charlottesville, in the county of Albemarle, in Virginia, of one of the distinguished families of that state. John Lewis, one of his father's uncles, was a member of the king's council, before the revolution. Another of them, Fielding Lewis, married a sister of general Washington. His father, William Lewis, was the youngest of five sons of colonel Robert Lewis, of Albemarle, the fourth of whom, Charles, was one of the early patriots who stepped forward in the commencement of the revolution, and commanded one of the regiments first raised in Virginia, and placed on continental establishment. Happily situated at home, with a wife and young family, and a fortune placing him at ease, he left all to aid in the liberation of his country from foreign usurpations, then first unmasking their ultimate end and aim. His good sense, integrity, bravery, enterprise, and remarkable bodily powers, marked him as an officer of great promise; but he unfortunately died early in the revolution. Nicholas Lewis, the second of his father's brothers, commanded a regiment of militia in the successful expedition of 1776, against the Cherokee Indians; who, seduced by the agents of the British government to take up the hatchet against us, had committed great havoc on our Southern frontier, by murdering and scalping helpless women and children, according to their cruel and cowardly principles of warfare. The chastisement they then received closed the history of their wars, and prepared them for receiving the elements of civilization, which, zealously inculcated by the present government of the United States, have rendered them an industrious, peaceable, and happy people. This member of the family of Lewises, whose bravery was so usefully proved on this occasion, was endeared to all who knew him by his inflexible probity, courteous disposition, benevolent heart, and engaging modesty and manners. He was the umpire of all the private differences of his county—selected always by both parties. He was also the guardian of Meriwether Lewis, of whom we are now to speak, and who had lost his father at an early age.

He [Meriwether] continued some years under the fostering care of a tender mother, of the respectable family of Meriwethers, of the same county; and was remarkable even in infancy for enterprise, boldness, and discretion. When only eight years of age he habitually went out, in the dead of night, alone with his dogs, into the forest to hunt the raccoon and opossum, which, seeking their food in the night, can then only be taken. In this exercise, no season or circumstance could obstruct his purpose—plunging through the winter's snows and frozen streams in pursuit of his object.

At thirteen he was put to the Latin school, and continued at that until eighteen, when he returned to his mother, and entered on the cares of his farm; having, as well as a younger brother, been left by his father with a competency for all the correct and comfortable purposes of temperate life. His talent for observation, which had led him to an accurate knowledge of the plants and animals of his own country, would have distinguished him as a farmer; but at the age of twenty, yielding to the ardour of youth, and a passion for more dazzling pursuits, he engaged as a volunteer in the body of militia which were called out by general Washington, on occasion of the discontents produced by the excise taxes in the western parts of the United States; and from that situation he was removed to the regular service as a lieutenant in the line. At twenty-three [in 1797] he was promoted to a captaincy; and, always attracting the first attention where punctuality and fidelity were requisite, he was appointed paymaster to his regiment. About this time a circumstance occurred which, leading to the transaction which is the subject of this book, will justify a recurrence to its original idea.

While I resided in Paris, John Ledyard, of Connecticut, arrived there, well known in the United States for energy of body and mind. He had accompanied captain Cook on his voyage to the Pacific ocean; and distinguished himself on that voyage by his intrepidity. Being of a roaming disposition, he was now panting for some new enterprise. His immediate object at Paris was to engage a mercantile company in the fur-trade of the western coast of America, in which, however, he failed. I then proposed to him to go by land to Kamschatka, cross in some of the Russian vessels to Nootka Sound, fall down into the latitude of the Missouri, and penetrate to, and through, that to the United States. He eagerly seized the idea, and only asked to be assured of the permission of the Russian government. I interested, in obtaining that, M. de Simoulin, minister plenipotentiary of the empress at Paris, but more especially the baron de Grimm, minister plenipotentiary of Saxe-Gotha, her more special agent and correspondent there in matters not immediately diplomatic. Her permission was obtained, and an assurance of protection while the course of the voyage should be through her territories.

Ledyard set out from Paris, and arrived at St. Petersburgh after the empress had left that place to pass the winter, I think, at Moscow. His finances not permitting him to make unnecessary stay at St. Petersburgh, he left it with a passport from one of the ministers; and at two hundred miles from Kamschatka, was obliged to take up his winter quarters. He was preparing, in the spring, to resume his journey, when he was arrested by an officer of the empress, who by this time had changed her mind, and forbidden his proceeding. He was put into a close carriage, and conveyed day and night, without ever stopping, till they reached Poland; where he was set down and left to himself. The fatigue of this journey broke down his constitution; and when he returned to Paris his bodily strength was much impaired. His mind, however, remained firm, and he after this undertook the journey to Egypt. I received a letter from him, full of sanguine hopes, dated at Cairo, the 15th of November, 1788, the day before he was to set out for the head of the Nile; on which day, however, he ended his career and life: and thus failed the first attempt to explore the western part of our Northern continent.

In 1792, I proposed to the American Philosophical Society that we should set on foot a subscription to engage some competent person to explore that region in the opposite direction; that is, by ascending the Missouri, crossing the Stony [Rocky] Mountains, and descending the nearest river to the Pacific. Captain Lewis being then stationed at Charlottesville, on the recruiting service, warmly solicited me to obtain for him the execution of that object. I told him it was proposed that the person engaged should be attended by a single companion only, to avoid exciting alarm among the Indians. This did not deter him; but Mr. André Michaux, a professed botanist, author of "Flora Boreali-Americana" and of the "Histoire des Chesnes d'Amérique," offering his services, they were accepted. He received his instructions, and when he had reached Kentucky in the prosecution of his journey, he was overtaken by an order from the Minister of France, then at Philadelphia, to relinquish the expedition, and to pursue elsewhere the botanical inquiries on which he was employed by that government: and thus failed the second attempt for exploring that region.

In 1803, the act for establishing trading houses with the Indian tribes being about to expire, some modifications of it were recommended to congress by a confidential message of January 18th, and an extension of its views to the Indians on the Missouri. In order to prepare the way, the message proposed the sending an exploring party to trace the Missouri to its source, to cross the Highlands, and follow the best water-communication which offered itself from thence to the Pacific ocean. Congress approved the proposition, and voted a sum of money for carrying it into execution.

Captain Lewis, who had then been near two years with me as private secretary, immediately renewed his solicitations to have the direction of the party. I had now had opportunities of knowing him intimately. Of courage undaunted; possessing a firmness and perseverance of purpose which nothing but impossibilities could divert from its direction; careful as a father of those committed to his charge, yet steady in the maintenance of order and discipline; intimate with the Indian character, customs, and principles; habituated to the hunting life; guarded, by exact observation of the vegetables and animals of his own country, against losing time in the description of objects already possessed; honest, disinterested, liberal, of sound understanding, and a fidelity to truth so scrupulous, that whatever he should report would be as certain as if seen by ourselves; with all these qualifications, as if selected and implanted by nature in one body for this express purpose, I could have no hesitation in confiding the enterprise to him. To fill up the measure desired, he wanted nothing but a greater familiarity with the technical language of the natural sciences, and readiness in the astronomical observations necessary for the geography of his route.

To acquire these he repaired immediately to Philadelphia, and placed himself under the tutorage of the distinguished professors of that place, who with a zeal and emulation, enkindled by an ardent devotion to science, communicated to him freely the information requisite for the purposes of the journey. While attending too, at Lancaster, the fabrication of the arms with which he chose that his men should be provided, he had the benefit of daily communication with Mr. Andrew Ellicot, whose experience in astronomical observation, and practice of it in the woods, enabled him to apprise captain Lewis of the wants and difficulties he would encounter, and of the substitutes and resources offered by a woodland and uninhabited country.

Deeming it necessary he should have some person with him of known competence to the direction of the enterprise, in the event of accident to himself, he proposed William Clark, brother of general George Rogers Clark, who was approved, and, with that view, received a commission of captain.

In April, 1803, a draught of his instructions was sent to captain Lewis, and on the 20th of June they were signed in the following form:

THE COMMISSION "To Meriwether Lewis, esquire, captain of the first regiment of infantry of the United States of America:

"Your situation as secretary of the president of the United States, has made you acquainted with the objects of my confidential message of January 18, 1803, to the legislature; you have seen the act they passed, which, though expressed in general terms, was meant to sanction those objects, and you are appointed to carry them into execution.

"Instruments for ascertaining, by celestial observations, the geography of the country through which you will pass, have been already provided. Light articles for barter and presents among the Indians, arms for your attendants, say for from ten to twelve men, boats, tents, and other travelling apparatus, with ammunition, medicine, surgical instruments, and provisions, you will have prepared, with such aids as the secretary at war can yield in his department; and from him also you will receive authority to engage among our troops, by voluntary agreement, the number of attendants abovementioned; over whom you, as their commanding officer, are invested with all the powers the laws give in such a case.

"As your movements, while within the limits of the United States, will be better directed by occasional communications, adapted to circumstances as they arise, they will not be noticed here. What follows will respect your proceedings after your departure from the United States.

"Your mission has been communicated to the ministers here from France, Spain, and Great Britain, and through them to their governments;

and such assurances given them as to its objects, as we trust will satisfy them. The country of Louisiana having been ceded by Spain to France, the passport you have from the minister of France, the representative of the present sovereign of the country, will be a protection with all its subjects; and that from the minister of England will entitle you to the friendly aid of any traders of that allegiance with whom you may happen to meet.

"The object of your mission is to explore the Missouri river, and such principal streams of it, as, by its course and communication with the waters of the Pacific ocean, whether the Columbia, Oregan [sic], Colorado, or any other river, may offer the most direct and practicable water-communication across the continent, for the purposes of commerce.

"Beginning at the mouth of the Missouri, you will take observations of latitude and longitude, at all remarkable points on the river, and especially at the mouths of rivers, at rapids, at islands, and other places and objects distinguished by such natural marks and characters, of a durable kind, as that they may with certainty be recognised hereafter. The courses of the river between these points of observation may be supplied by the compass, the log-line, and by time, corrected by the observations themselves. The variations of the needle, too, in different places, should be noticed.

"The interesting points of the portage between the heads of the Missouri, and of the water offering the best communication with the Pacific ocean, should also be fixed by observation; and the course of that water to the ocean, in the same manner as that of the Missouri.

"Your observations are to be taken with great pains and accuracy; to be entered distinctly and intelligibly for others as well as yourself; to comprehend all the elements necessary, with the aid of the usual tables, to fix the latitude and longitude of the places at which they were taken; and are to be rendered to the war-office, for the purpose of having the calculations made concurrently by proper persons within the United States. Several copies of these, as well as of your other notes, should be made at leisure times, and put into the care of the most trustworthy of your attendants to guard, by multiplying them against the accidental losses to which they will be exposed. A further guard would be, that one of these copies be on the cuticular membranes of the paper-birch, as less liable to injury from damp than common paper.

"The commerce which may be carried on with the people inhabiting the line you will pursue, renders a knowledge of those people important. You will therefore endeavour to make yourself acquainted, as far as a diligent pursuit of your journey shall admit, with the names of the nations and their numbers;

"The extent and limits of their possessions;

"Their relations with other tribes or nations;

"Their language, traditions, monuments;

"Their ordinary occupations in agriculture, fishing, hunting, war, arts, and the implements for these;

"Their food, clothing, and domestic accommodations:

"The diseases prevalent among them, and the remedies they use;

"Moral and physical circumstances which distinguish them from the tribes we know;

"Peculiarities in their laws, customs, and dispositions;

"And articles of commerce they may need or furnish, and to what extent.

"And, considering the interest which every nation has in extending and strengthening the authority of reason and justice among the people around them, it will be useful to acquire what knowledge you can of the state of morality, religion, and information among them; as it may better enable those who may endeavour to civilize and instruct them, to adapt their measures to the existing notions and practices of those on whom they are to operate.

"Other objects worthy of notice will be—

"The soil and face of the country, its growth and vegetable productions, especially those not of the United States;

"The animals of the country generally, and especially those not known in the United States;

"The remains and accounts of any which may be deemed rare or extinct;

"The mineral productions of every kind, but more particularly metals, lime-stone, pit-coal, and saltpetre; salines and mineral waters, noting the temperature of the last, and such circumstances as may indicate their character;

"Volcanic appearances;

"Climate, as characterized by the thermometer, by the proportion of rainy, cloudy, and clear days; by lightning, hail, snow, ice; by the access and recess of frost; by the winds prevailing at different seasons; the dates at which particular plants put forth, or lose their flower or leaf; times of appearance of particular birds, reptiles or insects.

"Although your route will be along the channel of the Missouri, yet you will endeavour to inform yourself, by inquiry, of the character and extent of the country watered by its branches, and especially on its southern side. The North river, or Rio Bravo, which runs into the gulf of Mexico, and the North river, or Rio Colorado, which runs into the gulf of California, are understood to be the principal streams heading opposite to the waters of the Missouri, and running southwardly. Whether the dividing grounds between the Missouri and them are mountains or flat lands, what are their distance from the Missouri, the character of the intermediate country, and the people inhabiting it, are worthy of particular inquiry. The northern waters of the Missouri are less to be inquired after, because they have been ascertained to a considerable degree, and are still in a course of ascertainment by English traders and travellers; but if you can learn any thing certain of the most northern source of the Missisipi [*sic*], and of its position relatively to the Lake of the Woods, it will be interesting to us. Some account too of the path of the Canadian traders from the Missisipi, at the mouth of the Ouisconsing [Wisconsin] to where it strikes the Missouri, and of the soil and rivers in its course, is desirable.

"In all your intercourse with the natives, treat them in the most friendly and conciliatory manner which their own conduct will admit; allay all jealousies as to the object of your journey; satisfy them of its innocence; make them acquainted with the position, extent, character, peaceable and commercial dispositions of the United States; of our wish to be neighbourly, friendly, and useful to them, and of our dispositions to a commercial intercourse with them; confer with them on the points most convenient as mutual emporiums, and the articles of most desirable interchange for them and us. If a few of their influential chiefs, within practicable distance, wish to visit us, arrange such a visit with them, and furnish them with authority to call on our officers on their entering the United States, to have them conveyed to this place at the public expense. If any of them should wish to have some of their young people brought up with us, and taught such arts as may be useful to them, we will receive, instruct, and take care of them. Such a mission, whether of influential chiefs, or of young people, would give some security to your own party. Carry with you some matter of the kine-pox; inform those of them with whom you may be of its efficacy as a preservative from the small-pox, and instruct and encourage them in the use of it. This may be especially done wherever you winter.

"As it is impossible for us to foresee in what manner you will be received by those people, whether with hospitality or hostility, so is it impossible to prescribe the exact degree of perseverance with which you are to pursue your journey. We value too much the lives of citizens to offer them to probable destruction. Your numbers will be sufficient to secure you against the unauthorized opposition of individuals, or of small parties; but if a superior force, authorized, or not authorized, by a nation, should be arrayed against your further passage, and inflexibly determined to arrest it, you must decline its further pursuit and return. In the loss of yourselves we should lose also the information you will have acquired. By returning safely with that, you may enable us to renew the essay with better calculated means. To your own discretion, therefore, must be left the degree of danger you may risk, and the point at which you should decline, only saying, we wish you to err on the side of your safety, and to bring back your party safe, even if it be with less information.

"As far up the Missouri as the white settlements extend, an intercourse will probably be found to exist between them and the Spanish posts of St. Louis opposite Cahokia, or St. Genevieve opposite Kaskaskia. From still further up the river the traders may furnish a conveyance for letters. Beyond that you may perhaps be able to engage Indians to bring letters for the government to Cahokia, or Kaskaskia, on promising that they shall there receive such special compensation as you shall have stipulated with them. Avail yourself of these means to communicate to us, at seasonable intervals, a copy of your journal, notes and observations of every kind, putting into cypher whatever might do injury if betrayed.

"Should you reach the Pacific ocean, inform yourself of the circumstances which may decide whether the furs of those parts may not be collected as advantageously at the head of the Missouri (convenient as is supposed to the waters of the Colorado and Oregan or Columbia) as at Nootka Sound, or any other point of that coast; and that trade be consequently conducted through the Missouri and United States more beneficially than by the circumnavigation now practised.

"On your arrival on that coast, endeavour to learn if there be any port within your reach frequented by the sea vessels of any nation, and to send two of your trusty people back by sea, in such way as shall appear practicable, with a copy of your notes; and should you be of opinion that the return of your party by the way they went will be imminently dangerous, then ship the whole, and return by sea, by the way either of Cape Horn, or the Cape of Good Hope, as you shall be able. As you will be without money, clothes, or provisions, you must endeavour to use the credit of the United States to obtain them; for which purpose open letters of credit shall be furnished you, authorizing you to draw on the executive of the United States, or any of its officers, in any part of the world, on which draughts can be disposed of, and to apply with our recommendations to the consuls, agents, merchants, or citizens of any nation with which we have intercourse, assuring them, in our name, that any aids they may furnish you shall be honourably repaid, and on demand. Our consuls, Thomas Hewes, at Batavia, in Java, William Buchanan, in the Isles of France and Bourbon, and John Elmslie, at the Cape of Good Hope, will be able to supply your necessities, by draughts on us.

"Should you find it safe to return by the way you go, after sending two of your party round by sea, or with your whole party, if no conveyance by sea can be found, do so; making such observations on your return as may serve to supply [supplement], correct, or confirm those made on your outward journey.

"On reëntering the United States and reaching a place of safety, discharge any of your attendants who may desire and deserve it, procuring for them immediate payment of all arrears of pay and clothing which may have [been] incurred since their departure, and assure them that they shall be recommended to the liberality of the legislature for the grant of a soldier's portion of land each, as proposed in my message to congress, and repair yourself, with your papers, to the seat of government.

"To provide, on the accident of your death, against anarchy, dispersion, and the consequent danger to your party, and total failure of the enterprise, you are hereby authorized, by any instrument signed and written in your own hand, to name the person among them who shall succeed to the command on your decease, and by like instruments to change the nomination, from time to time, as further experience of the characters accompanying you shall point out superior fitness; and all the powers and authorities given to yourself are, in the event of your death, transferred to, and vested in the successor so named, with further power to him and his successors, in like manner to name each his successor, who, on the death of his predecessor, shall be invested with all the powers and authorities given to yourself. Given under my hand at the city of Washington, this twentieth day of June, 1803.

"THOMAS JEFFERSON.

"President of the United States of America."

While these things were going on here, the country of Louisiana, lately ceded by Spain to France, had been the subject of negotiation at Paris between us and this last power; and had actually been transferred to us by treaties executed at Paris on the 30th of April. This information, received about the 1st day of July, increased infinitely the interest we felt in the expedition, and lessened the apprehensions of interruption from other powers. Every thing in this quarter being now prepared, captain Lewis left Washington on the 5th of July, 1803, and proceeded to Pittsburg, where other articles had been ordered to be provided for him. The men too were to be selected from the military stations on the Ohio. Delays of preparation, difficulties of navigation down the Ohio, and other untoward obstructions, retarded his arrival at Cahokia until the season was so far advanced as to render it prudent to suspend his entering the Missouri before the ice should break up in the succeeding spring.

From this time his journal, now published, will give the history of his journey to and from the Pacific ocean, until his return to St. Louis on the 23d of September, 1806. Never did a similar event excite more joy through the United States. The humblest of its citizens had taken a lively interest in the issue of this journey, and looked forward with impatience for the information it would furnish. Their anxieties too for the safety of the corps had been kept in a state of excitement by lugubrious rumours, circulated from time to time on uncertain authorities, and uncontradicted by letters, or other direct information, from the time they had left the Mandan towns, on their ascent up the river in April of the preceding year, 1805, until their actual return to St. Louis.

It was the middle of February, 1807, before captain Lewis, with his companion captain Clark, reached the city of Washington, where congress was then in session. That body granted to the two chiefs and their followers the donation of lands which they had been encouraged to expect in reward of their toil and dangers. Captain Lewis was soon after appointed governor of Louisiana, and captain Clark a general of its militia, and agent of the United States for Indian affairs in that department.

A considerable time intervened before the governor's arrival at St. Louis. He found the territory distracted by feuds and contentions among the officers of the government, and the people themselves divided by these into factions and parties. He determined at once to take no side with either; but to use every endeavour to conciliate and harmonize them. The even-handed justice he administered to all soon established a respect for his person and authority; and perseverance and time wore down animosities, and reunited the citizens again into one family.

Governor Lewis had, from early life, been subject to hypochondriac affections. It was a constitutional disposition in all the nearer branches of the family of his name, and was more immediately inherited by him from his father. They had not, however, been so strong as to give uneasiness to his family. While he lived with me in Washington I observed at times sensible depressions of mind: but knowing their constitutional source, I estimated their course by what I had seen in the family. During his western expedition, the constant exertion which that required of all the faculties of body and mind, suspended these distressing affections; but after his establishment at St. Louis in sedentary occupations, they returned upon him with redoubled vigour, and began seriously to alarm his friends. He was in a paroxysm of one of these, when his affairs rendered it necessary for him to go to Washington. He proceeded to the Chickasaw Bluffs, where he arrived on the 16th of September, 1809, with a view of continuing his journey thence by water. Mr. Neely, agent of the United States with the Chickasaw Indians, arriving there two days after, found him extremely indisposed, and betraying at times some symptoms of a derangement of mind. The rumours of a war with England, and apprehensions that he might lose the papers he was bringing on, among which were the vouchers of his public accounts, and the journals and papers of his western expedition, induced him here to change his mind, and to take his course by land through the Chickasaw country. Although he appeared somewhat relieved, Mr. Neely kindly determined to accompany and watch over him. Unfortunately, at their encampment, after having passed the Tennessee one day's journey, they lost two horses, which obliging Mr. Neely to halt for their recovery, the governor proceeded, under a promise to wait for him at the house of the first white inhabitant on his road. He stopped at the house of a Mr. Grinder, who not being at home, his wife, alarmed at the symptoms of derangement she discovered, gave him up the house and retired to rest herself in an outhouse, the governor's and Neely's servants lodging in another. About three o'clock in the night he did the deed which plunged his friends into affliction, and deprived his country of one of her most valued citizens, whose valour and intelligence would have been now employed in avenging the wrongs of his country, and in emulating by land the splendid deeds which have honoured her arms on the ocean. It lost too to the nation the benefit of receiving from his own hand the narrative now offered them of his sufferings and successes, in endeavouring to extend for them the boundaries of science, and to present to their knowledge that vast and fertile country, which their sons are destined to fill with arts, with science, with freedom and happiness.

To this melancholy close of the life of one, whom posterity will declare not to have lived in vain, I have only to add, that all the facts I have stated are either known to myself, or communicated by his family or others, for whose truth I have no hesitation to make myself responsible; and I conclude with tendering you the assurances of my respect and consideration.

Th Jefferson

Mr. Paul Allen, *Philadelphia.*

One of the Indian Peace Medals that Lewis and Clark distributed to friendly chiefs.

CONTENTS OF VOLUME ONE

Introduction BY JOHN BAKELESS … vii

Letter of Thomas Jefferson Relating to Captain Meriwether Lewis … xvii

The Route from St. Louis to the Great Divide … xxxviii

CHAPTER 1 *Up the Missouri to the Platte* … 1

The party set out on the expedition and pass Wood river. Description of the town of St. Charles. Osage Woman river. Gasconade and Osage rivers described. Character of the Osage Indians; curious traditionary account of their origin. The party proceed and pass the Mine river. The two Charitons. The Kanzas, Nodawa, Newahaw, Neeshnabatona, Little Nemahar, each of which are particularly described. They encamp at the mouth of the river Platte. A particular description of the surrounding country. The various creeks, bays, islands, prairies, &c., given in the course of the route.

CHAPTER 2 *From the Platte to the Vermilion River* … 20

Some account of the Pawnee Indians. Council held with the Otto and Missouri Indians. Council held with another party of the Ottoes. Death of serjeant Floyd. The party encamp near the mouth of Whitestone river. The character of the Missouri, with the rivers that enter it. The surrounding country. The various islands, bays, creeks, &c., given in the course of the expedition.

CHAPTER 3 *From the Vermilion to the Teton River* … 33

Whimsical instance of superstition of the Sioux Indians. Council held with the Sioux. Character of that tribe, their manners, &c. A ridiculous instance of their heroism. Ancient fortifications. Quicurre river described. Vast herds of Buffalo. Account of the Petit Chien or Little Dog. Narrow escape of George Shannon. Description of White river. Surprising fleetness of the antelope. Pass the river of the Sioux. Description of the Grand Detour, or Great Bend. Encamp on the Teton river.

CHAPTER 4 *From the Teton River to the Mandans* … 52

Council held with the Tetons. Their manners, dances, &c. Chayenne river described. Council held with the Ricara Indians. Their manners and habits. Strange instance of Ricara idolatry. Another instance. Cannon-ball river. Arrival among the Mandans. Character of the surrounding country, and of the creeks, islands, &c.

CHAPTER 5 *Wintering with the Mandans* … 74

Council held with the Mandans. A prairie on fire, and a singular instance of preservation. Peace established between the Mandans and Ricaras. The party encamp for the winter. Indian mode of catching goats. Beautiful appearance of northern lights. Friendly character of the Indians. Some account of the Mandans. The Anahaways and the Minnetarees.

The party acquire the confidence of the Mandans by taking part in their controversy with the Sioux. Religion of the Mandans, and their singular conception of the term medicine. Their tradition. The sufferings of the party from the severity of the season. Indian game of billiards described. Character of the Missouri, of the surrounding country, and of the rivers, creeks, islands, &c.

CHAPTER 6 *Still with the Mandans* 92

The party increase in the favour of the Mandans. Description of a buffalo dance. Medicine dance. The fortitude with which the Indians bear the severity of the season. Distress of the party for want of provisions. The great importance of the blacksmith in procuring it. Depredations of the Sioux. The homage paid to the medicine stone. Summary act of justice among the Minnetarees. The process by which the Mandans and Ricaras make beads. Character of the Missouri, of the surrounding country, and of the rivers, creeks, islands, &c.

CHAPTER 7 *From Fort Mandan to the Yellowstone* 108

Indian method of attacking the buffalo on the ice. An enumeration of the presents sent to the president of the United States. The party are visited by a Ricara chief. They leave their encampment, and proceed on their journey. Description of the Little Missouri. Some account of the Assiniboins. Their mode of burying the dead. White earth river described. Great quantity of salt discovered on its banks. Yellowstone river described. A particular account of the country at the confluence of the Yellowstone and Missouri. Description of the Missouri, the surrounding country, and of the rivers, creeks, islands, &c.

CHAPTER 8 *From the Yellowstone to the Musselshell* 123

Unusual appearance of salt. The formidable character of the white bear. Porcupine river described. Beautiful appearance of the surrounding country. Immense quantities of game. Milk river described. Extraordinary character of Bigdry river. An instance of uncommon tenacity of life in a white bear. Narrow escape of one of the party from that animal. A still more remarkable instance. Musselshell river described.

CHAPTER 9 *From the Musselshell to Maria's River* 139

The party continue their route. Description of Judith river. Indian mode of taking the buffalo. Slaughter river described. Phenomena of nature. Of walls on the banks of the Missouri. The party encamp on the banks of the river to ascertain which of the streams constitute the Missouri. Captain Lewis leaves the party to explore the northern fork, and captain Clark explores the southern. The surrounding country described in the route of captain Lewis. Narrow escape of one of his party.

CHAPTER 10 *From Maria's River to the Great Falls* 154

Return of captain Lewis. Account of captain Clark's researches with his exploring party. Perilous situation of one of his party. Tansy river described. The party still believing the southern fork the Missouri, captain Lewis resolves to ascend it. Mode of making a place to deposit provisions, called cache. Captain Lewis explores the southern fork. Falls of the Missouri discovered, which ascertains the question. Romantic scenery of the surrounding country. Narrow escape of captain Lewis. The main body under captain Clark approach within five miles of the falls, and prepare for making a portage over the rapids.

CHAPTER 11 *Portaging Around the Great Falls* 170

Description and romantic appearance of the Missouri at the junction of the Medicine river. The difficulty of transporting the baggage at the falls. The party employed in the construction of a boat of skins. The embarrassments they had to encounter for want of proper materials. During the work the party much troubled by white bears. Violent hail-storm, and providential escape of captain Clark and his party. Description of a remarkable fountain. Singular explosion heard from the Black mountains. The boat found to be insufficient, and the serious disappointment of the party. Captain Clark undertakes to repair the damage by building canoes, and accomplishes the task.

CHAPTER 12 *From the Great Falls to the Three Forks* 186

The party embark on board the canoes. Description of Smith's river. Character of the country, &c. Dearborne's river described. Captain Clark precedes the party for the purpose of discovering the Indians of the Rocky mountains. Magnificent rocky appearances on the borders of the river denominated the Gates of the Rocky mountains. Captain Clark arrives at the three forks of the Missouri without overtaking the Indians. The party arrive at the three forks, of which a particular and interesting description is given.

CHAPTER 13 *From the Three Forks to Beaver's Head* 202

The name of the Missouri changed, as the river now divides itself into three forks, one of which is called after Jefferson, the other Madison, and the other after Gallatin. Their general character. The party ascend the Jefferson branch. Description of the river Philosophy which enters into the Jefferson. Captain Lewis and a small party go in advance in search of the Shoshonees. Description of the country, &c., bordering on the river. Captain Lewis still preceding the main party in quest of the Shoshonees. A singular accident which prevented captain Clark from following captain Lewis's advice, and ascending the middle fork of the river. Description of Philanthropy river, another stream running into the Jefferson. Captain Lewis and a small party having been unsuccessful in their first attempt, set off a second time in quest of the Shoshonees.

CHAPTER 14 *From Beaver's Head to the Great Divide* 217

Captain Lewis proceeds before the main body in search of the Shoshonees; his ill success on the first interview. The party with captain Lewis at length discover the source of the Missouri. Captain Clark with the main body still employed in ascending the Missouri or Jefferson river. Captain Lewis's second interview with the Shoshonees attended with success. The interesting ceremonies of his first introduction to the natives, detailed at large. Their hospitality. Their mode of hunting the antelope. The difficulties encountered by captain Clark and the main body in ascending the river. The suspicions entertained of Captain Lewis by the Shoshonees, and his mode of allaying them. The ravenous appetites of the savages illustrated by a singular adventure. The Indians still jealous, and the great pains taken by captain Lewis to preserve their confidence. Captain Clark arrives with the main body exhausted by the difficulties which they underwent.

CONTENTS OF VOLUME TWO

The Route from the Great Divide to the Pacific and Back to St. Louis xvi

CHAPTER 15 *Crossing the Great Divide* 233

Affecting interview between the wife of Chaboneau and the chief of the Shoshonees. Council held with that nation, and favourable result. The extreme navigable point of the Missouri mentioned. General character of the river and of the country through which it passes. Captain Clark in exploring the source of the Columbia falls in company with another party of Shoshonees. The geographical information acquired from one of that party. Their manner of catching fish. The party reach Lewis river. The difficulties which captain Clark had to encounter in his route. Friendship and hospitality of the Shoshonees. The party with captain Lewis employed in making saddles, and preparing for the journey.

CHAPTER 16 *Among the Shoshonee Indians* 248

Contest between Drewyer and a Shoshonee. The fidelity and honour of that tribe. The party set out on their journey. The conduct of Cameahwait reproved, and himself reconciled. The easy parturition of the Shoshonee women. History of this nation. Their terror of the Pawkees. Their government and family economy in their treatment of their women. Their complaint of Spanish treachery. Description of their weapons of warfare. Their curious mode of making a shield. The caparison of their horses. The dress of the man and of the women particularly described. Their mode of acquiring new names.

CHAPTER 17 *Down the Kooskooskee River* 264

The party, after procuring horses from the Shoshonees, proceed on their journey through the mountains. The difficulties and dangers of the route. A council held with another band of the Shoshonees, of whom some account is given. They are reduced to the necessity of killing their horses for food. Captain Clark with a small party precedes the main body in quest of food, and is hospitably received by the Pierced-nose Indians. Arrival of the main body amongst this tribe, with whom a council is held. They resolve to perform the remainder of their journey in canoes. Sickness of the party. They descend the Kooskooskee to its junction with Lewis river, after passing several dangerous rapids. Short description of the Pierced-nose Indians. Their manners and dress.

CHAPTER 18 *Down the Snake and Columbia Rivers* 285

The party proceed in canoes. Description of an Indian sweating bath and burial place. Many dangerous rapids passed. Narrow escape of one of the canoes. In the passage down they are visited by several Indians, all of whom manifest pacific dispositions. Description of the Sokulk tribe. Their dress, and manner of building houses. Their pacific character. Their habits of living. Their mode of boiling salmon. Vast quantities of salmon amongst the Sokulk. Council held with this tribe. The terror and consternation excited by captain Clark, concerning which an interesting cause is related. Some account of the Pisquitpaws. Their mode of burying the dead.

CHAPTER 19 *Down the Columbia to the Great Rapids* 300

The party in their passage still visited by the Indians. Lepage's river described. Immense quantities of salmon caught by the Indians. Description of the river Towahnahiooks. Indian mode of stacking fish, and preparing them for market. Description of the great falls. Description of an Indian canoe. Alarm excited by an anticipated attack from the Eheltoots. A very dangerous rapid passed in safety, called by the Indians the Falls. Account of the Indian houses in the neighbourhood. Another dreadful rapid passed without injury. Some account of the Chilluckittequaw Indians. Captain Clark examines the great rapids. Description of an Indian burial place. The rapids passed in safety.

CHAPTER 20 *From Tidewater to the Pacific Ocean* 320

First appearance of tide water in the Columbia river. Description of the Quicksand river. Some account of the Skilloot Indians. The party pass the river Coweliskee. Some account of the Wahkiacum Indians. Arrival on the borders of the Pacific. Disagreeable and critical situation of the party when first encamped. Their distress occasioned by the incessant torrents of rain. Exposed for thirty days to this drenching deluge, during which time their provisions are spoiled, and most of their few articles of merchandise destroyed. Distress of the party. Adventure of Shannon and his danger from the Wahkiacums. Difficulty of finding a place suitable for a permanent encampment. Visited by several Indians of different tribes, on whom medals are bestowed.

CHAPTER 21 *The Establishment of Fort Clatsop* 336

Extravagant passion of the natives for blue beads, which constitute amongst them the circulating medium of the country. The party still in search of a suitable place for winter quarters. Still suffering from the constant deluges of rain. Are visited by the Indians, with whom they traffic but little, on account of the extravagant prices they ask for every article. Return of captain Lewis who reports that he has found a suitable place for winter quarters. The rain still continues. They prepare to form an encampment on a point of high land on the banks of the river Nutel. Captain Clark goes with a party to find a place suitable for the manufacture of salt. He is hospitably entertained by the Clatsops. This tribe addicted to the vice of gambling. Sickness of some of the party, occasioned by the incessant rains. They form, notwithstanding a permanent encampment for their winter quarters.

CHAPTER 22 *At Fort Clatsop* 353

A party, headed by captain Clark, go in quest of a whale driven on the shore of the Pacific to obtain some of the oil. They pass Clatsop river, which is described. The perilous nature of this jaunt, and the grandeur of the scenery described. Indian mode of extracting whale oil. The life of one of captain Clark's party preserved by the kindness of an Indian woman. A short account of the Chinnooks, of the Clatsops, Killamucks, the Lucktons, and an enumeration of several other tribes. The manner of sepulchre among the Chinnooks, Clatsops, &c. Description of their weapons of war and hunting. Their mode of building houses. Their manufactures, and cookery. Their mode of making canoes. Their great dexterity in managing that vehicle.

CHAPTER 23 *Indians of the Vicinity* 367

An account of the Clatsops, Killamucks, Chinnooks and Cathlamahs. Their uniform custom of flattening the forehead. The dress of these savages, and their ornaments, described. The licensed prostitution of the women, married and unmarried, of which a ludicrous instance is given.

The character of their diseases. The common opinion, that the treatment of women is the standard by which the virtues of an Indian may be known, combatted, and disproved by examples. The respect entertained by these Indians for old age, compared with the different conduct of those nations who subsist by the chase. Their mode of government. Their ignorance of ardent spirits, and their fondness for gambling. Their dexterity in traffic. In what articles their traffic consists. Their extraordinary attachment to blue beads, which forms their circulating medium.

CHAPTER 24 *Botany and Zoology* 379

A general description of the beasts, birds, and plants, &c. found by the party in this expedition.

CHAPTER 25 *Homeward Bound* 410

Difficulty of procuring means of subsistence for the party. They determine to resume their journey to the mountains. They leave in the hands of the Indians a written memorandum, importing their having penetrated to the Pacific, through the route of the Missouri and Columbia, and through the Rocky mountains. The party commence their return route. Dexterity of the Cathlamah Indians in carving. Description of the Coweliskee river. They experience much hospitality from the natives. An instance of the extreme voracity of the vulture. The party are visited by many strange Indians, all of whom are kind and hospitable. Scarcity of game, and embarrassments of the party on that account. Captain Clark discovers a tribe not seen in the descent down the Columbia. Singular adventure to obtain provisions from them. Particular description of the Multnomah village and river. Description of mount Jefferson. Some account by captain Clark of the Neerchokio tribe, and of their architecture. Their sufferings by the small-pox.

CHAPTER 26 *Up the Columbia to the Dalles* 422

Description of Wappatoo island, and the mode in which the nations gather wappatoo. The character of the soil and its productions. The numerous tribes residing in its vicinity. The probability that they were all of the tribe of the Multnomahs originally, inferred from similarity of dress, manners, language, &c. Description of their dress, weapons of war, their mode of burying the dead. Description of another village, called the Wahclellah village. Their mode of architecture. Extraordinary height of Beacon rock. Unfriendly character of the Indians at that place. The party, alarmed for their safety, resolve to inflict summary vengeance, in case the Wahclellah tribe persist in their outrages and insults. Interview with the chief of that tribe, and confidence restored. Difficulty of drawing the canoes over the rapids. Visited by a party of the Yehugh tribe. Short notice of the Weocksockwillackum tribe. Curious phenomenon observed in the Columbia, from the rapids to the Chilluckittequaws.

CHAPTER 27 *From the Dalles to Walla Walla River* 434

Captain Clark procures four horses for the transportation of the baggage. Some further account of the Skilloot tribe. Their joy at the first appearance of salmon in the Columbia. Their thievish propensities. The party arrive at the village of the Eneeshurs, where the natives are found alike unfriendly. The party now provided with horses. The party prevented from the exercise of hostility against this nation by a friendly adjustment. The scarcity of timber so great that they are compelled to buy wood to cook their provisions. Arrive at the Wahhowpum village. Dance of the natives. Their ingenuity in declining to purchase the canoes, on the supposition that the party would be compelled to leave them behind defeated. The party having obtained a complement of horses, proceed by land. Arrive at the Pishquitpah village, and some account of that people. Their frank and hospitable treatment from the Wollawollahs. Their mode of dancing described. Their mode of making fish-weirs. Their amiable character, and their unusual affection for the whites.

CHAPTER 28 *From the Walla Walla to Commearp Creek* 446

The party still pursue their route towards the Kooskooskee on horseback with Wollawollah guides. Character of the country. The quamash and other flowering shrubs in bloom. The party reach the Kinnooenim creek. They meet with an old acquaintance called the Bighorn Indian. They arrive at the mouth of the Kooskooskee. Singular custom among the Chopunnish women. Difficulty of purchasing provisions from the natives, and the new resort of the party to obtain them. The Chopunnish style of architecture. Captain Clark turns physician, and performs several experiments with success upon the natives, which they reward. An instance of their honesty. The distress of the Indians for want of provisions during the winter. The party finally meet the Twistedhair, to whom was entrusted their horses during their journey down. The quarrel between that chief and another of his nation, on the subject of his horses. The causes of this controversy stated at large. The two chiefs reconciled by the interference of the party, and the horses restored. Extraordinary instance of Indian hospitality towards strangers. A council held with the Chopunnish, and the object of the expedition explained in a very circuitous route of explanation. The party again perform medical cures. The answer of the Chopunnish to the speech delivered at the council, confirmed by a singular ceremony of acquiescence. They promise faithfully to follow the advice of their visitors.

CHAPTER 29 *Encamped on the Upper Kooskooskee* 458

The party encamp amongst the Chopunnish, and receive further evidences of their hospitality. The Indian mode of boiling bear-flesh. Of gelding horses. Their mode of decoying the deer within reach of their arrows. Character of the soil and climate in the Rocky mountains. Varieties of climate. Character of the natives. Their dress and ornaments. Mode of burying the dead. The party administer medical relief to the natives. One of the natives restored to the use of his limbs by sweating, and the curious process by which perspiration was excited. Another proof of Chopunnish hospitality. Success of their sweating prescription on the Indian chief. Description of the horned lizard, and a variety of insects. The attachment of the friends of a dying Indian to a tomahawk which he had stolen from the party, and which they desired to bury with the body. Description of the river Tommanamah. The Indians return an answer to a proposition made by the party.

CHAPTER 30 *In the Bitter Root Mountains Again* 471

The party mingle in the diversions of the Willetpos Indians, a tribe hitherto unnoticed. Their joy on the prospect of a return. Description of the vegetables growing on the Rocky mountains. Various preparations made to resume their journey. The party set out, and arrive at Hungry creek. The serious and desponding difficulties that obstructed their progress. They are compelled to return and wait for a guide across the mountains. Their distress for want of provisions. They resolve to return to the Quamash flats. They are at last so fortunate as to procure Indian guides, with whom they resume their journey to the falls of the Missouri. The danger of the route described. Their scarcity of provisions, and the danger of their journey. Their course lying along the ridges of mountains. Description of the warm springs, where the party encamp. The fondness of the Indians for bathing in them.

CHAPTER 31 *Captain Lewis Seeks a Short-Cut* 482

The party proceed on their journey with their Indian guides, and at length agree to divide, to take several routes, and to meet again at the mouth of Yellowstone river. The route of captain Lewis is to pursue the most direct road to the falls of the Missouri, then to ascend Maria's river, explore the country, and to descend that river to its mouth. Captain Lewis, accordingly, with nine men proceed up the eastern branch of Clark's river, and take leave of their Indian guides. Description of that branch, and character of the surrounding country. Description of the Cokalahishkit river. They arrive at the ridge dividing the Missouri from the Columbia rivers. Meet once more with the buffalo and brown bear. Immense herds of buffalo discovered on the borders of Medicine river. The party encamp on Whitebear islands. Singular adventure that befel M'Neil. Captain Lewis, with three of his party proceed to explore the source of Maria's river. Tansy river described. He reaches the dividing line of these two streams. General character of the surrounding country.

CHAPTER 32 *Lewis Completes His Separate Exploration* 493

Captain Lewis and his party still proceed on the route mentioned in the last chapter, and arrive at the forks of Maria's river; of which river a particular description is given. Alarmed by the evidence that they are in the neighbourhood of unfriendly Indians, and much distressed for want of provisions, the weather proving unfavourable, they are compelled to return. The face of the country described. Interview with the unfriendly Indians, called Minnetarees of Fort de Prairie. Mutual consternation. Resolution of captain Lewis. They encamp together for the night, apparently with amicable dispositions. The conversation that ensued between these new visitants. The conflict occasioned by the Indians attempting to seize the rifles and horses of the party, in which one is mortally wounded. Captain Lewis kills another Indian, and his narrow escape. Having taken four horses belonging to the Indians, they hastened with all expedition to join the party attached to captain Clark. Arriving near the Missouri they are alarmed by the sound of rifles, which proves fortunately to be from the party of their friends, under the command of sergeant Ordway. The two detachments thus fortunately united, leave their horses, and descend the Missouri in canoes. They continue their route down the river to form a junction with captain Clark. Vast quantities of game found in their passage down the river. Captain Lewis accidentally wounded by one of his own party. They proceed down the Missouri, and at length join captain Clark.

CHAPTER 33 *Captain Clark Explores the Yellowstone* 505

The party commanded by captain Clark, previous to his being joined by captain Lewis, proceed along Clark's river, in pursuance of the route mentioned in a preceding chapter. Their sorry commemoration of our national anniversary. An instance of Sacajawea's strength of memory. Description of the river and of the surrounding country as the party proceed. Several of the horses belonging to the party supposed to be stolen by their Indian neighbours. They reach Wisdom river. Extraordinary heat of a spring. The strong attachment of the party for tobacco, which they find on opening a cache. Sergeant Ordway recovers the horses. Captain Clark divides his party, one detachment of which was to descend the river: they reach Gallatin and Jefferson rivers, of which a description is given. Arrive at the Yellowstone river. Some account of Otter and Beaver rivers. An example of Indian fortification. One of the party seriously and accidentally wounded. Engaged in the construction of canoes. Twenty-four horses stolen, probably by the Indians, in one night.

CHAPTER 34   *Down the Yellowstone; Reunion of the Parties*   516

Captain Clark proceeds with his party down the river. Description of an Indian lodge. Sergeant Pryor arrives with the horses left by the party when they embarked in their canoes; his difficulty in bringing them on. Remarkable rock discovered by captain Clark, and the beauty of the prospect from the summit. They continue their route down the river, of which a particular description is given, as well as of the surrounding country. Yellowstone and Bighorn rivers compared. Great quantities of game found on the banks of the rivers. Immense herds of buffalo. Fierceness of the white bear. Encamp at the junction of the Yellowstone and Missouri. A general outline given of Yellowstone river, comprehending the shoals; its entrance recommended for the formation of a trading establishment. The sufferings of the party from the mosquitoes. Sergeant Pryor, who, with a detachment of the party, was to have brought on the horses, arrives and reports that they were all stolen by the Indians; deprived of these animals, they form for themselves Indian canoes of the skins of beasts, and of curious structure, with which they descend the river over the most difficult shoals and dangerous rapids. Meet with two white men unexpectedly, from whom they procure intelligence of the Indians formerly visited by the party.

CHAPTER 35   *Down the Missouri to White River*   527

The party, while descending the river in their skin canoes, are overtaken by the detachment under captain Lewis, and the whole party, now once more happily united, descend the Missouri together. They once more visit the Minnetaree Indians, and hold a council with that nation as well as with the Mahahas. Captain Clark endeavours to persuade their chiefs to accompany him to the United States, which invitation they decline, on account of their fears of the Sioux, in their passage down the river. Colter, one of the party, requests and obtains liberty to remain among the Indians, for the purpose of hunting beaver. Friendly deportment of the Mandans; council held by captain Clark with the chiefs of the different villages; the chief named the Bigwhite, with his wife and son, agree to accompany the party to the United States, who takes an affecting farewell of his nation. Chaboneau, with his wife and child, decline visiting the United States, and are left among the Indians. The party at length proceed on their journey, and find that the course of the Missouri has, in some places, changed since their passage up that river. They arrive among the Ricaras. Character of the Chayennes; their dress, habits, &c. Captain Clark offers to the chief of this nation a medal, which he at first refuses, believing it to be medicine, but which he is afterwards prevailed on to accept. The party proceed rapidly down the river. Prepare to defend themselves against the Tetons, but receive no injury from them. Incredible numbers of buffalo seen near White river. They meet, at last, with the Tetons, and refuse their invitations to land. Intrepidity of captain Clark.

CHAPTER 36   *The Expedition Returns in Safety to St. Louis*   539

The party are hailed by a group of Indians and fear an attack, but are relieved to learn that they are friendly Yanktons. A flagstaff that had been erected by the party in September, 1804, opposite Calumet bluff, is found still standing. They meet Mr. James Airs, a trader from Mackinaw, who presents the party with tobacco and flour. Next they meet a party on the way to trade with the Yanktons, and obtain their first whiskey in more than a year. Encounter with Mr. Gravelines, who reports the death of the Ricara chief at Washington. Learn of the opinion in the United States that the expedition had perished. They are met with a great welcome at Lacharette and St. Louis.

Acknowledgments   547

PORTRAITS & COLOR PLATES

VOLUME ONE

Meriwether Lewis (*Charles Willson Peale*)   PAGE ii

William Clark (*Charles Willson Peale*)   iii

Mandan Chief (*Carl Bodmer*)   FACING PAGE 10
    "Four Bears" (Mato-Topé) was a renowned chief of this Siouan tribe. Among the symbolic objects in his hair is a red wooden knife, a token of his having slain a Cheyenne chief. The yellow hand signifies that he has captured prisoners, and the stripes represent heroic deeds of war.

Funeral Scaffold of a Sioux Chief (*Carl Bodmer*)   50
    After being painted, dressed, and sewed up in blankets, the bodies of the dead were exposed on a high stage until decomposed.

Mandan Village (*Carl Bodmer*)   78
    The Mandan village Mih-Tutta-Hang-Kush, viewed from the Missouri River near Fort Clark. High scaffolds for drying meat and corn can be seen among the huts. The circular "bull boats" were constructed of buffalo hide.

Buffalo Dance of the Mandan Indians (*Carl Bodmer*)   110
    The pair considered the bravest wear the complete buffalo head with horns and with metal rings around the eyeholes; others wear parts of the skin and mane, and the horns.

On the Upper Missouri (*Carl Bodmer*)   154
    "These hills and river cliffs exhibit a most extraordinary and romantic appearance.... There seems no end to the visionary enchantment which surrounds us." (See Chapter 9.)

Osage Chief (*George Bird King?*)   174
    "The Soldier of Oak," who signed several treaties with the whites.

Woman of the Snake Tribe (*Carl Bodmer*)   218
    It was the Snake or Shoshone tribe to which Sacagawea, the expedition's interpreter, belonged.

The Route of the Expedition (*copied by Samuel Lewis*)   BACK OF VOLUME ONE
    The route is superimposed on a map copied from the original drawing made by Captain Clark.

VOLUME TWO

Meriwether Lewis (*after Charles de St.-Memin*)   PAGE ii

William Clark (*Chester Harding and John J. Douberman*)   iii

Indian Painting of a Combat (*copied by Carl Bodmer*)   FACING PAGE 242

    In the scene painted on a buffalo robe by Mato-Topé, the Mandan chief is depicted fighting a Cheyenne chief, distinguished by the otter skin on his head. Mato-Topé's hand has been cut in seizing the knife with which he is about to stab his enemy.

Indian Utensils and Weapons (*Carl Bodmer*)   274

    Tools, weapons, and apparel of various midwestern Indian tribes: 1. Bone tool for scraping wood. 2. Horn ladle. 3. Horseman's short spear. 4. Gunstock club with spear blade. 5. Feathered bonnet. 6. Shield belonging to Mato-Topé. 7. Roached deertail decorated with rattlesnake rattle. 8. Parfleche—painted rawhide envelope for carrying food. 9. Moccasins (left, man's; right, woman's). 10. Quiver, with two types of bows. 11. Coup stick, used in close fighting to win acclaim as an act of bravery. 12. Pipe with catlinite (red clay) stem, inlaid with slate and lead. 13. Calumet, or ceremonial peace pipe. 14. Woman's game ball. 15. Game hoop and spear. 16. Double bone whistle. 17. Dance drum. 18. Man's moccasin. 19. Bundle of tobacco.

Iowa Warrior (*George Bird King*)   298

    Tah-Ro-Hon, famed from his youth for his combats with the Sioux and Osage. A signer of the treaty of St. Louis, he visited Washington, where his portrait was painted.

Assiniboin and Yanktonai Indians (*Carl Bodmer*)   338

    The Assiniboin's headdress combines antelope horns and a crest of trimmed feathers; a rosette of porcupine quills decorates his breast.

Muskwaki (Fox) Indian (*Carl Bodmer*)   390

    Wakusaase's tribe belonged to the Algonquian group and was allied to the Sacs.

Oto Warrior (*George Bird King*)   430

    The "Ottoes" are described in Chapter 2 as among the first with whom the expedition had contact. This warrior's name, No-Way-Ke-Sug-Ga, means "He who strikes two at once."

Interior of the Hut of a Mandan Chief (*Carl Bodmer*)   462

    Between the four center posts that support the roof are shorter posts forming the wall, which is covered on the outside with matting, hay, and earth. Smoke from the central fire escapes through the roof. These large circular houses were warm and spacious.

Blackfoot Indian on Horseback (*Carl Bodmer*)   494

    It was an armed Indian of this tribe who barely missed killing Captain Lewis in July 1806 (see Chapter 32).

Hunting the Bison (*Carl Bodmer*) 530
Big-game hunting was an easier task for the Indians after the white men brought horses to the New World. With the introduction of fire-arms, the buffalo herds were reduced almost to extinction.

VOLUME ONE

From St. Louis to the Great Divide

———

MAY 14, 1804 TO AUGUST 16, 1805

THE ROUTE

The camp in which the Lewis and Clark expedition passed the winter of 1803–04 was on the eastern side of the Mississippi, at the mouth of Wood, now Du Bois River, near St. Louis. It was on Monday, May 14, 1804, that they left this camp; they were to ascend the Missouri and the Yellowstone, cross the Rocky Mountains, and descend Lewis's (now Salmon) River, the Clearwater, and the Columbia to the Pacific Coast. In the course of this journey they were to pass through or by the present States of Missouri, Kansas, Iowa, Nebraska, South Dakota, North Dakota, Montana, Idaho, Washington, and Oregon. Altogether, between May, 1804, and the return to St. Louis in September, 1806, they were to travel in boats, on horses, and on foot some 8000 miles.

When the expedition was finally ready to start it was nearly four in the afternoon, and the first day's journey was a short one. Camp was made near Cold Water Creek, a little above Bellefontaine, Missouri. On May 21 Captain Lewis, who had been detained at St. Louis, overtook them at the little settlement of St. Charles, which bears the same name to-day, and the expedition was then finally under way.

The opening chapter tells the story of the journey as far as the mouth of the Platte River in Nebraska. While ascending the river through the State of Missouri they camped, on June 3, on Moreau Creek, near Jefferson City, and on the 10th they reached the country of the Ayauway, or Iowa Indians, not far from the centre of Missouri. A more important landmark was reached on June 26, when they reached the mouth of the Kansas River and saw the future site of Kansas City, Missouri. As they ascended the Missouri from this point their course became more nearly northerly. Above Kansas City they passed the sites of Leavenworth, Atchison, and St. Joseph. The middle of July brought them to Nebraska and Iowa, and the chapter closes at the mouth of the Platte.

The camp described in Chapter 2 as some ten miles from the Platte was on the east side of the Missouri, probably about ten miles below the cities of Council Bluffs and Omaha. While the former city is named from the council described in this chapter, the council was held several miles above the city on the west bank of the river. The death of Sergeant Floyd occurred near Sioux City, Iowa.

In late August the explorers entered South Dakota. The "Mountain of Little Spirits," described at the beginning of Chapter 3, is in Clay County, South Dakota, and has kept the name of Spirit Mound. The Yankton River, noted here, is now the Dakota, and at its mouth, near which the council was held, is situated the city of Yankton. A little above Yankton near Bon Homme Island, which keeps its name, the explorers found the sand dunes, described and pictured, which they mistook for fortifications. The "backbone of a fish" (p. 44) was the remains of a giant reptile of the Cretaceous period, and the "white bear" mentioned frequently from this time on was the grizzly bear.

In Chapter 4 the explorers, in their ascent through the Dakotas, leave the country of the Teton Sioux for that of the Arikaras. They passed the mouth of Dog River, which rises in the Black Hills. "Stone Idol Creek" is now Spring River, in Campbell County, South Dakota. Passing on into North Dakota, on October 21, they reached "Chisshetaw," now Heart River, which enters the Missouri near Bismarck, where the Northern Pacific Railroad crosses the river.

The villages of the Mandan Indians then occupied the site of the future city of Bismarck, and it was near them, not far from the mouth of Big Knife River, that Lewis and Clark, in early November, 1804, established the winter camp described in Chapter 5. They had now travelled 1600 miles from St. Louis.

On April 7, 1805 (Chapter 7), the explorers re-embarked to continue their journey, taking with them an interpreter, Chaboneau, his child, and his wife, the faithful Sacajawea, the only woman of the party, whose courage and resourcefulness make a touching and vivid part of the narrative. From the Mandan villages Lewis and Clark sent back reports which furnished the only news of the explorers until their return in September, 1806. The finding of the Yellowstone River, described in the later pages of Chapter 7, was not an original discovery, since the river was already known to the French trappers as *La Roche Jaune*.

The journey through Montana is described in Chapter 8, where the "salts" referred to are the alkali of the plains. "Porcupine River" is Poplar River, at whose mouth an Indian agency was established. Note the discoveries of Milk and Big Dry Rivers, which preserve their names, although the important "Muscleshell" River of the explorers has become the Musselshell.

The experiences described in the opening pages of Chapter 9 occurred while the party were to the westward of the present town of Carroll, Montana. Their first glimpse of the Rocky Mountains, on May 26, 1805, was near Cow Creek, Montana. The specimens of Montana's natural wonders sketched in the accounts of the "Cathedral Rocks," as they have sometimes been termed, are to the eastward of the town of Ophir, Montana, where the explorers, two days later, found the mouth of Maria's River.

In Chapters 10 and 11 a more important discovery is described, that of the Great Falls of the Missouri; the surveys and measurements made by Captain Clark have been proved accurate. The bears which then disturbed the travellers have now given place to the town of Great Falls.

When the journey was continued (Chapter 12), the travellers were puzzled by the crookedness of the Missouri. Its general course was northward, and they were therefore journeying south. Their reference to the "north bank" therefore should be understood as the west, while the "south bank" is the east. As to Dearborn's River, it may be noted that the secretary's name was afterward given to Fort Dearborn, which was the nucleus of Chicago. In this southward progress the party had the main Rocky

Mountain Range on their right and the Big Belt Mountains on their left, and their route was in part between Meagher County on the east, and Lewis and Clark County on the west. On July 25 they reached the Three Forks of the Missouri. They were approaching the mountains dividing the headwaters of the Missouri and the Columbia, and at the end of the chapter are seeking a way through these mountain barriers.

At the opening of Chapter 13 we find the explorers, late in July, 1805, at the forks of the Missouri, much in doubt as to whether the Jefferson, Madison, or Gallatin, as they named the three uniting streams, was the true Missouri and their proper route. After they had made a correct choice and had begun to ascend the Jefferson, Captain Lewis went ahead, skirting the base of the Bitter Root Mountains, between Montana and Idaho. It was in a gap in these mountains that, as described in Chapter 14, Captain Lewis found the actual source of the Missouri. The explorers were seeking anxiously for a way through the mountains to the Pacific side, and in this chapter Lewis succeeds in his quest. He reaches the headwaters of the Lemhi River on the western side of the Divide, a river which empties into the Salmon. He also encounters friendly Indians and tastes a salmon, another assurance that he had reached the headwaters of the Columbia.

The map seems to indicate a very short distance between the headwaters of the Jefferson and the Lemhi River, but the unknown and mountainous country and the difficulty of transportation made it a serious matter finally to take the entire party across the Divide.

August 30th 1803.

Left Pittsburgh this day at 11 ock. with a party of 11 hands 7 of which are soldiers, a pilot and three young men on trial they having proposed to go with me throughout the voyage arrived at Bruno's Island 3 miles below halted a few minutes. went on shore and being invited on by some of the gentlemen present to try my airgun which I had purchased brought it on shore charged it and fired myself seven times fifty five yards with pretty good success; after which a Mr. Blaze Cenas being unacquainted with the management of the gun suffered her to discharge herself accidentally

A page from Captain Lewis's Journal for his Ohio River trip, which was undertaken in preparation for the expedition to the West.

Chapter 1
UP THE MISSOURI TO THE PLATTE

On the acquisition of Louisiana, in the year *1803*, the attention of the government of the United States, was early directed towards exploring and improving the new territory. Accordingly in the summer of the same year, an expedition was planned by the president for the purpose of discovering the courses and sources of the Missouri, and the most convenient water communication thence to the Pacific ocean. His private secretary, captain Meriwether Lewis, and captain William Clark, both officers of the army of the United States, were associated in the command of this enterprise. After receiving the requisite instructions, captain Lewis left the seat of government, and being joined by captain Clark at Louisville, in Kentucky, proceeded to St. Louis, where they arrived in the month of December. Their original intention was to pass the winter at La Charrette, the highest settlement on the Missouri. But the Spanish commandant of the province, not having received an official account of its transfer to the United States, was obliged by the general policy of his government, to prevent strangers from passing through the Spanish territory. They therefore encamped at the mouth of Wood river, on the eastern side of the Mississippi, out of his jurisdiction, where they passed the winter in disciplining the men, and making the necessary preparations for setting out early in the Spring, before which the cession was officially announced.

The party consisted of nine young men from Kentucky, fourteen soldiers of the United States army who volunteered their services, two French watermen—an interpreter and hunter—and a black servant belonging to captain Clark. All these, except the last, were enlisted to serve as privates during the expedition, and three sergeants appointed from amongst them by the captains. In addition to these were engaged a corporal and six soldiers, and nine watermen to accompany the expedition as far as the Mandan nation, in order to assist in carrying the stores, or repelling an attack which was most to be apprehended between Wood river and that tribe. The necessary stores were subdivided into seven bales, and one box, containing a small portion of each article in case of accident. They consisted of a great variety of clothing, working utensils, locks, flints, powder, ball, and articles of the greatest use. To these were added fourteen bales and one box of Indian presents, distributed in the same manner, and composed of richly laced coats and other articles of dress, medals, flags, knives, and tomahawks for the chiefs—ornaments of different kinds, particularly beads, looking-glasses, handkerchiefs, paints, and generally such articles as were deemed best calculated for the taste of the Indians.

The party was to embark on board of three boats; the first was a keel boat fifty-five feet long, drawing three feet water, carrying one large squaresail and twenty-two oars, a deck of ten feet in the bow, and stern formed a forecastle and cabin, while the middle was covered by lockers, which might be raised so as to form a breastwork in case of attack. This was accompanied by two periogues [pirogues] or open boats, one of six and the other of seven oars. Two horses were at the same time to be led along the banks of the river for the purpose of bringing home game, or hunting in case of scarcity.

Of the proceedings of this expedition, the following is a succinct and circumstantial narrative.

Monday, May 14th, 1804

All the preparations being completed, we left our encampment. This spot is at the mouth of Wood river, a small stream which empties itself into the Mississippi, opposite to the entrance of the Missouri. It is situated in latitude 38° 55′ 19″ $\frac{6}{10}$ north, and longitude from Greenwich, 89° 57′ 45″. On both sides of the Mississippi the land for two or three miles is rich and level, but gradually swells into a high pleasant country, with less timber on the western than on the eastern side, but all susceptible of cultivation. The point which separates the two rivers on the north, extends for fifteen or twenty miles, the greater part of which is an open level plain, in which the people of the neighbourhood cultivate what little grain they raise. Not being able to set sail before four o'clock P.M., we did not make more than four miles, and encamped on the first island opposite a small creek called Cold Water.

MAY 15TH The rain, which had continued yesterday and last night, ceased this morning. We then proceeded, and after passing two small islands about ten miles further, stopped for the night at Piper's landing, opposite another island. The water is here very rapid and the banks falling in. We found that our boat was too heavily laden in the stern, in consequence of which she ran on logs three times to-day. It became necessary to throw the greatest weight on the bow of the boat, a precaution very necessary in ascending both the Missouri and Mississippi rivers, in the beds of which, there lie great quantities of concealed timber.

The next morning we set sail at five o'clock. At the distance of a few miles, we passed a remarkably large coal hill on the north side, called by the French La Charbonnière, and arrived at the town of St. Charles. Here we remained a few days.

St. Charles is a small town on the north bank of the Missouri, about twenty-one miles from its confluence with the Mississippi. It is situated in a narrow plain, sufficiently high to protect it from the annual risings of the river in the month of June, and at the foot of a range of small hills, which have occasioned its being called Petite Côte, a name by which it is more known to the French than by that of St. Charles. One principal street, about a mile in length and running parallel with the river, divides the town, which is composed of nearly one hundred small wooden houses, besides a chapel. The inhabitants, about four hundred and fifty in number, are chiefly descendants from the French of Canada; and, in their manners, they unite all the careless gayety, and the amiable hospitality of the best times of France: yet, like most of their countrymen in America, they are but ill qualified for the rude life of a frontier; not that they are without talent, for they possess much natural genius and vivacity; nor that they are destitute of enterprise, for their hunting excursions are long, laborious, and hazardous: but their exertions are all desultory; their industry is without system, and without perseverance. The surrounding country, therefore, though rich, is not, in general, well cultivated; the inhabitants chiefly subsisting by hunting and trade with the Indians, and confine their culture to gardening, in which they excel.

Being joined by captain Lewis, who had been detained by business at St. Louis, we again set sail on *Monday, May 21st*, in the afternoon, but were prevented by wind and rain from going more than about three miles, when we encamped on the upper point of an island, nearly opposite a creek which falls in on the south side.

On the 22d we made about eighteen miles, passing several small farms on the bank of the river, a number of islands, and a large creek on the south side, called Bonhomme, or Goodman's river. A small number of emigrants from the United States have settled on the sides of this creek, which are very fertile. We also passed some high lands, and encamped, on the north side, near a small creek. Here we met with a camp of Kickapoo Indians who had left us at St. Charles, with a promise of procuring us some provisions by the time we overtook them. They now made us a present of four deer, and we gave them in return two quarts of whiskey. This tribe reside on the heads of the Kaskaskia and Illinois river, on the other side of the Mississippi, but occasionally hunt on the Missouri.

MAY 23D

Two miles from our camp of last night, we reached a river emptying itself on the north side, called Osage Woman river. It is about thirty yards wide, and has now a settlement of thirty or forty families from the United States. About a mile and a half beyond this is a large cave, on the south side at the foot of cliffs nearly three hundred feet high, overhanging the water, which becomes very swift at this place. The cave is one hundred and twenty feet wide, forty feet deep, and twenty high, it is known by the name of the Tavern, among the traders who have written their names on the rock, and painted some images which command the homage of the Indians and French. About a mile further we passed a small creek called Tavern creek, and encamped on the south side of the river, having gone nine miles.

Early the next morning we ascended a very difficult rapid, called the Devil's Race Ground, where the current sets for half a mile against some projecting rocks on the south side. We were less fortunate in attempting a second place of equal difficulty. Passing near the southern shore, the bank fell in so fast as to oblige us to cross the river instantly, between the northern side and a sandbar which is constantly moving and banking with the violence of the current. The boat struck on it, and would have upset immediately, if the men had not jumped into the water and held her, till the sand washed from under her. We encamped on the south side, having ascended ten miles, and the next day, *May 25th*, passed on the south side the mouth of Wood river, on the north, two small creeks and several islands, and stopped for the night at the entrance of a creek on the north side, called by the French La Charrette, ten miles from our last encampment, and a little above a small village of the same name. It consists of seven small houses, and as many poor families who have fixed themselves here for the convenience of trade, and form the last establishment of whites on the Missouri. It rained last night, yet we found this morning that the river had fallen several inches.

MAY 26TH

The wind being favourable we made eighteen miles to-day. We passed in the morning several islands, the largest of which is Buffalo island, separated from the southern side by a small channel which receives the waters of Buffalo creek. On the same side is Shepherd's creek, a little beyond which we encamped on the northern side. The next day we sailed along a large island called Otter island, on the northern side, extending nearly ten miles in length, narrow but high in its situation, and one of the most fertile in the whole river. Between it and the northern shore, three small creeks, one of which has the same name with the island, empty themselves. On the southern shore is a creek twenty yards wide, called Ash creek. In the course of the day we met two canoes loaded with furs, which had been two months on their route from the Mahar [Omaha] nation, residing more than seven hundred miles up the river—one large raft from the Pawnees on the river Platte, and three others from the Grand Osage river. At the distance of fifteen miles we encamped on a willow island, at the entrance of the river Gasconade. This river falls into the Missouri from the south, one hundred miles from the Mississippi. Its length is about one hundred and fifty miles in a course generally northeast through a hilly country. On its banks are a number of saltpetre caves, and it is believed some mines of lead in the vicinity. Its width at the mouth is one hundred and fifty-seven yards, and its depth nineteen feet.

Here we halted for the purpose of hunting and drying our provisions, and making the necessary celestial observations. This being completed, we set sail on the *29th* at four o'clock, and at four miles distance encamped on the south side, above a small creek, called Deer creek. The next day, *30th*, we set out early, and at two miles distant reached a large cave, on the north, called Montbrun's tavern, after a French trader of that name, just above a creek called after the same person. Beyond this is a large island, and at the distance of four miles, Rush creek coming in from the south, at eleven, Big-muddy river on the north, about fifty yards wide; three miles further, is Little-muddy river on the same side, opposite to which we encamped at the mouth of Grindstone creek. The rain which began last night continued through the day, accompanied with high wind and some hail. The river has been rising fast for two days, and the country around appears full of water. Along the sides of the river to-day we observe much timber, the cotton wood, the sycamore, hickory, white walnut, some grapevines, and rushes—the high west wind and rain compelled us to remain all the next day, *May 31st*. In the afternoon a boat came down from the Grand Osage river, bringing a letter from a person sent to the Osage nation on the Arkansaw river, which mentioned that the letter announcing the cession of Louisiana was committed to the flames—that the Indians would not believe that the Americans were owners of that country, and disregarded St. Louis and its supplies. The party was occupied in hunting, in the course of which, they caught in the woods several very large rats.

Friday, June 1st, 1804

We set sail early the next morning, and at six miles distant passed Bear creek, a stream of about twenty-five yards width: but the wind being ahead and the current rapid, we were unable to make more than thirteen miles to the mouth of the Osage river; where we encamped and remained the following day, for the purpose of making celestial observations.

The Osage river empties itself into the Missouri, at one hundred and thirty-three miles distance from the mouth of the latter river. Its general course is west and west southwest through a rich and level country. At the junction the Missouri is about eight hundred and seventy-five yards wide, and the Osage three hundred and ninety-seven. The low point of junction is in latitude 38° 31′ 16″, and at a short distance from it is a high commanding position, whence we enjoyed a delightful prospect of the country.

The Osage river gives or owes its name to a nation inhabiting its banks at a considerable distance from this place. Their present name however, seems to have originated from the French traders, for both among themselves and their neighbours they are called the Wasbashas. They number between twelve and thirteen hundred warriors, and consist of three tribes: the Great Osages of about five hundred warriors, living in a village on the south bank of the river—the Little Osages, of nearly half that number, residing at the distance of six miles from them—and the Arkansaw band, a colony of Osages, of six hundred warriors, who left them some years ago, under the command of a chief called the Bigfoot, and settled on the Vermillion river, a branch of the Arkansaw. In person the Osages are among the largest and best formed Indians, and are said to possess fine military capacities; but residing as they do in villages, and having made considerable advance in agriculture, they seem less addicted to war, than their northern neighbours, to whom the use of rifles gives a great superiority.

Among the peculiarities of this people, there is nothing more remarkable than the tradition relative to their origin. According to universal belief, the founder of the nation was a snail passing a quiet existence along the banks of the Osage, till a high flood swept him down to the Missouri, and left him exposed on the shore. The heat of the sun at length ripened him into a man, but with the change of his nature, he had not forgotten his native seats on the Osage, towards which, he immediately bent his way. He was however soon overtaken by hunger, and fatigue, when happily the Great Spirit appeared, and giving him a bow and arrow, showed him how to kill and cook deer, and cover himself with the skin. He then proceeded to his original residence, but as he approached the river, he was met by a beaver, who inquired haughtily who he was, and by what authority he came to disturb his possession. The Osage answered that the river was his own, for he had once lived on its borders. As they stood disputing, the daughter of the beaver came, and having by her entreaties reconciled her father to this young stranger, it was proposed that the Osage should marry the young beaver, and share with her family the enjoyment of the river. The Osage readily consented, and from this happy union there soon came the village and the nation of the Wasbasha, or Osages, who have ever since preserved a pious reverence for their ancestors, abstaining from the chase of the beaver, because in killing that animal, they killed a brother of the Osage. Of late years, however, since the trade with the whites has rendered beaver skins more valuable, the sanctity of these maternal relatives has visibly reduced, and the poor animals have nearly lost all the privileges of kindred.

On the afternoon of *June 3d*, we proceeded, and at three miles distant, reached a creek called Cupboard creek, from a rock of that appearance near its entrance. Two miles further we encamped at Moreau creek, a stream of twenty yards width, on the southern side. The next morning, we passed at an early hour, Cedar island on the north, so called from the abundance of the tree of that name; near which is a small creek, named Nightingale creek, from a bird of that species, who sang for us during the night. Beyond Cedar island, are some others of a smaller extent, and at seven miles distance a creek fifteen or twenty yards wide, entering from the north, and known by the name of Cedar creek. At seven and a half miles further we passed on the south side another creek, which we called Mast creek, from the circumstance of our mast being broken by running under a concealed tree; a little above is another creek on the left, one mile beyond which we encamped on the southern shore under high projecting cliffs. The French had reported that lead ore was to be found in this place, but on examining the hills, we could discern no appearance of that mineral. Along the river on the south, is a low land covered with rushes, and high nettles, and near the mouths of the creeks, supplied with oak, ash, and walnut timber. On the north the land is rich and well situated. We made seventeen and a half miles this day. The river is falling slowly.

We continued our route the next morning early: a small creek called Lead creek, on the south; another on the north, known to the French by the name of Little Good Woman's creek, and again Big Rock creek on the south were the only streams we passed this morning. At eleven o'clock we met a raft made of two canoes joined together, in which two French traders were descending, from eighty leagues up the river Kanzas, where they had wintered, and caught great quantities of beaver, but had lost much of their game by fires from the prairies. They told us that the Kanzas nation is now hunting buffalo in the plains, having passed the last winter in this river. Two miles further, we reached on the south Little Manitou creek, which takes its name from a strange figure resembling the bust of a man, with the horns of a stag, painted on a projecting rock, which may represent some spirit or deity. Near this is a sandbar extending several miles, which renders the navigation difficult, and a small creek called Sand creek on the south, where we stopped for dinner, and gathered wild cresses and tongue grass from the sandbar. The rapidity of the currents, added to our having broken our mast, prevented our going more than twelve and a half miles. The scouts and hunters whom we always kept out, report that they have seen fresh tracks of Indians.

The next morning we left our camp, which was on the south side, opposite to a large island in the middle of the river, and at five miles reached a creek on the north side, of about twenty yards wide, called Split Rock creek, from a fissure in the point of a neighbouring rock. Three miles beyond this, on the south is Saline river, it is about thirty yards wide, and has its name from the number of salt licks, and springs, which render its water brackish; the river is very rapid and the banks falling in. After leaving Saline creek, we passed one large island and several smaller ones, having made fourteen miles. The water rose a foot during the last night.

The next day, *June 7th*, we passed at four and a half miles Big Manitou creek, near which is a limestone rock inlaid with flint of various colours, and embellished, or at least covered with uncouth paintings of animals and inscriptions. We landed to examine it, but found the place occupied by a nest of rattlesnakes, of which we killed three. We also examined some licks and springs of salt water, two or three miles up this creek. We then proceeded by some small willow islands, and encamped at the mouth of Good

Woman river on the north. It is about thirty-five yards wide, and said to be navigable for boats several leagues. The hunters, who had hitherto given us only deer, brought in this evening three bears, and had seen some indication of buffalo. We had come fourteen miles.

JUNE 8TH

We saw several small willow islands, and a creek on the south, near which are a number of deer licks; at nine miles distance we came to Mine river. This river, which falls into the Missouri from the south, is said to be navigable for boats eighty or ninety miles, and is about seventy yards wide at its mouth. It forks about five or six leagues from the Missouri, and at the point of junction are some very rich salt springs; the west branch in particular, is so much impregnated, that, for twenty miles, the water is not palatable: several branches of the Manitou and Good Woman are equally tinctured. The French report also, that lead ore has been found on different parts of the river. We made several excursions near the river through the low rich country on its banks, and after dinner went on to the island of Mills, where we encamped. We met with a party of three hunters from the Sioux river; they had been out for twelve months, and collected about nine hundred dollars worth of peltries and furs. We ascended this river twelve miles.

On the *9th*, we set out early, and reached a cliff of rocks, called the Arrow Rock, near to which is a prairie called the Prairies of Arrows, and Arrow creek, a small stream about eight yards wide, whose source is in the adjoining prairies on the south. At this cliff the Missouri is confined within a bed of two hundred yards; and about four miles to the south-east is a large lick and salt spring of great strength. About three miles further is Blackbird creek on the north side, opposite to which, is an island and a prairie inclosing a small lake. Five miles beyond this we encamped on the south side, after making, in the course of the day, thirteen miles. The land on the north is a high rich plain. On the south it is also even, of a good quality, and rising from fifty to one hundred feet.

The next morning, *10th*, we passed Deer creek, and at the distance of five miles, the two rivers called by the French the two Charatons, a corruption of Thieraton, the first of which is thirty, the second seventy yards wide, and enter the Missouri together. They are both navigable for boats: the country through which they pass is broken, rich, and thickly covered with timber. The Ayauway [Iowa] nation, consisting of three hundred men, have a village near its head-waters on the river De Moines. Farther on we passed a large island called *Chicot* or Stump Island, and encamped on the south, after making ten miles.

A head wind forced us to remain there all the next day, during which we dried the meat we had killed, and examined the surrounding country, which consists of good land, well watered, and supplied with timber: the prairies also differ from those eastward of the Mississippi, inasmuch as the latter are generally without any covering except grass, whilst the former abound with hazel, grapes and other fruits, among which is the Osage plum of a superior size and quality. On the morning of the *12th*, we passed through difficult places in the river, and reached Plum creek on the south side.

At one o'clock, we met two rafts loaded, the one with furs, the other with the tallow of buffalo; they were from the Sioux nation, and on their

7

way to St. Louis; but we were fortunate enough to engage one of them, a Mr. Durion, who had lived with that nation more than twenty years, and was high in their confidence, to accompany us thither. We made nine miles.

On the *13th*, we passed at between four and five miles, a bend of the river, and two creeks on the north, called the Round Bend creeks. Between these two creeks is the prairie, in which once stood the ancient village of the Missouris. Of this village there remains no vestige, nor is there any thing to recall this great and numerous nation, except a feeble remnant of about thirty families. They were driven from their original seats by the invasions of the Sauks [Sacs] and other Indians from the Mississippi, who destroyed at this village two hundred of them in one contest, and sought refuge near the Little Osage, on the other side of the river. The encroachment of the same enemies forced, about thirty years since, both these nations from the banks of the Missouri. A few retired with the Osage, and the remainder found an asylum on the river Platte, among the Ottoes, who are themselves declining. Opposite the plain there was an island and a French fort, but there is now no appearance of either, the successive inundations having probably washed them away, as the willow island which is in the situation described by Du Pratz, is small and of recent formation. Five miles from this place is the mouth of Grand River, where we encamped. This river follows a course nearly south, or southeast, and is between eighty and a hundred yards wide where it enters the Missouri, near a delightful and rich plain. A racoon, a bear, and some deer were obtained to-day.

We proceeded at six o'clock the next morning. The current was so rapid and the banks on the north falling in so constantly, that we were obliged to approach the sandbars on the south. These were moving continually, and formed the worst passage we had seen, and which we surmounted with much difficulty. We met a trading raft from the Pawnee nation on the river Platte, and attempted unsuccessfully to engage one of their party to return with us. At the distance of eight miles, we came to some high cliffs, called the Snake bluffs, from the number of that animal in the neighbourhood, and immediately above these bluffs, Snake creek, about eighteen yards wide, on which we encamped. One of our hunters, a half Indian, brought us an account of his having to-day passed a small lake, near which a number of deer were feeding, and in the pond he heard a snake making a guttural noise like a turkey. He fired his gun, but the noise became louder. He adds, that he has heard the Indians mention this species of snake, and this story is confirmed by a Frenchman of our party.

All the next day, the river being very high, the sandbars were so rolling and numerous, and the current so strong, that we were unable to stem it even with oars added to our sails; this obliged us to go nearer the banks, which were falling in, so that we could not make, though the boat was occasionally towed, more than fourteen miles. We passed several islands and one creek on the south side, and encamped on the north opposite a beautiful plain, which extends as far back as the Osage river, and some miles up the Missouri. In front of our encampment are the remains of an old village of the Little Osage, situated at some distance from the river, and at the foot of a small hill. About three miles above them, in view of our camp is the situation of the old village of the Missouris after they fled from the Sauks. The inroads of the same tribe compelled the Little Osage to retire from the Missouri a few years ago, and establish themselves near the Great Osages. The river, which is here about one mile wide, had risen in the morning, but fell towards evening.

Early this morning, *June 16th*, we joined the camp of our hunters, who had provided two deer and two bear, and then passing an island and a prairie on the north covered with a species of timothy, made our way through bad sandbars and a swift current, to an encampment for the evening, on the north side, at ten miles distance. The timber which we examined to-day was not sufficiently strong for oars; the mosquitoes and ticks are exceedingly troublesome. On the *17th*, we set out early, and having come to a convenient place at one mile distance, for procuring timber and making oars, we occupied ourselves in that way on this and the following day. The country on the north of the river is rich and covered with timber; among which we procured the ash for oars. At two miles it changes into extensive prairies, and at seven or eight miles distance becomes higher and waving. The prairie and high lands on the south commence more immediately on the river; the whole is well watered and provided with game, such as deer, elk, and bear. The hunters brought in a fat horse which was probably lost by some war party—this being the crossing place for the Sauks, Ayauways, and Sioux, in their excursions against the Osage.

JUNE 19TH

The oars being finished, we proceeded under a gentle breeze by two large and some smaller islands. The sandbars are numerous and so bad, that at one place we were forced to clear away the driftwood in order to pass: the water too was so rapid that we were under the necessity of towing the boat for half a mile round a point of rocks on the south side. We passed two creeks, one called Tiger creek on the north, twenty-five yards wide at the extremity of a large island called Panther Island; the other Tabo creek on the south, fifteen yards wide. Along the shores are gooseberries and raspberries in great abundance. At the distance of seventeen and a half miles we encamped on the south, near a lake about two miles from the river and several in circumference; and much frequented by deer and all kinds of fowls. On the north the land is higher and better calculated for farms than that on the south, which ascends more gradually, but is still rich and pleasant. The mosquitoes and other animals are so troublesome that mosquito biers or nets were distributed to the party.

The next morning we passed a large island, opposite to which on the north is a large and beautiful prairie, called Sauk prairie, the land being fine and well timbered on both sides the river. Pelicans were seen to-day. We made six and three quarter miles, and encamped at the lower point of a small island, along the north side of which we proceeded the next day, *June 21st*, but not without danger in consequence of the sands and the rapidity of the water which rose three inches last night. Behind another island come in from the south two creeks, called Eau, Beau, or Clear Water creeks; on the north is a very remarkable bend, where the high lands approach the river, and form an acute angle at the head of a large island produced by a narrow channel through the point of the bend. We passed several other islands, and encamped at seven and a half miles on the south.

JUNE 22D   The river rose during the night four inches. The water is very rapid and crowded with concealed timber. We passed two large islands and an extensive prairie on the south, beginning with a rich low land, and rising to the distance of seventy or eighty feet of rolling clear country. The thermometer at three o'clock P.M. was at 87°. After coming ten and a half miles we encamped on the south, opposite a large creek called Fire Prairie river.

JUNE 23D   The wind was against us this morning, and became so violent that we made only three and a half miles, and were obliged to lie to during the day at a small island. This is separated from the northern side by a narrow channel which cannot be passed by boats, being choked by trees and drifted wood. Directly opposite on the south, is a high commanding position, more than seventy feet above high water mark, and overlooking the river which is here of but little width; this spot has many advantages for a fort, and trading house with the Indians. The river fell eight inches last night.

    The next day, *24th*, we passed at eight miles distance, Hay Cabin creek coming in from the south, about twenty yards wide, and so called from camps of straw built on it; to the north are some rocks projecting into the river, and a little beyond them a creek on the same side, called Charaton Scarty; that is, Charaton like the Otter. We halted, after making eleven and a half miles, the country on both sides being fine and interspersed with prairies, in which we now see numerous herds of deer, pasturing in the plains or feeding on the young willows of the river.

JUNE 25TH   A thick fog detained us till eight o'clock, when we set sail, and at three miles reached a bank of stone coal on the north, which appeared to be very abundant: just below it is a creek called after the bank La Charbonnière. Four miles further, and on the southern side, comes in a small creek, called La Bénite. The prairies here approach the river and contain many fruits, such as plums, raspberries, wild apples, and nearer the river vast quantities of mulberries. Our encampment was at thirteen miles distance on an island to the north, opposite some hills higher than usual, and almost one hundred and sixty or one hundred and eighty feet.

JUNE 26TH   At one mile we passed at the end of a small island, Blue Water creek, which is about thirty yards wide at its entrance from the south. Here the Missouri is confined within a narrow bed, and the current still more so by counter currents or whirls on one side and a high bank on the other. We passed a small island and a sandbar, where our tow rope broke twice, and we rowed round with great exertions. We saw a number of parroquets, and killed some deer; after nine and three-quarter miles we encamped at the upper point of the mouth of the river Kanzas: here we remained two days, during which we made the necessary observations, recruited the party, and repaired the boat.

    The river Kanzas takes its rise in the plains between the Arkansaw and Platte rivers, and pursues a course generally east till its junction with the Missouri which is in latitude 38° 31′ 13″; here it is three hundred and forty and a quarter yards wide, though it is wider a short distance above the mouth. The Missouri itself is about five hundred yards in width; the point of union is low and subject to inundations for two hundred and fifty yards, it then rises a little above high water mark, and continues so as far back as

MANDAN CHIEF (Bodmer)

the hills. On the south of the Kanzas the hills or highlands come within one mile and a half of the river; on the north of the Missouri they do not approach nearer than several miles; but on all sides the country is fine. The comparative specific gravities of the two rivers is, for the Missouri seventy-eight, the Kansas seventy-two degrees; the waters of the latter have a very disagreeable taste; the former has risen during yesterday and to-day about two feet. On the banks of the Kanzas reside the Indians of the same name, consisting of two villages, one at about twenty, the other forty leagues from its mouth, and amounting to about three hundred men. They once lived twenty-four leagues higher than the Kanzas, on the south bank of the Missouri, and were then more numerous, but they have been reduced and banished by the Sauks and Ayauways, who being better supplied with arms have an advantage over the Kanzas, though the latter are not less fierce or warlike than themselves. This nation is now hunting in the plains for the buffalo which our hunters have seen for the first time.

JUNE 29TH

We set out late in the afternoon, and having passed a sandbar, near which the boat was almost lost, and a large island on the north, we encamped at seven and a quarter miles on the same side in the low lands, where the rushes are so thick that it is troublesome to walk through them. Early the next morning, *30th*, we reached, at five miles distance, the mouth of a river coming in from the north, and called by the French, Petite Rivière Platte, or Little Shallow river; it is about sixty yards wide at its mouth. A few of the party who ascended informed us, that the lands on both sides are good, and that there are several falls well calculated for mills; the wind was from the south west, and the weather oppressively warm, the thermometer standing at 96° above 0 at three o'clock P.M. One mile beyond this is a small creek on the south, at five miles from which we encamped on the same side, opposite the lower point of an island called Diamond island. The land on the north between the Little Shallow river and the Missouri is not good and subject to overflow—on the south it is higher and better timbered.

Sunday, July 1st, 1804

We proceeded along the north side of Diamond island, where a small creek called Biscuit creek empties itself. One and a half miles above the island is a large sandbar in the middle of the river, beyond which we stopped to refresh the men, who suffered very much from the heat. Here we observed great quantities of grapes and raspberries. Between one and two miles further are three islands and a creek on the south known by the French name of Remore. The main current, which is now on the south side of the largest of the three islands, ran three years [ago], as we were told, on the north, and there was then no appearance of the two smaller islands. At the distance of four and a half miles we reached the lower point of a cluster of small islands, two large and two small, called Isles des Parcs or Field Islands. Paccaun [pecan] trees were this day seen, and large quantities of deer and turkies on the banks. We had advanced twelve miles.

JULY 2D We left our encampment, opposite to which is a high and beautiful prairie on the southern side, and passed up the south of the islands, which are high meadows, and a creek on the north called Parc creek. Here for half an hour the river became covered with drift wood, which rendered the navigation dangerous, and was probably caused by the giving way of some sandbar, which had detained the wood. After making five miles we passed a stream on the south called Turky creek, near a sandbar, where we could scarcely stem the current with twenty oars, and all the poles we had. On the north at about two miles further is a large island called by the Indians, Wau-car-da-war-card-da, or the Bear Medicine island. Here we landed and replaced our mast, which had been broken three days ago, by running against a tree, overhanging the river. Thence we proceeded, and after night stopped on the north side, above the island, having come eleven and a half miles. Opposite our camp is a valley, in which was situated an old village of the Kanzas, between two high points of land, and on the bank of the river. About a mile in the rear of the village was a small fort, built by the French on an elevation. There are now no traces of the village, but the situation of the fort may be recognized by some remains of chimnies, and the general outline of the fortification, as well as by the fine spring which supplied it with water. The party, who were stationed here, were probably cut off by the Indians, as there are no accounts of them.

JULY 3D A gentle breeze from the south carried us eleven and a quarter miles this day, past two islands, one a small willow island, the other large, and called by the French Isle des Vaches, or Cow island. At the head of this island, on the northern shore, is a large pond containing beaver, and fowls of different kinds. After passing a bad sandbar, we stopped on the south side at an old trading house, which is now deserted, and half a mile beyond it encamped on the south. The land is fine along the rivers, and some distance back. We observed the black walnut and oak, among the timber; and the honey-suckle and the buck's-eye, with the nuts on them.

The morning of the *4th July* was announced by the discharge of our gun. At one mile we reached the mouth of a bayeau or creek, coming from a large lake on the north side, which appears as if it had once been the bed of the river, to which it runs parallel for several miles. The water of it is clear and supplied by a small creek and several springs, and the number of goslings which we saw on it, induced us to call it the Gosling lake. It is about three-quarters of a mile wide, and seven or eight miles long. One of our men was bitten by a snake, but a poultice of bark and gunpowder was sufficient to cure the wound. At ten and a quarter miles we reached a creek on the south about twelve yards wide and coming from an extensive prairie, which approached the borders of the river. To this creek, which had no name, we gave that of Fourth of July creek; above it is a high mound, where three Indian paths centre, and from which is a very extensive prospect. After fifteen miles sail we came to on the north a little above a creek on the southern side, about thirty yards wide, which we called Independence creek, in honour of the day, which we could celebrate only by an evening gun, and an additional gill of whiskey to the men.

The next day, *5th*, we crossed over to the south and came along the bank of an extensive and beautiful prairie, interspersed with copses of timber, and watered by Independence creek. On this bank formerly stood the second village of the Kanzas; from the remains it must have been once a large town. We passed several bad sandbars, and a small creek to the south, which we called Yellow Ochre creek, from a bank of that mineral a little above it. The river continues to fall. On the shores are great quantities of summer and fall grapes, berries and wild roses. Deer is not so abundant as usual, but there are numerous tracks of elk around us. We encamped at ten miles distance on the south side under a high bank, opposite to which was a low land covered with tall rushes, and some timber.

JULY 6TH

We set sail, and at one mile passed a sandbar, three miles further an island, a prairie to the north, at the distance of four miles, called Reevey's prairie, after a man who was killed there; at which place the river is confined to a very narrow channel, and by a sandbar from the south. Four miles beyond is another sandbar terminated by a small willow island, and forming a very considerable bend in the river towards the north. The sand of the bar is light, intermixed with small pebbles and some pit coal. The river falls slowly, and, owing either to the muddiness of its water, or the extreme heat of the weather, the men perspire profusely. We encamped on the south having made twelve miles. The bird called whip-poor-will sat on the boat for some time.

In the morning, *July 7th*, the rapidity of the water obliged us to draw the boat along with ropes. At six and three quarter miles, we came to a sandbar, at a point opposite a fine rich prairie on the north, called St. Michael's. The prairies of this neighbourhood have the appearance of distinct farms, divided by narrow strips of woodland, which follow the borders of the small runs leading to the river. Above this, about a mile, is a cliff of yellow clay on the north. At four o'clock we passed a narrow part of the channel, where the water is confined within a bed of two hundred yards wide, the current running directly against the southern bank with no sand on the north to confine it or break its force. We made fourteen miles, and halted on the north, after which we had a violent gust about seven o'clock. One of the hunters saw in a pond to the north which we passed yesterday a number of young swans. We saw a large rat, and killed a wolf. Another of our men had a stroke of the sun; he was bled, and took a preparation of nitre which relieved him considerably.

JULY 8TH

We set out early, and soon passed a small creek on the north, which we called Ordway's creek, from our sergeant of that name who had been sent on shore with the horses, and went up it. On the same side are three small islands, one of which is the Little Nodawa, and a large island called the Great Nodawa extending more than five miles, and containing seven or eight thousand acres of high good land, rarely overflowed, and one of the largest islands of the Missouri. It is separated from the northern shore by a small channel of from forty-five to eighty yards wide, up which we passed, and found near the western extremity of the island the mouth of the river Nodawa.

This river pursues nearly a southern course, is navigable for boats to some distance, and about seventy yards wide above the mouth, though not so wide immediately there, as the mud from the Missouri contracts its chan-

13

nel. At twelve and a quarter miles, we encamped on the north side, near the head of Nodawa island, and opposite a smaller one in the middle of the river. Five of the men were this day sick with violent headaches. The river continues to fall.

JULY 9TH　We passed the island opposite to which we last night encamped, and saw near the head of it a creek falling in from a pond on the north, to which we gave the name of Pike pond, from the numbers of that animal which some of our party saw from the shore. The wind changed at eight from N. E. to S. W. and brought rain. At six miles we passed the mouth of Monter's creek on the south, and two miles above a few cabins, where one of our party had encamped with some Frenchmen about two years ago. Further on we passed an island on the north, opposite some cliffs on the south side, near which Loup or Wolf river falls into the Missouri. This river is about sixty yards wide, it heads near the same sources as the Kanzas, and is navigable for boats, at some distance up. At fourteen miles we encamped on the south side.

JULY 10TH　*Tuesday.* We proceeded on by a prairie on the upper side of Wolf river, and at four miles passed a creek fifteen yards wide on the south, called Pape's creek after a Spaniard of that name, who killed himself there. At six miles we dined on an island called by the French Isle de Salomon, or Solomon's island, opposite to which on the south is a beautiful plain covered with grass, intermixed with wild rye and a kind of wild potato. After making ten miles we stopped for the night on the northern side, opposite a cliff of yellow clay. The river has neither risen nor fallen to-day. On the north the low land is very extensive, and covered with vines; on the south, the hills approach nearer the river, and back of them commence the plains. There are a great many goslings along the banks.

JULY 11TH　*Wednesday.* After three miles sailing we came to a willow island on the north side, behind which enters a creek called by the Indians Tarkio. Above this creek on the north the low lands are subject to overflow, and further back the undergrowth of vines particularly, is so abundant that they can scarcely be passed. Three miles from the Tarkio we encamped on a large sand island on the north, immediately opposite the river Nemahaw.

JULY 12TH　*Thursday.* We remained here to-day for the purpose of refreshing the party, and making lunar observations. The Nemahaw empties itself into the Missouri from the south, and is eighty yards wide at the confluence, which is in lat. 39° 55′ 56″. Captain Clark ascended it in the periogue about two miles to the mouth of a small creek on the lower side. On going ashore he found in the level plain several artificial mounds or graves, and on the adjoining hills others of a larger size. This appearance indicates sufficiently the former population of this country, the mounds being certainly intended as tombs; the Indians of the Missouri still preserving the custom of interring the dead on high ground. From the top of the highest mound a delightful prospect presented itself—the level and extensive meadows watered by the Nemahaw, and enlivened by the few trees and shrubs skirting the borders of the river and its tributary streams—the lowland of the Missouri covered with undulating grass, nearly five feet high, gradually rising into a second plain, where rich weeds and flowers are interspersed with copses of the Osage plum; further back are seen small groves of trees; an abundance of grapes; the wild cherry of the Missouri, resembling our own, but larger, and growing on a small bush; and the chokecherry, which we observed for the first time. Some of the grapes gathered to-day are nearly ripe. On the south of the Nemahaw, and about a quarter of a mile from its mouth, is a cliff of freestone, in which are various inscriptions and marks made by the Indians. The sand island where we are encamped, is covered with the two species of willow, broad and narrow leaf.

JULY 13TH We proceeded at sunrise with a fair wind from the south, and at two miles, passed the mouth of a small river on the north, called Big Tarkio. A channel from the bed of the Missouri once ran into this river, and formed an island called St. Joseph's, but the channel is now filled up, and the island is added to the northern shore. Further on to the south, is situated an extensive plain, covered with a grass resembling timothy in its general appearance, except the seed, which is like flax-seed, and also a number of grape-vines. At twelve miles, we passed an island on the north, above which is a large sandbar covered with willows: and at twenty and a half miles, stopped on a large sandbar, in the middle of the river opposite a high handsome prairie, which extends to the hills four or five miles distant, though near the bank the land is low, and subject to be overflowed. This day was exceedingly fine and pleasant, a storm of wind and rain from north northeast, last night, having cooled the air.

JULY 14TH We had some hard showers of rain before seven o'clock, when we set out. We had just reached the end of the sand island, and seen the opposite banks falling in, and so lined with timber that we could not approach it without danger, when a sudden squall, from the northeast, struck the boat on the starboard quarter, and would have certainly dashed her to pieces on the sand island, if the party had not leaped into the river, and with the aid of the anchor and cable kept her off: the waves dashing over her for the space of forty minutes; after which, the river became almost instantaneously calm and smooth. The two periogues were ahead, in a situation nearly similar, but fortunately no damage was done to the boats or the loading. The wind having shifted to the southeast, we came at the distance of two miles, to an island on the north, where we dined. One mile above, on the same side of the river, is a small factory, where a merchant of St. Louis traded with the Ottoes and Pawnees two years ago. Near this is an extensive lowland, part of which is overflowed occasionally, the rest is rich and well timbered. The wind again changed to northwest by north. At seven and a half miles, we reached the lower point of a large island, on the north side. A small distance above this point is a river, called by the Maha [Omaha] Indians Nishnahbatona. This is a considerable creek, nearly as large as the Mine river, and runs parallel to the Missouri the greater part of its course, being fifty yards wide at the mouth. In the prairies or glades, we saw wild-timothy, lambsquarter, cuckleberries, and on the edges of the river, summer-grapes, plums, and gooseberries. We also saw to-day, for the first time, some elk, at which some of the party shot, but at too great a distance. We encamped on the north side of the island, a little above Nishnahbatona, having made nine miles. The river fell a little.

JULY 15TH   A thick fog prevented our leaving the encampment before seven. At about four miles, we reached the extremity of the large island, and crossing to the south, at the distance of seven miles, arrived at the Little Nemaha, a small river from the south, forty yards wide a little above its mouth, but contracting, as do almost all the waters emptying into the Missouri, at its confluence. At nine and three-quarter miles, we encamped on a woody point, on the south. Along the southern bank, is a rich lowland covered with peavine, and rich weeds, and watered by small streams rising in the adjoining prairies. They too, are rich, and though with abundance of grass, have no timber except what grows near the water: interspersed through both are grapevines, plums of two kinds, two species of wild-cherries, hazelnuts, and gooseberries. On the south there is one unbroken plain; on the north the river is skirted with some timber, behind which the plain extends four or five miles to the hills, which seem to have little wood.

A page from Sergeant Floyd's diary.

JULY 16TH   We continued our route between a large island opposite to our last night's encampment, and an extensive prairie on the south. About six miles, we came to another large island, called Fairsun [Fair Sun] island, on the same side; above which is a spot, where about twenty acres of the hill have fallen into the river. Near this, is a cliff of sandstone for two miles, which is much frequented by birds. At this place the river is about one mile wide, but not deep; as the timber, or sawyers, may be seen, scattered across the whole of its bottom. At twenty miles distance, we saw on the south, an island called by the French, l'Isle Chauve, or Bald island, opposite to a large prairie, which we called Baldpated prairie, from a ridge of naked hills which bound

16

it, running parallel with the river as far as we could see, and from three to six miles distance. To the south the hills touch the river. We encamped a quarter of a mile beyond this, in a point of woods on the north side. The river continues to fall.

Tuesday. We remained here this day, in order to make observations and correct the chronometer, which ran down on Sunday. The latitude we found to be 40° 27′ 5$\frac{4}{10}$″. The observation of the time proved our chronometer too slow, by 6′ 51$\frac{6}{10}$″. The highlands bear from our camp, north 25° west, up the river. Captain Lewis rode up the country, and saw the Nishnahbatona, about ten or twelve miles from its mouth, at a place not more than three hundred yards from the Missouri, and a little above our camp. It then passes near the foot of the Baldhills, and is at least six feet below the level of the Missouri. On its banks are the oak, walnut, and mulberry. The common current of the Missouri, taken with the log, is 50 fathoms in 40″, at some places, and even 20″.

JULY 17TH

Wednesday. The morning was fair, and a gentle wind from southeast by south, carried us along between the prairie on the north, and Bald island to the south: opposite the middle of which, the Nishnahbatona approaches the nearest to the Missouri. The current here ran fifty fathoms in 41″. At thirteen and a half miles, we reached an island on the north, near to which the banks overflow; while on the south, the hills project over the river and form high cliffs. At one point a part of the cliff, nearly three-quarters of a mile in length, and about two hundred feet in height, has fallen into the river. It is composed chiefly of sandstone intermixed with an iron ore of bad quality; near the bottom is a soft slatestone with pebbles. We passed several bad sandbars in the course of the day, and made eighteen miles, and encamped on the south, opposite to the lower point of the Oven islands. The country around is generally divided into prairies, with little timber, except on low points, islands, and near creeks, and that consisting of cottonwood, mulberry, elm, and sycamore. The river falls fast. An Indian dog came to the bank; he appeared to have been lost and was nearly starved: we gave him some food, but he would not follow us.

JULY 18TH

Thursday. The Oven islands are small, and two in number; one near the south shore, the other in the middle of the river. Opposite to them is the prairie, called Terrien's Oven, from a trader of that name. At four and a half miles, we reached some high cliffs of a yellow earth, on the south, near which are two beautiful runs of water, rising in the adjacent prairies, and one of them with a deer-lick, about two hundred yards from its mouth. In this neighbourhood we observed some iron ore in the bank. At two and a half miles above the runs, a large portion of the hill, for nearly three-quarters of a mile, has fallen into the river. We encamped on the western extremity of an island, in the middle of the river, having made ten and three-quarter miles. The river falls a little. The sandbars which we passed to-day, are more numerous, and the rolling sands more frequent and dangerous, than any we have seen; these obstacles increasing as we approach the river Platte. The Missouri here is wider also than below, where the timber on the banks resists the current; while here the prairies which approach, are more easily

JULY 19TH

washed and undermined. The hunters have brought for the last few days, no quadruped, but deer: great quantities of young geese are seen to-day: one of them brought calamus, which he had gathered opposite our encampment, and a large quantity of sweet-flag.

JULY 20TH   *Friday.* There was a heavy dew last night, and this morning was foggy and cool. We passed at about three miles distance, a small willow island to the north, and a creek on the south, about twenty-five yards wide, called by the French, L'Eau qui Pleure, or the Weeping Water, and emptying itself just above a cliff of brown clay. Thence we made two and a half miles to another island; three miles further to a third: six miles beyond which is a fourth island; at the head of which we encamped on the southern shore; in all eighteen miles. The party, who walked on the shore to-day, found the plains to the south, rich, but much parched with frequent fires, and with no timber, except the scattering trees about the sources of the runs, which are numerous and fine. On the north, is a similar prairie country. The river continues to fall. A large yellow wolf was this day killed.

For a month past the party have been troubled with boils, and occasionally with the dysentery. These boils were large tumours which broke out under the arms, on the legs, and, generally, in the parts most exposed to action, which sometimes became too painful to permit the men to work. After remaining some days, they disappeared without any assistance, except a poultice of the bark of the elm, or of Indian meal. This disorder, which we ascribe to the muddiness of the river water, has not affected the general health of the party, which is quite as good, if not better, than that of the same number of men in any other situation.

JULY 21ST   *Saturday.* We had a breeze from the southeast, by the aid of which we passed, at about ten miles, a willow island on the south, near high lands covered with timber, at the bank, and formed of limestone with cemented shells: on the opposite side is a bad sandbar, and the land near it is cut through at high water, by small channels forming a number of islands. The wind lulled at seven o'clock, and we reached, in the rain, the mouth of the great river Platte, at the distance of fourteen miles. The highlands which had accompanied us on the south, for the last eight or ten miles, stopped at about three quarters of a mile from the entrance of the Platte. Captains Lewis and Clark ascended the river in a periogue, for about one mile, and found the current very rapid; rolling over sands, and divided into a number of channels; none of which are deeper than five or six feet. One of our Frenchmen, who spent two winters on it, says that it spreads much more at some distance from the mouth; that its depth is generally not more than five or six feet; that there are many small islands scattered through it, and that from its rapidity and the quantity of its sand, it cannot be navigated by boats or periogues, though the Indians pass it in small flat canoes made of hides. That the Saline or Salt river, which in some seasons is too brackish to be drank, falls into it from the south about thirty miles up, and a little above it Elkhorn river from the north, running nearly parallel with the Missouri. The river is, in fact, much more rapid than the Missouri, the bed of which it fills with moving sands, and drives the current on the northern shore, on which it is constantly encroaching. At its junction the Platte is about six hundred yards wide, and the same number of miles from the Mississippi. With much difficulty we worked round the sandbars near the mouth, and came to above the point, having made fifteen miles. A number of wolves were seen and heard around us in the evening.

The next morning we set sail, and having found at the distance of ten miles from the Platte, a high and shaded situation on the north, we encamped there, intending to make the requisite observations, and to send for the neighbouring tribes, for the purpose of making known the recent change in the government, and the wish of the United States to cultivate their friendship. JULY 22D

Chapter 2

FROM THE PLATTE TO THE VERMILION RIVER

Our camp is by observation in latitude 41° 3′ 11″. Immediately behind it is a plain about five miles wide, one half covered with wood, the other dry and elevated. The low grounds on the south near the junction of the two rivers, are rich, but subject to be overflowed. Farther up, the banks are higher, and opposite our camp the first hills approach the river, and are covered with timber, such as oak, walnut, and elm. The intermediate country is watered by the Papillon, or Butterfly creek, of about eighteen yards wide, and three miles from the Platte; on the north are high open plains and prairies, and at nine miles from the Platte, the Mosquito creek, and two or three small willow islands.

We stayed here several days, during which we dried our provisions, made new oars, and prepared our despatches and maps of the country we had passed, for the president of the United States, to whom we intend to send them by a periogue from this place. The hunters have found game scarce in this neighbourhood; they have seen deer, turkeys, and grouse; we have also an abundance of ripe grapes; and one of our men caught a white catfish, the eyes of which were small, and its tail resembling that of a dolphin. The present season is that in which the Indians go out into the prairies to hunt the buffalo; but as we discovered some hunter's tracks, and observed the plains on fire in the direction of their villages, we hoped that they might have returned to gather the green Indian corn, and therefore despatched two men to the Ottoes or Pawnee villages with a present of tobacco, and an invitation to the chiefs to visit us. They returned after two days absence. Their first course was through an open prairie to the south, in which they crossed Butterfly creek. They then reached a small beautiful river, called Corne de Cerf, or Elkhorn river, about one hundred yards wide, with clear water and a gravelly channel. It empties a little below the Ottoe village into the Platte, which they crossed, and arrived at the town about forty-five miles from our camp. They found no Indians there, though they saw some fresh tracks of a small party.

The Ottoes were once a powerful nation, and lived about twenty miles above the Platte, on the southern bank of the Missouri. Being reduced, they migrated to the neighbourhood of the Pawnees, under whose protection they now live. Their village is on the south side of the Platte, about thirty miles from its mouth; and their number is two hundred men, including about thirty families of Missouri Indians, who are incorporated with them.

Five leagues above them, on the same side of the river, resides the nation of Pawnees. This people were among the most numerous of the Missouri Indians, but have gradually been dispersed and broken, and even since the year 1797, have undergone some sensible changes. They now consist of four bands; the first is the one just mentioned, of about five hundred men, to whom of late years have been added the second band, who are called republican Pawnees, from their having lived on the republican branch of the river Kanzas, whence they emigrated to join the principal band of Pawnees: the republican Pawnees amount to nearly two hundred and fifty men. The third, are the Pawnees Loups, or Wolf Pawnees, who reside on the Wolf fork of the Platte, about ninety miles from the principal Pawnees, and number two hundred and eighty men. The fourth band originally resided on the Kanzas and Arkansaw, but in their wars with the Osages, they were so often defeated, that they at last retired to their present position on the Red river, where they form a tribe of four hundred men. All these tribes live in villages, and raise corn; but during the intervals of culture rove in the plains in quest of buffalo.

Beyond them on the river, and westward of the Black mountains, are the Kaninaviesch, consisting of about four hundred men. They are supposed to have emigrated originally from the Pawnees nation; but they have degenerated from the improvements of the parent tribe, and no longer live in villages, but rove through the plains.

Still further to the westward, are several tribes, who wander and hunt on the sources of the river Platte, and thence to Rock Mountain. These tribes, of which little more is known than the names and the population, are first, the Staitan, or Kite Indians, a small tribe of one hundred men. They have acquired the name of Kites, from their flying; that is, their being always on horseback; and the smallness of their numbers is to be attributed to their extreme ferocity; they are the most warlike of all the western Indians; they never yield in battle; they never spare their enemies; and the retaliation of this barbarity has almost extinguished the nation. Then come the Wetapahato, and Kiawa tribes, associated together, and amounting to two hundred men; the Castahana, of three hundred men, to which are to be added the Cataka of seventy-five men, and the Dotami. These wandering tribes, are conjectured to be the remnants of the Great Padouca nation, who occupied the country between the upper parts of the river Platte, and the river Kanzas. They were visited by Bourgemont, in 1724, and then lived on the Kanzas river. The seats, which he describes as their residence, are now occupied by the Kanzas nation; and of the Padoucas, there does not now exist even the name.

JULY 27TH Having completed the object of our stay, we set sail, with a pleasant breeze from the N. W. The two horses swam over to the southern shore, along which we went, passing by an island, at three and a half miles, formed by a pond, fed by springs: three miles further is a large sand island, in the middle of the river; the land on the south being high, and covered with timber; that on the north, a high prairie. At ten and a half miles from our encampment, we saw and examined a curious collection of graves or mounds, on the south side of the river. Not far from a low piece of land and a pond, is a tract of about two hundred acres in circumference, which is covered with mounds of different heights, shapes, and sizes: some of sand, and some of both earth and sand; the largest being nearest the river. These mounds indicate the position of the ancient village of the Ottoes, before they retired to the protection of the Pawnees. After making fifteen miles, we encamped on the south, on the bank of a high handsome prairie, with lofty cottonwood in groves, near the river.

JULY 28TH At one mile, this morning we reached a bluff, on the north, being the first highlands, which approach the river on that side, since we left the Nodawa. Above this, is an island and a creek, about fifteen yards wide, which, as it has no name, we called Indian Knob creek, from a number of round knobs bare of timber, on the highlands, to the north. A little below the bluff, on the north, is the spot where the Ayauway Indians formerly lived. They were a branch of the Ottoes, and emigrated from this place to the river Desmoines. At ten and three-quarter miles, we encamped on the north, opposite an island, in the middle of the river. The land, generally, on the north, consists of high prairie and hills, with timber: on the south, low and covered with cottonwood. Our hunter brought to us in the evening, a Missouri Indian, whom he had found, with two others, dressing an elk; they were perfectly friendly, gave him some of the meat, and one of them agreed to accompany him to the boat. He is one of the few remaining Missouris, who live with the Ottoes: he belongs to a small party, whose camp is four miles from the river; and he says, that the body of the nation is now hunting buffalo in the plains: he appeared quite sprightly, and his language resembled that of the Osage, particularly in his calling a chief, inca.

We sent him back with one of our party next morning, *Sunday, July 29th*, with an invitation to the Indians, to meet us above on the river, and then proceeded. We soon came to a northern bend in the river, which runs within twenty yards of Indian Knob creek, the water of which is five feet higher than that of the Missouri. In less than two miles, we passed Boyer's creek on the north, of twenty-five yards width. We stopped to dine under a shade, near the highland on the south, and caught several large catfish, one of them nearly white, and all very fat. Above this highland, we observed the traces of a great hurricane, which passed the river obliquely from N. W. to S. E. and tore up large trees, some of which perfectly sound, and four feet in diameter, were snapped off near the ground. We made ten miles to a wood on the north, where we encamped. The Missouri is much more crooked, since we passed the river Platte, though generally speaking, not so rapid; more of prairie, with less timber, and cottonwood in the low grounds, and oak, black walnut, hickory, and elm.

JULY 30TH We went early in the morning, three and a quarter miles, and encamped on the south, in order to wait for the Ottoes. The land here consists of a plain, above the highwater level, the soil of which is fertile, and covered with a grass from five to eight feet high, interspersed with copses of large plums, and a currant, like those of the United States. It also furnishes two species of honeysuckle; one growing to a kind of shrub, common about Harrodsburgh (Kentucky), the other is not so high: the flowers grow in clusters, are short, and of a light pink colour; the leaves too, are distinct, and do not surround the stalk, as do those of the common honeysuckle of the United States. Back of this plain, is a woody ridge about seventy feet above it, at the end of which we formed our camp. This ridge separates the lower from a higher prairie, of a good quality, with grass, of ten or twelve inches in height, and extending back about a mile, to another elevation, of eighty or ninety feet, beyond which is one continued plain. Near our camp, we enjoy from the bluffs a most beautiful view of the river, and the adjoining country. At a distance, varying from four to ten miles, and of a height between seventy and three hundred feet, two parallel ranges of highland affords a passage to the Missouri, which enriches the low grounds between them. In its winding course, it nourishes the willow islands, the scattered cottonwood, elm, sycamore, lynn, and ash, and the groves are interspersed with hickory, walnut, coffeenut, and oak.

The meridian altitude of this day made the latitude of our camp 41° 18′ 1$\frac{4}{10}$″. The hunters supplied us with deer, turkeys, geese, and beaver; one of the last was caught alive, and in a very short time was perfectly tamed. Catfish are very abundant in the river, and we have also seen a buffalo fish. One of our men brought in yesterday an animal called, by the Pawnees, chocartoosh, and, by the French, blaireau, or badger. The evening is cool, yet the mosquitoes are still very troublesome.

JULY 31ST

We waited with much anxiety the return of our messenger to the Ottoes. The men whom we despatched to our last encampment, returned without having seen any appearance of its having been visited. Our horses too had strayed; but we were so fortunate as to recover them at the distance of twelve miles. Our apprehensions were at length relieved by the arrival of a party of about fourteen Ottoe and Missouri Indians, who came at sunset, on the second of August, accompanied by a Frenchman, who resided among them, and interpreted for us. Captains Lewis and Clark went out to meet them, and told them that we would hold a council in the morning. In the mean time we sent them some roasted meat, pork, flour, and meal; in return for which they made us a present of watermelons. We learnt that our man Liberté had set out from their camp a day before them; we were in hopes that he had fatigued his horse, or lost himself in the woods, and would soon return; but we never saw him again.

Captain Lewis addresses a tribal council (from the journal of Patrick Gass).

Friday, August 3d, 1804

The next morning the Indians, with their six chiefs, were all assembled under an awning, formed with the mainsail, in presence of all our party, paraded for the occasion. A speech was then made, announcing to them the change in the government, our promises of protection, and advice as to their future conduct. All the six chiefs replied to our speech, each in his turn, according to rank: they expressed their joy at the change in the government; their hopes that we would recommend them to their great father (the president), that they might obtain trade and necessaries; they wanted arms as well for hunting as for defence, and asked our mediation between them and the Mahas, with whom they are now at war. We promised to do so, and wished some of them to accompany us to that nation, which they declined, for fear of being killed by them. We then proceeded to distribute our presents. The grand chief of the nation not being of the party, we sent him a flag, a medal, and some ornaments for clothing. To the six chiefs who were present, we gave a medal of the second grade to one Ottoe chief, and one Missouri chief; a medal of the third grade to two inferior chiefs of each nation: the customary mode of recognizing a chief, being to place a medal round his neck, which is considered among his tribe as a proof of his consideration abroad. Each of these medals was accompanied by a present of paint, garters, and cloth ornaments of dress; and to this we added a canister of powder, a bottle of whiskey, and a few presents to the whole, which appeared to make them perfectly satisfied. The air-gun too was fired, and astonished them greatly. The absent grand chief was an Ottoe, named Weahrushhah, which, in English, degenerates into Little Thief. The two principal chieftains present were, Shongotongo, or Big Horse; and Wethea, or Hospitality; also Shosguscan, or White Horse, an Ottoe; the first an Ottoe, the second a Missouri. The incidents just related, induced us to give to this place the name of the Council-bluff; the situation of it is exceedingly favourable for a fort and trading factory, as the soil is well calculated for bricks, and there is an abundance of wood in the neighbourhood, and the air being pure and healthy. It is also central to the chief resorts of the Indians: one day's journey to the Ottoes; one and a half to the great Pawnees; two days from the Mahas; two and a quarter from the Pawnees Loups village; convenient to the hunting grounds of the Sioux; and twenty-five days journey to Santa Fee [sic].

The ceremonies of the council being concluded, we set sail in the afternoon, and encamped at the distance of five miles, on the south side, where we found the mosquitoes very troublesome.

AUGUST 4TH   A violent wind, accompanied by rain, purified and cooled the atmosphere last night; we proceeded early, and reached a very narrow part of the river, where the channel is confined within a space of two hundred yards, by a sand point on the north, and a bend on the south; the banks in the neighbourhood washing away, the trees falling in, and the channel filled with buried logs. Above this is a trading house, on the south, where one of our party passed two years, trading with the Mahas. At nearly four miles, is a creek on the south, emptying opposite a large island of sand; between this creek and our last night's encampment, the river has changed its bed, and encroached on the southern shore. About two miles further, is another creek on the south, which, like the former, is the outlet of three ponds, communicating with each other, and forming a small lake, which is fed by streams from the highlands. At fifteen miles, we encamped on the south. The hills on both sides of the river are nearly twelve or fifteen miles from each other; those of the north containing some timber, while the hills of the south are without any covering, except some scattering wood in the ravines, and near where the creeks pass into the hills, rich plains and prairies occupying the intermediate space, and partially covered, near the water, with cottonwood. There has been a great deal of pumice-stone on the shore to-day.

AUGUST 5TH

We set out early, and, by means of our oars, made twenty and a half miles, though the river was crowded with sandbars. On both sides the prairies extend along the river; the banks being covered with great quantities of grapes, of which three different species are now ripe; one large and resembling the purple grape. We had some rain this morning, attended by high wind; but generally speaking, have remarked that thunder storms are less frequent than in the Atlantic states, at this season. Snakes too are less frequent, though we killed one to-day of the shape and size of the rattlesnake, but of a lighter colour. We fixed our camp on the north side.

In the evening, Captain Clark, in pursuing some game, in an eastern direction, found himself at the distance of three hundred and seventy yards from the camp, at a point of the river whence we had come twelve miles. When the water is high, this peninsula is overflowed, and judging from the customary and notorious changes in the river, a few years will be sufficient to force the main current of the river across, and leave the great bend dry. The whole lowland between the parallel range of hills seems formed of mud or ooze of the river, at some former period, mixed with sand and clay. The sand of the neighbouring banks accumulates with the aid of that brought down the stream, and forms sandbars, projecting into the river; these drive the channel to the opposite banks, the loose texture of which it undermines, and at length deserts its ancient bed for a new and shorter passage; it is thus that the banks of the Missouri are constantly falling, and the river changing its bed.

AUGUST 6TH

In the morning, after a violent storm of wind and rain from N. W. we passed a large island to the north. In the channel separating it from the shore, a creek called Soldier's river enters; the island kept it from our view, but one of our men who had seen it, represents it as about forty yards wide at its mouth. At five miles, we came to a bend of the river towards the north, a sandbar, running in from the south, had turned its course so as to leave the old channel quite dry. We again saw the same appearance at our encampment, twenty and a half miles distant on the north side. Here the channel of the river had encroached south, and the old bed was without water, except a few ponds. The sandbars are still very numerous.

AUGUST 7TH

We had another storm from the N. W. in the course of the last evening; in the morning we proceeded, having the wind from the north, and encamped on the northern shore, having rowed seventeen miles. The river is here encumbered with sandbars, but no islands, except two small ones, called Detachment islands, and formed on the south side by a small stream.

We despatched four men back to the Ottoes village in quest of our man, Liberté, and to apprehend one of the soldiers, who left us on the *4th*, under pretence of recovering a knife which he had dropped a short distance behind, and who we fear has deserted. We also sent small presents to the Ottoes and Missouris, and requested that they would join us at the Maha village, where a peace might be concluded between them.

AUGUST 8TH

At two miles distance, this morning we came to a part of the river, where there was concealed timber difficult to pass. The wind was from the N. W. and we proceeded in safety. At six miles, a river empties on the northern side, called by the Sioux Indians, Eaneahwadepon, or Stone river; and by the French, Petite Rivière des Sioux, or Little Sioux river. At its confluence it is eighty yards wide. Our interpreter, Mr. Durion, who has been to the sources of it, and knows the adjoining country, says that it rises within about nine miles of the river Desmoines; that within fifteen leagues of that river it passes through a large lake nearly sixty miles in circumference, and divided into two parts by rocks which approach each other very closely: its width is various: it contains many islands, and is known by the name of the Lac d'Esprit: it is near the Dog-plains [Prairie du Chien], and within four days march of the Mahas. The country watered by it, is open and undulating, and may be visited in boats up the river for some distance. The Desmoines, he adds, is about eighty yards wide where the Little Sioux river approaches it: it is shoaly, and one of its principal branches is called Cat river. Two miles beyond this river is a long island which we called Pelican island, from the numbers of that animal which were feeding on it: one of these being killed, we poured into his bag five gallons of water. An elk, too, was shot, and we had again to remark that snakes are rare in this part of the Missouri. A meridian altitude near the Little Sioux river made the latitude 41° 42′ 34″. We encamped on the north, having come sixteen miles.

AUGUST 9TH A thick fog detained us until past seven o'clock, after which we proceeded with a gentle breeze from the southeast. After passing two sandbars we reached, at seven and a half miles, a point of highland on the left, near which the river has forced itself a channel across a peninsula, leaving on the right a circuit of twelve or eighteen miles, which is now recognized by the ponds and islands it contains. At seventeen and a half miles, we reached a point on the north, where we encamped. The hills are at a great distance from the river for the last several days; the land on both sides low, and covered with cottonwood and abundance of grape vines. An elk was seen to-day, a turkey also shot, and near our camp is a beaver den: the mosquitoes have been more troublesome than ever for the two last days.

AUGUST 10TH At two and a half miles, we came to a place, called Coupée à Jacques, where the river has found a new bed, and abridged a circuit of several miles: at twelve and a half miles, a cliff of yellow stone on the left. This is the first highland near the river above the Council-bluff. After passing a number of sandbars we reached a willow island at the distance of twenty-two and a half miles, which we were enabled to do with our oars and a wind from the S. W. and encamped on the north side.

AUGUST 11TH After a violent wind from the N. W. attended with rain, we sailed along the right of the island. At nearly five miles, we halted on the south side for the purpose of examining a spot where one of the great chiefs of the Mahas named Blackbird, who died about four years ago of the small-pox, was buried. A hill of yellow soft sandstone rises from the river in bluffs of various heights, till it ends in a knoll about three hundred feet above the water; on the top of this a mound, of twelve feet diameter at the base and six feet high, is raised over the body of the deceased king; a pole of about eight feet high is fixed in the centre; on which we placed a white flag, bordered with red, blue, and white. The Blackbird seems to have been a personage of great consideration; for ever since his death he is supplied with provisions, from time to time, by the superstitious regard of the Mahas. We descended to the river and passed a small creek on the south, called, by the Mahas, Waucandipeeche (Great Spirit is bad). Near this creek and the adjoining hills the Mahas had a village, and lost four hundred of their nation by the dreadful malady which destroyed the Blackbird. The meridian altitude made the latitude 42° 1′ 3$\frac{8}{10}$″ north. We encamped, at seventeen miles distance, on the north side in a bend of the river. During our day's course it has been crooked; we observed a number of places in it where the old channel is filled up, or gradually becoming covered with willow and cottonwood; great numbers of *herons* are observed to-day, and the mosquitoes annoy us very much.

AUGUST 12TH
A gentle breeze from the south, carried us along about ten miles, when we stopped to take a meridian altitude, and sent a man across to our place of observation: yesterday he stepped nine hundred and seventy-four yards, and the distance we had come round, was eighteen miles and three-quarters. The river is wider and shallower than usual. Four miles beyond this bend a bluff begins, and continues several miles; on the south it rises from the water at different heights, from twenty to one hundred and fifty feet, and higher as it recedes on the river: it consists of yellow and brown clay, with soft sandstone imbedded in it, and is covered with timber, among which may be observed some red cedar: the lands on the opposite side are low and subject to inundation, but contain willows, cottonwood, and many grapes. A prairie-wolf came near the bank and barked at us; we attempted unsuccessfully to take him. This part of the river abounds in beaver. We encamped on a sand-island in a bend to the north, having made twenty miles and a quarter.

AUGUST 13TH
Set out at daylight with a breeze from the southeast, and passed several sandbars. Between ten and eleven miles, we came to a spot on the south, where a Mr. Mackay had a trading establishment in the year 1795 and 1796, which he called Fort Charles. At fourteen miles, we reached a creek on the south, on which the Mahas reside, and at seventeen miles and a quarter, formed a camp on a sandbar, to the south side of the river, opposite the lower point of a large island. From this place sergeant Ordway and four men were detached to the Maha village with a flag and a present, in order to induce them to come and hold a council with us. They returned at twelve o'clock the next day, *August 14th*. After crossing a prairie covered with high grass, they reached the Maha creek, along which they proceeded to its three forks, which join near the village: they crossed the north branch and went along the south; the walk was very fatiguing, as they were forced to break their way through grass, sunflowers and thistles, all above ten feet high, and interspersed with wild pea. Five miles from our camp they reached the position of the ancient Maha village: it had once consisted of three hundred cabins, but was burnt about four years ago, soon after the smallpox had destroyed four hundred men, and a proportion of women and children. On a hill, in the rear of the village, are the graves of the nation; to the south of which runs the fork of the Maha creek: this they crossed where it was about ten yards wide, and followed its course to the Missouri, passing along a ridge of hill for one and a half mile, and a long pond between that and the Missouri: they then recrossed the Maha creek, and arrived at the

camp, having seen no tracks of Indians nor any sign of recent cultivation.

In the morning, *15th*, some men were sent to examine the cause of a large smoke from the northeast, and which seemed to indicate that some Indians were near; but they found that a small party, who had lately passed that way, had left some trees burning, and that the wind from that quarter blew the smoke directly towards us: Our camp lies about three miles northeast from the old Maha village, and is in latitude 42° 13′ 41″. The accounts we have had of the effects of the smallpox on that nation are most distressing; it is not known in what way it was first communicated to them, though probably by some war party. They had been a military and powerful people; but when these warriors saw their strength wasting before a malady which they could not resist, their frenzy was extreme; they burnt their village, and many of them put to death their wives and children, to save them from so cruel an affliction, and that all might go together to some better country.

On the *16th* we still waited for the Indians: a party had gone out yesterday to the Maha creek, which was dammed up by the beaver between the camp and the village: a second went to-day. They made a kind of drag with small willows and bark, and swept the creek: the first company brought three hundred and eighteen, the second upwards of eight hundred, consisting of pike, bass, fish resembling salmon, trout, redhorse, buffalo, one rockfish, one flatback, perch, catfish, a small species of perch called, on the Ohio, silverfish, a shrimp of the same size, shape and flavour of those about New Orleans, and the lower part of the Mississippi. We also found very fat mussels; and on the river as well as the creek, are different kinds of ducks and plover. The wind, which in the morning had been from the northwest, shifted round in the evening to the southeast, and as usual we had a breeze, which cooled the air and relieved us from the mosquitoes, who generally give us great trouble.

AUGUST 17TH *Friday*. The wind continued from the southeast, and the morning was fair. We observe about us a grass resembling wheat, except that the grain is like rye, also some similar to both rye and barley, and a kind of timothy, the seed of which branches from the main stock, and is more like a flaxseed than a timothy. In the evening, one of the party sent to the Ottoes, returned with the information that the rest were coming on with the deserter: they had also caught Liberté, but, by a trick, he made his escape: they were bringing three of the chiefs in order to engage our assistance in making peace with the Mahas. This nation having left their village, that desirable purpose cannot be effected; but in order to bring in any neighbouring tribes, we set the surrounding prairies on fire. This is the customary signal made by traders to apprise the Indians of their arrival: it is also used between different nations as an indication of any event which they have previously agreed to announce in that way; and as soon as it is seen collects the neighbouring tribes, unless they apprehend that it is made by their enemies.

AUGUST 18TH In the afternoon the party arrived with the Indians, consisting of the Little Thief and the Big Horse, whom we had seen on the third, together with six other chiefs, and a French interpreter. We met them under a shade, and after they had finished a repast with which we supplied them, we inquired into the origin of the war between them and the Mahas, which they related with great frankness. It seems that two of the Missouris went to the Mahas to steal horses, but were detected and killed; the Ottoes and Missouris thought themselves bound to avenge their companions, and the whole nations were at last obliged to share in the dispute; they are also in fear of a war from the Pawnees, whose village they entered this summer, while the inhabitants were hunting, and stole their corn. This ingenuous confession did not make us the less desirous of negotiating a peace for them; but no Indians have as yet been attracted by our fire. The evening was closed by a dance; and the next day, *August 19th*, the chiefs and warriors being assembled at ten o'clock, we explained the speech we had already sent from the Council-bluffs, and renewed our advice. They all replied in turn, and the presents were then distributed: we exchanged the small medal we had formerly given to the Big Horse for one of the same size with that of Little Thief: we also gave a small medal to a third chief, and a kind of certificate or letter of acknowledgment to five of the warriors expressive of our favour and their good intentions: one of them, dissatisfied, returned us the certificate; but the chief, fearful of our being offended, begged that it might be restored to him; this we declined, and rebuked them severely for having in view mere traffic instead of peace with their neighbours. This displeased them at first; but they at length all petitioned that it should be given to the warrior, who then came forward and made an apology to us; we then delivered it to the chief to be given to the most worthy, and he bestowed it on the same warrior, whose name was Great Blue Eyes. After a more substantial present of small articles and tobacco, the council was ended with a dram to the Indians. In the evening we exhibited different objects of curiosity, and particularly the airgun, which gave them great surprise. Those people are almost naked, having no covering, except a sort of breechcloth round the middle, with a loose blanket or buffalo robe painted, thrown over them. The names of these warriors, besides those already mentioned, were Karkapaha (or Crow's Head) and Nenasawa (or Black Cat), Missouris; and Sananona (or Iron Eyes), Neswaunja (or Big Ox), Stageaunja (or Big Blue Eyes), and Wasashaco (or Brave Man), all Ottoes. These two tribes speak very nearly the same language: they all begged us to give them whiskey.

    The next morning, *August 20th*, the Indians mounted their horses and left us, having received a canister of whiskey at parting. We then set sail, and after passing two islands on the north, came to on that side under some bluffs; the first near the river since we left the Ayauwa village.

    Here we had the misfortune to lose one of our sergeants, Charles Floyd. He was yesterday seized with a bilious colic, and all our care and attention were ineffectual to relieve him: a little before his death, he said to Captain Clark, "I am going to leave you," his strength failed him as he added, "I want you to write me a letter;" but he died with a composure which justified the high opinion we had formed of his firmness and good conduct. He was buried on the top of the bluff with the honours due to a brave soldier; and the place of his interment marked by a cedar post, on which his name and the day of his death were inscribed. About a mile beyond this place, to which we gave his name, is a small river about thirty yards wide, on the north, which we called Floyd's river, where we encamped. We had a breeze from the southeast, and made thirteen miles.

> 20th August Monday 1804
> Sergeant Floyd much weaker and no better. Made Mr. Faufon the interpeter a few presents, and the Indians a Canister of Whiskey we Set out under a gentle braize from the S.E. and proceeded on verry well — Sergeant Floyd as bad as he can be no pulse & nothing will Stay a moment on his Stomach or bowels — Passed two Islands on the S.S. and at the first Bluff on the S.d Sergt Floyd Died with a great deel of Composure, before his death he Said to me, "I am going away" I want you to write me a letter" — We buried him on the top of the bluff ½ Mile below a Small river to which we gave his name, he was buried with the Honors of War much

The expedition's only casualty, Sergeant Floyd's illness and death, as Captain Clark reported it in his journal.

The same breeze from the southeast carried us by a small willow creek on the north, about one mile and a half above Floyd's river. Here began a range of bluffs which continued till near the mouth of the great Sioux river, three miles beyond Floyd's. This river comes in from the north, and is about one hundred and ten yards wide. Mr. Durion, our Sioux interpreter, who is well acquainted with it, says that it is navigable upwards of two hundred miles to the falls, and even beyond them; that its sources are near those of the St. Peter's [Minnesota river]. He also says, that below the falls a creek falls in from the eastward, after passing through cliffs of red rock: of this the Indians make their pipes; and the necessity of procuring that article, has introduced a sort of law of nations, by which the banks of the creek are sacred, and even tribes at war meet without hostility at these quarries, which possess a right of asylum. Thus we find even among savages certain principles deemed sacred, by which the rigours of their merciless system of warfare are mitigated. A sense of common danger, where stronger ties are wanting, gives all the binding force of more solemn obligations. The importance of preserving the known and settled rules of warfare among civilized nations, in all their integrity, becomes strikingly evident; since even savages, with their few precarious wants, cannot exist in a state of peace or war where this faith is once violated.

AUGUST 21ST

The wind became southerly, and blew with such violence that we took a reef in our sail: it also blew the sand from the bars in such quantities, that we could not see the channel at any distance ahead. At four and a quarter miles, we came to two willow islands, beyond which are several sandbars; and at twelve miles, a spot where the Mahas once had a village, now no longer existing. We again passed a number of sandbars, and encamped on the south; having come twenty-four and three-quarter miles. The country through which we passed has the same uniform appearance ever since we left the river Platte: rich low-grounds near the river, succeeded by undulating prairies, with timber near the waters. Some wolves were seen to-day on the sandbeaches to the south; we also procured an excellent fruit, resembling a red currant, growing on a shrub like the privy, and about the height of a wild plum.

About three miles distance, we joined the men who had been sent from the Maha village with our horses, and who brought us two deer. The bluffs or hills which reach the river at this place, on the south, contain alum, copperas, cobalt which had the appearance of soft isinglass, pyrites, and sandstone, the two first very pure. Above this bluff comes in a small creek on the south, which we call Rologe creek. Seven miles above is another cliff, on the same side, of alum rock, of a dark brown colour, containing in its crevices great quantities of cobalt, cemented shells, and red earth. From this the river bends to the eastward, and approaches the Sioux river within three or four miles. We sailed the greater part of the day, and made nineteen miles to our camp on the north side. The sandbars are as usual numerous: there are also considerable traces of elk; but none are yet seen.

AUGUST 22D

Captain Lewis in proving the quality of some of the substances in the first cliff, was considerably injured by the fumes and taste of the cobalt, and took some strong medicine to relieve him from its effects. The appearance of these mineral substances enable us to account for disorders of the

31

stomach, with which the party had been affected since they left the river Sioux. We had been in the habit of dipping up the water of the river inadvertently and making use of it, till, on examination, the sickness was thought to proceed from a scum covering the surface of the water along the southern shore, and which, as we now discovered, proceeded from these bluffs. The men had been ordered, before we reached the bluffs, to agitate the water, so as to disperse the scum, and take the water, not at the surface, but at some depth. The consequence was, that these disorders ceased: the boils too which had afflicted the men, were not observed beyond the Sioux river.

In order to supply the place of sergeant Floyd, we permitted the men to name three persons, and Patrick Gass having the greatest number of votes was made a sergeant.

AUGUST 23D   We set out early, and at four miles came to a small run between cliffs of yellow and blue earth: the wind, however, soon changed, and blew so hard from the west, that we proceeded very slowly; the fine sand from the bar being driven in such clouds, that we could scarcely see. Three and a quarter miles beyond this run, we came to a willow island, and a sand island opposite, and encamped on the south side, at ten and a quarter miles. On the north side is an extensive and delightful prairie, which we called Buffalo prairie, from our having here killed the first buffalo. Two elk swam the river to-day and were fired at, but escaped: a deer was killed from the boat; one beaver was killed; and several prairie wolves were seen.

AUGUST 24TH   It began to rain last night, and continued this morning: we proceeded, however, two and a quarter miles, to the commencement of a bluff of blue clay, about one hundred and eighty, or one hundred and ninety feet on the south side: it seems to have been lately on fire; and even now the ground is so warm that we cannot keep our hands in it at any depth: there are strong appearances of coal, and also great quantities of cobalt, or a crystallized substance resembling it. There is a fruit now ripe which looks like a currant, except that it is double the size, and grows on a bush like a privy, the size of a damson, and of a delicious flavour; its Indian name means rabbit-berries. We then passed, at the distance of about seven miles, the mouth of a creek on the north side, called by an Indian name, meaning Whitestone river. The beautiful prairie of yesterday, has changed into one of greater height, and very smooth and extensive. We encamped on the south side, at ten and a quarter miles, and found ourselves much annoyed by the mosquitoes.

Chapter 3
FROM THE VERMILION TO THE TETON RIVER

SATURDAY, AUGUST 25TH, 1804 Captains Lewis and Clark, with ten men, went to see an object deemed very extraordinary among all the neighbouring Indians. They dropped down to the mouth of Whitestone river, about thirty yards wide, where they left the boat, and at the distance of two hundred yards, ascended a rising ground, from which a plain extended itself as far as the eye could discern. After walking four miles, they crossed the creek where it is twenty-three yards wide, and waters an extensive valley. The heat was so oppressive that we were obliged to send back our dog to the creek, as he was unable to bear the fatigue; and it was not till after four hours march that we reached the object of our visit. This was a large mound in the midst of the plain about N. 20° W. from the mouth of Whitestone river, from which it is nine miles distant. The base of the mound is a regular parallelogram, the longest side being about three hundred yards, the shorter sixty or seventy: from the longest side it rises with a steep ascent from the north and south to the height of sixty-five or seventy feet, leaving on the top a level plain of twelve feet in breadth and ninety in length. The north and south extremities are connected by two oval borders which serve as new bases, and divide the whole side into three steep but regular gradations from the plain.

The only thing characteristic in this hill is its extreme symmetry, and this, together with its being totally detached from the other hills which are at the distance of eight or nine miles, would induce a belief that it was artificial; but, as the earth and the loose pebbles which compose it, are arranged exactly like the steep grounds on the borders of the creek, we concluded from this similarity of texture that it might be natural. But the Indians have made it a great article of their superstition: it is called the mountain of Little People, or Little Spirits, and they believe that it is the abode of little devils, in the human form, of about eighteen inches high and with remarkably large heads; they are armed with sharp arrows, with which they are very skilful, and are always on the watch to kill those who should have the hardihood to approach their residence. The tradition is, that many have suffered from these little evil spirits, and among others, three Maha Indians fell a sacrifice to them a few years since. This has inspired all the neighbouring nations, Sioux, Mahas, and Ottoes, with such terror, that no consideration could tempt them to visit the hill. We saw none of these wicked little spirits; nor any place for them, except some small holes scattered over the top: we were happy enough to escape their vengeance, though we remained some time on the mound to enjoy the delightful prospect of the plain, which spreads itself out till the eye rests upon the N. W. hills at a great distance, and those of the N. E. still farther off, enlivened by large herds of buffalo feeding at a distance.

The soil of these plains is exceedingly fine; there is, however, no timber except on the Missouri: all the wood of the Whitestone river not being sufficient to cover thickly one hundred acres. The plain country which surrounds this mound has contributed not a little to its bad reputation: the wind driving from every direction over the level ground obliges the insects to seek shelter on its leeward side, or be driven against us by the wind. The small birds, whose food they are, resort of course in great numbers in quest of subsistence; and the Indians always seem to discover an unusual assemblage of birds as produced by some supernatural cause: among them we observed the brown martin employed in looking for insects, and so gentle that they did not fly until we got within a few feet of them. We have also distinguished among the numerous birds of the plain, the blackbird, the wren or prairie bird, and a species of lark about the size of a partridge, with a short tail.

The excessive heat and thirst forced us from the hill, about one o'clock, to the nearest water, which we found in the creek, at three miles distance, and remained an hour and a half. We then went down the creek, through a lowland about one mile in width, and crossed it three times, to the spot where we first reached it in the morning. Here we gathered some delicious plums, grapes and blue currants, and afterwards arrived at the mouth of the river about sunset. To this place the course from the mound is S. twenty miles, E. nine miles; we there resumed our periogue, and on reaching our encampment of last night set the prairies on fire, to warn the Sioux of our approach.

In the mean time, the boat under sergeant Pryor had proceeded in the afternoon one mile, to a bluff of blue clay on the south, and after passing a sandbar and two sand islands fixed their camp at the distance of six miles on the south. In the evening some rain fell. We had killed a duck and several birds: in the boat, they had caught some large catfish.

AUGUST 26TH *Sunday.* We rejoined the boat at nine o'clock before she set out, and then passing by an island, and under a cliff on the south, nearly two miles in extent and composed of white and blue earth, encamped at nine miles distance, on a sandbar towards the north. Opposite to this, on the south, is a small creek called Petit Arc or Little Bow, and a short distance above it, an old village of the same name. This village, of which nothing remains but the mound of earth about four feet high surrounding it, was built by a Maha chief named Little Bow, who being displeased with Blackbird, the late king, seceded with two hundred followers and settled at this spot, which is now abandoned, as the two villages have reunited since the death of Blackbird. We have great quantities of grapes, and plums of three kinds; two of a yellow colour, and distinguished by one of the species being longer than the other; and a third round and red: all have an excellent flavour, particularly those of the yellow kind.

AUGUST 27TH The morning star appeared much larger than usual. A gentle breeze from the southeast carried us by some large sandbars, on both sides and in the middle of the river, to a bluff, on the south side, at seven and a half miles distant: this bluff is of white clay or chalk, under which is much stone, like lime, incrusted with a clear substance, supposed to be cobalt, and some dark ore. Above this bluff we set the prairie on fire, to invite the Sioux. After twelve and a half miles, we had passed several other sandbars, and now reached the mouth of a river called by the French Jacques (James river) or Yankton, from the tribe which inhabits its banks. It is about ninety yards wide at the confluence: the country which it waters is rich prairie, with little timber: it becomes deeper and wider above its mouth, and may be navigated a great distance; as its sources rise near those of St. Peter's, of the Mississippi, and the Red river of lake Winnipeg. As we came to the mouth of the river, an Indian swam to the boat; and, on our landing, we were met by two others, who informed us that a large body of Sioux were encamped near us: they accompanied three of our men, with an invitation to meet us at a spot above the river: the third Indian remained with us: he is a Maha boy, and says that his nation have gone to the Pawnees to make peace with them. At fourteen miles, we encamped on a sandbar to the north. The air was cool, the evening pleasant, the wind from the southeast, and light. The river has fallen gradually, and is now low.

Tuesday. We passed, with a stiff breeze from the south, several sandbars. On the south is a prairie which rises gradually from the water to the height of a bluff, which is, at four miles distance, of a whitish colour, and about seventy or eighty feet high. Further on is another bluff, of a brownish colour, on the north side; and at the distance of eight and a half miles is the beginning of Calumet bluff, on the south side, under which we formed our camp, in a beautiful plain, to wait the arrival of the Sioux. At the first bluff the young Indian left us and joined their camp. Before reaching Calumet bluff one of the periogues ran upon a log in the river, and was rendered unfit for service; so that all our loading was put into the second periogue. On both sides of the river are fine prairies, with cotton wood; and near the bluff there is more timber in the points and valleys than we have been accustomed to see. AUGUST 28TH

Wednesday. We had a violent storm of wind and rain last evening; and were engaged during the day in repairing the periogues, and other necessary occupations; when, at four o'clock in the afternoon, sergeant Pryor and his party arrived on the opposite side, attended by five chiefs, and about seventy men and boys. We sent a boat for them, and they joined us, as did also Mr. Durion, the son of our interpreter, who happened to be trading with the Sioux at this time. He returned with sergeant Pryor to the Indians, with a present of tobacco, corn, and a few kettles; and told them that we would speak to their chiefs in the morning. Sergeant Pryor reported, that on reaching their village, which is at twelve miles distance from our camp, he was met by a party with a buffalo robe, on which they desired to carry their visitors: an honour which they declined, informing the Indians that they were not the commanders of the boats: as a great mark of respect, they were then presented with a fat dog, already cooked, of which they partook heartily, and found it well flavoured. The camps [lodges or tepees] of the Sioux are of a conical form, covered with buffalo robes, painted with various figures and colours, with an aperture in the top for the smoke to pass through. The lodges contain from ten to fifteen persons, and the interior arrangement is compact and handsome, each lodge having a place for cooking detached from it. AUGUST 29TH

Thursday. The fog was so thick that we could not see the Indian camp on the opposite side, but it cleared off about eight o'clock. We prepared a speech, and some presents, and then sent for the chiefs and warriors, whom we received, at twelve o'clock, under a large oak tree, near to which the flag of the United States was flying. Captain Lewis delivered a speech, with the usual advice and counsel for their future conduct. We then acknowledged their chiefs, by giving to the grand chief a flag, a medal, a certificate, with a string of wampum; to which we added a chief's coat; that is, a richly laced AUGUST 30TH

35

uniform of the United States artillery corps, and a cocked hat and red feather. One second chief and three inferior ones were made or recognised by medals, and a suitable present of tobacco, and articles of clothing. We then smoked the pipe of peace, and the chiefs retired to a bower, formed of bushes, by their young men, where they divided among each other the presents, and smoked and eat, and held a council on the answer which they were to make us to-morrow. The young people exercised their bows and arrows in shooting at marks for beads, which we distributed to the best marksmen; and in the evening the whole party danced until a late hour, and in the course of their amusement we threw among them some knives, tobacco, bells, tape, and binding, with which they were much pleased. Their musical instruments were the drum, and a sort of little bag made of buffalo hide, dressed white, with small shot or pebbles in it, and a bunch of hair tied to it. This produces a sort of rattling music, with which the party was annoyed by four musicians during the council this morning.

AUGUST 31ST In the morning, after breakfast, the chiefs met, and sat down in a row, with pipes of peace, highly ornamented, and all pointed towards the seats intended for captains Lewis and Clark. When they arrived and were seated, the grand chief, whose Indian name, Weucha, is, in English, Shake Hand, and, in French, is called Le Liberateur (the deliverer) rose, and spoke at some length, approving what we had said, and promising to follow our advice:

"I see before me," said he, "my great father's two sons. You see me, and the rest of our chiefs and warriors. We are very poor; we have neither powder nor ball, nor knives; and our women and children at the village have no clothes. I wish that as my brothers have given me a flag and a medal, they would give something to those poor people, or let them stop and trade with the first boat which comes up the river. I will bring chiefs of the Pawnees and Mahas together, and make peace between them; but it is better that I should do it than my great father's sons, for they will listen to me more readily. I will also take some chiefs to your country in the spring; but before that time I cannot leave home. I went formerly to the English, and they gave me a medal and some clothes: when I went to the Spanish they gave me a medal, but nothing to keep it from my skin; but now you give me a medal and clothes. But still we are poor; and I wish, brothers, you would give us something for our squaws."

When he sat down, Mahtoree, or White Crane, rose:

"I have listened," said he, "to what our father's words were yesterday; and I am, to-day, glad to see how you have dressed our old chief. I am a young man, and do not wish to take much: my fathers have made me a chief: I had much sense before, but now I think I have more than ever. What the old chief has declared I will confirm, and do whatever he and you please: but I wish that you would take pity on us, for we are very poor."

Another chief, called Pawnawneahpahbe, then said:

"I am a young man, and know but little: I cannot speak well; but I have listened to what you have told the old chief, and will do whatever you agree."

The same sentiments were then repeated by Aweawechache.

We were surprised at finding that the first of these titles means

"Struck by the Pawnee," and was occasioned by some blow which the chief had received in battle, from one of the Pawnee tribe. The second is, in English, "Half Man," which seems a singular name for a warrior, till it was explained to have its origin, probably, in the modesty of the chief; who, on being told of his exploits, would say, "I am no warrior: I am only half a man."

The other chiefs spoke very little; but after they had finished, one of the warriors delivered a speech, in which he declared he would support them. They promised to make peace with the Ottoes and Missouris, the only nations with whom they are at war. All these harangues concluded by describing the distress of the nation: they begged us to have pity on them: to send them traders: that they wanted powder and ball; and seemed anxious that we should supply them with some of their great father's milk, the name by which they distinguished ardent spirits. We then gave some tobacco to each of the chiefs, and a certificate to two of the warriors who attended the chief. We prevailed on Mr. Durion to remain here, and accompany as many of the Sioux chiefs as he could collect, down to the seat of government. We also gave his son a flag, some clothes, and provisions, with directions to bring about a peace between the surrounding tribes, and to convey some of their chiefs to see the president. In the evening they left us, and encamped on the opposite bank, accompanied by the two Durions. During the evening and night we had much rain, and observed that the river rises a little.

The Indians who have just left us are the Yanktons, a tribe of the great nation of Sioux. These Yanktons are about two hundred men in number; and inhabit the Jacques, Desmoines, and Sioux rivers. In person they are stout, well proportioned, and have a certain air of dignity and boldness. In their dress they differ nothing from the other bands of the nation whom we saw, and will describe afterwards: they are fond of decorations, and use paint, and porcupine quills, and feathers. Some of them wore a kind of necklace of white bear's claws, three inches long, and closely strung together round their necks. They have only a few fowling pieces, being generally armed with bows and arrows, in which, however, they do not appear as expert as the more northern Indians.

What struck us most was an institution, peculiar to them, and to the Kite Indians, further to the westward, from whom it is said to have been copied. It is an association of the most active and brave young men, who are bound to each other by attachment, secured by a vow, never to retreat before any danger, or give way to their enemies. In war they go forward without sheltering themselves behind trees, or aiding their natural valour by any artifice. This punctilious determination, not to be turned from their course, became heroic, or ridiculous, a short time since, when the Yanktons were crossing the Missouri on the ice. A hole lay immediately in their course, which might easily have been avoided, by going round. This the foremost of the band disdained to do; but went straight forward, and was lost. The others would have followed his example, but were forcibly prevented by the rest of the tribe. These young men sit, and encamp, and dance together, distinct from the rest of the nation: they are generally about thirty or thirty-five years old; and such is the deference paid to courage, that their seats in council are superior to those of the chiefs, and their persons more respected. But, as may be supposed, such indiscreet bravery will soon diminish the numbers of those who practise it; so that the band is now reduced to four warriors, who were among our visitors. These were the remains of twenty-two, who composed the society not long ago; but, in a battle with the Kite Indians, of the Black Mountains, eighteen of them were killed, and these four were dragged from the field by their companions.

Whilst these Indians remained with us we made very minute inquiries relative to their situation and numbers, and trade, and manners. This we did very satisfactorily, by means of two different interpreters; and from their accounts, joined to our interviews with other bands of the same nation, and much intelligence acquired since, we were enabled to understand, with some accuracy, the condition of the Sioux, hitherto so little known.

The Sioux or Dacorta [Dakota] Indians, originally settled on the Mississippi, and called by Carver, Madowesians, are now subdivided into tribes, as follow:

First, the Yanktons: this tribe inhabits the Sioux, Desmoines, and Jacques rivers, and number about two hundred warriors.

Second, the Tetons of the Burnt Woods [Bois Brulés]. This tribe numbers about three hundred men, who rove on both sides of the Missouri, the White, and Teton rivers.

Third, the Tetons Okandandas, a tribe consisting of about one hundred and fifty men, who inhabit both sides of the Missouri below the Chayenne river.

Fourth, Tetons Minnakenozzo, a nation inhabiting both sides of the Missouri, above the Chayenne river, and containing about two hundred and fifty men.

Fifth, Tetons Saone; these inhabit both sides of the Missouri below the Warreconne river, and consist of about three hundred men.

Sixth, Yanktons of the Plains, or Big Devils; who rove on the heads of the Sioux, Jacques, and Red river; the most numerous of all the tribes, and number about five hundred men.

Seventh, Wahpatone; a nation residing on the St. Peter's, just above the mouth of that river, and numbering two hundred men.

Eighth, Mindawarcarton, or proper Dacorta or Sioux Indians. These possess the original seat of the Sioux, and are properly so denominated. They rove on both sides of the Mississippi, about the falls of St. Anthony, and consist of three hundred men.

Ninth, the Wahpatoota, or Leaf Beds. This nation inhabits both sides of the river St. Peter's, below Yellow wood river, amounting to about one hundred and fifty men.

Tenth, Sistasoone: this nation numbers two hundred men, and reside at the head of the St. Peter's. Of these several tribes, more particular notice will be taken hereafter.

Saturday, September 1st, 1804

We proceeded this morning under a light southern breeze, and passed the Calumet bluffs; these are composed of a yellowish red, and brownish clay as hard as chalk, which it much resembles, and are one hundred and seventy, or one hundred and eighty feet high. At this place the hills on each side come

The Missouri River at Bon Homme Island. What the explorers took to be the remains of aboriginal earthwork fortifications were actually the typical configurations of islands in this area of high winds and strong currents.

to the verge of the river, those on the south being higher than on the north. Opposite the bluffs is a large island covered with timber; above which the highlands form a cliff over the river on the north side, called White Bear cliff; an animal of that kind being killed in one of the holes in it, which are numerous and apparently deep. At six miles we came to a large sand island covered with cottonwood; the wind was high, and the weather rainy and cloudy during the day. We made fifteen miles to a place on the north side, at the lower point of a large island called Bonhomme, or Goodman's island. The country on both sides has the same character of prairies, with no timber; with occasional lowlands covered with cottonwood, elm, and oak: our hunters had killed an elk and a beaver: the catfish too are in great abundance.

SEPTEMBER 2D It rained last night, and this morning we had a high wind from the N. W. We went three miles to the lower part of an ancient fortification on the south side, and passed the head of Bonhomme island, which is large and well timbered: after this the wind became so violent, attended by a cold rain, that we were compelled to land at four miles on the northern side, under a high bluff of yellow clay, about one hundred and ten feet in height. Our hunters supplied us with four elk; and we had grapes and plums on the banks: we also saw the beargrass and rue, on the side of the bluffs. At this place there are highlands on both sides of the river which become more level at some distance back, and contain but few streams of water. On the southern bank, during this day, the grounds have not been so elevated. Captain Clark crossed the river to examine the remains of the fortification we had just passed.

This interesting object is on the south side of the Missouri, opposite the upper extremity of Bonhomme island, and in a low level plain, the hills being three miles from the river. It begins by a wall composed of earth, rising immediately from the bank of the river and running in a direct course S. 76°, W. ninety-six yards; the base of this wall or mound is seventy-five feet, and its height about eight. It then diverges in a course S. 84° W. and continues at the same height and depth to the distance of fifty-three yards, the angle being formed by a sloping descent; at the junction of these two is an appearance of a hornwork of the same height with the first angle: the same wall then pursues a course N. 69° W. for three hundred yards: near its western extremity is an opening or gateway at right angles to the wall, and projecting inwards; this gateway is defended by two nearly semicircular walls placed before it, lower than the large walls; and from the gateway there seems to have been a covered way communicating with the interval between these two walls: westward of the gate, the wall becomes much larger, being about one hundred and five feet at its base, and twelve feet high: at the end of this high ground the wall extends for fifty-six yards on a course N. 32° W.; it then turns N. 23° W. for seventy-three yards: these two walls seem to have had a double or covered way; they are from ten to fifteen feet eight inches in height, and from seventy-five to one hundred and five feet in width at the base; the descent inwards being steep, whilst outwards it forms a sort of glacis. At the distance of seventy-three yards, the wall ends abruptly at a large hollow place much lower than the general level of the plain, and from which is some indication of a covered way to the water. The space between them is occupied by several mounds scattered promiscuously through the gorge, in the centre of which is a deep round hole.

From the extremity of the last wall, in a course N. 32° W. is a distance of ninety-six yards over the low ground, where the wall recommences and crosses the plain in a course N. 81° W. for eighteen hundred and thirty yards to the bank of the Missouri. In this course its height is about eight feet, till it enters, at the distance of five hundred and thirty-three yards, a deep circular pond of seventy-three yards diameter; after which it is gradually lower, towards the river: it touches the river at a muddy bar, which bears every mark of being an encroachment of the water, for a considerable distance; and a little above the junction, is a small circular redoubt. Along the bank of the river, and at eleven hundred yards distance, in a straight line from this wall, is a second, about six feet high, and of considerable width: it rises abruptly from the bank of the Missouri, at a point where the river bends, and goes straight forward, forming an acute angle with the last wall, till it enters the river again, not far from the mounds just described, towards which it is obviously tending.

At the bend the Missouri is five hundred yards wide; the ground on the opposite side highlands, or low hills on the bank; and where the river passes between this fort and Bonhomme island, all the distance from the bend, it is constantly washing the banks into the stream, a large sandbank being already taken from the shore near the wall. During the whole course of this wall, or glacis, it is covered with trees, among which are many large cotton trees, two or three feet in diameter. Immediately opposite the citadel, or the part most strongly fortified, on Bonhomme island, is a small work in a circular form, with a wall surrounding it, about six feet in height. The young willows along the water, joined to the general appearance of the two shores, induce a belief that the bank of the island is encroaching, and the Missouri indemnifies itself by washing away the base of the fortification. The citadel contains about twenty acres, but the parts between the long walls must embrace nearly five hundred acres.

These are the first remains of the kind which we have had an opportunity of examining; but our French interpreters assure us, that there are great numbers of them on the Platte, the Kanzas, the Jacques, &c., and some of our party say, that they observed two of those fortresses on the upper side of the Petit Arc creek, not far from its mouth; that the wall was about six feet high, and the sides of the angles one hundred yards in length.

SEPTEMBER 3D

The morning was cold, and the wind from the northwest. We passed at sunrise, three large sandbars, and at the distance of ten miles reached a small creek, about twelve yards wide, coming in from the north, above a white bluff: this creek has obtained the name of Plum creek, from the number of that fruit which are in the neighbourhood, and of a delightful quality. Five miles further, we encamped on the south near the edge of a plain; the river is wide, and covered with sandbars to-day: the banks are high and of a whitish colour; the timber scarce, but an abundance of grapes. Beaver houses too have been observed in great numbers on the river, but none of the animals themselves.

SEPTEMBER 4TH   We set out early, with a very cold wind from S. S. E. and at one mile and a half, reached a small creek, called Whitelime creek, on the south side. Just above this is a cliff, covered with cedar trees, and at three miles a creek, called Whitepaint creek, of about thirty yards wide: on the same side, and at four and a half miles distance from the Whitepaint creek, is the Rapid river, or, as it is called by the French, la Rivière qui Court; this river empties into the Missouri, in a course S. W. by W. and is one hundred and fifty-two yards wide, and four feet deep at the confluence. It rises in the Black mountains, and passes through a hilly country, with a poor soil. Captain Clark ascended three miles to a beautiful plain, on the upper side, where the Pawnees once had a village: he found that the river widened above its mouth, and much divided by sands and islands, which, joined to the great rapidity of the current, makes the navigation very difficult, even for small boats. Like the Platte its waters are of a light colour; like that river too it throws out into the Missouri great quantities of sand, coarser even than that of the Platte, which form sandbars and shoals near its mouth.

We encamped just above it, on the south, having made only eight miles, as the wind shifted to the south, and blew so hard that in the course of the day we broke our mast: we saw some deer, a number of geese, and shot a turkey and a duck: the place in which we halted is a fine low-ground, with much timber, such as red cedar, honeylocust, oak, arrowwood, elm and coffeenut.

SEPTEMBER 5TH   *Wednesday*. The wind was again high from the south. At five miles, we came to a large island, called Pawnee island, in the middle of the river; and stopped to breakfast at a small creek on the north, which has the name of Goat creek, at eight and a half miles. Near the mouth of this creek the beaver had made a dam across so as to form a large pond, in which they built their houses. Above this island the river Poncara falls into the Missouri from the south, and is thirty yards wide at the entrance. Two men whom we despatched to the village of the same name, returned with information that they had found it on the lower side of the creek; but as this is the hunting season, the town was so completely deserted that they had killed a buffalo in the village itself. This tribe of Poncaras, who are said to have once numbered four hundred men, are now reduced to about fifty, and have associated for mutual protection with the Mahas, who are about two hundred in number. These two nations are allied by a similarity of misfortune; they were once both numerous, both resided in villages, and cultivated Indian corn; their common enemies, the Sioux and small-pox, drove them from their towns, which they visit only occasionally for the purposes of trade; and they now wander over the plains on the sources of the Wolf and Quicurre rivers. Between the Pawnee island and Goat creek on the north, is a cliff of blue earth, under which are several mineral springs, impregnated with salts: near this we observed a number of goats [antelopes], from which the creek derives its name. At three and a half miles from the creek, we came to a large island on the south, along which we passed to the head of it, and encamped about four o'clock. Here we replaced the mast we had lost, with a new one of cedar: some bucks and an elk were procured to-day, and a black tailed deer was seen near the Poncara's village.

Thursday. There was a storm this morning from the N. W. and though it moderated, the wind was still high, and the weather very cold; the number of sandbars too, added to the rapidity of the current, obliged us to have recourse to the towline: with all our exertions we did not make more than eight and a half miles, and encamped on the north, after passing high cliffs of soft, blue, and red coloured stone, on the southern shore. We saw some goats, and great numbers of buffalo, in addition to which the hunters furnished us with elk, deer, turkies, geese, and one beaver: a large catfish too was caught in the evening. The ground near the camp was a low prairie, without timber, though just below is a grove of cottonwood.

SEPTEMBER 6TH

Friday. The morning was very cold and the wind southeast. At five and a half miles, we reached and encamped at the foot of a round mountain, on the south, having passed two small islands. This mountain, which is about three hundred feet at the base, forms a cone at the top, resembling a dome at a distance, and seventy feet or more above the surrounding highlands.

SEPTEMBER 7TH

As we descended from this dome, we arrived at a spot, on the gradual descent of the hill, nearly four acres in extent, and covered with small holes: these are the residence of a little animal [prairie dog], called by the French petit chien (little dog), who sit erect near the mouth, and make a whistling noise, but when alarmed take refuge in their holes. In order to bring them out, we poured into one of the holes five barrels of water without filling it, but we dislodged and caught the owner. After digging down another of the holes for six feet, we found, on running a pole into it, that we had not yet dug half way to the bottom: we discovered, however, two frogs in the hole, and near it we killed a dark rattlesnake, which had swallowed a small prairie dog: we were also informed, though we never witnessed the fact, that a sort of lizard, and a snake, live habitually with these animals. The petit chien are justly named, as they resemble a small dog in some particulars, though they have also some points of similarity to the squirrel. The head resembles the squirrel in every respect, except that the ear is shorter, the tail like that of the ground-squirrel, the toe-nails are long, the fur is fine, and the long hair is gray.

Saturday. The wind still continued from the southeast, but moderately. At seven miles we reached a house on the north side, called the Pawnee house, where a trader, named Trudeau, wintered in the year 1796–7: behind this, hills, much higher than usual, appear to the north, about eight miles off. Before reaching this house, we came by three small islands, on the north side, and a small creek on the south; and after leaving it, reached another, at the end of seventeen miles, on which we encamped, and called it Boat island: we here saw herds of buffalo, and some elk, deer, turkies, beaver, a squirrel, and a prairie dog. The party on the north represent the country through which they passed, as poor, rugged, and hilly, with the appearance of having been lately burnt by the Indians; the broken hills, indeed, approach the river on both sides, though each is bordered by a strip of woodland near the water.

SEPTEMBER 8TH

Sunday. We coasted along the island on which we had encamped, and then passed three sand and willow islands, and a number of smaller sandbars. The river is shallow, and joined by two small creeks from the north, and one

SEPTEMBER 9TH

from the south. In the plains, to the south, are great numbers of buffalo, in herds of nearly five hundred; all the copses of timber appear to contain elk or deer. We encamped on a sandbar, on the southern shore, at the distance of fourteen and a quarter miles.

SEPTEMBER 10TH *Monday.* The next day we made twenty miles. The morning was cloudy and dark, but a light breeze from the southeast carried us past two small islands on the south, and one on the north; till, at the distance of ten and a half miles, we reached an island, extending for two miles in the middle of the river, covered with red cedar, from which it derives its name of Cedar island. Just below this island, on a hill, to the south, is the backbone of a fish, forty-five feet long, tapering towards the tail, and in a perfect state of petrification, fragments of which were collected and sent to Washington. On both sides of the river are high dark-coloured bluffs. About a mile and a half from the island, on the southern shore, the party on that side discovered a large and very strong impregnated spring of water; and another, not so strongly impregnated, half a mile up the hill. Three miles beyond Cedar island is a large island on the north, and a number of sandbars. After which is another, about a mile in length, lying in the middle of the river, and separated by a small channel, at its extremity, from another above it, on which we encamped. These two islands are called Mud islands. The river is shallow during this day's course, and is falling a little. The elk and buffalo are in great abundance, but the deer have become scarce.

SEPTEMBER 11TH *Tuesday.* At six and a half miles we passed the upper extremity of an island on the south; four miles beyond which is another on the same side of the river; and about a quarter of a mile distant we visited a large village of the barking-squirrel [prairie dog]. It was situated on a gentle declivity, and covered a space of nine hundred and seventy yards long, and eight hundred yards wide; we killed four of them. We then resumed our course, and during five and a half miles passed two islands on the north, and then encamped at the distance of sixteen miles, on the south side of the river, and just above a small run. The morning had been cloudy, but in the afternoon it began raining, with a high northwest wind, which continued during the greater part of the night. The country seen to-day consists of narrow strips of lowland, rising into uneven grounds, which are succeeded, at the distance of three miles, by rich and level plains, but without any timber. The river itself is wide, and crowded with sandbars. Elk, deer, squirrels, a pelican, and a very large porcupine, were our game this day; some foxes too were seen, but not caught.

In the morning we observed a man riding on horseback down towards the boat, and we were much pleased to find that it was George Shannon, one of our party, for whose safety we had been very uneasy. Our two horses having strayed from us on the *26th of August*, he was sent to search for them. After he had found them he attempted to rejoin us, but seeing some other tracks, which must have been those of Indians, and which he mistook for our own, he concluded that we were ahead, and had been for sixteen days following the bank of the river above us. During the first four days he exhausted his bullets, and was then nearly starved, being obliged to subsist, for twelve days, on a few grapes, and a rabbit which he killed by making use of a hard piece of stick for a ball. One of his horses gave out, and was left behind; the other he kept as a last resource for food. Despairing of overtaking us, he was returning down the river, in hopes of meeting some other boat; and was on the point of killing his horse, when he was so fortunate as to join us.

Wednesday. The day was dark and cloudy; the wind from the northwest. At a short distance we reached an island in the middle of the river, which is covered with timber, a rare object now. We with great difficulty were enabled to struggle through the sandbars, the water being very rapid and shallow, so that we were several hours in making a mile. Several times the boat wheeled on the bar, and the men were obliged to jump out and prevent her from upsetting; at others, after making a way up one channel, the shoalness of the water forced us back to seek the deep channel. We advanced only four miles in the whole day and encamped on the south. Along both sides of the river are high grounds; on the southern side particularly, they form dark bluffs, in which may be observed slate and coal intermixed. We saw also several villages of barking-squirrels; great numbers of grouse, and three foxes. SEPTEMBER 12TH

Thursday. We made twelve miles to-day through a number of sandbars, which make it difficult to find the proper channel. The hills on each side are high, and separated from the river by a narrow plain on its borders. On the north, these lowlands are covered in part with timber, and great quantities of grapes, which are now ripe: on the south we found plenty of plums, but they are not yet ripe; and near the dark bluffs, a run tainted with alum and copperas; the southern side being more strongly impregnated with minerals than the northern. Last night four beaver were caught in the traps; a porcupine was shot as it was upon a cottontree, feeding on its leaves and branches. We encamped on the north side, opposite to a small willow island. At night the mosquitoes were very troublesome, though the weather was cold and rainy and the wind from the northwest. SEPTEMBER 13TH

Friday. At two miles we reached a round island on the northern side; at about five, a run on the south; two and a half miles further, a small creek; and at nine miles encamped near the mouth of a creek, on the same side. The sandbars are very numerous, and render the river wide and shallow, and obliged the crew to get into the water and drag the boat over the bars several times. During the whole day we searched along the southern shore, and at some distance into the interior, to find an ancient volcano which we heard at St. Charles was somewhere in this neighbourhood; but we could not discern the slightest appearance of any thing volcanic. In the course of their search the party shot a buck-goat and a hare. SEPTEMBER 14TH

    The hills, particularly on the south, continue high, but the timber is confined to the islands and banks of the river. We had occasion here to observe the rapid undermining of these hills by the Missouri: the first attacks seem to be on the hills which overhang the river; as soon as the violence of the current destroys the grass at the foot of them, the whole texture appears loosened, and the ground dissolves and mixes with the water: the muddy mixture is then forced over the low-grounds, which it covers sometimes to the depth of three inches, and gradually destroys the herbage; after which it can offer no resistance to the water, and becomes at last covered with sand.

SEPTEMBER 15TH   *Saturday.* We passed, at an early hour, the creek near our last night's encampment; and at two miles distance reached the mouth of White river, coming in from the south. We ascended a short distance, and sent a sergeant and another man to examine it higher up. This river has a bed of about three hundred yards, though the water is confined to one hundred and fifty: in the mouth is a sand island, and several sandbars. The current is regular and swift, with sandbars projecting from the points. It differs very much from the Platte, and Quicurre, in throwing out, comparatively, little sand, but its general character is like that of the Missouri. This resemblance was confirmed by the sergeant, who ascended about twelve miles; at which distance it was about the same width as near the mouth, and the course, which was generally west, had been interrupted by islands and sandbars. The timber consisted chiefly of elm; they saw pine burrs, and sticks of birch were seen floating down the river; they had also met with goats, such as we have heretofore seen; great quantities of buffalo, near to which were wolves, some deer, and villages of barking-squirrels.

At the confluence of White river with the Missouri is an excellent position for a town; the land rising by three gradual ascents, and the neighbourhood furnishing more timber than is usual in this country.

After passing high dark bluffs on both sides, we reached the lower point of an island towards the south, at the distance of six miles. The island bears an abundance of grapes, and is covered with red cedar: it also contains a number of rabbits. At the end of this island, which is small, a narrow channel separates it from a large sand island, which we passed, and encamped, eight miles on the north, under a high point of land opposite a large creek to the south, on which we observe an unusual quantity of timber. The wind was from the northwest this afternoon, and high, the weather cold, and its dreariness increased by the howlings of a number of wolves around us.

SEPTEMBER 16TH   *Sunday.* Early this morning, having reached a convenient spot on the south side, and at one mile and a quarter distance, we encamped just above a small creek, which we called Corvus, having killed an animal [magpie] of that genus near it. Finding that we could not proceed over the sandbars, as fast as we desired, while the boat was so heavily loaded, we concluded not to send back, as we originally intended, our third periogue, but to detain the soldiers until spring, and in the mean time lighten the boat by loading the periogue: this operation, added to that of drying all our wet articles, detained us during the day. Our camp is in a beautiful plain, with timber thinly scattered for three-quarters of a mile, and consisting chiefly of elm, cottonwood, some ash of an indifferent quality, and a considerable quantity of a small species of white oak: this tree seldom rises higher than thirty feet, and branches very much; the bark is rough, thick and of a light colour; the leaves small, deeply indented, and of a pale green; the cup which contains the acorn is fringed on the edges, and embraces it about one half; the acorn itself, which grows in great profusion, is of an excellent flavour, and has none of the roughness which most other acorns possess; they are now falling, and have probably attracted the number of deer which we saw on this place, as all the animals we have seen are fond of that food. The ground having been recently burnt by the Indians, is covered with young green grass, and in the neighbourhood are great quantities of fine plums. We killed a few deer for the sake of their skins, which we wanted to cover the periogues, the meat being too poor for food: the cold season coming on, a flannel shirt was given to each man, and fresh powder to those who had exhausted their supply.

Monday. Whilst some of the party were engaged in the same way as yesterday, others were employed in examining the surrounding country. About a quarter of a mile behind our camp, and at an elevation of twenty feet above it, a plain extends nearly three miles parallel to the river, and about a mile back to the hills, towards which it gradually ascends. Here we saw a grove of plum-trees loaded with fruit, now ripe, and differing in nothing from those of the Atlantic states, except that the tree is smaller and more thickly set. The ground of the plain is occupied by the burrows of multitudes of barking squirrels, who entice hither the wolves of a small kind, hawks, and polecats, all of which animals we saw, and presumed that they fed on the squirrel. This plain is intersected nearly in its whole extent by deep ravines and steep irregular rising grounds from one to two hundred feet. On ascending the range of hills which border the plain, we saw a second high level plain stretching to the south as far as the eye could reach. To the westward, a high range of hills about twenty miles distant runs nearly north and south, but not to any great extent, as their rise and termination is embraced by one view, and they seemed covered with a verdure similar to that of the plains. The same view extended over the irregular hills which border the northern side of the Missouri: all around the country had been recently burnt, and a young green grass about four inches high covered the ground, which was enlivened by herds of antelopes and buffalo; the last of which were in such multitudes, that we cannot exaggerate in saying that at a single glance we saw three thousand of them before us.

Of all the animals we had seen the antelope seems to possess the most wonderful fleetness: shy and timorous they generally repose only on the ridges, which command a view of all the approaches of an enemy: the acuteness of their sight distinguishes the most distant danger, the delicate sensibility of their smell defeats the precautions of concealment, and when alarmed their rapid career seems more like the flight of birds than the movements of an earthly being. After many unsuccessful attempts, captain Lewis at last, by winding around the ridges, approached a party of seven, which were on an eminence, towards which the wind was unfortunately blowing. The only male of the party frequently encircled the summit of the hill, as if to announce any danger to the females, who formed a group at the top. Although they did not see captain Lewis, the smell alarmed them, and they fled when he was at the distance of two hundred yards: he immediately ran to the spot where they had been, a ravine concealed them from him, but the next moment they appeared on a second ridge at the distance of three miles. He doubted whether it could be the same, but their number and the extreme rapidity with which they continued their course, convinced him that they must have gone with a speed equal to that of the most distinguished racehorse.

SEPTEMBER 17TH

Among our acquisitions to-day was a mule-deer, a magpie, the common deer, and buffalo: captain Lewis also saw a hare, and killed a rattle-snake near the burrows of the barking squirrels.

SEPTEMBER 18TH *Tuesday.* Having every thing in readiness we proceeded, with the boat much lightened, but the wind being from the N. W. we made but little way. At one mile we reached an island in the middle of the river, nearly a mile in length, and covered with red cedar; at its extremity a small creek comes in from the north; we then met some sandbars, and the wind being very high and ahead, we encamped on the south, having made only seven miles. In addition to the common deer, which were in great abundance, we saw goats, elk, buffalo, the black tailed deer; the large wolves too are very numerous, and have long hair with coarse fur, and are of a light colour. A small species of wolf about the size of a gray fox was also killed, and proved to be the animal [coyote] which we had hitherto mistaken for a fox: there are also many porcupines, rabbits, and barking squirrels in the neighbourhood.

SEPTEMBER 19TH We this day enjoyed a cool clear morning, and a wind from the southeast. We reached at three miles a bluff on the south, and four miles further, the lower point of Prospect island, about two and a half miles in length; opposite to this are high bluffs, about eighty feet above the water, beyond which are beautiful plains gradually rising as they recede from the river: these are watered by three streams which empty near each other: the first is about thirty-five yards wide, the ground on its sides high and rich, with some timber; the second about twelve yards wide, but with less timber; the third is nearly of the same size, and contains more water, but it scatters its waters over the large timbered plain, and empties itself into the river at three places. These rivers are called by the French Les trois rivières des Sioux, the three Sioux rivers; and as the Sioux generally cross the Missouri at this place, it is called the Sioux pass of the three rivers. These streams have the same right of asylum, though in a less degree than Pipestone creek already mentioned.

Two miles from the island we passed a creek fifteen yards wide; eight miles further, another twenty yards wide; three miles beyond which, is a third of eighteen yards width, all on the south side: the second which passes through a high plain we called Elm creek; to the third we gave the name of Night creek, having reached it late at night. About a mile beyond this is a small island on the north side of the river, and is called Lower island, as it is situated at the commencement of what is known by the name of the Grand Détour, or Great Bend of the Missouri. Opposite is a creek on the south about ten yards wide, which waters a plain where there are great numbers of the prickly pear, which name we gave to the creek. We encamped on the south, opposite the upper extremity of the island, having made an excellent day's sail of twenty-six and a quarter miles. Our game this day consisted chiefly of deer, of these four were black tails, one a buck with two main prongs of horns on each side and forked equally. Large herds of buffalo, elk and goats, were also seen.

SEPTEMBER 20TH *Thursday.* Finding we had reached the Big Bend, we despatched two men with our only horse across the neck, to hunt there and wait our arrival at the first creek beyond it. We then set out with fair weather and the wind from S. E. to make the circuit of the bend. Near the lower island the sandbars are numerous, and the river shallow. At nine and a half miles is a sand island, on the southern side. About ten miles beyond it is a small island on the south, opposite to a small creek on the north. This island, which is near the N. W. extremity of the bend, is called Solitary island. At about eleven miles further, we encamped on a sandbar, having made twenty-seven and a half miles. Captain Clark, who early this morning had crossed the neck of the bend, joined us in the evening. At the narrowest part, the gorge is composed of high and irregular hills of about one hundred and eighty or one hundred and ninety feet in elevation; from this descends an unbroken plain over the whole of the bend, and the country is separated from it by this ridge. Great numbers of buffalo, elk, and goats are wandering over these plains, accompanied by grouse and larks. Captain Clark saw a hare also, on the Great Bend. Of the goats killed to-day, one is a female, differing from the male in being smaller in size; its horns too are smaller and straighter, having one short prong, and no black about the neck: none of these goats have any beard, but are delicately formed, and very beautiful.

Friday. Between one and two o'clock the sergeant on guard alarmed us, by crying that the sandbar on which we lay was sinking; we jumped up, and found that both above and below our camp the sand was undermined and falling in very fast: we had scarcely got into the boats and pushed off, when the bank under which they had been lying, fell in, and would certainly have sunk the two periogues if they had remained there. By the time we reached the opposite shore the ground of our encampment sunk also. We formed a second camp for the rest of the night, and at daylight proceeded on to the gorge or throat of the Great Bend, where we breakfasted. A man, whom we had despatched to step off the distance across the bend, made it two thousand yards: the circuit is thirty miles. During the whole course, the land of the bend is low, with occasional bluffs; that on the opposite side, high prairie ground, and long ridges of dark bluffs. After breakfast, we passed through a high prairie on the north side, and a rich cedar lowland and cedar bluff on the south, till we reached a willow island below the mouth of a small creek. This creek, called Tyler's river, is about thirty-five yards wide, comes in on the south, and is at the distance of six miles from the neck of the Great Bend.

Here we found a deer, and the skin of a white wolf, left us by our hunters ahead: large quantities of different kinds of plover and brants are in this neighbourhood, and seen collecting and moving towards the south: the catfish are small, and not in such plenty as we had found them below this place. We passed several sandbars, which make the river very shallow and about a mile in width, and encamped on the south, at the distance of eleven and a half miles. On each side the shore is lined with hard rough gulley-stones, rolled from the hills and small brooks. The most common timber is the cedar, though, in the prairies, there are great quantities of the prickly pear. From this place we passed several sandbars, which make the river shallow, and about a mile in width. At the distance of eleven and a half miles, we encamped on the north at the lower point of an ancient island, which has since been connected with the main land by the filling up of the northern channel, and is now covered with cottonwood. We here saw some tracks of Indians, but they appeared three or four weeks old. This day was warm.

SEPTEMBER 22D A thick fog detained us until seven o'clock; our course was through inclined prairies on each side of the river, crowded with buffalo. We halted at a point on the north side, near a high bluff on the south, and took a meridian altitude, which gave us the latitude of 44° 11′ 33$\frac{3}{10}$″. On renewing our course, we reached first a small island on the south, at the distance of four and a half miles, immediately above which is another island opposite to a creek fifteen yards wide. This creek, and the two islands, one of which is half a mile long, and the second three miles, are called the Three Sisters: a beautiful plain extending on both sides of the river. This is followed by an island on the north, called Cedar island, about one mile and a half in length and the same distance in breadth, and deriving its name from the quality of the timber.

On the south side of this island is a fort and a large trading-house, built by a Mr. Loisel, who wintered here during the last year, in order to trade with the Sioux, the remains of whose camps are in great numbers about this place. The establishment is sixty or seventy feet square, built with red cedar and picketted in with the same materials. The hunters who had been sent ahead joined us here. They mention that the hills are washed in gullies, in passing over which, some mineral substances had rotted and destroyed their moccasins; they had killed two deer and a beaver. At sixteen miles distance we came to on the north side at the mouth of a small creek. The large stones which we saw yesterday on the shores are now some distance in the river, and render the navigation dangerous. The mosquitoes are still numerous in the low grounds.

SEPTEMBER 23D *Sunday.* We passed, with a light breeze from the southeast, a small island on the north, called Goat island; above which is a small creek, called by the party Smoke creek, as we observed a great smoke to the southwest on approaching it. At ten miles we came to the lower point of a large island, having passed two small willow islands with sandbars projecting from them. This island, which we called Elk island, is about two and a half miles long, and three-quarters of a mile wide, situated near the south, and covered with cottonwood, the red currant, and grapes. The river is here almost straight for a considerable distance, wide and shallow, with many sandbars. A small creek on the north, about sixteen yards wide, we called Reuben's creek; as Reuben Fields, one of our men, was the first of the party who reached it. At a short distance above this we encamped for the night, having made twenty miles.

The country, generally, consists of low, rich, timbered ground on the north, and high barren lands on the south: on both sides great numbers of buffalo are feeding.

In the evening three boys of the Sioux nation [Tetons] swam across the river, and informed us that two parties of Sioux were encamped on the next river, one consisting of eighty, and the second of sixty lodges, at some distance above. After treating them kindly we sent them back, with a present of two carrots of tobacco to their chiefs, whom we invited to a conference in the morning.

FUNERAL SCAFFOLD OF A SIOUX CHIEF (Bodmer)

Monday. The wind was from the east, and the day fair; we soon passed a handsome prairie on the north side, covered with ripe plums, and the mouth of a creek on the south, called Highwater creek, a little above our encampment. At about five miles we reached an island two and a half miles in length, and situated near the south. Here we were joined by one of our hunters, who procured four elk, but whilst he was in pursuit of the game the Indians had stolen his horse. We left the island, and soon overtook five Indians on the shore: we anchored, and told them from the boat we were friends and wished to continue so, but were not afraid of any Indians; that some of their young men had stolen the horse which their great father had sent for their great chief, and that we could not treat with them until he was restored. They said that they knew nothing of the horse, but if he had been taken he should be given up. We went on, and at eleven and a half miles, passed an island on the north, which we called Good-humoured island; it is about one and a half miles long, and abounds in elk. At thirteen and a half-miles, we anchored one hundred yards off the mouth of a river on the south side, where we were joined by both the periogues and encamped; two-thirds of the party remained on board, and the rest went as a guard on shore with the cooks and one periogue; we have seen along the sides of the hills on the north a great deal of stone; besides the elk, we also observed a hare; the five Indians whom we had seen followed us, and slept with the guard on shore. Finding one of them was a chief we smoked with him, and made him a present of tobacco. This river is about seventy yards wide and has a considerable current. As the tribe of the Sioux which inhabit it are called Teton, we gave it the name of Teton river.

SEPTEMBER 24TH

Chapter 4

FROM THE TETON RIVER TO THE MANDANS

TUESDAY, SEPTEMBER 25TH, 1804 The morning was fine, and the wind continued from the southeast. We raised a flagstaff and an awning, under which we assembled at twelve o'clock, with all the party parading under arms. The chiefs and warriors from the camp two miles up the river, met us, about fifty or sixty in number, and after smoking delivered them a speech; but as our Sioux interpreter, Mr. Durion, had been left with the Yanktons, we were obliged to make use of a Frenchman who could not speak fluently, and therefore we curtailed our harangue. After this we went through the ceremony of acknowledging the chiefs, by giving to the grand chief a medal, a flag of the United States, a laced uniform coat, a cocked hat and feather: to the two other chiefs a medal and some small presents; and to two warriors of consideration certificates. The name of the great chief is Untongasabaw, or Black Buffalo; the second Tortohonga, or the Partisan; the third Tartongawaka, or Buffalo Medicine: the name of one of the warriors was Wawzinggo; that of the second Matocoquepa, or Second Bear.

We then invited the chiefs on board, and showed them the boat, the airgun, and such curiosities as we thought might amuse them: in this we succeeded too well; for after giving them a quarter of a glass of whiskey, which they seemed to like very much, and sucked the bottle, it was with much difficulty that we could get rid of them. They at last accompanied captain Clark on shore in a periogue with five men; but it seems they had formed a design to stop us; for no sooner had the party landed than three of the Indians seized the cable of the periogue, and one of the soldiers of the chief put his arms round the mast: the second chief who affected intoxication, then said, that we should not go on, that they had not received presents enough from us: captain Clark told him that he would not be prevented from going on; that we were not squaws, but warriors; that we were sent by our great father, who could in a moment exterminate them: the chief replied, that he too had warriors, and was proceeding to offer personal violence to captain Clark, who immediately drew his sword, and made a signal to the boat to prepare for action. The Indians who surrounded him, drew their arrows from their quivers and were bending their bows, when the swivel in the boat was instantly pointed towards them, and twelve of our most determined men jumped into the periogue and joined captain Clark. This movement made an impression on them, for the grand chief ordered the young men away from the periogue, and they withdrew and held a short council with the warriors. Being unwilling to irritate them, captain Clark then went forward and offered his hand to the first and second chiefs, who refused to take it. He then turned from them and got into the periogue, but had not gone more than ten paces when both the chiefs and two of the warriors waded in after him, and he brought them on board. We then proceeded on for a mile and anchored off a willow island, which from the circumstances which had just occurred, we called Badhumoured island.

SEPTEMBER 26TH *Wednesday.* Our conduct yesterday seemed to have inspired the Indians with fear of us, and as we were desirous of cultivating their acquaintance, we complied with their wish that we should give them an opportunity of treating us well, and also suffer their squaws and children to see us and our boat, which would be perfectly new to them. Accordingly, after passing at one and a half mile a small willow island and several sandbars, we came to on the south side, where a crowd of men, women and children were waiting to receive us. Captain Lewis went on shore and remained several hours, and observing that their disposition was friendly we resolved to remain during the night to a dance, which they were preparing for us.

Captains Lewis and Clark, who went on shore one after the other, were met on landing by ten well dressed young men, who took them up in a robe highly decorated and carried them to a large council house, where they were placed on a dressed buffalo skin by the side of the grand chief. The hall or council-room was in the shape of three-quarters of a circle, covered at the top and sides with skins well dressed and sewed together. Under this shelter sat about seventy men, forming a circle round the chief, before whom were placed a Spanish flag and the one we had given them yesterday. This left a vacant circle of about six feet diameter, in which the pipe of peace was raised on two forked sticks, about six or eight inches from the ground, and under it the down of the swan was scattered: a large fire, in which they were cooking provisions, stood near, and in the centre about four hundred pounds of excellent buffalo meat as a present for us. As soon as we were seated, an old man got up, and after approving what we had done, begged us to take pity on their unfortunate situation. To this we replied with assurances of protection. After he had ceased, the great chief rose and delivered an harangue to the same effect: then with great solemnity he took some of the most delicate parts of the dog, which was cooked for the festival, and held it to the flag by way of sacrifice: this done, he held up the pipe of peace, and first pointed it towards the heavens, then to the four quarters of the globe, and then to the earth, made a short speech, lighted the pipe, and presented it to us. We smoked, and he again harangued his people, after which the repast was served up to us. It consisted of the dog which they had just been cooking, this being a great dish among the Sioux, and used on all festivals; to this were added, pemitigon, a dish made of buffalo meat, dried or jerked, and then pounded and mixed raw with grease and a kind of ground potato, dressed like the preparation of Indian corn called hominy, to which it is little inferior. Of all these luxuries which were placed before us in platters with horn spoons, we took the pemitigon [pemmican] and the potato, which we found good, but we could as yet partake but sparingly of the dog. We eat and smoked for an hour, when it became dark: every thing was then cleared away for the dance, a large fire being made in the centre of the house, giving at once light and warmth to the ballroom.

The orchestra was composed of about ten men who played on a sort of tambourin, formed of skin stretched across a hoop; and made a jingling noise with a long stick to which the hoofs of deer and goats were hung; the third instrument was a small skin bag with pebbles in it: these, with five or six young men for the vocal part, made up the band. The women then came forward highly decorated; some with poles in their hands, on which were hung the scalps of their enemies; others with guns, spears or different trophies, taken in war by their husbands, brothers, or connexions. Having arranged themselves in two columns, one on each side of the fire, as soon as the music began they danced towards each other till they met in the centre, when the rattles were shaken, and they all shouted and returned back to their places. They have no step, but shuffle along the ground; nor does the music appear to be any thing more than a confusion of noises, distinguished only by hard or gentle blows upon the buffalo skin: the song is perfectly extemporaneous.

In the pauses of the dance, any man of the company comes forward and recites, in a sort of low guttural tone, some little story or incident, which is either martial or ludicrous; or, as was the case this evening, voluptuous and indecent; this is taken up by the orchestra and the dancers, who repeat it in a higher strain and dance to it. Sometimes they alternate; the orchestra first performing, and when it ceases, the women raise their voices and make a music more agreeable, that is, less intolerable than that of the musicians. The dances of the men, which are always separate from those of the women, are conducted very nearly in the same way, except that the men jump up and down instead of shuffling; and in the war dances the recitations are all of a military cast. The harmony of the entertainment had nearly been disturbed by one of the musicians, who thinking he had not received a due share of the tobacco we had distributed during the evening, put himself into a passion, broke one of the drums, threw two of them into the fire, and left the band. They were taken out of the fire: a buffalo robe held in one hand and beaten with the other, by several of the company, supplied the place of the lost drum or tambourin, and no notice was taken of the offensive conduct of the man. We staid till twelve o'clock at night, when we informed the chiefs that they must be fatigued with all these attempts to amuse us, and retired accompanied by four chiefs, two of whom spent the night with us on board.

While on shore we saw twenty-five squaws, and about the same number of children, who had been taken prisoners two weeks ago, in a battle with their countrymen the Mahas. In this engagement the Sioux destroyed forty lodges, killed seventy-five men, of which we saw many of the scalps, and took these prisoners; their appearance is wretched and dejected; the women too seem low in stature, coarse and ugly; though their present condition may diminish their beauty. We gave them a variety of small articles, such as awls and needles, and interceded for them with the chiefs, to whom we recommended to follow the advice of their great father, to restore the prisoners and live in peace with the Mahas, which they promised to do.

The tribe which we this day saw, are a part of the great Sioux nation, and are known by the name of the Teton Okandandas: they are about two hundred men in number, and their chief residence is on both sides of the Missouri, between the Chayenne and Teton rivers. In their persons they are rather ugly and ill made, their legs and arms being too small, their cheekbones high, and their eyes projecting. The females, with the same character of form, are more handsome; and both sexes appear cheerful and sprightly; but in our intercourse with them we discovered that they were cunning and vicious.

The men shave the hair off their heads, except a small tuft on the top, which they suffer to grow and wear in plaits over the shoulders; to this they seem much attached, as the loss of it is the usual sacrifice at the death of near relations. In full dress, the men of consideration wear a hawk's feather, or calumet feather worked with porcupine quills, and fastened to the top of the head, from which it falls back. The face and body are generally painted with a mixture of grease and coal. Over the shoulders is a loose robe or mantle of buffalo skin dressed white, adorned with porcupine quills loosely fixed so as to make a jingling noise when in motion, and painted with various uncouth figures unintelligible to us, but to them emblematic of military exploits, or any other incident; the hair of the robe is worn next the skin in fair weather, but when it rains the hair is put outside, and the robe is either thrown over the arm, or wrapped round the body, all of which it may cover. Under this in the winter season they wear a kind of shirt resembling ours, and made either of skin or cloth, and covering the arms and body. Round the middle is fixed a girdle of cloth or procured dressed elk-skin, about an inch in width and closely tied to the body, to this is attached a piece of cloth or blanket or skin about a foot wide, which passes between the legs and is tucked under the girdle both before and behind; from the hip to the ancle he is covered by leggings of dressed antelope skins, with seams at the sides two inches in width, and ornamented by little tufts of hair the produce of the scalps they have made in war, which are scattered down the leg. The winter moccasins are of dressed buffalo-skin, the hair being worn inwards, and soled with thick elk-skin parchment: those for summer are of deer or elk-skin, dressed without the hair, and with soles of elk-skin.

On great occasions, or wherever they are in full dress, the young men drag after them the entire skin of a polecat fixed to the heel of the moccasin. Another skin of the same animal is either tucked into the girdle or carried in the hand, and serves as a pouch for their tobacco, or what the French traders call the bois roulé: this is the inner bark of a species of red willow, which being dried in the sun or over the fire, is rubbed between the hands and broken into small pieces, and is used alone or mixed with tobacco. The pipe is generally of red earth, the stem made of ash, about three or four feet long, and highly decorated with feathers, hair and porcupine quills.

The hair of the women is suffered to grow long, and is parted from the forehead across the head, at the back of which it is either collected into a kind of bag, or hangs down over the shoulders. Their moccasins are like those of the men, as are also the leggings, which do not however reach beyond the knee, where it is met by a long loose shift of skin which reaches nearly to the ancles: this is fastened over the shoulders by a string and has no sleeves, but a few pieces of the skin hang a short distance down the arm. Sometimes a girdle fastens this skin round the waist, and over all is thrown a robe like that worn by the men. They seem fond of dress.

Their lodges are very neatly constructed, in the same form as those of the Yanktons; they consist of about one hundred cabins, made of white buffalo hide dressed, with a larger one in the centre for holding councils and dances. They are built round with poles about fifteen or twenty feet high, covered with white skins; these lodges may be taken to pieces, packed up, and carried with the nation wherever they go, by dogs which bear great burdens. The women are chiefly employed in dressing buffalo skins: they seem perfectly well disposed, but are addicted to stealing any thing which they can take without being observed. This nation, although it makes so many ravages among its neighbours, is badly supplied with guns. The water which they carry with them is contained chiefly in the paunches of deer and other animals, and they make use of wooden bowls. Some had their heads shaved, which we found was a species of mourning for relations. Another usage, on these occasions, is to run arrows through the flesh both above and below the elbow.

While on shore to-day we witnessed a quarrel between two squaws, which appeared to be growing every moment more boisterous, when a man came forward, at whose approach every one seemed terrified and ran. He took the squaws, and without any ceremony whipped them severely; on inquiring into the nature of such summary justice, we learnt that this man was an officer well known to this and many other tribes. His duty is to keep the peace, and the whole interior police of the village is confided to two or three of these officers, who are named by the chief and remain in power some days, at least till the chief appoints a successor; they seem to be a sort of constable or sentinel, since they are always on the watch to keep tranquillity during the day, and guarding the camp in the night. The short duration of their office is compensated by its authority: his power is supreme, and in the suppression of any riot or disturbance no resistance to him is suffered: his person is sacred, and if in the execution of his duty he strikes even a chief of the second class, he cannot be punished for this salutary insolence. In general they accompany the person of the chief, and when ordered to any duty, however dangerous, it is a point of honour rather than to refuse obedience. Thus, when they attempted to stop us yesterday, the chief ordered one of these men to take possession of the boat; he immediately put his arms round the mast, and, as we understood, no force except the command of the chief would have induced him to release his hold. Like the other men their bodies are blackened, but their distinguishing mark is a collection of two or three raven skins fixed to the girdle behind the back in such a way, that the tails stick out horizontally from the body. On his head too is a raven skin split into two parts, and tied so as to let the beak project from the forehead.

SEPTEMBER 27TH *Thursday*. We rose early, and the two chiefs took off, as a matter of course and according to their custom, the blanket on which they had slept. To this we added a peck of corn as a present to each. Captain Lewis and the chiefs went on shore to see a part of the nation that was expected, but did not come. He returned at two o'clock, with four of the chiefs and a warrior of distinction, called Wadrapa (or, on his guard); they examined the boat and admired whatever was strange, during half an hour, when they left it with great reluctance. Captain Clark accompanied them to the lodge of the grand chief, who invited them to a dance, where, being joined by captain Lewis, they remained till a late hour. The dance was very similar to that of yesterday. About twelve we left them, taking the second chief and one principal warrior on board; as we came near the boat the man who steered the periogue, by mistake, brought her broadside against the boat's cable, and broke it. We called up all hands to their oars; but our noise alarmed the two Indians: they called out to their companions, and immediately the whole camp crowded to the shore; but after half an hour they returned, leaving about sixty men near us. The alarm given by the chiefs was said to be that the Mahas had attacked us, and that they were desirous of assisting us to repel it; but we suspected that they were afraid we meant to set sail, and intended to prevent us from doing so; for in the night the Maha prisoners had told one of our men, who understood the language, that we were to be stopped. We therefore, without giving any indication of our suspicion, prepared every thing for an attack, as the loss of our anchor obliged to come to near a falling bank, very unfavourable for defence.

We were not mistaken in these opinions; for when in the morning,

56

Friday, September 28th, after dragging unsuccessfully for the anchor, we wished to set sail, it was with great difficulty that we could make the chiefs leave the boat. At length we got rid of all except the great chief; when just as we were setting out, several of the chief's soldiers sat on the rope which held the boat to the shore. Irritated at this, we got every thing ready to fire on them if they persisted, but the great chief said that these were his soldiers and only wanted some tobacco. We had already refused a flag and some tobacco to the second chief, who had demanded it with great importunity; but willing to leave them without going to extremities, we threw him a carrot of tobacco, saying to him, "You have told us that you were a great man, and have influence; now show your influence, by taking the rope from those men, and we will then go without any further trouble."

This appeal to his pride had the desired effect; he went out of the boat, gave the soldiers the tobacco, and pulling the rope out of their hands delivered it on board, and we then set sail under a breeze from the S. E. After sailing about two miles we observed the third chief beckoning to us: we took him on board, and he informed us that the rope had been held by the order of the second chief, who was a double-faced man. A little farther on we were joined by the son of the chief, who came on board to see his father. On his return we sent a speech to the nation, explaining what we had done, and advising them to peace; but if they persisted in their attempts to stop us, we were willing and able to defend ourselves. After making six miles, during which we passed a willow island on the south and one sandbar, we encamped on another in the middle of the river. The country on the south side was a low prairie, that on the north highland.

SEPTEMBER 29TH

We set out early, but were again impeded by sandbars, which made the river shallow; the weather was however fair; the land on the north side low and covered with timber contrasted with the bluffs to the south. At nine o'clock we saw the second chief and two women and three men on shore, who wished us to take two women offered by the second chief to make friends, which was refused; he then requested us to take them to the other band of their nation, who were on the river not far from us: this we declined; but in spite of our wishes they followed us along shore. The chief asked us to give them some tobacco; this we did, and gave more as a present for that part of the nation which we did not see. At seven and a half miles we came to a small creek on the southern side, where we saw great numbers of elk, and which we called Notimber creek from its bare appearance. Above the mouth of this stream, a Ricara [Arikara] band of Pawnees had a village five years ago: but there are no remains of it except the mound which encircled the town. Here the second chief went on shore. We then proceeded, and at the distance of eleven miles encamped on the lower part of a willow island, in the middle of the river, being obliged to substitute large stones in the place of the anchor which we lost.

SEPTEMBER 30TH

The wind was this morning very high from the southeast, so that we were obliged to proceed under a double-reefed mainsail, through the rain. The country presented a large low prairie covered with timber on the north side; on the south, we first had high barren hills, but after some miles it became of the same character as that on the opposite side. We had not gone far when an Indian ran after us, and begged to be carried on board as far as the Ricaras, which we refused: soon after, we discovered on the hills at a distance, a great number of Indians, who came towards the river and encamped ahead of us. We stopped at a sandbar, at about eleven miles, and after breakfasting proceeded on a short distance to their camp, which consisted of about four hundred souls.

We anchored one hundred yards from the shore, and discovering that they were Tetons belonging to the band which we had just left, we told them that we took them by the hand, and would make each chief a present of tobacco; that we had been badly treated by some of their band, and that having waited for them two days below, we could not stop here, but referred them to Mr. Durion for our talk and an explanation of our views: they then apologized for what had past, assured us that they were friendly, and very desirous that we should land and eat with them: this we refused, but sent the periogue on shore with the tobacco, which was delivered to one of the soldiers of the chief, whom we had on board. Several of them now ran along the shore after us, but the chief threw them a twist of tobacco, and told them to go back and open their ears to our counsels; on which they immediately returned to their lodges.

We then proceeded past a continuation of the low prairie on the north, where we had large quantities of grapes, and on the south saw a small creek and an island. Six miles above this, two Indians came to the bank, looked at us about half an hour, and then went without speaking over the hills to the southwest. After some time, the wind rose still higher, and the boat struck a log, turned, and was very near taking in water. The chief became so much terrified at the danger, that he hid himself in the boat, and as soon as we landed got his gun and told us that he wanted to return, that we would now see no more Tetons, and that we might proceed unmolested: we repeated the advice we had already given, presented him with a blanket, a knife, some tobacco, and after smoking with him he set out. We then continued to a sandbar on the north side, where we encamped, having come twenty and a half miles. In the course of the day we saw a number of sandbars which impede the navigation. The only animal which we observed was the white gull, then in great abundance.

Monday, October 1st, 1804

The weather was very cold and the wind high from the southeast during the night, and continued so this morning. At three miles distance, we had passed a large island in the middle of the river, opposite to the lower end of which the Ricaras once had a village on the south side of the river: there are, however, no remnants of it now, except a circular wall three or four feet in height, which encompassed the town. Two miles beyond this island is a river coming in from the southwest, about four hundred yards wide; the current gentle, and discharging not much water, and very little sand: it takes its rise in the second range of the Côte Noire or Black mountains, and its general course is nearly east: this river has been occasionally called Dog river, under a mistaken opinion that its French name was Chien, but its true appellation is Chayenne, and it derives this title from the Chayenne Indians:

their history is the short and melancholy relation of the calamities of almost all the Indians. They were a numerous people and lived on the Chayenne, a branch of the Red river of Lake Winnipeg. The invasion of the Sioux drove them westward; in their progress they halted on the southern side of the Missouri below the Warreconne, where their ancient fortifications still exist; but the same impulse again drove them to the heads of the Chayenne, where they now rove, and occasionally visit the Ricaras. They are now reduced, but still number three hundred men.

Although the river did not seem to throw out much sand, yet near and above its mouth we find a great many sandbars difficult to pass. On both sides of the Missouri, near the Chayenne, are rich thinly timbered lowlands, behind which are bare hills. As we proceeded, we found that the sandbars made the river so shallow, and the wind was so high, that we could scarcely find the channel, and at one place were forced to drag the boat over a sandbar, the Missouri being very wide and falling a little. At seven and a half miles we came to at a point, and remained three hours, during which time the wind abated: we then passed within four miles two creeks on the south, one of which we called Centinel creek, and the other Lookout creek. This part of the river has but little timber; the hills are not so high as we have hitherto seen, and the number of sandbars extends the river to more than a mile in breadth. We continued about four and a half miles further, to a sandbar in the middle of the river, where we spent the night, our progress being sixteen miles. On the opposite shore, we saw a house among the willows and a boy, to whom we called, and brought him on board. He proved to be a young Frenchman in the employ of a Mr. Vallé, a trader, who is now here pursuing his commerce with the Sioux.

Tuesday. There had been a violent wind from the S. E. during the night, which having moderated we set sail with Mr. Vallé, who visited us this morning and accompanied us for two miles. He is one of three French traders who have halted here, expecting the Sioux who are coming down from the Ricaras, where they now are, for the purposes of traffic. Mr. Vallé tells us that he passed the last winter three hundred leagues up the Chayenne under the Black mountains. That river he represents as very rapid, liable to sudden swells, the bed and shores formed of coarse gravel, and difficult of ascent even for canoes. One hundred leagues from its mouth it divides into two branches, one coming from the south, the other at forty leagues from the junction enters the Black mountains. The land which it waters from the Missouri to the Black mountains, resembles the country on the Missouri, except that the former has even less timber, and of that the greater proportion is cedar. The Chayennes reside chiefly on the heads of the river, and steal from the Spanish settlement, a plundering excursion which they perform in a month's time. The Black mountains he observes are very high, covered with great quantities of pine, and in some parts the snow remains during the summer. There are also great quantities of goats, white bear [grizzly], prairie cocks, and a species of animal which from his description must resemble a small elk, with large circular horns [Rocky Mountain sheep, or bighorn].

OCTOBER 2D

At two and a half miles we had passed a willow island on the south, on the north side of the river were dark bluffs, and on the south low rich prairies. We took a meridian altitude on our arrival at the upper end of the isthmus of the bend, which we called the Lookout bend, and found the latitude to be 44° 19′ 36″. This bend is nearly twenty miles round, and not more than two miles across.

In the afternoon we heard a shot fired, and not long after observed some Indians on a hill: one of them came to the shore and wished us to land, as there were twenty lodges of Yanktons or Boisbrulé there; we declined doing so, telling him that we had already seen his chiefs, and that they might learn from Mr. Durion the nature of the talk we had delivered to them. At nine miles we came to the lower point of a long island on the north, the banks of the south side of the river being high, those of the north forming a low rich prairie. We coasted along this island, which we called Caution island, and after passing a small creek on the south encamped on a sandbar in the middle of the river, having made twelve miles. The wind changed to the northwest, and became very high and cold. The current of the river is less rapid, and the water though of the same colour contains less sediment than below the Chayenne, but its width continues the same. We were not able to hunt to-day; for as there are so many Indians in the neighbourhood, we were in constant expectation of being attacked, and were therefore forced to keep the party together and be on our guard.

OCTOBER 3D *Wednesday.* The wind continued so high from the northwest, that we could not set out till after seven: we then proceeded till twelve o'clock, and landed on a bar towards the south, where we examined the periogues, and the forecastle of the boat, and found that the mice had cut several bags of corn, and spoiled some of our clothes: about one o'clock an Indian came running to the shore with a turkey on his back: several others soon joined him, but we had no intercourse with them. We then went on for three miles, but the ascent soon became so obstructed by sandbars and shoal water, that after attempting in vain several channels, we determined to rest for the night under some high bluffs on the south, and send out to examine the best channel. We had made eight miles along high bluffs on each side. The birds we saw were the white gulls and the brant which were flying to the southward in large flocks.

OCTOBER 4TH *Thursday.* On examination we found that there was no outlet practicable for us in this channel, and that we must retread our steps. We therefore returned three miles, and attempted another channel in which we were more fortunate. The Indians were in small numbers on the shore, and seemed willing had they been more numerous to molest us. They called to desire that we would land, and one of them gave three yells and fired a ball ahead of the boat: we however took no notice of it, but landed on the south to breakfast. One of these Indians swam across and begged for some powder, we gave him a piece of tobacco only. At eight and a half miles we had passed an island in the middle of the river, which we called Goodhope island. At one and a half mile we reached a creek on the south side about twelve yards wide, to which we gave the name of Teal creek. A little above this is an island on the north side of the current, about one and a half mile in length and three-quarters of a mile in breadth. In the centre of this island is an old village of the Ricaras, called Lahoocat; it was surrounded by a circular wall, containing seventeen lodges. The Ricaras are known to have lived there in

1797, and the village seems to have been deserted about five years since: it does not contain much timber. We encamped on a sandbar making out from the upper end of this island; our journey to-day being twelve miles.

Friday. The weather was very cold: yesterday evening and this morning there was a white frost. We sailed along the highlands on the north side, passing a small creek on the south, between three and four miles. At seven o'clock we heard some yells and saw three Indians of the Teton band, who asked us to come on shore and begged for some tobacco, to all which we gave the same answer as hitherto. At eight miles we reached a small creek on the north. At fourteen we passed an island on the south, covered with wild rye, and at the head a large creek comes in from the south, which we named Whitebrant creek, from seeing several white brants [snow geese] among flocks of dark-coloured ones. At the distance of twenty miles we came to on a sandbar towards the north side of the river, with a willow island opposite; the hills or bluffs come to the banks of the river on both sides, but are not so high as they are below: the river itself however continues of the same width, and the sandbars are quite as numerous. The soil of the banks is dark coloured, and many of the bluffs have the appearance of being on fire. Our game this day was a deer, a prairie wolf, and some goats [antelope] out of a flock that was swimming across the river.

OCTOBER 5TH

Saturday. The morning was still cold, the wind being from the north. At eight miles we came to a willow island on the north, opposite a point of timber, where there are many large stones near the middle of the river, which seem to have been washed from the hills and high plains on both sides, or driven from a distance down the stream. At twelve miles we halted for dinner at a village which we suppose to have belonged to the Ricaras: it is situated in a low plain on the river, and consists of about eighty lodges, of an octagon form, neatly covered with earth, placed as close to each other as possible, and picketed round. The skin canoes, mats, buckets, and articles of furniture found in the lodges, induce us to suppose that it had been left in the spring. We found three different sorts of squashes growing in the village; we also killed an elk near it, and saw two wolves. On leaving the village the river became shallow, and after searching a long time for the main channel, which was concealed among sandbars, we at last dragged the boat over one of them rather than go back three miles for the deepest channel. At fourteen and a half miles we stopped for the night on a sandbar, opposite a creek on the north, called Otter creek, twenty-two yards in width, and containing more water than is common for creeks of that size. The sides of the river during the day are variegated with high bluffs and low timbered grounds on the banks: the river is very much obstructed by sandbars. We saw geese, swan, brants and ducks of different kinds on the sandbars, and on shore numbers of the prairie hen; the magpie too is very common, but the gulls and plover, which we saw in such numbers below, are now quite rare.

OCTOBER 6TH

Sunday. There was frost again last evening, and this morning was cloudy and attended with rain. At two miles we came to the mouth of a river; called by the Ricaras, Sawawkawna, or Pork river; the party who examined it for about three miles up, say that its current is gentle, and that it does not seem

OCTOBER 7TH

61

to throw out much sand. Its sources are in the first range of the Black mountains, and though it has now only water of twenty yards width, yet when full it occupies ninety. Just below the mouth is another village or wintering camp of the Ricaras, composed of about sixty lodges, built in the same form as those passed yesterday, with willow and straw mats, baskets and buffalo-skin canoes remaining entire in the camp. We proceeded under a gentle breeze from the southwest: at ten o'clock we saw two Indians on the north side, who told us they were a part of the lodge of Tartongawaka, or Buffalo Medicine, the Teton chief whom we had seen on the twenty-fifth, that they were on the way to the Ricaras, and begged us for something to eat, which we of course gave them. At seven and a half miles is a willow island on the north, and another on the same side five miles beyond it, in the middle of the river between highlands on both sides. At eighteen and a half miles is an island called Grouse island, on which are the walls of an old village: the island has no timber, but is covered with grass and wild rye, and owes its name to the number of grouse that frequent it. We then went on till our journey for the day was twenty-two miles: the country presented the same appearance as usual. In the low timbered ground near the mouth of the Sawawkawna, we saw the tracks of large white bear, and on Grouse island killed a female blaireau [badger], and a deer of the black-tailed species, the largest we have ever seen.

OCTOBER 8TH *Monday.* We proceeded early with a cool northwest wind, and at two and a half miles above Grouse island, reached the mouth of a creek on the south, then a small willow island, which divides the current equally; and at four and a half miles came to a river on the southern side where we halted. This river, which our meridian altitude fixes at 45° 39′ 5″ north latitude, is called by the Ricaras Wetawhoo; it rises in the Black mountains, and its bed, which flows at the mouth over a low soft slate stone, is one hundred and twenty yards wide, but the water is now confined within twenty yards, and is not very rapid, discharging mud with a small proportion of sand: here as in every bend of the river, we again observe the red berries resembling currants, which we mentioned before. Two miles above the Wetawhoo, and on the same side, is a small river called Maropa by the Indians; it is twenty yards in width, but so dammed up by mud that the stream creeps through a channel of not more than an inch in diameter, and discharges no sand. One mile further we reached an island close to the southern shore, from which it is separated by a deep channel of sixty yards. About half way a number of Ricara Indians came out to see us. We stopped and took a Frenchman on board, who accompanied us past the island to our camp on the north side of the river, which is at the distance of twelve miles from that of yesterday.

Captain Lewis then returned with four of the party to see the village; it is situated in the centre of the island, near the southern shore, under the foot of some high, bald, uneven hills, and contains about sixty lodges. The island itself is three miles long, and covered with fields in which the Indians raise corn, beans, and potatoes. Several Frenchmen living among these Indians as interpreters, or traders, came back with captain Lewis, and particularly a Mr. Gravelines, a man who has acquired the language. On setting out we had a low prairie covered with timber on the north, and on the south highlands, but at the mouth of the Wetawhoo the southern country changes, and a low timbered plain extends along the south, while the north has a ridge of barren hills during the rest of the day's course.

Tuesday. The wind was so cold and high last night and during all the day, that we could not assemble the Indians in council; but some of the party went to the village. We received the visits of the three principal chiefs with many others, to whom we gave some tobacco, and told them that we would speak to them to-morrow. The names of these chiefs were first, Kakawissassa or Lighting Crow; second chief Pocasse or Hay; third chief Piaheto or Eagle's Feather. Notwithstanding the high waves, two or three squaws rowed to us in little canoes made of a single buffalo skin, stretched over a frame of boughs interwoven like a basket, and with the most perfect composure. The object which appeared to astonish the Indians most, was captain Clark's servant York, a remarkable stout strong negro. They had never seen a being of that colour, and therefore flocked round him to examine the extraordinary monster. By way of amusement he told them that he had once been a wild animal, and caught and tamed by his master, and to convince them, showed them feats of strength which added to his looks made him more terrible than we wished him to be. Opposite our camp is a small creek on the south, which we distinguished by the name of the chief Kakawissassa.

OCTOBER 9TH

Wednesday. The weather was this day fine, and as we were desirous of assembling the whole nation at once, we despatched Mr. Gravelines, who with Mr. Tabeau another French trader had breakfasted with us, to invite the chiefs of the two upper villages to a conference. They all assembled at one o'clock, and after the usual ceremonies we addressed them in the same way in which we had already spoken to the Ottoes and Sioux: we then made or acknowledged three chiefs, one for each of the three villages; giving to each a flag, a medal, a red coat, a cocked hat and feather, also some goods, paint and tobacco, which they divided among themselves: after this the airgun was exhibited, very much to their astonishment, nor were they less surprised at the colour and manner of York. On our side we were equally gratified at discovering that these Ricaras made use of no spirituous liquors of any kind, the example of the traders who bring it to them so far from tempting having in fact disgusted them. Supposing that it was as agreeable to them as to the other Indians, we had at first offered them whiskey; but they refused it with this sensible remark, that they were surprised that their father should present to them a liquor which would make them fools. On another occasion they observed to Mr. Tabeau, that no man could be their friend who tried to lead them into such follies.

OCTOBER 10TH

    The council being over they retired to consult on their answer, and the next morning, *Thursday, 11th*, at eleven o'clock we again met in council at our camp. The grand chief made a short speech of thanks for the advice we had given, and promised to follow it; adding that the door was now open and no one dare shut it, and that we might depart whenever we pleased, alluding to the treatment we had received from the Sioux: they also brought us some corn, beans, and dried squashes, and in return we gave them a steel mill with which they were very much pleased. At one o'clock we left our camp with the grand chief and his nephew on board, and at about two miles anchored below a creek on the south, separating the second and third village of the Ricaras, which are about half a mile distant from each other. We visited both the villages, and sat conversing with the chiefs for some time, during which they presented us with a bread made of corn and beans, also corn and beans boiled, and a large rich bean which they take from the mice of the prairie, who discover and collect it. These two villages are placed near each other in a high smooth prairie; a fine situation, except that having no wood the inhabitants are obliged to go for it across the river to a timbered lowland opposite to them. We told them that we would speak to them in the morning at their villages separately.

OCTOBER 12TH *Friday.* Accordingly after breakfast we went on shore to the house of the chief of the second village named Lassel, where we found his chiefs and warriors. They made us a present of about seven bushels of corn, a pair of leggings, a twist of their tobacco, and the seeds of two different species of tobacco. The chief then delivered a speech expressive of his gratitude for the presents and the good counsels which we had given him; his intention of visiting his great father but for fear of the Sioux; and requested us to take one of the Ricara chiefs up to the Mandans and negociate a peace between the two nations. To this we replied in a suitable way, and then repaired to the third village. Here we were addressed by the chief in nearly the same terms as before, and entertained with a present of ten bushels of corn, some beans, dried pumpkins, and squashes. After we had answered and explained the magnitude and power of the United States, the three chiefs came with us to the boat. We gave them some sugar, a little salt, and a sunglass. Two of them then left us, and the chief of the third, by name Ahketahnasha or Chief of the Town, accompanied us to the Mandans. At two o'clock we left the Indians, who crowded to the shore to take leave of us, and after making seven and a half miles landed on the north side, and had a clear, cool, pleasant evening.

The three villages which we have just left, are the residence of a nation called the Ricaras [Arikaras]. They were originally colonies of Pawnees, who established themselves on the Missouri, below the Chayenne, where the traders still remember that twenty years ago they occupied a number of villages. From that situation a part of the Ricaras emigrated to the neighbourhood of the Mandans, with whom they were then in alliance. The rest of the nation continued near the Chayenne till the year *1797*, in the course of which, distressed by their wars with the Sioux, they joined their countrymen near the Mandans. Soon after a new war arose between the Ricaras and the Mandans, in consequence of which the former came down the river to their present position. In this migration those who had first gone to the Mandans kept together, and now live in the two lower villages, which may thence be considered as the Ricaras proper. The third village was composed of such remnants of the villages as had survived the wars, and as these were nine in number a difference of pronunciation and some difference of language may be observed between them and the Ricaras proper, who do not understand all the words of these wanderers. The villages are within the distance of four miles of each other, the two lower ones consisting of between one hundred and fifty and two hundred men each, the third of three hundred.

The Ricaras are tall and well proportioned, the women handsome and lively, and as among other savages to them falls all the drudgery of the field and the labours of procuring subsistence, except that of hunting: both sexes are poor, but kind and generous, and although they receive with thankfulness what is given to them, do not beg as the Sioux did, though this praise should be qualified by mentioning that an axe was stolen last night from our cooks. The dress of the men is a simple pair of moccasins, leggings, and a cloth round the middle, over which a buffalo robe is occasionally thrown, with their hair, arms and ears decorated with different ornaments. The women wear moccasins, leggings, a long shirt made of goats' skins, generally white and fringed, which is tied round the waist; to these they add, like the men, a buffalo robe without the hair, in summer.

These women are handsomer than the Sioux; both of them are however, disposed to be amorous, and our men found no difficulty in procuring companions for the night by means of the interpreters. These interviews were chiefly clandestine, and were of course to be kept a secret from the husband or relations. The point of honour indeed, is completely reversed among the Ricaras; that the wife or the sister should submit to a stranger's embraces without the consent of her husband or brother, is a cause of great disgrace and offence, especially as for many purposes of civility or gratitude the husband and brother will themselves present to a stranger these females, and be gratified by attentions to them. The Sioux had offered us squaws, but while we remained there having declined, they followed us with offers of females for two days. The Ricaras had been equally accommodating; we had equally withstood their temptation; but such was their desire to oblige that two very handsome young squaws were sent on board this evening, and persecuted us with civilities. The black man York participated largely in these favours; for instead of inspiring any prejudice, his colour seemed to procure him additional advantages from the Indians, who desired to preserve among them some memorial of this wonderful stranger. Among other instances of attention, a Ricara invited him into his house and presenting his wife to him, retired to the outside of the door: while there one of York's comrades who was looking for him came to the door, but the gallant husband would permit no interruption before a reasonable time had elapsed.

The Ricara lodges are in a circular or octagonal form, and generally about thirty or forty feet in diameter: they are made by placing forked posts about six feet high round the circumference of the circle; these are joined by poles from one fork to another, which are supported also by other forked poles slanting from the ground: in the centre of the lodge are placed four higher forks, about fifteen feet in length, connected together by beams; from these to the lower poles the rafters of the roof are extended so as to leave a vacancy in the middle for the smoke: the frame of the building is then covered with willow branches, with which is interwoven grass, and over this mud or clay: the aperture for the door is about four feet wide, and before it is a sort of entry about ten feet from the lodge. They are very warm and compact.

They cultivate maize or Indian corn, beans, pumpkins, watermelons, squashes, and a species of tobacco peculiar to themselves.

Their commerce is chiefly with the traders who supply them with goods in return for peltries, which they procure not only by their own hunting, but in exchange for corn from their less civilized neighbours. The object chiefly in demand seemed to be red paint, but they would give any thing they had to spare for the most trifling article. One of the men to-day gave an Indian a hook made out of a pin, and he gave him in return a pair of moccasins.

They express a disposition to keep at peace with all nations, but they are well armed with fusils, and being much under the influence of the Sioux, who exchanged the goods which they get from the British for Ricara corn, their minds are sometimes poisoned and they cannot be always depended on. At the present moment they are at war with the Mandans.

We are informed by Mr. Gravelines, who had passed through that country, that the Yankton or Jacques river rises about forty miles to the east or northeast of this place, the Chayenne branch of the Red river about twenty miles further, passing the Sioux, and the St. Peter's about eighty.

OCTOBER 13TH *Saturday.* In the morning our visitors left us, except the brother of the chief who accompanies us and one of the squaws. We passed at an early hour a camp of Sioux on the north bank, who merely looked at us without saying a word, and from the character of the tribe we did not solicit a conversation. At ten and a half miles we reached the mouth of a creek on the north, which takes its rise from some ponds a short distance to the northeast: to this stream we gave the name of Stone Idol creek, for after passing a willow and sand island just above its mouth, we discovered that a few miles back from the Missouri there are two stones resembling human figures, and a third like a dog; all which are objects of great veneration among the Ricaras.

Their history would adorn the metamorphoses of Ovid. A young man was deeply enamoured with a girl whose parents refused their consent to the marriage. The youth went out into the fields to mourn his misfortunes; a sympathy of feeling led the lady to the same spot, and the faithful dog would not cease to follow his master. After wandering together and having nothing but grapes to subsist on, they were at last converted into stone, which beginning at the feet gradually invaded the nobler parts, leaving nothing unchanged but a bunch of grapes which the female holds in her hands to this day. Whenever the Ricaras pass these sacred stones, they stop to make some offering of dress to propitiate these deities. Such is the account given by the Ricara chief which we had no mode of examining, except that we found one part of the story very agreeably confirmed; for on the river near where the event is said to have occurred, we found a greater abundance of fine grapes than we had yet seen.

Above this is a small creek four and a half miles from Stone Idol creek, which is fifteen yards wide, comes in from the south, and received from us the name of Pocasse or Hay Creek, in honour of the chief of the second village. Above the Ricara island, the Missouri becomes narrow and deeper, the sandbars being generally confined to the points; the current too is much more gentle; the timber on the lowlands is also in much greater quantities, though the high grounds are still naked. We proceeded on under a fine breeze from the southeast, and after making eighteen miles encamped on the north near a timbered low plain, after which we had some rain and the evening was cold. The hunters killed one deer only.

Sunday. We set out in the rain which continued during the day. At five miles we came to a creek on the south, about fifteen yards wide, and named by us Piaheto or Eagle's Feather, in honour of the third chief of the Ricaras. After dinner we stopped on a sandbar, and executed the sentence of a court martial which inflicted corporal punishment on one of the soldiers. This operation affected the Indian chief very sensibly, for he cried aloud during the punishment: we explained the offence and the reasons of it. He acknowledged that examples were necessary, and that he himself had given them by punishing with death; but his nation never whipped even children from their birth. After this we continued with the wind from the northeast, and at the distance of twelve miles, encamped in a cove of the southern bank. Immediately opposite our camp on the north side are the ruins of an ancient fortification, the greater part of which is washed into the river: nor could we distinguish more than that the walls were eight or ten feet high. The evening is wet and disagreeable, and the river which is somewhat wider than yesterday, continues to have an unusual quantity of timber. The country was level on both sides in the morning, but afterwards we passed some black bluffs of the south.

OCTOBER 14TH

Monday. We stopped at three miles on the north a little above a camp of Ricaras who are hunting, where we were visited by about thirty Indians. They came over in their skin canoes, bringing us meat, for which we returned them beads and fishhooks. About a mile higher we found another encampment of Ricaras on the south, consisting of eight lodges: here we again ate and exchanged a few presents. As we went we discerned numbers of other Indians on both sides of the river; and at about nine miles we came to a creek on the south, where we saw many high hills resembling a house with a slanting roof; and a little below the creek an old village of the Sharha or Chayenne Indians. The morning had been cloudy, but the evening became pleasant, the wind from the northeast, and at sunset we halted, after coming ten miles over several sandbars and points, above a camp of ten Ricara lodges on the north side.

OCTOBER 15TH

We visited their camp, and smoked and eat with several of them; they all appeared kind and pleased with our attentions, and the fair sex received our men with more than hospitality. York was here again an object of astonishment; the children would follow him constantly, and if he chanced to turn towards them, run with great terror.

The country of to-day is generally low and covered with timber on both sides, though in the morning we passed some barren hills on the south.

Tuesday. At this camp the squaw who accompanied the chief left us; two others were very anxious to go on with us. Just above our camp we passed a circular work or fort where the Sharha or Chayennes formerly lived: and a short distance beyond, a creek which we called Chayenne creek. At two miles is a willow island with a large sandbar on both sides above it, and a creek, both on the south, which we called Sohawch, the Ricara name for girl; and two miles above a second creek, to which we gave the name of Chapawt, which means woman in the same language. Three miles further is an island situated in a bend to the north, about a mile and a half long, and covered with cottonwood. At the lower end of this island comes in a small creek

OCTOBER 16TH

67

A page of "celestial observations" from the journal of Captain Lewis.

from the north, called Keetooshsahawna or Place of Beaver. At the upper extremity of the island a river empties itself from the north: it is called Warreconne, or Elk Shed their Horns, and is about thirty-five yards wide: the island itself is named Carp island by Evans, a former traveller.

As we proceeded there were great numbers of goats [antelopes] on the banks of the river, and we soon after saw large flocks of them in the water: they had been gradually driven into the river by the Indians who now

68

lined the shore so as to prevent their escape, and were firing on them, while sometimes boys went into the river and killed them with sticks: they seemed to be very successful, for we counted fifty-eight which they had killed. We ourselves killed some, and then passing the lodges to which these Indians belonged, encamped at the distance of half a mile on the south, having made fourteen and a half miles. We were soon visited by numbers of these Ricaras, who crossed the river hallooing and singing: two of them then returned for some goats' flesh and buffalo meat dried and fresh, with which they made a feast that lasted till late at night, and caused much music and merriment.

Wednesday. The weather was pleasant: we passed a low ground covered with small timber on the south, and barren hills on the north which came close to the river; the wind from the northwest then became so strong that we could not move after ten o'clock, until late in the afternoon, when we were forced to use the towline, and we therefore made only six miles. We all went out hunting and examining the country. The goats, of which we see large flocks coming to the north bank of the river, spend the summer, says Mr. Gravelines, in the plains east of the Missouri, and at the present season are returning to the Black mountains, where they subsist on leaves and shrubbery during the winter, and resume their migrations in the spring. We also saw buffalo, elk, and deer, and a number of snakes; a beaver house too was seen, and we caught a whip-poor-will of a small and uncommon kind: the leaves are fast falling; the river wider than usual and full of sandbars; and on the sides of the hills are large stones, and some rock of a brownish colour in the southern bend below us. Our latitude by observation was 46° 23′ 57″.

OCTOBER 17TH

Thursday. After three miles we reached the mouth of Le Boulet or Cannonball river: this stream rises in the Black mountains, and falls into the Missouri on the south; its channel is about one hundred and forty yards wide, though the water is now confined within forty, and its name is derived from the numbers of perfectly round large stones on the shore and in the bluffs just above. We here met with two Frenchmen in the employ of Mr. Gravelines, who had been robbed by the Mandans of their traps, furs, and other articles, and were descending the river in a periogue, but they turned back with us in expectation of obtaining redress through our means. At eight miles is a creek on the north, about twenty-eight yards wide, rising in the northeast, and called Chewah or Fish river; one mile above this is another creek on the south: we encamped on a sandbar to the south, at the distance of thirteen miles, all of which we had made with oars and poles. Great numbers of goats are crossing the river and directing their course to the westward; we also saw a herd of buffalo and of elk; a pelican too was killed, and six fallow deer, having found, as the Ricaras informed us, that there are none of the black-tail species as high up as this place. The country is in general level and fine, with broken short high grounds, low timbered mounds on the river, and a rugged range of hills at a distance.

OCTOBER 18TH

Friday. We set sail with a fine morning, and a southeast wind, and at two and a half miles passed a creek on the north side: at eleven and a half miles

OCTOBER 19TH

we came to a lake or large pond on the same side, in which were some swans. On both banks of the Missouri are low grounds which have much more timber than lower down the river: the hills are at one or two miles distance from the banks, and the streams which rise in them are brackish, and the mineral salts appear on the sides of the hills and edges of the runs. In walking along the shore we counted fifty-two herds of buffalo, and three of elk, at a single view. Besides these we also observed elk, deer, pelicans, and wolves. After seventeen and a half miles we encamped on the north, opposite to the uppermost of a number of round hills, forming a cone at the top, one being about ninety, another sixty feet in height, and some of less elevation. Our chief tells us that the calumet bird [golden eagle] lives in the holes formed by the filtration of the water from the top of these hills through the sides. Near to one of these holes, on a point of a hill ninety feet above the plain, are the remains of an old village which is high, strong, and has been fortified; this our chief tells us is the remains of one of the Mandan villages, and are the first ruins which we have seen of that nation in ascending the Missouri: opposite to our camp is a deep bend to the south, at the extremity of which is a pond.

OCTOBER 20TH *Saturday.* We proceeded early with a southeast wind, which continued high all day, and came to a creek on the north at two miles distance, twenty yards wide. At eight miles we reached the lower point of an island in the middle of the river, though there is no current on the south. This island is covered with willows and extends about two miles, there being a small creek coming in from the south at its lower extremity. After making twelve miles we encamped on the south, at the upper part of a bluff containing stone-coal of an inferior quality; immediately below this bluff and on the declivity of a hill, are the remains of a village covering six or eight acres, formerly occupied by the Mandans, who, says our Ricara chief, once lived in a number of villages on each side of the river, till the Sioux forced them forty miles higher; whence, after a few years residence, they moved to their present position. The country through which we passed has wider bottoms and more timber than those we have been accustomed to see, the hills rising at a distance and by gradual ascents. We have seen great numbers of elk, deer, goats, and buffalo, and the usual attendants of these last, the wolves, who follow their movements and feed upon those who die by accident, or who are too poor to keep pace with the herd; we also wounded a white bear, and saw some fresh tracks of those animals which are twice as large as the track of a man.

OCTOBER 21ST *Sunday.* Last night the weather was cold, the wind high from the northeast, and the rain which fell froze on the ground. At daylight it began to snow, and continued till the afternoon, when it remained cloudy and the ground was covered with snow. We however, set out early, and just above our camp came to a creek on the south, called Chisshetaw, about thirty yards wide and with a considerable quantity of water.

Our Ricara chief tells us, that at some distance up this river is situated a large rock which is held in great veneration, and visited by parties who go to consult it as to their own or their nations' destinies, all of which they discern in some sort of figures or paintings with which it is covered. About two miles off from the mouth of the river the party on shore saw another of the objects of Ricara superstition: it is a large oak tree, standing alone in the open prairie, and as it alone has withstood the fire which has consumed every thing around, the Indians naturally ascribe to it extraordinary powers. One of their ceremonies is to make a hole in the skin of their necks through which a string is passed and the other end tied to the body of the tree; and after remaining in this way for some time they think they become braver.

At two miles from our encampment we came to the ruins of a second Mandan village, which was in existence at the same time with that just mentioned. It is situated on the north at the foot of a hill in a beautiful and extensive plain, which is now covered with herds of buffalo: nearly opposite are remains of a third village on the south of the Missouri; and there is another also about two miles further on the north, a little off the river. At the distance of seven miles we encamped on the south, and spent a cold night. We procured to-day a buffalo and an otter only. The river is wide and the sandbars numerous, and a low island near our encampment.

Monday. In the morning we passed an old Mandan village on the south, near our camp; at four miles another on the same side. About seven o'clock we came to at a camp of eleven Sioux of the Teton tribe, who are almost perfectly naked, having only a piece of skin or cloth round the middle, though we are suffering from the cold. From their appearance, which is warlike, and from their giving two different accounts of themselves, we believe that they are either going to or returning from the Mandans, to which nations the Sioux frequently make excursions to steal horses. As their conduct displeased us, we gave them nothing. At six we reached an island about one mile in length, at the head of which is a Mandan village on the north in ruins, and two miles beyond a bad sandbar. At eight miles are remains of another Mandan village on the south; and at twelve miles encamped on the south. The hunters brought in a buffalo bull, and mentioned that of about three hundred which they had seen, there was not a single female. The beaver is here in plenty, and the two Frenchmen who are returning with us catch several every night. OCTOBER 22D

These villages which are nine in number are scattered along each side of the river within a space of twenty miles; almost all that remains of them is the wall which surrounded them, the fallen heaps of earth which covered the houses, and occasionally human skulls and the teeth and bones of men, and different animals, which are scattered on the surface of the ground.

Tuesday. The weather was cloudy and we had some snow; we soon arrived at five lodges where the two Frenchmen had been robbed, but the Indians had left it lately as we found the fires still burning. The country consists as usual of timbered low grounds, with grapes, rushes, and great quantities of a small red acid fruit, known among the Indians by a name signifying rabbit-berries, and called by the French graisse de buffle or buffalo fat. The river too, is obstructed by many sandbars. At twelve miles we passed an old village on the north, which was the former residence of the Ahnahaways who now live between the Mandans and Minnetarees. After making thirteen miles we encamped on the south. OCTOBER 23D

OCTOBER 24TH *Wednesday.* The day was again dark and it snowed a little in the morning. At three miles we came to a point on the south, where the river by forcing a channel across a former bend has formed a large island on the north. On this island we found one of the grand chiefs of the Mandans, who with five lodges was on a hunting excursion. He met his enemy the Ricara chief, with great ceremony and apparent cordiality, and smoked with him. After visiting his lodges, the grand chief and his brother came on board our boat for a short time; we then proceeded and encamped on the north, at seven miles from our last night's station and below the old village of the Mandans and Ricaras. Here four Mandans came down from a camp above, and our Ricara chief returned with them to their camp, from which we augur favourably of their pacific views towards each other. The land is low and beautiful, and covered with oak and cottonwood, but has been too recently hunted to afford much game.

OCTOBER 25TH The morning was cold and the wind gentle from the southeast: at three miles we passed a handsome high prairie on the south, and on an eminence about forty feet above the water and extending back for several miles in a beautiful plain, was situated an old village of the Mandan nation which has been deserted for many years. A short distance above it, on the continuation of the same rising ground are two old villages of Ricaras, one on the top of the hill, the other in the level plain, which have been deserted only five years ago. Above these villages is an extensive low ground for several miles, in which are situated, at three or four miles from the Ricara villages, three old villages of Mandans near together. Here the Mandans lived when the Ricaras came to them for protection, and from this they moved to their present situation above. In the low ground the squaws raised their corn, and the timber, of which there was little near the villages, was supplied from the opposite side of the river, where it was and still is abundant.

As we proceeded several parties of Mandans both on foot and horseback came along the river to view us, and were very desirous that we should land and talk to them: this we could not do on account of the sandbreaks on the shore, but we sent our Ricara chief to them in a periogue. The wind too having shifted to the southwest and being very high it required all our precautions on board, for the river was full of sandbars which made it very difficult to find the channel. We got aground several times, and passed a very bad point of rocks, after which we encamped on a sandpoint to the north, above a handsome plain covered with timber, and opposite to a high hill on the south side at the distance of eleven miles. Here we were joined by our Ricara chief, who brought an Indian to the camp where he remained all night.

OCTOBER 26TH We set out early with a southwest wind, and after putting the Ricara chief on shore to join the Mandans who were in great numbers along it, we proceeded to the camp of the grand chiefs four miles distant. Here we met a Mr. M'Cracken one of the northwest or Hudson Bay company, who arrived with another person about nine days ago to trade for horses and buffalo robes. Two of the chiefs came on board with some of their household furniture, such as earthen pots and a little corn and went on with us; the rest of the Indians following on shore. At one mile beyond the camp we passed a small creek, and at three more a bluff of coal of an inferior quality on the south. After making eleven miles we reached an old field where the Mandans had cultivated grain last summer, and encamped for the night on the south side, about half a mile below the first village of the Mandans. In the morning we had a low willow ground on the south and highland on the north, which occasionally varied in the course of the day. There is but little wood on this part of the river, which is here subdivided into many channels and obstructed by sandbars.

As soon as we arrived a crowd of men, women, and children came down to see us. Captain Lewis returned with the principal chiefs to the village, while the others remained with us during the evening; the object which seemed to surprise them most, was a corn-mill fixed to the boat which we had occasion to use, and delighted them by the ease with which it reduced the grain to powder. Among others who visited us was the son of the grand chief of the Mandans, who had his two little fingers cut off at the second joints. On inquiring into this accident, we found that it was customary to express grief for the death of relations by some corporeal suffering, and that the usual mode was to lose two joints of the little fingers, or sometimes the other fingers. The wind blew very cold in the evening from the southwest. Two of the party are affected with rheumatic complaints.

Chapter 5
WINTERING WITH THE MANDANS

SATURDAY, OCTOBER 27TH, 1804 At an early hour we proceeded and anchored off the village. Captain Clark went on shore, and after smoking a pipe with the chiefs, was desired to remain and eat with them. He declined on account of his being unwell; but his refusal gave great offence to the Indians, who considered it disrespectful not to eat when invited, till the cause was explained to their satisfaction. We sent them some tobacco, and then proceeded to the second village on the north, passing by a bank containing coal, and a second village, and encamped at four miles on the north, opposite to a village of Ahnahaways. We here met with a Frenchman, named Jesseaume, who lives among the Indians with his wife and children, and who we take as an interpreter. The Indians had flocked to the bank to see us as we passed, and they visited in great numbers the camp, where some of them remained all night. We sent in the evening three young Indians with a present of tobacco for the chiefs of the three upper villages, inviting them to come down in the morning to a council with us. Accordingly the next day,

OCTOBER 28TH *Sunday.* We were joined by many of the Minnetarees and Ahnahaways from above, but the wind was so violent from the southwest that the chiefs of the lower villages could not come up, and the council was deferred till tomorrow. In the mean while we entertained our visitors by showing them what was new to them in the boat; all which, as well our black servant, they called Great Medicine, the meaning of which we afterwards learnt. We also consulted the grand chief of the Mandans, Black Cat, and Mr. Jesseaume, as to the names, characters, &c., of the chiefs with whom we are to hold the council. In the course of the day we received several presents from the women, consisting of corn, boiled hominy, and garden stuffs: in our turn we gratified the wife of the great chief with a gift of a glazed earthen jar. Our hunter brought us two beaver. In the afternoon we sent the Minnetaree chiefs to smoke for us with the great chief of the Mandans, and told them we would speak in the morning.

Finding that we shall be obliged to pass the winter at this place, we went up the river about one and a half miles to-day, with a view of finding a convenient spot for a fort, but the timber was too scarce and small for our purposes.

OCTOBER 29TH *Monday.* The morning was fine and we prepared our presents and speech for the council. After breakfast we were visited by an old chief of the Ahnahaways, who finding himself growing old and weak had transferred his power to his son, who is now at war against the Shoshonees. At ten o'clock the chiefs were all assembled under an awning of our sails, stretched so as to exclude the wind which had become high; that the impression might be the more forcible, the men were all paraded, and the council opened by a discharge from the swivel of the boat. We then delivered a speech, which like those we had already made intermingled advice with assurances of friendship and trade: while we were speaking the old Ahnahaway chief grew very restless, and observed that he could not wait long as his camp was exposed to the hostilities of the Shoshonees; he was instantly rebuked with great dignity by one of the chiefs for this violation of decorum at such a moment, and remained quiet during the rest of the council. Towards the end of our speech we introduced the subject of our Ricara chief, with whom we recommended a firm peace: to this they seemed well disposed, and all smoked with him very amicably. We all mentioned the goods which had been taken from the Frenchmen, and expressed a wish that they should be restored. This being over, we proceeded to distribute the presents with great ceremony: one chief of each town was acknowledged by a gift of a flag, a medal with the likeness of the president of the United States, a uniform coat, hat and feather: to the second chiefs we gave a medal representing some domestic animals, and a loom for weaving; to the third chiefs medals with the impressions of a farmer sowing grain. A variety of other presents were distributed, but none seemed to give them more satisfaction than an iron corn mill which we gave to the Mandans.

The chiefs who were made to-day are: Shahaka or Big White, a first chief, and Kagohami or Little Raven, a second chief of the lower village of the Mandans, called Matootonha: the other chiefs of an inferior quality who were recommended were, 1. Ohheenaw, or Big Man, a Chayenne taken prisoner by the Mandans who adopted him, and he now enjoys great consideration among the tribe. 2. Shotahawrora, or Coal, of the second Mandan village which is called Rooptahee. We made Poscopsahe, or Black Cat, the first chief of the village, and the grand chief of the whole Mandan nation: his second chief is Kagonomokshe, or Raven man Chief; inferior chiefs of this village were, Tawnuheo, and Bellahsara, of which we did not learn the translation.

In the third village which is called Mahawha, and where the Ahwahhaways reside, we made one first chief, Tetuckopinreha, or White Buffalo robe unfolded, and recognized two of an inferior order: Minnissurraree, or Neighing Horse, and Locongotiha, or Old woman at a distance.

Of the fourth village where the Minnetarees live, and which is called Metaharta, we made a first chief, Ompsehara, or Black Moccasin: a second chief, Ohhaw, or Little Fox. Other distinguished chiefs of this village were, Mahnotah, or Big Thief, a man whom we did not see as he is out fighting, and was killed soon after; and Mahserassa, or Tail of the Calumet Bird. In the fifth village we made a first chief Eapanopa, or Red Shield; a second chief Wankerassa, or Two Tailed Calumet Bird, both young chiefs; other persons of distinction are, Shahakohopinnee, or Little Wolf's Medicine; Ahrattanamockshe, or Wolfman chief, who is now at war, and is the son of the old chief we have mentioned, whose name is Caltahcota, or Cherry on a Bush.

The presents intended for the grand chief of the Minnetarees, who was not at the council, were sent to him by the old chief Caltahcota; and we delivered to a young chief those intended for the chief of the lower village. The council was concluded by a shot from our swivel, and after firing the airgun for their amusement, they retired to deliberate on the answer which they are to give to-morrow.

In the evening the prairie took fire, either by accident or design, and burned with great fury, the whole plain being enveloped in flames: so rapid was its progress that a man and a woman were burnt to death before they could reach a place of safety; another man with his wife and child were much burnt, and several other persons narrowly escaped destruction. Among the rest a boy of the half white breed escaped unhurt in the midst of the flames; his safety was ascribed to the great medicine spirit, who had preserved him on account of his being white. But a much more natural cause was the presence of mind of his mother, who seeing no hopes of carrying off her son, threw him on the ground, and covering him with the fresh hide of a buffalo, escaped herself from the flames; as soon as the fire had passed, she returned and found him untouched, the skin having prevented the flame from reaching the grass on which he lay.

OCTOBER 30TH *Tuesday.* We were this morning visited by two persons from the lower village, one the Big White the chief of the village, the other the Chayenne called the Big Man; they had been hunting, and did not return yesterday early enough to attend the council. At their request we repeated part of our speech of yesterday, and put the medal round the neck of the chief. Captain Clark took a periogue and went up the river in search of a good wintering place, and returned after going seven miles to the lower point of an island on the north side, about one mile in length; he found the banks on the north side high, with coal occasionally, and the country fine on all sides; but the want of wood and the scarcity of game up the river, induced us to decide on fixing ourselves lower down during the winter. In the evening our men danced among themselves to the great amusement of the Indians.

OCTOBER 31ST *Wednesday.* A second chief arrived this morning with an invitation from the grand chief of the Mandans, to come to his village where he wished to present some corn to us and to speak with us. Captain Clark walked down to his village; he was first seated with great ceremony on a robe by the side of the chief, who then threw over his shoulders another robe handsomely ornamented. The pipe was then smoked with several of the old men who were seated around the chief; after some time he began his discourse, by observing that he believed what we had told him, and that they should soon enjoy peace, which would gratify him as well as his people, because they could then hunt without fear of being attacked, and the women might work in the fields without looking every moment for the enemy, and at night put off their moccasins, a phrase by which is conveyed the idea of security when the women could undress at night without fear of attack. As to the Ricaras, he continued, in order to show you that we wish peace with all men, that chief (pointing to his second chief) will go with some warriors back to the Ricaras with their chief now here and smoke with that nation. When we heard of your coming all the nations around returned from their hunting to see you, in hopes of receiving large presents; all are disappointed and some discontented; for his part he was not much so, though his village was. He added that he would go and see his great father the president. Two of the steel traps stolen from the Frenchmen were then laid before captain Clark, and the women brought about twelve bushels of corn. After the chief had finished, captain Clark made an answer to the speech and then returned to the boat, where he found the chief of the third village and Kagohami (the Little Raven) who smoked and talked about an hour. After they left the boat the grand chief of the Mandans came dressed in the clothes we had given him, with his two children, and begged to see the men dance, in which they willingly gratified him.

Captain Clark and his men building a line of huts (from Sergeant Gass's diary).

Thursday, November 1st, 1804

Mr. M'Cracken, the trader whom we found here, set out to-day on his return to the British fort and factory on the Assiniboin river, about one hundred and fifty miles from this place. He took a letter from captain Lewis to the Northwest company, inclosing a copy of the passport granted by the British minister in the United States.

At ten o'clock the chiefs of the lower village arrived; they requested that we would call at their village for some corn, that they were willing to make peace with the Ricaras, that they had never provoked the war between them, but as the Ricaras had killed some of their chiefs they had retaliated on them; that they had killed them like birds, till they were tired of killing them, so that they would send a chief and some warriors to smoke with them. In the evening we dropped down to the lower village where captain Lewis went on shore, and captain Clark proceeded to a point of wood on the north side.

Friday. He therefore went up to the village where eleven bushels of corn were presented to him. In the meantime captain Clark went down with the boats three miles, and having found a good position where there was plenty of timber, encamped and began to fell trees to build our huts. Our Ricara chief set out with one Mandan chief and several Minnetaree and Mandan warriors; the wind was from the southeast, and the weather being fine a crowd of Indians came down to visit us.

NOVEMBER 2D

Saturday. We now began the building of our cabins, and the Frenchmen who are to return to St. Louis are building a periogue for the purpose. We sent six men in a periogue to hunt down the river. We were also fortunate enough to engage in our service a Canadian Frenchman, who had been with the Chayenne Indians on the Black mountains, and last summer descended thence by the Little Missouri. Mr. Jesseaume our interpreter also came down with his squaw and children to live at our camp. In the evening we re-

NOVEMBER 3D

77

ceived a visit from Kagohami or Little Raven, whose wife accompanied him, bringing about sixty [pounds'] weight of dried meat, a robe and a pot of meal. We gave him in return a piece of tobacco, to his wife an axe and a few small articles, and both of them spent the night at our camp. Two beavers were caught in traps this morning.

NOVEMBER 4TH *Sunday.* We continued our labours: the timber which we employ is large and heavy, and chiefly consists of cottonwood and elm with some ash of an inferior size. Great numbers of the Indians pass our camp on their hunting excursions: the day was clear and pleasant, but last night was very cold and there was a white frost.

NOVEMBER 5TH *Monday.* The Indians are all out on their hunting parties: a camp of Mandans caught within two days one hundred goats a short distance below us: their mode of hunting them is to form a large strong pen or fold, from which a fence made of bushes gradually widens on each side: the animals are surrounded by the hunters and gently driven towards this pen, in which they imperceptibly find themselves inclosed and are then at the mercy of the hunters. The weather is cloudy and the wind moderate from the northwest. Late at night we were awaked by the sergeant on guard to see the beautiful phenomenon called the northern light: along the northern sky was a large space occupied by a light of a pale but brilliant white colour: which rising from the horizon extended itself to nearly twenty degrees above it. After glittering for some time its colours would be overcast, and almost obscured, but again it would burst out with renewed beauty; the uniform colour was pale light, but its shapes were various and fantastic: at times the sky was lined with light coloured streaks rising perpendicularly from the horizon, and gradually expanding into a body of light in which we could trace the floating columns sometimes advancing, sometimes retreating and shaping into infinite forms, the space in which they moved. It all faded away before the morning.

At daylight, *Tuesday 6th*, the clouds to the north were darkening and the wind rose high from the northwest at eight o'clock, and continued cold during the day. Mr. Gravelines and four others who came with us returned to the Ricaras in a small periogue, we gave him directions to accompany some of the Ricara chiefs to the seat of government in the spring.

NOVEMBER 7TH *Wednesday.* The day was temperate but cloudy and foggy, and we were enabled to go on with our work with much expedition.

NOVEMBER 8TH *Thursday.* The morning again cloudy; our huts advance very well, and we are visited by numbers of Indians who come to let their horses graze near us: in the day the horses are let loose in quest of grass, in the night they are collected and receive an armfull of small boughs of the cottonwood, which being very juicy, soft and brittle, form nutritious and agreeable food: the frost this morning was very severe, the weather during the day cloudy and the wind from the northwest. We procured from an Indian a weasel perfectly white except the extremity of the tail which was black: great numbers of wild geese are passing to the south, but their flight is too high for us to procure any of them.

MANDAN VILLAGE (Bodmer)

NOVEMBER 10TH

We had again a raw day, a northwest wind, but rose early in hopes of finishing our works before the extreme cold begins. A chief who is a half Pawnee came to us and brought a present of half a buffalo, in return for which we gave him some small presents and a few articles to his wife and son: he then crossed the river in a buffalo skin canoe; his wife took the boat on her back and carried it to the village three miles off. Large flocks of geese and brant, and also a few ducks are passing towards the south.

NOVEMBER 11TH

Sunday. The weather is cold. We received the visit of two squaws, prisoners from the Rock [Rocky] mountains, and purchased by Chaboneau. The Mandans at this time are out hunting the buffalo.

NOVEMBER 12TH

Monday. The last night had been cold and this morning we had a very hard frost: the wind changeable during the day, and some ice appears on the edges of the rivers; swans too are passing to the south. The Big White came down to us, having packed on the back of his squaw about one hundred pounds of very fine meat: for which we gave him as well as the squaw some presents, particularly an axe to the woman with which she was very much pleased.

NOVEMBER 13TH

Tuesday. We this morning unloaded the boat and stowed away the contents in a storehouse which we have built. At half past ten ice began to float down the river for the first time: in the course of the morning we were visited by the Black Cat, Poscapsahe, who brought an Assiniboin chief and seven warriors to see us. This man, whose name is Chechawk, is a chief of one out of three bands of Assiniboins who wander over the plains between the Missouri and Assiniboin during the summer, and in the winter carry the spoils of their hunting to the traders on the Assiniboin river, and occasionally come to this place: the whole three bands consist of about eight hundred men. We gave him a twist of tobacco to smoke with his people, and a gold cord for himself: the Sioux also asked for whiskey which we refused to give them. It snowed all day and the air was very cold.

NOVEMBER 14TH

Wednesday. The river rose last night half an inch, and is now filled with floating ice. This morning was cloudy with some snow: about seventy lodges of Assiniboins and some Knistenaux are at the Mandan village, and this being the day of adoption and exchange of property between them all, it is accompanied by a dance, which prevents our seeing more than two Indians to-day: these Knistenaux [or Crees] are a band of Chippeways whose language they speak; they live on the Assiniboin and Saskashawan rivers, and are about two hundred and forty men. We sent a man down on horseback to see what had become of our hunters, and as we apprehend a failure of provisions we have recourse to our pork this evening. Two Frenchmen who had been below returned with twenty beaver which they had caught in traps.

NOVEMBER 15TH

Thursday. The morning again cloudy, and the ice running thicker than yesterday, the wind variable. The man came back with information that our hunters were about thirty miles below, and we immediately sent an order to them to make their way through the floating ice, to assist them in which we sent some tin for the bow of the periogue and a towrope. The ceremony of yesterday seem to continue still, for we were not visited by a single Indian. The swan are still passing to the south.

NOVEMBER 16TH *Friday.* We had a very hard white frost this morning, the trees are all covered with ice, and the weather cloudy. The men this day moved into the huts, although they are not finished. In the evening some horses were sent down to the woods near us in order to prevent their being stolen by the Assiniboins, with whom some difficulty is now apprehended. An Indian came down with four buffalo robes and some corn, which he offered for a pistol, but was refused.

NOVEMBER 17TH *Saturday.* Last night was very cold, and the ice in the river to-day is thicker than hitherto. We are totally occupied with our huts, but received visits from several Indians.

NOVEMBER 18TH *Sunday.* To-day we had a cold windy morning; the Black Cat came to see us, and occupied us for a long time with questions on the usages of our country. He mentioned that a council had been held yesterday to deliberate on the state of their affairs. It seems that not long ago, a party of Sioux fell in with some horses belonging to the Minnetarees, and carried them off; but in their flight they were met by some Assiniboins, who killed the Sioux and kept the horses: a Frenchman too who had lived many years among the Mandans, was lately killed on his route to the British factory on the Assiniboin; some smaller differences existed between the two nations, all of which being discussed, the council decided that they would not resent the recent insults from the Assiniboins and Knistenaux, until they had seen whether we had deceived them or not in our promises of furnishing them with arms and ammunition. They had been disappointed in their hopes of receiving them from Mr. Evans and were afraid that we too, like him, might tell them what was not true. We advised them to continue at peace, that supplies of every kind would no doubt arrive for them, but that time was necessary to organize the trade. The fact is that the Assiniboins treat the Mandans as the Sioux do the Ricaras; by their vicinity to the British they get all the supplies, which they withhold or give at pleasure to the remoter Indians: the consequence is, that however badly treated, the Mandans and Ricaras are very slow to retaliate lest they should lose their trade altogether.

NOVEMBER 19TH *Monday.* The ice continues to float in the river, the wind high from the northwest, and the weather cold. Our hunters arrived from their excursion below, and bring a very fine supply of thirty-two deer, eleven elk, and five buffalo, all of which was hung in a smokehouse.

NOVEMBER 20TH *Tuesday.* We this day moved into our huts which are now completed. This place which we call Fort Mandan, is situated in a point of low ground, on the north side of the Missouri, covered with tall and heavy cotton wood. The works consist of two rows of huts or sheds, forming an angle where they joined each other; each row containing four rooms, of fourteen feet square and seven feet high, with plank ceiling, and the roof slanting so as to form a loft above the rooms, the highest part of which is eighteen feet from the ground: the backs of the huts formed a wall of that height, and opposite the angle the place of the wall was supplied by picketing: in the area were two rooms for stores and provisions. The latitude by observation is 47° 21′ 47″, and the computed distance from the mouth of the Missouri sixteen hundred miles.

In the course of the day several Indians came down to partake of our fresh meat; among the rest, three chiefs of the second Mandan village. They inform us that the Sioux on the Missouri above the Chayenne river, threaten to attack them this winter; that these Sioux are much irritated at the Ricaras for having made peace through our means with the Mandans, and have lately ill treated three Ricaras who carried the pipe of peace to them, by beating them and taking away their horses. We gave them assurances that we would protect them from all their enemies.

NOVEMBER 21ST

The weather was this day fine: the river clear of ice and rising a little: we are now settled in our new winter habitation, and shall wait with much anxiety the first return of spring to continue our journey.

The villages near which we are established are five in number, and are the residence of three distinct nations: the Mandans, the Ahnahaways, and the Minnetarees. The history of the Mandans, as we received it from our interpreters and from the chiefs themselves, and as it is attested by existing monuments, illustrates more than that of any other nation the unsteady movements and the tottering fortunes of the American nations. Within the recollection of living witnesses, the Mandans were settled forty years ago in nine villages, the ruins of which we passed about eighty miles below, and situated seven on the west and two on the east side of the Missouri. The two finding themselves wasting away before the smallpox and the Sioux, united into one village, and moved up the river opposite to the Ricaras. The same causes reduced the remaining seven to five villages, till at length they emigrated in a body to the Ricara nation, where they formed themselves into two villages, and joined those of their countrymen who had gone before them. In their new residence they were still insecure, and at length the three villages ascended the Missouri to their present position. The two who had emigrated together still settled in the two villages on the northwest side of the Missouri, while the single village took a position on the southeast side. In this situation they were found by those who visited them in *1796;* since which the two villages have united into one. They are now in two villages, one on the southeast of the Missouri, the other on the opposite side, and at the distance of three miles across. The first, in an open plain, contains about forty or fifty lodges, built in the same way as those of the Ricaras: the second, the same number, and both may raise about three hundred and fifty men.

On the same side of the river, and at the distance of four miles from the lower Mandan village, is another called Mahaha. It is situated in a high plain at the mouth of Knife river, and is the residence of the Ahnahaways. This nation, whose name indicates that they were "people whose village is on a hill," formerly resided on the Missouri, about thirty miles below where they now live. The Assiniboins and Sioux forced them to a spot five miles higher, where the greatest part of them were put to death, and the rest emigrated to their present situation, in order to obtain an asylum near the Min-

81

netarees. They are called by the French, Soulier Noir or [Black] Shoe Indians; by the Mandans, Wattasoons, and their whole force is about fifty men.

On the south side of the same Knife river, half a mile above the Mahaha and in the same open plain with it, is a village of Minnetarees surnamed Metaharta, who are about one hundred and fifty men in number. On the opposite side of Knife river, and one and a half mile above this village is a second of Minnetarees, who may be considered as the proper Minnetaree nation. It is situated in a beautiful low plain, and contains four hundred and fifty warriors.

The accounts which we received of the Minnetarees were contradictory. The Mandans say that this people came out of the water to the east, and settled near them in their former establishment in nine villages; that they were very numerous, and fixed themselves in one village on the southern side of the Missouri. A quarrel about a buffalo divided the nation, of which two bands went into the plains, and were known by the name of Crow and Paunch Indians, and the rest moved to their present establishment. The Minnetarees proper assert, on the contrary, that they grew where they now live, and will never emigrate from the spot; the great spirit having declared that if they moved they would all die. They also say that the Minnetarees Metaharta, that is Minnetarees of the Willows, whose language with very little variation is their own, came many years ago from the plains and settled near them, and perhaps the two traditions may be reconciled by the natural presumption that these Minnetarees were the tribe known to the Mandans below, and that they ascended the river for the purpose of rejoining the Minnetarees proper. These Minnetarees are part of the great nation called Fall Indians, who occupy the intermediate country between the Missouri and the Saskaskawan, and who are known by the name of Minnetarees of the Missouri, and Minnetarees of Fort de Prairie; that is, residing near or rather frequenting the establishment in the prairie on the Saskaskawan. These Minnetarees indeed, told us that they had relations on the Saskaskawan, whom they had never known till they met them in war, and having engaged in the night were astonished at discovering that they were fighting with men who spoke their own language. The name of Grosventres, or Bigbellies, is given to these Minnetarees, as well as to all the Fall Indians.

The inhabitants of these five villages, all of which are within the distance of six miles, live in harmony with each other. The Ahnahaways understand in part the language of the Minnetarees: the dialect of the Mandans differs widely from both; but their long residence together has insensibly blended their manners, and occasioned some approximation in language, particularly as to objects of daily occurrence and obvious to the senses.

NOVEMBER 22D The morning was fine, and the day warm. We purchased from the Mandans a quantity of corn of a mixed colour, which they dug up in ears from holes made near the front of their lodges, in which it is buried during the winter.

This morning the sentinel informed us that an Indian was about to kill his wife near the fort; we went down to the house of our interpreter where we found the parties, and after forbidding any violence, inquired into the cause of his intending to commit such an atrocity. It appeared that some days ago a quarrel had taken place between him and his wife, in consequence of which she had taken refuge in the house where the two squaws of our interpreter lived: by running away she forfeited her life, which might have been lawfully taken by the husband. About two days ago she had returned to the village, but the same evening came back to the fort much beaten and stabbed in three places, and the husband now came for the purpose of completing his revenge. He observed that he had lent her to one of our serjeants for a night, and that if he wanted her he would give her to him altogether: we gave him a few presents and tried to persuade him to take his wife home; the grand chief too happened to arrive at the same moment, and reproached him with his violence, till at length they went off together, but by no means in a state of much apparent love.

NOVEMBER 23D Again we had a fair and warm day, with the wind from the southeast: the river is now at a stand having risen four inches in the whole.

NOVEMBER 24TH The wind continued from the same quarter and the weather was warm: we were occupied in finishing our huts and making a large rope of elk-skin to draw our boat on the bank.

NOVEMBER 25TH *Sunday.* The weather is still fine, warm and pleasant, and the river falls one inch and a half. Captain Lewis went on an excursion to the villages accompanied by eight men. A Minnetaree chief, the first who has visited us, came down to the fort: his name was Waukerassa, but as both the interpreters had gone with captain Lewis we were obliged to confine our civilities to some presents with which he was much pleased.

We now completed our huts, and fortunately too, for the next day, *Monday, November 26th,* before daylight the wind shifted to the northwest, and blew very hard, with cloudy weather and a keen cold air, which confined us much and prevented us from working. The night continued very cold, and, *Tuesday 27th,* the weather cloudy, the wind continuing from the northwest and the river crowded with floating ice.

Captain Lewis returned with two chiefs Mahnotah, an Ahnahaway, and Minnessurraree a Minnetaree, and a third warrior: they explained to us that the reason of their not having come to see us, was that the Mandans had told them that we meant to combine with the Sioux and cut them off in the course of the winter: a suspicion increased by the strength of the fort, and the circumstance of our interpreters having been removed there with their families: these reports we did not fail to disprove to their entire satisfaction, and amused them by every attention, particularly by the dancing of the men which diverted them highly. All the Indians whom captain Lewis had visited were very well disposed, and received him with great kindness, except a principal chief of one of the upper villages, named Mahpahpaparapassatoo or Horned Weasel, who made use of the civilized indecorum of refusing to be seen, and when captain Lewis called he was told the chief was not at home. In the course of the day seven of the Northwest company's traders arrived from the Assiniboin river, and one of their interpreters having undertaken to circulate among the Indians unfavourable reports, it becomes necessary to warn them of the consequences if they did not desist from such proceedings. The river fell two inches to-day and the weather became very cold.

NOVEMBER 28TH *Wednesday.* About eight o'clock last evening it began to snow and continued till daybreak, after which it ceased till seven o'clock, but then resumed and continued during the day, the weather being cold and the river full of floating ice: about eight o'clock Poscopsahe came down to visit us, with some warriors; we gave them presents and entertained them with all that might amuse their curiosity, and at parting we told them that we had heard of the British trader, Mr. Laroche, having attempted to distribute medals and flags among them, but that those emblems could not be received from any other than the American nation without incurring the displeasure of their great father the president. They left us much pleased with their treatment. The river fell one inch to-day.

NOVEMBER 29TH *Thursday.* The wind is again from the northwest, the weather cold, and the snow which fell yesterday and last night is thirteen inches in depth. The river closed during the night at the village above, and fell two feet; but this afternoon it began to rise a little. Mr. Laroche, the principal of the seven traders, came with one of his men to see us; we told him that we should not permit him to give medals and flags to the Indians; he declared that he had no such intention, and we then suffered him to make use of one of our interpreters, on his stipulating not to touch any subject but that of his traffic with them. An unfortunate accident occurred to sergeant Pryor, who in taking down the boat's mast dislocated his shoulder, nor was it till after four trials that we replaced it.

NOVEMBER 30TH *Friday.* About eight o'clock an Indian came to the opposite bank of the river, calling out that he had something important to communicate, and on sending for him, he told us that five Mandans had been met about eight leagues to the southwest by a party of Sioux, who had killed one of them, wounded two, and taken nine horses; that four of the Wattasoons were missing, and that the Mandans expected an attack. We thought this an excellent opportunity to discountenance the injurious reports against us, and to fix the wavering confidence of the nation.

Captain Clark therefore instantly crossed the river with twenty-three men strongly armed, and circling the town approached it from behind. His unexpected appearance surprised and alarmed the chiefs, who came out to meet him, and conducted him to the village. He then told them that having heard of the outrage just committed, he had come to assist his dutiful children; that if they would assemble their warriors and those of the nation, he would lead them against the Sioux and avenge the blood of their countrymen. After some minutes conversation, Oheenaw the Chayenne arose:

"We now see," said he, "that what you have told us is true, since as soon as our enemies threaten to attack us you come to protect us and are ready to chastise those who have spilt our blood. We did indeed listen to your good talk, for when you told us that the other nations were inclined to peace with us, we went out carelessly in small parties, and some have been killed by the Sioux and Ricaras. But I knew that the Ricaras were liars, and I told their chief who accompanied you, that his whole nation were liars and bad men; that we had several times made a peace with them which they were the first to break; that whenever we pleased we might shoot them like buffalo, but that we had no wish to kill them; that we would not suffer them to kill us, nor steal our horses; and that although we agreed to make peace with them, because our two fathers [Lewis and Clark] desired it, yet we did not believe that they would be faithful long. Such, father, was my language to them in your presence, and you see that instead of listening to your good counsels they have spilt our blood. A few days ago two Ricaras came here and told us that two of their villages were making moccasins, that the Sioux were stirring them up against us, and that we ought to take care of our horses; yet these very Ricaras we sent home as soon as the news reached us to-day, lest our people should kill them in the first moment of grief for their murdered relatives. Four of the Wattasoons whom we expected back in sixteen days have been absent twenty-four, and we fear have fallen. But father the snow is now deep, the weather cold, and our horses cannot travel through the plains: the murderers have gone off: if you will conduct us in the spring, when the snow has disappeared, we will assemble all the surrounding warriors and follow you."

Captain Clark replied that we were always willing and able to defend them; that he was sorry that the snow prevented their marching to meet the Sioux, since he wished to show them that the warriors of their great father would chastise the enemies of his obedient children who opened their ears to his advice; that if some Ricaras had joined the Sioux, they should remember that there were bad men in every nation, and that they should not be offended at the Ricaras till they saw whether these ill-disposed men were countenanced by the whole tribe; that the Sioux possessed great influence over the Ricaras, whom they supplied with military stores, and sometimes led them astray, because they were afraid to oppose them: but that this should be the less offensive since the Mandans themselves were under the same apprehensions from the Assiniboins and Knistenaux, and that while they were thus dependant, both the Ricaras and Mandans ought to keep on terms with their powerful neighbours, whom they may afterwards set at defiance, when we shall supply them with arms, and take them under our protection.

After two hours' conversation captain Clark left the village. The chief repeatedly thanked him for the fatherly protection he had given them, observing that the whole village had been weeping all night and day for the brave young man who had been slain, but now they would wipe their eyes and weep no more as they saw that their father would protect them. He then crossed the river on the ice and returned on the north side to the fort. The day as well as the evening was cold, and the river rose to its former height.

Saturday, December 1st, 1804

The wind was from the northwest, and the whole party engaged in picketing the fort. About ten o'clock the half-brother of the man who had been killed, came to inform us that six Sharhas or Chayenne Indians had arrived, bringing a pipe of peace, and that their nation was three days march behind them. Three Pawnees had accompanied the Sharhas, and the Mandans being afraid of the Sharhas on account of their being at peace with the Sioux, wished to put both them and the three Pawnees to death; but the chiefs had forbidden it as it would be contrary to our wishes. We gave him a present of tobacco, and although from his connexion with the sufferer, he was more embittered against the Pawnees than any other Mandan, yet he seemed perfectly satisfied with our pacific counsels and advice. The Mandans, we observe, call all the Ricaras by the name of Pawnees; the name of Ricaras being that by which the nation distinguishes itself.

In the evening we were visited by a Mr. Henderson, who came from the Hudson Bay Company to trade with the Minnetarees. He had been about eight days on his route in a direction nearly south, and brought with him tobacco, beads, and other merchandise to trade for furs, and a few guns which are to be exchanged for horses.

DECEMBER 2D *Sunday.* The latter part of the evening was warm, and a thaw continued till the morning, when the wind shifted to the north. At eleven o'clock the chiefs of the lower village brought down four of the Sharhas. We explained to them our intentions, and advised them to remain at peace with each other: we also gave them a flag, some tobacco, and a speech for their nation. These were accompanied by a letter to messrs. Tabeau and Gravelines at the Ricara village, requesting them to preserve peace if possible, and to declare the part which we should be forced to take if the Ricaras and Sioux made war on those whom we had adopted. After distributing a few presents to the Sharhas and Mandans, and showing them our curiosities we dismissed them, apparently well pleased at their reception.

DECEMBER 3D *Monday.* The morning was fine, but in the afternoon the weather became cold with the wind from the northwest. The father of the Mandan who was killed brought us a present of dried pumpkins and some pemitigon, for which we gave him some small articles. Our offer of assistance to avenge the death of his son seemed to have produced a grateful respect from him, as well as from the brother of the deceased, which pleased us much.

DECEMBER 4TH *Tuesday.* The wind continues from the northwest, the weather cloudy and raw, and the river rose one inch. Poscapsahe and two young chiefs pass the day with us.

The whole religion of the Mandans consists in the belief of one great spirit presiding over their destinies. This being must be in the nature of a good genius since it is associated with the healing art, and the great spirit is synonymous with great medicine, a name also applied to every thing which they do not comprehend. Each individual selects for himself the particular object of his devotion, which is termed his medicine, and is either some invisible being or more commonly some animal, which thenceforward becomes his protector or his intercessor with the great spirit; to propitiate whom every attention is lavished, and every personal consideration is sacrificed. "I was lately owner of seventeen horses," said a Mandan to us one day, "but I have offered them all up to my medicine and am now poor." He had in reality taken all his wealth, his horses, into the plain, and turning them loose committed them to the care of his medicine and abandoned them forever. The horses less religious took care of themselves, and the pious votary travelled home on foot.

Their belief in a future state is connected with this tradition of their origin: the whole nation resided in one large village under ground near a

86

subterraneous lake: a grape-vine extended its roots down to their habitation and gave them a view of the light: some of the most adventurous climbed up the vine and were delighted with the sight of the earth, which they found covered with buffalo and rich with every kind of fruits: returning with the grapes they had gathered, their countrymen were so pleased with the taste of them that the whole nation resolved to leave their dull residence for the charms of the upper region; men, women, and children ascended by means of the vine; but when about half the nation had reached the surface of the earth, a corpulent woman who was clambering up the vine broke it with her weight, and closed upon herself and the rest of the nation the light of the sun. Those who were left on earth made a village below where we saw the nine villages; and when the Mandans die they expect to return to the original seats of their forefathers; the good reaching the ancient village by means of the lake, which the burden of the sins of the wicked will not enable them to cross.

Wednesday. The morning was cold and disagreeable, the wind from the southeast accompanied with snow: in the evening there was snow again and the wind shifted to the northeast: we were visited by several Indians with a present of pumpkins, and by two of the traders of the Northwest company. DECEMBER 5TH

Thursday. The wind was violent from the north northwest with some snow, the air keen and cold. At eight o'clock A.M. the thermometer stood at ten degrees above 0, and the river rose an inch and a half in the course of the day. DECEMBER 6TH

Friday. The wind still continued from the northwest and the day is very cold: Shahaka [Big White] the chief of the lower village came to apprise us that the buffalo were near, and that his people were waiting for us to join them in the chase: captain Clark with fifteen men went out and found the Indians engaged in killing the buffalo, the hunters mounted on horseback and armed with bows and arrows encircle the herd, and gradually drive them into a plain or an open place fit for the movement of horse; they then ride in among them, and singling out a buffalo, a female being preferred, go as close as possible and wound her with arrows till they think they have given the mortal stroke; when they pursue another till the quiver is exhausted. If, which rarely happens, the wounded buffalo attacks the hunter, he evades his blow by the agility of his horse which is trained for the combat with great dexterity. When they have killed the requisite number they collect their game, and the squaws and attendants come up from the rear and skin and dress the animals. Captain Clark killed ten buffalo, of which five only were brought to the fort, the rest which could not be conveyed home being seized by the Indians, among whom the custom is that whenever a buffalo is found dead without an arrow or any particular mark, he is the property of the finder; so that often a hunter secures scarcely any of the game he kills if the arrow happens to fall off; whatever is left out at night falls to the share of the wolves, who are the constant and numerous attendants of the buffalo. The river closed opposite the fort last night, [with ice] an inch and a half in thickness. In the morning the thermometer stood at one degree below 0. Three men were badly frostbitten in consequence of their exposure. DECEMBER 7TH

DECEMBER 8TH *Saturday.* The thermometer stood at twelve degrees below 0, that is at forty-two degrees below the freezing point: the wind was from the northwest. Captain Lewis with fifteen men went out to hunt the buffalo; great numbers of which darkened the prairies for a considerable distance: they did not return till after dark, having killed eight buffalo and one deer. The hunt was, however, very fatiguing, as they were obliged to make a circuit at the distance of more than seven miles: the cold too, was so excessive that the air was filled with icy particles resembling a fog, and the snow generally six or eight inches deep and sometimes eighteen, in consequence of which two of the party were hurt by falls, and several had their feet frostbitten.

DECEMBER 9TH *Sunday.* The wind was this day from the east, the thermometer at seven degrees above 0, and the sun shone clear: two chiefs visited us, one in a sleigh drawn by a dog and loaded with meat.

DECEMBER 10TH *Monday.* Captain Clark who had gone out yesterday with eighteen men to bring in the meat we had killed the day before, and to continue the hunt, came in at twelve o'clock. After killing nine buffalo and preparing that already dead, he had spent a cold disagreeable night on the snow, with no covering but a small blanket, sheltered by the hides of the buffalo they had killed. We observe large herds of buffalo crossing the river on the ice, the men who were frostbitten are recovering, but the weather is still exceedingly cold, the wind being from the north, and the thermometer at ten and eleven degrees below 0: the rise of the river is one inch and a half.

DECEMBER 11TH *Tuesday.* The weather became so intensely cold that we sent for all the hunters who had remained out with captain Clark's party, and they returned in the evening several of them frostbitten. The wind was from the north and the thermometer at sunrise stood at twenty-one below 0, the ice in the atmosphere being so thick as to render the weather hazy and give the appearance of two suns reflecting each other. The river continued at a stand. Poscapsahe made us a visit to-day.

DECEMBER 12TH *Wednesday.* The wind is still from the north, the thermometer being at sunrise thirty-eight degrees below 0. One of the Ahnahaways brought us down the half of an antelope killed near the fort; we had been informed that all these animals return to the Black mountains, but there are great numbers of them about us at this season which we might easily kill, but are unwilling to venture out before our constitutions are hardened gradually to the climate. We measured the river on the ice, and find it five hundred yards wide immediately opposite the fort.

DECEMBER 13TH *Thursday.* Last night was clear and a very heavy frost covered the old snow, the thermometer at sunrise being twenty degrees below 0, and followed by a fine day. The river falls.

DECEMBER 14TH *Friday.* The morning was fine, and the weather having moderated so far, that the mercury stood at 0, captain Lewis went down with a party to hunt; they proceeded about eighteen miles, but the buffalo having left the banks of the river they saw only two, which were so poor as not to be worth killing, and shot two deer. Notwithstanding the snow we were visited by a large number of the Mandans.

Saturday. Captain Lewis finding no game returned to the fort hunting on both sides of the river, but with no success. The wind being from the north, the mercury at sunrise eight degrees below 0, and the snow of last night an inch and a half in depth. The Indian chiefs continue to visit us to-day with presents of meat. DECEMBER 15TH

Sunday. The morning is clear and cold, the mercury at sunrise 22° below 0. A Mr. Haney with two other persons from the British establishment on the Assiniboin, arrived in six days with a letter from Mr. Charles Chabouilles, one of the company, who with much politeness offered to render us any service in his power. DECEMBER 16TH

Monday. The weather to-day was colder than any we had yet experienced, the thermometer at sunrise being 45° below 0, and about eight o'clock it fell to 74° below the freezing point. From Mr. Haney, who is a very sensible intelligent man, we obtained much geographical information with regard to the country between the Missouri and Mississippi, and the various tribes of Sioux who inhabit it. DECEMBER 17TH

Tuesday. The thermometer at sunrise was 32° below 0. The Indians had invited us yesterday to join their chase to-day, but the seven men whom we sent returned in consequence of the cold, which was so severe last night that we were obliged to have the sentinel relieved every half hour. The northwest traders however left us on their return home. DECEMBER 18TH

Wednesday. The weather moderated, and the river rose a little, so that we were enabled to continue the picketing of the fort. Notwithstanding the extreme cold, we observe the Indians at the village engaged out in the open air at a game which resembled billiards more than any thing we had seen, and which we inclined to suspect may have been acquired by ancient intercourse with the French of Canada. From the first to the second chief's lodge, a distance of about fifty yards, was covered with timber smoothed and joined so as to be as level as the floor of one of our houses, with a battery at the end to stop the rings: these rings were of clay-stone and flat like the chequers for drafts, and the sticks were about four feet long, with two short pieces at one end in the form of a mace, so fixed that the whole will slide along the board. Two men fix themselves at one end, each provided with a stick, and one of them with a ring; they then run along the board, and about half way slide the sticks after the ring. DECEMBER 19TH

Thursday. The wind was from the N. W. the weather moderate, the thermometer 24° above 0 at sunrise. We availed ourselves of this change to picket the fort near the river. DECEMBER 20TH

Friday. The day was fine and warm, the wind N. W. by W. The Indian who had been prevented a few days ago from killing his wife, came with both his wives to the fort, and was very desirous of reconciling our interpreter, a DECEMBER 21ST jealousy against whom on account of his wife's taking refuge in his house, had been the cause of his animosity. A woman brought her child with an abscess in the lower part of the back, and offered as much corn as she could carry for some medicine; we administered to it of course very cheerfully.

DECEMBER 22D *Saturday.* A number of squaws and men dressed like squaws brought corn to trade for small articles with the men. Among other things we procured two horns of the animal called by the French the Rock [Rocky] mountain sheep, and known to the Mandans by the name of ahsahta. The animal itself is about the size of a small elk or large deer: the horns winding like those of a ram which they resemble also in texture, though larger and thicker.

DECEMBER 23D *Sunday.* The weather was fine and warm like that of yesterday: we were again visited by crowds of Indians of all descriptions, who came either to trade or from mere curiosity. Among the rest Kogahami, the Little Raven, brought his wife and son loaded with corn, and she then entertained us with a favourite Mandan dish, a mixture of pumpkins, beans, corn, and choke-cherries with the stones, all boiled together in a kettle, and forming a composition by no means unpalatable.

DECEMBER 24TH *Monday.* The day continued warm and pleasant, and the number of visitors became troublesome. As a present to three of the chiefs, we divided a fillet of sheep-skin which we brought for spunging into three pieces each of two inches in width; they were delighted at the gift, which they deemed of equal value with a fine horse. We this day completed our fort, and the next morning being Christmas, *Tuesday, 25th,* we were awakened before day by a discharge of three platoons from the party. We had told the Indians not to visit us as it was one of our great medicine days; so that the men remained at home and amused themselves in various ways, particularly with dancing in which they take great pleasure. The American flag was hoisted for the first time in the fort; the best provisions we had were brought out, and this, with a little brandy, enabled them to pass the day in great festivity.

DECEMBER 26TH *Wednesday.* The weather is again temperate, but no Indians have come to see us. One of the northwest traders who came down to request the aid of our Minnetaree interpreter, informs us that a party of Minnetarees who had gone in pursuit of the Assiniboins who lately stole their horses had just returned. As is their custom, they came back in small detachments, the last of which brought home eight horses which they had captured or stolen from an Assiniboin camp on Mouse river.

DECEMBER 27TH *Thursday.* A little fine snow fell this morning and the air was colder than yesterday, with a high northwest wind. We were fortunate enough to have among our men a good blacksmith, whom we set to work to make a variety of articles: his operations seemed to surprise the Indians who came to see us, but nothing could equal their astonishment at the bellows, which they considered as a very great medicine.

Having heretofore promised a more particular account of the Sioux, the following may serve as a general outline of their history:

Almost the whole of that vast tract of country comprised between the Mississippi, the Red river of Lake Winnipeg, the Saskaskawan, and the Missouri, is loosely occupied by a great nation whose primitive name is Darcota, but who are called Sioux by the French, Sues by the English. Their original seats were on the Mississippi, but they have gradually spread themselves abroad and become subdivided into numerous tribes. Of these, what may be considered as the Darcotas are the Mindawarcarton, or Minowakanton, known to the French by the name of the Gens du Lac, or People of the Lake. Their residence is on both sides of the Mississippi near the falls of St. Anthony, and the probable number of their warriors about three hundred. Above them, on the river St. Peter's, is the Wahpatone, a smaller band of nearly two hundred men; and still further up the same river below Yellowwood river are the Wahpatootas or Gens de Feuilles, an inferior band of not more than one hundred men; while the sources of the St. Peter's are occupied by the Sisatoones, a band consisting of about two hundred warriors.

These bands rarely if ever approach the Missouri, which is occupied by their kinsmen the Yanktons and the Tetons. The Yanktons are of two tribes, those of the plains, or rather of the north, a wandering race of about five hundred men, who roam over the plains at the heads of the Jacques, the Sioux, and the Red river; and those of the south, who possess the country between the Jacques and Sioux rivers and the Desmoine. But the bands of Sioux most known on the Missouri are the Tetons. The first who are met on ascending the Missouri is the tribe called by the French the Tetons of the Bois Brulé or Burntwood, who reside on both sides of the Missouri, about White and Teton rivers, and number two hundred warriors. Above them on the Missouri are the Teton Okandandas, a band of one hundred and fifty men living below the Chayenne river, between which and the Wetarhoo river is a third band, called Teton Minnakenozzo, of nearly two hundred and fifty men; and below the Warreconne is the fourth and last tribe of Tetons of about three hundred men, and called Teton Saone. Northward of these, between the Assiniboin and the Missouri, are two bands of Assiniboins, one on Mouse river of about two hundred men, and called Assiniboin Menatopa; the other, residing on both sides of White river, called by the French Gens de Feuilles, and amounting to two hundred and fifty men. Beyond these a band of Assiniboins of four hundred and fifty men, and called the Big Devils, wander on the heads of Milk, Porcupine, and Martha's rivers; while still farther to the north are seen two bands of the same nation, one of five hundred and the other of two hundred, roving on the Saskaskawan. Those Assiniboins are recognized by a similarity of language, and by tradition as descendants or seceders from the Sioux; though often at war are still acknowledged as relations. The Sioux themselves, though scattered, meet annually on the Jacques, those on the Missouri trading with those on the Mississippi.

Chapter 6
STILL WITH THE MANDANS

FRIDAY, DECEMBER 28TH, 1804 The wind continued high last night, the frost severe, and the snow drifting in great quantities through the plains.

Saturday, 29th. There was a frost fell last night nearly one quarter of an inch in depth, which continued to fall till the sun had gained some height: the mercury at sunrise stood at 9° below 0: there were a number of Indians at the fort in the course of the day.

Sunday, 30th. The weather was cold, and the thermometer 20° below 0. We killed one deer, and yesterday one of the men shot a wolf. The Indians brought corn, beans, and squashes, which they very readily gave for getting their axes and kettles mended. In their general conduct during these visits they are honest, but will occasionally pilfer any small article.

DECEMBER 31ST *Monday.* During the night there was a high wind which covered the ice with hillocks of mixed sand and snow; the day was however fine, and the Indians came in great numbers for the purpose of having their utensils repaired.

Tuesday, January 1st, 1805

The new year was welcomed by two shots from the swivel and a round of small arms. The weather was cloudy but moderate; the mercury which at sunrise was at 18°, in the course of the day rose to 34° above 0: towards evening it began to rain, and at night we had snow, the temperature for which is about 0. In the morning we permitted sixteen men with their music to go up to the first village, where they delighted the whole tribe with their dances, particularly with the movements of one of the Frenchmen who danced on his head. In return they presented the dancers with several buffalo robes and quantities of corn. We were desirous of showing this attention to the village, because they had received an impression that we had been wanting in regard for them, and because they had in consequence circulated invidious comparisons between us and the northern traders; all these, however, they declared to captain Clark, who visited them in the course of the morning, were made in jest.

As captain Clark was about leaving the village, two of their chiefs returned from a mission to the Grosventres or wandering Minnetarees. These people were encamped about ten miles above, and while there one of the Ahnahaways had stolen a Minnetaree girl: the whole nation immediately espoused the quarrel, and one hundred and fifty of their warriors were marching down to revenge the insult on the Ahnahaways. The chief of that nation took the girl from the ravisher, and giving her to the Mandans requested their intercession. The messengers went out to meet the warriors, and delivered the young damsel into the hands of her countrymen, smoked the pipe of peace with them, and were fortunate enough to avert their indignation and induce them to return. In the evening some of the men came to the fort and the rest slept in the village. Poscapsahe also visited us and brought some meat on his wife's back.

Wednesday. It snowed last night, and during this day the same scene of gayety was renewed at the second village, and all the men returned in the evening.

JANUARY 2D

Thursday. Last night it became very cold, and this morning we had some snow: our hunters were sent out for buffalo, but the game had been frightened from the river by the Indians, so that they obtained only one: they however killed a hare and a wolf. Among the Indians who visited us was a Minnetaree who came to seek his wife: she had been much abused and came here for protection, but returned with him, as we had no authority to separate those whom even the Mandan rites had united.

JANUARY 3D

Friday. The morning was cloudy and warm, the mercury being 28° above 0: but towards evening the wind changed to northwest, and the weather became cold. We sent some hunters down the river, but they killed only one buffalo and a wolf. We received the visit of Kagohami who is very friendly, and to whom we gave a handkerchief and two files.

JANUARY 4TH

Saturday. We had high and boisterous winds last night and this morning: the Indians continue to purchase repairs with grain of different kinds. In the first village there has been a buffalo dance for the last three nights, which has put them all into commotion, and the description which we received from those of the party who visited the village and from other sources, is not a little ludicrous:

JANUARY 5TH

> The buffalo dance is an institution originally intended for the benefit of the old men, and practised at their suggestion. When buffalo becomes scarce they send a man to harangue the village, declaring that the game is far off and that a feast is necessary to bring it back, and if the village be disposed a day and place is named for the celebration of it. At the appointed hour the old men arrive, and seat themselves crosslegged on skins round a fire in the middle of the lodge with a sort of doll or small image, dressed like a female, placed before them. The young men bring with them a platter of provisions, a pipe of tobacco, and their wives, whose dress on the occasion is only a robe or mantle loosely thrown round the body. On their arrival each youth selects the old man whom he means to distinguish by his favour, and spreads before him the provisions, after which he presents the pipe and smokes with him. Mox senex vir simulacrum parvae puellae ostensit. Tunc egrediens caetu, jecit effigium solo et superincumbens, senili ardore veneris complexit. Hoc est signum. Denique uxor e turba recessit, et jactu corporis, fovet amplexus viri solo recubante. Maritus appropinquans senex vir dejecto vultu, et honorem et dignitatem ejus conservare amplexu uxoris illum oravit. Forsitan imprimis ille refellit; dehinc, maritus multus precibus, multis lachrymis, et multis donis vehementer intercessit. Tunc senex amator perculsus miserecordia, tot precibus, tot lachrymis, et tot donis, conjugali amplexu submisit. Multum ille jactatus est, sed debilis et effoetus senectute, frustra jactatus est. Maritus interdum stans juxta guadit multum honore, et ejus dignitati sic conservata. Unus nostrum sodalium multum alacrior et potentior juventute, hac nocte honorem quartuor maritorum custodivit.
>
> [The young men, who have their wives back of the circle, go each to one of the old men with a whining tone and request the old man to take his

wife (who presents herself naked except a robe) and ——— (or, sleep with her). The girl then takes the old man (who very often can scarcely walk) and leads him to a convenient place for the business, after which they return to the lodge. If the old man (or a white man) returns to the lodge without gratifying the man and his wife, he offers her again and again. It is often the case that after the second time without kissing, the husband throws a new robe over the old man and begs him not to despise him and his wife. (We sent a man to this Medicine Dance last night; they gave him four girls.) All this is to cause the buffalo to come near so that they may kill them.—*Clark's Journal.*]

JANUARY 6TH *Sunday.* A clear cold morning with high wind: we caught in a trap a large gray wolf, and last night obtained in the same way a fox who had for some time infested the neighbourhood of the fort. Only a few Indians visited us to-day.

JANUARY 7TH *Monday.* The weather was again clear and cold with a high northwest wind, and the thermometer at sunrise 22° below 0: the river fell an inch. Shahaka the Big White chief dined with us, and gave a connected sketch of the country as far as the mountains.

JANUARY 8TH *Tuesday.* The wind was still from the northwest, the day cold, and we received few Indians at the fort. Besides the buffalo dance we have just described, there is another called medicine dance, an entertainment given by any person desirous of doing honour to his medicine or genius. He announces, that on such a day he will sacrifice his horses, or other property, and invites the young females of the village to assist in rendering homage to his medicine; all the inhabitants may join in the solemnity, which is performed in the open plain and by daylight, but the dance is reserved for the virgins or at least the unmarried females, who disdain the incumbrance or the ornament of dress. The feast is opened by devoting the goods of the master of the feast to his medicine, which is represented by a head of the animal itself, or by a medicine bag if the deity be an invisible being. The young women then begin the dance, in the intervals of which each will prostrate herself before the assembly to challenge or reward the boldness of the youth, who are often tempted by feeling or the hopes of distinction to achieve the adventure.

A medicine bag.

JANUARY 9TH *Wednesday.* The weather is cold, the thermometer at sunrise 21° below 0. Kagohami breakfasted with us, and captain Clark with three or four men accompanied him and a party of Indians to hunt, in which they were so fortunate as to kill a number of buffalo: but they were incommoded by snow, by high and squally winds, and by extreme cold: several of the Indians came to the fort nearly frozen, others are missing, and we are uneasy, for one of our men who was separated from the rest during the chase has not returned.

JANUARY 10TH *Thursday.* In the morning, however, he came back just as we were sending out five men in search of him. The night had been excessively cold, and this morning at sunrise the mercury stood at 40° below 0, or 72 below the freezing point. He had, however, made a fire and kept himself tolerably warm. A young Indian, about thirteen years of age, also came in soon after. His father who came last night to inquire after him very anxiously, had sent him in the afternoon to the fort: he was overtaken by the night, and was obliged to sleep on the snow with no covering except a pair of antelope-skin moccasins and leggings and a buffalo-robe: his feet being frozen we put them into cold water, and gave him every attention in our power. About the same time an Indian who had also been missing returned to the fort, and although his dress was very thin, and he had slept on the snow without a fire, he had not suffered the slightest inconvenience. We have indeed observed that these Indians support the rigours of the season in a way which we had hitherto thought impossible. A more pleasing reflection occurred at seeing the warm interest which the situation of these two persons had excited in the village, the boy had been a prisoner and adopted from charity, yet the distress of the father proved that he felt for him the tenderest affection, the man was a person of no distinction, yet the whole village was full of anxiety for his safety, and when they came to us, borrowed a sleigh to bring them home with ease, if they survived, or to carry their bodies if they had perished.

Friday. We despatched three hunters to join the same number whom we had sent below about seven miles to hunt elk. Like that of yesterday the weather to-day was cold and clear, the thermometer standing at 38° below 0. Poscopsahe and Shotahawrora visited us, and passed the night at the fort. JANUARY 11TH

Saturday. The weather continues very cold, the mercury at sunrise being 20° below 0. Three of the hunters returned, having killed three elk. JANUARY 12TH

Sunday. We have a continuation of clear weather, and the cold has increased, the mercury having sunk to 34° below 0. Nearly one half of the Mandan nation passed down the river to hunt for several days; in these excursions men, women and children, with their dogs, all leave the village together, and after discovering a spot convenient for the game, fix their tents; all the family bear their part in the labour, and the game is equally divided among the families of the tribe. When a single hunter returns from the chase with more than is necessary for his own immediate consumption, the neighbours are entitled by custom to a share of it: they do not however ask for it, but send a squaw, who without saying any thing, sits down by the door of the lodge till the master understands the hint, and gives her gratuitously a part for her family. Chaboneau who with one man had gone to some lodges of Minnetarees near the Turtle mountain, returned with their faces much frostbitten. They had been about ninety miles distant, and procured from the inhabitants some meat and grease, with which they loaded the horses. He informs us that the agent of the Hudson Bay company at that place, had been endeavouring to make unfavourable impressions with regard to us on the mind of the great chief, and that the N. W. company intend building a fort there. The great chief had in consequence spoken slightly of the Americans, but said that if we would give him our great flag he would come and see us. JANUARY 13TH

Monday. The Mandans continue to pass down the river on their hunting party, and were joined by six of our men. One of those sent on Thursday re- JANUARY 14TH turned, with information that one of his companions had his feet so badly frostbitten that he could not walk home. In their excursion they had killed a buffalo, a wolf, two porcupines and a white hare. The weather was more moderate to-day, the mercury being at 16° below 0, and the wind from the S.E. We had however some snow, after which it remained cloudy.

JANUARY 15TH *Tuesday.* The morning is much warmer than yesterday, and the snow begins to melt, though the wind after being for some time from the S. E. suddenly shifted to N. W. Between twelve and three o'clock A.M. there was a total eclipse of the moon, from which we obtained a part of the observation necessary for ascertaining the longitude.

We were visited by four of the most distinguished men of the Minnetarees, to whom we showed marked attentions, as we knew that they had been taught to entertain strong prejudices against us; these we succeeded so well in removing, that when in the morning, *Wednesday, 16th*, about thirty Mandans, among whom six were chiefs came to see us, the Minnetarees reproached them with their falsehoods, declaring that they were bad men and ought to hide themselves. They had told the Minnetarees that we would kill them if they came to the fort, yet on the contrary they had spent a night there and been treated with kindness by the whites, who had smoked with them and danced for their amusement. Kagohami visited us and brought us a little corn, and soon afterwards one of the first war chiefs of the Minnetarees came accompanied by his squaw, a handsome woman, whom he was desirous we should use during the night. He favoured us with a more acceptable present, a draft of the Missouri in his manner, and informed us of his intention to go to war in the spring against the Snake Indians; we advised him to reflect seriously before he committed the peace of his nation to the hazards of war; to look back on the numerous nations whom war has destroyed, that if he wished his nation to be happy he should cultivate peace and intercourse with all his neighbours, by which means they would procure more horses, increase in numbers, and that if he went to war he would displease his great father the president, and forfeit his protection. We added that we had spoken thus to all the tribes whom we had met, that they had all opened their ears, and that the president would compel those who did not voluntarily listen to his advice. Although a young man of only twenty-six years of age, this discourse seemed to strike him. He observed that if it would be displeasing to us he would not go to war, since he had horses enough, and that he would advise all the nation to remain at home, until we had seen the Snake Indians, and discovered whether their intentions were pacific. The party who went down with the horses for the man who was frostbitten returned, and we are glad to find his complaint not serious.

JANUARY 17TH *Thursday.* The day was very windy from the north; the morning clear and cold, the thermometer at sunrise being at 0: we had several Indians with us.

JANUARY 18TH *Friday.* The weather is fine and moderate. Messrs. Laroche and M'Kenzie, two of the N. W. company's traders, visited us with some of the Minnetarees. In the afternoon two of our hunters returned, having killed four wolves and a blaireau.

Saturday. Another cloudy day. The two traders set out on their return, and we sent two men with the horses thirty miles below to the hunting camp. JANUARY 19TH

Sunday. The day fair and cold. A number of Indians visit us with corn to exchange for articles, and to pay for repairs to their household utensils. JANUARY 20TH

Monday. The weather was fine and moderate. The hunters all returned, having killed during their absence three elk, four deer, two porcupines, a fox and a hare. JANUARY 21ST

Tuesday. The cold having moderated and the day pleasant, we attempted to cut the boats out of the ice, but at the distance of eight inches came to water, under which the ice became three feet thick, so that we were obliged to desist. JANUARY 22D

Wednesday. The cold weather returned, the mercury having sunk 2° below 0, and the snow fell four inches deep. JANUARY 23D

Thursday. The day was colder than any we have had lately, the thermometer being at 12° below 0. The hunters whom we sent out returned unsuccessful, and the rest were occupied in cutting wood to make charcoal. JANUARY 24TH

Friday. The thermometer was at 25° below 0, the wind from N. W. and the day fair, so that the men were employed in preparing coal, and cutting the boats out of the ice. A band of Assiniboins headed by their chief, called by the French, Son of the Little Calf, have arrived at the villages. JANUARY 25TH

Saturday. A fine warm day: a number of Indians dine with us: and one of our men is attacked with a violent pleurisy. JANUARY 26TH

Sunday. Another warm and pleasant day: we again attempted to get the boat out of the ice. The man who has the pleurisy was blooded and sweated, and we were forced to take off the toes of the young Indian who was frostbitten some time since. Our interpreter returned from the villages, bringing with him three of Mr. Laroche's horses which he had sent in order to keep them out of the way of the Assiniboins, who are very much disposed to steal, and who have just returned to their camp. JANUARY 27TH

Monday. The weather to-day is clear and cold: we are obliged to abandon the plan of cutting the boat through the ice, and therefore made another attempt the next day, *Tuesday 29th*, by heating a quantity of stones so as to warm the water in the boat, and thaw the surrounding ice: but in this too we were disappointed, as all the stones on being put into the fire cracked into pieces: the weather warm and pleasant: the man with the pleurisy is recovering. JANUARY 28TH

Wednesday. The morning was fair, but afterwards became cloudy. Mr. Laroche, the trader from the Northwest company, paid us a visit, in hopes of being able to accompany us on our journey westward, but this proposal we thought it best to decline. JANUARY 30TH

JANUARY 31ST　*Thursday.* It snowed last night, and the morning is cold and disagreeable, with a high wind from the northwest: we sent five hunters down the river. Another man is taken with the pleurisy.

Friday, February 1st, 1805

A cold windy day: our hunters returned having killed only one deer. One of the Minnetaree war chiefs, a young man named Maubuksheahokeah or Seeing Snake, came to see us and procure a war hatchet: he also requested that we would suffer him to go to war against the Sioux and Ricaras who had killed a Mandan some time ago: this we refused for reasons which we explained to him. He acknowledged that we were right, and promised to open his ears to our counsels.

FEBRUARY 2D　*Saturday.* The day is fine: another deer was killed. Mr. Laroche who has been very anxious to go with us left the fort to-day, and one of the squaws of the Minnetaree interpreter is taken ill.

FEBRUARY 3D　*Sunday.* The weather is again pleasant: disappointed in all our efforts to get the boats free, we occupied ourselves in making iron spikes so as to prize them up by means of long poles.

FEBRUARY 4TH　*Monday.* The morning fair and cold, the mercury at sunrise being 18° below 0, and the wind from the northwest. The stock of meat which we had procured in November and December being now nearly exhausted, it became necessary to renew our supply; captain Clark therefore took eighteen men, and with two sleighs and three horses descended the river for the purpose of hunting, as the buffalo has disappeared from our neighbourhood, and the Indians are themselves suffering for want of meat. Two deer were killed to-day but they were very lean.

FEBRUARY 5TH　*Tuesday.* A pleasant fair morning with the wind from northwest: a number of the Indians come with corn for the blacksmith, who being now provided with coal has become one of our greatest resources for procuring grain. They seem particularly attached to a battle axe, of a very inconvenient figure: it is made wholly of iron, the blade extremely thin, and from seven to nine inches long; it is sharp at the point and five or six inches on each side, whence they converge towards the eye, which is circular and about an inch in diameter, the blade itself being not more than an inch wide, the handle is straight, and twelve or fifteen inches long; the whole weighing about a pound. By way of ornament, the blade is perforated with several circular holes. The length of the blade compared with the shortness of the handle render it a weapon of very little strength, particularly as it is always used on horseback: there is still however another form which is even worse, the same sort of handle being fixed to a blade resembling an espontoon.

FEBRUARY 6TH　*Wednesday.* The morning was fair and pleasant, the wind N. W. A number of Indian chiefs visited us and withdrew after we had smoked with them contrary to their custom, for after being once introduced into our apartment they are fond of lounging about during the remainder of the day. One of the men killed three antelopes. Our blacksmith has his time completely occupied, so great is the demand for utensils of different kinds. The Indians are particularly fond of sheet iron, out of which they form points for arrows and instruments for scraping hides, and when the blacksmith cut up an old cambouse of that metal, we obtained for every piece of four inches square seven or eight gallons of corn from the Indians, who were delighted at the exchange.

Thursday. The morning was fair and much warmer than for some days, the thermometer being at 18° above 0, and the wind from the S. E. A number of Indians continue to visit us; but learning that the interpreter's squaws had been accustomed to unbar the gate during the night, we ordered a lock put on it, and that no Indian should remain in the fort all night, nor any person admitted during the hours when the gate is closed, that is from sunset to sunrise. — FEBRUARY 7TH

Friday. A fair pleasant morning, with S.E. winds. Poscopsahe came down to the fort with a bow, and apologized for his not having finished a shield which he had promised captain Lewis, and which the weather had prevented him from completing. This chief possesses more firmness, intelligence, and integrity, than any Indian of this country, and he might be rendered highly serviceable in our attempts to civilize the nation. He mentioned that the Mandans are very much in want of meat, and that he himself had not tasted any for several days. To this distress they are often reduced by their own improvidence, or by their unhappy situation. Their principal article of food is buffalo-meat, their corn, beans, and other grain being reserved for summer, or as a last resource against what they constantly dread, an attack from the Sioux, who drive off the game and confine them to their villages. The same fear too prevents their going out to hunt in small parties to relieve their occasional wants, so that the buffalo is generally obtained in large quantities, and wasted by carelessness. — FEBRUARY 8TH

Saturday. The morning was fair and pleasant, the wind from the S. E. Mr. M'Kenzie from the N. W. company establishment visited us. — FEBRUARY 9TH

Sunday. A slight snow fell in the course of the night, the morning was cloudy, and the northwest wind blew so high that although the thermometer was 18° above 0, the day was cooler than yesterday, when it was only 10° above the same point. Mr. M'Kenzie left us, and Chaboneau returned with information that our horses loaded with meat were below, but could not cross the ice not being shod. — FEBRUARY 10TH

Monday. We sent down a party with sleds, to relieve the horses from their loads; the weather fair and cold, with a N. W. wind. About five o'clock one of the wives of Chaboneau was delivered of a boy; this being her first child she was suffering considerable, when Mr. Jessaume told captain Lewis that he had frequently administered to persons in her situation, a small dose of the rattle of the rattlesnake which had never failed to hasten the delivery. Having some of the rattle, captain Lewis gave it to Mr. Jessaume who crum- — FEBRUARY 11TH

99

bled two of the rings of it between his fingers, and mixing it with a small quantity of water gave it to her. What effect it may really have had it might be difficult to determine, but captain Lewis was informed that she had not taken it more than ten minutes before the delivery took place.

FEBRUARY 12TH *Tuesday*. The morning is fair though cold, the mercury being 14° below 0, the wind from the S. E. About four o'clock the horses were brought in much fatigued; on giving them meal bran moistened with water they would not eat it, but preferred the bark of the cottonwood, which as is already observed forms their principal food during the winter. The horses of the Mandans are so often stolen by the Sioux, Ricaras, and Assiniboins, that the invariable rule now is to put the horses every night in the same lodge with the family. In the summer they ramble in the plains in the vicinity of the camp, and feed on the grass, but during cold weather the squaws cut down the cottonwood trees as they are wanted, and the horses feed on the boughs and bark of the tender branches, which are also brought into the lodges at night and placed near them. These animals are very severely treated; for whole days they are pursuing the buffalo, or burdened with the fruits of the chase, during which they scarcely ever taste food, and at night return to a scanty allowance of wood; yet the spirit of this valuable animal sustains him through all these difficulties, and he is rarely deficient either in flesh or vigour.

FEBRUARY 13TH *Wednesday*. The morning was cloudy, the thermometer at 2° below 0, the wind from the southeast. Captain Clark returned last evening with all his hunting party: during their excursion they had killed forty deer, three buffalo, and sixteen elk; but most of the game was too lean for use, and the wolves, who regard whatever lies out at night as their own, had appropriated a large part of it. When he left the fort on the *4th* instant, he descended on the ice twenty-two miles to New Mandan island, near some of their old villages, and encamped, having killed nothing, and therefore without food for the night.

Early on the *5th*, the hunters went out and killed two buffalo and a deer, but the last only could be used, the others being too lean. After breakfast they proceeded down to an Indian lodge and hunted during the day: the next morning, *6th*, they encamped forty-four miles from the fort on a sand point near the mouth of a creek on the southwest side, which they call Hunting creek, and during this and the following day hunted through all the adjoining plains, with much success, having killed a number of deer and elk. On the *8th*, the best of the meat was sent with the horses to the fort, and such parts of the remainder as were fit for use were brought to a point of the river three miles below, and after the bones were taken out, secured in pens built of logs, so as to keep off the wolves, ravens and magpies, who are very numerous and constantly disappoint the hunter of his prey; they then went to the low grounds near the Chisshetaw river where they encamped, but saw nothing except some wolves on the hills, and a number of buffalo too poor to be worth hunting. The next morning, *9th*, as there was no game and it would have been inconvenient to send it back sixty miles to the fort, they returned up the river, and for three days hunted along the banks and plains, and reached the fort in the evening of the *12th* much fatigued, having walked thirty miles that day on the ice and through the snow in many places knee deep, the moccasins too being nearly worn out: the only game which they saw besides what is mentioned, was some grouse on the sandbars in the river.

Thursday. Last night the snow fell three inches deep; the day was, however, fine. Four men were despatched with sleds and three horses to bring up the meat which had been collected by the hunters. They returned however, with intelligence that about twenty-one miles below the fort a party of upwards of one hundred men, whom they supposed to be Sioux, rushed on them, cut the traces of the sleds, and carried off two of the horses, the third being given up by intercession of an Indian who seemed to possess some authority over them; they also took away two of the men's knives, and a tomahawk, which last however they returned. We sent up to the Mandans to inform them of it, and to know whether any of them would join a party which intended to pursue the robbers in the morning. About twelve o'clock two of their chiefs came down and said that all their young men were out hunting, and that there were few guns in the village. Several Indians however, armed some with bows and arrows, some with spears and battle-axes, and two with fusils [muskets], accompanied captain Lewis, who set out *Friday 15th* at sunrise with twenty-four men. FEBRUARY 14TH

The morning was fine and cool, the thermometer being at 16° below 0. In the course of the day one of the Mandan chiefs returned from captain Lewis's party, his eye-sight having become so bad that he could not proceed. At this season of the year the reflection from the ice and snow is so intense as to occasion almost total blindness. This complaint is very common, and the general remedy is to sweat the part affected by holding the face over a hot stone, and receiving the fumes from snow thrown on it. A large red fox was killed to-day.

Saturday. The morning was warm, mercury at 32° above 0, the weather cloudy: several of the Indians who went with captain Lewis returned, as did also one of our men, whose feet had been frostbitten. FEBRUARY 16TH

Sunday. The weather continued as yesterday, though in the afternoon it became fair. Shotawhorora and his son came to see us, with about thirty pounds of dried buffalo meat and some tallow. FEBRUARY 17TH

Monday. The morning was cloudy with some snow, but in the latter part of the day it cleared up. Mr. M'Kenzie who had spent yesterday at the fort now left us. Our stock of meat is exhausted, so that we must confine ourselves to vegetable diet, at least till the return of the party: for this, however, we are at no loss, since both on this and the following day, *Tuesday 19th*, our blacksmith got large quantities of corn from the Indians who came in great numbers to see us. The weather was fair and warm, the wind from the south. FEBRUARY 18TH

Wednesday. The day was delightfully fine; the mercury being at sunrise 2° and in the course of the day 22° above 0, the wind southerly. Kagohami came down to see us early: his village is afflicted by the death of one of their eldest men, who from his account to us must have seen one hundred and FEBRUARY 20TH

101

twenty winters. Just as he was dying, he requested his grandchildren to dress him in his best robe when he was dead, and then carry him on a hill and seat him on a stone, with his face down the river towards their old villages, that he might go straight to his brother who had passed before him to the ancient village under ground. We have seen a number of Mandans who have lived to a great age; chiefly however the men, whose robust exercises fortify the body, while the laborious occupations of the women shorten their existence.

FEBRUARY 21ST *Thursday*. We had a continuation of the same pleasant weather. Oheenaw and Shahaka came down to see us, and mentioned that several of their countrymen had gone to consult their medicine stone as to the prospects of the following year. This medicine stone is the great oracle of the Mandans, and whatever it announces is believed with implicit confidence. Every spring, and on some occasions during the summer, a deputation visits the sacred spot, where there is a thick porous stone twenty feet in circumference, with a smooth surface. Having reached the place the ceremony of smoking to it is performed by the deputies, who alternately take a whiff themselves and then present the pipe to the stone; after this they retire to an adjoining wood for the night, during which it may be safely presumed that all the embassy do not sleep; and in the morning they read the destinies of the nation in the white marks on the stone, which those who made them are at no loss to decipher. The Minnetarees have a stone of a similar kind, which has the same qualities and the same influence over the nation.

      Captain Lewis returned from his excursion in pursuit of the Indians. On reaching the place where the Sioux had stolen our horses, they found only one sled, and several pair of moccasins which were recognized to be those of the Sioux. The party then followed the Indian tracks till they reached two old lodges where they slept, and the next morning pursued the course of the river till they reached some Indian camps, where captain Clark passed the night some time ago, and which the Sioux had now set on fire, leaving a little corn near the place in order to induce a belief that they were Ricaras. From this point the Sioux tracks left the river abruptly and crossed into the plains; but perceiving that there was no chance of overtaking them, captain Lewis went down to the pen where captain Clark had left some meat, which he found untouched by the Indians, and then hunted in the low grounds on the river, till he returned with about three thousand pounds of meat, some drawn in a sled by fifteen of the men, and the rest on horseback; having killed thirty-six deer, fourteen elk, and one wolf.

FEBRUARY 22D *Friday*. The morning was cloudy and a little snow fell, but in the afternoon the weather became fair. We were visited by a number of Indians, among whom was Shotawhorora, a chief of much consideration among the Mandans, although by birth a Ricara.

FEBRUARY 23D *Saturday*. The day is warm and pleasant. Having worked industriously yesterday and all this morning we were enabled to disengage one of the periogues and haul it on shore, and also nearly to cut out the second. The father of the boy whose foot had been so badly frozen, and whom we had now cured, came to-day and carried him home in a sleigh.

Sunday. The weather is again fine. We succeeded in loosening the second periogue and barge, though we found a leak in the latter. The whole of the next day, *Monday, 25th,* we were occupied in drawing up the boats on the bank: the smallest one we carried there with no difficulty, but the barge was too heavy for our elk-skin ropes which constantly broke. We were visited by Orupsehara, or Black Moccasin, and several other chiefs, who brought us presents of meat on the backs of their squaws, and one of the Minnetarees requested and obtained permission for himself and his two wives to remain all night in the fort. The day was exceedingly pleasant.

FEBRUARY 24TH

Tuesday. The weather is again fine. By great labour during the day we got all the boats on the bank by sunset, an operation which attracted a great number of Indians to the fort.

FEBRUARY 26TH

Wednesday. The weather continues fine. All of us employed in preparing tools to build boats for our voyage, as we find that small periogues will be much more convenient than the barge in ascending the Missouri.

FEBRUARY 27TH

Thursday. The day is clear and pleasant. Sixteen men were sent out to examine the country for trees suitable for boats, and were successful in finding them. Two of the N. W. company traders arrived with letters; they had likewise a root which is used for the cure of persons bitten by mad dogs, snakes, and other venomous animals: it is found on high grounds and the sides of hills, and the mode of using it is to scarify the wound, and apply to it an inch or more of the chewed or pounded root, which is to be renewed twice a day; the patient must not however chew or swallow any of the root, as an inward application might be rather injurious than beneficial.

FEBRUARY 28TH

    Mr. Gravelines with two Frenchmen and two Indians arrived from the Ricara nation, with letters from Mr. Anthony Tabeau. This last gentleman informs us that the Ricaras express their determination to follow our advice, and to remain at peace with the Mandans and Minnetarees, whom they are desirous of visiting; they also wish to know whether these nations would permit the Ricaras to settle near them, and form a league against their common enemies the Sioux. On mentioning this to the Mandans they agreed to it, observing that they always desired to cultivate friendship with the Ricaras, and that the Ahnahaways and Minnetarees have the same friendly views. Mr. Gravelines states that the band of Tetons we had seen was well disposed to us, owing to the influence of their chief the Black Buffalo; but that the three upper bands of Tetons, with the Sisatoons, and the Yanktons of the north, mean soon to attack the Indians in this quarter, with a resolution to put to death every white man they encounter. Moreover, that Mr. Cameron of St. Peter's has armed the Sioux against the Chippeways, who have lately put to death three of his men. The men who had stolen our horses we found to be all Sioux, who after committing the outrage went to the Ricara villages, where they said that they had hesitated about killing our men who were with the horses, but that in future they would put to death any of us they could, as we were bad medicines and deserved to be killed. The Ricaras were displeased at their conduct and refused to give them any thing to eat, which is deemed the greatest act of hostility short of actual violence.

Friday, March 1st, 1805

The day is fine, and the whole party is engaged, some in making ropes and periogues, others in burning coal, and making battle-axes to sell for corn.

MARCH 2D *Saturday.* Mr. Laroche one of the N. W. company's traders has just arrived with merchandise from the British establishments on the Assiniboin. The day is fine, and the river begins to break up in some places, the mercury being between 28° and 36° above 0, and the wind from the N. E. We were visited by several Indians.

MARCH 3D *Sunday.* The weather pleasant, the wind from the E. with clouds; in the afternoon the clouds disappeared and the wind came from the N. W. The men are all employed in preparing the boats; we are visited by Poscapsahe and several other Indians with corn. A flock of ducks passed up the river to-day.

MARCH 4TH *Monday.* A cloudy morning with N. W. wind, the latter part of the day clear. We had again some Indian visitors with a small present of meat. The Assiniboins, who a few days since visited the Mandans, returned, and attempted to take horses from the Minnetarees, who fired on them; a circumstance which may occasion some disturbance between the two nations.

MARCH 5TH *Tuesday.* About four o'clock in the morning there was a slight fall of snow, but the day became clear and pleasant with the mercury 40° above 0. We sent down an Indian and a Frenchman to the Ricara villages with a letter to Mr. Tabeau.

MARCH 6TH *Wednesday.* The day was cloudy and smoky in consequence of the burning of the plains by the Minnetarees; they have set all the neighbouring country on fire in order to obtain an early crop of grass which may answer for the consumption of their horses, and also as an inducement for the buffalo and other game to visit it. The horses stolen two days ago by the Assiniboins have been returned to the Minnetarees. Ohhaw second chief of the lower Minnetaree village came to see us. The river rose a little and overran the ice, so as to render the crossing difficult.

MARCH 7TH *Thursday.* The day was somewhat cloudy, and colder than usual; the wind from the northeast. Shotawhorora visited us with a sick child, to whom some medicine was administered. There were also other Indians who brought corn and dried buffalo meat in exchange for blacksmith's work.

MARCH 8TH *Friday.* The day cold and fair with a high easterly wind: we were visited by two Indians who gave us an account of the country and people near the Rocky mountains where they had been.

MARCH 9TH *Saturday.* The morning cloudy and cool, the wind from the north. The grand chief of the Minnetarees, who is called by the French Le Borgne, from his having but one eye, came down for the first time to the fort. He was received with much attention, two guns were fired in honour of his arrival, the curiosities were exhibited to him, and as he said that he had not received the presents which we had sent to him on his arrival, we again gave him a flag, a medal, shirt, armbraces and the usual presents on such occasions, with all which he was much pleased. In the course of the conversation, the chief observed that some foolish young men of his nation had told him there was a person among us who was quite black, and he wished to know if it could be true. We assured him that it was true, and sent for York: the Borgne was very much surprised at his appearance, examined him closely, and spit on his finger and rubbed the skin in order to wash off the paint; nor was it until the negro uncovered his head, and showed his short hair, that the Borgne could be persuaded that he was not a painted white man.

Sunday. A cold windy day. Tetuckopinreha, chief of the Ahnahaways, and the Minnetaree chief Ompschara, passed the day with us, and the former remained during the night. We had occasion to see an instance of the summary justice of the Indians: a young Minnetaree had carried off the daughter of Cagonomokshe, the Raven Man, second chief of the upper village of the Mandans; the father went to the village and found his daughter, whom he brought home, and took with him a horse belonging to the offender: this reprisal satisfied the vengeance of the father and of the nation, as the young man would not dare to reclaim his horse, which from that time became the property of the injured party.

MARCH 10TH

The stealing of young women is one of the most common offences against the police of the village, and the punishment of it always measured by the power or the passions of the kindred of the female. A voluntary elopement is of course more rigorously chastised. One of the wives of the Borgne deserted him in favour of a man who had been her lover before the marriage, and who after some time left her, and she was obliged to return to her father's house. As soon as he heard it the Borgne walked there and found her sitting near the fire: without noticing his wife, he began to smoke with the father; when they were joined by the old men of the village, who knowing his temper had followed in hopes of appeasing him. He continued to smoke quietly with them, till rising to return, he took his wife by the hair, led her as far as the door, and with a single stroke of his tomahawk put her to death before her father's eyes: then turning fiercely upon the spectators, he said that if any of her relations wished to avenge her, they might always find him at his lodge; but the fate of the woman had not sufficient interest to excite the vengeance of the family. The caprice or the generosity of the same chief gave a very different result to a similar incident which occurred some time afterwards. Another of his wives eloped with a young man, who not being able to support her as she wished they both returned to the village, and she presented herself before the husband, supplicating his pardon for her conduct: the Borgne sent for the lover: at the moment when the youth expected that he would be put to death, the chief mildly asked them if they still preserved their affection for each other; and on their declaring that want, and not a change of affection had induced them to return, he gave up his wife to her lover, with the liberal present of three horses, and restored them both to his favour.

MARCH 11TH *Monday.* The weather was cloudy in the morning and a little snow fell, the wind then shifted from southeast to northwest and the day became fair. It snowed again in the evening, but the next day, *Tuesday 12th*, was fair with the wind from the northwest.

MARCH 13TH *Wednesday.* We had a fine day, and a southwest wind. Mr. M'Kenzie came to see us, as did also many Indians who are so anxious for battle-axes that our smiths have not a moment's leisure, and procure us an abundance of corn. The river rose a little to-day, and so continued.

MARCH 14TH *Thursday.* The wind being from the west, and the day fine, the whole party were employed in building boats and in shelling corn.

MARCH 15TH *Friday.* The day is clear, pleasant and warm. We take advantage of the fine weather to hang all our Indian presents and other articles out to dry before our departure.

MARCH 16TH *Saturday.* The weather is cloudy, the wind from the southeast. A Mr. Garrow, a Frenchman who has resided a long time among the Ricaras and Mandans, explained to us the mode in which they make their large beads, an art which they are said to have derived from some prisoners of the Snake Indian nation, and the knowledge of which is a secret even now confined to a few among the Mandans and Ricaras. The process is as follows:

    Glass of different colours is first pounded fine and washed, till each kind, which is kept separate, ceases to stain the water thrown over it: some well seasoned clay, mixed with a sufficient quantity of sand to prevent its becoming very hard when exposed to heat, and reduced by water to the consistency of dough, is then rolled on the palm of the hand, till it becomes of the thickness wanted for the hole in the bead: these sticks of clay are placed upright, each on a little pedestal or ball of the same material about an ounce in weight, and distributed over a small earthen platter, which is laid on the fire for a few minutes, when they are taken off to cool: with a little paddle or shovel three or four inches long and sharpened at the end of the handle, the wet pounded glass is placed in the palm of the hand: the beads are made of an oblong form wrapped in a cylindrical form round the stick of clay which is laid crosswise over it, and gently rolled backwards and forwards till it becomes perfectly smooth. If it be desired to introduce any other colour, the surface of the bead is perforated with the pointed end of the paddle and the cavity filled with pounded glass of that colour. The sticks with the string of beads are then replaced on their pedestals, and the platter deposited on burning coals or hot embers. Over the platter an earthen pot containing about three gallons, with a mouth large enough to cover the platter, is reversed, being completely closed except a small aperture at the top, through which are watched the beads. A quantity of old dried wood formed into a sort of dough or paste is placed round the pot so as almost to cover it, and afterwards set on fire.

    The manufacturer then looks through the small hole in the pot, till he sees the beads assume a deep red colour, to which succeeds a paler or whitish red, or they become pointed at the upper extremity; on which the fire is removed and the pot suffered to cool gradually: at length it is removed, the beads taken out, the clay in the hollow of them picked out with an awl or needle, and it is then fit for use. The beads thus formed are in great demand among the Indians, and used as pendants to their ears and hair, and are sometimes worn round the neck.

MARCH 17TH

Sunday. A windy but clear and pleasant day, the river rising a little and open in several places. Our Minnetaree interpreter Chaboneau, whom we intended taking with us to the Pacific, had some days ago been worked upon by the British traders, and appeared unwilling to accompany us, except on certain terms: such as his not being subject to our orders, and do duty, or to return whenever he chose. As we saw clearly the source of his hesitation, and knew that it was intended as an obstacle to our views, we told him that the terms were inadmissible, and that we could dispense with his services: he had accordingly left us with some displeasure. Since then he had made an advance towards joining us, which we showed no anxiety to meet; but this morning he sent an apology for his improper conduct, and agreed to go with us and perform the same duties as the rest of the corps; we therefore took him again into our service.

MARCH 18TH

Monday. The weather was cold and cloudy, the wind from the north. We were engaged in packing up the goods into eight divisions, so as to preserve a portion of each in case of accident. We hear that the Sioux have lately attacked a party of Assiniboins and Knistenaux, near the Assiniboin river, and killed fifty of them.

MARCH 19TH

Tuesday. Some snow fell last night, and this morning was cold, windy, and cloudy. Shahaka and Kagohami came down to see us, as did another Indian with a sick child, to whom we gave some medicine. There appears to be an approaching war, as two parties have already gone from the Minnetarees, and a third is preparing.

MARCH 20TH

Wednesday. The morning was cold and cloudy, the wind high from the north, but the afternoon was pleasant. The canoes being finished, four of them were carried down to the river, at the distance of a mile and a half from where they were constructed.

MARCH 21ST

Thursday. The remaining periogues were hauled to the same place, and all the men except three, who were left to watch them returned to the fort. On his way down, which was about six miles, captain Clark passed along the points of the high hills, where he saw large quantities of pumicestone on the foot, sides and tops of the hills, which had every appearance of having been at some period on fire. He collected specimens of the stone itself, the pumicestone, and the hard earth; and on being put into the furnace the hard earth melted and glazed, the pumicestone melted, and the hardstone became a pumicestone glazed.

Chapter 7

FROM FORT MANDAN TO THE YELLOWSTONE

FRIDAY, MARCH 22D, 1805   This was a clear, pleasant day, with the wind from the S. S. W. We were visited by the second chief of the Minnetarees, to whom we gave a medal and some presents, accompanied by a speech. Mr. M'Kenzie and Mr. Laroche also came to see us. They all took their leave next day.

Saturday, 23d. Soon after their departure, a brother of the Borgne with other Indians came to the fort. The weather was fine, but in the evening we had the first rain that has fallen during the winter.

MARCH 24TH   *Sunday.* The morning cloudy, but the afternoon fair, the wind from the N. E. We are employed in preparing for our journey. This evening swans and wild-geese flew towards the N. E.

MARCH 25TH   *Monday.* A fine day, the wind S. W. The river rose nine inches, and the ice began breaking away in several places, so as to endanger our canoes which we are hauling down to the fort.

MARCH 26TH   *Tuesday.* The river rose only half an inch, and being choked up with ice near the fort, did not begin to run till towards evening. This day is clear and pleasant.

MARCH 27TH   *Wednesday.* The wind is still high from the S. W.: the ice which is occasionally stopped for a few hours is then thrown over shallow sandbars when the river runs. We had all our canoes brought down, and were obliged to calk and pitch very attentively the cracks so common in cottonwood.

MARCH 28TH   *Thursday.* The day is fair. Some obstacle above has prevented the ice from running. Our canoes are now nearly ready, and we expect to set out as soon as the river is sufficiently clear to permit us to pass.

MARCH 29TH   *Friday.* The weather clear, and the wind from N. W. The obstruction above gave way this morning, and the ice came down in great quantities; the river having fallen eleven inches in the course of the last twenty-four hours. We have had few Indians at the fort for the last three or four days, as they are now busy in catching the floating buffalo. Every spring as the river is breaking up the surrounding plains are set on fire, and the buffalo tempted to cross the river in search of the fresh grass which immediately succeeds to the burning: on their way they are often insulated on a large cake or mass of ice, which floats down the river: the Indians now select the most favourable points for attack, and as the buffalo approaches dart with astonishing agility across the trembling ice, sometimes pressing lightly a cake of not more than two feet square: the animal is of course unsteady, and his footsteps insecure on this new element, so that he can make but little resistance, and the hunter, who has given him his death wound, paddles his icy boat to the shore and secures his prey.

MARCH 30TH   *Saturday.* The day was clear and pleasant, the wind N. W. and the ice running in great quantities. All our Indian presents were again exposed to the air, and the barge made ready to descend the Missouri.

Sunday. Early this morning it rained, and the weather continued cloudy during the day; the river rose nine inches, the ice not running so much as yesterday. Several flocks of geese and ducks fly up the river.   MARCH 31ST

Monday, April 1st, 1805

This morning there was a thunder storm, accompanied with large hail, to which succeeded rain for about half an hour. We availed ourselves of this interval to get all the boats in the water. At four o'clock P.M. it began to rain a second time, and continued till twelve at night. With the exception of a few drops at two or three different times, this is the first rain we have had since the 15th of October last.

Tuesday. The wind was high last night and this morning from N. W. and the weather continued cloudy. The Mandans killed yesterday twenty-one elk, about fifteen miles below, but they were so poor as to be scarcely fit for use.   APRIL 2D

Wednesday. The weather is pleasant, though there was a white frost and some ice on the edge of the water. We were all engaged in packing up our baggage and merchandise.   APRIL 3D

Thursday. The day is clear and pleasant, though the wind is high from N. W. We now packed up in different boxes a variety of articles for the president, which we shall send in the barge. They consisted of a stuffed male and female antelope with their skeletons, a weasel, three squirrels from the Rocky mountains, the skeleton of the prairie wolf, those of the white and gray hare, a male and female blaireau, or burrowing dog of the prairie, with a skeleton of the female, two burrowing squirrels, a white weasel, and the skin of the louservia, the horns of the mountain ram, or big-horn, a pair of large elk horns, the horns and tail of the black-tailed deer, and a variety of skins, such as those of the red fox, white hare, martin, yellow bear obtained from the Sioux; also, a number of articles of Indian dress, among which was a buffalo robe, representing a battle fought about eight years since between the Sioux and Ricaras against the Mandans and Minnetarees, in which the combatants are represented on horseback.   APRIL 4TH

    It has of late years excited much discussion to ascertain the period when the art of painting was first discovered: how hopeless all researches of this kind are, is evident from the foregoing fact. It is indebted for its origin to one of the strongest passions of the human heart; a wish to preserve the features of a departed friend, or the memory of some glorious exploit: this inherits equally the bosoms of all men either civilized or savage. Such sketches, rude and imperfect as they are, delineate the predominant character of the savage nations. If they are peaceable and inoffensive, the drawings usually consist of local scenery, and their favourite diversions. If the band are rude and ferocious, we observe tomahawks, scalping-knives, bows, arrows, and all the engines of destruction.

    Also sent were a Mandan bow and quiver of arrows; also some Ricara tobacco-seed and an ear of Mandan corn; to these were added a box of plants, another of insects, and three cases containing a burrowing squirrel, a prairie hen, and four magpies, all alive.

APRIL 5TH *Friday.* Fair and pleasant, but the wind high from the northwest: we were visited by a number of Mandans, and are occupied in loading our boats in order to proceed on our journey.

APRIL 6TH *Saturday.* Another fine day with a gentle breeze from the south. The Mandans continue to come to the fort; and in the course of the day informed us of the arrival of a party of Ricaras on the other side of the river. We sent our interpreter to inquire into their reason for coming; and in the morning, *Sunday 7th*, he returned with a Ricara chief and three of his nation. The chief, whose name is Kagohweto, or Brave Raven, brought a letter from Mr. Tabeau, mentioning the wish of the grand chiefs of the Ricaras to visit the president, and requesting permission for himself and four men to join our boat when it descends; to which we consented, as it will then be manned with fifteen hands and be able to defend itself against the Sioux. After presenting the letter, he told us that he was sent with ten warriors by his nation to arrange their settling near the Mandans and Minnetarees, whom they wished to join; that he considered all the neighbouring nations friendly except the Sioux, whose persecution they would no longer withstand, and whom they hoped to repel by uniting with the tribes in this quarter: he added that the Ricaras intended to follow our advice and live in peace with all nations, and requested that we would speak in their favour to the Assiniboin Indians. This we willingly promised to do, and assured them that their great father would protect them and no longer suffer the Sioux to have good guns, or to injure his dutiful children. We then gave him a small medal, a certificate of his good conduct, a carrot of tobacco, and some wampum, with which he departed for the Mandan village well satisfied with his reception. Having made all our arrangements, we left the fort about five o'clock in the afternoon.

The party now consisted of thirty-two persons. Besides ourselves were sergeants John Ordway, Nathaniel Pryor, and Patrick Gass: the privates were William Bratton, John Colter, John Collins, Peter Cruzatte, Robert Frazier, Reuben Fields, Joseph Fields, George Gibson, Silas Goodrich, Hugh Hall, Thomas P. Howard, Baptiste Lapage, Francis Labiche, Hugh M'Neal, John Potts, John Shields, George Shannon, John B. Thompson, William Werner, Alexander Willard, Richard Windsor, Joseph Whitehouse, Peter Wiser, and captain Clark's black servant York. The two interpreters, were George Drewyer and Toussaint Chaboneau. The wife [Sacajawea] of Chaboneau also accompanied us with her young child, and we hope may be useful as an interpreter among the Snake Indians. She was herself one of that tribe, but having been taken in war by the Minnetarees, by whom she was sold as a slave to Chaboneau, who brought her up and afterwards married her. One of the Mandans likewise embarked with us, in order to go to the Snake Indians and obtain a peace with them for his countrymen. All this party with the baggage was stowed in six small canoes and two large periogues.

We left the fort with fair pleasant weather though the northwest wind was high, and after making about four miles encamped on the north

BUFFALO DANCE (Bodmer)

side of the Missouri, nearly opposite the first Mandan village. At the same time that we took our departure, our barge manned with seven soldiers, two Frenchmen, and Mr. Gravelines as pilot, sailed for the United States loaded with our presents and despatches.

Monday. The day was clear and cool, the wind from the northwest, so that we travelled slowly. After breakfasting at the second Mandan village, we passed the Mahaha at the mouth of Knife river, a handsome stream about eighty yards wide. Beyond this we reached the island which captain Clark had visited on the *30th October*. This island has timber as well as the lowlands on the north, but its distance from the water had prevented our encamping there during the winter. From the head of this island we made three and a half miles to a point of wood on the north, passing a high bluff on the south, and having come about fourteen miles. In the course of the day one of our boats filled and was near sinking; we however saved her with the loss of a little biscuit and powder. APRIL 8TH

Tuesday. We set off as soon as it was light, and proceeded five miles to breakfast, passing a low ground on the south, covered with groves of cottonwood timber. At the distance of six miles, we reached on the north a hunting camp of Minnetarees consisting of thirty lodges, and built in the usual form of earth and timber. Two miles and a quarter farther, comes in on the same side Miry creek, a small stream about ten yards wide, which, rising in some lakes near the Mouse river, passes through beautiful level fertile plains without timber in a direction nearly southwest; the banks near its entrance being steep, and rugged on both sides of the Missouri. Three miles above this creek we came to a hunting party of Minnetarees, who had prepared a park or inclosure and were waiting the return of the antelope: this animal, which in the autumn retires for food and shelter to the Black mountains during the winter, recross the river at this season of the year, and spread themselves through the plains on the north of the Missouri. We halted and smoked a short time with them, and then proceeded on through handsome plains on each side of the river, and encamped at the distance of twenty-three and a half miles on the north side: the day was clear and pleasant, the wind high from the south, but afterwards changed to a western steady breeze. APRIL 9TH

    The bluffs which we passed to-day are upwards of one hundred feet high, composed of a mixture of yellow clay and sand, with many horizontal strata of carbonated wood resembling pit-coal, from one to five feet in depth, and scattered through the bluff at different elevations, some as high as eighty feet above the water: the hills along the river are broken, and present every appearance of having been burned at some former period; great quantities of pumicestone and lava or rather earth, which seems to have been boiled and then hardened by exposure, being seen in many parts of these hills where they are broken and washed down into gullies by the rain and melting snow.

    A great number of brants pass up the river: there are some of them perfectly white, except the large feathers of the first and second joint of the wing which are black, though in every other characteristic they resemble common gray brant: we also saw but could not procure an animal [pouched

111

rat or pocket gopher] that burrows in the ground, and similar in every respect to the burrowing squirrel, except that it is only one third of its size. This may be the animal whose works we have often seen in the plains and prairies; they resemble the labours of the salamander [so called] in the sand hills of South Carolina and Georgia, and like him, the animals rarely come above ground; they consist of a little hillock of ten or twelve pounds of loose ground which would seem to have been reversed from a pot, though no aperture is seen through which it could have been thrown: on removing gently the earth, you discover that the soil has been broken in a circle of about an inch and a half diameter, where the ground is looser though still no opening is perceptible. When we stopped for dinner the squaw went out, and after penetrating with a sharp stick the holes of the mice [gophers] near some driftwood, brought to us a quantity of wild artichokes, which the mice collect and hoard in large numbers; the root is white, of an ovate form, from one to three inches long, and generally of the size of a man's finger, and two, four, and sometimes six roots are attached to a single stalk. Its flavour as well as the stalk which issues from it resemble those of the Jerusalem artichoke, except that the latter is much larger. A large beaver was caught in a trap last night, and the mosquitoes begin to trouble us.

APRIL 10TH *Wednesday.* We again set off early with clear pleasant weather, and halted about ten for breakfast, above a sandbank which was falling in, and near a small willow island. On both sides of the Missouri, after ascending the hills near the water, one fertile unbroken plain extends itself as far as the eye can reach, without a solitary tree or shrub, except in moist situations or in the steep declivities of hills where they are sheltered from the ravages of fire. At the distance of twelve miles we reached the lower point of a bluff on the south; which is in some parts on fire and throws out quantities of smoke which has a strong sulphurous smell, the coal and other appearances in the bluffs being like those described yesterday.

    At one o'clock we overtook three Frenchmen who left the fort a few days before us, in order to make the first attempt on this river of hunting beaver, which they do by means of traps: their efforts promise to be successful for they have already caught twelve which are finer than any we have ever seen: they mean to accompany us as far as the Yellowstone river in order to obtain our protection against the Assiniboins who might attack them.

    In the evening we encamped on a willow point to the south opposite to a bluff, above which a small creek falls in, and just above a remarkable bend in the river to the southwest, which we called the Little Basin. The low grounds which we passed to-day possess more timber than is usual, and are wider; the current is moderate, at least not greater than that of the Ohio in high tides; the banks too fall in but little; so that the navigation comparatively with that lower down the Missouri is safe and easy. We were enabled to make eighteen and a half miles: we saw the track of a large white bear, there were also a herd of antelopes in the plains; the geese and swan are now feeding in considerable quantities on the young grass in the low prairies; we shot a prairie hen, and a bald eagle of which there were many nests in the tall cottonwood trees; but could procure neither of two elk which were in the plain. Our old companions the mosquitoes have renewed their visit, and gave us much uneasiness.

Thursday. We set out at daylight, and after passing bare and barren hills on the south, and a plain covered with timber on the north, breakfasted at five miles distance: here we were regaled with a deer brought in by the hunters, which was very acceptable as we had been for several days without fresh meat; the country between this and fort Mandan being so frequently disturbed by hunters that the game has become scarce. We then proceeded with a gentle breeze from the south which carried the periogues on very well; the day was however so warm that several of the men worked with no clothes except round the waist, which is the less inconvenient as we are obliged to wade in some places owing to the shallowness of the river. At seven miles we reached a large sandbar making out from the north. We again stopped for dinner, after which we went on to a small plain on the north covered with cottonwood where we encamped, having made nineteen miles.

APRIL 11TH

The country around is much the same as that we passed yesterday: on the sides of the hills, and even on the banks of the rivers, as well as on the sandbars, is a white substance [alkali] which appears in considerable quantities on the surface of the earth, and tastes like a mixture of common salt with glauber salts: many of the streams which come from the foot of the hills, are so strongly impregnated with this substance, that the water has an unpleasant taste and a purgative effect. A beaver was caught last night by one of the Frenchmen; we killed two geese, and saw some cranes, the largest bird of that kind common to the Missouri and Mississippi, and perfectly white except the large feathers on the two first joints of the wing which are black. Under a bluff opposite to our encampment we discovered some Indians with horses, whom we supposed were Minnetarees, but the width of the river prevented our speaking to them.

Friday. We set off early and passed a high range of hills on the south side, our periogues being obliged to go over to the south, in order to avoid a sandbank which was rapidly falling in. At six miles we came to at the lower side of the entrance of the Little Missouri, where we remained during the day for the purpose of making celestial observations.

APRIL 12TH

This river empties itself on the south side of the Missouri, one thousand six hundred and ninety-three miles from its confluence with the Mississippi. It rises to the west of the Black mountains, across the northern extremity of which it finds a narrow rapid passage along high perpendicular banks, then seeks the Missouri in a northeastern direction, through a broken country with highlands bare of timber, and the low grounds particularly supplied with cottonwood, elm, small ash, box-elder, and an undergrowth of willow, redwood, sometimes called red or swamp-willow, the redberry and chokecherry. In its course it passes near the northwest side of the Turtle mountain, which is said to be only twelve or fifteen miles from its mouth in a straight line a little to the south of west, so that both the Little Missouri and Knife river have been laid down too far southwest. It enters the Missouri with a bold current, and is one hundred and thirty-four yards wide, but its greatest depth is two feet and a half, and this joined to its rapidity and its sandbars, make the navigation difficult except for canoes, which may ascend it for a considerable distance. At the mouth, and as far as we could discern from the hills between the two rivers about three miles from their junction, the country is much broken, the soil consisting of a deep rich dark coloured loam, intermixed with a small proportion of fine sand and covered generally with a short grass resembling blue grass. In its colour, the nature of its bed, and its general appearance, it resembles so much the Missouri as to induce a belief that the countries they water are similar in point of soil. From the Mandan villages to this place the country is hilly and irregular, with the same appearance of glauber salts and carbonated wood, the low grounds smooth, sandy, and partially covered with cottonwood and small ash; at some distance back there are extensive plains of a good soil, but without timber or water.

We found great quantities of small onions which grow single, the bulb of an oval form, white, about the size of a bullet with a leaf resembling that of the shive [chive]. On the side of a neighbouring hill, there is a species of dwarf cedar: it spreads its limbs along the surface of the earth, which it almost conceals by its closeness and thickness, and is sometimes covered by it, having always a number of roots on the under side, while on the upper are a quantity of shoots which with their leaves seldom rise higher than six or eight inches; it is an evergreen, its leaf more delicate than that of the common cedar, though the taste and smell is the same.

The country around has been so recently hunted that the game are extremely shy, so that a white rabbit, two beaver, a deer, and a bald eagle were all that we could procure. The weather had been clear, warm, and pleasant in the morning, but about three we had a squall of high wind and rain with some thunder, which lasted till after sunset when it again cleared.

APRIL 13TH *Saturday.* We set out at sunrise, and at nine o'clock having the wind in our favour went on rapidly past a timbered low ground on the south, and a creek on the north at the distance of nine miles, which we called Onion creek, from the quantity of that plant which grows in the plains near it: this creek is about sixteen yards wide at a mile and a half above its mouth, it discharges more water than is usual for creeks of that size in this country, but the whole plain which it waters is totally destitute of timber. The Missouri itself widens very remarkably just above the junction with the Little Missouri: immediately at the entrance of the latter, it is not more than two hundred yards wide, and so shallow that it may be passed in canoes with setting poles, while a few miles above it is upwards of a mile in width: ten miles beyond Onion creek we came to another, discharging itself on the north in the centre of a deep bend: on ascending it for about a mile and a half, we found it to be the discharge of a pond or small lake, which seemed to have been once the bed of the Missouri: near this lake were the remains of forty-three temporary lodges which seem to belong to the Assiniboins, who are now on the river of the same name.

A great number of swan and geese were also in it, and from this circumstance we named the creek Goose creek, and the lake by the same name: these geese we observe do not build their nests on the ground or in sandbars, but in the tops of lofty cottonwood trees: we saw some elk and buffalo to-day but at too great a distance to obtain any of them, though a number of the carcases of the latter animal are strewed along the shore, having fallen through the ice, and been swept along when the river broke up. More bald eagles are seen on this part of the Missouri than we have previously met with; the small or common hawk, common in most parts of the United States, are also found here: great quantities of geese are feeding in the prairies, and one flock of white brant or geese with black wings, and some gray brant with them pass up the river, and from their flight they seem to proceed much farther to the northwest. We killed two antelopes which were very lean, and caught last night two beaver: the French hunters who had procured seven, thinking the neighbourhood of the Little Missouri a convenient hunting ground for that animal, remained behind there: in the evening we encamped in a beautiful plain on the north thirty feet above the river, having made twenty-two and a half miles.

Sunday. We set off early with pleasant and fair weather: a dog joined us, which we suppose had strayed from the Assiniboin camp on the lake. At two and a half miles we passed timbered low grounds and a small creek: in these low grounds are several uninhabited lodges built with the boughs of the elm, and the remains of two recent encampments, which from the hoops of small kegs found in them we judged could belong to Assiniboins only, as they are the only Missouri Indians who use spirituous liquors: of these they are so passionately fond that it forms their chief inducement to visit the British on the Assiniboin, to whom they barter for kegs of rum their dried and pounded meat, their grease, and the skins of large and small wolves, and small foxes. The dangerous exchange is transported to their camps with their friends and relations, and soon exhausted in brutal intoxication: so far from considering drunkenness as disgraceful, the women and children are permitted and invited to share in these excesses with their husbands and fathers, who boast how often their skill and industry as hunters has supplied them with the means of intoxication: in this, as in their other habits and customs, they resemble the Sioux from whom they are descended: the trade with the Assiniboins and Knistenaux is encouraged by the British, because it procures provision for their *engagés* on their return from Rainy lake to the English river and the Athabasky country where they winter; these men being obliged during that voyage to pass rapidly through a country but scantily supplied with game.

APRIL 14TH

    We halted for dinner near a large village of burrowing squirrels [gophers], who we observe generally select a southeasterly exposure, though they are sometimes found in the plains. At ten and a quarter miles we came to the lower point of an island, which from the day of our arrival there we called Sunday island: here the river washes the bases of the hills on both sides and above the island, which with its sandbar extends a mile and a half: two small creeks fall in from the south; the uppermost of these, which is the largest, we called Chaboneau's creek, after our interpreter who once encamped on it several weeks with a party of Indians. Beyond this no white man had ever been except two Frenchmen, one of whom Lapage is with us, and who having lost their way straggled a few miles further, though to what point we could not ascertain: about a mile and a half beyond this island we encamped on a point of woodland on the north, having made in all fourteen miles.

    The Assiniboins have so recently left the river that game is scarce and shy. One of the hunters shot at an otter last evening; a buffalo too was killed, and an elk, both so poor as to be almost unfit for use; two white bear were also seen, and a muskrat swimming across the river. The river continues wide and of about the same rapidity as the ordinary current of the Ohio. The low grounds are wide, the moister parts containing timber, the upland extremely broken, without wood, and in some places seem as if they had slipped down in masses of several acres in surface. The mineral appearances of salts, coal, and sulphur, with the burnt hill and pumicestone continue, and a bituminous water about the colour of strong lye, with the taste of glauber salts and a slight tincture of alum. Many geese were feeding in the prairies, and a number of magpies who build their nests much like those of the blackbird in trees, and composed of small sticks, leaves and grass, open at top: the egg is of a bluish brown colour, freckled with reddish brown spots. We also killed a large hooting owl resembling that of the United States, except that is was more booted and clad with feathers. On the hills are many aromatic herbs, resembling in taste, smell and appearance the sage, hyssop, wormwood, southern wood, juniper and dwarf cedar; a plant also about two or three feet high, similar to the camphor in smell and taste, and another plant of the same size, with a long, narrow, smooth, soft leaf, of an agreeable smell and flavour, which is a favourite food of the antelope, whose necks are often perfumed by rubbing against it.

APRIL 15TH *Monday.* We proceeded under a fine breeze from the south, and clear pleasant weather. At seven miles we reached the lower point of an island in a bend to the south, which is two miles in length. Captain Clark, who went about nine miles northward from the river reached the high grounds, which, like those we have seen, are level plains without timber; here he observed a number of drains, which descending from the hills pursue a northeast course, and probably empty into the Mouse river, a branch of the Assiniboin, which from Indian accounts approaches very near to the Missouri at this place. Like all the rivulets of this neighbourhood these drains were so strongly impregnated with mineral salts that they are not fit to drink. He saw also the remains of several camps of Assiniboins: the low grounds on both sides of the river are extensive, rich, and level. In a little pond on the north, we heard for the first time this season the croaking of frogs, which exactly resembles that of the small frogs in the United States: there are also in these plains great quantities of geese, and many of the grouse, or prairie hen, as they are called by the N. W. company traders; the note of the male, as far as words can represent it, is cook, cook, cook, coo, coo, coo, the first part of which both male and female use when flying; the male too drums with his wings when he flies in the same way, though not so loud as the pheasant; they appear to be mating. Some deer, elk, and goats were in the low grounds, and buffalo on the sand beaches, but they were uncommonly shy; we also saw a black bear, and two white ones. At fifteen miles we passed on the north side a small creek twenty yards wide, which we called Goatpen creek, from a park or enclosure for the purpose of catching that animal, which those who went up the creek found, and which we presume to have been left by the Assiniboins. Its water is impregnated with mineral salts, and the country through which it flows consists of wide and very fertile plains, but without any trees. We encamped at the distance of twenty-three miles, on a sandpoint to the south; we passed in the evening a rock in the middle of the river, the channel of which a little above our camp, is confined within eighty yards.

Tuesday. The morning was clear, the wind light from the S. E. The country presents the same appearance of low plains and meadows on the river, bounded a few miles back by broken hills, which end in high level fertile lands, the quantity of timber is however increasing. The appearance of minerals continues as usual, and to-day we found several stones which seemed to have been wood, first carbonated and then petrified by the water of the Missouri, which has the same effect on many vegetable substances. There is indeed reason to believe that the strata of coal in the hills cause the fire and appearances which they exhibit of being burned. Whenever these marks present themselves in the bluffs on the river, the coal is seldom seen, and when found in the neighbourhood of the strata of burnt earth, the coal with the sand and sulphurous matter usually accompanying it, is precisely at the same height and nearly of the same thickness with those strata. We passed three small creeks or rather runs, which rise in the hills to the north. Numbers of geese, and a few ducks chiefly of the mallard and bluewinged teal, many buffalo, elk and deer were also observed, and in the timbered low grounds this morning we were surprised to observe a great quantity of old hornets' nests: we encamped in a point of woods on the south, having come eighteen miles, though the circuits which we were obliged to make round sandbars very much increased the real distance.

APRIL 16TH

Wednesday. We set off early, the weather being fine, and the wind so favourable as to enable us to sail the greater part of the course. At ten and three quarter miles we passed a creek ten yards wide on the south; at eighteen miles a little run on the north, and at night encamped in a woody point on the south. We had travelled twenty-six miles through a country similar to that of yesterday, except that there were greater appearances of burnt hills, furnishing large quantities of lava and pumicestone, of the last of which we observe some pieces floating down the river, as we had previously done, as low as the Little Missouri. In all the copses of wood are the remains of the Assiniboin encampments; around us are great quantities of game, such as herds of buffalo, elk, antelopes, some deer and wolves, the tracks of bear, a curlew was also seen, and we obtained three beaver, the flesh of which is more relished by the men than any other food which we have. Just before we encamped we saw some tracks of Indians, who had passed twenty-four hours before, and left four rafts, and whom we supposed to be a band of Assiniboins on their return from war against the Indians on the Rocky mountains.

APRIL 17TH

Thursday. We had again a pleasant day, and proceeded on with a westerly wind, which however changed to N. W. and blew so hard that we were obliged to stop at one o'clock and remain four hours, when it abated and we then continued our course.

APRIL 18TH

We encamped about dark on a woody bank having made thirteen miles. The country presented the usual variety of highlands interspersed with rich plains. In one of these we observed a species of pea bearing a yellow flower, which is now in blossom, the leaf and stalk resembling the common pea. It seldom rises higher than six inches, and the root is perennial. On the rose bushes we also saw a quantity of the hair of the buffalo, which had become perfectly white by exposure, and resembled the wool of the sheep, except that it was much finer and more soft and silky. A buffalo which we killed yesterday had shed his long hair, and that which remained was about two inches long, thick, fine, and would have furnished five pounds of wool, of which we have no doubt an excellent cloth may be made. Our game to-day was a beaver, a deer, an elk, and some geese. The river has been crooked all day and bearing towards the south.

On the hills we observed considerable quantities of dwarf juniper, which seldom grows higher than three feet. We killed in the course of the day an elk, three geese and a beaver. The beaver on this part of the Missouri are in greater quantities, larger and fatter, and their fur is more abundant and of a darker colour than any we had hitherto seen: their favourite food seems to be the bark of the cottonwood and willow, as we have seen no other species of tree that has been touched by them, and these they gnaw to the ground through a diameter of twenty inches.

The next day, *Friday, 19th*, the wind was so high from northwest that we could not proceed, but being less violent on *Saturday 20th*, we set off about seven o'clock, and had nearly lost one of the canoes as we left the shore, by the falling in of a large part of the bank. The wind too became again so strong that we could scarcely make one mile an hour, and the sudden squalls so dangerous to the small boats, that we stopped for the night among some willows on the north, not being able to advance more than six and a half miles. In walking through the neighbouring plains we found a fine fertile soil covered with cottonwood, some box, alder, ash, red elm, and an undergrowth of willow, rosebushes, honeysuckle, red willow, gooseberry, currant, and serviceberries, and along the foot of the hills great quantities of hyssop. Our hunters procured elk and deer which are now lean, and six beaver which are fatter and more palatable.

Along the plain there were also some Indian camps; near one of these was a scaffold about seven feet high, on which were two sleds with their harness, and under it the body of a female, carefully wrapped in several dressed buffalo skins; near it lay a bag made of buffalo skin, containing a pair of moccasins, some red and blue paint, beaver's nails, scrapers for dressing hides, some dried roots, several plaits of sweet grass, and a small quantity of Mandan tobacco. These things as well as the body itself had probably fallen down by accident, as the custom is to place them on the scaffold. At a little distance was the body of a dog not yet decayed, who had met this reward for having dragged thus far in the sled the corpse of his mistress, to whom according to the Indian usage he had been sacrificed.

APRIL 21ST *Sunday*. Last night there was a hard white frost, and this morning the weather cold, but clear and pleasant: in the course of the day however it became cloudy and the wind rose. The country is of the same description as within the last few days. We saw immense quantities of buffalo, elk, deer, antelopes, geese, and some swan and ducks, out of which we procured three deer, four buffalo calves, which last are equal in flavour to the most delicious veal; also two beaver, and an otter. We passed one large and two small creeks on the south side, and reached at sixteen miles the mouth of Whiteearth river, coming in from the north.

This river before it reaches the low grounds near the Missouri, is a fine bold stream sixty yards wide, and is deep and navigable, but it is so much choked up at the entrance by the mud of the Missouri, that its mouth is not more than ten yards wide. Its course, as far as we could discern from the neighbouring hills, is nearly due north, passing through a beautiful and fertile valley, though without a tree or bush of any description. Half a mile beyond this river we encamped on the same side below a point of highland, which from its appearance we call Cut bluff.

Monday. The day clear and cold: we passed a high bluff on the north and plains on the south, in which were large herds of buffalo, till breakfast, when the wind became so strong ahead that we proceeded with difficulty even with the aid of the towline. Some of the party now walked across to the White-earth river, which here at the distance of four miles from its mouth approaches very near to the Missouri. It contains more water than is usual in streams of the same size at this season, with steep banks about ten or twelve feet high, and the water is much clearer than that of the Missouri; the salts which have been mentioned as common on the Missouri, are here so abundant that in many places the ground appears perfectly white, and from this circumstance it may have derived its name; it waters an open country and is navigable almost to its source, which is not far from the Saskaskawan, and judging from its size and course, it is probable that it extends as far north as the fiftieth degree of latitude. After much delay in consequence of the high wind, we succeeded in making eleven miles, and encamped in a low ground on the south covered with cottonwood and rabbit berries.

APRIL 22D

    The hills of the Missouri near this place exhibit large irregular broken masses of rocks and stones, some of which, although two hundred feet above the water, seem at some remote period to have been subject to its influence, being apparently worn smooth by the agitation of the water. These rocks and stones consist of white and gray granite, a brittle black rock, flint, limestone, freestone, some small specimens of an excellent pebble, and occasionally broken stratas of a black coloured stone like petrified wood, which make good whetstones. The usual appearances of coal, or carbonated wood, and pumicestone still continue, the coal being of a better quality and when burnt affords a hot and lasting fire, emitting very little smoke or flame. There are large herds of deer, elk, buffalo, and antelopes in view of us: the buffalo are not so shy as the rest, for they suffer us to approach within one hundred yards before they run, and then stop and resume their pasture at a very short distance. The wolves to-day pursued a herd of them, and at length caught a calf that was unable to keep up with the rest; the mothers on these occasions defending their young as long as they can retreat as fast as the herd, but seldom returning any distance to seek for them.

Tuesday. A clear and pleasant morning, but at nine o'clock the wind became so high that the boats were in danger of upsetting; we therefore were forced to stop at a place of safety till about five in the afternoon, when the wind being lower we proceeded and encamped on the north at the distance of thirteen and a half miles: the party on shore brought us a buffalo calf and three black-tailed deer: the sand on the river has the same appearances as usual, except that the quantity of wood increases.

APRIL 23D

APRIL 24TH *Wednesday.* The wind blew so high during the whole day that we were unable to move; such indeed was its violence, that although we were sheltered by high timber the waves wet many articles in the boats: the hunters went out and returned with four deer, two elk, and some young wolves of the small kind.

The party are very much afflicted with sore eyes, which we presume are occasioned by the vast quantities of sand which are driven from the sandbars in such clouds as often to hide from us the view of the opposite bank. The particles of this sand are so fine and light that it floats for miles in the air like a column of thick smoke, and is so penetrating that nothing can be kept free from it, and we are compelled to eat, drink, and breathe it very copiously. To the same cause we attribute the disorder of one of our watches, although her cases are double and tight; since without any defect in its works, that we can discover, it will not run for more than a few minutes without stopping.

APRIL 25TH *Thursday.* The wind moderated this morning, but was still high; we therefore set out early, the weather being so cold that the water froze on the oars as we rowed, and about ten o'clock the wind increased so much that we were obliged to stop. This detention from the wind and the reports from our hunters of the crookedness of the river, induced us to believe that we were at no great distance from the Yellowstone river. In order therefore to prevent delay as much as possible, captain Lewis determined to go on by land in search of that river, and make the necessary observations, so as to be enabled to proceed on immediately after the boats should join him: he therefore landed about eleven o'clock on the south side, accompanied by four men; the boats were prevented from going until five in the afternoon, when they went on a few miles further and encamped for the night at the distance of fourteen and a half miles.

APRIL 26TH *Friday.* We continued our voyage in the morning and by twelve o'clock encamped at eight miles distance, at the junction of the Missouri and Yellowstone rivers; where we were soon joined by captain Lewis.

On leaving us yesterday he pursued his route along the foot of the hills, which he ascended at the distance of eight miles; from these the wide plains watered by the Missouri and the Yellowstone spread themselves before the eye, occasionally varied with the wood of the banks, enlivened by the irregular windings of the two rivers, and animated by vast herds of buffalo, deer, elk, and antelope. The confluence of the two rivers was concealed by the wood, but the Yellowstone itself was only two miles distant to the south. He therefore descended the hills and encamped on the bank of the river, having killed as he crossed the plain four buffaloes; the deer alone are shy and retire to the woods, but the elk, antelope, and buffalo suffered him to approach them without alarm, and often followed him quietly for some distance.

This morning he sent a man up the river to examine it, while he proceeded down to the junction: the ground on the lower side of the Yellowstone near its mouth, is flat, and for about a mile seems to be subject to inundation, while that at the point of junction, as well as on the opposite side of the Missouri, is at the usual height of ten or eighteen feet above the water, and therefore not overflown. There is more timber in the neighbourhood of this place, and on the Missouri, as far below as the White-earth river, than on any other part of the Missouri on this side of the Chayenne: the timber consists principally of cottonwood, with some small elm, ash, and box-elder. On the sandbars and along the margin of the river grows the small-leafed willow; in the low grounds adjoining are scattered rosebushes three or four feet high, the redberry, serviceberry and redwood. The higher plains are either immediately on the river—in which case they are generally timbered, and have an undergrowth like that of the low grounds, with the addition of the broad-leafed willow, gooseberry, chokecherry, purple currant, and honeysuckle—or they are between the low grounds and the hills, and for the most part without wood or any thing except large quantities of wild hyssop; this plant rises about two feet high, and like the willow of the sandbars is a favourite food of the buffalo, elk, deer, grouse, porcupine, hare, and rabbit.

This river which had been known to the French as the Roche jaune, or as we have called it the Yellowstone, rises according to Indian information in the Rocky mountains; its sources are near those of the Missouri and the Platte, and it may be navigated in canoes almost to its head. It runs first through a mountainous country, but in many parts fertile and well timbered; it then waters a rich delightful land, broken into vallies and meadows, and well supplied with wood and water till it reaches near the Missouri open meadows and low grounds, sufficiently timbered on its borders. In the upper country its course is represented as very rapid, but during the two last and largest portions, its current is much more gentle than that of the Missouri, which it resembles also in being turbid though with less sediment.

The man who was sent up the river, reported in the evening that he had gone about eight miles, that during that distance the river winds on both sides of a plain four or five miles wide, that the current was gentle and much obstructed by sandbars, that at five miles he had met with a large timbered island, three miles beyond which a creek falls in on the S. E. above a high bluff, in which are several strata of coal. The country as far as he could discern, resembled that of the Missouri, and in the plain he met several of the bighorn animals, but they were too shy to be obtained.

The bed of the Yellowstone, as we observed it near the mouth, is composed of sand and mud, without a stone of any kind. Just above the confluence we measured the two rivers, and found the bed of the Missouri five hundred and twenty yards wide, the water occupying only three hundred and thirty, and the channel deep: while the Yellowstone, including its sandbar, occupied eight hundred and fifty-eight yards, with two hundred and ninety-seven yards of water: the deepest part of the channel is twelve feet, but the river is now falling and seems to be nearly at its summer height.

APRIL 27TH We left the mouth of the Yellowstone. From the point of junction a wood occupies the space between the two rivers, which at the distance of a mile comes within two hundred and fifty yards of each other. There a beautiful low plain commences, and widening as the rivers recede, extends along each of them for several miles, rising about half a mile from the Missouri into a plain twelve feet higher than itself. The low plain is a few inches above high water mark, and where it joins the higher plain there is a channel of sixty or seventy yards in width, through which a part of the Missouri when at its greatest height passes into the Yellowstone. At two and a half miles above the junction and between the high and low plain is a small lake, two hundred yards wide, extending for a mile parallel with the Missouri along the edge of the upper plain.

At the lower extremity of this lake, about four hundred yards from the Missouri, and twice that distance from the Yellowstone, is a situation highly eligible for a trading establishment; it is in the high plain which extends back three miles in width, and seven or eight miles in length, along the Yellowstone, where it is bordered by an extensive body of woodland, and along the Missouri with less breadth, till three miles above it is circumscribed by the hills within a space four yards in width. A sufficient quantity of limestone for building may easily be procured near the junction of the rivers; it does not lie in regular stratas, but is in large irregular masses, of a light colour and apparently of an excellent quality. Game too is very abundant, and as yet quite gentle; above all, its elevation recommends it as preferable to the land at the confluence of the rivers, which their variable channels may render very insecure.

The N. W. wind rose so high at eleven o'clock, that we were obliged to stop till about four in the afternoon, when we proceeded till dusk. On the south a beautiful plain separates the two rivers, till at about six miles there is a timbered piece of low ground, and a little above it bluffs, where the country rises gradually from the river; the situations on the north more high and open. We encamped on that side, the wind, the sand which it raised, and the rapidity of the current having prevented our advancing more than eight miles; during the latter part of the day the river becomes wider and crowded with sandbars: although the game is in such plenty we kill only what is necessary for our subsistence. For several days past we have seen great numbers of buffalo lying dead along the shore, and some of them partly devoured by the wolves; they have either sunk through the ice during the winter, or been drowned in attempting to cross, or else, after crossing to some high bluff, found themselves too much exhausted either to ascend or swim back again, and perished for want of food; in this situation we found several small parties of them. There are geese too in abundance, and more bald-eagles than we had hitherto observed; the nests of these last being always accompanied by those of two or three magpies, who are their inseparable attendants.

SUNDAY, APRIL 28TH, 1805   The day was clear and pleasant, and the wind having shifted to southeast, we could employ our sails, and went twenty-four miles to a low ground on the north opposite to steep bluffs: the country on both sides is much broken, the hills approaching nearer to the river, and forming bluffs, some of a white and others of a red colour, and exhibiting the usual appearances of minerals, and some burnt hills though without any pumicestone; the salts are in greater quantities than usual, and the banks and sandbars are covered with a white incrustation like frost. The low grounds are level, fertile and partially timbered, but are not so wide as for a few days past. The woods are now green, but the plains and meadows seem to have less verdure than those below: the only streams which we met to-day are two small runs on the north and one on the south, which rise in the neighbouring hills, and have very little water. At the distance of eighteen miles the Missouri makes a considerable bend to the southeast: the game is very abundant, the common, and mule or blacktailed deer, elk, buffalo, antelope, brown bear, beaver, and geese. The beaver have committed great devastation among the trees, one of which, nearly three feet in diameter, had been gnawed through by them.

Monday. We proceeded early with a moderate wind: captain Lewis who was on shore with one hunter met about eight o'clock two white [grizzly] bears: of the strength and ferocity of this animal, the Indians had given us dreadful accounts: they never attack him but in parties of six or eight persons, and even then are often defeated with the loss of one or more of the party. Having no weapons but bows and arrows, and the bad guns with which the traders supply them, they are obliged to approach very near to the bear; and as no wound except through the head or heart is mortal, they frequently fall a sacrifice if they miss their aim. He rather attacks than avoids a man, and such is the terror which he has inspired, that the Indians who go in quest of him paint themselves and perform all the superstitious rites customary when they make war on a neighbouring nation. Hitherto those we had seen did not appear desirous of encountering us, but although to a skilful rifleman the danger is very much diminished, yet the white bear is still a terrible animal: on approaching these two, both captain Lewis and the hunter fired and each wounded a bear: one of them made his escape; the other turned upon captain Lewis and pursued him seventy or eighty yards, but being badly wounded he could not run so fast as to prevent him from reloading his piece, which he again aimed at him, and a third shot from the hunter brought him to the ground: he was a male not quite full grown, and weighed about three hundred pounds: the legs are somewhat longer than those of the black bear, and the talons and tusks much larger and stronger. The testicles are also placed much farther forward and suspended in separate pouches from two to four inches asunder, while those of the black bear are situated back between the thighs and in a single pouch like those of the dog: its colour is a yellowish brown, the eyes small, black, and piercing, the front of the fore legs near the feet is usually black, and the fur is finer, thicker, and deeper than that of the black bear: add to which, it is a more furious animal, and remarkable for the wounds which it will bear without dying. We are surrounded with deer, elk, buffalo, antelopes, and their companions the wolves, who have become more numerous and make great rav-

Chapter 8
FROM THE
YELLOWSTONE TO
THE MUSSELSHELL

APRIL 29TH

ages among them: the hills are here much more rough and high, and almost overhang the banks of the river. There are greater appearances of coal than we have hitherto seen, the stratas of it being in some places six feet thick, and there are stratas of burnt earth, which are always on the same level with those of coal.

In the evening after coming twenty-five miles we encamped at the entrance of a river which empties itself into a bend on the north side of the Missouri: this stream which we called Martha's river, is about fifty yards wide, with water for fifteen yards, the banks are of earth, and steep, though not high, and the bed principally of mud. Captain Clark, who ascended it for three miles, found that it continued of the same width with a gentle current, and pursuing its course about north 30° west, through an extensive, fertile, and beautiful valley, but without a single tree. The water is clear, and has a brownish yellow tint; at this place the highlands which yesterday and to-day had approached so near the river became lower, and receding from the water left a valley seven or eight miles wide.

APRIL 30TH *Tuesday*. The wind was high from the north during last evening and continued so this morning: we however continued, and found the river more winding than usual and with a number of sand islands and bars, on one of which last we encamped at the distance of twenty-four miles. The low grounds are fertile and extensive but with very little timber, and that cottonwood, very bad of its kind, being too small for planks, and broken and dead at the top and unsound in the centre of the trunk. We passed some ancient lodges of driftwood which do not appear to have been lately inhabited.

The game continues abundant: we killed the largest male elk we have yet seen; on placing it in its natural erect position, we found that it measured five feet three inches from the point of the hoof to the top of the shoulder. The antelopes are yet lean and the females are with young: this fleet and quick-sighted animal is generally the victim of its curiosity: when they first see the hunters they run with great velocity; if he lies down on the ground and lifts up his arm, his hat, or his foot, the antelope returns on a light trot to look at the object, and sometimes goes and returns two or three times till they approach within reach of the rifle: so too they sometimes leave their flock to go and look at the wolves who crouch down, and if the antelope be frightened at first repeat the same manoeuvre, and sometimes relieve each other till they decoy it from the party when they seize it. But generally the wolves take them as they are crossing the rivers, for although swift of foot they are not good swimmers.

Wednesday, May 1st, 1805

The wind was in our favour and we were enabled to use the sails till twelve o'clock, when the wind became so high and squally that we were forced to come-to at the distance of ten miles on the south, in a low ground stocked with cottonwood, and remain there during the day; one of the canoes being separated from us, and not able to cross over in consequence of the high waves. The country around is more pleasant than that through which we had passed for several days, the hills being lower, the low grounds wider and better supplied with timber, which consists principally of cottonwood: the undergrowth willow on the banks and sandbars, rosebushes, red willow, and the broadleafed willow in the low plains, while the high country on both sides is one extensive plain without wood, though the soil is a dark, rich, mellow loam. Our hunters killed a buffalo, an elk, a goat, and two beaver, and also a bird [avocet] of the plover kind.

Thursday. The wind continued high during the night, and at daylight it began to snow and did not stop till ten o'clock, when the ground was covered an inch deep, forming a striking contrast with the vegetation which is now considerably advanced; some flowers having put forth, and the cottonwood leaves as large as a dollar. The wind lulled about five o'clock in the afternoon, and we then proceeded along wide fertile low grounds and high level plains, and encamped at the distance of four miles. Our game to-day was deer, elk, and buffalo: we also procured three beaver who are quite gentle, as they have not been hunted, but when the hunters are in pursuit they never leave their huts during the day: this animal we esteem a great delicacy, particularly the tail, which when boiled resembles in flavour the flesh tongues and sounds of the codfish, and is generally so large as to afford a plentiful meal for two men. One of the hunters in passing near an old Indian camp found several yards of scarlet cloth, suspended on the boughs of a tree as a sacrifice to the deity by the Assiniboins: the custom of making these offerings being common among that people as indeed among all the Indians on the Missouri.

MAY 2D

The air was sharp this evening; the water froze on the oars as we rowed, and in the morning, *Friday, 3d*, the weather became quite cold, the ice was a quarter of an inch thick in the kettle, and the snow still continued on the hills though it has melted from the plains. The wind too continued high from the west, but not so violently as to prevent our going on. At two miles from our encampment we passed a curious collection of bushes about thirty feet high and ten or twelve in diameter, tied in the form of a fascine and standing on end in the middle of the low ground: this too we supposed to have been left by the Indians as a religious sacrifice: at twelve o'clock the usual hour we halted for dinner. The low grounds on the river are much wider than common, sometimes extending from five to nine miles to the highlands, which are much lower than heretofore, not being more than fifty or sixty feet above the lower plain: through all this valley traces of the ancient bed of the river are every where visible, and since the hills have become lower, the stratas of coal, burnt earth, and pumicestone have in a great measure ceased, there being in fact none to-day.

At the distance of fourteen miles we reached the mouth of a river on the north, which from the unusual number of porcupines near it, we called Porcupine river. This is a bold and beautiful stream one hundred and twelve yards wide, though the water is only forty yards at its entrance: captain Clark who ascended it several miles and passed it above where it enters the highlands, found it continued nearly of the same width and about knee deep, and as far as he could distinguish for twenty miles from the hills, its course was from a little to the east of north. There was much timber on the low grounds: he found some limestone also on the surface of the earth in the course of his walk, and saw a range of low mountains at a distance to the west of north, whose direction was northwest; the adjoining country being every where level, fertile, open, and exceedingly beautiful. The water of this river is transparent, and is the only one that is so of all those that fall into the Missouri: before entering a large sandbar through which it discharges itself, its low grounds are formed of a stiff blue and black clay, and its banks which are from eight to ten feet high and seldom if ever overflow are composed of the same materials. From the quantity of water which this river contains, its direction, and the nature of the country through which it passes, it is not improbable that its sources may be near the main body of the Saskaskawan, and as in high water it can be no doubt navigated to a considerable distance, it may be rendered the means of intercourse with the Athabasky country, from which the Northwest company derive so many of their valuable furs.

A quarter of a mile beyond this river a creek falls in on the south, to which on account of its distance from the mouth of the Missouri, we gave it the name of Two-thousand mile creek: it is a bold stream with a bed thirty yards wide. Three miles and a half above Porcupine river, we reached some high timber on the north, and encamped just above an old channel of the river, which is now dry. We saw vast quantities of buffaloe, elk, deer, principally of the long tailed kind, antelopes, beaver, geese, ducks, brant, and some swan. The porcupines too are numerous, and so careless and clumsy that we can approach very near without disturbing them as they are feeding on the young willows; towards evening we also found for the first time, the nest of a goose among some driftwood, all that we have hitherto seen being on the top of a broken tree on the forks, and invariably from fifteen to twenty feet or more in height.

MAY 4TH *Saturday.* We were detained till nine in order to repair the rudder of one of the boats, and when we set out the wind was ahead; at six and a half miles we passed a small creek in a deep bend on the south with a sand island opposite to it, and then passing along an extensive plain which gradually rises from the north side of the river, encamped at the distance of eighteen miles in a point of woodland on the north: the river is this day wider than usual, and crowded with sandbars on all sides: the country is level, fertile, and beautiful, the low grounds extensive and contain a much greater portion of timber than is common: indeed all the forepart of the day the river was bordered with timber on both sides, a circumstance very rare on the Missouri, and the first that has occurred since we left the Mandans. There are as usual vast quantities of game, and extremely gentle; the male buffalo particularly will scarcely give way to us, and as we approach will merely look at us for a moment, as something new, and then quietly resume their feeding.

In the course of the day we passed some old Indian hunting camps, one of which consisted of two large lodges fortified with a circular fence, twenty or thirty feet in diameter, and made of timber laid horizontally, the beams overlaying each other to the height of five feet, and covered with the trunks and limbs of trees that have drifted down the river: the lodges themselves are formed by three or more strong sticks about the size of a man's leg or arm, and twelve feet long, which are attached at the top by a withe of small willows, and spreading out so as to form at the base a circle of ten or fourteen feet in diameter: against these are placed pieces of driftwood and fallen timber, usually in three ranges one on the other, and the interstices are covered with leaves, bark, and straw, so as to form a conical figure about ten feet high, with a small aperture in one side for the door. It is, however, at best a very imperfect shelter against the inclemencies of the season.

Sunday. We had a fine morning, and the wind being from the east we used our sails. At the distance of five miles we came to a small island, and twelve miles farther encamped on the north, at the distance of seventeen miles. The country like that of yesterday is beautiful in the extreme. Among the vast quantities of game around us, we distinguish a small species of goose differing considerably from the common Canadian goose; its neck, head, and beak, being much thicker, larger, and shorter in proportion to its size, which is nearly a third smaller; the noise too resembling more that of the brant or of a young goose that has not yet fully acquired its note; in other respects its colour, habits, and the number of feathers in the tail, the two species correspond; this species also associates in flocks with the large geese, but we have not seen it pair off with them. The white brant is about the size of the common brown brant, or two thirds of the common goose, than which it is also six inches shorter from the extremity of the wings, though the beak, head, and neck are larger and stronger: the body and wings are of a beautiful pure white, except the black feathers of the first and second joints of the wings; the beak and legs are of a reddish or flesh-coloured white, the eye of a moderate size, the pupil of a deep sea-green incircled with a ring of yellowish brown, the tail consists of sixteen feathers equally long, the flesh is dark and as well as its note differs but little from those of the common brant, whom in form and habits it resembles, and with whom it sometimes unites in a common flock; the white brant also associate by themselves in large flocks, but as they do not seem to be mated or paired off, it is doubtful whether they reside here during the summer for the purpose of rearing their young.

MAY 5TH

The wolves are also very abundant, and are of two species. First, the small wolf or burrowing dog of the prairies [coyote], which are found in almost all the open plains. It is of an intermediate size between the fox and dog, very delicately formed, fleet and active. The ears are large, erect, and pointed; the head long and pointed, like that of the fox; the tail long and bushy; the hair and fur of a pale reddish brown colour, though much coarser than that of the fox; the eye of a deep sea-green colour, small and piercing; the talons rather longer than those of the wolf of the Atlantic states, which animal as far as we can perceive is not to be found on this side of the river Platte. These wolves usually associate in bands of ten or twelve, and are rarely if ever seen alone, not being able singly to attack a deer or antelope. They live and rear their young in burrows, which they fix near some pass or spot much frequented by game, and sally out in a body against any animal which they think they can overpower, but on the slightest alarm retreat to their burrows making a noise exactly like that of a small dog.

The second species is lower, shorter in the legs and thicker than the Atlantic wolf; their colour, which is not affected by the seasons, is of every variety of shade, from a gray or blackish brown to a cream coloured white. They do not burrow, nor do they bark, but howl, and they frequent the woods and plains, and skulk along the skirts of the buffalo herds, in order to attack the weary or wounded.

Captain Clark and one of the hunters met this evening the largest brown bear we have seen. As they fired he did not attempt to attack, but fled with a most tremendous roar, and such was its extraordinary tenacity of life, that although he had five balls passed through his lungs and five other wounds, he swam more than half across the river to a sandbar, and survived twenty minutes. He weighed between five and six hundred pounds at least, and measured eight feet seven inches and a half from the nose to the extremity of the hind feet, five feet ten inches and a half round the breast, three feet eleven inches round the neck, one foot eleven inches round the middle of the foreleg, and his talons, five on each foot, were four inches and three eighths in length. It differs from the common black bear in having its talons much longer and more blunt; its tail shorter; its hair of a reddish or bay brown, longer, finer, and more abundant; his liver, lungs, and heart, much larger even in proportion to his size, the heart particularly being equal to that of a large ox; his maw ten times larger; his testicles pendant from the belly and in separate pouches four inches apart: besides fish and flesh he feeds on roots, and every kind of wild fruit.

The antelope are now lean and with young, so that they may readily be caught at this season, as they cross the river from S. W. to N. E.

Private M'Neal's escape from a bear, as related in Sergeant Gass's diary.

MAY 6TH *Monday.* The morning being fair and the wind favourable, we set sail, and proceeded on very well the greater part of the day. The country continues level, rich, and beautiful; the low grounds wide and comparatively with the other parts of the Missouri, well supplied with wood. The appearances of coal, pumicestone, and burnt earth have ceased, though the salts of tartar or vegetable salts continue on the banks and sandbars, and sometimes in the little ravines at the base of the low hills. We passed three streams on the south; the first at the distance of one mile and a half from our camp was about twenty-five yards wide, but although it contained some water in standing pools it discharges none; this we called Littledry creek, about eight miles beyond which is Bigdry creek, fifty yards wide, without any water; the third is six miles further, and has the bed of a large river two hundred yards wide, yet without a drop of water: like the other two this stream,

128

which we called Big Dry [Little Dry] river, continues its width undiminished as far as we can discern. The banks are low, the channel formed of a fine brown sand, intermixed with a small proportion of little pebbles of various colours, and the country around flat and without trees. They had recently discharged their waters, and from their appearance and the nature of the country through which they pass, we concluded that they rose in the Black mountains, or in the level low plains which are probably between this place and the mountains; that the country being nearly of the same kind and of the same latitude, the rains of spring melting the snows about the same time, conspire with them to throw at once vast quantities of water down these channels, which are then left dry during the summer, autumn, and winter, when there is very little rain. We had to-day a slight sprinkling, but it lasted a very short time. The game is in such plenty that it has become a mere amusement to supply the party with provisions. We made twenty-five miles to a clump of trees on the north where we passed the night.

Tuesday. The morning was pleasant and we proceeded at an early hour. There is much driftwood floating, and what is contrary to our expectation, although the river is rising, the water is somewhat clearer than usual. At eleven o'clock the wind became so high that one of the boats was nearly sunk, and we were obliged to stop till one, when we proceeded on, and encamped on the south, above a large sandbar projecting from the north, having made fifteen miles. On the north side of the river are the most beautiful plains we have yet seen; they rise gradually from the low grounds on the water to the height of fifty or sixty feet, and then extend in an unbroken level as far as the eye can reach: the hills on the south are more broken and higher, though at some distance back the country becomes level and fertile. There are no more appearances of burnt earth, coal, or pumicestone, though that of salt still continues, and the vegetation seems to have advanced but little since the twenty-eighth of last month: the game is as abundant as usual. The bald-eagles, of whom we see great numbers, probably feed on the carcases of dead animals, for on the whole Missouri we have seen neither the blue-crested fisher, nor the fishing-hawks, to supply them with their favourite food, and the water of the river is so turbid that no bird which feeds exclusively on fish can procure a subsistence.

MAY 7TH

Wednesday. A light breeze from the east carried us sixteen miles, till we halted for dinner at the entrance of a river on the north. Captain Clark who had walked on the south, on ascending a high point opposite to its entrance discovered a level and beautiful country which it watered; that its course for twelve or fifteen miles was N. W. when it divided into two nearly equal branches, one pursuing a direction nearly north, the other to the W. of N.W.: its width at the entrance is one hundred and fifty yards, and on going three miles up, captain Lewis found it to be of the same breadth, and sometimes more; it is deep, gentle, and has a large quantity of water; its bed is principally of mud, the banks abrupt, about twelve feet in height, and formed of a dark, rich loam and blue clay; the low grounds near it are wide and fertile, and possess a considerable proportion of cottonwood and willow. It seems to be navigable for boats and canoes, and this circumstance joined to its course and the quantity of water, which indicates that it passes through

MAY 8TH

a large extent of country, we are led to presume that it may approach the Saskashawan and afford a communication with that river. The water has a peculiar whiteness, such as might be produced by a tablespoon full of milk in a dish of tea, and this circumstance induced us to call it Milk river. In the evening we had made twenty-seven miles, and encamped on the south. The country on that side consists in general of high broken hills, with much gray, black and brown granite scattered over the surface of the ground. At a little distance from the river there is no timber on either side, the wood being confined as below to the margin of the river; so that unless the contrary is particularly mentioned, it is always understood that the upland is perfectly naked, and that we consider the low grounds well timbered if even a fifth be covered with wood. The wild liquorice is found in great abundance on these hills, as is also the white apple. As usual we are surrounded by buffalo, elk, common and blacktailed deer, beaver, antelopes and wolves. We observed a place where an Indian had recently taken the hair off an antelope's skin, and some of the party thought they distinguished imperfectly some smoke and Indian lodges up Milk river, marks which we are by no means desirous of realizing, as the Indians are probably Assiniboins, and might be very troublesome.

MAY 9TH *Thursday.* We again had a favourable wind and sailed along very well. Between four and five miles we passed a large island in a deep bend to the north, and a large sandbar at the upper point. At fifteen and a quarter miles we reached the bed of a most extraordinary river which presents itself on the south: though as wide as the Missouri itself, that is about half a mile, it does not discharge a drop of water and contains nothing but a few standing pools. On ascending it three miles we found an eminence from which we saw the direction of the channel, first south for [nine] or ten miles, then turning to the east of southeast as far as we could see: it passes through a wide valley without timber, and the surrounding country consists of waving low hills interspersed with some handsome level plains; the banks are abrupt and consist of a black or yellow clay, or of a rich sandy loam, but though they do not rise more than six or eight feet above the bed, they exhibit no appearance of being overflowed: the bed is entirely composed of a light brown sand, the particles of which like those of the Missouri are extremely fine. Like the dry rivers we passed before, this seemed to have discharged its waters recently, but the watermark indicated that its greatest depth had not been more than two feet: this stream, if it deserve the name, we called Big Dry river.

About a mile below is a large creek on the same side, which is also perfectly dry: the mineral salts and quartz are in large quantities near this neighbourhood. The sand of the Missouri from its mouth to this place has been mixed with a substance which we had presumed to be a granulated talc, but which is most probably this quartz. The game is now in great quantities, particularly the elk and buffalo, which last is so gentle that the men are obliged to drive them out of the way with sticks and stones. The ravages of the beaver are very apparent: in one place the timber was entirely prostrated for a space of three acres in front on the river and one in depth, and great part of it removed, although the trees were in large quantities, and some of them as thick as the body of a man. At the distance of twenty-four miles we encamped, after making twenty-five and a half miles, at the entrance of a small creek in a bend on the north, to which we gave the name of Werner's creek after one of our men.

For several days past the river has been as wide as it generally is near its mouth, but as it is much shallower, crowded with sandbars, and the colour of the water has become much clearer, we do not yet despair of reaching the Rock mountains, for which we are very anxious.

Friday. We had not proceeded more than four and a quarter miles when the violence of the wind forced us to halt for the day under some timber in a bend on the south side. The wind continued high, the clouds thick and black, and we had a slight sprinkling of rain several times in the course of the day. Shortly after our landing a dog came to us, and as this induced us to believe that we are near the hunting grounds of the Assiniboins, who are a vicious ill-disposed people, it was necessary to be on our guard: we therefore inspected our arms which we found in good order, and sent several hunters to scour the country, but they returned in the evening having seen no tents, nor any recent tracks of Indians. Boils and imposthumes [abscesses] are very common among the party, and sore eyes continue in a greater or less degree with all of us; for the imposthumes we use emollient poultices, and apply to the eyes a solution of two grains of white vitriol and one of sugar of lead with one ounce of water.

MAY 10TH

Saturday. The wind blew very hard in the night, but having abated this morning we went on very well, till in the afternoon the wind arose and retarded our progress; the current too was strong, the river very crooked, and the banks as usual constantly precipitating themselves in large masses into the water. The highlands are broken and approach nearer the river than they do below. The soil however of both hills and low grounds appear as fertile as that further down the river: it consists of a black looking loam with a small portion of sand, which cover the hills and bluffs to the depth of twenty or thirty feet, and when thrown in the water dissolves as readily as loaf-sugar, and effervesces like marl. There are also great appearances of quartz and mineral salts: the first is most commonly seen in the faces of the bluffs, the second is found on the hills as well as the low grounds, and in the gullies which come down from the hills; it lies in a crust of two or three inches in depth, and may be swept up with a feather in large quantities. There is no longer any appearance of coal, burnt earth or pumicestone.

MAY 11TH

We saw and visited some high hills on the north side about three miles from the river, whose tops were covered with the pitch-pine: this is the first pine we have seen on the Missouri, and it is like that of Virginia, except that the leaves are somewhat longer: among this pine is also a dwarf cedar, sometimes between three or four feet high, but generally spreading itself like a vine along the surface of the earth, which it covers very closely, putting out roots from the under side. The fruit and smell resemble those of the common red cedar, but the leaf is finer and more delicate. The tops of the hills where these plants grow have a soil quite different from that just described, the basis of it is usually yellow or white clay, and the general appearance light coloured, sandy, and barren, some scattering tufts of sedge being almost its only herbage.

About five in the afternoon one of our men who had been afflicted with boils, and suffered to walk on shore, came running to the boats with loud cries and every symptom of terror and distress: for some time after we had taken him on board he was so much out of breath as to be unable to describe the cause of his anxiety, but he at length told us that about a mile and a half below he had shot a brown bear which immediately turned and was in close pursuit of him; but the bear being badly wounded could not overtake him. Captain Lewis with seven men immediately went in search of him, and having found his track followed him by the blood for a mile, and found him concealed in some thick brushwood, and shot him with two balls through the skull. Though somewhat smaller than that killed a few days ago, he was a monstrous animal and a most terrible enemy: our man had shot him through the centre of the lungs, yet he had pursued him furiously for half a mile, then returned more than twice that distance, and with his talons had prepared himself a bed in the earth two feet deep and five feet long, and was perfectly alive when they found him, which was at least two hours after he received the wound. The wonderful power of life which these animals possess render them dreadful: their very track in the mud or sand, which we have sometimes found eleven inches long and seven and a quarter wide, exclusive of the talons, is alarming; and we had rather encounter two Indians than meet a single brown bear. There is no chance of killing them by a single shot unless the ball goes through the brains, and this is very difficult on account of two large muscles which cover the side of the forehead, and the sharp projection of the centre of the frontal bone, which is also thick.

Our encampment was on the south at the distance of sixteen miles from that of last night: the fleece and skin of the bear were a heavy burden for two men, and the oil amounted to eight gallons.

MAY 12TH *Sunday*. The weather being clear and calm, we set out early. Within a mile we came to a small creek, about twenty yards wide, emptying itself on the south. At eleven and three quarter miles we reached a point of woodland on the south, opposite to which is a creek of the same width as the last, but with little water, which we called Pine creek. At eighteen and three quarter miles we came to on the south opposite to the lower point of a willow island, situated in a deep bend of the river to the southeast. Here we remained during the day, the wind having risen at twelve so high that we could not proceed. It continued to blow violently all night, with occasional sprinklings of rain from sunset till midnight. On both sides of the river the country is rough and broken, the low grounds becoming narrower; the tops of the hills on the north exhibits some scattered pine and cedar, on the south the pine has not yet commenced, though there is some cedar on the sides of the hills and in the little ravines. The chokecherry, the wild hyssop, sage, fleshy-leafed thorn, and particularly the aromatic herb on which the antelope and hare feed, are to be found on the plains and hills. The soil of the hills has now altered its texture considerably: their bases, like that of the river plains, is as usual a rich, black loam, while from the middle to the summits they are composed of a light brown-coloured earth, poor and sterile, and intermixed with a coarse white sand.

MAY 13TH *Monday*. The wind was so strong that we could not proceed till about one o'clock, when we had to encounter a current rather stronger than usual. In the course of a mile and a half we passed two small creeks on the south, one of eighteen the other of thirty yards width, but neither of them containing any water, and encamped on the south at a point of woodland, having made only seven miles. The country is much the same as yesterday, with little timber in the low grounds, and a small quantity of pine and cedar on the northern hills. The river however continues to grow clearer, and this as well as the increased rapidity induces us to hope for some change of country. The game is as usual so abundant that we can get without difficulty all that is necessary.

Tuesday. There was some fog on the river this morning, which is a very rare occurrence. At the distance of a mile and a half we reached an island in a bend on the north, which continued for about half a mile, when at the head of it a large creek comes in on the north, to which we gave the name of Gibson's creek. At seven and a half miles is a point of rocks on the south, above a creek on the same side, which we called Sticklodge creek: five miles further is a large creek on the south, which like the two others has no running water; and at sixteen and a half miles a timbered point on the north, where we encamped for the night. The country is like that of yesterday, except that the low grounds are wider: there are also many high black bluffs along the banks: the game too is in great abundance.

MAY 14TH

Towards evening the men in the hindmost canoes discovered a large brown bear lying in the open grounds, about three hundred paces from the river: six of them, all good hunters, immediately went to attack him, and concealing themselves by a small eminence came unperceived within forty paces of him: four of the hunters now fired, and each lodged a ball in his body, two of them directly through the lungs: the furious animal sprung up and ran openmouthed upon them; as he came near, the two hunters who had reserved their fire gave him two wounds, one of which breaking his shoulder retarded his motion for a moment; but before they could reload he was so near that they were obliged to run to the river, and before they reached it he had almost overtaken them: two jumped into the canoe; the other four separated, and concealing themselves in the willows fired as fast as each could reload: they struck him several times, but instead of weakening the monster each shot seemed only to direct him towards the hunter, till at last he pursued two of them so closely, that they threw aside their guns and pouches, and jumped down a perpendicular bank of twenty feet into the river; the bear sprang after them, and was within a few feet of the hindmost, when one of the hunters on shore shot him in the head and finally killed him. They dragged him to the shore, and found that eight balls had passed through him in different directions; the bear was old and the meat tough, so that they took the skin only, and rejoined us at camp, where we had been as much terrified by an accident of a different kind.

This was the narrow escape of one of our canoes containing all our papers, instruments, medicine, and almost every article indispensable for the success of our enterprise. The canoe being under sail, a sudden squall of wind struck her obliquely, and turned her considerably. The man at the helm, who was unluckily the worst steersman of the party, became alarmed, and instead of putting her before the wind luffed her up into it. The wind was so high that it forced the brace of the squaresail out of the hand of the

133

man who was attending it, and instantly upset the canoe, which would have been turned bottom upwards but for the resistance made by the awning. Such was the confusion on board, and the waves ran so high, that it was half a minute before she righted, and then nearly full of water, but by baling out she was kept from sinking until they rowed ashore: besides the loss of the lives of three men who not being able to swim would probably have perished, we should have been deprived of nearly every thing necessary for our purposes, at a distance of between two and three thousand miles from any place where we could supply the deficiency.

MAY 15TH *Wednesday.* As soon as a slight shower of rain had passed, we spread out the articles to dry; but the weather was so damp and cloudy that they derived little benefit from exposure. Our hunters procured us deer, buffalo, and beaver.

MAY 16TH *Thursday.* The morning was fair and we were enabled to dry and repack our stores: the loss we sustained is chiefly in the medicines, many articles of which are completely spoiled, and others considerably injured. At four o'clock we embarked, and after making seven miles encamped on the north near some wood: the country on both sides is broken, the low grounds narrower and with less timber, though there are some scattered pine and cedar on the steep declivities of the hills, which are now higher than usual. A white bear tore the coat of one of the men which he had left on shore; and two of the party wounded a large panther [cougar] who was feasting on a deer. We caught some lean antelopes as they were swimming the river, and killed two buffalo.

MAY 17TH *Friday.* We set out early and proceeded on very well; the banks being firm and the shore bold we were enabled to use the towline, which, whenever the banks will permit it, is the safest and most expeditious mode of ascending the river, except under a sail with a steady breeze. At the distance of ten and a half miles we came to the mouth of a small creek on the south, below which the hills approach the river, and continue near it during the day: three miles further is a large creek on the north, and again six and three quarter miles beyond it, another large creek to the south, which contain a small quantity of running water of a brackish taste. The last we called Rattlesnake creek from our seeing that animal near it. Although no timber can be observed on it from the Missouri, it throws out large quantities of driftwood, among which were some pieces of coal brought down by the stream. We continued on one mile and a quarter, and encamped on the south after making twenty and a half miles.

    The country in general is rugged, the hills high, with their summits and sides partially covered with pine and cedar, and their bases on both sides washed by the river: like those already mentioned the lower part of these hills is a dark rich loam, while the upper region for one hundred and fifty feet consists of a whitish brown sand, so hard as in many places to resemble stone, though in fact very little stone or rock of any kind is to be seen on the hills. The bed of the Missouri is much narrower than usual, being not more than between two and three hundred yards in width, with an uncommonly large proportion of gravel; but the sandbars, and low points covered with willows have almost entirely disappeared: the timber on the river consists of scarcely any thing more than a few scattered cottonwood trees. The saline incrustations along the banks and the foot of the hills are more abundant than usual.

The game is in great quantities, but the buffalo are not so numerous as they were some days ago: two rattlesnakes were seen to-day, and one of them killed: it resembles those of the middle Atlantic states, being about two feet six inches long, of a yellowish brown on the back and sides, variegated with a row of oval dark brown spots lying transversely on the back from the neck to the tail, and two other rows of circular spots of the same colour on the sides along the edge of the scuta: there are one hundred and seventy-six scuta on the belly, and seventeen on the tail.

Captain Clark saw in his excursions a fortified Indian camp which appeared to have been recently occupied, and was, we presumed, made by a party of Minnetarees who went to war last March.

Late at night we were roused by the sergeant of the guard in consequence of a fire which had communicated to a tree overhanging our camp. The wind was so high, that we had not removed the camp more than a few minutes when a large part of the tree fell precisely on the spot it had occupied, and would have crushed us if we had not been alarmed in time.

Saturday. The wind continued high from the west, but by means of the towline we were able to make nineteen miles, the sandbars being now few in number, the river narrow and the current gentle; the willow has in a great measure disappeared, and even the cottonwood, almost the only timber remaining, is growing scarce. At twelve and three quarter miles we came to a creek on the north, which was perfectly dry. We encamped on the south opposite the lower point of an island. MAY 18TH

Sunday. The last night was disagreeably cold; and in the morning there was a very heavy fog which obscured the river so much as to prevent our seeing the way. This is the first fog of any degree of thickness which we have experienced: there was also last evening a fall of dew, the second which we have seen since entering this extensive open country. About eight o'clock the fog dispersed, and we proceeded with the aid of the towline: the island near which we were encamped, was three quarters of a mile in length. The country resembles that of yesterday, high hills closely bordering the river. In the afternoon the river became crooked, and contained more sawyers or floating timber than we have seen in the same space since leaving the Platte. Our game consisted of deer, beaver, and elk: we also killed a brown bear, who, although shot through the heart, ran at his usual pace nearly a quarter of a mile before he fell. At twenty-one miles is a willow island half a mile in length, on the north side, a quarter of a mile beyond which is a shoal of rapid water under a bluff: the water continued very strong for some distance beyond it: at half a mile we came to a sandbar on the north, from which to our place of encampment was another half mile, making in all twenty-two and a quarter miles. The saline substances which we have mentioned continue to appear; and the men are much afflicted with sore eyes and imposthumes. MAY 19TH

MAY 20TH *Monday.* As usual we set out early, and the banks being convenient for that purpose, we used the towline: the river is narrow and crooked, the water rapid, and the country much like that of yesterday: at the distance of two and a quarter miles we passed a large creek with but little water, to which we gave the name of Blowingfly creek, from the quantity of those insects found in its neighbourhood. They are extremely troublesome, infesting our meat whilst cooking and at our meals. After making seven miles we reached by eleven o'clock the mouth of a large river on the south, and encamped for the day at the upper point of its junction with the Missouri.

This stream which we suppose to be that called by the Minnetarees the Muscleshell river, empties into the Missouri two thousand two hundred and seventy miles above the mouth of the latter river, and in latitude 47° 0′ 24.6″ north. It is one hundred and ten yards wide, and contains more water than streams of that size usually do in this country: its current is by no means rapid, and there is every appearance of its being susceptible of navigation by canoes for a considerable distance: its bed is chiefly formed of coarse sand and gravel, with an occasional mixture of black mud; the banks abrupt and nearly twelve feet high, so that they are secure from being overflowed: the water is of a greenish yellow cast and much more transparent than that of the Missouri, which itself, though clearer than below, still retains its whitish hue and a portion of its sediment. Opposite to the point of junction the current of the Missouri is gentle, and two hundred and twenty-two yards in width, the bed principally of mud (the little sand remaining being wholly confined to the points) and still too deep to use the settingpole.

If this be, as we suppose, the Muscleshell, our Indian information is, that it rises in the first chain of the Rocky mountains not far from the sources of the Yellowstone, whence in its course to this place it waters a high broken country, well timbered particularly on its borders, and interspersed with handsome fertile plains and meadows. We have reason, however, to believe, from their giving a similar account of the timber where we now are, that the timber of which they speak is similar to that which we have seen for a few days past, which consists of nothing more than a few straggling small pine and dwarf cedar, on the summits of the hills, nine-tenths of the ground being totally destitute of wood, and covered with a short grass, aromatic herbs, and an immense quantity of prickly pears: though the party who explored it for eight miles represented low grounds on the river as well supplied with cottonwood of a tolerable size, and of an excellent soil. They also reported that the country is broken and irregular like that near our camp; that about five miles up a handsome river about fifty yards wide, which we named after Chaboneau's wife, Sahcajahweah, or Birdwoman's river, discharges itself into the Muscleshell on the north or upper side.

Another party found at the foot of the southern hills, about four miles from the Missouri, a fine bold spring, which in this country is so rare that since we left the Mandans we have found only one of a similar kind, and that was under the bluffs on the south side of the Missouri, at some distance from it, and about five miles below the Yellowstone: with this exception all the small fountains of which we have met a number are impregnated with the salts which are so abundant here, and with which the Missouri is itself most probably tainted, though to us who have been so much accustomed to it, the taste is not perceptible.

Among the game to-day we observed two large owls, with remarkably long feathers resembling ears on the sides of the head, which we presume are the hooting owls, though they are larger and their colours are brighter than those common in the United States.

Tuesday. The morning being very fine we were able to employ the rope, and made twenty miles to our camp on the north. The shores of the river are abrupt, bold and composed of a black and yellow clay, the bars being formed of black mud, and a small proportion of fine sand; the current strong. In its course the Missouri makes a sudden and extensive bend towards the south, to receive the waters of the Muscleshell. The neck of land thus formed, though itself high is lower than the surrounding country, and makes a waving valley extending for a great distance to the northward, with a fertile soil which, though without wood, produces a fine turf of low grass, some herbs and vast quantities of prickly pear. The country on the south is high, broken, and crowned with some pine and dwarf cedar; the leaf of this pine is longer than that of the common pitch or red pine of Virginia, the cone is longer and narrower, the imbrications wider and thicker, and the whole frequently covered with rosin. During the whole day the bends of the river are short and sudden; and the points covered with some cottonwood, large or broad leaved willow, and a small quantity of redwood; the undergrowth consisting of wild roses, and the bushes of the small honeysuckle.

MAY 21ST

The mineral appearances on the river are as usual. We do not find the grouse or prairie hen so abundant as below, and think it probable that they retire from the river to the plains during this season.

The wind had been moderate during the fore part of the day, but continued to rise towards evening, and about dark veered to northwest, and blew a storm all night. We had encamped on a bar on the north, opposite the lower point of an island, which from this circumstance we called Windy island; but we were so annoyed by clouds of dust and sand that we could neither eat nor sleep, and were forced to remove our camp at eight o'clock to the foot of an adjoining hill, which shielded us in some degree from the wind: we procured elk, deer, and buffalo.

Wednesday. The wind blew so violently that it was deemed prudent to wait till it had abated, so that we did not leave the camp till ten o'clock, when we proceeded principally by the towline. We passed Windy island which is about three quarters of a mile in length: and five and a half miles above it a large island in a bend to the north: three miles beyond this we came to the entrance of a creek twenty yards wide, though with little water, which we called Grouse creek, from observing near its mouth a quantity of the prairie hen with pointed tails, the first we have seen in such numbers for several days: the low grounds are somewhat wider than usual and apparently fertile, though the short and scanty grass on the hills does not indicate much richness of soil. The country around is not so broken as that of yesterday, but is still waving, the southern hills possessing more pine than usual, and some appearing on the northern hills, which are accompanied by the usual salt and mineral appearances.

MAY 22D

The river continues about two hundred and fifty yards wide, with fewer sandbars, and the current more gentle and regular. Game is no longer in such abundance, since leaving the Muscleshell. We have caught very few fish on this side of the Mandans, and these were the white catfish of two to five pounds. We killed a deer and a bear: we have not seen in this quarter the black bear, common in the United States and on the lower parts of the Missouri, nor have we discerned any of their tracks, which may easily be distinguished by the shortness of its talons from the brown, grizzly, or white bear, all of which seem to be of the same family, which assumes those colours at different seasons of the year. We halted earlier than usual, and encamped on the north, in a point of woods, at the distance of sixteen and a half miles.

THURSDAY, MAY 23D, 1805   Last night the frost was severe, and this morning the ice appeared along the edges of the river, and the water froze on our oars. At the distance of a mile we passed the entrance of a creek on the north, which we named Teapot creek; it is fifteen yards wide, and although it has running water at a small distance from its mouth, yet it discharges none into the Missouri, resembling, we believe, most of the creeks in this hilly country, the waters of which are absorbed by the thirsty soil near the river. They indeed afford but little water in any part, and even that is so strongly tainted with salts that it is unfit for use, though all the wild animals are very fond of it. On experiment it was found to be moderately purgative, but painful to the intestines in its operation. This creek seems to come from a range of low hills, which run from east to west for seventy miles, and have their eastern extremity thirty miles to the north of Teapot creek. Just above its entrance is a large assemblage of the burrowing squirrels on the north side of the river. At nine miles we reached the upper point of an island in a bend on the south, and opposite the centre of the island, a small dry creek on the north. Half a mile further a small creek falls in on the same side; and six and a half miles beyond this another on the south. At four and a half we passed a small island in a deep bend to the north, and on the same side in a deep northeastern bend of the river another small island. None of these creeks however possessed any water, and at the entrances of the islands, the two first are covered with tall cottonwood timber, and the last with willows only. The river has become more rapid, the country much the same as yesterday, except that there is rather more rocks on the face of the hills, and some small spruce pine appears among the pitch. The wild roses are very abundant and now in bloom; they differ from those of the United States only in having the leaves and the bush itself of a somewhat smaller size. We find the mosquitoes troublesome, notwithstanding the coolness of the morning. The buffalo is scarce to-day, but the elk, deer, and antelope, are very numerous. The geese begin to lose the feathers of the wings, and are unable to fly. We saw five bears, one of which we wounded, but in swimming from us across the river, he became entangled in some driftwood and sank. We formed our camp on the north opposite to a hill and a point of wood in a bend to the south, having made twenty-seven miles.

Friday. The water in the kettles froze one eighth of an inch during the night; the ice appears along the margin of the river, and the cottonwood trees which have lost nearly all their leaves by the frost, are putting forth other buds. We proceeded with the line principally till about nine o'clock, when a fine breeze sprung up from the S. E. and enabled us to sail very well, notwithstanding the rapidity of the current. At one mile and a half is a large creek thirty yards wide, and containing some water which it empties on the north side, over a gravelly bed, intermixed with some stone. A man who was sent up to explore the country returned in the evening, after having gone ten miles directly towards the ridge of mountains to the north, which is the source of this as well as of Teapot creek. The air of these highlands is so pure, that objects appear much nearer than they really are, so that although our man went ten miles without thinking himself by any means half way to the mountains, they do not from the river appear more than fifteen miles distant; this stream we called Northmountain creek. Two and a half miles

Chapter 9
FROM THE
MUSSELSHELL TO
MARIA'S RIVER

MAY 24TH

higher is a creek on the south which is fifteen yards wide, but without any water, and to which we gave the name of Littledog creek, from a village of burrowing squirrels opposite to its entrance, that being the name given by the French watermen to those animals. Three miles from this a small creek enters on the north, five beyond which is an island a quarter of a mile in length, and two miles further a small river: this falls in on the south, is forty yards wide, and discharges a handsome stream of water; its bed rocky with gravel and sand, and the banks high: we called it Southmountain creek, as from its direction it seemed to rise in a range of mountains about fifty or sixty miles to the S. W. of its entrance.

The low grounds are narrow and without timber; the country high and broken; a large portion of black rock, and brown sandy rock appears in the face of the hills, the tops of which are covered with scattered pine, spruce and dwarf cedar; the soil is generally poor, sandy near the tops of the hills, and nowhere producing much grass, the low grounds being covered with little else than the hyssop, or southern wood, and the pulpy-leafed thorn. Game is more scarce, particularly beaver, of which we have seen but few for several days, and the abundance or scarcity of which seems to depend on the greater or less quantity of timber. At twenty-four and a half miles we reached a point of woodland on the south, where we observed that the trees had no leaves, and encamped for the night.

The high country through which we have passed for some days, and where we now are, we suppose to be a continuation of what the French traders called the Côte Noire or Black hills. The country thus denominated consists of high broken irregular hills and short chains of mountains, sometimes one hundred and twenty miles in width, sometimes narrower, but always much higher than the country on either side. They commence about the head of the Kanzas, where they diverge; the first ridge going westward, along the northern shore of the Arkansaw; the second approaches the Rock mountains obliquely in a course a little to the W. of N. W. and after passing the Platte above its forks, and intersecting the Yellowstone near the Bigbend, crosses the Missouri at this place, and probably swell the country as far as the Saskashawan, though as they are represented much smaller here than to the south, they may not reach that river.

MAY 25TH *Saturday.* Two canoes which were left behind yesterday to bring on the game, did not join us till eight o'clock this morning, when we set out with the towline, the use of which the banks permitted. The wind was, however, ahead, the current strong, particularly round the points against which it happened to set, and the gullies from the hills having brought down quantities of stone, these projected into the river, forming barriers for forty or fifty feet round, which it was very difficult to pass. At the distance of two and three quarter miles we passed a small island in a deep bend on the south, and on the same side a creek twenty yards wide, but with no running water. About a mile further is an island between two and three miles in length, separated from the northern shore by a narrow channel, in which is a sand island at the distance of half a mile from its lower extremity. To this large island we gave the name of Teapot island; two miles above which is an island a mile long, and situated on the south. At three and a half miles is another small island, and one mile beyond it a second three quarters of a mile in length, on the north side. In the middle of the river two miles above this is an island with no timber, and of the same extent as this last.

The country on each side is high, broken, and rocky; the rock being either a soft brown sandstone, covered with a thin stratum of limestone, or else a hard black rugged granite, both usually in horizontal stratas, and the sandrock overlaying the other. Salts and quartz as well as some coal and pumicestone still appear: the bars of the river are composed principally of gravel; the river low grounds are narrow, and afford scarcely any timber; nor is there much pine on the hills. The buffalo have now become scarce: we saw a polecat this evening, which was the first for several days: in the course of the day we also saw several herds of the big-horned animals among the steep cliffs on the north, and killed several of them. At the distance of eighteen miles we encamped on the south, and the next morning, *Sunday, 26th*, proceeded on at an early hour by means of the towline, using our oars merely in passing the river, to take advantage of the best banks. There are now scarcely any low grounds on the river, the hills being high and in many places pressing on both sides to the verge of the water. The black rock has given place to a very soft sandstone, which seems to be washed away fast by the river, and being thrown into the river renders its navigation more difficult than it was yesterday: above this sandstone, and towards the summits of the hills, a hard freestone of a yellowish brown colour shows itself in several stratas of unequal thickness, frequently overlaid or incrusted by a thin stratum of limestone, which seems to be formed of concreted shells. At eight and a quarter miles we came to the mouth of a creek on the north, thirty yards wide, with some running water and a rocky bed: we called it Windsor creek, after one of the party. Four and three-quarter miles beyond this we came to another creek in a bend to the north, which is twenty yards wide, with a handsome little stream of water: there is however no timber on either side of the river except a few pines on the hills. Here we saw for the first time since we left the Mandans several soft shelled turtles, though this may be owing rather to the season of the year than to any scarcity of the animal.

It was here that after ascending the highest summits of the hills on the north side of the river, that captain Lewis first caught a distant view of the Rock [Rocky] mountains, the object of all our hopes, and the reward of all our ambition. On both sides of the river and at no great distance from it, the mountains followed its course: above these, at the distance of fifty miles from us, an irregular range of mountains spread themselves from west to northwest from his position. To the north of these a few elevated points, the most remarkable of which bore north 65° west, appeared above the horizon, and as the sun shone on the snows of their summits he obtained a clear and satisfactory view of those mountains which close on the Missouri the passage to the Pacific.

Four and a half miles beyond this creek we came to the upper point of a small sand island. At the distance of five miles between high bluffs, we passed a very difficult rapid, reaching quite across the river, where the water is deep, the channel narrow, and gravel obstructing it on each side: we had great difficulty in ascending it, although we used both the rope and the pole, and doubled the crews. This is the most considerable rapid on the Missouri, and in fact the only place where there is a sudden descent. As we were labouring over them, a female elk with its fawn swam down through the waves, which ran very high, and obtained for the place the name of the Elk Rapids. Just above them is a small low ground of cottonwood trees, where at twenty-two and a quarter miles we fixed our encampment, and were joined by captain Lewis, who had been on the hills during the afternoon.

The country has now become desert and barren: the appearances of coal, burnt earth, pumicestone, salts, and quartz, continue as yesterday: but there is no timber except the thinly scattered pine and spruce on the summits of the hills, or along the sides. The only animals we have observed are the elk, the bighorn, and the hare, common in this country. In the plain where we lie are two Indian cabins [wickiups] made of sticks, and during the last few days we have passed several others in the points of timber on the river.

MAY 27TH *Monday.* The wind was so high that we did not start till ten o'clock, and even then were obliged to use the line during the greater part of the day. The river has become very rapid with a very perceptible descent: its general width is about two hundred yards: the shoals too are more frequent, and the rocky points at the mouth of the gullies more troublesome to pass: great quantities of this stone lie in the river and on its banks, and seem to have fallen down as the rain washed away the clay and sand in which they were imbedded. The water is bordered by high rugged bluffs, composed of irregular but horizontal stratas of yellow and brown or black clay, brown and yellowish white sand, soft yellowish white sandstone: hard dark brown freestone; and also large round kidney formed irregular separate masses of a hard black ironstone, imbedded in the clay and sand; some coal or carbonated wood also makes its appearance in the cliffs, as do also its usual attendants the pumicestone and burnt earth. The salts and quartz are less abundant, and generally speaking the country is if possible more rugged and barren than that we passed yesterday; the only growth of the hills being a few pine, spruce, and dwarf cedar, interspersed with an occasional contrast once in the course of some miles, of several acres of level ground, which supply a scanty subsistence for a few little cottonwood trees.

Soon after setting out we passed a small untimbered island on the south: at about seven miles we reached a considerable bend which the river makes towards the southeast, and in the evening, after making twelve and a half miles, encamped on the south near two dead cottonwood trees, the only timber for fuel which we could discover in the neighbourhood.

MAY 28TH *Tuesday.* The weather was dark and cloudy; the air smoky, and there fell a few drops of rain. At ten o'clock we had again a slight sprinkling of rain, attended with distant thunder, which is the first we have heard since leaving the Mandans. We employed the line generally, with the addition of the pole at the ripples and rocky points, which we find more numerous and troublesome than those we passed yesterday. The water is very rapid round these points, and we are sometimes obliged to steer the canoes through the points of sharp rocks rising a few inches above the surface of the water, and so near to each other that if our ropes give way the force of the current drives the sides of the canoe against them, and must inevitably upset them or dash them to pieces. These cords are very slender, being almost all made of elk-skin, and much worn and rotted by exposure to the weather: several times they gave way, but fortunately always in places where there was room for the canoe to turn without striking the rock; yet with all our precautions it was with infinite risk and labour that we passed these points. An Indian pole for building floated down the river, and was worn at one end as if dragged along the ground in travelling; several other articles were also brought down by the current, which indicate that the Indians are probably at no great distance above us, and judging from a football which resembles those used by the Minnetarees near the Mandans, we conjecture that they must be a band of the Minnetarees of fort de Prairie.

The appearance of the river and the surrounding country continued as usual, till towards evening, at about fifteen miles, we reached a large creek on the north thirty-five yards wide, discharging some water, and named after one of our men Thompson's creek. Here the country assumed a totally different aspect; the hills retired on both sides from the river which now spreads to more than three times its former size, and is filled with a number of small handsome islands covered with cottonwood. The low grounds on the river are again wide, fertile, and enriched with trees; those on the north are particularly wide, the hills being comparatively low and opening into three large vallies, which extend themselves for a considerable distance towards the north: these appearances of vegetation are delightful after the dreary hills over which we have passed, and we have now to congratulate ourselves at having escaped from the last ridges of the Black mountains. On leaving Thompson's creek we passed two small islands, and at twenty-three miles distance encamped among some timber on the north, opposite to a small creek, which we named Bull creek. The bighorn is in great quantities, and must bring forth their young at a very early season, as they are now half grown. One of the party saw a large bear also, but being at a distance from the river, and having no timber to conceal him, he would not venture to fire.

Wednesday. Last night we were alarmed by a new sort of enemy. A buffalo swam over from the opposite side and to the spot where lay one of our canoes, over which he clambered to the shore; then taking fright he ran full speed up the bank towards our fires, and passed within eighteen inches of the heads of some of the men, before the sentinel could make him change his course: still more alarmed he ran down between four fires and within a few inches of the heads of a second row of the men, and would have broken into our lodge if the barking of the dog had not stopped him. He suddenly turned to the right and was out of sight in a moment, leaving us all in confusion, every one seizing his rifle and inquiring the cause of the alarm. On learning what had happened, we had to rejoice at suffering no more injury than the damage to some guns which were in the canoe which the buffalo crossed.

MAY 29TH

In the morning early we left our camp, and proceeded as usual by the cord. We passed an island and two sandbars, and at the distance of two and a half miles we came to a handsome river which discharges itself on the south, and which we ascended to the distance of a mile and a half: we called it Judith's river: it rises in the Rock mountains in about the same place with the Muscleshell and near the Yellowstone river. Its entrance is one hundred yards wide from one bank to the other, the water occupying about seventy-five yards, and in greater quantity than that of the Muscleshell river, and though more rapid equally navigable, there being no stones or rocks in the bed, which is composed entirely of gravel and mud with some sand: the water too is clearer than any which we have yet seen; and the low grounds, as far as we could discern, wider and more woody than those of the Missouri: along its banks we observed some box-alder intermixed with the cottonwood and the willow; the undergrowth consisting of rosebushes, honeysuckles, and a little red willow. There was a great abundance of the argalea or bighorned animals in the high country through which it passes, and a great number of the beaver in its waters.

Just above the entrance of it we saw the fires of one hundred and twenty-six lodges, which appeared to have been deserted about twelve or fifteen days, and on the other side of the Missouri a large encampment, apparently made by the same nation. On examining some moccasins which we found there, our Indian woman said that they do not belong to her own nation the Snake Indians, but she thought that they indicated a tribe on this side of the Rocky mountains, and to the north of the Missouri; indeed it is probable that these are the Minnetarees of fort de Prairie.

At the distance of six and a half miles the hills again approached the brink of the river, and the stones and rocks washed down from them form a very bad rapid, with rocks and ripples more numerous and difficult than those we passed on the *27th* and *28th*: here the same scene was renewed, and we had again to struggle and labour to preserve our small craft from being lost. Near this spot are a few trees of the ash, the first we have seen for a great distance, and from which we named the place Ash Rapids. On these hills there is but little timber, but the salts, coal, and other mineral appearances continue.

On the north we passed a precipice about one hundred and twenty feet high, under which lay scattered the fragments of at least one hundred carcasses of buffaloes, although the water which had washed away the lower part of the hill must have carried off many of the dead. These buffaloes had been chased down the precipice in a way very common on the Missouri, and by which vast herds are destroyed in a moment. The mode of hunting is to select one of the most active and fleet young men, who is disguised by a buffalo skin round his body; the skin of the head with the ears and horns fastened on his own head in such a way as to deceive the buffalo: thus dressed, he fixes himself at a convenient distance between a herd of buffalo and any of the river precipices, which sometimes extend for some miles. His companions in the meantime get in the rear and side of the herd, and at a given signal show themselves, and advance towards the buffalo: they instantly take the alarm, and finding the hunters beside them, they run towards the disguised Indian or decoy, who leads them on at full speed towards the river, when suddenly securing himself in some crevice of the cliff which he had previously fixed on, the herd is left on the brink of the precipice: it is then in vain for the foremost to retreat or even to stop; they are pressed on by the hindmost rank, who, seeing no danger but from the hunters, goad on those before them till the whole are precipitated and the shore is strewed with their dead bodies. Sometimes in this perilous seduction the Indian is himself either trodden underfoot by the rapid movements of the buffalo, or missing his footing in the cliff is urged down the precipice by the falling herd. The Indians then select as much meat as they wish, and the rest is abandoned to the wolves, and creates a most dreadful stench. The wolves who had been feasting on these carcases were very fat, and so gentle that one of them was killed with a spontoon.

Above this place we came to for dinner at the distance of seventeen miles, opposite to a bold running river of twenty yards wide, and falling in on the south. From the objects we had just passed we called this stream Slaughter river. Its low grounds are narrow, and contain scarcely any timber. Soon after landing it began to blow and rain, and as there was no prospect of getting wood for fuel farther on, we fixed our camp on the north, three quarters of a mile above Slaughter river. After the labours of the day we gave to each man a dram, and such was the effect of long abstinence from spirituous liquors, that from the small quantity of half a gill of rum, several of the men were considerably affected by it, and all very much exhilarated. Our game to-day consisted of an elk and two beaver.

Thursday. The rain which commenced last evening continued with little intermission till eleven this morning, when the high wind which accompanied it having abated, we set out. More rain has now fallen than we have had since the 1st of September last, and many circumstances indicate our approach to a climate differing considerably from that of the country through which we have been passing: the air of the open country is astonishingly dry and pure. Observing that the case of our sextant, though perfectly seasoned, shrank and the joints opened, we tried several experiments, by which it appeared that a tablespoonful of water exposed in a saucer to the air would evaporate in thirty-six hours, when the mercury did not stand higher than the temperate point at the greatest heat of the day. The river, notwithstanding the rain, is much clearer than it was a few days past; but we advance with great labour and difficulty; the rapid current, the ripples and rocky points rendering the navigation more embarrassing than even that of yesterday, in addition to which the banks are now so slippery after the rain, that the men who draw the canoes can scarcely walk, and the earth and stone constantly falling down the high bluffs make it dangerous to pass under them; still however we are obliged to make use of the cord, as the wind is strong ahead, the current too rapid for oars, and too deep for the pole. In this way we passed at the distance of five and a half miles a small rivulet in a bend on the north, two miles further an island on the same side, half a mile beyond which came to a grove of trees at the entrance of a run in a bend to the south, and encamped for the night on the northern shore. The eight miles which we made to-day cost us much trouble. The air was cold and rendered more disagreeable by the rain, which fell in several slight showers in the course of the day; our cords too broke several times, but fortunately without injury to the boats.

MAY 30TH

On ascending the hills near the river, one of the party found that there was snow mixed with the rain on the heights: a little back of these the country becomes perfectly level on both sides of the river. There is now no timber on the hills, and only a few scattering cottonwood, ash, box-alder, and willows, along the water. In the course of the day we passed several encampments of Indians, the most recent of which seemed to have been evacuated about five weeks since, and from the several apparent dates we supposed that they were made by a band of about one hundred lodges who were travelling slowly up the river. Although no part of the Missouri from the Minnetarees to this place exhibit signs of permanent settlements, yet none seem exempt from the transient visits of hunting parties. We know that the Minnetarees of the Missouri extend their excursions on the south side of the river, as high as the Yellowstone; and the Assiniboins visit the northern side, most probably as high as Porcupine river. All the lodges between that place and the Rocky mountains we supposed to belong to the Minnetarees of fort de Prairie, who live on the south fork of the Saskashawan.

MAY 31ST *Friday.* We proceeded in two periogues, leaving the canoes to bring on the meat of two buffaloes killed last evening. Soon after we set off it began to rain, and though it ceased at noon, the weather continued cloudy during the rest of the day. The obstructions of yesterday still remain and fatigue the men excessively: the banks are so slippery in some places and the mud so adhesive that they are unable to wear their moccasins; one fourth of the time they are obliged to be up to their armpits in the cold water, and sometimes walk for several yards over the sharp fragments of rocks which have fallen from the hills: all this added to the burden of dragging the heavy canoes is very painful, yet the men bear it with great patience and good humour. Once the rope of one of the periogues, the only one we had made of hemp, broke short, and the periogue swung and just touched a point of rock which almost overset her.

At nine miles we came to a high wall of black rock rising from the water's edge on the south, above the cliffs of the river: this continued about a quarter of a mile, and was succeeded by a high open plain, till three miles further a second wall two hundred feet high rose on the same side. Three miles further a wall of the same kind about two hundred feet high and twelve in thickness, appeared to the north. These hills and river cliffs exhibit a most extraordinary and romantic appearance: they rise in most places nearly perpendicular from the water, to the height of between two and three hundred feet, and are formed of very white sandstone, so soft as to yield readily to the impression of water, in the upper part of which lie imbedded two or three thin horizontal strata of white freestone insensible to the rain, and on the top is a dark rich loam, which forms a gradually ascending plain, from a mile to a mile and a half in extent, when the hills again rise abruptly to the height of about three hundred feet more. In trickling down the cliffs, the water has worn the soft sandstone into a thousand grotesque figures, among which with a little fancy may be discerned elegant ranges of freestone buildings, with columns variously sculptured, and supporting long and elegant galleries, while the parapets are adorned with statuary: on a nearer approach they represent every form of elegant ruins; columns, some with pedestals and capitals entire, others mutilated and prostrate, and some rising pyramidally over each other till they terminate in a sharp point. These are varied by niches, alcoves, and the customary appearances of desolated magnificence: the illusion is increased by the number of martins, who have built their globular nests in the niches and hover over these columns; as in our country they are accustomed to frequent large stone structures.

As we advance there seems no end to the visionary enchantment which surrounds us. In the midst of this fantastic scenery are vast ranges of walls, which seem the productions of art, so regular is the workmanship:

146

they rise perpendicularly from the river, sometimes to the height of one hundred feet, varying in thickness from one to twelve feet, being equally broad at the top as below. The stones of which they are formed are black, thick, and durable, and composed of a large portion of earth, intermixed and cemented with a small quantity of sand, and a considerable proportion of talc or quartz. These stones are almost invariably regular parallelipeds of unequal sizes in the wall, but equally deep, and laid regularly in ranges over each other like bricks, each breaking and covering the interstice of the two on which it rests; but though the perpendicular interstice be destroyed, the horizontal one extends entirely through the whole work: the stones too are proportioned to the thickness of the wall in which they are employed, being largest in the thickest walls. The thinner walls are composed of a single depth of the paralleliped, while the thicker ones consist of two or more depths: these walls pass the river at several places, rising from the water's edge much above the sandstone bluffs which they seem to penetrate; thence they cross in a straight line on either side of the river, the plains over which they tower to the height of from ten to seventy feet, until they lose themselves in the second range of hills: sometimes they run parallel in several ranges near to each other, sometimes intersect each other at right angles, and have the appearance of walls of ancient houses or gardens.

The face of some of these river hills, is composed of very excellent freestone of a light yellowish brown colour, and among the cliffs we found a species of pine which we had not yet seen, and differing from the Virginia pitch-pine in having a shorter leaf, and a longer and more pointed cone. The coal appears only in small quantities, as do the burnt earth and pumicestone: the mineral salts have abated. Among the animals are a great number of the bighorn, a few buffalo and elk, and some mule-deer, but none of the common deer nor any antelopes. We saw but could not procure a beautiful fox, of a colour varied with orange, yellow, white, and black, rather smaller than the common fox of this country, and about the same size as the red fox of the United States.

The river to-day has been from about one hundred and fifty to two hundred and fifty yards wide, with but little timber. At the distance of two miles and a half from the last stone wall, is a stream on the north side, twenty-eight yards in width, and with some running water. We encamped just above its mouth, having made eighteen miles.

Saturday, June 1st, 1805

The weather was cloudy with a few drops of rain. As we proceeded by the aid of our cord we found the river cliffs and bluffs not so high as yesterday, and the country more level. The timber too is in greater abundance on the river, though there is no wood on the high ground; coal however appears in the bluffs. The river is from two hundred to two hundred and fifty feet wide, the current more gentle, the water becoming still clearer and fewer rocky points and shoals than we met yesterday, though those which we did encounter were equally difficult to pass. Game is by no means in such plenty as below; all that we obtained were one bighorn, and a mule-deer, though we saw in the plains a quantity of buffalo, particularly near a small lake about eight miles from the river to the south. Notwithstanding the wind was ahead all day, we dragged the canoes along the distance of twenty-three miles. At fourteen and a quarter miles, we came to a small island opposite a bend of the river to the north: two and a half miles to the upper point of a small island on the north; five miles to another island on the south side and opposite to a bluff. In the next two miles we passed an island on the south, a second beyond it on the north, and reached near a high bluff on the north a third on which we encamped.

In the plains near the river are the chokecherry, yellow and red currant-bushes, as well as the wild rose and prickly pear, both of which are now in bloom. From the tops of the river hills, which are lower than usual, we enjoyed a delightful view of the rich fertile plains on both sides, in many places extending from the river cliffs to a great distance back. In these plains we meet occasionally large banks of pure sand, which were driven apparently by the southwest winds, and there deposited. The plains are more fertile some distance from the river than near its banks, where the surface of the earth is very generally strewed with small pebbles, which appear to be smoothed and worn by the agitation of the waters with which they were no doubt once covered. A mountain or part of the North mountain approaches the river within eight or ten miles, bearing north from our encampment of last evening; and this morning a range of high mountains bearing S. W. from us and apparently running to the westward, are seen at a great distance covered with snow. In the evening we had a little more rain.

JUNE 2D *Sunday.* The wind blew violently last night, and a slight shower of rain fell, but this morning was fair. We set out at an early hour, and although the wind was ahead by means of the cord went on much better than for the last two days, as the banks were well calculated for towing. The current of the river is strong but regular, its timber increases in quantity, the low grounds become more level and extensive, and the bluffs on the rivers are lower than usual. In the course of the day we had a small shower of rain, which lasted a few minutes only.

As the game is very abundant we think it necessary to begin a collection of hides for the purpose of making a leathern boat, which we intend constructing shortly. The hunters who were out the greater part of the day brought in six elk, two buffalo, two mule-deer and a bear. This last animal had nearly cost us the lives of two of our hunters who were together when he attacked them; one of them narrowly escaped being caught, and the other after running a considerable distance, concealed himself in some thick bushes, and while the bear was in quick pursuit of his hiding place, his companion came up and fortunately shot the animal through the head.

At six and a half miles we reached an island on the northern side; one mile and a quarter thence is a timbered low ground on the south: and in the next two and three quarter miles we passed three small islands, and came to a dark bluff on the south: within the following mile are two small islands on the same side. At three and a quarter miles we reached the lower part of a much larger island near a northern point, and as we coasted along its side, within two miles passed a smaller island, and half a mile above reached the head of another. All these islands are small, and most of them contain some timber. Three quarters of a mile beyond the last, and at the distance of eighteen miles from our encampment, we came to for the night in a handsome low cottonwood plain on the south, where we remained for the purpose of making some celestial observations during the night, and of examining in the morning a large river which comes in opposite to us.

Monday. Accordingly at an early hour, we crossed and fixed our camp in the point, formed by the junction of the river with the Missouri. It now became an interesting question which of these two streams is what the Minnetarees call Ahmateahza or the Missouri, which they described as approaching very near to the Columbia. On our right decision much of the fate of the expedition depends; since if after ascending to the Rocky mountains or beyond them, we should find that the river we were following did not come near the Columbia, and be obliged to return, we should not only lose the travelling season, two months of which had already elapsed, but probably dishearten the men so much as to induce them either to abandon the enterprise, or yield us a cold obedience instead of the warm and zealous support which they had hitherto afforded us. We determined, therefore, to examine well before we decided on our future course; and for this purpose despatched two canoes with three men up each of the streams with orders to ascertain the width, depth, and rapidity of the current, so as to judge of their comparative bodies of water. At the same time parties were sent out by land to penetrate the country, and discover from the rising grounds, if possible, the distant bearings of the two rivers; and all were directed to return towards evening.

JUNE 3D

While they were gone we ascended together the high grounds in the fork of these two rivers, whence we had a very extensive prospect of the surrounding country: on every side it was spread into one vast plain covered with verdure, in which innumerable herds of buffalo were roaming, attended by their enemies the wolves: some flocks of elk also were seen, and the solitary antelopes were scattered with their young over the face of the plain. To the south was a range of lofty mountains, which we supposed to be a continuation of the South mountain, stretching themselves from southeast to northwest, and terminating abruptly about southwest from us. These were partially covered with snow; but at a great distance behind them was a more lofty ridge completely covered with snow, which seemed to follow the same direction as the first, reaching from west to the north of northwest, where their snowy tops were blended with the horizon. The direction of the rivers could not however be long distinguished, as they were soon lost in the extent of the plain. On our return we continued our examination; the width of the north branch is two hundred yards, that of the south is three hundred and seventy-two. The north, although narrower and with a gentler current, is deeper than the south: its waters too are of the same whitish brown colour, thickness, and turbidness: they run in the same boiling and rolling manner which has uniformly characterized the Missouri; and its bed is composed of some gravel, but principally mud. The south fork is deeper, but its waters are perfectly transparent: its current is rapid, but the surface smooth and unruffled; and its bed too is composed of round and flat smooth stones like those of rivers issuing from a mountainous country.

The air and character of the north fork so much resemble those of the Missouri that almost all the party believe that to be the true course to be pursued. We however, although we have given no decided opinion, are inclined to think otherwise, because, although this branch does give the colour and character to the Missouri, yet these very circumstances induce an opinion that it rises in and runs through an open plain country, since if it came from the mountains it would be clearer, unless, which from the position of the country is improbable, it passed through a vast extent of low ground after leaving them: we thought it probable that it did not even penetrate the Rocky mountains, but drew its sources from the open country towards the lower and middle parts of the Saskashawan, in a direction north of this place. What embarrasses us most is, that the Indians who appeared to be well acquainted with the geography of the country, have not mentioned this northern river; for "the river which scolds at all others," as it is termed, must be according to their account one of the rivers which we have passed; and if this north fork be the Missouri, why have they not designated the south branch which they must also have passed, in order to reach the great falls which they mention on the Missouri?

In the evening our parties returned, after ascending the rivers in canoes for some distance, then continuing on foot, just leaving themselves time to return by night. The north fork was less rapid, and therefore afforded the easiest navigation: the shallowest water of the north was five feet deep, that of the south six feet. At two and a half miles up the north fork is a small river coming in on the left or western side, sixty feet wide, with a bold current three feet in depth. The party by land had gone up the south fork in a straight line, somewhat north of west for seven miles, where they discovered that this little river came within one hundred yards of the south fork, and on returning down it found it a handsome stream, with as much timber as either of the larger rivers, consisting of the narrow and wide-leafed cottonwood, some birch and box-alder, and undergrowth of willows, rose-bushes, and currants: they also saw on this river a great number of elk and some beaver.

All these accounts were however very far from deciding the important question of our future route, and we therefore determined each of us to ascend one of the rivers during a day and a half's march, or farther if necessary, for our satisfaction. Our hunters killed two buffalo, six elk, and four deer to-day. Along the plains near the junction are to be found the prickly pear in great quantities; the chokecherry is also very abundant in the river low grounds, as well as the ravines along the river bluffs; the yellow and red currants are not yet ripe; the gooseberry is beginning to ripen, and the wild rose which now covers all the low grounds near the rivers is in full bloom. The fatigues of the last few days have occasioned some falling off in the appearance of the men, who not having been able to wear moccasins, had their feet much bruised and mangled in passing over the stones and rough ground. They are however perfectly cheerful, and have an undiminished ardour for the expedition.

JUNE 4TH *Tuesday.* At the same hour this morning captain Lewis and captain Clark set out to explore the two rivers; captain Lewis with six men crossed the north fork near the camp, below a small island from which he took a course N. 30° W. for four and a half miles to a commanding eminence. Here he observed that the North mountain, changing its direction parallel to the Missouri, turned towards the north and terminated abruptly at the distance of about thirty miles, the point of termination bearing N. 48° E. The South mountain too diverges to the south, and terminates abruptly, its extremity bearing S. 8° W. distant about twenty miles: to the right of, and retreating from this extremity, is a separate mountain at the distance of thirty-five miles in a direction S. 38° W. which from its resemblance to the roof of a barn, we called the Barn mountain. The north fork, which is now on the left, makes a considerable bend to the northwest, and on its western border a range of hills about ten miles long, and bearing from this spot N. 60° W. runs parallel with it: north of this range of hills is an elevated point of the river bluff on its south side, bearing N. 72° W. about twelve miles from us; towards this he directed his course across a high, level, dry open plain; which in fact embraces the whole country to the foot of the mountains. The soil is dark, rich, and fertile, yet the grass by no means so luxuriant as might have been expected, for it is short and scarcely more than sufficient to cover the ground. There are vast quantities of prickly pears, and myriads of grasshoppers, which afford food for a species of curlew which is in great numbers in the plain.

    He then proceeded up the river to the point of observation they had fixed on; from which he went two miles N. 15° W. to a bluff point on the north side of the river: thence his course was N. 30° W. for two miles to the entrance of a large creek on the south. The part of the river along which he passed is from forty to sixty yards wide, the current strong, the water deep and turbid, the banks falling in, the salts, coal and mineral appearances are as usual, and in every respect, except as to size, this river resembles the Missouri. The low grounds are narrow but well supplied with wood: the bluffs are principally of dark brown yellow, and some white clay with freestone in some places. From this point the river bore N. 20° E. to a bluff on the south, at the distance of twelve miles: towards this he directed his course, ascending the hills which are about two hundred feet high, and passing through plains for three miles, till he found the dry ravines so steep and numerous that he resolved to return to the river and follow its banks. He reached it about four miles from the beginning of his course, and encamped on the north in a bend among some bushes which sheltered the party from the wind: the air was very cold, the northwest wind high, and the rain wet them to the skin. Besides the game just mentioned, he observed buffalo, elk, wolves, foxes, and we got a blaireau and a weasel, and wounded a large brown bear, whom it was too late to pursue. Along the river are immense quantities of roses which are now in full bloom, and which make the low grounds a perfect garden.

Wednesday. The rain fell during the greater part of the last night, and in the morning the weather was cloudy and cold, with a high northwest wind: at sunrise he proceeded up the river eight miles to the bluff on the left side, towards which he had been directing his course yesterday. Here he found the bed of a creek twenty-five yards wide at the entrance, with some timber, but no water, notwithstanding the rain: it is, indeed, astonishing to observe the vast quantities of water absorbed by the soil of the plains, which being opened in large crevices presents a fine rich loam: at the mouth of this stream (which he called Lark creek) the bluffs are very steep and approach the river so that he ascended them, and crossing the plains reached the river, JUNE 5TH which from the last point bore N. 50° W.: four miles from this place it extended north two miles. Here he discovered a lofty mountain standing alone at the distance of more than eighty miles in the direction of N. 30° W. and which from its conical figure he called Tower mountain.

He then proceeded on these two hills and afterwards in different courses six miles, when he again changed for a western course across a deep bend along the south side: in making this passage over the plains he found them like those of yesterday, level and beautiful, with great quantities of buffalo, and some wolves, foxes, and antelopes, and intersected near the river by deep ravines. Here at the distance of from one to nine miles from the river, he met the largest village of barking squirrels which we had yet seen: for he passed a skirt of their territory for seven miles. He also saw near the hills a flock of the mountain cock or a large species of heath hen with a long pointed tail, which the Indians below had informed us were common among the Rock mountains. Having finished his course of ten miles west across a bend, he continued two miles N. 80° W. and from that point discovered some lofty mountains to the northwest of Tower mountain and bearing N. 65° W. at eighty or one hundred miles distance: here he encamped on the north side in a handsome low ground, on which were several old stick lodges: there had been but little timber on the river in the forepart of the day, but now there is a greater quantity than usual. The river itself is about eighty yards wide, from six to ten feet deep, and has a strong steady current. The party had killed five elk, and a mule-deer; and by way of experiment roasted the burrowing squirrels, which they found to be well flavoured and tender.

JUNE 6TH *Thursday.* Captain Lewis was now convinced that this river pursued a direction too far north for our route to the Pacific, and therefore resolved to return; but waited till noon to take a meridian altitude. The clouds, however, which had gathered during the latter part of the night continued and prevented the observation: part of the men were sent forward to a commanding eminence, six miles S. 70° W.; from which they saw at the distance of about fifteen miles S. 80° W. a point of the south bluff of the river, which thence bore northwardly. In their absence two rafts had been prepared, and when they returned about noon, the party embarked: but they soon found that the rafts were so small and slender that the baggage was wet, and therefore it was necessary to abandon them, and go by land. They therefore crossed the plains, and at the distance of twelve miles came to the river, through a cold storm from the northeast, accompanied by showers of rain. The abruptness of the cliffs compelled them, after going a few miles, to leave the river and meet the storm in the plains. Here they directed their course too far northward, in consequence of which they did not meet the river till late at night, after having travelled twenty-three miles since noon, and halted at a little below the entrance of Lark creek.

They had the good fortune to kill two buffalo which supplied them with supper: but spent a very uncomfortable night without any shelter from the rain, which continued till morning, *Friday, 7th,* when at an early hour they continued down the river. The route was extremely unpleasant, as the wind was high from the N. E. accompanied with rain, which made the ground so slippery that they were unable to walk over the bluffs which they had passed on ascending the river. The land is the most thirsty we have ever seen; notwithstanding all the rain which has fallen, the earth is not wet for more than two inches deep, and resembles thawed ground; but if it requires more water to saturate it than the common soils, on the other hand it yields its moisture with equal difficulty.

In passing along the side of one of these bluffs at a narrow pass thirty yards in length, captain Lewis slipped, and but for a fortunate recovery, by means of his spontoon, would have been precipitated into the river over a precipice of about ninety feet. He had just reached a spot where by the assistance of his spontoon he could stand with tolerable safety, when he heard a voice behind him cry out, "Good God, captain, what shall I do?" He turned instantly and found it was Windsor, who had lost his foothold about the middle of the narrow pass, and had slipped down to the very verge of the precipice, where he lay on his belly, with his right arm and leg over the precipice, while with the other leg and arm he was with difficulty holding on to keep himself from being dashed to pieces below. His dreadful situation was instantly perceived by captain Lewis, who stifling his alarm, calmly told him that he was in no danger; that he should take his knife out of his belt with the right hand, and dig a hole in the side of the bluff to receive his right foot. With great presence of mind he did this, and then raised himself on his knees; captain Lewis then told him to take off his moccasins and come forward on his hands and knees, holding the knife in one hand and his rifle in the other. He immediately crawled in this way till he came to a secure spot. The men who had not attempted this passage were ordered to return and wade the river at the foot of the bluff, where they found the water breast high.

This adventure taught them the danger of crossing the slippery heights of the river; but as the plains were intersected by deep ravines almost as difficult to pass, they continued down the river, sometimes in the mud of the low grounds, sometimes up to their arms in the water, and when it became too deep to wade, they cut footholds with their knives in the sides of the banks. In this way they travelled through the rain, mud, and water, and having made only eighteen miles during the whole day, encamped in an old Indian lodge of sticks, which afforded them a dry shelter. Here they cooked part of six deer they had killed in the course of their walk, and having eaten the only morsel they had tasted during the whole day slept comfortably on some willow boughs.

Chapter 10

FROM MARIA'S RIVER TO THE GREAT FALLS

SATURDAY, JUNE 8TH, 1805   It continued to rain moderately all last night, and the morning was cloudy till about ten o'clock, when it cleared off, and became a fine day. They breakfasted about sunrise and then proceeded down the river in the same way as they had done yesterday, except that the travelling was somewhat better, as they had not so often to wade, though they passed some very dangerous bluffs. The only timber to be found is in the low grounds which are occasionally on the river, and these are the haunts of innumerable birds, who, when the sun began to shine, sang very delightfully. Among these birds they distinguished the brown thrush, robin, turtledove, linnet, goldfinch, the large and small blackbird, the wren, and some others. As they came along, the whole of the party were of opinion that this river was the true Missouri; but captain Lewis being fully persuaded that it was neither the main stream, nor that which it would be advisable to ascend, gave it the name of Maria's river. After travelling all day they reached the camp at five o'clock in the afternoon, and found captain Clark and the party very anxious for their safety, as they had staid two days longer than had been expected, and as captain Clark had returned at the appointed time, it was feared that they had met with some accident.

Captain Clark on setting out with five men on the *4th*, went seven miles on a course S. 25° W. to a spring; thence he went S. 20° W. for eight miles to the river where was an island, from which he proceeded in a course N. 45° W. and approached the river at the distance of three, five, and thirteen miles, at which place they encamped in an old Indian lodge made of sticks and bark. In crossing the plains they observed several herds of buffalo, some mule-deer, antelopes and wolves. The river is rapid and closely hemmed in by high bluffs, crowded with bars of gravel, with little timber on the low grounds, and none on the highlands. Near the camp this evening, a white bear attacked one of the men, whose gun happening to be wet, would not go off; he instantly made towards a tree, but was so closely pursued, that as he ascended the tree he struck the bear with his foot. The bear not being able to climb, waited till he should be forced to come down; and as the rest of the party were separated from him by a perpendicular cliff of rocks, which they could not descend, it was not in their power to give him any assistance: fortunately however at last the bear became affrighted at their cries and firing, and released the man.

In the afternoon it rained, and during the night there fell both rain and snow, and in the morning, *June 5th*, the hills to the S. E. were covered with snow, and the rain continued. They proceeded on in a course N. 20° W. near the river several miles, till at the distance of eleven miles they reached a ridge, from the top of which on the north side they could plainly discern a mountain to the S. and W. at a great distance covered with snow; a high ridge projecting from the mountains to the southeast approaches the river on the southeast side, forming some cliffs of dark hard stone. They also saw that the river ran for a great distance west of south, with a rapid current, from which as well as its continuing of the same width and depth, captain Clark thought it useless to advance any further, and therefore returned across the level plain in a direction north 30° east, and reached at the distance of twenty miles the little river which is already mentioned as falling into the north fork, and to which they gave the name of Tansy river, from

ON THE UPPER MISSOURI (Bodmer)

the great quantity of that herb growing on its banks. Here they dined, and then proceeded on a few miles by a place where the Tansy breaks through a high ridge on its north side and encamped.

The next day, *6th*, the weather was cold, raw and cloudy, with a high northeast wind. They set out early, down the Tansy, whose low grounds resemble precisely, except as to extent, those of the Missouri before it branches, containing a great proportion of a species of cottonwood, with a leaf like that of the wild cherry. After halting at twelve o'clock for dinner, they ascended the plain, and at five o'clock reached the camp through the rain, which had fallen without intermission since noon. During his absence the party had been occupied in dressing skins, and being able to rest themselves were nearly freed from their lameness and swollen feet. All this night and the whole of the following day, *7th*, it rained, the wind being from the southwest off the mountains: yet the rivers are falling, and the thermometer 40° above 0. The rain continued till the next day, *8th*, at ten o'clock, when it cleared off, and the weather became fine, the wind high from the southwest. The rivers at the point have now fallen six inches since our arrival, and this morning the water of the south fork became of a reddish brown colour, while the north branch continued of its usual whitish appearance. The mountains to the south are covered with snow.

Sunday, June 9th, 1805

We now consulted upon the course to be pursued. On comparing our observations we were more than ever convinced of what we already suspected, that Mr. Arrowsmith is incorrect in laying down in the chain of Rocky mountains one remarkable mountain called the Tooth, nearly as far south as 45°, and said to be so marked from the discoveries of a Mr. Fidler. We are now within one hundred miles of the Rocky mountains and in the latitude of 47° 24′ 12.8″, and therefore it is highly improbable that the Missouri should make such a bend to the south before it reaches the Rocky mountains, as to have suffered Mr. Fidler to come as low as 45° along the eastern borders without touching that river: yet the general course of Maria's river from this place for fifty-nine miles, as far as captain Lewis ascended, was north 69° west, and the south branch, or what we consider the Missouri, which captain Clark had examined as far as forty-five miles in a straight line, ran in a course south 29° west, and as far as it could be seen went considerably west of south, whence we conclude that the Missouri itself enters the Rocky mountains to the north of 45°.

In writing to the President from our winter quarters, we had already taken the liberty of advancing the southern extremity of Mr. Fidler's discoveries about a degree to the northward, and this from Indian information as to the bearing of the point at which the Missouri enters the mountain; but we think actual observation will place it one degree still further to the northward. This information of Mr. Fidler however, incorrect as it is, affords an additional reason for not pursuing Maria's river; for if he came as low even as 47° and saw only small streams coming down from the mountains, it is to be presumed that these rivulets do not penetrate the Rocky mountains so far as to approach any navigable branch of the Columbia, and they are most probably the remote waters of some northern branch of the Missouri. In short, being already in latitude 47° 24′ we cannot reasonably hope by going farther to the northward to find between this place and the Saskashawan any stream which can, as the Indians assure us the Missouri does, possess a navigable current for some distance in the Rocky mountains: the Indians had assured us also that the water of the Missouri was nearly transparent at the falls; this is the case with the southern branch; that the falls lay a little to the south of sunset from them; this too is in favour of the southern fork, for it bears considerably south of this place, which is only a few minutes to the northward of fort Mandan; that the falls are below the Rocky mountains and near the northern termination of one range of those mountains: now there is a ridge of mountains which appear behind the South mountains and terminates to the southwest of us, at a sufficient distance from the unbroken chain of the Rocky mountains to allow space for several falls, indeed we fear for too many of them. If too the Indians had ever passed any stream as large as this southern fork on their way up the Missouri, they would have mentioned it; so that their silence seems to prove that this branch must be the Missouri. The body of water also which it discharges must have been acquired from a considerable distance in the mountains, for it could not have been collected in the parched plains between the Yellowstone and the Rocky mountains, since that country could not supply nourishment for the dry channels which we passed on the south, and the travels of Mr. Fidler forbid us to believe that it could have been obtained from the mountains towards the northwest.

These observations, which satisfied our minds completely, we communicated to the party: but every one of them were of a contrary opinion; and much of their belief depended on Crusatte, an experienced waterman on the Missouri, who gave it as his decided judgment that the north fork was the genuine Missouri. The men therefore mentioned that although they would most cheerfully follow us wherever we should direct, yet they were afraid that the south fork would soon terminate in the Rocky mountains and leave us at a great distance from the Columbia. In order that nothing might be omitted which could prevent our falling into an error, it was agreed that one of us should ascend the southern branch by land until we reached either the falls or the mountains. In the meantime in order to lighten our burdens as much as possible, we determined to deposit here one of the periogues and all the heavy baggage which we could possibly spare, as well as some provision, salt, powder, and tools: this would at once lighten the other boats, and give them the crew which had been employed on board the periogue.

JUNE 10TH *Monday.* The weather being fair and pleasant we dried all our baggage and merchandise and made our deposit. These holes, or caches as they are called by the Missouri traders, are very common, particularly among those who deal with the Sioux, as the skins and merchandise will keep perfectly sound for years, and are protected from robbery: our cache is built in this manner: In the high plain on the north side of the Missouri and forty yards from a steep bluff, we chose a dry situation, and then describing a small circle of about twenty inches diameter, removed the sod as gently and carefully as possible: the hole is then sunk perpendicularly for a foot deep, or more if the ground be not firm. It is now worked gradually wider as they descend, till at length it becomes six or seven feet deep, shaped nearly like a kettle or the lower part of a large still, with the bottom somewhat sunk at the centre. As the earth is dug it is handed up in a vessel and carefully laid on a skin or cloth, in which it is carried away and usually thrown into the river or concealed so as to leave no trace of it. A floor of three or four inches in thickness is then made of dry sticks, on which is thrown hay or a hide perfectly dry. The goods being well aired and dried are laid on this floor, and prevented from touching the wall by other dried sticks in proportion as the merchandise is stowed away: when the hole is nearly full, a skin is laid over the goods, and on this earth is thrown and beaten down until with the addition of the sod first removed the whole is on a level with the ground, and there remains not the slightest appearance of an excavation. In addition to this we made another of smaller dimensions, in which we placed all the baggage, some powder, and our blacksmith's tools, having previously repaired such of the tools we carry with us as require mending. To guard against accident, we hid two parcels of lead and powder in the two distinct places.

The red periogue was drawn up on the middle of a small island at the entrance of Maria's river, and secured by being fastened to the trees from the effect of any floods. In the evening there was a high wind from the southwest accompanied with thunder and rain. We now made another observation of the meridian altitude of the sun, and found that the mean latitude of the entrance of Maria's river, as deduced from three observations, is 47° 25′ 17.2″ north. We saw a small bird like the blue thrush or catbird which we had not before met, and also observed that the bee-martin or kingbird is common to this country although there are no bees here, and in fact we have not met with the honey-bee since leaving the Osage river.

Tuesday. This morning captain Lewis with four men set out on their expedition up the south branch. They soon reached the point where the Tansy river approaches the Missouri, and observing a large herd of elk before them, descended and killed several, which they hung up along the river so that the party in the boats might see them as they came along. They then halted for dinner; but captain Lewis who had been for some days afflicted with the dysentery, was now attacked with violent pains attended by a high fever and was unable to go on. He therefore encamped for the night under some willow boughs: having brought no medicine he determined to try an experiment with the small twigs of the chokecherry, which being stripped of their leaves and cut into pieces about two inches long were boiled in pure water, till they produced a strong black decoction of an astringent bitter taste; a pint of this he took at sunset, and repeated the dose an hour afterwards. By ten o'clock he was perfectly relieved from pain, a gentle perspiration ensued, his fever abated, and in the morning he was quite recovered.

JUNE 11TH

One of the men caught several dozen fish of two species: the first is about nine inches long, of a white colour, round in shape; the mouth is beset both above and below with a rim of fine sharp teeth, the eye moderately large, the pupil dark, and the iris narrow, and of a yellowish brown colour: in form and size it resembles the white chub of the Potomac, though its head is proportionably smaller; they readily bite at meat or grasshoppers; but the flesh though soft and of a fine white colour is not highly flavoured. The second species is precisely of the form and about the size of the fish known by the name of the hickory shad or old wife, though it differs from it in having the outer edge of both the upper and lower jaw set with a rim of teeth, and the tongue and palate also are defended by long sharp teeth bending inwards, the eye is very large, the iris wide and of a silvery colour; they do not inhabit muddy water, and the flavour is much superior to that of the former species. Of the first kind we had seen a few before we reached Maria's river; but had found none of the last before we caught them in the Missouri above its junction with that river. The white cat continues as high as Maria's river, but they are scarce in this part of the river, nor have we caught any of them since leaving the Mandans which weighed more than six pounds.

Of other game they saw a great abundance even in their short march of nine miles.

JUNE 12TH *Wednesday.* This morning captain Lewis left the bank of the river in order to avoid the steep ravines which generally run from the shore to the distance of one or two miles in the plain: having reached the opened country he went for twelve miles in a course a little to the west of southwest, when the sun becoming warm by nine o'clock, he returned to the river in quest of water and to kill something for breakfast, there being no water in the plain, and the buffalo discovering them before they came within gunshot took to flight. They reached the banks in a handsome open low ground with cottonwood, after three miles walk. Here they saw two large brown bears, and killed them both at the first fire, a circumstance which has never before occurred since we have seen that animal. Having made a meal of a part and hung the remainder on a tree with a note for captain Clark, they again ascended the bluffs into the open plains. Here they saw great numbers of the burrowing squirrel, also some wolves, antelopes, mule-deer, and vast herds of buffalo. They soon crossed a ridge considerably higher than the surrounding plains, and from its top had a beautiful view of the Rocky mountains, which are now completely covered with snow: their general course is from southeast to the north of northwest, and they seem to consist of several ranges which successively rise above each other till the most distant mingles with the clouds. After travelling twelve miles they again met the river, where there was a handsome plain of cottonwood; and although it was not sunset, and they had only come twenty-seven miles, yet captain Lewis felt weak from his late disorder, and therefore determined to go no further that night.

In the course of the day they killed a quantity of game, and saw some signs of otter as well as beaver, and many tracks of the brown bear: they also caught great quantities of the white fish mentioned yesterday. With the broad-leafed cottonwood, which has formed the principal timber of the Missouri, is here mixed another species differing from the first only in the narrowness of its leaf and the greater thickness of its bark. The leaf is long, oval, acutely pointed, about two and a half or three inches long and from three quarters of an inch to an inch in width; it is smooth and thick, sometimes slightly grooved or channeled, with the margin a little serrate, the upper disk of a common, the lower of a whitish green. This species seems to be preferred by the beaver to the broadleaved, probably because the former affords a deeper and softer bark.

Thursday. They left their encampment at sunrise, and ascending the river hills went for six miles in a course generally southwest, over a country which though more waving than that of yesterday may still be considered level. At the extremity of this course they overlooked a most beautiful plain, where were infinitely more buffalo than we had ever before seen at a single view. To the southwest arose from the plain two mountains of a singular appearance and more like ramparts of high fortifications than works of nature. They are square figures with sides rising perpendicularly to the height of two hundred and fifty feet, formed of yellow clay, and the tops seemed to be level plains. Finding that the river here bore considerably to the south, and fearful of passing the falls before reaching the Rocky mountains, they now changed their course to the south, and leaving those insulated hills to the right proceeded across the plain.

JUNE 13TH

In this direction captain Lewis had gone about two miles when his ears were saluted with the agreeable sound of a fall of water, and as he advanced a spray which seemed driven by the high southwest wind arose above the plain like a column of smoke and vanished in an instant. Towards this point he directed his steps, and the noise increasing as he approached soon became too tremendous to be mistaken for any thing but the great falls of the Missouri. Having travelled seven miles after first hearing the sound he reached the falls about twelve o'clock; the hills as he approached were difficult of access and two hundred feet high: down these he hurried with impatience and seating himself on some rocks under the centre of the falls, enjoyed the sublime spectacle of this stupendous object which since the creation had been lavishing its magnificence upon the desert unknown to civilization.

The river immediately at its cascade is three hundred yards wide, and is pressed in by a perpendicular cliff on the left, which rises to about one hundred feet and extends up the stream for a mile; on the right the bluff is also perpendicular for three hundred yards above the falls. For ninety or a hundred yards from the left cliff, the water falls in one smooth even sheet, over a precipice of at least eighty feet. The remaining part of the river precipitates itself with a more rapid current, but being received as it falls by the irregular and somewhat projecting rocks below, forms a splendid prospect of perfectly white foam two hundred yards in length, and eighty in perpendicular elevation. This spray is dissipated into a thousand shapes, sometimes flying up in columns of fifteen or twenty feet, which are then oppressed by larger masses of the white foam, on all which the sun impresses the brightest colours of the rainbow. As it rises from the fall it beats with fury against a ledge of rocks which extend across the river at one hundred and fifty yards from the precipice. From the perpendicular cliff on the north, to the distance of one hundred and twenty yards, the rocks rise only a few feet above the water, and when the river is high the stream finds a channel across them forty yards wide, and near the higher parts of the ledge which then rise about twenty feet, and terminate abruptly within eighty or ninety yards of the southern side. Between them and the perpendicular cliff on the south, the whole body of water runs with great swiftness. A few small cedars grow near this ridge of rocks which serves as a barrier to defend a small plain of about three acres shaded with cottonwood, at the lower extremity of which is a grove of the same tree, where are several Indian cabins of sticks;

below the point of them the river is divided by a large rock, several feet above the surface of the water, and extending down the stream for twenty yards. At the distance of three hundred yards from the same ridge is a second abutment of solid perpendicular rock about sixty feet high, projecting at right angles from the small plain on the north for one hundred and thirty-four yards into the river. After leaving this, the Missouri again spreads itself to its usual distance of three hundred yards, though with more than its ordinary rapidity.

The hunters who had been sent out now returned loaded with buffalo meat, and captain Lewis encamped for the night under a tree near the falls. The men were again despatched to hunt for food against the arrival of the party, and captain Lewis walked down the river to discover if possible some place where the canoes might be safely drawn on shore, in order to be transported beyond the falls. He returned however without discovering any such spot, the river for three miles below being one continued succession of rapids and cascades, overhung with perpendicular bluffs from one hundred and fifty to two hundred feet high; in short, it seems to have worn itself a channel through the solid rock. In the afternoon they caught in the falls some of both kinds of the white fish, and half a dozen trout from sixteen to twenty-three inches long, precisely resembling in form and the position of its fins the mountain or speckled trout of the United States, except that the specks of the former are of a deep black, while those of the latter are of a red or gold colour: they have long sharp teeth on the palate and tongue, and generally a small speck of red on each side behind the front ventral fins; the flesh is of a pale yellowish red, or when in good order of a rose-coloured red.

JUNE 14TH *Friday.* This morning one of the men was sent to captain Clark with an account of the discovery of the falls, and after employing the rest in preserving the meat which had been killed yesterday, captain Lewis proceeded to examine the rapids above. From the falls he directed his course southwest up the river: after passing one continued rapid, and three small cascades, each three or four feet high, he reached at the distance of five miles a second fall. The river is about four hundred yards wide, and for the distance of three hundred throws itself over to the depth of nineteen feet, and so irregularly that he gave it the name of the Crooked falls. From the southern shore it extends obliquely upwards about one hundred and fifty yards, and then forms an acute angle downwards nearly to the commencement of four small islands close to the northern side. From the perpendicular pitch to these islands, a distance of more than one hundred yards, the water glides down a sloping rock with a velocity almost equal to that of its fall.

Above this fall the river bends suddenly to the northward: while viewing this place captain Lewis heard a loud roar above him, and crossing the point of a hill for a few hundred yards, he saw one of the most beautiful objects in nature: the whole Missouri is suddenly stopped by one shelving rock, which without a single niche and with an edge as straight and regular as if formed by art, stretches itself from one side of the river to the other for at least a quarter of a mile. Over this it precipitates itself in an even uninterrupted sheet to the perpendicular depth of fifty feet, whence dashing against the rocky bottom it rushes rapidly down, leaving behind it a spray of the purest foam across the river. The scene which it presented was indeed singularly beautiful, since without any of the wild irregular sublimity of the lower falls, it combined all the regular elegances which the fancy of a painter would select to form a beautiful waterfall. The eye had scarcely been regaled with this charming prospect, when at the distance of half a mile captain Lewis observed another of a similar kind: to this he immediately hastened, and found a cascade stretching across the whole river for a quarter of a mile with a descent of fourteen feet, though the perpendicular pitch was only six feet. This too in any other neighbourhood would have been an object of great magnificence, but after what he had just seen it became of secondary interest: his curiosity being however awakened, he determined to go on even should night overtake him to the head of the falls.

He therefore pursued the southwest course of the river, which was one constant succession of rapids and small cascades, at every one of which the bluffs grew lower, or the bed of the river became more on a level with the plains. At the distance of two and a half miles he arrived at another cataract of twenty-six feet. The river is here six hundred yards wide, but the descent is not immediately perpendicular, though the river falls generally with a regular and smooth sheet; for about one third of the descent a rock protrudes to a small distance, receives the water in its passage and gives it a curve. On the south side is a beautiful plain a few feet above the level of the falls; on the north the country is more broken, and there is a hill not far from the river. Just below the falls is a little island in the middle of the river well covered with timber. Here on a cottonwood tree an eagle had fixed its nest, and seemed the undisputed mistress of a spot, to contest whose dominion neither man nor beast would venture across the gulfs that surround it, and which is further secured by the mist rising from the falls. This solitary bird could not escape the observation of the Indians who made the eagle's nest a part of their description of the falls, which now proves to be correct in almost every particular, except that they did not do justice to their height. Just above this is a cascade of about five feet, beyond which, as far as could be discerned, the velocity of the water seemed to abate.

Captain Lewis now ascended the hill which was behind him, and saw from its top a delightful plain extending from the river to the base of the Snow [Rocky] mountains to the south and southwest. Along this wide level country the Missouri pursued its winding course, filled with water to its even and grassy banks, while about four miles above it was joined by a large river flowing from the northwest through a valley three miles in width, and distinguished by the timber which adorned its shores; the Missouri itself stretches to the south in one unruffled stream of water as if unconscious of the roughness it must soon encounter, and bearing on its bosom vast flocks of geese, while numerous herds of buffalo are feeding on the plains which surround it.

Captain Lewis then descended the hill, and directed his course towards the river falling in from the west. He soon met a herd of at least a thousand buffalo, and being desirous of providing for supper shot one of them; the animal immediately began to bleed, and captain Lewis who had forgotten to reload his rifle, was intently watching to see him fall, when he beheld a large brown bear who was stealing on him unperceived, and was already within twenty steps. In the first moment of surprise he lifted his rifle, but remembering instantly that it was not charged, and that he had not time to reload, he felt that there was no safety but in flight. It was in the open level plain, not a bush nor a tree within three hundred yards, the bank of the river sloping and not more than three feet high, so that there was no possible mode of concealment; captain Lewis therefore thought of retreating in a quick walk as fast as the bear advanced towards the nearest tree; but as soon as he turned the bear ran open mouth and at full speed upon him. Captain Lewis ran about eighty yards, but finding that the animal gained on him fast, it flashed on his mind that by getting into the water to such a depth that the bear would be obliged to attack him swimming, there was still some chance of his life; he therefore turned short, plunged into the river about waist deep, and facing about presented the point of his spontoon. The bear arrived at the water's edge within twenty feet of him, but as soon as he put himself in this position of defence, he seemed frightened, and wheeling about, retreated with as much precipitation as he had pursued. Very glad to be released from this danger, captain Lewis returned to the shore, and observed him run with great speed, sometimes looking back as if he expected to be pursued, till he reached the woods. He could not conceive the cause of the sudden alarm of the bear, but congratulated himself on his escape when he saw his own track torn to pieces by the furious animal, and learnt from the whole adventure never to suffer his rifle to be a moment unloaded.

He now resumed his progress in the direction which the bear had taken towards the western river, and found it a handsome stream about two hundred yards wide, apparently deep, with a gentle current; its waters clear, and its banks, which were formed principally of dark brown and blue clay, are about the same height as those of the Missouri, that is from three to five feet. What was singular was that the river does not seem to overflow its banks at any season, while it might be presumed from its vicinity to the mountains, that the torrents arising from the melting of the snows would sometimes cause it to swell beyond its limits. The contrary fact would induce a belief that the Rocky mountains yield their snows very reluctantly and equably to the sun, and are not often drenched by very heavy rains. This river is no doubt that which the Indians call Medicine river, which they mentioned as emptying into the Missouri, just above the falls.

After examining Medicine river, captain Lewis set out at half after six o'clock in the evening on his return towards the camp, which he estimated at the distance of twelve miles. In going through the low grounds on Medicine river he met an animal which at a distance he thought was a wolf, but on coming within sixty paces, it proved to be some brownish yellow animal standing near its burrow, which, when he came nigh, crouched and seemed as if about to spring on him. Captain Lewis fired and the beast disappeared in its burrow. From the track and the general appearance of the animal he supposed it to be of the tiger kind. He then went on, but as if the beasts of the forests had conspired against him, three buffalo bulls which were feeding with a large herd at the distance of half a mile, left their companions and ran at full speed towards him. He turned round, and unwilling to give up the field advanced towards them: when they came within a hundred yards, they stopped, looked at him for some time, and then retreated as they came. He now pursued his route in the dark, reflecting on the strange adventures and sights of the day, which crowded on his mind so rapidly that he should have been inclined to believe it all enchantment if the thorns of the prickly pear piercing his feet did not dispel at every moment the illusion. He at last reached the party, who had been very anxious for his safety, and who had already decided on the route which each should take in the morning to look for him. Being much fatigued he supped and slept well during the night.

Saturday. The men were again sent out to bring in the game killed yesterday and to procure more: they also obtained a number of fine trout and several small catfish weighing about four pounds, and differing from the white catfish lower down the Missouri. On awaking this morning captain Lewis found a large rattlesnake coiled on the trunk of a tree under which he had been sleeping. He killed it, and found it like those we had seen before, differing from those of the Atlantic states, not in its colours but in the form and arrangement of them; it had one hundred and seventy-six scuta on the abdomen, and seventeen half-formed scuta on the tail. There is a heavy dew on the grass about the camp every morning, which no doubt proceeds from the mist of the falls, as it takes place nowhere in the plains nor on the river except here. The messenger sent to captain Clark returned with information of his having arrived five miles below at a rapid, which he did not think it prudent to ascend and would wait till captain Lewis and his party rejoined him.

JUNE 15TH

On *Tuesday, 11th*, the day when captain Lewis left us, we remained at the entrance of Maria's river and completed the deposits of all the articles with which we could dispense. The morning had been fair with a high wind from the southwest, which shifted in the evening to northwest, when the weather became cold and the wind high. The next morning, *Wednesday, 12th*, we left our encampment with a fair day and a southwest wind.

WITH CAPTAIN CLARK'S PARTY

The river was now so crowded with islands that within the distance of ten miles and a half we passed eleven of different dimensions before reaching a high black bluff in a bend on the left, where we saw a great number of swallows. Within one mile and a half further we passed four small islands, two on each side, and at fifteen miles from our encampment reached a spring which the men called Grog spring: it is on the northern shore, and at the point where Tansy river approaches within one hundred yards of the Missouri. From this place we proceeded three miles to a low bluff on the north opposite to an island, and spent the night in an old Indian encampment. The bluffs under which we passed were composed of a blackish clay and coal for about eighty feet, above which for thirty or forty feet is a brownish yellow earth. The river is very rapid and obstructed by bars of gravel and stone of different shapes and sizes, so that three of our canoes were in great danger in the course of the day. We had a few drops of rain about two o'clock in the afternoon. The only animals we killed were elk and deer; but we saw great numbers of rattlesnakes.

Thursday, 13th. The morning was fair and there was some dew on the ground. After passing two islands we reached at the distance of a mile and a half a small rapid stream fifty yards wide, emptying itself on the south, rising in a mountain to the southeast about twelve or fifteen miles distant, and at this time covered with snow. As it is the channel for the melted snow of that mountain we called it Snow river: opposite to its entrance is another

THE FALLS AND PORTAGE.

Left, map based on one made by Captain Clark after the explorer discovered the Great Falls of the Missouri, in what is now central Montana; his measurements have been proved to be accurate. Note the eighteen-mile line of portage. Above, Captain Clark's sketch-map and detailed observations.

island: at one mile and three quarters is a black bluff of slate on the south, nine miles beyond which, after passing ten islands, we came to on the southern shore near an old Indian fortified camp, opposite the lower point of an island, having made thirteen miles. The number of islands and shoals, the rapidity of the river, and the quantity of large stones, rendered the navigation very disagreeable: along the banks we distinguished several low bluffs or cliffs of slate. There were great numbers of geese and goslings; the geese not being able to fly at this season. Gooseberries are ripe and in great abundance; the yellow currant is also common, but not yet ripe. Our game consisted of buffalo and goats.

A contemporary conception of the Great Falls in Montana.

Friday, 14th. Again the day is fine. We made two miles to a small island in the southern bend, after passing several bad rapids. The current becomes indeed swifter as we ascend, and the canoes frequently receive water as we drag them with difficulty along. At the distance of six miles we reached captain Clark's camp on the fourth, which is on the north side and opposite to a large gravelly bar. Here the man sent by captain Lewis joined us with the pleasing intelligence that he had discovered the falls, and was convinced that the course we were pursuing was that of the true Missouri. At a mile and a half we reached the upper point of an island, three-quarters of a mile beyond which we encamped on the south, after making only ten and a quarter miles. Along the river was but little timber, but much hard slate in the bluffs.

Saturday, 15th. The morning being warm and fair we set out at the usual hour, but proceeded with great difficulty in consequence of the increased rapidity of the current. The channel is constantly obstructed by rocks and dangerous rapids. During the whole progress the men are in the water hauling the canoes, and walking on sharp rocks and round stones which cut their feet or cause them to fall. The rattlesnakes too are so numerous that the men are constantly on their guard against being bitten by them; yet they bear the fatigues with the most undiminished cheerfulness. We hear the roar of the falls very distinctly this morning. At three and three quarter miles we came to a rock in a bend to the south, resembling a tower. At six and three quarter miles we reached a large creek on the south, which after one of our men we called Shields's creek. It is rapid in its course, about thirty yards wide, and on sending a person five miles up it proved to have a fall of fifteen feet, and some timber on its low ground. Above this river the bluffs of the Missouri are of red earth mixed with stratas of black stone; below it we passed some white clay in the banks which mixes with water in every respect like flour. At three and three quarter miles we reached a point on the north opposite an island and a bluff; and one mile and a quarter further, after passing some red bluffs, came to on the north side, having made twelve miles. Here we found a rapid so difficult that we did not think proper to attempt the passage this evening, and therefore sent to captain Lewis to apprise him of our arrival. We saw a number of geese, ducks, crows, and blackbirds to-day, the two former with their young. The river rose a little this evening, but the timber is still so scarce that we could not procure enough for our use during the night.

Sunday. Some rain fell last night, and this morning the weather was cloudy and the wind high from the southwest. We passed the rapid by doubly manning the periogue and canoes, and halted at the distance of a mile and a quarter to examine the rapids above, which we found to be a continued succession of cascades as far as the view extended, which was about two miles. About a mile above where we halted was a large creek falling in on the south, opposite to which is a large sulphur spring falling over the rocks on the north: captain Lewis arrived at two from the falls about five miles above us, and after consulting upon the subject of the portage, we crossed the river and formed a camp on the north, having come three quarters of a mile today. JUNE 16TH

From our own observation we had deemed the south side to be the most favourable for a portage, but two men sent out for the purpose of examining it, reported that the creek and the ravines intersected the plain so deeply that it was impossible to cross it. Captain Clark therefore resolved to examine more minutely what was the best route: the four canoes were unloaded at the camp and then sent across the river, where by means of strong cords they were hauled over the first rapid, whence they may be easily drawn into the creek. Finding too, that the portage would be at all events too long to enable us to carry the boats on our shoulders, six men were set to work to make wheels for carriages to transport them. Since leaving Maria's river the wife of Chaboneau, our interpreter, has been dangerously ill, but she now found great relief from the mineral water of the sulphur spring. It is situated about two hundred yards from the Missouri, into which it empties over a precipice of rock about twenty-five feet high. The water is perfectly transparent, strongly impregnated with sulphur, and we suspect iron also, as the colour of the hills and bluffs in the neighbourhood indicates the presence of that metal. In short the water to all appearance is precisely similar to that of Bowyer's sulphur spring in Virginia.

Monday. Captain Clark set out with five men to explore the country; the rest were employed in hunting, making wheels and in drawing the five canoes JUNE 17TH and all the baggage up the creek, which we now called Portage creek: from this creek there is a gradual ascent to the top of the high plain, while the bluffs of the creek lower down and of the Missouri, both above and below its entrance, were so steep as to have rendered it almost impracticable to drag them up from the Missouri. We found great difficulty and some danger in even ascending the creek thus far, in consequence of the rapids and rocks of the channel of the creek, which just above where we brought the canoes has a fall of five feet, and high and steep bluffs beyond it: we were very fortunate in finding just below Portage creek a cottonwood tree about twenty-two inches in diameter, and large enough to make the carriage wheels: it was perhaps the only one of the same size within twenty miles; and the cottonwood, which we are obliged to employ in the other parts of the work, is extremely soft and brittle. The mast of the white periogue which we mean to leave behind, supplied us with two axletrees.

There are vast quantities of buffalo feeding on the plains or watering in the river, which is also strewed with the floating carcases and limbs of these animals. They go in large herds to water about the falls, and as all the passages to the river near that place are narrow and steep, the foremost are pressed into the river by the impatience of those behind. In this way we have seen ten or a dozen disappear over the falls in a few minutes. They afford excellent food for the wolves, bears, and birds of prey; and this circumstance may account for the reluctance of the bears to yield their dominion over the neighbourhood.

JUNE 18TH *Tuesday.* The periogue was drawn up a little below our camp and secured in a thick copse of willow bushes. We now began to form a cache or place of deposit and to dry our goods and other articles which required inspection. The wagons too are completed. Our hunters brought us ten deer, and we shot two out of a herd of buffalo that came to water at the sulphur spring. There is a species of gooseberry growing abundantly among the rocks on the sides of the cliffs: it is now ripe, of a pale red colour, about the size of the common gooseberry, and like it is an ovate pericarp of soft pulp enveloping a number of small whitish coloured seeds, and consisting of a yellowish slimy mucilaginous substance, with a sweet taste; the surface of the berry is covered with a glutinous adhesive matter, and its fruit though ripe retains its withered corolla. The shrub itself seldom rises more than two feet high, is much branched, and has no thorns. The leaves resemble those of the comman gooseberry except in being smaller, and the berry is supported by separate peduncles or footstalks half an inch long. There are also immense quantities of grasshoppers of a brown colour in the plains, and they no doubt contribute to the lowness of the grass, which is not generally more than three inches high, though it is soft, narrow-leafed and affords a fine pasture for the buffalo.

JUNE 19TH *Wednesday.* The wind blew violently to-day, as it did yesterday, and as it does frequently in this open country, where there is not a tree to break or oppose its force. Some men were sent for the meat killed yesterday which fortunately had not been discovered by the wolves. Another party went to Medicine river in quest of elk, which we hope may be induced to resort there, from there being more wood in that neighbourhood than on the Missouri.

All the rest were occupied in packing the baggage and mending their moccasins, in order to prepare for the portage. We caught a number of the whitefish, but no catfish or trout. Our poor Indian woman, who had recovered so far as to walk out, imprudently ate a quantity of the white apple, which with some dried fish occasioned a return of her fever.

The meridian altitude of the sun's lower limb, as observed with octant by back observation, was 53° 12′, giving as the latitude of our camp, 47° 8′ 59.5″.

JUNE 20TH

Thursday. As we were desirous of getting meat enough to last us during the portage, so that the men might not be diverted from their labour to look for food, we sent out four hunters to-day: they killed eleven buffalo. This was indeed an easy labour, for there are vast herds coming constantly to the opposite bank of the river to water; they seem also to make much use of the mineral water of the sulphur spring, but whether from choice, or because it is more convenient than the river, we cannot determine, as they sometimes pass near the spring and go on to the river. Besides this spring, brackish water or that of a dark colour impregnated with mineral salts, such as we have frequently met on the Missouri, may be found in small quantities in some of the steep ravines on the north side of the river opposite to us and at the falls.

CAPTAIN CLARK'S TOUR

Captain Clark returned this evening, having examined the whole course of the river and fixed the route most practicable for the portage. The first day, *17th*, he was occupied in measuring the heights and distances along the banks of the river, and slept near a ravine at the foot of the Crooked falls, having very narrowly escaped falling into the river, where he would have perished inevitably, in descending the cliffs near the grand cataract. The next day, *18th*, he continued the same occupation, and arrived in the afternoon at the junction of Medicine and Missouri rivers; up the latter he ascended, and passed at the distance of a mile an island and a little timber in an eastwardly bend of the river. One mile beyond this he came to the lower point of a large island; another small island in the middle of the river, and one near the left shore at the distance of three miles, opposite to the head of which he encamped near the mouth of a creek which appeared to rise in the South mountain. These three islands are opposite to each other, and we gave them the name of the Whitebear islands from observing some of those animals on them. He killed a beaver, an elk and eight buffalo. One of the men who was sent a short distance from the camp to bring home some meat, was attacked by a white bear, and closely pursued within forty paces of the camp, and narrowly escaped being caught. Captain Clark immediately went with three men in quest of the bear, which he was afraid might surprise another of the hunters who was out collecting the game. The bear was however too quick, for before captain Clark could reach the man, the bear had attacked him and compelled him to take refuge in the water. He now ran off as they approached, and it being late they deferred pursuing him till the next morning.

Chapter 11
PORTAGING AROUND THE GREAT FALLS

On the *19th*, captain Clark not being able to find the bear mentioned in the last chapter, spent the day in examining the country both above and below the Whitebear islands, and concluded that the place of his encampment would be the best point for the extremity of the portage. The men were therefore occupied in drying the meat to be left here. Immense numbers of buffalo are every where round, and they saw a summer duck which is now sitting. The next morning, *20th*, he crossed the level plain, fixed stakes to mark the route of the portage, till he passed a large ravine which would oblige us to make the portage farther from the river: after this there being no other obstacle he went to the river where he had first struck it, and took its courses and distances down to the camp. From the draught and survey of captain Clark, we had now a clear and connected view of the falls, cascades, and rapids of the Missouri.

    This river is three hundred yards wide at the point where it receives the waters of Medicine river, which is one hundred and thirty-seven yards in width. The united current continues three hundred and twenty-eight poles to a small rapid on the north side, from which it gradually widens to one thousand four hundred yards, and at the distance of five hundred and forty-eight poles reaches the head of the rapids, narrowing as it approaches them. Here the hills on the north which had withdrawn from the bank closely border the river, which, for the space of three hundred and twenty poles, makes its way over the rocks with a descent of thirty feet: in this course the current is contracted to five hundred and eighty yards, and after throwing itself over a small pitch of five feet, forms a beautiful cascade of twenty-six feet five inches; this does not however fall immediately perpendicular, being stopped by a part of the rock which projects at about one third of the distance. After descending this fall, and passing the cottonwood island on which the eagle has fixed its nest, the river goes on for five hundred and thirty-two poles over rapids and little falls, the estimated descent of which is thirteen feet six inches till it is joined by a large fountain boiling up underneath the rocks near the edge of the river, into which it falls with a cascade of eight feet. It is of the most perfect clearness and rather of a bluish cast: and even after falling into the Missouri it preserves its colour for half a mile. From this fountain the river descends with increased rapidity for the distance of two hundred and fourteen poles, during which the estimated descent is five feet: from this for a distance of one hundred and thirty-five poles, the river descends fourteen feet seven inches including a perpendicular fall of six feet seven inches. The river has now become pressed into a space of four hundred and seventy-three yards, and here forms a grand cataract by falling over a plain rock the whole distance across the river to the depth of forty-seven feet eight inches. After recovering itself the Missouri then proceeds with an estimated descent of three feet, till at the distance of one hundred and two poles it again is precipitated down the Crooked falls of nineteen feet perpendicular; below this at the mouth of a deep ravine is a fall of five feet, after which for the distance of nine hundred and seventy poles the descent is much more gradual, not being more than ten feet, and then succeeds a handsome level plain for the space of one hundred and seventy-eight poles with a computed descent of three feet, making a bend towards the north. Thence it descends during four hundred and eighty poles, about eighteen feet and a half, when it makes a perpendicular fall of two feet, which is ninety poles beyond the great cataract, in approaching which it descends thirteen feet within two hundred yards, and gathering strength from its confined channel, which is only two hundred and eighty yards wide, rushes over the fall to the depth of eighty-seven feet and three quarters of an inch. After raging among the rocks and losing itself in foam, it is compressed immediately into a bed of ninety-three yards in width: it continues for three hundred and forty poles to the entrance of a run or deep ravine where there is a fall of three feet, which, joined to the decline of the river during that course, makes the descent six feet. As it goes on the descent within the next two hundred and forty poles is only four feet: from this passing a run or deep ravine the descent for four hundred poles is thirteen feet; within two hundred and forty poles a second descent of eighteen feet; thence one hundred and sixty poles a descent of six feet; after which to the mouth of Portage creek, a distance of two hundred and eighty poles, the descent is ten feet. From this survey and estimate it results that the river experiences a descent of three hundred and fifty-two feet in the course of two and three quarter miles, from the commencement of the rapids to the mouth of Portage creek, exclusive of the almost impassable rapids which extend for a mile below its entrance.

The latitude of our camp below the entrance of Portage creek was found to be 47° 7′ 10.3″, as deduced from a meridian altitude of the sun's lower limb taken with octant by back observation giving 53° 10′.

Friday, June 21st, 1805

Having made the necessary preparations for continuing our route, a part of the baggage was carried across the creek into the high plain, three miles in advance and placed on one of the carriages with truck wheels: the rest of the party was employed in drying meat and dressing elk skins. We killed several mule-deer and an elk, and observed as usual vast quantities of buffalo who came to drink at the river. For the first time on the Missouri we have seen near the falls a species of fishing duck, the body of which is brown and white, the wings white, and the head and upper part of the neck of a brick red, with a narrow beak, which seems to be of the same kind common in the Susquehanna, Potomac and James river. The little wood which this neighbourhood affords consists of the broad and narrow-leafed cottonwood, the box-alder, the narrow and broad-leafed willow, the large or sweet willow, which was not common below Maria's river, but which here attains the same size and has the same appearance as in the Atlantic states. The undergrowth consists of roses, gooseberries, currants, small honeysuckles, and the redwood, the inner part of which the *engagés* or watermen are fond of smoking when mixed with tobacco.

Saturday. We now set out to pass the portage and halted for dinner at eight miles distance near a little stream. The axletrees of our carriage, which had been made of an old mast, and the cottonwood tongues broke before we came there: but we renewed them with the timber of the sweet willow, which lasted till within half a mile of our intended camp, when the tongues gave way and we were obliged to take as much baggage as we could carry on our backs down to the river, where we formed an encampment in a small grove of timber opposite to the Whitebear islands.

Here the banks on both sides of the river are handsome, level, and extensive; that near our camp is not more than two feet above the surface of the water. The river is about eight hundred yards wide just above these islands, ten feet deep in most places, and with a very gentle current. The plains however on this part of the river are not so fertile as those from the mouth of the Muscleshell and thence downwards; there is much more stone on the sides of the hills and on the broken lands than is to be found lower down. We saw in the plains vast quantities of buffalo, a number of small birds, and the large brown curlew, which is now sitting, and lays its eggs, which are of a pale blue with black specks, on the ground without any nest. There is also a species of lark much resembling the bird called the oldfield lark, with a yellow breast and a black spot on the croup; though it differs from the latter in having its tail formed of feathers of an unequal length and pointed; the beak too is somewhat longer and more curved, and the note differs considerably. The prickly pear annoyed us very much to-day by sticking through our moccasins. As soon as we had kindled our fires we examined the meat which captain Clark had left here, but found that the greater part of it had been taken by the wolves.

JUNE 23D *Sunday.* After we had brought up the canoe and baggage captain Clark went down to the camp at Portage creek, where four of the men had been left with the Indian woman. Captain Lewis during the morning prepared the camp, and in the afternoon went down in a canoe to Medicine river to look after the three men who had been sent thither to hunt on the *19th*, and from whom nothing had as yet been heard. He went up the river about half a mile and then walked along on the right bank, hallooing as he went, till at the distance of five miles he found one of them who had fixed his camp on the opposite bank, where he had killed seven deer and dried about six hundred pounds of buffalo meat, but had killed no elk, the animal chiefly wanted. He knew nothing of his companions except that on the day of their departure from camp he had left them at the falls and come on to Medicine river, not having seen them since.

As it was too late to return captain Lewis passed over on a raft which he made for the purpose and spent the night at Shannon's camp, and the next morning, *Monday 24th*, sent J. Fields up the river with orders to go four miles and return, whether he found the two absent hunters or not; then descending the southwest side of Medicine river, he crossed the Missouri in the canoe, and sent Shannon back to his camp to join Fields and bring the meat which they had killed. This they did, and arrived in the evening at the camp on Whitebear islands. A part of the men from Portage creek also arrived with two canoes and baggage.

On going down yesterday captain Clark cut off several angles of the former route so as to shorten the Portage considerably, and marked it with stakes: he arrived there in time to have two of the canoes carried up in the high plain about a mile in advance. Here they all repaired their moccasins, and put on double soles to protect them from the prickly pear and from the sharp points of earth which have been formed by the trampling of the buffalo during the late rains: this of itself is sufficient to render the portage disagreeable to one who had no burden; but as the men are loaded as heavily as their strength will permit, the crossing is really painful: some are limping with the soreness of their feet, others are scarcely able to stand for more than a few minutes from the heat and fatigue: they are all obliged to halt and rest frequently, and at almost every stopping place they fall and many of them are asleep in an instant; yet no one complains and they go on with cheerfulness. At their camp Drewyer and Fields joined them, and while captain Lewis was looking for them at Medicine river, they returned to report the absence of Shannon about whom they had been very uneasy. They had killed several buffalo at the bend of the Missouri above the falls: and dried about eight hundred pounds of meat and got one hundred pounds of tallow: they had also killed some deer, but had seen no elk. After getting the party in motion with the canoes captain Clark returned to his camp at Portage creek.

We were now occupied in fitting up a boat of skins, the frame of which had been prepared for the purpose at Harper's ferry. It was made of iron, thirty-six feet long, four feet and a half in the beam, and twenty-six inches wide in the bottom. Two men had been sent this morning for timber to complete it, but they could find scarcely any even tolerably straight sticks four and a half feet long, and as the cottonwood is too soft and brittle we were obliged to use the willow and box-alder.

JUNE 25TH

Tuesday. The party returned to the lower camp. Two men were sent on the large island to look for timber. J. Fields was sent up the Missouri to hunt elk; but he returned about noon and informed us that a few miles above he saw two white bear near the river, and in attempting to fire at them came suddenly on a third, who being only a few steps off immediately attacked him; that in running to escape from the monster he leaped down a steep bank of the river, where falling on a bar of stone he cut his hand and knee and bent his gun; but fortunately for him the bank concealed him from his antagonist or he would have been most probably lost. The other two returned with a small quantity of bark and timber, which was all they could find on the island; but they had killed two elk: these were valuable, as we are desirous of procuring the skins of that animal in order to cover the boat, as they are more strong and durable than those of the buffalo, and do not shrink so much in drying. The party that went to the lower camp had one canoe and the baggage carried into the high plain to be ready in the morning, and then all who could make use of their feet had a dance on the green to the music of a violin.

We have been unsuccessful in our attempt to catch fish, nor does there seem to be any in this part of the river. We observe a number of water terrapins. There are great quantities of young blackbirds in these islands just beginning to fly. Among the vegetable productions we observe a species of wild rye which is now heading: it rises to the height of eighteen or twenty inches, the beard remarkably fine and soft; the culm is jointed, and in every respect except in height it resembles the wild rye. Great quantities of mint too, like the peppermint, are found here.

The winds are sometimes violent in these plains. The men inform us that as they were bringing one of the canoes along on truck-wheels, they hoisted the sail and the wind carried her along for some distance.

JUNE 26TH *Wednesday.* Two men were sent on the opposite side of the river for bark and timber, of which they procured some, but by no means enough for our purposes. The bark of the cottonwood is too soft, and our only dependence is on the sweet willow, which has a tough strong bark; the two hunters killed seven buffalo. A party arrived from below with two canoes and baggage, and the wind being from the southeast, they had made considerable progress with the sails. On their arrival one of the men who had been considerably heated and fatigued, swallowed a very hearty draught of water, and was immediately taken ill; captain Lewis bled him with a penknife, having no other instrument at hand, and succeeded in restoring him to health the next day. Captain Clark formed a second cache or deposit near the camp, and placed the swivel under the rocks near the river.

The antelopes are still scattered through the plains; the females with their young, which are generally two in number, and the males by themselves.

JUNE 27TH *Thursday.* The party were employed in preparing timber for the boat, except two who were sent to hunt. About one in the afternoon a cloud arose from the southwest and brought with it violent thunder, lightning, and hail: soon after it passed the hunters came in from about four miles above us. They had killed nine elk, and three bear. As they were hunting on the river they saw a low ground covered with thick brushwood, where from the tracks along shore they thought a bear had probably taken refuge: they therefore landed, without making a noise, and climbed a tree about twenty feet above the ground. Having fixed themselves securely, they raised a loud shout, and a bear instantly rushed towards them. These animals never climb, and therefore when he came to the tree and stopped to look at them, Drewyer shot him in the head; he proved to be the largest we have yet seen, his nose appeared to be like that of a common ox, his fore feet measured nine inches across, and the hind feet were seven inches wide, and eleven and three quarters long, exclusive of the talons. One of these animals came within thirty yards of the camp last night, and carried off some buffalo meat which we had placed on a pole.

In the evening after the storm the water on this side of the river became of a deep crimson colour, probably caused by some stream above washing down a kind of soft red stone, which we observe in the neighbouring bluffs and gullies. At the camp below, the men who left us in the morning were busy in preparing their load for to-morrow, which were impeded by the rain, hail, and the hard wind from the northwest.

JUNE 28TH *Friday.* The party all occupied in making the boat; they obtained a sufficient quantity of willow bark to line her, and over these were placed the elk skins, and when they failed we were obliged to use the buffalo hide. The white bear have now become exceedingly troublesome; they constantly infest our camp during the night, and though they have not attacked us, as our dog who patrols all night gives us notice of their approach, yet we are obliged to sleep with our arms by our sides for fear of accident, and we cannot send one man alone to any distance, particularly if he has to pass through brushwood. We saw two of them to-day on the large island opposite to us, but as we are all so much occupied now, we mean to reserve ourselves for some leisure moment,

OSAGE CHIEF (King?)

and then make a party to drive them from the islands. The river has risen nine inches since our arrival here.

At Portage creek captain Clark completed the cache, in which we deposited whatever we could spare from our baggage; some ammunition, provisions, books, the specimens of plants and minerals, and a draught of the river from its entrance to fort Mandan. After closing it he broke up the encampment, and took on all the remaining baggage to the high plain, about three miles. Portage creek has risen considerably in consequence of the rain, and the water had become of a deep crimson colour, and ill tasted; on overtaking the canoe he found that there was more baggage than could be carried on the two carriages, and therefore left some of the heavy articles which could not be injured, and proceeded on to Willow-run where he encamped for the night. Here they made a supper on two buffalo which they killed on the way; but passed the night in the rain, with a high wind from the southwest.

In the morning, finding it impossible to reach the end of the portage with their present load, in consequence of the state of the road after the rain, he sent back nearly all his party to bring on the articles which had been left yesterday. Having lost some notes and remarks which he had made on first ascending the river, he determined to go up to the Whitebear islands along its banks, in order to supply the deficiency. He there left one man to guard the baggage, and went on to the falls accompanied by his servant York, Chaboneau and his wife with her young child. JUNE 29TH

On his arrival there he observed a very dark cloud rising in the west which threatened rain, and looked around for some shelter, but could find no place where they would be secure from being blown into the river if the wind should prove as violent as it sometimes does in the plains. At length about a quarter of a mile above the falls he found a deep ravine where there were some shelving rocks, under which he took refuge. They were on the upper side of the ravine near the river, perfectly safe from the rain, and therefore laid down their guns, compass, and other articles which they carried with them. The shower was at first moderate; it then increased to a heavy rain, the effects of which they did not feel: soon after a torrent of rain and hail descended; the rain seemed to fall in a solid mass, and instantly collecting in the ravine come rolling down in a dreadful current, carrying the mud and rocks, and every thing that opposed it. Captain Clark fortunately saw it a moment before it reached them, and springing up with his gun and shotpouch in his left hand, with his right clambered up the steep bluff, pushing on the Indian woman with her child in her arms; her husband too had seized her hand, and was pulling her up the hill, but he was so terrified at the danger that but for captain Clark, himself and his wife and child would have been lost. So instantaneous was the rise of the water, that before captain Clark had reached his gun and began to ascend the bank, the water was up to his waist, and he could scarce get up faster than it rose, till it reached the height of fifteen feet with a furious current, which had they waited a moment longer would have swept them into the river just above the great falls, down which they must inevitably have been precipitated. They reached the plain in safety, and found York who had separated from them just before the storm to hunt some buffalo, and was now returning to find his master. They had been obliged to escape so rapidly that captain Clark lost his compass and umbrella, Chaboneau left his gun, shotpouch, and tomahawk, and the Indian woman had just time to grasp her child, before the net in which it lay at her feet was carried down the current.

He now relinquished his intention of going up the river and returned to the camp at Willow-run. Here he found that the party sent this morning for the baggage had all returned to camp in great confusion, leaving their loads in the plain. On account of the heat they generally go nearly naked, and with no covering on their heads. The hail was so large and driven so furiously against them by the high wind, that it knocked several of them down; one of them particularly was thrown on the ground three times, and most of them bleeding freely and complained of being much bruised. Willow-run had risen six feet since the rain, and as the plains were so wet that they could not proceed, they passed the night at their camp.

At the Whitebear camp also, we had not been insensible to the hailstorm, though less exposed. In the morning there had been a heavy shower of rain, after which it became fair. After assigning to the men their respective employments, captain Lewis took one of them and went to see the large fountain near the falls. For about six miles he passed through a beautiful level plain, and then on reaching the break of the river hills, was overtaken by the gust of wind from the southwest attended by lightning, thunder, and rain: fearing a renewal of the scene on the 27th, they took shelter in a little gully where there were some broad stones with which they meant to protect themselves against the hail; but fortunately there was not much, and that of a small size; so that they felt no inconvenience except that of being exposed without shelter for an hour, and being drenched by the rain: after it was over they proceeded to the fountain which is perhaps the largest in America. It is situated in a pleasant level plain, about twenty-five yards from the river, into which it falls over some steep irregular rocks with a sudden ascent of about six feet in one part of its course. The water boils up among the rocks and with such force near the centre, that the surface seems higher there than the earth on the sides of the fountain, which is a handsome turf of fine green grass. The water is extremely pure, cold and pleasant to the taste, not being impregnated with lime or any foreign substance. It is perfectly transparent and continues its bluish cast for half a mile down the Missouri, notwithstanding the rapidity of the river. After examining it for some time captain Lewis returned to the camp.

JUNE 30TH *Sunday.* In the morning captain Clark sent the men to bring up the baggage left in the plains yesterday. On their return the axletrees and carriages were repaired, and the baggage conveyed on the shoulders of the party across Willow-run which had fallen as low as three feet. The carriages being then taken over, a load of baggage was carried to the six-mile stake, deposited there, and the carriages brought back. Such is the state of the plains that this operation consumed the day. Two men were sent to the falls to look for the articles lost yesterday; but they found nothing but the compass covered with mud and sand at the mouth of the ravine; the place at which captain Clark had been caught by the storm, was filled with large rocks. The men complain much of the bruises received yesterday from the hail. A more than usual number of buffalo appeared about the camp to-day, and furnished plenty of meat: captain Clark thought that at one view he must have seen at least ten thousand. In the course of the day there was a heavy gust of wind from the southwest, after which the evening was fair.

At the Whitebear camp we had a heavy dew this morning, which is quite a remarkable occurrence. The party continues to be occupied with the boat, the crossbars for which are now finished, and there remain only the strips to complete the wood work: the skins necessary to cover it have already been prepared and they amount to twenty-eight elk skins and four buffalo skins. Among our game were two beaver, which we have had occasion to observe always are found wherever there is timber. We also killed a large bat or goatsucker of which there are many in this neighbourhood, resembling in every respect those of the same species in the United States. We have not seen the leather-winged bat for some time, nor are there any of the small goatsucker in this part of the Missouri. We have not seen either that species of goatsucker or nighthawk called the whippoorwill, which is commonly confounded in the United States with the large goatsucker which we observe here; this last prepares no nest but lays its eggs in the open plains; they generally begin to sit on two eggs, and we believe raise only one brood in a season: at the present moment they are just hatching their young.

Monday, July 1st, 1805

After a severe day's work captain Clark reached our camp in the evening, accompanied by his party and all the baggage except that left at the six-mile stake, for which they were too much fatigued to return. The route from the lower camp on Portage creek to that near Whitebear island, having been now measured and examined by captain Clark was as follows:

From our camp opposite the last considerable rapid to the entrance of Portage creek south 9° east for three quarters of a mile: thence on a course south 10° east for two miles, though for the canoes the best route is to the left of this course, and strikes Portage one mile and three-quarters from its entrance, avoiding in this way a very steep hill which lies above Portage creek: from this south 18° west for four miles, passing the head of a drain or ravine which falls into the Missouri below the great falls, and to the Willow-run which has always a plentiful supply of good water and some timber: here the course turns to south 45° west for four miles further; then south 66° west three miles, crossing at the beginning of the course the head of a drain which falls into the Missouri at the Crooked falls, and reaching an elevated point of the plain from which south 42° west. On approaching the river on this course there is a long and gentle descent from the high plain, after which the road turns a little to the right of the course up the river to our camp. The whole portage is seventeen and three quarter miles.

At the Whitebear camp we were occupied with the boat and digging a pit for the purpose of making some tar. The day has been warm, and the mosquitoes troublesome. We were fortunate enough to observe equal altitudes of the sun with sextant, which since our arrival here we have been prevented from doing, by flying clouds and storms in the evening.

JULY 2D *Tuesday.* A shower of rain fell very early this morning. We then despatched some men for the baggage left behind yesterday, and the rest were engaged in putting the boat together. This was accomplished in about three hours, and then we began to sew on the leather over the crossbars of iron on the inner side of the boat which form the ends of the sections. By two o'clock the last of the baggage arrived, to the great delight of the party who were anxious to proceed. The mosquitoes we find very troublesome.

A bear hunt, as shown in Sergeant Gass's diary.

Having completed our celestial observations we went over to the large island to make an attack upon its inhabitants the bears, who have annoyed us very much of late, and who were prowling about our camp all last night. We found that the part of the island frequented by the bear forms an almost impenetrable thicket of the broad-leafed willow: into this we forced our way in parties of three; but could see only one bear, who instantly attacked Drewyer. Fortunately as he was rushing on the hunter shot him through the heart within twenty paces and he fell, which enabled Drewyer to get out of his way: we then followed him one hundred yards and found that the wound had been mortal.

Not being able to discover any more of these animals we returned to camp: here in turning over some of the baggage we caught a rat [pack-rat] somewhat larger than the common European rat, and of a lighter colour; the body and outer parts of the legs and head of a light lead colour; the inner side of the legs as well as the belly, feet and ears are white; the ears are not covered with hair, and are much larger than those of the common rat; the toes also are longer, the eyes black and prominent, the whiskers very long and full; the tail rather longer than the body, and covered with fine fur and hair of the same size with that on the back, which is very close, short, and silky in its texture. This was the first we had met, although its nests are very frequent among the cliffs of rocks and hollow trees, where we also found large quantities of the shells and seed of the prickly pear, on which we conclude they chiefly subsist. The mosquitoes are uncommonly troublesome.

The wind was again high from the southwest: these winds are in fact always the coldest and most violent which we experience, and the hypothesis which we have formed on that subject is, that the air coming in contact with the Snowy mountains immediately becomes chilled and condensed, and being thus rendered heavier than the air below it descends into the rarified air below or into the vacuum formed by the constant action of the sun on the open unsheltered plains. The clouds rise suddenly near these mountains and distribute their contents partially over the neighbouring plains. The same cloud will discharge hail alone in one part, hail and rain in another, and rain only in a third, and all within the space of a few miles; while at the same time there is snow falling on the mountains to the southeast of us. There is at present no snow on those mountains; that which covered them on our arrival as well as that which has since fallen having disappeared. The mountains to the north and northwest of us are still entirely covered with snow, and indeed there has been no perceptible diminution of it since we first saw them, which induces a belief either that the clouds prevailing at this season do not reach their summits or that they deposit their snow only. They glisten with great beauty when the sun shines on them in a particular direction, and most probably from this glittering appearance have derived the name of the Shining mountains.

JULY 3D

Wednesday. Nearly the whole party were employed in different labours connected with the boat, which is now almost completed: but we have not as yet been able to obtain tar from our kiln, a circumstance that will occasion us not a little embarrassment. Having been told by the Indians that on leaving the falls we should soon pass the buffalo country, we have before us the prospect of fasting occasionally; but in order to provide a supply we sent out the hunters who killed only a buffalo and two antelopes, which added to six beaver and two otter have been all our game for two or three days. At ten in the morning we had a slight shower which scarcely wet the grass.

JULY 4TH

Thursday. The boat was now completed except what is in fact the most difficult part, the making her seams secure. We had intended to despatch a canoe with part of our men to the United States early this spring; but not having yet seen the Snake Indians, or knowing whether to calculate on their friendship or enmity, we have decided not to weaken our party which is already scarcely sufficient to repel any hostility. We were afraid too that such a measure might dishearten those who remain; and as we have never suggested it to them, they are all perfectly and enthusiastically attached to the enterprise, and willing to encounter any danger to ensure its success. We had a heavy dew this morning.

Since our arrival at the falls we have repeatedly heard a strange noise coming from the mountains in a direction a little to the north of west. It is heard at different periods of the day and night, sometimes when the air is perfectly still and without a cloud, and consists of one stroke only, or of five or six discharges in quick succession. It is loud and resembles precisely the sound of a six pound piece of ordnance at the distance of three miles. The Minnetarees frequently mentioned this noise like thunder, which they said the mountains made; but we had paid no attention to it, believing it to have been some superstition or perhaps a falsehood. The watermen also of the party say that the Pawnees and Ricaras give the same account of a noise heard in the Black mountains to the westward of them. The solution of the

Captain Clark's sketch map of the Handsom Falls of the Missouri.

mystery given by the philosophy of the watermen is, that it is occasioned by the bursting of the rich mines of silver confined within the bosom of the mountain.

An elk and a beaver are all that were killed to-day: the buffalo seem to have withdrawn from our neighbourhood, though several of the men who went to-day to visit the falls for the first time, mention that they are still abundant at that place. We contrived however to spread not a very sumptuous but a comfortable table in honour of the day, and in the evening gave the men a drink of spirits, which was the last of our stock. Some of them appeared sensible to the effects of even so small a quantity, and as is usual among them on all festivals, the fiddle was produced and a dance begun, which lasted till nine o'clock, when it was interrupted by a heavy shower of rain. They continued however their merriment till a late hour.

Friday. The boat was brought up into a high situation and fires kindled under her in order to dry her more expeditiously. Despairing now of procuring any tar, we formed a composition of pounded charcoal with beeswax and buffalo tallow to supply its place; should this resource fail us it will be very unfortunate, as in every other respect the boat answers our purposes completely. Although not quite dry she can be carried with ease by five men; her form is as complete as could be wished; very strong, and will carry at least eight thousand pounds with her complement of hands. Besides our want of tar, we have been unlucky in sewing the skins with a needle which had sharp edges instead of a point merely, although a large thong was used in order to fill the hole, yet it shrinks in drying and leaves the hole open, so that we fear the boat will leak. JULY 5TH

    A large herd of buffalo came near us and we procured three of them: besides which were killed two wolves and three antelopes. In the course of the day other herds of buffalo came near our camp on their way down the river: these herds move with great method and regularity. Although ten or twelve herds are seen scattered from each other over a space of many miles, yet if they are undisturbed by pursuit they will be uniformly travelling in the same direction.

Saturday. Last night there were several showers of rain and hail, attended with thunder and lightning: and about daybreak a heavy storm came on from the southwest with one continued roar of thunder, and rain and hail. The hail which was as large as musket balls, covered the ground completely; and on collecting some of it, it lasted during the day and served to cool the water. The red and yellow currant is abundant and now ripe, although still a little acid. We have seen in this neighbourhood what we have not met before, a remarkably small fox which associates in bands and burrows in the prairie, like the small wolf [coyote], but have not yet been able to obtain any of them, as they are extremely vigilant, and betake themselves on the slightest alarm to their burrows which are very deep. JULY 6TH

Sunday. The weather is warm but cloudy, so that the moisture retained by the bark after the rain leaves it slowly, though we have small fires constantly under the boat. We have no tents, and therefore are obliged to use the sails to keep off the bad weather. Our buffalo skins too, are scarcely sufficient to cover our baggage, but the men are now dressing others to replace their present leather clothing, which soon rots by being so constantly exposed to water. In the evening the hunters returned with the skins of only three buffalo, two antelope, four deer, and three wolf skins, and reported that the buffalo had gone further down the river; two other hunters who left us this morning could find nothing except one elk: in addition to this we caught a beaver. The mosquitoes still disturb us very much, and the blowing-flies JULY 7TH [blowflies] swarm in vast numbers round the boat. At four in the afternoon we had a light shower of rain attended with some thunder and lightning.

JULY 8TH *Monday.* In order more fully to replace the notes of the river which he had lost, and which he was prevented from supplying by the storm of the twenty-ninth ult. captain Clark set out after breakfast, taking with him nearly the whole party with a view of shooting buffalo if there should be any near the falls. After getting some distance in the plains the men were divided into squads, and he with two others struck the Missouri at the entrance of Medicine river, and thence proceeded down to the great cataract. He found that the immense herds of buffalo have entirely disappeared, and he thought had gone below the falls. Having made the necessary measurements, he returned through the plains and reached camp late in the evening; the whole party had killed only three buffalo, three antelopes and a deer; they had also shot a small fox, and brought a living ground-squirrel somewhat larger than those of the United States.

The day was warm and fair, but a slight rain fell in the afternoon. The boat having now become sufficiently dry, we gave it a coat of the composition, which after a proper interval was repeated, and the next morning, *Tuesday 9th,* she was launched into the water, and swam perfectly well.

The seats were then fixed and the oars fitted; but after we had loaded her, as well as the canoes, and were on the point of setting out a violent wind caused the waves to wet the baggage, so that we were forced to unload them. The wind continued high till evening, when to our great disappointment we discovered that nearly all the composition had separated from the skins, and left the seams perfectly exposed; so that the boat now leaked very much. To repair this misfortune without pitch is impossible, and as none of that article is to be procured, we therefore, however reluctantly, are obliged to abandon her, after having had so much labour in the construction. We now saw that the section of the boat covered with buffalo skins on which hair had been left, answered better than the elk skins and leaked but little; while that part which was covered with hair about one-eighth of an inch, retained the composition perfectly, and remained sound and dry. From this we perceived that had we employed buffalo instead of elk skins, and not singed them so closely as we have done, carefully avoiding to cut the leather in sewing, the boat would have been sufficient even with the present composition, or had we singed instead of shaving the elk skins we might have succeeded. But we discovered our error too late: the buffalo had deserted us, the travelling season was so fast advancing that we had no time to spare for experiments, and therefore finding that she could be no longer useful she was sunk in the water, so as to soften the skins and enable us the more easily to take her to pieces. It now became necessary to provide other means for transporting the baggage which we had intended to stow in her. For this purpose we shall want two canoes, but for many miles below the mouth of the Muscleshell river to this place, we have not seen a single tree fit to be used in that way. The hunters however who had hitherto been sent after timber, mention that there is a low ground on the opposite side of the river, about eight miles above us by land, and more than twice that distance by water, in which we may probably find trees large enough for our purposes. Captain Clark therefore determined to set out by land for that place with ten of the best workmen who would be occupied in building the canoes till the rest of the party, after taking the boat to pieces and making the necessary deposits, should transport the baggage and join them with the other six canoes.

Wednesday. He accordingly passed over to the opposite side of the river with his party, and proceeded on eight miles by land, the distance by water being twenty-three and three quarter miles. Here he found two cottonwood trees, but on cutting them down, one proved to be hollow, split at the top in falling, and both were much damaged at the bottom. He searched the neighbourhood but could find none which would suit better, and therefore was obliged to make use of those which he had felled, shortening them in order to avoid the cracks, and supplying the deficiency by making them as wide as possible. They were equally at a loss for wood of which they might make handles for their axes, the eyes of which not being round they were obliged to split the timber in such a manner that thirteen of the handles broke in the course of the day, though made of the best wood they could find for the purpose, which was the chokecherry. JULY 10TH

    The rest of the party took the frame of the boat to pieces, deposited it in a cache or hole, with a draught of the country from fort Mandan to this place, and also some other papers and small articles of less importance. After this we amused ourselves with fishing, and although we had thought on our arrival that there were none in this part of the river, we caught some of a species of white chub below the falls, but few in number, and small in size. Serjeant Ordway with four canoes and eight men had set sail in the morning, with part of the baggage to the place where captain Clark had fixed his camp, but the wind was so high that he only reached within three miles of that place, and encamped for the night.

Thursday. In the morning one of the canoes joined captain Clark: the other three having on board more valuable articles, which would have been injured by the water, went on more cautiously, and did not reach the camp till the evening. Captain Clark then had the canoes unloaded and sent back, but the high wind prevented their floating down nearer than about eight miles above us. His party were busily engaged with the canoes, and their hunters supplied them with three fat deer and a buffalo, in addition to two deer and an antelope killed yesterday. The few men who were with captain Lewis were occupied in hunting, but with not much success, having killed only one buffalo. They heard about sunset two discharges of the tremendous mountain artillery: they also saw several very large gray eagles, much larger than those of the United States, and most probably a distinct species, though the bald eagle of this country is not quite so large as that of the United States. The men have been much afflicted with painful whitlows, and one of them disabled from working by this complaint in his hand. JULY 11TH

Friday. In consequence of the wind the canoes did not reach the lower camp till late in the afternoon, before which time captain Lewis sent all the men he could spare up the river to assist in building the boats, and the day was too far advanced to reload and send them up before morning. The mosquitoes are very troublesome, and they have a companion not less so, a large black gnat which does not sting, but attacks the eyes in swarms. JULY 12TH

183

The party with captain Clark are employed on the canoes. In the course of the work sergeant Pryor dislocated his shoulder yesterday, but it was replaced immediately, and though painful does not threaten much injury. The hunters brought in three deer and two otter. This last animal has been numerous since the water has become sufficiently clear for them to take fish. The blue-crested fisher, or as it is sometimes called, the king-fisher, is an inhabitant of this part of the river; it is a bird rare on the Missouri; indeed we had not seen more than three or four of them from its entrance to Maria's river, and even those did not seem to reside on the Missouri but on some of the clearer streams which empty into it, as they were seen near the mouths of those streams.

JULY 13TH *Saturday.* The morning being fair and calm captain Lewis had all the remaining baggage embarked on board the six canoes, which sailed with two men in each for the upper camp. Then with a sick man and the Indian woman, he left the encampment, and crossing over the river went on by land to join captain Clark. From the head of the Whitebear islands he proceeded in a southwest direction, at the distance of three miles, till he struck the Missouri, which he then followed till he reached the place where all the party were occupied in boat-building.

On his way he passed a very large Indian lodge, which was probably designed as a great council-house, but it differs in its construction from all that we have seen lower down the Missouri or elsewhere. The form of it was a circle two hundred and sixteen feet in circumference at the base, and composed of sixteen large cottonwood poles about fifty feet long, and at their thicker ends, which touched the ground, about the size of a man's body: they were distributed at equal distances, except that one was omitted to the east, probably for the entrance. From the circumference of this circle the poles converged towards the centre where they were united and secured by large withes of willow brush. There was no covering over this fabric, in the centre of which were the remains of a large fire, and round it the marks of about eighty leathern lodges. He also saw a number of turtledoves, and some pigeons, of which he shot one differing in no respect from the wild pigeon of the United States.

The country exhibits its usual appearances, the timber confined to the river, the country on both sides as far as the eye can reach being entirely destitute of trees or brush. In the low ground in which we are building the canoes, the timber is larger and more abundant than we have seen it on the Missouri for several hundred miles. The soil too is good, for the grass and weeds reach about two feet high, being the tallest we have observed this season, though on the high plains and prairies the grass is at no season above three inches in height. Among these weeds are the sandrush, and nettle in small quantities; the plains are still infested by great numbers of the small birds already mentioned, among whom is the brown curlew. The current of the river is here extremely gentle; the buffalo have not yet quite gone, for the hunters brought in three in very good order. It requires some diligence to supply us plentifully, for as we reserve our parched meal for the Rocky mountains, where we do not expect to find much game, our principal article of food is meat, and the consumption of the whole thirty-two persons belonging to the party, amounts to four deer, an elk and a deer, or one buffalo every twenty-four hours. The mosquitoes and gnats persecute us as violently as before, so that we can get no sleep unless defended by biers [nets], with which we are all provided. We here found several plants hitherto unknown to us, and of which we preserved specimens.

Sergeant Ordway proceeded with the six canoes five miles up the river, but the wind becoming so high as to wet the baggage he was obliged to unload and dry it. The wind abated at five o'clock in the evening, when he again proceeded eight miles and encamped. The next morning, *Sunday, July 14th,* he joined us about noon. On leaving the Whitebear camp he passed at a short distance a little creek or run coming in on the left. This had been already examined and called Flattery run; it contains back water only, with very extensive low grounds, which rising into large plains reach the mountains on the east; then passed a willow island on the left within one mile and a half, and reached two miles further a cliff of rocks in a bend on the same side. In the course of another mile and a half he passed two islands covered with cottonwood, box-alder, sweet-willow, and the usual undergrowth, like that of the Whitebear islands. At thirteen and three quarter miles he came to the mouth of a small creek on the left; within the following nine miles he passed three timbered islands, and after making twenty-three and a quarter miles from the lower camp, arrived at the point of woodland on the north where the canoes were constructed.

The day was fair and warm; the men worked very industriously, and were enabled by the evening to launch the boats, which now want only seats and oars to be complete. One of them is twenty-five, the other thirty-three feet in length and three feet wide. Captain Lewis walked out between three and four miles over the rocky bluffs to a high situation, two miles from the river, a little below Fort Mountain creek. The country which he saw was in most parts level, but occasionally became varied by gentle rises and descents, but with no timber except along the water. From this position, the point at which the Missouri enters the first chain of the Rocky mountains bore south 28° west about twenty-five miles, according to our estimate.

The northern extremity of that chain north 73° west at the distance of eighty miles.

To the same extremity of the second chain north 65° west one hundred and fifty miles.

To the most remote point of a third and continued chain of these mountains north 50° west about two hundred miles.

The direction of the first chain was from south 20° east to north 20° west; of the second, from south 45° east to north 45° west; but the eye could not reach their southern extremities, which most probably may be traced to Mexico. In a course south 75° west, and at the distance of eight miles is a mountain, which from its appearance we shall call Fort Mountain. It is situated in the level plain, and forms nearly a square, each side of which is a mile in extent. These sides, which are composed of a yellow clay with no mixture of rock or stone whatever, rise perpendicularly to the height of three hundred feet, where the top becomes a level plain covered, as captain Lewis now observed, with a tolerably fertile mould two feet thick, on which was a coat of grass similar to that of the plain below: it has the appearance of being perfectly inaccessible, and although the mounds near the falls somewhat resemble it, yet none of them are so large.

Chapter 12

FROM THE GREAT FALLS TO THE THREE FORKS

MONDAY, JULY 15TH, 1805 We rose early, embarked all our baggage on board the canoes, which though light in number are still heavily loaded, and at ten o'clock set out on our journey. At the distance of three miles we passed an island, just above which is a small creek coming in from the left, which we called Fort Mountain creek, the channel of which is ten yards wide but now perfectly dry. At six miles we came to an island opposite to a bend towards the north side; and reached at seven and a half miles the lower point of a woodland at the entrance of a beautiful river, which in honour of the secretary of the navy we called Smith's river. This stream falls into a bend on the south side of the Missouri, and is eighty yards wide. As far as we could discern its course it wound through a charming valley towards the southeast, in which many herds of buffalo were feeding, till at the distance of twenty-five miles it entered the Rocky mountains, and was lost from our view. After dining near this place we proceeded on four and three quarter miles to the head of an island; four and a quarter miles beyond which is a second island on the left; three and a quarter miles further in a bend of the river towards the north, is a wood where we encamped for the night, after making nineteen and three quarter miles.

We find the prickly pear, one of the greatest beauties as well as the greatest inconveniences of the plains, now in full bloom. The sunflower too, a plant common on every part of the Missouri from its entrance to this place, is here very abundant and in bloom. The lambs-quarter, wild-cucumber, sandrush, and narrowdock are also common. Two elk, a deer, and an otter, were our game to-day.

The river has now become so much more crooked than below that we omit taking all its short meanders, but note only its general course, and lay down the small bends on our daily chart by the eye. The general width is from one hundred to one hundred and fifty yards. Along the banks are large beds of sand raised above the plains, and as they always appear on the sides of the river opposite to the southwest exposure, seem obviously brought there from the channel of the river by the incessant winds from that quarter: we find also more timber than for a great distance below the falls.

JULY 16TH *Tuesday*. There was a heavy dew last night. We soon passed about forty little booths, formed of willow bushes as a shelter against the sun. These seemed to have been deserted about ten days, and as we supposed by the Snake Indians, or Shoshonees, whom we hope soon to meet, as they appeared from the tracks to have a number of horses with them. At three and three quarter miles we passed a creek or run in a bend on the left side, and four miles further another run or small rivulet on the right. After breakfasting on a buffalo shot by one of the hunters, captain Lewis resolved to go on ahead of the party to the point where the river enters the Rocky mountains and make the necessary observations before our arrival. He therefore set out with Drewyer and two of the sick men to whom he supposed the walk would be useful: he travelled on the north side of the river through a handsome level plain, which continued on the opposite side also, and at the distance of eight miles passed a small stream on which he observed a considerable quantity of the aspen tree. A little before twelve o'clock he halted on a bend to the north in a low ground well covered with timber, about four and a half miles below the mountains, and obtained a meridian altitude, by which he found the latitude was N. 46° 46′ 50.2″. His route then lay through a high waving plain to a rapid where the Missouri first leaves the Rocky mountains, and here he encamped for the night.

In the meantime we had proceeded after breakfast one mile to a bend in the left, opposite to which was the frame of a large lodge situated in the prairie, constructed like that already mentioned above the Whitebear islands, but only sixty feet in diameter: round it were the remains of about eighty leathern lodges, all which seemed to have been built during the last autumn; within the next fifteen and a quarter miles we passed ten islands, on the last of which we encamped near the right shore, having made twenty-three miles.

JULY 17TH

The next morning we set out early, and at four miles distance joined captain Lewis at the foot of the rapids, and after breakfast began the passage of them: some of the articles most liable to be injured by the water were carried round. We then double manned the canoes, and with the aid of the towing-line got them up without accident. For several miles below the rapids the current of the Missouri becomes stronger as you approach, and the spurs of the mountain advance towards the river, which is deep and not more than seventy yards wide: at the rapids the river is closely hemmed in on both sides by the hills, and foams for half a mile over the rocks which obstruct its channel. The low grounds are now not more than a few yards in width, but they furnish room for an Indian road which winds under the hills on the north side of the river. The general range of these hills is from southeast to northwest, and the cliffs themselves are about eight hundred feet above the water, formed almost entirely of a hard black granite, on which are scattered a few dwarf pine and cedar trees. Immediately in the gap is a large rock four hundred feet high, which on one side is washed by the Missouri, while on its other sides a handsome little plain separates it from the neighbouring mountains. It may be ascended with some difficulty nearly to its summit, and affords a beautiful prospect of the plains below, in which we could observe large herds of buffalo. After ascending the rapids for half a mile we came to a small island at the head of them, which we called Pine island from a large pine tree at the lower end of it, which is the first we have seen near the river for a great distance. A mile beyond captain Lewis's camp we had a meridian altitude which gave us the latitude of 46° 42′ 14.7″. As the canoes were still heavily loaded all those not employed in working them walked on shore.

The navigation is now very laborious. The river is deep but with little current and from seventy to one hundred yards wide; the low grounds are very narrow, with but little timber and that chiefly the aspen tree. The cliffs are steep and hang over the river so much that often we could not cross them, but were obliged to pass and repass from one side of the river to the other in order to make our way. In some places the banks are formed of rocks, of dark black granite rising perpendicularly to a great height, through which the river seems in the progress of time to have worn its channel. On these mountains we see more pine than usual, but it is still in small quantities.

Along the bottoms, which have a covering of high grass, we observe the sunflower blooming in great abundance. The Indians of the Missouri, and more especially those who do not cultivate maize, make great use of the seed of this plant for bread or in thickening their soup. They first parch and then pound it between two stones until it is reduced to a fine meal. Sometimes they add a portion of water, and drink it thus diluted: at other times they add a sufficient proportion of marrow grease to reduce it to the consistency of common dough and eat it in that manner. This last composition we preferred to all the rest, and thought it at that time a very palatable dish.

There is however little of the broad-leafed cottonwood on this side of the falls, much the greater part of what we see being of the narrow-leafed species. There are also great quantities of red, purple, yellow and black currants. The currants are very pleasant to the taste, and much preferable to those of our common garden. The bush rises to the height of six or eight feet; the stem simple, branching and erect. These shrubs associate in corps either in upper or timbered lands near the water courses. The leaf is petiolate, of a pale green, and in form resembles the red currant so common in our gardens. The perianth of the fruit is one leaved, five cleft, abbreviated and tubular. The corolla is monopetallous, funnel-shaped, very long, and of a fine orange colour. There are five stamens and one pistillum of the first, the filaments are capillar, inserted in the corolla, equal and converging, the anther ovate and incumbent. The germ of the second species is round, smooth, inferior and pedicelled: the style long and thicker than the stamens, simple, cylindrical, smooth and erect. It remains with the corolla until the fruit is ripe; the stamen is simple and obtuse, and the fruit much the size and shape of our common garden currants, growing like them in clusters supported by a compound footstalk. The peduncles are longer in this species, and the berries are more scattered. The fruit is not so acid as the common currant, and has a more agreeable flavour.

The other species differs in no respect from the yellow currant excepting in the colour and flavour of the berries.

The serviceberry differs in some points from that of the United States. The bushes are small, sometimes not more than two feet high, and rarely exceed eight inches. They are proportionably small in their stems, growing very thickly, associated in clumps. The fruit is of the same form, but for the most part larger and of a very dark purple. They are now ripe and in great perfection. There are two species of gooseberry here, but neither of them yet ripe: nor are the chokecherry, though in great quantities. Besides there are also at that place the box-alder, red willow and a species of sumach.

In the evening we saw some mountain rams or big-horned animals, but no other game of any sort. After leaving Pine island we passed a small run on the left, which is formed by a large spring rising at the distance of half a mile under the mountain. One mile and a half above the island is another, and two miles further a third island, the river making small bends constantly to the north. From this last island to a point of rocks on the south side the low grounds become rather wider, and three quarters of a mile beyond these rocks, in a bend on the north, we encamped opposite to a very high cliff, having made during the day eleven and a half miles.

JULY 18TH *Thursday.* This morning early before our departure we saw a large herd of the big-horned animals, who were bounding among the rocks in the opposite cliff with great agility. These inaccessible spots secure them from all their enemies, and the only danger is in wandering among these precipices, where we should suppose it scarcely possible for any animal to stand; a single false step would precipitate them at least five hundred feet into the water.

At one mile and a quarter we passed another single cliff on the left; at the same distance beyond which is the mouth of a large river emptying itself from the north. It is a handsome, bold, and clear stream, eighty yards wide, that is nearly as broad as the Missouri, with a rapid current over a bed of small smooth stones of various figures. The water is extremely transparent, the low grounds are narrow, but possess as much wood as those of the Missouri: and it has every appearance of being navigable, though to what distance we cannot ascertain, as the country which it waters is broken and mountainous. In honour of the secretary of war we called it Dearborn's river.

Being now very anxious to meet with the Shoshonees or Snake Indians, for the purpose of obtaining the necessary information of our route, as well as to procure horses, it was thought best for one of us to go forward with a small party and endeavour to discover them, before the daily discharge of our guns, which is necessary for our subsistence, should give them notice of our approach: if by an accident they hear us, they will most probably retreat to the mountains, mistaking us for their enemies who usually attack them on this side.

Accordingly captain Clark set out with three men, and followed the course of the river on the north side; but the hills were so steep at first that he was not able to go much faster than ourselves. In the evening however he cut off many miles of the circuitous course of the river, by crossing a mountain over which he found a wide Indian road which in many places seems to have been cut or dug down in the earth. He passed also two branches of a stream which he called Ordway's creek, where he saw a number of beaver-dams extending in close succession towards the mountains as far as he could distinguish: on the cliffs were many of the big-horned animals. After crossing this mountain he encamped near a small stream of running water, having travelled twenty miles.

On leaving Dearborn's river we passed at three and a half miles a small creek, and at six beyond it an island on the north side of the river, which makes within that distance many small bends. At two and a half miles further is another island: three quarters of a mile beyond this is a small creek on the north side. At a mile and a half above the creek is a much larger stream thirty yards wide, and discharging itself with a bold current on the north side: the banks are low, and the bed formed of stones altogether. To this stream we gave the name of Ordway's creek, after sergeant John Ordway. At two miles beyond this the valley widens: we passed several bends of the river, and encamped in the centre of one on the south, having made twenty-one miles.

Here we found a small grove of the narrow-leafed cottonwood, there being no longer any of the broad-leafed kind since we entered the mountains. The water of these rivulets which come down from the mountains is very cold, pure, and well tasted. Along their banks as well as on the Missouri the aspen is very common, but of a small kind. The river is somewhat wider than we found it yesterday; the hills more distant from the river and not so high: there are some pines on the mountains, but they are principally confined to the upper regions of them: the low grounds are still narrower and have little or no timber. The soil near the river is good, and produces a luxuriant growth of grass and weeds: among these productions the sunflower holds a very distinguished place.

For several days past we have observed a species of flax in the low grounds, the leaf-stem and pericarp of which resemble those of the flax commonly cultivated in the United States: the stem rises to the height of two and a half or three feet, and spring to the number of eight or ten from the same root, with a strong thick bark apparently well calculated for use: the root seems to be perennial, and it is probable that the cutting of the stems may not at all injure it, for although the seeds are not yet ripe, there are young suckers shooting up from the root, whence we may infer that the stems which are fully grown and in the proper stage of vegetation to produce the best flax, are not essential to the preservation or support of the root, a circumstance which would render it a most valuable plant. To-day we have met with a second species of flax smaller than the first, as it seldom obtains a greater height than nine or twelve inches: the leaf and stem resemble those of the species just mentioned, except that the latter is rarely branched, and bears a single monopetallous bell-shaped blue flower, suspended with its limb downwards.

We saw several herds of the big-horn, but they were in the cliffs beyond our reach. We killed an elk this morning and found part of a deer which had been left for us by captain Clark. He pursued his route, *Friday, 19th*, early in the morning, and soon passed the remains of several Indian camps formed of willow brush, which seemed to have been deserted this spring. At the same time he observed that the pine trees had been stripped of their bark about the same season, which our Indian woman says her countrymen do in order to obtain the sap and the soft parts of the wood and bark for food. About eleven o'clock he met a herd of elk and killed two of them, but such was the want of wood in the neighbourhood that he was unable to procure enough to make a fire, and he was therefore obliged to substitute the dung of the buffalo, with which he cooked his breakfast. They then resumed their course along an old Indian road. In the afternoon they reached a handsome valley watered by a large creek, both of which extend a considerable distance into the mountain: this they crossed, and during the evening travelled over a mountainous country covered with sharp fragments of flintrock; these bruised and cut their feet very much, but were scarcely less troublesome than the prickly pear of the open plains, which have now become so abundant that it is impossible to avoid them, and the thorns are so strong that they pierce a double sole of dressed deer skin: the best resource against them is a sole of buffalo hide in parchment. At night they reached the river much fatigued, having passed two mountains in the course of the day and having travelled thirty miles. Captain Clark's first employment on lighting a fire was to extract from his feet the briars, which he found seventeen in number.

In the meantime we proceeded on very well, though the water appears to increase in rapidity as we advance: the current has indeed been strong during the day and obstructed by some rapids, which are not however much broken by rocks, and are perfectly safe: the river is deep, and its general width is from one hundred to one hundred and fifty yards wide. For more than thirteen miles we went along the numerous bends of the river and then reached two small islands; three and three quarter miles beyond which is a small creek in a bend to the left, above a small island on the right side of the river. We were regaled about ten o'clock P.M. with a thunderstorm of rain and hail which lasted for an hour, but during the day in this confined valley, through which we are passing, the heat is almost insupportable; yet whenever we obtain a glimpse of the lofty tops of the mountains we are tantalized with a view of the snow. These mountains have their sides and summits partially varied with little copses of pine, cedar, and balsam fir.

A mile and a half beyond this creek the rocks approach the river on both sides, forming a most sublime and extraordinary spectacle. For five and three quarter miles these rocks rise perpendicularly from the water's edge to the height of nearly twelve hundred feet. They are composed of a black granite near its base, but from its lighter colour above and from the fragments we suppose the upper part to be flint of a yellowish brown and cream colour. Nothing can be imagined more tremendous than the frowning darkness of these rocks, which project over the river and menace us with destruction. The river, of one hundred and fifty yards in width, seems to have forced its channel down this solid mass, but so reluctantly has it given way that during the whole distance the water is very deep even at the edges, and for the first three miles there is not a spot except one of a few yards, in which a man could stand between the water and the towering perpendicular of the mountain: the convulsion of the passage must have been terrible, since at its outlet there are vast columns of rock torn from the mountain which are strewed on both sides of the river, the trophies as it were of the victory. Several fine springs burst out from the chasms of the rock, and contribute to increase the river, which has now a strong current, but very fortunately we are able to overcome it with our oars, since it would be impossible to use either the cord or the pole. We were obliged to go on some time after dark, not being able to find a spot large enough to encamp on, but at length about two miles above a small island in the middle of the river we met with a spot on the left side, where we procured plenty of lightwood and pitchpine. This extraordinary range of rocks we called the Gates of the Rocky mountains. We had made twenty-two miles; and four and a quarter miles from the entrance of the Gates. The mountains are higher to-day than they were yesterday. We saw some big-horns, a few antelopes and beaver, but since entering the mountains have found no buffalo: the otter are however in great plenty: the mosquitoes have become less troublesome than they were.

Saturday. By employing the towrope whenever the banks permitted the use of it, the river being too deep for the pole, we were enabled to overcome the current which is still strong. At the distance of half a mile we came to a high rock in a bend to the left in the Gates. Here the perpendicular rocks cease, the hills retire from the river, and the valleys suddenly widen to a greater extent than they have been since we entered the mountains. At this place was some scattered timber, consisting of the narrow-leafed cottonwood, the aspen, and pine. There are also vast quantities of gooseberries, serviceberries, and several species of currant, among which is one of a black colour,

JULY 20TH

the flavour of which is preferable to that of the yellow, and would be deemed superior to that of any currant in the United States. We here killed an elk which was a pleasant addition to our stock of food. At a mile from the Gates, a large creek comes down from the mountains and empties itself behind an island in the middle of a bend to the north. To this stream which is fifteen yards wide we gave the name of Potts's creek, after John Potts, one of our men. Up this valley about seven miles we discovered a great smoke, as if the whole country had been set on fire; but were at a loss to decide whether it had been done accidentally by captain Clark's party, or by the Indians as a signal on their observing us. We afterwards learnt that this last was the fact; for they had heard a gun fired by one of captain Clark's men, and believing that their enemies were approaching had fled into the mountains, first setting fire to the plains as a warning to their countrymen.

We continued our course along several islands, and having made in the course of the day fifteen miles, encamped just above an island, at a spring on a high bank on the left side of the river. In the latter part of the evening we had passed through a low range of mountains, and the country became more open, though still unbroken and without timber, and the lowlands not very extensive: and just above our camp the river is again closed in by the mountains. We found on the banks an elk which captain Clark had left us, with a note mentioning that he should pass the mountains just above us and wait our arrival at some convenient place. We saw but could not pursue some redheaded ducks and sandhill cranes along the sides of the river, and a woodpecker about the size of the lark-woodpecker, which seems to be a distinct species: it is as black as a crow with a long tail, and flies like a jay-bird. The whole country is so infested by the prickly pear that we could scarcely find room to lie down at our camp.

Captain Clark on setting out this morning had gone through the valley about six miles to the right of the river. He soon fell into an old Indian road which he pursued till he reached the Missouri, at the distance of eighteen miles from his last encampment, just above the entrance of a large creek, which we afterwards called White Earth creek. Here he found his party so much cut and pierced with the sharp flint and the prickly pear that he proceeded only a small distance further, and then halted to wait for us. Along his track he had taken the precaution to strew signals, such as pieces of cloth, paper and linen, to prove to the Indians, if by accident they met his track, that we were white men. But he observed a smoke some distance ahead, and concluded that the whole country had now taken the alarm.

JULY 21ST *Sunday.* On leaving our camp we passed an island at half a mile, and reached at one mile a bad rapid at the place where the river leaves the mountain: here the cliffs are high and covered with fragments of broken rocks, the current is also strong, but although more rapid the river is wider and shallower, so that we are able to use the pole occasionally, though we principally depend on the towline. On leaving the rapid which is about half a mile in extent, the country opens on each side; the hills become lower; at one mile is a large island on the left side, and four and a half beyond it a large and bold creek twenty-eight yards wide, coming in from the north, where it waters a handsome valley: we called it Pryor's creek after one of the sergeants, John Pryor. At a mile above this creek on the left side of the Missouri we obtained a meridian altitude, which gave 46° 10′ 32.9″ as the latitude of the place.

For the following four miles, the country, like that through which we passed during the rest of the day, is rough and mountainous as we found it yesterday; but at the distance of twelve miles, we came towards evening into a beautiful plain ten or twelve miles wide, and extending as far as the eye could reach. This plain or rather valley is bounded by two nearly parallel ranges of high mountains whose summits are partially covered with snow, below which the pine is scattered along the sides down to the plain in some places, though the greater part of their surface has no timber and exhibits only a barren soil with no covering except dry parched grass or black rugged rocks. On entering the valley the river assumes a totally different aspect: it spreads to more than a mile in width, and though more rapid than before, is shallow enough in almost every part for the use of the pole, while its bed is formed of smooth stones and some large rocks, as it has been indeed since we entered the mountains: it is also divided by a number of islands some of which are large near the northern shore. The soil of the valley is a rich black loam apparently very fertile, and covered with a fine green grass about eighteen inches or two feet in height; while that of the high grounds is perfectly dry and seems scorched by the sun. The timber though still scarce is in greater quantities in this valley than we have seen it since entering the mountains, and seems to prefer the borders of the small creeks to the banks of the river itself. We advanced three and a half miles in this valley and encamped on the left side, having made in all fifteen and a half miles.

Our only large game to-day was one deer. We saw however two pheasants of a dark brown colour, much larger than the same species of bird in the United States. In the morning too, we saw three swans which, like the geese, have not yet recovered the feathers of the wing, and were unable to fly: we killed two of them, and the third escaped by diving and passing down the current. These are the first we have seen on the river for a great distance, and as they had no young with them, we presume that they do not breed in this neighbourhood. Of the geese we daily see great numbers, with their young perfectly feathered except on the wings, where both young and old are deficient; the first are very fine food, but the old ones are poor and unfit for use. Several of the large brown or sandhill crane are feeding in the low grounds on the grass which forms their principal food. The young crane cannot fly at this season: they are as large as a turkey, of a bright reddish bay colour. Since the river has become shallow we have caught a number of trout to-day, and a fish, white on the belly and sides, but of a bluish cast on the back, and a long pointed mouth opening somewhat like that of the shad.

This morning captain Clark wishing to hunt but fearful of alarming the Indians, went up the river for three miles, when finding neither any of them nor of their recent tracks returned, and then his little party separated to look for game. They killed two bucks and a doe, and a young curlew nearly feathered: in the evening they found the mosquitoes as troublesome as we did: these animals attack us as soon as the labours and fatigues of the day require some rest, and annoy us till several hours after dark, when the coldness of the air obliges them to disappear; but such is their persecution that were it not for our biers [nets] we should obtain no repose.

JULY 22D *Monday.* We set out at an early hour. The river being divided into so many channels by both large and small islands, that it was impossible to lay it down accurately by following in a canoe any single channel, captain Lewis walked on shore, took the general courses of the river, and from the rising grounds laid down the situation of the islands and channels, which he was enabled to do with perfect accuracy, the view not being obstructed by much timber. At one mile and a quarter we passed an island somewhat larger than the rest, and four miles further reached the upper end of another, on which we breakfasted. This is a large island forming in the middle of a bend to the north a level fertile plain ten feet above the surface of the water and never overflowed. Here we found great quantities of a small onion about the size of a musket ball, though some were larger; it is white, crisp, and as well flavoured as any of our garden onions, the seed is just ripening, and as the plant bears a large quantity to the square foot, and stands the rigours of the climate, it will no doubt be an acquisition to settlers. From this production we called it Onion island.

During the next seven and three quarter miles we passed several long circular bends, and a number of large and small islands which divide the river into many channels, and then reached the mouth of a creek on the north side. It is composed of three creeks which unite in a handsome valley about four miles before they discharge themselves into the Missouri, where it is about fifteen feet wide and eight feet deep, with clear transparent water. Here we halted for dinner, but as the canoes took different channels in ascending it was some time before they all joined.

Here we were delighted to find that the Indian woman recognizes the country; she tells us that to this creek her countrymen make excursions to procure a white paint on its banks, and we therefore call it White Earth creek. She says also that the three forks of the Missouri are at no great distance, a piece of intelligence which has cheered the spirits of us all, as we hope soon to reach the head of that river. This is the warmest day except one we have experienced this summer. In the shade the mercury stood at 80° above 0, which is the second time it has reached that height during this season. We encamped on an island after making nineteen and three quarter miles.

In the course of the day we saw many geese, cranes, small birds common to the plains, and a few pheasants: we also observed a small plover or curlew of a brown colour, about the size of the yellow-legged plover or jack curlew, but of a different species. It first appeared near the mouth of Smith's river, but is so shy and vigilant that we were unable to shoot it. Both the broad and narrow-leafed willow continue, though the sweet willow has become very scarce. The rosebush, small honeysuckle, the pulpy-leafed thorn, southern wood, sage and box-alder, narrow-leafed cottonwood, redwood, and a species of sumach, are all abundant. So too are the red and black gooseberries, serviceberries, chokecherry, and the black, red, yellow, and purple currant, which last seems to be a favourite food of the bear. Before encamping we landed and took on board captain Clark with the meat he had collected during this day's hunt, which consisted of one deer and an elk: we had ourselves shot a deer and an antelope. The mosquitoes and gnats were unusually fierce this evening.

Tuesday. Captain Clark again proceeded with four men along the right bank. During the whole day the river is divided by a number of islands, which spread it out sometimes to the distance of three miles: the current is very rapid and has many ripples; and the bed formed of gravel and smooth stones. The banks along the low grounds are of a rich loam, followed occasionally by low bluffs of yellow and red clay, with a hard red slatestone intermixed. The low grounds are wide, and have very little timber but a thick underbrush of willow, and rose and currant bushes: these are succeeded by high plains extending on each side to the base of the mountains, which lie parallel to the river about eight or twelve miles apart, and are high and rocky, with some small pine and cedar interspersed on them. At the distance of seven miles a creek twenty yards wide, after meandering through a beautiful low ground on the left for several miles parallel to the river, empties itself near a cluster of small islands: the stream we called Whitehouse creek after Joseph Whitehouse, one of the party, and the islands from their number received the name of the "Ten islands."

JULY 23D

About ten o'clock we came up with Drewyer, who had gone out to hunt yesterday, and not being able to find our encampment had staid out all night: he now supplied us with five deer. Three and a quarter miles beyond Whitehouse creek we came to the lower point of an island where the river is three hundred yards wide, and continued along it for one mile and a quarter, and then passed a second island just above it. We halted rather early for dinner in order to dry some part of the baggage which had been wet in the canoes: we then proceeded, and at five and a half miles had passed two small islands. Within the next three miles we came to a large island, which from its figure we called Broad island. From that place we made three and a half miles, and encamped on an island to the left, opposite to a much larger one on the right. Our journey to-day was twenty-two and a quarter miles, the greater part of which was made by means of our poles and cords, the use of which the banks much favoured. During the whole time we had the small flags hoisted in the canoes to apprise the Indians, if there were any in the neighbourhood, of our being white men and their friends; but we were not so fortunate as to discover any of them.

Along the shores we saw great quantities of the common thistle, and procured a further supply of wild onions and a species of garlic growing on the highlands, which is now green and in bloom: it has a flat leaf, and is strong, tough, and disagreeable. There was also much of the wild flax, of which we now obtained some ripe seed, as well as some bullrush and cattail flag. Among the animals we met with a black snake about two feet long, with the belly as dark as any other part of the body, which was perfectly black, and which had one hundred and twenty-eight scuta on the belly and sixty-three on the tail: we also saw antelopes, crane, geese, ducks, beaver, and otter; and took up four deer which had been left on the water side by captain Clark. He had pursued all day an Indian road on the right side of the river, and encamped late in the evening at the distance of twenty-five miles from our camp of last night. In the course of his walk he met besides deer a number of antelopes and a herd of elk, but all the tracks of Indians, though numerous, were of an old date.

JULY 24TH *Wednesday.* We proceeded for four and a quarter miles along several islands to a small run, just above which the low bluffs touch the river. Within three and a half miles further we came to a small island on the north, and a remarkable bluff composed of earth of a crimson colour, intermixed with stratas of slate, either black or of a red resembling brick. The following six and three-quarter miles brought us to an assemblage of islands, having passed four at different distances; and within the next five miles we met the same number of islands, and encamped on the north after making nineteen and a half miles.

The current of the river was strong and obstructed, as indeed it has been for some days by small rapids or ripples which descend from one to three feet in the course of one hundred and fifty yards, but they are rarely incommoded by any fixed rocks, and therefore, though the water is rapid, the passage is not attended with danger. The valley through which the river passes is like that of yesterday; the nearest hills generally concealing the most distant from us; but when we obtain a view of them they present themselves in amphitheatre, rising above each other as they recede from the river till the most remote are covered with snow.

We saw many otter and beaver to-day: the latter seem to contribute very much to the number of islands and the widening of the river. They begin by damming up the small channels of about twenty yards between the islands; this obliges the river to seek another outlet, and as soon as this is effected the channel stopped by the beaver becomes filled with mud and sand. The industrious animal is then driven to another channel which soon shares the same fate, till the river spreads on all sides, and cuts the projecting points of the land into islands. We killed a deer and saw great numbers of antelopes, cranes, some geese, and a few redheaded ducks. The small birds of the plains and the curlew are still abundant: we saw but could not come within gunshot of a large bear. There is much of the track of elk but none of the animals themselves, and from the appearance of bones and old excrement, we suppose that buffalo have sometimes strayed into the valley, though we have as yet seen no recent sign of them.

Along the water are a number of snakes, some of a brown uniform colour, others black, and a third speckled on the abdomen, and striped with black and a brownish yellow on the back and sides. The first, which are the largest, are about four feet long; the second is of the kind mentioned yesterday, and the third resembles in size and appearance the garter-snake of the United States. On examining the teeth of all these several kinds we found them free from poison: they are fond of the water, in which they take shelter on being pursued. The mosquitoes, gnats, and prickly pear, our three persecutors, still continue with us, and joined with the labour of working the canoes have fatigued us all excessively.

Captain Clark continued along the Indian road which led him up a creek. About ten o'clock he saw at the distance of six miles a horse feeding in the plains. He went towards him, but the animal was so wild that he could not get within several hundred paces of him: he then turned obliquely to the river where he killed a deer and dined, having passed in this valley five handsome streams, only one of which had any timber; another had some willows, and was very much dammed up by the beaver. After dinner he continued his route along the river and encamped at the distance of thirty miles.

As he went along he saw many tracks of Indians, but none of recent date.

The next morning, at the distance of a few miles he arrived at the three forks of the Missouri. Here he found that the plains had been recently burnt on the north side, and saw the track of a horse which seemed to have passed about four or five days since. After breakfast he examined the rivers, and finding that the north branch, although not larger, contained more water than the middle branch, and bore more to the westward, he determined to ascend it. He therefore left a note informing captain Lewis of his intention, and then went up that stream on the north side for about twenty-five miles. Here Chaboneau was unable to proceed any further, and the party therefore encamped, all of them much fatigued, their feet blistered and wounded by the prickly pear.

JULY 25TH

In the meantime we left our camp, and proceeded on very well, though the water is still rapid and has some occasional ripples. The country is much like that of yesterday: there are however fewer islands, for we passed only two. Behind one of them is a large creek twenty-five yards wide, to which we gave the name of Gass's creek, from one of our sergeants, Patrick Gass: it is formed by the union of five streams, which descend from the mountains and join in the plain near the river. On this island we saw a large brown bear, but he retreated to the shore and ran off before we could approach him. These animals seem more shy than they were below the mountains. The antelopes have again collected in small herds, composed of several females with their young, attended by one or two males, though some of the males are still solitary or wander in parties of two over the plains, which the antelope invariably prefers to the woodlands, and to which it always retreats if by accident it is found straggling in the hills, confiding no doubt in its wonderful fleetness. We also killed a few young geese, but as this game is small and very incompetent to the subsistence of the party, we have forbidden the men any longer to waste their ammunition on them.

About four and a half miles above Gass's creek, the valley in which we have been travelling ceases, the high craggy cliffs again approach the river, which now enters or rather leaves what appears to be a second great chain of the Rocky mountains. About a mile after entering these hills or low mountains we passed a number of fine bold springs, which burst out near the edge of the river under the cliffs on the left, and furnished a fine freestone water: near these we met with two of the worst rapids we have seen since entering the mountains; a ridge of sharp pointed rocks stretching across the river, leaving but small and dangerous channels for the navigation. The cliffs are of a lighter colour than those we have already passed, and in the bed of the river is some limestone which is small and worn smooth, and seems to have been brought down by the current. We went about a mile further and encamped under a high bluff on the right opposite to a cliff of rocks, having made sixteen miles.

All these cliffs appeared to have been undermined by the water at some period, and fallen down from the hills on their sides, the stratas of rock sometimes lying with their edges upwards, others not detached from the hills are depressed obliquely on the side next the river as if they had sunk to fill up the cavity formed by the washing of the river.

In the open places among the rocky cliffs are two kinds of gooseberry, one yellow and the other red. The former species was observed for the first time near the falls, the latter differs from it in no respect except in colour and in being of a larger size: both have a sweet flavour, and are rather indifferent fruit.

JULY 26TH *Friday.* We again found the current strong and the ripples frequent: these we were obliged to overcome by means of the cord and the pole, the oar being scarcely ever used except in crossing to take advantage of the shore. Within three and three quarter miles we passed seven small islands and reached the mouth of a large creek which empties itself in the centre of a bend on the left side: it is a bold running stream fifteen yards wide, and received the name of Howard creek after John P. Howard one of the party. One mile beyond it is a small run which falls in on the same side just above a rocky cliff. Here the mountains recede from the river, and the valley widens to the extent of several miles. The river now becomes crowded with islands of which we passed ten in the next thirteen and three quarter miles, then at the distance of eighteen miles we encamped on the left shore near a rock in the centre of a bend towards the left, and opposite to two more islands.

This valley has wide low grounds covered with high grass, and in many with a fine turf of green sward. The soil of the highlands is thin and meagre, without any covering except a low sedge and a dry kind of grass which is almost as inconvenient as the prickly pear. The seeds of it are armed with a long twisted hard beard at their upper extremity, while the lower part is a sharp firm point, beset at its base with little stiff bristles, with the points in a direction contrary to the subulate point to which they answer as a barb. We see also another species of prickly pear. It is of a globular form, composed of an assemblage of little conic leaves springing from a common root to which their small points are attached as a common centre, and the base of the cone forms the apex of the leaf which is garnished with a circular range of sharp thorns like the cochineal plant, and quite as stiff and even more keen than those of the common flat-leafed species.

Between the hills the river had been confined within one hundred and fifty or two hundred yards, but in the valley it widens to two hundred or two hundred and fifty yards, and sometimes is spread by its numerous islands to the distance of three quarters of a mile. The banks are low, but the river never overflows them. On entering the valley we again saw the snow-clad mountains before us, but the appearance of the hills as well as of the timber near us is much as heretofore.

Finding Chaboneau unable to proceed, captain Clark left him with one of the men, and accompanied by the other went up the river about twelve miles to the top of a mountain. Here he had an extensive view of the river valley upwards and saw a large creek which flowed in on the right side. He however discovered no fresh sign of the Indians, and therefore determined to examine the middle branch and join us by the time we reached the forks: he descended the mountain by an Indian path which wound through a deep valley, and at length reached a fine cold spring. The day had been very warm, the path unshaded by timber, and his thirst was excessive; he was therefore tempted to drink: but although he took the precaution of previously wetting his head, feet and hands, he soon found himself very unwell: he continued his route, and after resting with Chaboneau at his camp, resumed his march across the north fork near a large island. The first part was knee-deep, but on the other side of the island the water came to their waists and was so rapid that Chaboneau was on the point of being swept away, and not being able to swim would have perished if captain Clark had not rescued him. While crossing the island they killed two brown bear and saw great quantities of beaver. He then went on to a small river which falls into the north fork some miles above its junction with the two others: here, finding himself grow more unwell, he halted for the night at the distance of four miles from his last encampment.

Saturday. We proceeded on but slowly, the current being still so rapid as to require the utmost exertions of us all to advance, and the men are losing their strength fast in consequence of their constant efforts. At half a mile we passed an island, and a mile and a quarter further again entered a ridge of hills which now approach the river with cliffs apparently sinking like those of yesterday. They are composed of a solid limestone of a light lead colour when exposed to the air, though when freshly broken it is of a deep blue, and of an excellent quality and very fine grain. On these cliffs were numbers of the big-horn. At two and a half miles we reached the centre of a bend towards the south passing a small island, and at one mile and a quarter beyond this reached about nine in the morning the mouth of a river seventy yards wide, which falls in from the southeast. Here the country suddenly opens into extensive and beautiful meadows and plains, surrounded on every side with distant and lofty mountains.

 Captain Lewis went up this stream for about half a mile, and from the height of a limestone cliff could observe its course about seven miles, and the three forks of the Missouri, of which this river is one. Its extreme point bore S. 65° E. and during the seven miles it passes through a green extensive meadow of fine grass dividing itself into several streams, the largest passing near the ridge of hills on which he stood. On the right side of the Missouri a high, wide and extensive plain succeeds to this low meadow

JULY 27TH

A rocky eminence on the upper Missouri (from a watercolor by Charles Bodmer); on the water are keelboats similar to one used in the expedition.

which reaches the hills. In the meadow a large spring rises about a quarter of a mile from this southeast fork, into which it discharges itself on the right side about four hundred paces from where he stood. Between the southeast and middle forks a distant range of snow-topped mountains spread from east to south above the irregular broken hills nearer to this spot: the middle and southwest forks unite at half a mile above the entrance of the southeast fork. The extreme point at which the former can be seen, bears S. 15° E. and at the distance of fourteen miles, where it turns to the right round the point of a high plain and disappears from the view. Its low grounds are several miles in width, forming a smooth and beautiful green meadow, and like the southeast fork it divides itself into several streams.

Between these two forks and near their junction with that from the southwest, is a position admirably well calculated for a fort. It is a limestone rock of an oblong form, rising from the plain perpendicularly to the height of twenty-five feet on three of its sides; the fourth towards the middle fork being a gradual ascent and covered with a fine green sward, as is also the top which is level and contains about two acres.

An extensive plain lies between the middle and southwest forks, the last of which after watering a country like that of the other two branches, disappears about twelve miles off, at a point bearing south 30° west. It is also more divided and serpentine in its course than the other two, and possesses more timber in its meadows. This timber consists almost exclusively of the narrow-leafed cottonwood, with an intermixture of box-alder and sweet-willow, the underbrush being thick and like that of the Missouri lower down. A range of high mountains partially covered with snow is seen at a considerable distance running from south to west, and nearly all around us are broken ridges of country like that below, through which those united streams appear to have forced their passage: after observing the country captain Lewis descended to breakfast.

We then left the mouth of the southeast fork, to which in honour of the secretary of the treasury we called Gallatin's river, and at the distance of half a mile reached the confluence of the southwest and middle branch of the Missouris. Here we found the letter from captain Clark, and as we agreed with him that the direction of the southwest fork gave it a decided preference over the others, we ascended that branch of the river for a mile, and encamped in a level handsome plain on the left: having advanced only seven miles. Here we resolved to wait the return of captain Clark, and in the meantime make the necessary celestial observations, as this seems an essential point in the geography of the western world, and also to recruit the men and air the baggage. It was accordingly all unloaded and stowed away on shore.

Near the three forks we saw many collections of the mud-nests of the small martin attached to the smooth faces of the limestone rock, where they were sheltered by projections of the rock above it: and in the meadows were numbers of the duck or mallard with their young, who are now nearly grown. The hunters returned towards evening with six deer, three otter and a muskrat; and had seen great numbers of antelopes, and much sign of the beaver and elk.

During all last night captain Clark had a high fever and chills accompanied with great pain. He however pursued his route eight miles to the middle branch, where not finding any fresh Indian track he came down it

One of the "remarkable hills" along the Missouri (from a Bodmer drawing).

and joined us about three o'clock, very much exhausted with fatigue and the violence of his fever. Believing himself bilious he took a dose of Rush's pills, which we have always found sovereign in such cases, and bathing the lower extremities in warm water.

We are now very anxious to see the Snake Indians. After advancing for several hundred miles into this wild and mountainous country, we may soon expect that the game will abandon us. With no information of the route we may be unable to find a passage across the mountains when we reach the head of the river, at least such a one as will lead us to the Columbia, and even were we so fortunate as to find a branch of that river, the timber which we have hitherto seen in these mountains does not promise us any fit to make canoes, so that our chief dependence is on meeting some tribe from whom we may procure horses. Our consolation is, that this southwest branch can scarcely head with any other river than the Columbia, and that if any nation of Indians can live in the mountains we are able to endure as much as they, and have even better means of procuring subsistence.

Chapter 13

FROM THE
THREE FORKS TO
BEAVER'S HEAD

SUNDAY, JULY 28TH, 1805 Captain Clark continued very unwell during the night, but was somewhat relieved this morning. On examining the two streams it became difficult to decide which was the larger or the real Missouri; they are each ninety yards wide and so perfectly similar in character and appearance that they seem to have been formed in the same mould. We were therefore induced to discontinue the name of Missouri, and gave to the southwest branch the name of Jefferson in honour of the president of the United States, and the projector of the enterprise: and called the middle branch Madison, after James Madison secretary of state. These two, as well as Gallatin river, run with great velocity and throw out large bodies of water. Gallatin river is however the most rapid of the three, and though not quite as deep, yet navigable for a considerable distance. Madison river though much less rapid than the Gallatin, is somewhat more rapid than the Jefferson; the beds of all of them are formed of smooth pebble and gravel, and the waters are perfectly transparent. The timber in the neighbourhood would be sufficient for the ordinary uses of an establishment, which, however, it would be advisable to build of brick, as the earth appears calculated for that purpose, and along the shores are some bars of fine pure sand.

The greater part of the men, having yesterday put their deer skins in water, were this day engaged in dressing them, for the purpose of making clothing. The weather was very warm, the thermometer in the afternoon was at 90° above 0, and the mosquitoes more than usually inconvenient: we were, however, relieved from them by a high wind from the southwest, which came on at four o'clock, bringing a storm of thunder and lightning, attended by refreshing showers, which continued till after dark. In the evening the hunters returned with eight deer and two elk; and the party who had been sent up the Gallatin, reported that after passing the point, where it escaped from captain Lewis's view yesterday, it turned more towards the east, as far as they could discern the opening of the mountains, formed by the valley which bordered it. The low grounds were still wide but not so extensive as near its mouth, and though the stream is rapid and much divided by islands, it is still sufficiently deep for navigation with canoes.

The low grounds, although not more than eight or nine feet above the water, seem never to be overflowed, except a part on the west side of the middle fork, which is stony and seems occasionally inundated. They are furnished with great quantities of small fruit, such as currants and gooseberries, among the last of which is a black species, which we observe not only in the meadows but along the mountain rivulets. From the same root rise a number of stems to the height of five or six feet, some of them particularly branched and all reclining. The berry is attached by a long peduncle to the stem, from which they hang of a smooth ovate form, as large as the common garden gooseberry, and as black as jet, though the pulp is of a bright crimson colour. It is extremely acid: the form of the leaf resembles that of the common gooseberry, though larger. The stem is covered with very sharp thorns or briars: the grass too is very luxuriant and would yield fine hay in parcels of several acres. The sand-rushes will grow in many places as high as a man's breast, and as thick as stalks of wheat; it would supply the best food during the winter to cattle of any trading or military post.

Sacajawea, our Indian woman, informs us that we are encamped on the precise spot where her countrymen, the Snake Indians, had their huts five years ago, when the Minnetarees of Knife river first came in sight of them, and from which they hastily retreated three miles up the Jefferson, and concealed themselves in the woods. The Minnetarees, however, pursued and attacked them, killed four men, as many women, and a number of boys; and made prisoners of four other boys, and all the females, of whom Sacajawea was one: she does not, however, show any distress at these recollections, nor any joy at the prospect of being restored to her country; for she seems to possess the folly or the philosophy of not suffering her feelings to extend beyond the anxiety of having plenty to eat and a few trinkets to wear.

Monday. This morning the hunters brought in some fat deer of the long-tailed red kind, which are quite as large as those of the United States, and are, indeed, the only kind we have found at this place: there are numbers of the sandhill cranes feeding in the meadows; we caught a young one of the same colour as the red deer, which, though it had nearly attained its full growth could not fly; it is very fierce and strikes a severe blow with its beak. The kingfisher has become quite common on this side of the falls: but we have seen none of the summer duck since leaving that place. The mallard duck, which we saw for the first time on the *20th* instant, with their young, are now abundant, though they do not breed on the Missouri, below the mountains. The small birds already described are also abundant in the plains; here too, are great quantities of grasshoppers or crickets; and among other animals, a large ant with a reddish brown body and legs, and a black head and abdomen, who build little cones of gravel, ten or twelve inches high, without a mixture of sticks, and but little earth. In the river we see a great abundance of fish, but we cannot tempt them to bite by any thing on our hooks. The whole party have been engaged in dressing skins, and making them into moccasins and leggings. Captain Clark's fever has almost left him, but he still remains very languid and has a general soreness in his limbs. The latitude of our camp, as the mean of two observations of the meridian altitude of the sun's lower limb with octant by back observation, is N. 45° 24′ 8.5″.

JULY 29TH

Tuesday. Captain Clark was this morning much restored; and, therefore, having made all the observations necessary to fix the longitude, we reloaded our canoes, and began to ascend Jefferson river. The river now becomes very crooked, and forms bends on each side; the current too is rapid, and cut into a great number of channels, and sometimes shoals, the beds of which consist of coarse gravel. The islands are unusually numerous: on the right are high plains occasionally forming cliffs of rocks and hills; while the left was an extensive low ground and prairie intersected by a number of bayous or channels falling into the river. Captain Lewis, who had walked through it with Chaboneau, his wife, and two invalids, joined us at dinner, a few miles above our camp. Here the Indian woman said was the place where she had been made prisoner. The men being too few to contend with the Minnetarees, mounted their horses, and fled as soon as the attack began. The women and children dispersed, and Sacajawea as she was crossing at a shoal place, was overtaken in the middle of the river by her pursuers. As we proceeded, the low grounds were covered with cottonwood and a thick underbrush, and on both sides of the river, except where the high hills pre-

JULY 30TH

vented it, the ground was divided by bayous, which are dammed up by the beaver, which are very numerous here. We made twelve and a quarter miles, and encamped on the north side.

Captain Lewis proceeded after dinner, through an extensive low ground of timber and meadow land intermixed; but the bayous were so obstructed by beaver dams, that in order to avoid them he directed his course towards the high plain on the right. This he gained with some difficulty, after wading up to his waist through the mud and water of a number of beaver dams. When he desired to rejoin the canoes he found the underbrush so thick, and the river so crooked, that this, joined to the difficulty of passing the beaver dams, induced him to go on and endeavour to intercept the river at some point where it might be more collected into one channel and approach nearer to the high plain. He arrived at the bank about sunset, having gone only six miles in a direct course from the canoes: but he saw no traces of the men, nor did he receive any answer to his shouts nor the firing of his gun. It was now nearly dark; a duck lighted near him and he shot it. He then went on the head of a small island where he found some driftwood, which enabled him to cook his duck for supper, and he laid down to sleep on some willow brush. The night was cool, but the driftwood gave him a good fire, and he suffered no inconvenience except from the mosquitoes.

JULY 31ST *Wednesday.* The next morning he waited till after seven o'clock, when he became uneasy lest we should have gone beyond his camp last evening and determined to follow us. Just as he had set out with this intention, he saw one of the party in advance of the canoes; although our camp was only two miles below him, in a straight line, we could not reach him sooner, in consequence of the rapidity of the water and the circuitous course of the river. We halted for breakfast, after which captain Lewis continued his route. At the distance of one mile from our encampment we passed the principal entrance of a stream on the left, which rises in the snowy mountains to the southwest, between Jefferson and Madison rivers, and discharges itself by seven mouths, five below, and one three miles above this, which is the largest, and about thirty yards wide: we called it Philosophy river. The water of it is abundant and perfectly clear, and the bed like that of the Jefferson consists of pebble and gravel. There is some timber in the bottoms of the river, and vast numbers of otter and beaver, which build on its smaller mouths and the bayous of its neighbourhood. The Jefferson continues as yesterday, shoaly and rapid, but as the islands though numerous are small, it is however more collected into one current than it was below, and is from ninety to one hundred and twenty yards in width. The low ground has a fertile soil of rich black loam, and contains a considerable quantity of timber, with the bullrush and cattail flag very abundant in the moist parts, while the drier situations are covered with fine grass, tansy, thistles, onions, and flax. The uplands are barren, and without timber: the soil is a light yellow clay intermixed with small smooth pebble and gravel, and the only produce is the prickly-pear, the sedge, and the bearded grass, which is as dry and inflammable as tinder.

As we proceeded the low grounds became narrower, and the timber more scarce, till at the distance of ten miles the high hills approach and overhang the river on both sides, forming cliffs of a hard black granite, like almost all those below the limestone cliffs at the three forks of the Missouri: they continue so for a mile and three quarters, where we came to a point of rock on the right side, at which place the hills again retire, and the valley widens to the distance of a mile and a half. Within the next five miles we passed four islands, and reached the foot of a mountain in a bend of the river to the left: from this place we went a mile and a quarter to the entrance of a small run discharging itself on the left, and encamped on an island just above it, after making seventeen and three quarter miles. We observe some pine on the hills on both sides of our encampment, which are very lofty. The only game which we have seen are one bighorn, a few antelopes, deer, and one brown bear, which escaped from our pursuit. Nothing was, however, killed to-day, nor have we had any fresh meat except one beaver for the last two days, so that we are now reduced to an unusual situation, for we have hitherto always had a great abundance of flesh.

Thursday, August 1st, 1805

We left our encampment early, and at the distance of a mile, reached a point of rocks on the left side, where the river passes through perpendicular cliffs. Two and three quarter miles further we halted for breakfast under a cedar tree in a bend to the right: here as had been previously arranged, captain Lewis left us, with sergeant Gass, Chaboneau, and Drewyer, intending to go on in advance in search of the Shoshonees.

He began his route along the north side of the river over a high range of mountains, as captain Clark who ascended them on the *26th* had observed from them a large valley spreading to the north of west, and concluded that on leaving the mountain the river took that direction; but when he reached that valley, captain Lewis found it to be the passage of a large creek falling just above the mountain into the Jefferson, which bears to the southwest. On discovering his error, he bent his course towards that river, which he reached about two in the afternoon, very much exhausted with heat and thirst. The mountains were very bare of timber, and the route lay along the steep and narrow hollows of the mountain, exposed to the midday sun, without air, or shade, or water. Just as he arrived there a flock of elk passed, and they killed two of them, on which they made their dinner, and left the rest on the shore for the party in the canoes. After dinner they resumed their march, and encamped on the north side of the river, after making seventeen miles.

In crossing the mountains captain Lewis saw a flock of the black or dark brown pheasant, of which he killed one. This bird is one third larger than the common pheasant of the Atlantic States; its form is much the same. The male has not however the tufts of long black feathers on the sides of the neck so conspicuous in the Atlantic pheasant, and both sexes are booted nearly to the toes. The colour is a uniform dark brown with a small mixture of yellow or yellowish brown specks on some of the feathers, particularly those of the tail, though the extremities of these are perfectly black for about an inch. The eye is nearly black, and the iris has a small dash of yellowish brown; the feathers of the tail are somewhat longer than those of our pheasant, but the same in number, eighteen, and nearly equal in size, except that those of the middle are somewhat the longest; their flesh is white and agreeably flavoured.

He also saw among the scattered pine near the top of the mountain, a blue bird about the size of a robin, but in action and form something like a jay; it is constantly in motion, hopping from spray to spray, and its note which is loud and frequent, is, as far as letters can represent it, *char ah! char ah! char ah!*

After breakfast we proceeded on: at the distance of two and a quarter miles the river enters a high mountain, which forms rugged cliffs of nearly perpendicular rocks. These are of a black granite at the lower part, and the upper consists of a light coloured freestone; they continue from the point of rocks close to the river for nine miles, which we passed before breakfast, during which the current is very strong. At nine and a quarter miles we passed an island, and a rapid with a fall of six feet, and reached the entrance of a large creek on the left side. In passing this place the towline of one of the canoes broke just at the shoot of the rapids, swung on the rocks and had nearly upset. To the creek as well as the rapid we gave the name of Frazier, after Robert Frazier one of the party.

Here the country opens into a beautiful valley from six to eight miles in width. The river then becomes crooked and crowded with islands; its low grounds wide and fertile, but though covered with fine grass from nine inches to two feet high; possesses but a small proportion of timber, and that consists almost entirely of a few narrow-leafed cottonwood distributed along the verge of the river. The soil of the plain is tolerably fertile, and consists of a black or dark yellow loam. It gradually ascends on each side to the bases of two ranges of high mountains which lie parallel to the river; the tops of them are yet in part covered with snow, and while in the valley we are nearly suffocated with heat during the day, and at night the air is so cold that two blankets are not more than sufficient covering. In passing through the hills we observed some large cedar trees, and some juniper also. From Frazier's creek we went three and three quarter miles, and encamped on the left side, having come thirteen miles. Directly opposite our camp is a large creek which we call Field's creek, from Reuben Fields, one of our men. Soon after we halted two of the hunters went out and returned with five deer, which, with one bighorn, we killed in coming through the mountain on which we dined; and the elk left by captain Lewis. We were again well supplied with fresh meat. In the course of the day we saw a brown bear but were not able to shoot him.

AUGUST 2D *Friday.* Captain Lewis, who slept in the valley a few miles above us, resumed his journey early, and after making five miles and finding that the river still bore to the south, determined to cross it in hopes of shortening the route: for the first time therefore he waded across it, although there are probably many places above the falls where it might be attempted with equal safety. The river was about ninety yards wide, the current rapid, and about waist deep: the bottom formed of smooth pebble with a small mixture of coarse gravel. He then continued along the left bank of the river till sunset and encamped, after travelling twenty-four miles. He met no fresh tracks of Indians. Throughout the valley are scattered the bones and excrement of the buffalo of an old date, but there seems no hope of meeting the animals themselves in the mountains: he saw an abundance of deer and antelope, and many tracks of elk and bear. Having killed two deer they feasted sumptuously, with a dessert of currants of different colours; two species of red, others yellow, deep purple, and black: to these were added black gooseberries and deep purple serviceberries, somewhat larger than ours, from which it differs also in colour, size, and the superior excellence of its flavour. In the low grounds of the river were many beaver-dams formed of willow brush, mud, and gravel, so closely interwoven that they resist the water perfectly: some of them were five feet high and overflowed several acres of land.

In the meantime we proceeded on slowly, the current being so strong as to require the utmost exertions of the men to make any advance even with the aid of the cord and pole, the wind being from the northwest. The river is full of large and small islands, and the plain cut by great numbers of bayous or channels, in which are multitudes of beaver. In the course of the day we passed some villages of barking squirrels: we saw several rattlesnakes in the plain; young ducks, both of the duckon-mallard [duck-in-mallard] and red-headed fishing duck species; some geese; also the black woodpecker, and a large herd of elk. The channel, current, banks, and general appearance of the river, are like that of yesterday. At fourteen and three quarter miles we reached a rapid creek or bayou about thirty yards wide, to which we gave the name of Birth creek. After making seventeen miles we halted in a smooth plain in a bend towards the left.

Saturday. Captain Lewis continued his course along the river through the valley, which continued much as it was yesterday, except that it now widens to nearly twelve miles: the plains too are more broken and have some scattered pine near the mountains, where they rise higher than hitherto. In the level parts of the plains and the river bottoms there is no timber except small cottonwood near the margin, and an undergrowth of narrow-leafed willow, small honeysuckle, rosebushes, currants, serviceberry, and gooseberry, and a little of a small species of birch; it [the leaf] is a finely indented oval of a small size and a deep green colour; the stem is simple, ascending and branching, and seldom rises higher than ten or twelve feet. The mountains continue high on each side of the valley, but their only covering is a small species of pitch-pine with a short leaf, growing on the lower and middle regions, while for some distance below the snowy tops there is neither timber nor herbage of any kind.

About eleven o'clock Drewyer killed a doe on which they breakfasted, and after resting two hours continued till night, when they reached the river near a low ground more extensive than usual. From the appearance of the timber captain Lewis supposed that the river forked above him, and therefore encamped with an intention of examining it more particularly in the morning. He had now made twenty-three miles, the latter part of which were for eight miles through a high plain covered with prickly pears and bearded grass, which rendered the walking very inconvenient: but even this was better than the river bottoms we crossed in the evening, which, though apparently level, were formed into deep holes as if they had been rooted up by hogs, and the holes were so covered with thick grass that they were in danger of falling at every step. Some parts of these low grounds, however,

AUGUST 3D

contain turf or peat of an excellent quality for many feet deep apparently, as well as the mineral salts which we have already mentioned on the Missouri. They saw many deer, antelopes, ducks, geese, some beaver, and great traces of their work, and the small birds and curlews as usual. The only fish which they observed in this part of the river is the trout and a species of white fish with a remarkably long small mouth, which one of our men recognized as the fish called in the eastern states the bottlenose.

On setting out with the canoes we found the river as usual much crowded with islands, the current more rapid as well as shallower, so that in many places they were obliged to man the canoes double, and drag them over the stone and gravel of the channel. Soon after we set off captain Clark who was walking on shore observed a fresh track which he knew to be that of an Indian from the large toes being turned inwards, and on following it found that it led to the point of a hill from which our camp of last night could be seen. This circumstance strengthened the belief that some Indian had strayed thither, and had run off alarmed at the sight of us. At two and a quarter miles, is a small creek in a bend towards the right, which runs down from the mountains at a little distance; we called it Panther creek from an animal of that kind killed by Reuben Fields at its mouth. It is precisely the same animal common to the western parts of the United States, and measured seven and a half feet from the nose to the extremity of the tail. Six and three quarter miles beyond this stream is another on the left formed by the drains which convey the melted snows from a mountain near it, under which the river passes, leaving the low grounds on the right side, and making several bends in its course. On this stream are many large beaver dams. One mile above it is a small run on the left, after leaving which begins a very bad rapid, where the bed of the river is formed of solid rock: this we passed in the course of a mile, and encamped on the lower point of an island. Our journey had been only thirteen miles, but the badness of the river made it very laborious, as the men were compelled to be in the water during the greater part of the day. We saw only deer, antelopes, and the common birds of the country.

AUGUST 4TH   *Sunday.* This morning captain Lewis proceeded early, and after going southeast by east for four miles reached a bold running creek, twelve yards wide, with clear cold water, furnished apparently by four drains from the snowy mountains on the left: after passing this creek he changed his direction to southeast, and leaving the valley in which he had travelled for the last two days, entered another which bore east. At the distance of three miles on this course he passed a handsome little river, about thirty yards wide, which winds through the valley: the current is not rapid nor the water very clear, but it affords a considerable quantity of water, and appears as if it might be navigable for some miles. The banks are low, and the bed formed of stone and gravel. He now changed his route to southwest, and passing a high plain which separates the valleys, returned to the more southern or that which he had left: in passing this he found a river [the Jefferson] about forty-five yards wide, the water of which has a whitish blue tinge, with a gentle current, and a gravelly bottom. This he waded and found it waist deep. He then continued down it, till at the distance of three quarters of a mile he saw the entrance of the small river he had just passed; as he went on two miles lower down, he found the mouth of the creek he had seen in the morning. Proceeding further on three miles, he arrived at the junction of this river, with another which rises from the southwest, runs through the south valley about twelve miles before it forms its junction, where it is fifty yards wide: we now found that our camp of last night was about a mile and a half above the entrance of this large river, on the right side. This is a bold, rapid, clear stream, but its bed is so much obstructed by gravelly bars, and subdivided by islands, that the navigation must be very insecure, if not impracticable. The other or middle stream, has about two-thirds its quantity of water, and is more gentle, and may be safely navigated. As far as it could be observed, its course was about southwest, but the opening of the valley induced him to believe that farther above it turned more towards the west. Its water is more turbid and warmer than that of the other branch, whence it may be presumed to have its sources at a greater distance in the mountains, and to pass through a more open country. Under this impression he left a note recommending to captain Clark the middle fork, and then continued his course along the right side of the other, or more rapid branch. After travelling twenty-three miles he arrived near a place where the river leaves the valley and enters the mountains. Here he encamped for the night.

The country he passed is like that of the rest of this valley, though there is more timber in this part on the rapid fork than there has been on the river in the same extent since we entered it; for on some parts of the valley the Indians seem to have destroyed a great proportion of the little timber there was, by setting fire to the bottoms. He saw some antelopes, deer, cranes, geese and ducks of the two species common to this country, though the summer duck has ceased to appear, nor does it seem to be an inhabitant of this part of the river.

We proceeded soon after sunrise: the first five miles we passed four bends on the left, and several bayous on both sides. At eight o'clock we stopped to breakfast, and found the note captain Lewis had written on the *2d* instant. During the next four miles, we passed three small bends of the river to the right, two small islands, and two bayous on the same side. Here we reached a bluff on the left; our next course was six miles to our encampment. In this course we met six circular bends on the right, and several small bayous, and halted for the night in a low ground of cottonwood on the right. Our day's journey, though only fifteen miles in length, was very fatiguing. The river is still rapid and the water though clear is very much obstructed by shoals or ripples at every two or three hundred yards: at all these places we are obliged to drag the canoes over the stones as there is not a sufficient depth of water to float them, and in the other parts the currents obliges us to have recourse to the cord. But as the brushwood on the banks will not permit us to walk on shore, we are under the necessity of wading through the river as we drag the boats. This soon makes our feet tender, and sometimes occasions severe falls over the slippery stones; and the men by being constantly wet are becoming more feeble. In the course of the day the hunters killed two deer, some geese and ducks, and the party saw antelopes, cranes, beaver and otter.

Monday. This morning Chaboneau complained of being unable to march far to-day, and captain Lewis therefore ordered him and sergeant Gass to

AUGUST 5TH

pass the rapid river and proceed through the level low ground, to a point of high timber on the middle fork, seven miles distant, and wait his return. He then went along the north side of the rapid river about four miles, where he waded it, and found it so rapid and shallow that it would be impossible to navigate it. He continued along the left side for a mile and a half, when the mountains came close on the river, and rise to a considerable height with a partial covering of snow. From this place the course of the river was to the east of north. After ascending with some difficulty a high point of the mountain, he had a pleasing view of the valley he had passed, and which continued for about twenty miles further on each side of the middle fork, which then seemed to enter the mountains, and was lost to the view. In that direction, however, the hills which terminate the valley are much lower than those along either of the other forks, particularly the rapid one, where they continue rising in ranges above each other as far as the eye could reach. The general course too of the middle fork, as well as that of the gap which it forms on entering the mountains, is considerably to the south of west; circumstances which gave a decided preference to this branch as our future route.

Captain Lewis now descended the mountain, and crossed over to the middle fork, about five miles distant, and found it still perfectly navigable. There is a very large and plain Indian road leading up it, but it has at present no tracks, except those of horses which seem to have used it last spring. The river here made a great bend to the southeast, and he therefore directed his course, as well as he could, to the spot where he had directed Chaboneau and Gass to repair, and struck the river about three miles above their camp. It was now dark, and he, therefore, was obliged to make his way through the thick brush of the pulpy-leafed thorn and the prickly pear, for two hours before he reached their camp. Here he was fortunate enough to find the remains of some meat, which was his only food during the march of twenty-five miles to-day. He had seen no game of any sort except a few antelopes who were very shy.

The soil of the plains is a meagre clay, of a light yellow colour, intermixed with a large proportion of gravel, and producing nothing but twisted or bearded grass, sedge and prickly pears. The drier parts of the low grounds are also more indifferent in point of soil than those further down the river, and although they have but little grass, are covered with southern wood [sage-brush], pulpy-leafed thorn, and prickly pears, while the moist parts are fertile, and supplied with fine grass and sandrushes.

We passed within the first four and a quarter miles three small islands, and the same number of bad rapids. At the distance of three quarters of a mile is another rapid of difficult passage: three miles and three quarters beyond this are the forks of the river, in reaching which we had two islands and several bayous on different sides to pass. Here we had come nine miles and a quarter. The river was straighter and more rapid than yesterday, the labour of the navigation proportionally increased, and we therefore proceeded very slowly, as the feet of several of the men were swollen, and all were languid with fatigue. We arrived at the forks about four o'clock, but unluckily captain Lewis's note had been left on a green pole which the beaver had cut down and carried off with the note, an accident which deprived us of all information as to the character of the two branches of the river. Observing therefore that the northwest fork was most in our direction, and contained as much water as the other, we ascended it; we found it extremely rapid, and its waters were scattered in such a manner, that for a quarter of a mile we were forced to cut a passage through the willowbrush that leaned over the little channels and united at the top. After going up it for a mile we encamped on an island which had been overflowed, and was still so wet that we were compelled to make beds of brush to keep ourselves out of the mud. Our provision consisted of two deer which had been killed in the morning.

Tuesday. We proceeded up the northwest fork, which we found still very rapid, and divided by several islands, while the plains near it were intersected by bayous. After passing with much difficulty over stones and rapids, we reached a bluff on the right, at the distance of nine miles, our general course south 30° west, and halted for breakfast.

AUGUST 6TH

A water mishap, as depicted in the Gass diary.

Here we were joined by Drewyer, who informed us of the state of the two rivers and of captain Lewis's note, and we immediately began to descend the river in order to take the other branch. On going down one of the canoes upset, and two others filled with water, by which all the baggage was wet, and several articles irrevocably lost. As one of them swung round in a rapid current, Whitehouse was thrown out of her, and whilst down the canoe passed over him, and had the water been two inches shallower would have crushed him to pieces; but he escaped with a severe bruise of his leg. In order to repair these misfortunes we hastened to the forks, where we were joined by captain Lewis, and then passed over to the left side opposite to the entrance of the rapid fork, and encamped on a large gravelly bar, near which there was plenty of wood. Here we opened and exposed to dry all the articles which had suffered from the water; none of them were completely spoiled except a small keg of powder; the rest of the powder, which was distributed in the different canoes was quite safe, although it had been under the water upwards of an hour. The air is indeed so pure and dry that any wood-work immediately shrinks, unless it is kept filled with water; but we had placed our powder in small canisters of lead, each containing powder enough for the canister when melted into bullets, and secured with cork and wax, which answered our purpose perfectly.

Captain Lewis had risen very early, and having nothing to eat, sent out Drewyer to the woodland on the left in search of a deer, and directed sergeant Gass to keep along the middle branch to meet us if we were ascending it. He then set off with Chaboneau towards the forks, but five miles above them, hearing us on the left, struck the river as we were descending, and came on board at the forks.

In the evening we killed three deer and four elk, which furnished us once more with a plentiful supply of meat. Shannon, the same man who was lost before for fifteen days, was sent out this morning to hunt, up the northwest fork; when we decided on returning, Drewyer was directed to go in quest of him, but he returned with information that he had gone several miles up the river without being able to find Shannon. We now had the trumpet sounded, and fired several guns, but he did not return, and we fear he is again lost.

AUGUST 7TH *Wednesday.* We remained here this morning for the purpose of making some celestial observations, and also in order to refresh the men, and complete the drying of the baggage. We obtained a meridian altitude which gave the latitude of our camp as north 45° 2′ 43.8″. We were now completely satisfied that the middle branch was the most navigable, and the true continuation of the Jefferson. The northwest fork seems to be the drain of the melting snows of the mountains, its course cannot be so long as the other branch, and although it contains now as great a quantity of water, yet the water has obviously overflowed the old bed, and spread into channels which leave the low grounds covered with young grass, resembling that of the adjoining lands, which are not inundated; whence we readily infer that the supply is more precarious than that of the other branch, the waters of which though more gentle are more constant. This northwest fork we called Wisdom river.

As soon as the baggage was dried, it was reloaded on board the boats, but we now found it so much diminished, that we would be able to proceed with one canoe less. We therefore hauled up the superfluous one into a thicket of brush where we secured her against being swept away by the high tide. At one o'clock all set out, except captain Lewis who remained till the evening in order to complete the observation of equal altitudes: we passed several bends of the river both to the right and left, as well as a number of bayous on both sides, and made seven miles by water, though the distance by land is only three. We then encamped on a creek which rises in a high mountain to the northeast, and after passing through an open plain for several miles, discharges itself on the left, where it is a bold running stream twelve yards wide. We called it Turf creek, from the number of bogs and the quantity of turf on its waters. In the course of the afternoon there fell a shower of rain attended with thunder and lightning, which lasted about forty minutes, and the weather remained so cloudy all night that we were unable to take any lunar observations. Uneasy about Shannon, we sent R. Fields in search of him this morning, but we have as yet no intelligence of either of them. Our only game to-day was one deer.

Thursday. There was a heavy dew this morning. Having left one of the canoes, there are now more men to spare for the chase: and four were sent out at an early hour, after which we proceeded. We made five miles by water along two islands and several bayous, but as the river formed seven different bends towards the left, the distance by land was only two miles south of our encampment. At the end of that course we reached the upper principal entrance of a stream which we called Philanthropy river. This river empties itself into the Jefferson on the southeast side, by two channels a short distance from each other: from its size and its southeastern course, we presume that it rises in the Rocky mountains near the sources of the Madison. It is thirty yards wide at its entrance, has a very gentle current, and is navigable for some distance. One mile above this river we passed an island, a second at the distance of six miles further, during which the river makes a considerable bend to the east. Reuben Fields returned about noon with information that he had gone up Wisdom river till its entrance into the mountains, but could find nothing of Shannon. We made seven miles beyond the last island, and after passing some small bayous, encamped under a few high trees on the left, at the distance of fourteen miles above Philanthropy river by water, though only six by land.

The river has in fact become so very crooked that although by means of the pole which we now use constantly we make a considerable distance, yet being obliged to follow its windings, at the end of the day, we find ourselves very little advanced on our general course. It forms itself into smaller circular bends, which are so numerous that within the last fourteen miles we passed thirty-five of them, all inclining towards the right; it is however much more gentle and deep than below Wisdom river, and its general width is from thirty-five to forty-five yards. The general appearance of the surrounding country is that of a valley five or six miles wide, enclosed between two high mountains. The bottom is rich, with some small timber on the islands and along the river, which consists rather of underbrush, and a few cottonwood, birch, and willow-trees. The high grounds have some scattered pine, which just relieve the general nakedness of the hills and the plain, where there is nothing except grass. Along the bottoms we saw to-day a considerable quantity of the buffalo clover, the sunflower, flax, green sward, thistle and several species of rye grass, some of which rise to the height of three or four feet. There is also a grass with a soft smooth leaf which rises about three feet high, and bears its seed very much like the timothy, but it does not grow luxuriantly nor would it apparently answer so well in our meadows as that plant. We preserved some of its seed, which are now ripe, in order to make the experiment. Our game consisted of deer and antelope, and we saw a number of geese and ducks just beginning to fly, and some cranes. Among the inferior animals we have an abundance of the large biting or hare fly, of which there are two species, one black, the other smaller and brown, except the head which is green. The green or blowing flies unite with them in swarms to attack us, and seem to have relieved the eye-gnats who have now disappeared. The mosquitoes too are in large quantities, but not so troublesome as they were below. Through the valley are scattered bogs, and some very good turf, the earth of which the mud is composed is of a white or bluish white colour, and seems to be argillaceous. On all the three rivers, but particularly on the Philanthropy, are immense quantities of beaver, otter and muskrat. At our camp there was an abundance of rosebushes and briars, but so little timber that we were obliged to use willow brush for fuel. The night was again cloudy which prevented the lunar observations.

On our right is the point of a high plain, which our Indian woman recognizes as the place called the Beaver's-head from a supposed resemblance to that object. This she says is not far from the summer retreat of her countrymen, which is on a river beyond the mountains, and running to the west. She is therefore certain that we shall meet them either on this river, or on that immediately west of its source, which judging from its present size, cannot be far distant. Persuaded of the absolute necessity of procuring horses to cross the mountains, it was determined that one of us should proceed in the morning to the head of the river, and penetrate the mountains till he found the Shoshonees or some other nation who could assist us in transporting our baggage, the greater part of which we shall be compelled to leave without the aid of horses.

AUGUST 9TH

Friday. The morning was fair and fine. We set off early, and proceeded on very well, though there were more rapids in the river than yesterday. At eight o'clock we halted for breakfast, part of which consisted of two fine geese killed before we stopped.

Here we were joined by Shannon for whose safety we had been so uneasy. The day on which he left us on his way up Wisdom river, after hunting for some time and not seeing the party arrive, he returned to the place where he had left us. Not finding us there he supposed we had passed him, and he therefore marched up the river during all the next day, when he was convinced that we had not gone on, as the river was no longer navigable. He now followed the course of the river down to the forks, and then took the branch which we are pursuing. During the three days of his absence, he had been much wearied with his march, but had lived plentifully, and brought the skins of three deer. As far as he had ascended Wisdom river it kept its course obliquely down towards the Jefferson.

Immediately after breakfast, captain Lewis took Drewyer, Shields and M'Neal, and slinging their knapsacks they set out with a resolution to meet some nation of Indians before they returned, however long they might be separated from the party. He directed his course across the low ground to the plain on the right, leaving the Beaver's-head about two miles to the left. After walking eight miles to the river, which they waded, they went on to a commanding point from which he saw the place at which it enters the mountain, but as the distance would not permit his reaching it this evening, he descended towards the river, and after travelling eight miles further, encamped for the evening some miles below the mountain. They passed before reaching their camp a handsome little stream formed by some large springs which rise in the wide bottom on the left side of the river. In their way they killed two antelopes, and took with them enough of the meat for their supper and breakfast the next morning.

In the meantime we proceeded, and in the course of eleven miles from our last encampment passed two small islands, sixteen short round bends in the river, and halted in a bend towards the right where we dined. The river increases in rapidity as we advance, and is so crooked that the eleven miles, which have cost us so much labour, only bring us four miles in a direct line. The weather became overcast towards evening, and we experienced a slight shower attended with thunder and lightning. The three hunters who were sent out killed only two antelopes; game of every kind being scarce.

Saturday. Captain Lewis continued his route at an early hour through the wide bottom along the left bank of the river. At about five miles he passed a large creek, and then fell into an Indian road leading towards the point where the river entered the mountain. This he followed till he reached a high perpendicular cliff of rocks where the river makes its passage through the hills, and which he called the Rattlesnake cliff, from the number of that animal which he saw there: here he kindled a fire and waited the return of Drewyer, who had been sent out on the way to kill a deer: he came back about noon with the skin of three deer and the flesh of one of the best of them. After a hasty dinner they returned to the Indian road which they had left for a short distance to see the cliff. It led them sometimes over the hills, sometimes in the narrow bottoms of the river, till at the distance of fifteen miles from the Rattlesnake cliffs they reached a handsome open and level valley, where the river divided into two nearly equal branches.

AUGUST 10TH

The mountains over which they passed were not very high, but are rugged and continue close to the river side. The river, which before it enters the mountain was rapid, rocky, very crooked, much divided by islands, and shallow, now becomes more direct in its course as it is hemmed in by the hills, and has not so many bends nor islands, but becomes more rapid and rocky, and continues as shallow. On examining the two branches of the river it was evident that neither of them was navigable further. The road forked with the river; and captain Lewis therefore sent a man up each of them for a short distance, in order that by comparing their respective information he might be able to take that which seemed to have been most used this spring. From their account he resolved to choose that which led along the southwest branch of the river which was rather the smaller of the two: he accordingly wrote a note to captain Clark informing him of the route, and recommending his staying with the party at the forks till he should return: This he fixed on a dry willow pole at the forks of the river, and then proceeded up the southwest branch; but after going a mile and a half the road became scarcely distinguishable, and the tracks of the horses which he had followed along the Jefferson were no longer seen. Captain Lewis therefore returned to examine the other road himself, and found that the horses had in fact passed along the western or right fork which had the additional recommendation of being larger than the other.

This road he concluded to take, and therefore sent back Drewyer to the forks with a second letter to captain Clark apprising him of the change, and then proceeded on. The valley of the west fork through which he now passed, bears a little to the north of west, and is confined within the space of about a mile in width, by rough mountains and steep cliffs of rock. At the distance of four and a half miles it opens into a beautiful and extensive plain about ten miles long and five or six in width: this is surrounded on all sides by higher rolling or waving country, intersected by several little rivulets from the mountains, each bordered by its wide meadows. The whole prospect is bounded by these mountains, which nearly surround it, so as to form a beautiful cove about sixteen or eighteen miles in diameter. On entering this cove the river bends to the northwest, and bathes the foot of the hills to the right. At this place they halted for the night on the right side of the river, and having lighted a fire of dry willow brush, the only fuel which the country affords, supped on a deer. They had travelled to-day thirty miles by estimate: that is ten to the Rattlesnake cliff, fifteen to the forks of Jefferson river, and five to their encampment.

In this cove some parts of the low grounds are tolerably fertile, but much the greater proportion is covered with prickly pear, sedge, twisted grass, the pulpy-leafed thorn, southern-wood, and wild sage, and like the uplands have a very inferior soil. These last have little more than the prickly pear and the twisted or bearded grass, nor are there in the whole cove more than three or four cottonwood trees, and those are small. At the apparent extremity of the bottom above, and about ten miles to the westward, are two perpendicular cliffs rising to a considerable height on each side of the river, and at this distance seem like a gate.

In the meantime we proceeded at sunrise, and found the river not so rapid as yesterday, though more narrow and still very crooked, and so shallow that we were obliged to drag the canoes over many ripples in the course of the day. At six and a half miles we had passed eight bends on the north, and two small bayous on the left, and came to what the Indians call the Beaver's head, a steep rocky cliff about one hundred and fifty feet high, near the right side of the river. Opposite to this at three hundred yards from the water is a low cliff about fifty feet in height, which forms the extremity of a spur of the mountain about four miles distant on the left. At four o'clock we were overtaken by a heavy shower of rain, attended with thunder, lightning and hail. The party were defended from the hail by covering themselves with willow bushes, but they got completely wet, and in this situation, as soon as the rain ceased, continued till we encamped. This we did at a low bluff on the left, after passing in the course of six and a half miles, four islands and eighteen bends on the right, and a low bluff and several bayous on the same side. We had now come thirteen miles, yet were only four on our route towards the mountains. The game seems to be declining, for our hunters procured only a single deer, though we found another for us that had been killed three days before by one of the hunters during an excursion, and left for us on the river.

Chapter 14
FROM BEAVER'S HEAD TO THE GREAT DIVIDE

SUNDAY, AUGUST 11TH, 1805   Captain Lewis again proceeded on early, but had the mortification to find that the track which he followed yesterday soon disappeared. He determined therefore to go on to the narrow gate or pass of the river which he had seen from the camp, in hopes of being able to recover the Indian path. For this purpose he waded across the river, which was now about twelve yards wide, and barred in several places by the dams of the beaver, and then went straight forward to the pass, sending one man along the river to his left, and another on the right, with orders to search for the road, and if they found it to let him know by raising a hat on the muzzle of their guns.

In this order they went along for about five miles, when captain Lewis perceived with the greatest delight a man on horseback at the distance of two miles coming down the plain towards them. On examining him with the glass, captain Lewis saw that he was of a different nation from any Indians we had hitherto met: he was armed with a bow and a quiver of arrows; mounted on an elegant horse without a saddle, and a small string attached to the under jaw answered as a bridle. Convinced that he was a Shoshonee, and knowing how much of our success depended on the friendly offices of that nation, captain Lewis was full of anxiety to approach without alarming him, and endeavour to convince him that he was a white man. He therefore, proceeded on towards the Indian at his usual pace, when they were within a mile of each other the Indian suddenly stopped, captain Lewis immediately followed his example, took his blanket from his knapsack, and holding it with both hands at the two corners, threw it above his head and unfolded it as he brought it to the ground as if in the act of spreading it. This signal which originates in the practice of spreading a robe or a skin, as a seat for guests to whom they wish to show a distinguished kindness, is the universal sign of friendship among the Indians on the Missouri and the Rocky mountains. As usual, captain Lewis repeated this signal three times: still the Indian kept his position, and looked with an air of suspicion on Drewyer and Shields who were now advancing on each side.

Captain Lewis was afraid to make any signal for them to halt, lest he should increase the suspicions of the Indian, who began to be uneasy, and they were too distant to hear his voice. He, therefore, took from his pack some beads, a looking-glass and a few trinkets, which he had brought for the purpose, and leaving his gun advanced unarmed towards the Indian. He remained in the same position till captain Lewis came within two hundred yards of him, when he turned his horse, and began to move off slowly; captain Lewis then called out to him, in as loud a voice as he could, repeating the word, "tabba bone!" which in the Shoshonee language means white man; but looking over his shoulder the Indian kept his eyes on Drewyer and Shields, who were still advancing, without recollecting the impropriety of doing so at such a moment, till captain Lewis made a signal to them to halt: this Drewyer obeyed, but Shields did not observe it, and still went forward: seeing Drewyer halt the Indian turned his horse about as if to wait for captain Lewis who now reached within one hundred and fifty paces, repeating the word "tabba bone," and holding up the trinkets in his hand, at the same time stripping up the sleeve of his shirt to show the colour of his skin. The Indian suffered him to advance within one hundred paces, then suddenly turned his horse, and giving him the whip, leaped across the creek and disappeared in an instant among the willow bushes: with him vanished all the hopes which the sight of him had inspired of a friendly introduction to his countrymen.

Though sadly disappointed by the imprudence of his two men, captain Lewis determined to make the incident of some use, and therefore calling the men to him they all set off after the track of the horse, which they hoped might lead them to the camp of the Indian who had fled, or if he had given the alarm to any small party, their track might conduct them to the body of the nation. They now fixed a small flag of the United States on a pole, which was carried by one of the men as a signal of their friendly intentions, should the Indians observe them as they were advancing. The route lay across an island formed by a nearly equal division of the creek in the bottom: after reaching the open grounds on the right side of the creek, the track turned towards some high hills about three miles distant. Presuming that the Indian camp might be among these hills, and that by advancing hastily he might be seen and alarm them, captain Lewis sought an elevated situation near the creek, had a fire made of willow brush, and took breakfast. At the same time he prepared a small assortment of beads, trinkets, awls, some paint and a looking glass, and placed them on a pole near the fire, in order that if the Indians returned they might discover that the party were white men and friends. Whilst making these preparations a very heavy shower of rain and hail came on, and wet them to the skin: in about twenty minutes it was over, and captain Lewis then renewed his pursuit, but as the rain had made the grass which the horse had trodden down rise again, his track could with difficulty be distinguished. As they went along they passed several places where the Indians seemed to have been digging roots to-day, and saw the fresh track of eight or ten horses, but they had been wandering about in so confused a manner that he could not discern any particular path, and at last, after pursuing it about four miles along the valley to the left under the foot of the hills, he lost the track of the fugitive Indian. Near the head of the valley they had passed a large bog covered with moss and tall grass, among which were several springs of pure cold water: they now turned a little to the left along the foot of the high hills, and reached a small creek where they encamped for the night, having made about twenty miles, though not more than ten in a direct line from their camp of last evening.

AUGUST 11TH   The morning being rainy and wet we did not set out with the canoes till after an early breakfast. During the first three miles we passed three small islands, six bayous on different sides of the river, and the same number of bends towards the right. Here we reached the lower point of a large island which we called Three-thousand-mile island, on account of its being at that distance from the mouth of the Missouri. It is three miles and a half in length, and as we coasted along it we passed several small bends of the river towards the left, and two bayous on the same side. After leaving the upper point of Three-thousand-mile island, we followed the main channel on the left side, which led us by three small islands and several small bayous, and fifteen bends towards the right. Then at the distance of seven miles and a half we encamped on the upper end of a large island near the right. The river was shallow and rapid, so that we were obliged to be in the water during a

WOMAN OF THE SNAKE TRIBE (Bodmer)

great part of the day, dragging the canoes over the shoals and ripples. Its course too was so crooked, that notwithstanding we had made fourteen miles by water, we were only five miles from our encampment of last night.

The country consists of a low ground on the river about five miles wide, and succeeded on both sides by plains of the same extent which reach to the base of the mountains. These low grounds are very much intersected by bayous, and in those on the left side is a large proportion of bog covered with tall grass, which would yield a fine turf. There are very few trees, and those small narrow-leafed cottonwood: the principal growth being the narrow-leafed willow, and currant bushes, among which were some bunches of privet near the river. We saw a number of geese, ducks, beaver, otter, deer and antelopes, of all which one beaver was killed with a pole from the boat, three otters with a tomahawk, and the hunters brought in three deer and an antelope.

Monday. This morning as soon as it was light captain Lewis sent Drewyer to reconnoitre if possible the route of the Indians: in about an hour and a half he returned, after following the tracks of the horse which we had lost yesterday to the mountains, where they ascended and were no longer visible. Captain Lewis now decided on making the circuit along the foot of the mountains which formed the cove, expecting by that means to find a road across them, and accordingly sent Drewyer on one side, and Shields on the other. In this way they crossed four small rivulets near each other, on which were some bowers or conical lodges of willow brush, which seemed to have been made recently. From the manner in which the ground in the neighbourhood was torn up the Indians appeared to have been gathering roots; but captain Lewis could not discover what particular plant they were searching for, nor could he find any fresh track, till at the distance of four miles from his camp he met a large plain Indian road which came into the cove from the northeast, and wound along the foot of the mountains to the southwest, approaching obliquely the main stream he had left yesterday. Down this road he now went towards the southwest: at the distance of five miles it crossed a large run or creek, which is a principal branch of the main stream into which it falls, just above the high cliffs or gates observed yesterday, and which they now saw below them.

AUGUST 12TH

Here they halted and breakfasted on the last of the deer, keeping a small piece of pork in reserve against accident: they then continued through the low bottom along the main stream near the foot of the mountains on their right. For the first five miles the valley continues towards the southwest from two to three miles in width; then the main stream, which had received two small branches from the left in the valley, turns abruptly to the west through a narrow bottom between the mountains. The road was still plain, and as it led them directly on towards the mountain the stream gradually became smaller, till after going two miles it had so greatly diminished in width that one of the men in a fit of enthusiasm, with one foot on each side of the river, thanked God that he had lived to bestride the Missouri. As they went along their hopes of soon seeing the waters of the Columbia arose almost to painful anxiety, when after four miles from the last abrupt turn of the river, they reached a small gap formed by the high mountains which recede on each side, leaving room for the Indian road. From the foot of one of the lowest of these mountains, which rises with a gentle ascent of about half a mile, issues the remotest water of the Missouri.

They had now reached the hidden sources of that river, which had never yet been seen by civilized man; and as they quenched their thirst at the chaste and icy fountain—as they sat down by the brink of that little rivulet, which yielded its distant and modest tribute to the parent ocean, they felt themselves rewarded for all their labours and all their difficulties.

They left reluctantly this interesting spot, and pursuing the Indian road through the interval of the hills, arrived at the top of a ridge, from which they saw high mountains partially covered with snow still to the west of them. The ridge on which they stood formed the dividing line between the waters of the Atlantic and Pacific oceans.

They followed a descent much steeper than that on the eastern side, and at the distance of three quarters of a mile reached a handsome bold creek of cold clear water running to the westward. They stopped to taste for the first time the waters of the Columbia; and after a few minutes followed the road across steep hills and low hollows, till they reached a spring on the side of a mountain: here they found a sufficient quantity of dry willow brush for fuel, and therefore halted for the night; and having killed nothing in the course of the day supped on their last piece of pork, and trusted to fortune for some other food to mix with a little flour and parched meal, which was all that now remained of their provisions.

Before reaching the fountain of the Missouri they saw several large hawks nearly black, and some of the heath cocks: these last have a long pointed tail, and are of a uniform dark brown colour, much larger than the common dunghill fowl, and similar in habits and the mode of flying to the grouse or prairie hen. Drewyer also wounded at the distance of one hundred and thirty yards an animal which we had not yet seen, but which after falling recovered itself and escaped. It seemed to be of the fox kind, rather larger than the small wolf of the plains, and with a skin in which black, reddish brown, and yellow, were curiously intermixed.

On the creek of the Columbia they found a species of currant which does not grow as high as that of the Missouri, though it is more branching, and its leaf, the under disk of which is covered with a hairy pubescence, is twice as large. The fruit is of the ordinary size and shape of the currant, and supported in the usual manner, but is of a deep purple colour, acid, and of a very inferior flavour.

We proceeded on in the boats, but as the river was very shallow and rapid, the navigation is extremely difficult, and the men who are almost constantly in the water are getting feeble and sore, and so much wore down by fatigue that they are very anxious to commence travelling by land. We went along the main channel which is on the right side, and after passing nine bends in that direction, three islands and a number of bayous, reached at the distance of five and a half miles the upper point of a large island. At noon there was a storm of thunder which continued about half an hour; after which we proceeded, but as it was necessary to drag the canoes over the shoals and rapids, made but little progress. On leaving the island we passed a number of short bends, several bayous, and one run of water on the right side, and having gone by four small and two large islands, encamped on a smooth plain to the left near a few cottonwood trees: our journey by water was just twelve miles, and four in a direct line. The hunters supplied us with three deer and a fawn.

Tuesday. Very early in the morning captain Lewis resumed the Indian road, which led him in a western direction, through an open broken country; on the left was a deep valley at the foot of a high range of mountains running from southeast to northwest, with their sides better clad with timber than the hills to which we have been for some time accustomed, and their tops covered in part with snow. At five miles distance, after following the long descent of another valley, he reached a creek about ten yards wide, and on rising the hill beyond it had a view of a handsome little valley on the left, about a mile in width, through which they judged, from the appearance of the timber, that some stream of water most probably passed.

AUGUST 13TH

On the creek they had just left were some bushes of the white maple, the sumach of the small species with the winged rib, and a species of honey-suckle, resembling in its general appearance and the shape of its leaf the small honeysuckle of the Missouri, except that it is rather larger, and bears a globular berry, about the size of a garden pea, of a white colour, and formed of a soft white mucilaginous substance, in which are several small brown seeds irregularly scattered without any cell, and enveloped in a smooth thin pellicle.

They proceeded along a waving plain parallel to this valley for about four miles, when they discovered two women, a man and some dogs on an eminence at the distance of a mile before them. The strangers first viewed them apparently with much attention for a few minutes, and then two of them sat down as if to await captain Lewis's arrival. He went on till he reached within about half a mile, then ordered his party to stop, put down his knapsack and rifle, and unfurling the flag advanced alone towards the Indians. The females soon retreated behind the hill, but the man remained till captain Lewis came within a hundred yards from him, when he too went off, though captain Lewis called out "tabba bone!" loud enough to be heard distinctly. He hastened to the top of the hill, but they had all disappeared. The dogs however were less shy, and came close to him; he therefore thought of tying a handkerchief with some beads round their necks, and then let them loose to convince the fugitives of his friendly disposition, but they would not suffer him to take hold of them, and soon left him. He now made a signal to the men, who joined him, and then all followed the track of the Indians, which led along a continuation of the same road they had been already travelling. It was dusty and seemed to have been much used lately both by foot passengers and horsemen.

They had not gone along it more than a mile when on a sudden they saw three female Indians, from whom they had been concealed by the deep ravines which intersected the road, till they were now within thirty paces of each other; one of them a young woman immediately took to flight, the other two, an elderly woman and a little girl, seeing we were too near for them to escape, sat on the ground, and holding down their heads seemed as if reconciled to the death which they supposed awaited them. The same habit of holding down the head and inviting the enemy to strike, when all chance of escape is gone, is preserved in Egypt to this day.

Captain Lewis instantly put down his rifle, and advancing towards them, took the woman by the hand, raised her up, and repeated the word "tabba bone!" at the same time stripping up his shirt sleeve to prove that he was a white man, for his hands and face had become by constant exposure quite as dark as their own. She appeared immediately relieved from her alarm, and Drewyer and Shields now coming up, captain Lewis gave them some beads, a few awls, pewter mirrors, and a little paint, and told Drewyer to request the woman to recall her companion who had escaped to some distance, and by alarming the Indians might cause them to attack him without any time for explanation. She did as she was desired, and the young woman returned almost out of breath: captain Lewis gave her an equal portion of trinkets, and painted the tawny checks of all three of them with vermillion, a ceremony which among the Shoshonees is emblematic of peace.

After they had become composed, he informed them by signs of his wish to go to their camp in order to see their chiefs and warriors; they readily obeyed, and conducted the party along the same road down the river. In this way they marched two miles, when they met a troop of nearly sixty warriors mounted on excellent horses riding at full speed towards them. As they advanced captain Lewis put down his gun, and went with the flag about fifty paces in advance. The chief who with two men were riding in front of the main body, spoke to the women, who now explained that the party was composed of white men, and showed exultingly the presents they had received. The three men immediately leaped from their horses, came up to captain Lewis and embraced him with great cordiality, putting their left arm over his right shoulder and clasping his back, applying at the same time their left cheek to his, and frequently vociferating "ah hi e! ah hi e!—I am much pleased! I am much rejoiced!" The whole body of warriors now came forward, and our men received the caresses, and no small share of the grease and paint of their new friends. After this fraternal embrace, of which the motive was much more agreeable than the manner, captain Lewis lighted a pipe and offered it to the Indians who had now seated themselves in a circle around the party. But before they would receive this mark of friendship they pulled off their moccasins, a custom as we afterwards learnt, which indicates the sacred sincerity of their professions when they smoke with a stranger, and which imprecates on themselves the misery of going barefoot forever if they are faithless to their words, a penalty by no means light to those who rove over the thorny plains of their country.

It is not unworthy to remark the analogy which some of the customs of those wild children of the wilderness bear to those recorded in holy writ. Moses is admonished to pull off his shoes, for the place on which he stood was holy ground. Why this was enjoined as an act of peculiar reverence; whether it was from the circumstance that in the arid region in which the patriarch then resided, it was deemed a test of the sincerity of devotion to walk upon the burning sands barefooted, in some measure analogous to the pains inflicted by the prickly pear, does not appear.

After smoking a few pipes, some trifling presents were distributed amongst them, with which they seemed very much pleased, particularly with the blue beads and the vermillion. Captain Lewis then informed the chief that the object of his visit was friendly, and should be explained as soon as he reached their camp; but that in the meantime as the sun was oppressive, and no water near, he wished to go there as soon as possible. They now put on their moccasins, and their chief, whose name was Cameahwait, made a short speech to the warriors. Captain Lewis then gave him the flag, which he informed him was among white men the emblem of peace, and now that he had received it was to be in future the bond of union between them. The chief then moved on, our party followed him, and the rest of the warriors in a squadron, brought up the rear. After marching a mile they were halted by the chief, who made a second harangue, on which six or eight young men rode forward to their camp, and no further regularity was observed in the order of march. At the distance of four miles from where they had first met, they reached the Indian camp, which was in a handsome level meadow on the bank of the river.

Here they were introduced into an old leathern lodge which the young men who had been sent from the party had fitted up for their reception. After being seated on green boughs and antelope skins, one of the warriors pulled up the grass in the centre of the lodge so as to form a vacant circle of two feet diameter, in which he kindled a fire. The chief then produced his pipe and tobacco, the warriors all pulled off their moccasins, and our party was requested to take off their own. This being done, the chief lighted his pipe at the fire within the magic circle, and then retreating from it began a speech several minutes long, at the end of which he pointed the stem towards the four cardinal points of the heavens, beginning with the east and concluding with the north. After this ceremony he presented the stem in the same way to captain Lewis, who supposing it an invitation to smoke, put out his hand to receive the pipe, but the chief drew it back, and continued to repeat the same offer three times, after which he pointed the stem first to the heavens, then to the centre of the little circle, took three whiffs himself, and presented it again to captain Lewis. Finding that this last offer was in good earnest, he smoked a little, the pipe was then held to each of the white men, and after they had taken a few whiffs was given to the warriors.

This pipe was made of a dense transparent green stone, very highly polished, about two and half inches long, and of an oval figure, the bowl being in the same situation with the stem. A small piece of burnt clay is placed in the bottom of the bowl to separate the tobacco from the end of the stem, and is of an irregularly round figure, not fitting the tube perfectly close, in order that the smoke may pass with facility. The tobacco is of the same kind with that used by the Minnetarees, Mandans and Ricaras of the Missouri. The Shoshonees do not cultivate this plant, but obtain it from the Rocky mountain Indians, and some of the bands of their own nation who live further south.

The ceremony of smoking being concluded, captain Lewis explained to the chief the purposes of his visit, and as by this time all the women and children of the camp had gathered around the lodge to indulge in a view of the first white men they had ever seen, he distributed among them the remainder of the small articles he had brought with him.

It was now late in the afternoon, and our party had tasted no food since the night before. On apprising the chief of this circumstance, he said that he had nothing but berries to eat, and presented some cakes made of serviceberry and chokecherries which had been dried in the sun. On these captain Lewis made a hearty meal, and then walked down towards the river: he found it a rapid clear stream forty yards wide and three feet deep;

the banks were low and abrupt, like those of the upper part of the Missouri, and the bed formed of loose stones and gravel. Its course, as far as he could observe it, was a little to the north of west, and was bounded on each side by a range of high mountains, of which those on the east are the lowest and most distant from the river.

The chief informed him that this stream discharged itself at the distance of half a day's march, into another of twice its size, coming from the southwest; but added, on further inquiry, that there was scarcely more timber below the junction of those rivers than in this neighbourhood, and that the river was rocky, rapid, and so closely confined between high mountains, that it was impossible to pass down it, either by land or water to the great lake, where as he had understood the white men lived.

This information was far from being satisfactory; for there was no timber here that would answer the purpose of building canoes, indeed not more than just sufficient for fuel, and even that consisted of the narrow-leafed cottonwood, the red and the narrow-leafed willow, the chokecherry, serviceberry and a few currant bushes such as are common on the Missouri. The prospect of going on by land is more pleasant; for there are great numbers of horses feeding in every direction round the camp, which will enable us to transport our stores if necessary over the mountains. Captain Lewis returned from the river to his lodge, and on his way an Indian invited him into his bower and gave him a small morsel of boiled antelope and a piece of fresh salmon roasted. This was the first salmon he had seen, and perfectly satisfied him that he was now on the waters of the Pacific. On reaching this lodge, he resumed his conversation with the chief, after which he was entertained with a dance by the Indians.

It now proved, as our party had feared, that the men whom they had first met this morning had returned to the camp and spread the alarm that their enemies, the Minnetarees of fort de Prairie, whom they call Pahkees, were advancing on them. The warriors instantly armed themselves and were coming down in expectation of an attack, when they were agreeably surprised by meeting our party. The greater part of them were armed with bows and arrows, and shields, but a few had small fusils, such as are furnished by the Northwest company traders, and which they had obtained from the Indians on the Yellowstone, with whom they are now at peace. They had reason to dread the approach of the Pahkees, who had attacked them in the course of this spring and totally defeated them. On this occasion twenty of their warriors were either killed or made prisoners, and they lost their whole camp except the leathern lodge which they had fitted up for us, and were now obliged to live in huts of a conical figure made with willow brush. The music and dancing, which was in no respect different from those of the Missouri Indians, continued nearly all night; but captain Lewis retired to rest about twelve o'clock, when the fatigues of the day enabled him to sleep though he was awaked several times by the yells of the dancers.

Whilst all these things were occurring to captain Lewis we were slowly and laboriously ascending the river. For the first two and a half miles we went along the island opposite to which we encamped last evening, and soon reached a second island behind which comes in a small creek on the left side of the river. It rises in the mountains to the east and forms a handsome valley for some miles from its mouth, where it is a bold running stream about seven yards wide: we called it M'Neal's creek, after Hugh M'Neal one of our party. Just above this stream and at the distance of four miles from our camp is a point of limestone rock on the right, about seventy feet high, forming a cliff over the river. From the top of it the Beaver's-head bore north 24° east twelve miles distant, the course of Wisdom river, that is the direction of its valley through the mountains is north 25° west, while the gap through which the Jefferson enters the mountains is ten miles above us on a course south 18° west. From this limestone rock we proceeded along several islands, on both sides, and after making twelve miles arrived at a cliff of high rocks on the right, opposite to which we encamped in a smooth level prairie, near a few cottonwood trees; but were obliged to use the dry willow brush for fuel. The river is still very crooked, the bends short and abrupt, and obstructed by so many shoals, over which the canoes were to be dragged, that the men were in the water three-fourths of the day. They saw numbers of otter, some beaver, antelopes, ducks, geese, and cranes, but they killed nothing except a single deer. They, however, caught some very fine trout, as they have done for several days past. The weather had been cloudy and cool during the forepart of the day, and at eight o'clock a shower of rain fell.

Wednesday. In order to give time for the boats to reach the forks of Jefferson river, captain Lewis determined to remain here and obtain all the information he could collect with regard to the country. Having nothing to eat but a little flour and parched meal, with the berries of the Indians, he sent out Drewyer and Shields, who borrowed horses from the natives, to hunt for a few hours. About the same time the young warriors set out for the same purpose. There are but few elk or blacktailed deer in this neighbourhood, and as the common red-deer secrete themselves in the bushes when alarmed, they are soon safe from the arrows, which are but feeble weapons against any animals which the huntsmen cannot previously run down with their horses. The chief game of the Shoshonees, therefore, is the antelope, which when pursued retreats to the open plains, where the horses have full room for the chase. But such is its extraordinary fleetness and wind that a single horse has no possible chance of outrunning it, or tiring it down; and the hunters are therefore obliged to resort to stratagem. About twenty Indians, mounted on fine horses, and armed with bows and arrows, left the camp; in a short time they descried a herd of ten antelopes: they immediately separated into little squads of two or three, and formed a scattered circle round the herd for five or six miles, keeping at a wary distance, so as not to alarm them till they were perfectly enclosed, and usually selecting some commanding eminence as a stand. Having gained their positions, a small party rode towards the herd, and with wonderful dexterity the huntsman preserved his seat, and the horse his footing, as he ran at full speed over the hills, and down the steep ravines, and along the borders of the precipices. They were soon outstripped by the antelopes, which on gaining the other extremity of the circle were driven back and pursued by the fresh hunters. They turned and flew, rather than ran in another direction; but there too, they found new enemies. In this way they were alternately pursued backwards and forwards, till at length, notwithstanding the skill of the hunters, they all escaped, and the party after running for two hours returned without

AUGUST 14TH

having caught any thing, and their horses foaming with sweat. This chase, the greater part of which was seen from the camp, formed a beautiful scene; but to the hunters is exceedingly laborious, and so unproductive, even when they are able to worry the animal down and shoot him, that forty or fifty hunters will sometimes be engaged for half a day without obtaining more than two or three antelopes.

Soon after they returned, our two huntsmen came in with no better success. Captain Lewis therefore made a little paste with the flour, and the addition of some berries formed a very palatable repast. Having now secured the good will of Cameahwait, captain Lewis informed him of his wish that he would speak to the warriors and endeavour to engage them to accompany him to the forks of Jefferson river, where by this time another chief with a large party of white men were waiting his return: that it would be necessary to take about thirty horses to transport the merchandise; that they should be well rewarded for their trouble; and that when all the party should have reached the Shoshonee camp they would remain some time among them, and trade for horses, as well as concert plans for furnishing them in future with regular supplies of merchandise. He readily consented to do so, and after collecting the tribe together he made a long harangue, and in about an hour and a half returned, and told captain Lewis that they would be ready to accompany him in the morning.

As the early part of the day was cold, and the men stiff and sore from the fatigues of yesterday: we did not set out till seven o'clock. At the distance of a mile we passed a bold stream on the right, which comes from a snowy mountain to the north, and at its entrance is four yards wide, and three feet in depth: we called it Track creek: at six miles further we reached another stream which heads in some springs at the foot of the mountains on the left. After passing a number of bayous and small islands on each side, we encamped about half a mile by land below the Rattlesnake cliffs. The river was cold, shallow, and as it approached the mountains formed one continued rapid, over which we were obliged to drag the boats with great labour and difficulty. By using constant exertions we succeeded in making fourteen miles, but this distance did not carry us more than six and a half in a straight line: several of the men have received wounds and lamed themselves in hauling the boats over the stones. The hunters supplied them with five deer and an antelope.

AUGUST 15TH *Thursday.* Captain Lewis rose early, and having eaten nothing yesterday except his scanty meal of flour and berries felt the inconveniences of extreme hunger. On inquiry he found that his whole stock of provisions consisted of two pounds of flour. This he ordered to be divided into two equal parts, and one half of it boiled with the berries into a sort of pudding: and after presenting a large share to the chief, he and his three men breakfasted on the remainder. Cameahwait was delighted at this new dish: he took a little of the flour in his hand, tasted and examined it very narrowly, asking if it was made of roots; captain Lewis explained the process of preparing it, and he said it was the best thing he had eaten for a long time.

This being finished, captain Lewis now endeavoured to hasten the departure of the Indians who still hesitated, and seemed reluctant to move, although the chief addressed them twice for the purpose of urging them: on inquiring the reason, Cameahwait told him that some foolish person had suggested that he was in league with their enemies the Pahkees, and had come only to draw them into ambuscade, but that he himself did not believe it: captain Lewis felt uneasy at this insinuation: he knew the suspicious temper of the Indians, accustomed from their infancy to regard every stranger as an enemy, and saw that if this suggestion were not instantly checked, it might hazard the total failure of the enterprise. Assuming therefore a serious air, he told the chief that he was sorry to find they placed so little confidence in him, but that he pardoned their suspicions because they were ignorant of the character of white men, among whom it was disgraceful to lie or entrap even an enemy by falsehood; that if they continued to think thus meanly of us they might be assured no white men would ever come to supply them with arms and merchandise; that there was at this moment a party of white men waiting to trade with them at the forks of the river; and that if the greater part of the tribe entertained any suspicion, he hoped there were still among them some who were men, who would go and see with their own eyes the truth of what he said, and who, even if there was any danger, were not afraid to die. To doubt the courage of an Indian is to touch the tenderest string of his mind, and the surest way to rouse him to any dangerous achievement. Cameahwait instantly replied, that he was not afraid to die, and mounting his horse, for the third time harangued the warriors: he told them that he was resolved to go if he went alone, or if he were sure of perishing; that he hoped there were among those who heard him some who were not afraid to die, and who would prove it by mounting their horses and following him. This harangue produced an effect on six or eight only of the warriors, who now joined their chief. With these captain Lewis smoked a pipe, and then fearful of some change in their capricious temper set out immediately.

It was about twelve o'clock when his small party left the camp, attended by Cameahwait and the eight warriors: their departure seemed to spread a gloom over the village; those who would not venture to go were sullen and melancholy, and the women were crying and imploring the Great Spirit to protect their warriors as if they were going to certain destruction: yet such is the wavering inconstancy of these savages, that captain Lewis's party had not gone far when they were joined by ten or twelve more warriors, and before reaching the creek which they had passed on the morning of the *13th*, all the men of the nation and a number of women had overtaken them, and had changed from the surly ill temper in which they were two hours ago, to the greatest cheerfulness and gaiety. When they arrived at the spring on the side of the mountain where the party had encamped on the *12th*, the chief insisted on halting to let the horses graze; to which captain Lewis assented and smoked with them. They are excessively fond of the pipe, in which however they are not able to indulge much as they do not cultivate tobacco themselves, and their rugged country affords them but few articles to exchange for it. Here they remained for about an hour, and on setting out, by engaging to pay four of the party, captain Lewis obtained permission for himself and each of his men to ride behind an Indian; but he soon found riding without stirrups more tiresome than walking, and therefore dismounted, making the Indian carry his pack. About sunset they reached the upper part of the level valley in the cove through which he had passed, and which they now called Shoshonee cove. The grass being burnt on the north side of the river they crossed over to the south, and encamped about four miles above the narrow pass between the hills noticed as they traversed the cove before. The river was here about six yards wide, and frequently dammed up by the beaver. Drewyer had been sent forward to hunt, but he returned in the evening unsuccessful, and their only supper therefore was the remaining pound of flour stirred in a little boiling water, and then divided between the four white men and two of the Indians.

In order not to exhaust the strength of the men, captain Clark did not leave his camp till after breakfast. Although he was scarcely half a mile below the Rattlesnake cliffs he was obliged to make a circuit of two miles by water before he reached them. The river now passed between low and rugged mountains and cliffs formed of a mixture of limestone and a hard black rock, with no covering except a few scattered pines. At the distance of four miles is a bold little stream which throws itself from the mountains down a steep precipice of rocks on the left. One mile further is a second point of rocks, and an island, about a mile beyond which is a creek on the right, ten yards wide and three feet three inches in depth, with a strong current: we called it Willard's creek after one of our men, Alexander Willard. Three miles beyond this creek, after passing a high cliff on the right opposite to a steep hill, we reached a small meadow on the left bank of the river. During its passage through these hills to Willard's creek the river had been less tortuous than usual, so that in the first six miles to Willard's creek we had advanced four miles on our route. We continued on for two miles, till we reached in the evening a small bottom covered with clover and a few cottonwood trees: here we passed the night near the remains of some old Indian lodges of brush. The river is as it has been for some days shallow and rapid; and our men, who are for hours together in the river, suffer not only from fatigue, but from the extreme coldness of the water, the temperature of which is as low as that of the freshest springs in our country. In walking along the side of the river, captain Clark was very near being bitten twice by rattlesnakes, and the Indian woman narrowly escaped the same misfortune. We caught a number of fine trout; but the only game procured to-day was a buck, which had a peculiarly bitter taste, proceeding probably from its favourite food, the willow.

AUGUST 16TH *Friday.* As neither our party nor the Indians had any thing to eat, captain Lewis sent two of his hunters ahead this morning to procure some provision: at the same time he requested Cameahwait to prevent his young men from going out, lest by their noise they might alarm the game; but this measure immediately revived their suspicions: it now began to be believed that these men were sent forward in order to apprise the enemy of their coming, and as captain Lewis was fearful of exciting any further uneasiness, he made no objection on seeing a small party of Indians go on each side of the valley under pretence of hunting, but in reality to watch the movements of our two men: even this precaution however did not quiet the alarms of the Indians, a considerable part of whom returned home, leaving only twenty-eight men and three women.

After the hunters had been gone about an hour, captain Lewis again mounted with one of the Indians behind him, and the whole party set out; but just as they passed through the narrows they saw one of the spies coming back at full speed across the plain: the chief stopped and seemed uneasy, the whole band were moved with fresh suspicions, and captain Lewis himself was much disconcerted, lest by some unfortunate accident some of their enemies might have perhaps straggled that way. The young Indian had scarcely breath to say a few words as he came up, when the whole troop dashed forward as fast as their horses could carry them; and captain Lewis astonished at this movement was borne along for nearly a mile before he learnt with great satisfaction that it was all caused by the spy's having come to announce that one of the white men had killed a deer. Relieved from his anxiety he now found the jolting very uncomfortable; for the Indian behind him being afraid of not getting his share of the feast had lashed the horse at every step since they set off; he therefore reined him in and ordered the Indian to stop beating him. The fellow had no idea of losing time in disputing the point, and jumping off the horse ran for a mile at full speed.

Captain Lewis slackened his pace, and followed at a sufficient distance to observe them. When they reached the place where Drewyer had thrown out the intestines, they all dismounted in confusion and ran tumbling over each other like famished dogs: each tore away whatever part he could and instantly began to eat it; some had the liver, some the kidneys, in short no part on which we are accustomed to look with disgust escaped them: one of them who had seized about nine feet of the entrails was chewing at one end, while with his hand he was diligently clearing his way by discharging the contents at the other. It was indeed impossible to see these wretches ravenously feeding on the filth of animals, and the blood streaming from their mouths, without deploring how nearly the condition of savages approaches that of the brute creation: yet though suffering with hunger they did not attempt, as they might have done, to take by force the whole deer, but contented themselves with what had been thrown away by the hunter. Captain Lewis now had the deer skinned, and after reserving a quarter of it gave the rest of the animal to the chief to be divided among the Indians, who immediately devoured nearly the whole of it without cooking. They now went forward towards the creek where there was some brushwood to make a fire, and found Drewyer who had killed a second deer: the same struggle for the entrails was renewed here, and on giving nearly the whole deer to the Indians, they devoured it even to the soft part of the hoofs. A fire being made captain Lewis had his breakfast, during which Drewyer brought in a third deer: this too, after reserving one quarter, was given to the Indians, who now seemed completely satisfied and in good humour.

At this place they remained about two hours to let the horses graze, and then continued their journey, and towards evening reached the lower part of the cove, having on the way shot an antelope, the greater part of which was given to the Indians. As they were now approaching the place where they had been told by captain Lewis they would see the white men, the chief insisted on halting: they therefore all dismounted, and Cameahwait with great ceremony and as if for ornament, put tippets or skins round the necks of our party, similar to those worn by themselves. As this was obviously intended to disguise the white men, captain Lewis in order to inspire them with more confidence put his cocked hat and feather on the head of the chief, and as his own over-shirt was in the Indian form, and his skin browned by the sun, he could not have been distinguished from an Indian: the men followed his example, and the change seemed to be very agreeable to the Indians.

In order to guard however against any disappointment captain Lewis again explained the possibility of our not having reached the forks in consequence of the difficulty of the navigation, so that if they should not find us at that spot they might be assured of our not being far below. They again all mounted their horses and rode on rapidly, making one of the Indians carry their flag, so that we might recognize them as they approached us; but to the mortification and disappointment of both parties on coming within two miles of the forks, no canoes were to be seen. Uneasy lest at this moment he should be abandoned, and all his hopes of obtaining aid from the Indians be destroyed, captain Lewis gave the chief his gun, telling him that if the enemies of his nation were in the bushes he might defend himself with it; that for his own part he was not afraid to die, and that the chief might shoot him as soon as they discovered themselves betrayed. The other three men at the same time gave their guns to the Indians, who now seemed more easy, but still wavered in their resolutions.

As they went on towards the point, captain Lewis perceiving how critical his situation had become, resolved to attempt a stratagem which his present difficulty seemed completely to justify. Recollecting the notes he had left at the point for us, he sent Drewyer for them with an Indian who witnessed his taking them from the pole. When they were brought, captain Lewis told Cameahwait that on leaving his brother chief at the place where the river issues from the mountains, it was agreed that the boats should not be brought higher than the next forks we should meet; but that if the rapid water prevented the boats from coming on as fast as they expected, his brother chief was to send a note to the first forks above him to let him know where the boats were; that this note had been left this morning at the forks, and mentioned that the canoes were just below the mountains, and coming slowly up in consequence of the current. Captain Lewis added, that he would stay at the forks for his brother chief, but would send a man down the river, and that if Cameahwait doubted what he said, one of their young men would go with him whilst he and the other two remained at the forks. This story satisfied the chief and the greater part of the Indians, but a few did not conceal their suspicions, observing that we told different stories, and complaining that the chief exposed them to danger by a mistaken confidence.

Captain Lewis now wrote by the light of some willow brush a note to captain Clark, which he gave to Drewyer, with an order to use all possible expedition in ascending the river, and engaged an Indian to accompany him by a promise of a knife and some beads. At bedtime the chief and five others slept round the fire of captain Lewis, and the rest hid themselves in different parts of the willow brush to avoid the enemy, who they feared would attack them in the night. Captain Lewis endeavoured to assume a cheerfulness he did not feel to prevent the despondency of the savages: after conversing gayly with them he retired to his mosquito bier, by the side of which the chief now placed himself: he lay down, yet slept but little, being in fact scarcely less uneasy than his Indian companions. He was apprehensive that finding the ascent of the river impracticable, captain Clark might

have stopped below the Rattlesnake bluff, and the messenger would not meet him. The consequence of disappointing the Indians at this moment would most probably be, that they would retire and secrete themselves in the mountains, so as to prevent our having an opportunity of recovering their confidence: they would also spread a panic through all the neighbouring Indians, and cut us off from the supply of horses so useful and almost so essential to our success: he was at the same time consoled by remembering that his hopes of assistance rested on better foundations than their generosity—their avarice, and their curiosity. He had promised liberal exchanges for their horses; but what was still more seductive, he had told them that one of their countrywomen who had been taken with the Minnetarees accompanied the party below; and one of the men had spread the report of our having with us a man perfectly black, whose hair was short and curled. This last account had excited a great degree of curiosity, and they seemed more desirous of seeing this monster than of obtaining the most favourable barter for their horses.

In the meantime we had set out after breakfast, and although we proceeded with more ease than we did yesterday, the river was still so rapid and shallow as to oblige us to drag the large canoes during the greater part of the day. For the first seven miles the river formed a bend to the right so as to make our advance only three miles in a straight line; the stream is crooked, narrow, small, and shallow, with highlands occasionally on the banks, and strewed with islands, four of which are opposite to each other. Near this place we left the valley, to which we gave the name of Serviceberry valley, from the abundance of that fruit now ripe which is found in it. In the course of the four following miles we passed several more islands and bayous on each side of the river, and reached a high cliff on the right. Two and a half miles beyond this the cliffs approach on both sides and form a very considerable rapid near the entrance of a bold running stream on the left. The water was now excessively cold, and the rapids had been frequent and troublesome.

On ascending an eminence captain Clark saw the forks of the river and sent the hunters up. They must have left it only a short time before captain Lewis's arrival, but fortunately had not seen the note which enabled him to induce the Indians to stay with him. From the top of this eminence he could discover only three trees through the whole country, nor was there along the sides of the cliffs they had passed in the course of the day, any timber except a few small pines: the low grounds were supplied with willow, currant bushes, and serviceberries. After advancing half a mile further we came to the lower point of an island near the middle of the river, and about the centre of the valley: here we halted for the night, only four miles by land, though ten by water, below the point where captain Lewis lay. Although we had made only fourteen miles, the labours of the men had fatigued and exhausted them very much: we therefore collected some small willow brush for a fire, and lay down to sleep.

THE JOURNALS OF LEWIS & CLARK

Meriwether Lewis

THE
JOURNALS
OF THE EXPEDITION

UNDER THE COMMAND OF

Capt.ˢ LEWIS and CLARK

to the *sources* of the MISSOURI, thence *across*
the ROCKY MOUNTAINS and down
the river COLUMBIA to the PACIFIC Ocean,
performed during the YEARS 1804–5–6
by ORDER of the Government of the United States.

EDITED BY
NICHOLAS BIDDLE

with an introduction by JOHN BAKELESS

AND ILLUSTRATED WITH WATER COLORS AND DRAWINGS
BY CARL BODMER AND OTHER CONTEMPORARY ARTISTS

VOLUME TWO

THE HERITAGE PRESS

New York

The special contents of this edition are copyright © 1962 by The George Macy Companies, Inc.

CONTENTS OF VOLUME TWO

The Route from the Great Divide to the Pacific and Back to St. Louis xvi

CHAPTER 15 *Crossing the Great Divide* 233

Affecting interview between the wife of Chaboneau and the chief of the Shoshonees. Council held with that nation, and favourable result. The extreme navigable point of the Missouri mentioned. General character of the river and of the country through which it passes. Captain Clark in exploring the source of the Columbia falls in company with another party of Shoshonees. The geographical information acquired from one of that party. Their manner of catching fish. The party reach Lewis river. The difficulties which captain Clark had to encounter in his route. Friendship and hospitality of the Shoshonees. The party with captain Lewis employed in making saddles, and preparing for the journey.

CHAPTER 16 *Among the Shoshonee Indians* 248

Contest between Drewyer and a Shoshonee. The fidelity and honour of that tribe. The party set out on their journey. The conduct of Cameahwait reproved, and himself reconciled. The easy parturition of the Shoshonee women. History of this nation. Their terror of the Pawkees. Their government and family economy in their treatment of their women. Their complaint of Spanish treachery. Description of their weapons of warfare. Their curious mode of making a shield. The caparison of their horses. The dress of the man and of the women particularly described. Their mode of acquiring new names.

CHAPTER 17 *Down the Kooskooskee River* 264

The party, after procuring horses from the Shoshonees, proceed on their journey through the mountains. The difficulties and dangers of the route. A council held with another band of the Shoshonees, of whom some account is given. They are reduced to the necessity of killing their horses for food. Captain Clark with a small party precedes the main body in quest of food, and is hospitably received by the Pierced-nose Indians. Arrival of the main body amongst this tribe, with whom a council is held. They resolve to perform the remainder of their journey in canoes. Sickness of the party. They descend the Kooskooskee to its junction with Lewis river, after passing several dangerous rapids. Short description of the Pierced-nose Indians. Their manners and dress.

CHAPTER 18 *Down the Snake and Columbia Rivers* 285

The party proceed in canoes. Description of an Indian sweating bath and burial place. Many dangerous rapids passed. Narrow escape of one of the canoes. In the passage down they are visited by several Indians, all of whom manifest pacific dispositions. Description of the Sokulk tribe. Their dress, and manner of building houses. Their pacific character. Their habits of living. Their mode of boiling salmon. Vast quantities of salmon amongst the Sokulk. Council held with this tribe. The terror and consternation excited by captain Clark, concerning which an interesting cause is related. Some account of the Pisquitpaws. Their mode of burying the dead.

vii

CHAPTER 19 *Down the Columbia to the Great Rapids* 300

The party in their passage still visited by the Indians. Lepage's river described. Immense quantities of salmon caught by the Indians. Description of the river Towahnahiooks. Indian mode of stacking fish, and preparing them for market. Description of the great falls. Description of an Indian canoe. Alarm excited by an anticipated attack from the Eheltoots. A very dangerous rapid passed in safety, called by the Indians the Falls. Account of the Indian houses in the neighbourhood. Another dreadful rapid passed without injury. Some account of the Chilluckittequaw Indians. Captain Clark examines the great rapids. Description of an Indian burial place. The rapids passed in safety.

CHAPTER 20 *From Tidewater to the Pacific Ocean* 320

First appearance of tide water in the Columbia river. Description of the Quicksand river. Some account of the Skilloot Indians. The party pass the river Coweliskee. Some account of the Wahkiacum Indians. Arrival on the borders of the Pacific. Disagreeable and critical situation of the party when first encamped. Their distress occasioned by the incessant torrents of rain. Exposed for thirty days to this drenching deluge, during which time their provisions are spoiled, and most of their few articles of merchandise destroyed. Distress of the party. Adventure of Shannon and his danger from the Wahkiacums. Difficulty of finding a place suitable for a permanent encampment. Visited by several Indians of different tribes, on whom medals are bestowed.

CHAPTER 21 *The Establishment of Fort Clatsop* 336

Extravagant passion of the natives for blue beads, which constitute amongst them the circulating medium of the country. The party still in search of a suitable place for winter quarters. Still suffering from the constant deluges of rain. Are visited by the Indians, with whom they traffic but little, on account of the extravagant prices they ask for every article. Return of captain Lewis who reports that he has found a suitable place for winter quarters. The rain still continues. They prepare to form an encampment on a point of high land on the banks of the river Nutel. Captain Clark goes with a party to find a place suitable for the manufacture of salt. He is hospitably entertained by the Clatsops. This tribe addicted to the vice of gambling. Sickness of some of the party, occasioned by the incessant rains. They form, notwithstanding a permanent encampment for their winter quarters.

CHAPTER 22 *At Fort Clatsop* 353

A party, headed by captain Clark, go in quest of a whale driven on the shore of the Pacific to obtain some of the oil. They pass Clatsop river, which is described. The perilous nature of this jaunt, and the grandeur of the scenery described. Indian mode of extracting whale oil. The life of one of captain Clark's party preserved by the kindness of an Indian woman. A short account of the Chinnooks, of the Clatsops, Killamucks, the Lucktons, and an enumeration of several other tribes. The manner of sepulchre among the Chinnooks, Clatsops, &c. Description of their weapons of war and hunting. Their mode of building houses. Their manufactures, and cookery. Their mode of making canoes. Their great dexterity in managing that vehicle.

CHAPTER 23 *Indians of the Vicinity* 367

An account of the Clatsops, Killamucks, Chinnooks and Cathlamahs. Their uniform custom of flattening the forehead. The dress of these savages, and their ornaments, described. The licensed prostitution of the women, married and unmarried, of which a ludicrous instance is given.

The character of their diseases. The common opinion, that the treatment of women is the standard by which the virtues of an Indian may be known, combatted, and disproved by examples. The respect entertained by these Indians for old age, compared with the different conduct of those nations who subsist by the chase. Their mode of government. Their ignorance of ardent spirits, and their fondness for gambling. Their dexterity in traffic. In what articles their traffic consists. Their extraordinary attachment to blue beads, which forms their circulating medium.

CHAPTER 24 *Botany and Zoology* 379

A general description of the beasts, birds, and plants, &c. found by the party in this expedition.

CHAPTER 25 *Homeward Bound* 410

Difficulty of procuring means of subsistence for the party. They determine to resume their journey to the mountains. They leave in the hands of the Indians a written memorandum, importing their having penetrated to the Pacific, through the route of the Missouri and Columbia, and through the Rocky mountains. The party commence their return route. Dexterity of the Cathlamah Indians in carving. Description of the Coweliskee river. They experience much hospitality from the natives. An instance of the extreme voracity of the vulture. The party are visited by many strange Indians, all of whom are kind and hospitable. Scarcity of game, and embarrassments of the party on that account. Captain Clark discovers a tribe not seen in the descent down the Columbia. Singular adventure to obtain provisions from them. Particular description of the Multnomah village and river. Description of mount Jefferson. Some account by captain Clark of the Neerchokio tribe, and of their architecture. Their sufferings by the small-pox.

CHAPTER 26 *Up the Columbia to the Dalles* 422

Description of Wappatoo island, and the mode in which the nations gather wappatoo. The character of the soil and its productions. The numerous tribes residing in its vicinity. The probability that they were all of the tribe of the Multnomahs originally, inferred from similarity of dress, manners, language, &c. Description of their dress, weapons of war, their mode of burying the dead. Description of another village, called the Wahclellah village. Their mode of architecture. Extraordinary height of Beacon rock. Unfriendly character of the Indians at that place. The party, alarmed for their safety, resolve to inflict summary vengeance, in case the Wahclellah tribe persist in their outrages and insults. Interview with the chief of that tribe, and confidence restored. Difficulty of drawing the canoes over the rapids. Visited by a party of the Yehugh tribe. Short notice of the Weocksockwillackum tribe. Curious phenomenon observed in the Columbia, from the rapids to the Chilluckittequaws.

CHAPTER 27 *From the Dalles to Walla Walla River* 434

Captain Clark procures four horses for the transportation of the baggage. Some further account of the Skilloot tribe. Their joy at the first appearance of salmon in the Columbia. Their thievish propensities. The party arrive at the village of the Eneeshurs, where the natives are found alike unfriendly. The party now provided with horses. The party prevented from the exercise of hostility against this nation by a friendly adjustment. The scarcity of timber so great that they are compelled to buy wood to cook their provisions. Arrive at the Wahhowpum village. Dance of the natives. Their ingenuity in declining to purchase the canoes, on the supposition that the party would be compelled to leave them behind defeated. The party having obtained a complement of horses, proceed by land. Arrive at the Pishquitpah village, and some account of that people. Their frank and hospitable treatment from the Wollawollahs. Their mode of dancing described. Their mode of making fish-weirs. Their amiable character, and their unusual affection for the whites.

CHAPTER 28 *From the Walla Walla to Commearp Creek* 446

The party still pursue their route towards the Kooskooskee on horseback with Wollawollah guides. Character of the country. The quamash and other flowering shrubs in bloom. The party reach the Kinnooenim creek. They meet with an old acquaintance called the Bighorn Indian. They arrive at the mouth of the Kooskooskee. Singular custom among the Chopunnish women. Difficulty of purchasing provisions from the natives, and the new resort of the party to obtain them. The Chopunnish style of architecture. Captain Clark turns physician, and performs several experiments with success upon the natives, which they reward. An instance of their honesty. The distress of the Indians for want of provisions during the winter. The party finally meet the Twistedhair, to whom was entrusted their horses during their journey down. The quarrel between that chief and another of his nation, on the subject of his horses. The causes of this controversy stated at large. The two chiefs reconciled by the interference of the party, and the horses restored. Extraordinary instance of Indian hospitality towards strangers. A council held with the Chopunnish, and the object of the expedition explained in a very circuitous route of explanation. The party again perform medical cures. The answer of the Chopunnish to the speech delivered at the council, confirmed by a singular ceremony of acquiescence. They promise faithfully to follow the advice of their visitors.

CHAPTER 29 *Encamped on the Upper Kooskooskee* 458

The party encamp amongst the Chopunnish, and receive further evidences of their hospitality. The Indian mode of boiling bear-flesh. Of gelding horses. Their mode of decoying the deer within reach of their arrows. Character of the soil and climate in the Rocky mountains. Varieties of climate. Character of the natives. Their dress and ornaments. Mode of burying the dead. The party administer medical relief to the natives. One of the natives restored to the use of his limbs by sweating, and the curious process by which perspiration was excited. Another proof of Chopunnish hospitality. Success of their sweating prescription on the Indian chief. Description of the horned lizard, and a variety of insects. The attachment of the friends of a dying Indian to a tomahawk which he had stolen from the party, and which they desired to bury with the body. Description of the river Tommanamah. The Indians return an answer to a proposition made by the party.

CHAPTER 30 *In the Bitter Root Mountains Again* 471

The party mingle in the diversions of the Willetpos Indians, a tribe hitherto unnoticed. Their joy on the prospect of a return. Description of the vegetables growing on the Rocky mountains. Various preparations made to resume their journey. The party set out, and arrive at Hungry creek. The serious and desponding difficulties that obstructed their progress. They are compelled to return and wait for a guide across the mountains. Their distress for want of provisions. They resolve to return to the Quamash flats. They are at last so fortunate as to procure Indian guides, with whom they resume their journey to the falls of the Missouri. The danger of the route described. Their scarcity of provisions, and the danger of their journey. Their course lying along the ridges of mountains. Description of the warm springs, where the party encamp. The fondness of the Indians for bathing in them.

CHAPTER 31 *Captain Lewis Seeks a Short-Cut* 482

The party proceed on their journey with their Indian guides, and at length agree to divide, to take several routes, and to meet again at the mouth of Yellowstone river. The route of captain Lewis is to pursue the most direct road to the falls of the Missouri, then to ascend Maria's river, explore the country, and to descend that river to its mouth. Captain Lewis, accordingly, with nine men proceed up the eastern branch of Clark's river, and take leave of their Indian guides. Description of that branch, and character of the surrounding country. Description of the Cokalahishkit river. They arrive at the ridge dividing the Missouri from the Columbia rivers. Meet once more with the buffalo and brown bear. Immense herds of buffalo discovered on the borders of Medicine river. The party encamp on Whitebear islands. Singular adventure that befel M'Neil. Captain Lewis, with three of his party proceed to explore the source of Maria's river. Tansy river described. He reaches the dividing line of these two streams. General character of the surrounding country.

CHAPTER 32 *Lewis Completes His Separate Exploration* 493

Captain Lewis and his party still proceed on the route mentioned in the last chapter, and arrive at the forks of Maria's river; of which river a particular description is given. Alarmed by the evidence that they are in the neighbourhood of unfriendly Indians, and much distressed for want of provisions, the weather proving unfavourable, they are compelled to return. The face of the country described. Interview with the unfriendly Indians, called Minnetarees of Fort de Prairie. Mutual consternation. Resolution of captain Lewis. They encamp together for the night, apparently with amicable dispositions. The conversation that ensued between these new visitants. The conflict occasioned by the Indians attempting to seize the rifles and horses of the party, in which one is mortally wounded. Captain Lewis kills another Indian, and his narrow escape. Having taken four horses belonging to the Indians, they hastened with all expedition to join the party attached to captain Clark. Arriving near the Missouri they are alarmed by the sound of rifles, which proves fortunately to be from the party of their friends, under the command of sergeant Ordway. The two detachments thus fortunately united, leave their horses, and descend the Missouri in canoes. They continue their route down the river to form a junction with captain Clark. Vast quantities of game found in their passage down the river. Captain Lewis accidentally wounded by one of his own party. They proceed down the Missouri, and at length join captain Clark.

CHAPTER 33 *Captain Clark Explores the Yellowstone* 505

The party commanded by captain Clark, previous to his being joined by captain Lewis, proceed along Clark's river, in pursuance of the route mentioned in a preceding chapter. Their sorry commemoration of our national anniversary. An instance of Sacajawea's strength of memory. Description of the river and of the surrounding country as the party proceed. Several of the horses belonging to the party supposed to be stolen by their Indian neighbours. They reach Wisdom river. Extraordinary heat of a spring. The strong attachment of the party for tobacco, which they find on opening a cache. Sergeant Ordway recovers the horses. Captain Clark divides his party, one detachment of which was to descend the river: they reach Gallatin and Jefferson rivers, of which a description is given. Arrive at the Yellowstone river. Some account of Otter and Beaver rivers. An example of Indian fortification. One of the party seriously and accidentally wounded. Engaged in the construction of canoes. Twenty-four horses stolen, probably by the Indians, in one night.

CHAPTER 34 *Down the Yellowstone; Reunion of the Parties* 516

Captain Clark proceeds with his party down the river. Description of an Indian lodge. Sergeant Pryor arrives with the horses left by the party when they embarked in their canoes; his difficulty in bringing them on. Remarkable rock discovered by captain Clark, and the beauty of the prospect from the summit. They continue their route down the river, of which a particular description is given, as well as of the surrounding country. Yellowstone and Bighorn rivers compared. Great quantities of game found on the banks of the rivers. Immense herds of buffalo. Fierceness of the white bear. Encamp at the junction of the Yellowstone and Missouri. A general outline given of Yellowstone river, comprehending the shoals; its entrance recommended for the formation of a trading establishment. The sufferings of the party from the mosquitoes. Sergeant Pryor, who, with a detachment of the party, was to have brought on the horses, arrives and reports that they were all stolen by the Indians; deprived of these animals, they form for themselves Indian canoes of the skins of beasts, and of curious structure, with which they descend the river over the most difficult shoals and dangerous rapids. Meet with two white men unexpectedly, from whom they procure intelligence of the Indians formerly visited by the party.

CHAPTER 35 *Down the Missouri to White River* 527

The party, while descending the river in their skin canoes, are overtaken by the detachment under captain Lewis, and the whole party, now once more happily united, descend the Missouri together. They once more visit the Minnetaree Indians, and hold a council with that nation as well as with the Mahahas. Captain Clark endeavours to persuade their chiefs to accompany him to the United States, which invitation they decline, on account of their fears of the Sioux, in their passage down the river. Colter, one of the party, requests and obtains liberty to remain among the Indians, for the purpose of hunting beaver. Friendly deportment of the Mandans; council held by captain Clark with the chiefs of the different villages; the chief named the Bigwhite, with his wife and son, agree to accompany the party to the United States, who takes an affecting farewell of his nation. Chaboneau, with his wife and child, decline visiting the United States, and are left among the Indians. The party at length proceed on their journey, and find that the course of the Missouri has, in some places, changed since their passage up that river. They arrive among the Ricaras. Character of the Chayennes; their dress, habits, &c. Captain Clark offers to the chief of this nation a medal, which he at first refuses, believing it to be medicine, but which he is afterwards prevailed on to accept. The party proceed rapidly down the river. Prepare to defend themselves against the Tetons, but receive no injury from them. Incredible numbers of buffalo seen near White river. They meet, at last, with the Tetons, and refuse their invitations to land. Intrepidity of captain Clark.

CHAPTER 36 *The Expedition Returns in Safety to St. Louis* 539

The party are hailed by a group of Indians and fear an attack, but are relieved to learn that they are friendly Yanktons. A flagstaff that had been erected by the party in September, 1804, opposite Calumet bluff, is found still standing. They meet Mr. James Airs, a trader from Mackinaw, who presents the party with tobacco and flour. Next they meet a party on the way to trade with the Yanktons, and obtain their first whiskey in more than a year. Encounter with Mr. Gravelines, who reports the death of the Ricara chief at Washington. Learn of the opinion in the United States that the expedition had perished. They are met with a great welcome at Lacharette and St. Louis.

Acknowledgments 547

PORTRAITS & COLOR PLATES

VOLUME TWO

Meriwether Lewis (*after Charles de St.-Memin*)   PAGE ii

William Clark (*Chester Harding and John J. Douberman*)   iii

Indian Painting of a Combat (*copied by Carl Bodmer*)   FACING PAGE 242

    In the scene painted on a buffalo robe by Mato-Topé, the Mandan chief is depicted fighting a Cheyenne chief, distinguished by the otter skin on his head. Mato-Topé's hand has been cut in seizing the knife with which he is about to stab his enemy.

Indian Utensils and Weapons (*Carl Bodmer*)   274

    Tools, weapons, and apparel of various midwestern Indian tribes: 1. Bone tool for scraping wood. 2. Horn ladle. 3. Horseman's short spear. 4. Gunstock club with spear blade. 5. Feathered bonnet. 6. Shield belonging to Mato-Topé. 7. Roached deertail decorated with rattlesnake rattle. 8. Parfleche—painted rawhide envelope for carrying food. 9. Moccasins (left, man's; right, woman's). 10. Quiver, with two types of bows. 11. Coup stick, used in close fighting to win acclaim as an act of bravery. 12. Pipe with catlinite (red clay) stem, inlaid with slate and lead. 13. Calumet, or ceremonial peace pipe. 14. Woman's game ball. 15. Game hoop and spear. 16. Double bone whistle. 17. Dance drum. 18. Man's moccasin. 19. Bundle of tobacco.

Iowa Warrior (*George Bird King*)   298

    Tah-Ro-Hon, famed from his youth for his combats with the Sioux and Osage. A signer of the treaty of St. Louis, he visited Washington, where his portrait was painted.

Assiniboin and Yanktonai Indians (*Carl Bodmer*)   338

    The Assiniboin's headdress combines antelope horns and a crest of trimmed feathers; a rosette of porcupine quills decorates his breast.

Muskwaki (Fox) Indian (*Carl Bodmer*)   390

    Wakusaase's tribe belonged to the Algonquian group and was allied to the Sacs.

Oto Warrior (*George Bird King*)   430

    The "Ottoes" are described in Chapter 2 as among the first with whom the expedition had contact. This warrior's name, No-Way-Ke-Sug-Ga, means "He who strikes two at once."

Interior of the Hut of a Mandan Chief (*Carl Bodmer*) 462

    Between the four center posts that support the roof are shorter posts forming the wall, which is covered on the outside with matting, hay, and earth. Smoke from the central fire escapes through the roof. These large circular houses were warm and spacious.

Blackfoot Indian on Horseback (*Carl Bodmer*) 494

    It was an armed Indian of this tribe who barely missed killing Captain Lewis in July 1806 (see Chapter 32).

Hunting the Bison (*Carl Bodmer*) 530

    Big-game hunting was an easier task for the Indians after the white men brought horses to the New World. With the introduction of fire-arms, the buffalo herds were reduced almost to extinction.

VOLUME TWO

*From the Great Divide to the Pacific
and Back to St. Louis*

AUGUST 17, 1805 TO SEPTEMBER 23, 1806

THE ROUTE

Chapters 15, 16, and 17 are devoted largely to explorations of routes of passage across the mountains, investigations of waterways on the Pacific side, and interesting accounts of the Shoshones. From them they procured horses and made their way onward, seeking a water route to the Pacific. Captain Clark took his turn at path-seeking, and in Chapter 16 we find him, on August 21, 1805, passing the junction of the Salmon and Lemhi rivers, where Salmon City, Idaho, now stands. He travelled down the banks of Salmon River for some fifty miles, but found the route impossible for the party and returned. Meantime Lewis was awaiting him at the banks of the Jefferson. It was not until September 20, as related in Chapter 17, that the whole party finally reached the Pacific side of the Great Divide. Continuing their journey on horseback they reached a branch of the Kooskooskee River, now the Clearwater. Near this place is now Pierce City, the county seat of Shoshonee County, Idaho. Their land journey continued for only a few days, and then, encouraged by the assurances of the Indians as to a waterway to the Columbia, and also by the sight of navigable water, they began on September 27 to build canoes.

The latter part of Chapter 17 shows the explorers fairly on their way to the sea. They were descending the Kooskooskee, which they called the Clark, although, as we have seen, it is now the Clearwater.

At the junction of this river with the Kimooeenim near the Snake, described in the latter part of this chapter, they passed the present site of Lewiston, Idaho.

The adventurous journey down the Snake sketched in Chapter 18 carried them from Idaho into Washington and to the Columbia at the meeting point of Franklin, Walla Walla, and Yakima counties. The "western branch of the Columbia," described as the Tapteal, is now called the Yakima. The "conical mountain" (Mt. St. Helen's) is in Cowlitz County, Washington.

Chapter 19 continues the record of the voyage down the Columbia. "Le Page's River" is now John Day's River. "Timm Mountain" is Mt. Hood. Their descent of the "Great Falls," or Dalles and Chutes of the Columbia, is graphically described in this chapter and the next. For a part of the way they were travelling through Skamania County, Washington.

In Chapter 20 they pass the Willamette River without discovering it, and they presently catch a glimpse of Mt. St. Helen's. The Wahkiacum Indians whom they mention have disappeared, but the name has been given to the county of Washington west of Cowlitz. On November 7 the travellers obtained their first glimpse of the sea. They camped for the night near Gray's Bay, in the southwestern part of Wahkiakum County, and on the 15th moved to a camp on Baker's Bay. In Chapter 21 there is a description of their winter camp on the south side of the Columbia, some three miles up the Netul River, which empties into Meriwether's Bay.

The "Killamuck" Indians referred to in Chapter 22 are known as the Tillamooks, and the name has been given to Tillamook County, Oregon. Chapters 23 and 24 contain a detailed account of the Indians and the animals and birds observed by the explorers during the winter that they passed at the mouth of the Columbia.

It was on March 23, 1806, that the explorers started on their return (Chapter 25). They had encountered no white men at the mouth of the Columbia, and the scantiness of their remaining supplies increased the hardships of their journey.

Of the written lists and memoranda which they left with the Clatsops, one copy did reach the United States. In the summer of 1806 Captain Hill of the brig *Lydia* entered the Columbia to trade. He carried one of the explorers' papers to Canton, China, and then sent it to Philadelphia.

The vultures referred to in this chapter were the California condors, now nearly extinct. In this chapter and the next there is an account of the discovery of the Multnomah River, now the Willamette. Portland, Oregon, is near the Indian settlement described here. Wappatoo Inlet is now called Willamette Slough. The name "wappatoo" was the term in the Chinook jargon of the Northwest for the potato. The Multnomah Falls is the most noteworthy of the five cascades on the Oregon side of the river, which the explorers passed before they reached the head of tidewater, on April 9, and began the arduous portage around the Cascades of the Columbia and the Dalles.

On April 23 (Chapter 27) they passed the mouth of Rock River. The "Wollawollahs" encountered as they journeyed along the south or Oregon side of the Columbia are now the Walla Walla Indians, and the Youmalolam River is now the Umatilla. The end of this chapter finds the party travelling on horseback along the Walla Walla River through the county of that name. On May 1 they were between the present towns of Prescott and Waitesburg, in Washington. Their journey east of the Columbia continued along Touchet Creek, and, later, along the Kooskooskee, now the Clearwater, in Nez Percé County, Idaho.

The explorers were well to the eastward of the Bitter Root Mountains when they made the camp described in Chapter 29, to await the melting of the snow. The Quamash Flats of Chapter 30 were named for the camass root which was valued by the Indians. This chapter describes the difficult passage of the Bitter Root Mountains. Traveler's Rest Creek is near the summit of these mountains. The travellers had advanced from Idaho into Montana, but they had not yet passed the Great Divide.

Captain Lewis went ahead (Chapter 31), advancing between the Bitter Root and Rocky Mountain ranges, crossing the Missoula River and camping near the present site of Missoula, Montana. On July 7 they crossed the pass in the Rockies which brought them finally to the eastern side. They continued down the Medicine, now the Sun River, to the rendezvous at the Great Falls of the Missouri. Maria's River, which Lewis starts out to explore in Chapters 31 and 32, flows from near the northern boundary of Montana to the Missouri, near the town of Ophir. In Chapters 33 and 34 we can trace the journey of Captain Clark along Clark's or Bitter Root River to Ross' Hole, across the Rockies through Lewis' Pass, down Wisdom or Big Hole River to the forks of the Jefferson, down to the Missouri, and then up the Gallatin, crossing to the Yellowstone and following it to a meeting with Lewis on the Missouri.

The Divide was crossed on July 6, when Clark passed into Beaverhead County, Montana, travelling west of Bismarck City, Montana. A part of this journey followed the present line of the Northern Pacific Railroad from Gallatin City through Bozeman Pass to Livingston. On July 27 they passed from the Big Horn into the Yellowstone and "took a last look at the Rocky Mountains." It was not until August 12 (Chapter 35) that the party were reunited.

On their return to the Mandan villages, near Bismarck, they parted with the faithful Sacajawea, one of the most interesting figures of this expedition, and she and her husband and child remained behind. The hunter Colter, who turned back here to the wilderness, entered upon a dramatic series of adventures, which in 1807 included a flight from the Blackfeet that led to his discovery of the wonders of the Yellowstone National Park. The Indian chief Big White, who accompanied the explorers from this point, was prevented by the hostile Arikaras from returning the next year, and the Missouri Fur Company was paid $7000 to escort him back in 1809.

The return down the Missouri and Mississippi (Chapter 36) ended at St. Louis on September 23, 1806, closing a journey of 7689 miles. (The westward trip had been 4134 miles, the eastward 3555 miles, as the expedition saved 579 miles on their return by going from Traveler's Rest Creek directly to the Falls of the Missouri.)

Chapter 15
CROSSING THE GREAT DIVIDE

SATURDAY, AUGUST 17TH, 1805 Captain Lewis rose very early, and despatched Drewyer and the Indian down the river in quest of the boats. Shields was sent out at the same time to hunt, while M'Neal prepared a breakfast out of the remainder of the meat. Drewyer had been gone about two hours, and the Indians were all anxiously waiting for some news, when an Indian who had straggled a short distance down the river, returned with a report that he had seen the white men, who were only a short distance below, and were coming on. The Indians were all transported with joy, and the chief in the warmth of his satisfaction renewed his embrace to captain Lewis, who was quite as much delighted as the Indians themselves; the report proved most agreeably true.

On setting out at seven o'clock, captain Clark with Chaboneau and his wife walked on shore, but they had not gone more than a mile before captain Clark saw Sacajawea, who was with her husband one hundred yards ahead, begin to dance and show every mark of the most extravagant joy, turning round him and pointing to several Indians, whom he now saw advancing on horseback, sucking her fingers at the same time to indicate that they were of her native tribe. As they advanced captain Clark discovered among them Drewyer dressed like an Indian, from whom he learned the situation of the party. While the boats were performing the circuit, he went towards the forks with the Indians, who as they went along, sang aloud with the greatest appearance of delight.

We soon drew near to the camp, and just as we approached it a woman made her way through the crowd towards Sacajawea, and recognising each other, they embraced with the most tender affection. The meeting of these two young women had in it something peculiarly touching, not only in the ardent manner in which their feelings were expressed, but from the real interest of their situation. They had been companions in childhood, in the war with the Minnetarees they had both been taken prisoners in the same battle, they had shared and softened the rigours of their captivity, till one of them had escaped from the Minnetarees, with scarce a hope of ever seeing her friend relieved from the hands of her enemies. While Sacajawea was renewing among the women the friendships of former days, captain Clark went on, and was received by captain Lewis and the chief, who after the first embraces and salutations were over, conducted him to a sort of circular tent or shade of willows. Here he was seated on a white robe; and the chief immediately tied in his hair six small shells resembling pearls, an ornament highly valued by these people, who procured them in the course of trade from the seacoast. The moccasins of the whole party were then taken off, and after much ceremony the smoking began. After this the conference was to be opened, and glad of an opportunity of being able to converse more intelligibly, Sacajawea was sent for; she came into the tent, sat down, and was beginning to interpret, when in the person of Cameahwait she recognised her brother: she instantly jumped up, and ran and embraced him, throwing over him her blanket and weeping profusely: the chief was himself moved, though not in the same degree. After some conversation between them she resumed her seat, and attempted to interpret for us, but her new situation seemed to overpower her, and she was frequently interrupted by her tears. After the council was finished, the unfortunate woman learnt that all her family were dead except two brothers, one of whom was absent, and a son of her eldest sister, a small boy, who was immediately adopted by her. The canoes arriving soon after, we formed a camp in a meadow on the left side, a little below the forks; took out our baggage, and by means of our sails and willow poles formed a canopy for our Indian visitors. About four o'clock the chiefs and warriors were collected, and after the customary ceremony of taking off the moccasins and smoking a pipe, we explained to them in a long harangue the purposes of our visit, making themselves one conspicuous object of the good wishes of our government, on whose strength as well as its friendly disposition we expatiated. We told them of their dependence on the will of our government for all future supplies of whatever was necessary either for their comfort or defence; that as we were sent to discover the best route by which merchandise could be conveyed to them, and no trade would be begun before our return, it was mutually advantageous that we should proceed with as little delay as possible; that we were under the necessity of requesting them to furnish us with horses to transport our baggage across the mountains, and a guide to show us the route, but that they should be amply remunerated for their horses, as well as for every other service they should render us. In the meantime our first wish was, that they should immediately collect as many horses as were necessary to transport our baggage to their village, where, at our leisure we would trade with them for as many horses as they could spare.

The speech made a favourable impression: the chief in reply thanked us for our expressions of friendship towards himself and his nation, and declared their willingness to render us every service. He lamented that it would be so long before they should be supplied with firearms, but that till then they could subsist as they had heretofore done. He concluded by saying that there were not horses here sufficient to transport our goods, but that he would return to the village to-morrow, and bring all his own horses, and encourage his people to come over with theirs. The conference being ended to our satisfaction, we now enquired of Cameahwait what chiefs were among the party, and he pointed out two of them. We then distributed our presents: to Cameahwait we gave a medal of the small size, with the likeness of President Jefferson, and on the reverse a figure of hands clasped with a pipe and tomahawk: to this was added an uniform coat, a shirt, a pair of scarlet leggings, a carrot of tobacco, and some small articles. Each of the other chiefs received a small medal struck during the presidency of general Washington, a shirt, handkerchief, leggings, a knife, and some tobacco. Medals of the same sort were also presented to two young warriors, who though not chiefs were promising youths and very much respected in the tribe. These honorary gifts were followed by presents of paint, moccasins, awls, knives, beads and looking-glasses. We also gave them all a plentiful meal of Indian corn, of which the hull is taken off by being boiled in lye; and as this was the first they had ever tasted, they were very much pleased with it. They had indeed abundant sources of surprise in all they saw: the appearance of the men, their arms, their clothing, the canoes, the strange looks of the negro, and the sagacity of our dog, all in turn shared their admiration, which was raised to astonishment by a shot from the airgun: this operation was instantly considered as "a great medicine," by which they as well as the other Indians mean something emanating directly from the Great Spirit, or produced by his invisible and incomprehensible agency. The display of all

234

these riches had been intermixed with inquiries into the geographical situation of their country; for we had learnt by experience, that to keep the savages in good temper their attention should not be wearied with too much business; but that the serious affairs should be enlivened by a mixture of what is new and entertaining. Our hunters brought in very seasonably four deer and an antelope, the last of which we gave to the Indians, who in a very short time devoured it.

After the council was over, we consulted as to our future operations. The game does not promise to last here for a number of days, and this circumstance combined with many others to induce our going on as soon as possible. Our Indian information as to the state of the Columbia is of a very alarming kind, and our first object is of course to ascertain the practicability of descending it, of which the Indians discourage our expectations. It was therefore agreed that captain Clark should set off in the morning with eleven men, furnished, besides their arms, with tools for making canoes; that he should take Chaboneau and his wife to the camp of the Shoshonees, where he was to leave them, in order to hasten the collection of horses; that he was then to lead his men down to the Columbia, and if he found it navigable, and the timber in sufficient quantity, begin to build canoes. As soon as he had decided as to the propriety of proceeding down the Columbia or across the mountains, he was to send back one of the men with information of it to captain Lewis, who by that time would have brought up the whole party, and the rest of the baggage as far as the Shoshonee village.

Preparations were accordingly made this evening for such an arrangement. The sun is excessively hot in the day time, but the nights very cold, and rendered still more unpleasant from the want of any fuel except willow brush. The appearances too of game, for many days' subsistence, are not very favourable.

Sunday. In order to relieve the men of captain Clark's party from the heavy weight of their arms, provisions and tools, we exposed a few articles to barter for horses, and soon obtained three very good ones, in exchange for which we gave a uniform coat, a pair of leggings, a few handkerchiefs, three knifes and some other small articles, the whole of which did not in the United States cost more than twenty dollars: a fourth was purchased by the men for an old chequered shirt, a pair of old leggings and a knife. The Indians seemed to be quite as well pleased as ourselves at the bargains they had made. We now found that the two inferior chiefs were somewhat displeased at not having received a present equal to that given to the great chief, who appeared in a dress so much finer than their own. To allay their discontent, we bestowed on them two old coats, and promised them that if they were active in assisting us across the mountains they should have an additional present. This treatment completely reconciled them, and the whole Indian party, except two men and two women, set out in perfect good humour to return home with captain Clark.

AUGUST 18TH

After going fifteen miles through a wide level valley with no wood but willows and shrubs, he encamped in the Shoshonee cove near a narrow pass where the highlands approach within two hundred yards of each other, and the river is only ten yards wide. The Indians went on further, except the three chiefs and two young men, who assisted in eating two deer brought in by the hunters. After their departure every thing was prepared for the transportation of the baggage, which was now exposed to the air and dried. Our game was one deer and a beaver, and we saw an abundance of trout in the river for which we fixed a net in the evening.

We have now reached the extreme navigable point of the Missouri, which our observation places in latitude 43° 30′ 43″ north. It is difficult to comprise in any general description the characteristics of a river so extensive, and fed by so many streams which have their sources in a great variety of soils and climates. But the Missouri is still sufficiently powerful to give to all its waters something of a common character, which is of course decided by the nature of the country through which it passes. The bed of the river is chiefly composed of a blue mud from which the water itself derives a deep tinge. From its junction here to the place near which it leaves the mountains, its course is embarrassed by rapids and rocks which the hills on each side have thrown into its channel. From that place, its current, with the exception of the falls, is not difficult of navigation, nor is there much variation in its appearance till the mouth of the Platte. That powerful river throws out vast quantities of coarse sand which contribute to give a new face to the Missouri, which is now much more impeded by islands. The sand, as it is drifted down, adheres in time to some of the projecting points from the shore, and forms a barrier to the mud, which at length fills to the same height with the sandbar itself: as soon as it has acquired a consistency, the willow grows there the first year, and by its roots assists the solidity of the whole: as the mud and sand accumulate the cottonwood tree next appears; till the gradual excretion of soils raises the surface of the point above the highest freshets. Thus stopped in its course the water seeks a passage elsewhere, and as the soil on each side is light and yielding, what was only a peninsula, becomes gradually an island, and the river indemnifies itself for the usurpation by encroaching on the adjacent shore. In this way the Missouri like the Mississippi is constantly cutting off the projections of the shore, and leaving its ancient channel, which is then marked by the mud it has deposited and a few stagnant ponds.

The general appearance of the country as it presents itself on ascending may be thus described: From its mouth to the two Charletons, a ridge of highlands borders the river at a small distance, leaving between them fine rich meadows. From the mouth of the two Charletons the hills recede from the river, giving greater extent to the low grounds, but they again approach the river for a short distance near Grand river, and again at Snake creek. From that point they retire, nor do they come again to the neighbourhood of the river till above the Sauk prairie, where they are comparatively low and small. Thence they diverge and reappear at the Charaton Searty, after which they are scarcely if at all discernible, till they advance to the Missouri nearly opposite to the Kanzas.

The same ridge of hills extends on the south side, in almost one unbroken chain, from the mouth of the Missouri to the Kanzas, though decreasing in height beyond the Osage. As they are nearer the river than the hills on the opposite sides, the intermediate low grounds are of course narrower, but the general character of the soil is common to both sides.

In the meadows and along the shore, the tree most common is the cottonwood, which with the willow forms almost the exclusive growth of the Missouri. The hills or rather high grounds, for they do not rise higher than from one hundred and fifty to two hundred feet, are composed of a good rich black soil, which is perfectly susceptible of cultivation, though it becomes richer on the hills beyond the Platte, and are in general thinly covered with timber. Beyond these hills the country extends into high open plains, which are on both sides sufficiently fertile, but the south has the advantage of better streams of water, and may therefore be considered as preferable for settlements. The lands, however, become much better and the timber more abundant between the Osage and the Kanzas.

From the Kanzas to the Nadawa the hills continue at nearly an equal distance, varying from four to eight miles from each other, except that from the little Platte to nearly opposite the ancient Kanzas village, the hills are more remote, and the meadows of course wider on the north side of the river. From the Nadawa the northern hills disappear, except at occasional intervals, where they are seen at a distance, till they return about twenty-seven miles above the Platte near the ancient village of the Ayoways. On the south the hills continue close to the river from the ancient village of the Kanzas up to Council bluff, fifty miles beyond the Platte; forming high prairie lands. On both sides the lands are good, and perhaps this distance from the Osage to the Platte may be recommended as among the best districts on the Missouri for the purposes of settlers.

From the Ayoway village the northern hills again retire from the river, to which they do not return till three hundred and twenty miles above, at Floyd's river. The hills on the south also leave the river at Council bluffs, and reappear at the Mahar village, two hundred miles up the Missouri. The country thus abandoned by the hills is more open and the timber in smaller quantities than below the Platte, so that although the plain is rich and covered with high grass, the want of wood renders it less calculated for cultivation than below that river.

The northern hills after remaining near the Missouri for a few miles at Floyd's river, recede from it at the Sioux river, the course of which they follow; and though they again visit the Missouri at Whitestone river, where they are low, yet they do not return to it till beyond James river. The highlands on the south, after continuing near the river at the Mahar villages, again disappear, and do not approach it till the Cobalt bluffs, about forty-four miles from the villages, and then from those bluffs to the Yellowstone river, a distance of about one thousand miles, they follow the banks of the river with scarcely any deviation.

From the James river, the lower grounds are confined within a narrow space by the hills on both sides, which now continue near each other up to the mountains. The space between them however varies from one to three miles as high as the Muscleshell river, from which the hills approach so high as to leave scarcely any low grounds on the river, and near the falls reach the water's edge. Beyond the falls the hills are scattered and low to the first range of mountains.

The soil during the whole length of the Missouri below the Platte is generally speaking very fine, and although the timber is scarce, there is still sufficient for the purposes of settlers. But beyond that river, although the soil is still rich, yet the almost total absence of timber, and particularly the want of good water, of which there is but a small quantity in the creeks, and even that brackish, oppose powerful obstacles to its settlement. The difficulty becomes still greater between the Muscleshell river and the falls, where besides the greater scarcity of timber, the country itself is less fertile.

The elevation of these highlands varies as they pass through this extensive tract of country. From Wood river they are about one hundred and fifty feet above the water, and continue at that height till they rise near the Osage, from which place to the ancient fortification they again diminish in size. Thence they continue higher till the Mandan village, after which they are rather lower till the neighbourhood of Muscleshell river, where they are met by the Northern hills, which have advanced at a more uniform height, varying from one hundred and fifty to two hundred or three hundred feet. From this place to the mountains the height of both is nearly the same, from three hundred to five hundred feet, and the low grounds so narrow that the traveller seems passing through a range of high country. From Maria's river to the falls, the hills descend to the height of about two or three hundred feet.

AUGUST 19TH *Monday.* The morning was cold, and the grass perfectly whitened by the frost. We were engaged in preparing packs and saddles to load the horses as soon as they should arrive. A beaver was caught in a trap, but we were disappointed in trying to catch trout in our net; we therefore made a seine of willow brush, and by hauling it procured a number of fine trout, and a species of mullet which we had not seen before: it is about sixteen inches long, the scales small; the nose long, obtusely pointed, and exceeding the under jaw; the mouth opens with folds at the sides; it has no teeth, and the tongue and palate is smooth. The colour of its back and sides is a bluish brown while the belly is white: it has the faggot bones, whence we concluded it to be of the mullet species. It is by no means so well flavoured a fish as the trout, which are the same as those we first saw at the falls, larger than the speckled trout of the mountains in the Atlantic states, and equally well flavoured. In the evening the hunters returned with two deer.

Captain Clark, in the meantime, proceeded through a wide level valley, in which the chief pointed out a spot where many of his tribe were killed in battle a year ago. The Indians accompanied him during the day, and as they had nothing to eat, he was obliged to feed them from his own stores, the hunters not being able to kill any thing. Just as he was entering the mountains, he met an Indian with two mules and a Spanish saddle, who was so polite as to offer one of them to him to ride over the hills. Being on foot, captain Clark accepted his offer and gave him a waistcoat as a reward for his civility. He encamped for the night on a small stream, and the next morning, *Tuesday, August 20th,* he set out at six o'clock.

In passing through a continuation of the hilly broken country, he met several parties of Indians. On coming near the camp, which had been removed since we left them two miles higher up the river, Cameahwait requested that the party should halt. This was complied with: a number of Indians came out from the camp, and with great ceremony several pipes were smoked. This being over captain Clark was conducted to a large leathern lodge prepared for his party in the middle of the encampment, the Indians having only shelters of willow bushes. A few dried berries, and one salmon, the only food the whole village could contribute, were then pre-

238

sented to him; after which he proceeded to repeat in council, what had been already told them, the purposes of his visit; urged them to take their horses over and assist in transporting our baggage, and expressed a wish to obtain a guide to examine the river. This was explained and enforced to the whole village by Cameahwait, and an old man was pointed out who was said to know more of their geography to the north than any other person, and whom captain Clark engaged to accompany him. After explaining his views he distributed a few presents, the council was ended, and nearly half the village set out to hunt the antelope, but returned without success.

[Account of Capt. Clark's party]

Captain Clark in the meantime made particular inquiries as to the situation of the country, and the possibility of soon reaching a navigable water. The chief began by drawing on the ground a delineation of the rivers, from which it appeared that his information was very limited. The river on which the camp is he divided into two branches just above us, which, as he indicated by the opening of the mountains, were in view: he next made it discharge itself into a larger river ten miles below, coming from the southwest: the joint stream continued one day's march to the northwest, and then inclined to the westward for two days' march farther. At that place he placed several heaps of sand on each side, which, as he explained them, represented vast mountains of rock always covered with snow, in passing through which the river was so completely hemmed in by the high rocks, that there was no possibility of travelling along the shore; that the bed of the river was obstructed by sharp-pointed rocks, and such its rapidity, that as far as the eye could reach it presented a perfect column of foam. The mountains he said were equally inaccessible, as neither man nor horse could cross them; that such being the state of the country neither he nor any of his nation had ever attempted to go beyond the mountains. Cameahwait said also that he had been informed by the Chopunnish, or Pierced-nose Indians, who reside on this river west of the mountains, that it ran a great way towards the setting sun, and at length lost itself in a great lake of water which was ill-tasted, and where the white men lived.

An Indian belonging to a band of Shoshonees who live to the southwest, and who happened to be at camp, was then brought in, and enquiries made of him as to the situation of the country in that direction: this he described in terms scarcely less terrible than those in which Cameahwait had represented the west. He said that his relations lived at the distance of twenty days' march from this place, on a course a little to the west of south and not far from the whites, with whom they traded for horses, mules, cloth, metal, beads, and the shells here worn as ornaments, and which are those of a species of pearl oyster. In order to reach his country we should be obliged during the first seven days to climb over steep rocky mountains where there was no game, and we should find nothing but roots for subsistence. Even for these however we should be obliged to contend with a fierce warlike people, whom he called the Broken-moccasin, or moccasin with holes, who lived like bears in holes, and fed on roots and the flesh of such horses as they could steal or plunder from those who passed through the mountains. So rough indeed was the passage, that the feet of the horses would be wounded in such a manner that many of them would be unable to proceed. The next part of the route was for ten days through a dry parched desert of sand, inhabited by no animal which would supply us with subsistence, and as the sun had now scorched up the grass and dried up the small pools of water which are sometimes scattered through this desert in the spring, both ourselves and our horses would perish for want of food and water. About the middle of this plain a large river passes from southeast to northwest, which, though navigable, afforded neither timber nor salmon. Three or four days' march beyond this plain his relations lived, in a country tolerably fertile and partially covered with timber, on another large river running in the same direction as the former; that this last discharges itself into a third large river, on which resided many numerous nations, with whom his own were at war, but whether this last emptied itself into the great or stinking lake, as they called the ocean, he did not know; that from his country to the stinking lake was a great distance, and that the route to it, taken by such of his relations as had visited it, was up the river on which they lived, and over to that on which the white people lived, and which they knew discharged itself into the ocean. This route he advised us to take, but added, that we had better defer the journey till spring, when he would himself conduct us.

This account persuaded us that the streams of which he spoke were southern branches of the Columbia, heading with the Rio des Apostolos, and Rio Colorado, and that the route which he mentioned was to the gulf of California: captain Clark therefore told him that this road was too much towards the south for our purpose, and then requested to know if there was no route on the left of the river where we now are, by which we might intercept it below the mountains; but he knew of none except that through the barren plains, which he said joined the mountains on that side, and through which it was impossible to pass at this season, even if we were fortunate enough to escape the Broken-moccasin Indians. Captain Clark recompensed the Indian by a present of a knife, with which he seemed much gratified, and now inquired of Cameahwait by what route the Pierced-nose Indians, who he said lived west of the mountains, crossed over to the Missouri: this he said was towards the north, but that the road was a very bad one; that during the passage he had been told they suffered excessively from hunger, being obliged to subsist for many days on berries alone, there being no game in that part of the mountains, which were broken and rocky, and so thickly covered with timber that they could scarcely pass.

Surrounded by difficulties as all the other routes are, this seems to be the most practicable of all the passages by land, since, if the Indians can pass the mountains with their women and children, no difficulties which they could encounter could be formidable to us; and if the Indians below the mountains are so numerous as they are represented to be, they must have some means of subsistence equally within our power. They tell us indeed that the nations to the westward subsist principally on fish and roots, and that their only game were a few elk, deer, and antelope, there being no buffalo west of the mountain. The first inquiry however was to ascertain the truth of their information relative to the difficulty of descending the river: for this purpose captain Clark set out at three o'clock in the afternoon, accompanied by the guide and all his men, except one whom he left with orders to purchase a horse and join him as soon as possible.

At the distance of four miles he crossed the river, and eight miles from the camp halted for the night at a small stream. The road which he followed was a beaten path through a wide rich meadow, in which were several old lodges. On the route he met a number of men, women, and children, as well as horses, and one of the men who appeared to possess some consideration turned back with him, and observing a woman with three salmon obtained them from her, and presented them to the party. Captain Clark shot a mountain cock or cock of the plains, a dark brown bird larger than the dunghill fowl, with a long and pointed tail, and a fleshy protuberance about the base of the upper chop, something like that of the turkey though without the snout.

Wednesday. In the morning he resumed his march early, and at the distance of five miles reached an Indian lodge of brush, inhabited by seven families of Shoshonees. They behaved with great civility, gave the whole party as much boiled salmon as they could eat, and added as a present several dried salmon and a considerable quantity of chokecherries.

AUGUST 21ST

After smoking with them all he visited the fish weir, which was about two hundred yards distant; the river was here divided by three small islands, which occasioned the water to pass along four channels. Of these three were narrow, and stopped by means of trees which were stretched across, and supported by willow stakes, sufficiently near each other to prevent the passage of the fish. About the centre of each was placed a basket formed of willows, eighteen or twenty feet in length, of a cylindrical form, and terminating in a conic shape at its lower extremity; this was situated with its mouth upwards, opposite to an aperture in the weir. The main channel of the water was then conducted to this weir, and as the fish entered it they were so entangled with each other that they could not move, and were taken out by untying the small end of the willow basket. The weir in the main channel was formed in a manner somewhat different; there were in fact two distinct weirs formed of poles and willow sticks quite across the river, approaching each other obliquely with an aperture in each side near the angle. This is made by tying a number of poles together at the top, in parcels of three, which were then set up in a triangular form at the base, two of the poles being in the range desired for the weir, and the third down the stream. To these poles two ranges of other poles are next lashed horizontally, with willow bark and withes, and willow sticks joined in with these crosswise, so as to form a kind of wicker-work from the bottom of the river to the height of three or four feet above the surface of the water. This is so thick as to prevent the fish from passing, and even in some parts with the help of a little gravel and some stone enables them to give any direction which they wish to the water. These two weirs being placed near to each other, one for the purpose of catching the fish as they ascend, the other as they go down the river, is provided with two baskets made in the form already described, and which are placed at the apertures of the weir.

After examining these curious objects, he returned to the lodges, and soon passed the river to the left, where an Indian brought him a tomahawk which he said he had found in the grass, near the lodge where captain Lewis had stayed on his first visit to the village. This was a tomahawk which had been missed at the time, and supposed to be stolen; it was however the only article which had been lost in our intercourse with the nation, and as even that was returned the inference is highly honourable to the integrity of the Shoshonees.

On leaving the lodges captain Clark crossed to the left side of the river, and despatched five men to the forks of it, in search of the man left behind yesterday, who procured a horse and passed by another road as they learnt, to the forks. At the distance of fourteen miles they killed a very large salmon, two and a half feet long, in a creek six miles below the forks: and after travelling about twenty miles through the valley, following the course of the river, which runs nearly northwest, halted in a small meadow on the right side, under a cliff of rocks. Here they were joined by the five men who had gone in quest of Crusatte. They had been to the forks of the river, where the natives resort in great numbers for the purpose of gigging fish, of which they made our men a present of five fresh salmon. In addition to this food, one deer was killed to-day.

The western branch of this river is much larger than the eastern, and after we passed the junction we found the river about one hundred yards in width, rapid and shoaly, but containing only a small quantity of timber. As captain Lewis was the first white man who visited its waters, captain Clark gave it the name of Lewis's river. The low grounds through which he had passed to-day were rich and wide, but at his camp this evening the hills begin to assume a formidable aspect. The cliff under which he lay is of a reddish brown colour, the rocks which have fallen from it are a dark brown flintstone. Near the place are gulleys of white sandstone, and quantities of a fine sand, of a snowy whiteness: the mountains on each side are high and rugged, with some pine trees scattered over them.

AUGUST 22D *Thursday.* He soon began to perceive that the Indian accounts had not exaggerated: at the distance of a mile he passed a small creek, and the points of four mountains, which were rocky, and so high that it seemed almost impossible to cross them with horses. The road lay over the sharp fragments of rocks which had fallen from the mountains, and were strewed in heaps for miles together, yet the horses altogether unshod, travelled across them as fast as the men, and without detaining them a moment. They passed two bold-running streams, and reached the entrance of a small river, where a few Indian families resided. They had not been previously acquainted with the arrival of the whites, the guide was behind, and the wood so thick that we came upon them unobserved, till at a very short distance. As soon as they saw us, the women and children fled in great consternation; the men offered us every thing they had, the fish on the scaffolds, the dried berries and the collars of elk's tushes worn by the children. We took only a small quantity of the food, and gave them in return some small articles which conduced very much to pacify them. The guide now coming up, explained to them who we were, and the object of our visit, which seemed to relieve the fears, but still a number of the women and children did not recover from their fright, but cried during our stay, which lasted about an hour. The guide, whom we found a very intelligent friendly old man, informed us that up this river there was a road which led over the mountains to the Missouri.

On resuming his route, he went along the steep side of a mountain about three miles, and then reached the river near a small island, at the lower part of which he encamped; he here attempted to gig some fish, but could only obtain one small salmon. The river is here shoal and rapid, with many rocks scattered in various directions through its bed. On the sides of

INDIAN PAINTING OF A COMBAT (copied by Bodmer)

the mountains are some scattered pines, and of those on the left the tops are covered with them; there are however but few in the low grounds through which they passed, indeed they have seen only a single tree fit to make a canoe, and even that was small. The country has an abundant growth of berries, and we met several women and children gathering them who bestowed them upon us with great liberality. Among the woods captain Clark observed a species of woodpecker, the beak and tail of which were white, the wings black, and every other part of the body of a dark brown; its size was that of the robin, and it fed on the seeds of the pine.

Friday. Captain Clark set off very early, but as his route lay along the steep side of a mountain, over irregular and broken masses of rocks, which wounded the horses' feet, he was obliged to proceed slowly. At the distance of four miles he reached the river, but the rocks here became so steep, and projected so far into the river, that there was no mode of passing, except through the water. This he did for some distance, though the river was very rapid, and so deep that they were forced to swim their horses. After following the edge of the water for about a mile under this steep cliff, he reached a small meadow, below which the whole current of the river beat against the right shore on which he was, and which was formed of a solid rock perfectly inaccessible to horses. Here too, the little track which he had been pursuing terminated. He therefore resolved to leave the horses and the greater part of the men at this place, and examine the river still further, in order to determine if there were any possibility of descending it in canoes. Having killed nothing except a single goose to-day, and the whole of our provision being consumed last evening, it was by no means advisable to remain any length of time where they were.

AUGUST 23D

He now directed the men to fish and hunt at this place till his return, and then with his guide and three men he proceeded, clambering over immense rocks, and along the sides of lofty precipices which bordered the river, when at about twelve miles distance he reached a small meadow, the first he had seen on the river since he left his party. A little below this meadow, a large creek twelve yards wide, and of some depth, discharges itself from the north. Here were some recent signs of an Indian encampment, and the tracks of a number of horses, who must have come along a plain Indian path, which he now saw following the course of the creek. This stream his guide said led towards a large river running to the north, and was frequented by another nation for the purpose of catching fish. He remained here two hours, and having taken some small fish, made a dinner on them with the addition of a few berries.

From the place where he had left the party, to the mouth of this creek, it presents one continued rapid, in which are five shoals, neither of which could be passed with loaded canoes; and the baggage must therefore be transported for a considerable distance over the steep mountains, where it would be impossible to employ horses for the relief of the men. Even the empty canoes must be let down the rapids by means of cords, and not even in that way without great risk both to the canoes as well as to the men. At one of these shoals, indeed the rocks rise so perpendicularly from the water as to leave no hope of a passage or even a portage without great labour in removing rocks, and in some instances cutting away the earth. To surmount these difficulties would exhaust the strength of the party, and what is equally discouraging would waste our time and consume our provisions, of neither of which have we much to spare. The season is now far advanced, and the Indians tell us we shall shortly have snow: the salmon too have so far declined that the natives themselves are hastening from the country, and not an animal of any kind larger than a pheasant or a squirrel, and of even these a few only will then be seen in this part of the mountains: after which we shall be obliged to rely on our own stock of provisions, which will not support us more than ten days. These circumstances combine to render a passage by water impracticable in our present situation.

To descend the course of the river on horseback is the other alternative, and scarcely a more inviting one. The river is so deep that there are only a few places where it can be forded, and the rocks approach so near the water as to render it impossible to make a route along the water's edge. In crossing the mountains themselves we should have to encounter, besides their steepness, one barren surface of broken masses of rock, down which in certain seasons the torrents sweep vast quantities of stone into the river. These rocks are of a whitish brown, and towards the base of a gray colour, and so hard, that on striking them with steel, they yield a fire like flint. This sombre appearance is in some places scarcely relieved by a single tree, though near the river and on the creeks there is more timber, among which are some tall pine: several of these might be made into canoes, and by lashing two of them together, one of tolerable size might be formed.

After dinner he continued his route, and at the distance of half a mile passed another creek about five yards wide. Here his guide informed him that by ascending the creek for some distance he would have a better road, and cut off a considerable bend of the river towards the south. He therefore pursued a well-beaten Indian track up this creek for about six miles, when leaving the creek to the right he passed over a ridge, and after walking a mile again met the river, where it flows through a meadow of about eighty acres in extent. This they passed and then ascended a high and steep point of a mountain, from which the guide now pointed out where the river broke through the mountains about twenty miles distant. Near the base of the mountains a small river falls in from the south.

This view was terminated by one of the loftiest mountains captain Clark had ever seen, which was perfectly covered with snow. Towards this formidable barrier the river went directly on, and there it was, as the guide observed, that the difficulties and dangers of which he and Cameahwait had spoken commenced. After reaching the mountain, he said, the river continues its course towards the north for many miles, between high perpendicular rocks, which were scattered through its bed: it then penetrated the mountain through a narrow gap, on each side of which arose perpendicularly a rock as high as the top of the mountain before them; that the river then made a bend which concealed its future course from view, and as it was alike impossible to descend the river or clamber over that vast mountain, eternally covered with snow, neither he nor any of his nation had ever been lower than at a place where they could see the gap made by the river on entering the mountain. To that place he said he would conduct captain Clark if he desired it by the next evening. But he was in need of no further evidence to convince him of the utter impracticability of the route before him.

He had already witnessed the difficulties of part of the road, yet after all these dangers his guide, whose intelligence and fidelity he could not doubt, now assured him that the difficulties were only commencing, and what he saw before him too clearly convinced him of the Indian's veracity.

He therefore determined to abandon this route, and returned to the upper part of the last creek we had passed, and reaching it an hour after dark encamped for the night: on this creek he had seen in the morning an Indian road coming in from the north. Disappointed in finding a route by water, captain Clark now questioned his guide more particularly as to the direction of this road which he seemed to understand perfectly. He drew a map on the sand, and represented this road as well as that we passed yesterday on Berry creek as both leading towards two forks of the same great river, where resided a nation called Tushepaws, who having no salmon on their river, came by these roads to the fish weirs on Lewis's river. He had himself been among these Tushepaws, and having once accompanied them on a fishing party to another river he had there seen Indians who had come across the rocky mountains. After a great deal of conversation, or rather signs, and a second and more particular map from his guide, captain Clark felt persuaded that his guide knew of a road from the Shoshonee village they had left, to the great river to the north, without coming so low down as this on a route impracticable for horses.

Saturday. He was desirous of hastening his return, and therefore set out early, and after descending the creek to the river, stopped to breakfast on berries in the meadow above the second creek. He then went on, but unfortunately fell from a rock and injured his leg very much; he however walked on as rapidly as he could, and at four in the afternoon rejoined his men. During his absence they had killed one of the mountain cocks, a few pheasants, and some small fish, on which with haws and serviceberries they had subsisted. Captain Clark immediately sent forward a man on horseback with a note to captain Lewis, apprising him of the result of his inquiries, and late in the afternoon set out with the rest of the party and encamped at the distance of two miles. The men were much disheartened at the bad prospect of escaping from the mountains, and having nothing to eat but a few berries which have made several of them sick, they all passed a disagreeable night, which was rendered more uncomfortable by a heavy dew. AUGUST 24TH

Sunday. The want of provisions urged captain Clark to return as soon as possible; he therefore set out early, and halted an hour in passing the Indian camp near the fish weirs. These people treated them with great kindness, and though poor and dirty they willingly give what little they possess; they gave the whole party boiled salmon and dried berries, which were not however in sufficient quantities to appease their hunger. They soon resumed their old road, but as the abstinence or strange diet had given one of the men a very severe illness, they were detained very much on his account, and it was not till late in the day they reached the cliff under which they had encamped on the *21st*. They immediately began to fish and hunt, in order to procure a meal. We caught several small fish, and by means of our guide, obtained two salmon from a small party of women and children, who, with one man, were going below to gather berries. This supplied us with AUGUST 25TH about half a meal, but after dark we were regaled with a beaver which one of the hunters brought in. The other game seen in the course of the day were one deer, and a party of elk among the pines on the sides of the mountains.

AUGUST 26TH   *Monday.* The morning was fine, and three men were despatched ahead to hunt, while the rest were detained until nine o'clock, in order to retake some horses which had strayed away during the night. They then proceeded along the route by the forks of the river, till they reached the lower Indian camp where they first were when we met them. The whole camp immediately flocked around him with great appearance of cordiality, but all the spare food of the village did not amount to more than two salmon, which they gave to captain Clark, who distributed them among his men. The hunters had not been able to kill any thing, nor had captain Clark or the greater part of the men any food during the twenty-four hours, till towards evening one of them shot a salmon in the river, and a few small fish were caught, which furnished them with a scanty meal. The only animals they had seen were a few pigeons, some very wild hares, a great number of the large black grasshopper, and a quantity of ground lizards.

AUGUST 27TH   *Tuesday.* The men, who were engaged last night in mending their moccasins, all except one, went out hunting, but no game was to be procured. One of the men however killed a small salmon, and the Indians made a present of another, on which the whole party made a very slight breakfast. These Indians, to whom this life is familiar, seem contented, although they depend for subsistence on the scanty productions of the fishery. But our men who are used to hardships, but have been accustomed to have the first wants of nature regularly supplied, feel very sensibly their wretched situation: their strength is wasting away; they begin to express their apprehensions of being without food in a country perfectly destitute of any means of supporting life, except a few fish. In the course of the day an Indian brought into the camp five salmon, two of which captain Clark bought, and made a supper for the party.

AUGUST 28TH   *Wednesday.* There was a frost again this morning. The Indians gave the party two salmon out of several which they caught in their traps, and having purchased two more, the party was enabled to subsist on them during the day. A camp of about forty Indians from the west fork passed us to-day, on their route to the eastward. Our prospect of provisions is getting worse every day: the hunters who had ranged through the country in every direction where game might be reasonably expected, have seen nothing. The fishery is scarcely more productive, for an Indian who was out all day with his gig killed only one salmon. Besides the four fish procured from the Indians, captain Clark obtained some fishroe in exchange for three small fishhooks, the use of which he taught them, and which they very readily comprehended. All the men who are not engaged in hunting, are occupied in making pack-saddles for the horses which captain Lewis informed us he had bought.

AUGUST 20TH

[*Account of Capt. Lewis's party*]

Two hunters were despatched early in the morning, but they returned without killing any thing, and the only game we procured was a beaver, who was caught last night in a trap which he carried off two miles before he was found. The fur of this animal is as good as any we have ever seen, nor does it in fact appear to be ever out of season on the upper branches of the Missouri. This beaver, with several dozen of fine trout, gave us a plentiful subsistence for the day. The party were occupied chiefly in making pack-saddles, in the manufacture of which we supply the place of nails and boards, by substituting for the first thongs of raw hide, which answer very well; and for boards we use the handles of our oars, and the plank of some boxes, the contents of which we empty into sacks of raw hides made for the purpose. The Indians who visit us behave with the greatest decorum, and the women are busily engaged in making and mending the moccasins of the party. As we had still some superfluous baggage which would be too heavy to carry across the mountains, it became necessary to make a cache or deposit. For this purpose we selected a spot on the bank of the river, three quarters of a mile below the camp, and three men were set to dig it, with a sentinel in the neighbourhood, who was ordered if the natives were to straggle that way, to fire a signal for the workmen to desist and separate. Towards evening the cache was completed without being perceived by the Indians, and the packages prepared for deposit.

Chapter 16

AMONG THE SHOSHONEE INDIANS

WEDNESDAY, AUGUST 21ST, 1805 The weather was very cold; the water which stood in the vessels exposed to the air being covered with ice a quarter of an inch thick: the ink freezes in the pen, and the low grounds are perfectly whitened with frost: after this the day proved excessively warm. The party were engaged in their usual occupations, and completed twenty saddles with the necessary harness, all prepared to set off as soon as the Indians should arrive. Our two hunters who were despatched early in the morning have not returned, so that we were obliged to encroach on our pork and corn, which we consider as the last resource when our casual supplies of game fail. After dark we carried our baggage to the cache, and deposited what we thought too cumbrous to carry with us: a small assortment of medicines, and all the specimens of plants, seeds, and minerals, collected since leaving the falls of the Missouri.

Late at night Drewyer, one of the hunters, returned with a fawn and a considerable quantity of Indian plunder, which he had taken by way of reprisal. While hunting this morning in the Shoshonee cove, he came suddenly upon an Indian camp, at which were an old man, a young one, three women, and a boy: they showed no surprise at the sight of him, and he therefore rode up to them, and after turning his horse loose to graze sat down and began to converse with them by signs. They had just finished a repast on some roots, and in about twenty minutes one of the women spoke to the rest of the party, who immediately went out, collected their horses and began to saddle them. Having rested himself, Drewyer thought that he would continue his hunt, and rising went to catch his horse who was at a short distance, forgetting at the moment to take up his rifle. He had scarcely gone more than fifty paces when the Indians mounted their horses, the young man snatched up the rifle, and leaving all their baggage, whipped their horses, and set off at full speed towards the passes of the mountains: Drewyer instantly jumped on his horse and pursued them.

After running about ten miles the horses of the women nearly gave out, and the women finding Drewyer gain on them raised dreadful cries, which induced the young man to slacken his pace, and being mounted on a very fleet horse rode round them at a short distance. Drewyer now came up with the women, and by signs persuaded them that he did not mean to hurt them: they then stopped, and as the young man came towards them Drewyer asked him for his rifle, but the only part of the answer which he understood was Pahkee, the name by which they call their enemies, the Minnetarees of fort de Prairie. While they were thus engaged in talking, Drewyer watched his opportunity, and seeing the Indian off his guard, galloped up to him and seized his rifle: the Indian struggled for some time, but finding Drewyer getting too strong for him, had the presence of mind to open the pan and let the priming fall out: he then let go his hold, and giving his horse the whip escaped at full speed, leaving the women to the mercy of the conqueror. Drewyer then returned to where he had first seen them, where he found that their baggage had been left behind, and brought it to camp with him.

AUGUST 22D *Thursday.* This morning early two men were sent to complete the covering of the cache, which could not be so perfectly done during the night as to elude the search of the Indians. On examining the spoils which Drewyer had obtained, they were found to consist of several dressed and undressed skins; two bags wove with the bark of the silk-grass, each containing a bushel of dried serviceberries, and about the same quantity of roots; an instrument made of bone for manufacturing the flints into heads for arrows; and a number of flints themselves: these were much of the same colour and nearly as transparent as common black glass, and when cut detached itself into flakes, leaving a very sharp edge.

[Account of Capt. Lewis's party]

The roots were of three kinds, and folded separate from each in hides of buffalo made into parchment. The first is a fusiform root six inches long, and about the size of a man's finger at the largest end, with radicles larger than is usual in roots of the fusiform sort: the rind is white and thin, the body is also white, mealy, and easily reducible, by pounding, to a substance resembling flour, like which it thickens by boiling, and is of an agreeable flavour: it is eaten frequently in its raw state either green or dried. The second species was much mutilated, but appeared to be fibrous; it is of a cylindrical form about the size of a small quill, hard and brittle. A part of the rind which had not been detached in the preparation was hard and black, but the rest of the root was perfectly white; this the Indians informed us was always boiled before eating; and on making the experiment we found that it became perfectly soft, but had a bitter taste, which was nauseous to our taste, but which the Indians seemed to relish; for on giving the roots to them they were very heartily swallowed.

The third species was a small nut about the size of a nutmeg, of an irregularly rounded form, something like the smallest of the Jerusalem artichokes, which, on boiling, we found them to resemble also in flavour, and is certainly the best root we have seen in use among the Indians. On inquiring of the Indians from what plant these roots were procured, they informed us that none of them grew near this place.

The men were chiefly employed in dressing the skins belonging to the party who accompanied captain Clark. About eleven o'clock Chaboneau and his wife returned with Cameahwait, accompanied by about fifty men with their women and children. After they had encamped near us and turned loose their horses, we called a council of all the chiefs and warriors and addressed them in a speech: additional presents were then distributed, particularly to the two second chiefs, who had agreeably to their promises exerted themselves in our favour. The council was then adjourned, and all the Indians were treated with an abundant meal of boiled Indian corn and beans. The poor wretches, who had no animal food and scarcely any thing but a few fish, had been almost starved, and received this new luxury with great thankfulness. Out of compliment to the chief we gave him a few dried squashes which we had brought from the Mandans, and he declared it was the best food he had ever tasted except sugar, a small lump of which he had received from his sister: he now declared how happy they should all be to live in a country which produced so many good things, and we told him that it would not be long before the white men would put it in their power to live below the mountains, where they might themselves cultivate all these kinds of food instead of wandering in the mountains. He appeared to be much pleased with this information, and the whole party being now in excellent temper after their repast, we began our purchase of horses. We soon obtained five very good ones on very reasonable terms; that is, by giving for

249

each merchandise which cost us originally about six dollars. We have again to admire the perfect decency and propriety of their conduct; for although so numerous, they do not attempt to crowd round our camp or take any thing which they see lying about, and whenever they borrow knives or kettles or any other article from the men, they return them with great fidelity.

Towards evening we formed a drag of bushes, and in about two hours caught five hundred and twenty-eight very good fish most of them large trout. Among them we observed for the first time ten or twelve trout of a white or silvery colour, except on the back and head where they are of a bluish cast: in appearance and shape they resemble exactly the speckled trout, except that they are not quite so large, though the scales are much larger, and the flavour equally good. The greater part of the fish was distributed among the Indians.

AUGUST 23D *Friday*. Our visitors seem to depend wholly on us for food, and as the state of our provisions obliges us to be careful of our remaining stock of corn and flour, this was an additional reason for urging our departure; but Cameahwait requested us to wait till the arrival of another party of his nation who were expected to-day. Knowing that it would be in vain to oppose his wish, we consented, and two hunters were sent out with orders to go further up the southeast fork than they had hitherto been. At the same time the chief was informed of the low state of our provisions, and advised to send out his young men to hunt. This he recommended them to do, and most of them set out: we then sunk our canoes by means of stones to the bottom of the river, a situation which better than any other secured them against the effects of the high waters, and the frequent fires of the plains; the Indians having promised not to disturb them during our absence, a promise we believe the more readily, as they are almost too lazy to take the trouble of raising them for fire-wood. We were desirous of purchasing some more horses, but they declined selling any until we reached their camp in the mountains.

Soon after starting the Indian hunters discovered a mule buck, and twelve of their horsemen pursued it, for four miles. We saw the chase, which was very entertaining, and at length they rode it down and killed it. This mule buck was the largest deer of any kind we have seen, being nearly as large as a doe elk. Besides this they brought in another deer and three goats; but instead of a general distribution of the meat, and such as we have hitherto seen among all tribes of Indians, we observed that some families had a large share, while others received none. On enquiring of Cameahwait the reason of this custom, he said that meat among them was scarce, that each hunter reserved what he killed for the use of himself and his own family, none of the rest having any claim on what he chose to keep. Our hunters returned soon after with two mule deer and three common deer, three of which we distributed among the families who had received none of the game of their own hunters. About three o'clock the expected party consisting of fifty men, women and children arrived. We now learnt that most of the Indians were on their way down the valley towards the buffalo country, and some anxiety to accompany them appeared to prevail among those who had promised to assist us in crossing the mountains. We ourselves were not without some apprehension that they might leave us, but as they continued to say that they would return with us nothing was said upon the subject. We were, however, resolved to move early in the morning, and therefore despatched two men to hunt in the cove and leave the game on the route we should pass to-morrow.

Saturday. As the Indians who arrived yesterday had a number of spare horses, we thought it probable they might be willing to dispose of them, and desired the chief to speak to them for that purpose. They declined giving any positive answer, but requested to see the goods which we proposed to exchange. We then produced some battle-axes which we had made at fort Mandan, and a quantity of knives; with both of which they appeared very much pleased; and we were soon able to purchase three horses by giving for each an axe, a knife, a handkerchief and a little paint. To this we were obliged to add a second knife, a shirt, a handkerchief and a pair of leggings; and such is the estimation in which those animals are held, that even at this price, which was double that for a horse, the fellow who sold him took upon himself great merit in having given away a mule to us. They now said that they had no more horses for sale, and as we had now nine of our own, two hired horses, and a mule, we began loading them as heavily as was prudent, and placing the rest on the shoulders of the Indian women, left our camp at twelve o'clock.

We were all on foot, except Sacajawea, for whom her husband had purchased a horse with some articles which we gave him for that purpose; an Indian however had the politeness to offer captain Lewis one of his horses to ride, which he accepted in order better to direct the march of the party. We crossed the river below the forks, directing our course towards the cove by the route already passed, and had just reached the lower part of the cove when an Indian rode up to captain Lewis to inform him that one of his men was very sick, and unable to come on. The party was immediately halted at a run which falls into the creek on the left, and captain Lewis rode back two miles, and found Wiser severely afflicted with the colic: by giving him some of the essence of peppermint and laudanum, he recovered sufficiently to ride the horse of captain Lewis, who then rejoined the party on foot. When he arrived he found that the Indians who had been impatiently expecting his return, at last unloaded their horses and turned them loose, and had now made their camp for the night. It would have been fruitless to remonstrate, and not prudent to excite any irritation, and therefore, although the sun was still high, and we had made only six miles, we thought it best to remain with them: after we had encamped there fell a slight shower of rain. One of the men caught several fine trout; but Drewyer had been sent out to hunt without having killed any thing. We therefore gave a little corn to those of the Indians who were actually engaged in carrying our baggage, and who had absolutely nothing to eat. We also advised Cameahwait, as we could not supply all his people with provisions, to recommend to all who were not assisting us, to go on before us to their camp. This he did: but in the morning, *Sunday 25th*, a few only followed his advice, the rest accompanying us at some distance on each side.

We set out at sunrise and after going seventeen miles halted for dinner within two miles of the narrow pass in the mountains. The Indians who were on the sides of our party had started some antelopes, but were obliged after a pursuit of several hours to abandon the chase: our hunters had in the

[Account of Capt. Lewis's party]

AUGUST 24TH

meantime brought in three deer, the greater part of which was distributed among the Indians.

Whilst at dinner we learnt by means of Sacajawea, that the young men who left us this morning, carried a request from the chief, that the village would break up its encampment and meet this party to-morrow, when they would all go down the Missouri into the buffalo country. Alarmed at this new caprice of the Indians which, if not counteracted, threatened to leave ourselves and our baggage on the mountains, or even if we reached the waters of the Columbia, prevent our obtaining horses to go on further, captain Lewis immediately called the three chiefs together.

After smoking a pipe he asked them if they were men of their words, and if we can rely on their promises. They readily answered in the affirmative. He then asked if they had not agreed to assist us in carrying our baggage over the mountains. To this they also answered yes. "And why then," said he, "have you requested your people to meet us to-morrow, where it will be impossible for us to trade for horses, as you promised we should? If," he continued, "you had not promised to help us in transporting our goods over the mountains, we should not have attempted it, but have returned down the river, after which no white men would ever have come into your country. If you wish the whites to be your friends, and to bring you arms and protect you from your enemies, you should never promise what you do not mean to perform: when I first met you, you doubted what I said, yet you afterwards saw that I told you the truth. How therefore can you doubt what I now tell you; you see that I have divided amongst you the meat which my hunters kill, and I promise to give all who assist us a share of whatever we have to eat. If therefore you intend to keep your promise, send one of the young men immediately to order the people to remain at the village till we arrive."

The two inferior chiefs then said, that they had wished to keep their words and to assist us; that they had not sent for the people, but on the contrary had disapproved of the measure which was done wholly by the first chief. Cameahwait remained silent for some time: at last he said that he knew he had done wrong, but that seeing his people all in want of provisions, he had wished to hasten their departure for the country where their wants might be supplied. He however now declared, that having passed his word he would never violate it, and counter orders were immediately sent to the village by a young man, to whom we gave a handkerchief in order to ensure despatch and fidelity.

This difficulty being now adjusted, our march was resumed with an unusual degree of alacrity on the part of the Indians. We passed a spot, where six years ago the Shoshonees suffered a very severe defeat from the Minnetarees; and late in the evening we reached the upper part of the cove where the creek enters the mountains. The part of the cove on the northeast side of the creek has lately been burnt, most probably as a signal on some occasion. Here we were joined by our hunters with a single deer, which captain Lewis gave, as a proof of his sincerity, to the women and children, and remained supperless himself. As we came along we observed several large hares, some ducks, and many of the cock of the plains: in the low grounds of the cove were also considerable quantities of wild onions.

Monday. The morning was excessively cold, and the ice in our vessels was nearly a quarter of an inch in thickness: we set out at sunrise, and soon reached the fountain of the Missouri, where we halted for a few minutes, and then crossing the dividing ridge reached the fine spring where captain Lewis had slept on the *12th* in his first excursion to the Shoshonee camp. The grass on the hill sides is perfectly dry and parched by the sun, but near the spring was a fine green grass: we therefore halted for dinner and turned our horses to graze. To each of the Indians who were engaged in carrying our baggage was distributed a pint of corn, which they parched, then pounded, and made a sort of soup.

AUGUST 26TH

[*Account of Capt. Lewis's party*]

One of the women who had been leading two of our pack horses halted at a rivulet about a mile behind, and sent on the two horses by a female friend: on inquiring of Cameahwait the cause of her detention, he answered with great appearance of unconcern, that she had just stopped to lie in, but would soon overtake us. In fact, we were astonished to see her in about an hour's time come on with her new born infant and pass us on her way to the camp, apparently in perfect health.

This wonderful facility with which the Indian women bring forth their children, seems rather some benevolent gift of nature, in exempting them from pains which their savage state would render doubly grievous, than any result of habit. If, as has been imagined, a pure dry air or a cold and elevated country are obstacles to easy delivery, every difficulty incident to that operation might be expected in this part of the continent: nor can another reason, the habit of carrying heavy burdens during pregnancy, be at all applicable to the Shoshonee women, who rarely carry any burdens, since their nation possesses an abundance of horses. We have indeed been several times informed by those conversant with Indian manners, and who asserted their knowledge of the fact, that Indian women pregnant by white men experience more difficulty in child-birth than when the father is an Indian. If this account be true, it may contribute to strengthen the belief, that the easy delivery of the Indian women is wholly constitutional.

The tops of the high irregular mountains to the westward are still entirely covered with snow; and the coolness which the air acquires in passing them, is a very agreeable relief from the heat, which has dried up the herbage on the sides of the hills. While we stopped, the women were busily employed in collecting the root of a plant with which they feed their children, who like their mothers are nearly half starved and in a wretched condition. It is a species of fennel which grows in the moist grounds; the radix is of the knob kind, of a long ovate form, terminating in a single radicle, the whole being three or four inches long, and the thickest part about the size of a man's little finger: when fresh, it is white, firm, and crisp; and when dried and pounded makes a fine white meal. Its flavour is not unlike that of aniseed, though less pungent. From one to four of these knobbed roots are attached to a single stem which rises to the height of three or four feet, and is jointed, smooth, cylindric, and has several small peduncles, one at each joint above the sheathing leaf. Its colour is a deep green, as is also that of the leaf, which is sheathing, sessile, and *polipartite*, the divisions being long and narrow. The flowers, which are now in bloom, are small and numerous, with white and umbelliferous petals: there are no root leaves. As soon as the seeds have matured, the roots of the present year as well as the stem decline, and are renewed in the succeeding spring from the little knot which unites the roots. The sunflower is also abundant here, and the seeds, which are now ripe, are gathered in considerable quantities, and after being pounded and rubbed between smooth stones, form a kind of meal, which is a favourite dish among the Indians.

After dinner we continued our route and were soon met by a party of young men on horseback, who turned with us and went to the village. As soon as we were within sight of it, Cameahwait requested that we would discharge our guns; the men were therefore drawn up in a single rank, and gave a running fire of two rounds, to the great satisfaction of the Indians. We then proceeded to the encampment where we arrived about six o'clock, and were conducted to the leathern lodge in the centre of thirty-two others made of brush. The baggage was arranged near this tent, which captain Lewis occupied, and surrounded by those of the men so as to secure it from pillage. This camp was in a beautiful smooth meadow near the river, and about three miles above their camp when we first visited the Indians. We here found Colter, who had been sent by captain Clark with a note apprising us that there were no hopes of a passage by water, and that the most practicable route seemed to be that mentioned by his guide, towards the north. Whatever road we meant to take, it was now necessary to provide ourselves with horses; we therefore informed Cameahwait of our intention of going to the great river beyond the mountains, and that we would wish to purchase twenty more horses: he said the Minnetarees had stolen a great number of their horses this spring, but he still hoped they could spare us that number. In order not to lose the present favourable moment, and to keep the Indians as cheerful as possible, the violins were brought out and our men danced to the great diversion of the Indians. This mirth was the more welcome because our situation was not precisely that which would most dispose us for gaiety, for we have only a little parched corn to eat, and our means of subsistence or of success, depend on the wavering temper of the natives, who may change their minds to-morrow.

The Shoshonees are a small tribe of the nation called Snake Indians, a vague denomination, which embraces at once the inhabitants of the southern parts of the Rocky mountains and of the plains on each side. The Shoshonees with whom we now are, amount to about one hundred warriors, and three times that number of women and children. Within their own recollection they formerly lived in the plains, but they have been driven into the mountains by the Pawkees, or the roving Indians of the Sascatchawain, and are now obliged to visit occasionally, and by stealth, the country of their ancestors. Their lives are indeed migratory. From the middle of May to the beginning of September, they reside on the waters of the Columbia, where they consider themselves perfectly secure from the Pawkees who have never yet found their way to that retreat. During this time they subsist chiefly on salmon, and as that fish disappears on the approach of autumn, they are obliged to seek subsistence elsewhere. They then cross the ridge to the waters of the Missouri, down which they proceed slowly and cautiously, till they are joined near the three forks by other bands, either of their own nation or of the Flatheads, with whom they associate against the common enemy. Being now strong in numbers, they venture to hunt buffalo in the plains eastward of the mountains, near which they spend the winter, till the return of the salmon invites them to the Columbia. But such is their terror of the Pawkees, that as long as they can obtain the scantiest subsistence, they do not leave the interior of the mountains; and as soon as they collect a large stock of dried meat, they again retreat, and thus alternately obtaining their food at the hazard of their lives, and hiding themselves to consume it.

In this loose and wandering existence they suffer the extremes of want; for two-thirds of the year they are forced to live in the mountains, passing whole weeks without meat, and with nothing to eat but a few fish and roots. Nor can any thing be imagined more wretched than their condition at the present time, when the salmon is fast retiring, when roots are becoming scarce, and they have not yet acquired strength to hazard an encounter with their enemies. So insensible are they however to these calamities, that the Shoshonees are not only cheerful but even gay; and their character, which is more interesting than that of any Indians we have seen, has in it much of the dignity of misfortune. In their intercourse with strangers they are frank and communicative, in their dealings perfectly fair, nor have we had during our stay with them, any reason to suspect that the display of all our new and valuable wealth, has tempted them into a single act of dishonesty. While they have generally shared with us the little they possess, they have always abstained from begging any thing from us. With their liveliness of temper, they are fond of gaudy dresses, and of all sorts of amusements, particularly to games of hazard; and like most Indians fond of boasting of their own warlike exploits, whether real or fictitious.

In their conduct towards ourselves, they were kind and obliging, and though on one occasion they seemed willing to neglect us, yet we scarcely knew how to blame the treatment by which we suffered, when we recollected how few civilised chiefs would have hazarded the comforts or the subsistence of their people for the sake of a few strangers. This manliness of character may cause or it may be formed by the nature of their government, which is perfectly free from any restraint. Each individual is his own master, and the only control to which his conduct is subjected, is the advice of a chief supported by his influence over the opinions of the rest of the tribe. The chief himself is in fact no more than the most confidential person among the warriors, a rank neither distinguished by any external honor, nor invested by any ceremony, but gradually acquired from the good wishes of his companions and by superior merit. Such an officer has therefore strictly no power; he may recommend or advise or influence, but his commands have no effect on those who incline to disobey, and who may at any time withdraw from their voluntary allegiance. His shadowy authority which cannot survive the confidence which supports it, often decays with the personal vigour of the chief, or is transferred to some more fortunate or favourite hero.

In their domestic economy, the man is equally sovereign. The man is the sole proprietor of his wives and daughters, and can barter them away, or dispose of them in any manner he may think proper. The children are seldom corrected; the boys, particularly, soon become their own masters; they are never whipped, for they say that it breaks their spirit, and that after being flogged they never recover their independence of mind, even when they grow to manhood. A plurality of wives is very common; but these are not generally sisters, as among the Minnetarees and Mandans, but are purchased of different fathers. The infant daughters are often betrothed by the father to men who are grown, either for themselves or for their sons, for whom they are desirous of providing wives. The compensation to the father is usually made in horses or mules; and the girl remains with her parents till the age of puberty, which is thirteen or fourteen, when she is surrendered to her husband. At the same time the father often makes a present to the husband equal to what he had formerly received as the price of his daughter, though this return is optional with her parent. Sacajawea had been contracted in this way before she was taken prisoner, and when we brought her back, her betrothed was still living. Although he was double the age of Sacajawea, and had two other wives, he claimed her, but on finding that she had a child by her new husband, Chaboneau, he relinquished his pretensions and said he did not want her.

The chastity of the women does not appear to be held in much estimation. The husband will for a trifling present lend his wife for a night to a stranger, and the loan may be protracted by increasing the value of the present. Yet strange as it may seem, notwithstanding this facility, any connection of this kind not authorised by the husband, is considered highly offensive and quite as disgraceful to his character as the same licentiousness in civilised societies. The Shoshonees are not so importunate in volunteering the services of their wives as we found the Sioux were; and indeed we observed among them some women who appeared to be held in more respect than those of any nation we had seen. But the mass of the females are condemned, as among all savage nations, to the lowest and most laborious drudgery. When the tribe is stationary, they collect the roots, and cook; they build the huts, dress the skins and make clothing; collect the wood, and assist in taking care of the horses on the route; they load the horses and have the charge of all the baggage. The only business of the man is to fight; he therefore takes on himself the care of his horse, the companion of his warfare; but he will descend to no other labour than to hunt and to fish. He would consider himself degraded by being compelled to walk any distance; and were he so poor as to possess only two horses, he would ride the best of them, and leave the other for his wives and children and their baggage; and if he has too many wives or too much baggage for the horse, the wives have no alternative but to follow him on foot; they are not however often reduced to those extremities, for their stock of horses is very ample.

Notwithstanding their losses this spring they still have at least seven hundred, among which are about forty colts, and half that number of mules. There are no horses here which can be considered as wild; we have seen two only on this side of the Muscleshell river which were without owners, and even those although shy, showed every mark of having been once in the possession of man. The original stock was procured from the Spaniards, but they now raise their own. The horses are generally very fine, of a good size, vigorous and patient of fatigue as well as hunger. Each warrior has one or two tied to a stake near his hut both day and night, so as to be always prepared for action. The mules are obtained in the course of trade from the Spaniards, with whose brands several of them are marked, or stolen from them by the frontier Indians. They are the finest animals of that kind we have ever seen, and at this distance from the Spanish colonies are very highly valued. The worst are considered as worth the price of two horses, and a good mule cannot be obtained for less than three and sometimes four horses. We also saw a bridle bit, stirrups and several other articles which, like the mules, came from the Spanish colonies. The Shoshonees say that they can reach those settlements in ten days' march by the route of the Yellowstone river; but we readily perceive that the Spaniards are by no means favourites. They complain that the Spaniards refuse to let them have fire arms under pretence that these dangerous weapons will only induce them to kill each other. In the meantime, say the Shoshonees, they are left to the mercy of the Minnetarees, who having arms, plunder them of their horses, and put them to death without mercy. "But this should not be," said Cameahwait fiercely, "if we had guns, instead of hiding ourselves in the mountains and living like the bears on roots and berries, we would then go down and live in the buffalo country in spite of our enemies, whom we never fear when we meet on equal terms."

Knife scabbard.

As war is the chief occupation, bravery is the first virtue among the Shoshonees. None can hope to be distinguished without having given proofs of it, nor can there be any preferment, or influence among the nation, without some warlike achievement. Those important events which give reputation to a warrior, and which entitle him to a new name, are killing a white bear, stealing individually the horses of the enemy, leading out a party who happen to be successful either in plundering horses or destroying the enemy, and lastly scalping a warrior. These acts seem of nearly equal dignity, but the last, that of taking an enemy's scalp, is an honour quite independent of the act of vanquishing him. To kill your adversary is of no importance unless the scalp is brought from the field of battle, and were a warrior to slay any number of his enemies in action, and others were to obtain the scalps or first touch the dead, they would have all the honours, since they have borne off the trophy.

Although thus oppressed by the Minnetarees, the Shoshonees are still a very military people. Their cold and rugged country inures them to fatigue; their long abstinence makes them support the dangers of mountain warfare, and worn down as we saw them, by want of sustenance, have a look of fierce and adventurous courage. The Shoshonee warrior always fights on horseback; he possesses a few bad guns, which are reserved exclusively for war, but his common arms are the bow and arrow, a shield, a lance and a weapon called by the Chippeways, by whom it was formerly used, the poggamoggon.

The bow is made of cedar or pine covered on the outer side with sinews and glue. It is about two and a half feet long, and does not differ in shape from those used by the Sioux, Mandans and Minnetarees. Sometimes, however, the bow is made of a single piece of the horn of an elk, covered on the back like those of wood with sinews and glue, and occasionally ornamented by a strand wrought of porcupine quills and sinews, which is wrapped round the horn near its two ends. The bows made of the horns of the bighorn, are still more prized, and are formed by cementing with glue flat pieces of the horn together, covering the back with sinews and glue, and loading the whole with an unusual quantity of ornaments. The arrows resemble those of the other Indians except in being more slender than any we have seen. They are contained, with the implements for striking fire, in a narrow quiver formed of different kinds of skin, though that of the otter seems to be preferred. It is just long enough to protect the arrows from the weather, and is worn on the back by means of a strap passing over the right shoulder and under the left arm. The shield is a circular piece of buffalo hide about two feet four or five inches in diameter, ornamented with feathers, and a fringe round it of dressed leather, and adorned or deformed with paintings of strange figures. The buffalo hide is perfectly proof against any arrow, but in the minds of the Shoshonees, its power to protect them is chiefly derived from the virtues which are communicated to it by the old men and jugglers.

To make a shield is indeed one of their most important ceremonies: it begins by a feast to which all the warriors, old men and jugglers are invited. After the repast a hole is dug in the ground about eighteen inches in depth and of the same diameter as the intended shield: into this hole red hot stones are thrown and water poured over them, till they emit a very strong hot steam. The buffalo skin, which must be the entire hide of a male two years old, and never suffered to dry since it was taken from the animal, is now laid across the hole, with the fleshy side to the ground, and stretched in every direction by as many as can take hold of it. As the skin becomes heated, the hair separates and is taken off by the hand; till at last the skin is contracted into the compass designed for the shield. It is then taken off and placed on a hide prepared into parchment, and then pounded during the rest of the festival by the bare heels of those who are invited to it. This operation sometimes continues for several days, after which it is delivered to the proprietor, and declared by the old men and jugglers to be a security against arrows; and provided the feast has been satisfactory, against even the bullets of their enemies. Such is the delusion, that many of the Indians implicitly believe that this ceremony has given to the shield supernatural powers, and that they have no longer to fear any weapons of their enemies.

The poggamoggon is an instrument, consisting of a handle twenty-two inches long, made of wood, covered with dressed leather about the size of a whip-handle: at one end is a thong of two inches in length, which is tied to a round stone weighing two pounds and held in a cover of leather: at the other end is a loop of the same material, which is passed round the wrist so as to secure the hold of the instrument, with which they strike a very severe blow.

Besides these, they have a kind of armour something like a coat of mail, which is formed by a great many folds of dressed antelope skins, united by means of a mixture of glue and sand. With this they cover their own bodies and those of their horses, and find it impervious to the arrow.

The caparison of their horses is a halter and a saddle: the first is either a rope of six or seven strands of buffalo hair plaited or twisted together, about the size of a man's finger and of great strength; or merely a thong of raw hide, made pliant by pounding and rubbing; though the first kind is much preferred. The halter is very long, and is never taken from the neck of the horse when in constant use. One end of it is first tied round the neck in a knot and then brought down to the under jaw, round which it is formed into a simple noose, passing through the mouth: it is then drawn up on the right side and held by the rider in his left hand, while the rest trails after him to some distance. At other times the knot is formed at a little distance from one of the ends, so as to let that end serve as a bridle, while the other trails on the ground. With these cords dangling along side of them the horse is put to his full speed without fear of falling, and when he is turned to graze the noose is merely taken from his mouth. The saddle is formed like the pack-saddles used by the French and Spaniards, of two flat thin boards which fit the sides of the horse, and are kept together by two cross pieces, one before and the other behind, which rise to a considerable height, ending sometimes in a flat point extending outwards, and always making the saddle deep and narrow. Under this a piece of buffalo skin, with the hair on, is placed so as to prevent the rubbing of the boards, and when they mount they throw a piece of skin or robe over the saddle, which has no permanent cover. When stirrups are used, they consist of wood covered with leather; but stirrups and saddles are conveniences reserved for old men and women.

The young warriors rarely use any thing except a small leather pad stuffed with hair, and secured by a girth made of a leathern thong. In this way they ride with great expertness, and they have a particular dexterity in catching the horse when he is running at large. If he will not immediately submit when they wish to take him, they make a noose in the rope, and although the horse may be at a distance, or even running, rarely fail to fix it on his neck; and such is the docility of the animal, that however unruly he may seem, he surrenders as soon as he feels the rope on him. This cord is so useful in this way that it is never dispensed with, even when they use the Spanish bridle, which they prefer, and always procure when they have it in their power. The horse becomes almost an object of attachment: a favourite is frequently painted and his ears cut into various shapes: the mane and tail, which are never drawn nor trimmed, are decorated with feathers of birds, and sometimes a warrior suspends at the breast of his horse the finest ornaments he possesses.

Thus armed and mounted the Shoshonee is a formidable enemy, even with the feeble weapons which he is still obliged to use. When they attack at full speed they bend forward and cover their bodies with the shield, while with the right hand they shoot under the horse's neck.

The only articles of metal which the Shoshonees possess are a few bad knives, some brass kettles, some bracelets or armbands of iron and brass, a few buttons worn as ornaments in their hair, one or two spears about a foot in length, and some heads for arrows made of iron and brass. All these they had obtained in trading with the Crow or Rocky mountain Indians, who live on the Yellowstone. The few bridle-bits and stirrups they procured from the Spanish colonies.

The instrument which supplies the place of a knife among them, is a piece of flint with no regular form, and the sharp part of it not more than one or two inches long: the edge of this is renewed, and the flint itself is formed into heads for arrows, by means of the point of a deer or elk horn, an instrument which they use with great art and ingenuity. There are no axes or hatchets; all the wood being cut with flint or elk-horn, the latter of which is always used as a wedge in splitting wood. Their utensils consist, besides the brass kettles, of pots in the form of a jar, made either of earth, or of a stone found in the hills between Madison and Jefferson rivers, which, though soft and white in its natural state, becomes very hard and black after exposure to the fire. The horns of the buffalo and the bighorn supply them with spoons.

The fire is always kindled by means of a blunt arrow, and a piece of well-seasoned wood of a soft spongy kind, such as the willow or cottonwood.

The Shoshonees are of a diminutive stature, with thick flat feet and ankles, crooked legs, and are, generally speaking, worse formed than any nation of Indians we have seen. Their complexion resembles that of the Sioux, and is darker than that of the Minnetarees, Mandans, or Shawnees. The hair in both sexes is suffered to fall loosely over the face and down the shoulders: some men, however, divide it by means of thongs of dressed leather or otter skin into two equal queues, which hang over the ears and are drawn in front of the body; but at the present moment, when the nation is afflicted by the loss of so many relations killed in war, most of them have the hair cut quite short in the neck, and Cameahwait has the hair cut short all over his head, this being the customary mourning for a deceased kindred.

The dress of the men consists of a robe, a tippet, a shirt, long leggings and moccasins. The robe is formed most commonly of the skins of antelope, bighorn, or deer, though when it can be procured, the buffalo hide is preferred. Sometimes too they are made of beaver, moonax [monax, or marmot], and small wolves, and frequently during the summer of elk skin. These are dressed with the hair on, and reach about as low as the middle of the leg. They are worn loosely over the shoulders, the sides being at pleasure either left open or drawn together by the hand, and in cold weather kept close by a girdle round the waist. This robe answers the purpose of a cloak during the day, and at night is their only covering.

The tippet is the most elegant article of Indian dress we have ever seen. The neck or collar of it is a strip about four or five inches wide, cut from the back of the otter skin, the nose and eyes forming one extremity, and the tail another. This being dressed with the fur on, they attach to one edge of it from one hundred to two hundred and fifty little rolls of ermine skin, beginning at the ear, and proceeding towards the tail. These ermine skins are the same kind of narrow strips from the back of that animal, which are sewed round a small cord of twisted silkgrass thick enough to make the skin taper towards the tail which hangs from the end, and are generally about the size of a large quill. These are tied at the head into little bundles, of two, three or more according to the caprice of the wearer, and then suspended from the collar, and a broad fringe of ermine skin is fixed so as to cover the parts where they unite, which might have a coarse appearance. Little tassels of fringe of the same materials are also fastened to the extremities of the tail, so as to show its black colour to greater advantage. The centre of the collar is further ornamented with the shells of the pearl oyster. Thus adorned, the collar is worn close round the neck, and the little rolls fall down over the shoulders nearly to the waist, so as to form a sort of short cloak, which has a very handsome appearance. These tippets are very highly esteemed, and are given or disposed of on important occasions only. The ermine is the fur known to the northwest traders by the name of the white weasel, but is the genuine ermine; and by encouraging the Indians to take them, might no doubt be rendered a valuable branch of trade. These animals must be very abundant, for the tippets are in great numbers, and the construction of each requires at least one hundred skins.

The shirt is a covering of dressed skin without the hair, and formed of the hide of the antelope, deer, bighorn, or elk, though the last is more rarely used than any other for this purpose. It fits the body loosely, and reaches half way down the thigh. The aperture at the top is wide enough to admit the head, and has no collar, but is either left square, or most frequently terminates in the tail of the animal, which is left entire, so as to fold outwards, though sometimes the edges are cut into a fringe, and ornamented with quills of the porcupine. The seams of the shirt are on the sides, and are richly fringed and adorned with porcupine quills, till within five or six inches of the sleeve, where it is left open, as is also the under side of the sleeve from the shoulder to the elbow, where it fits closely round the arm as low as the wrist, and has no fringe like the sides, and the under part of the sleeve above the elbow. It is kept up by wide shoulder straps, on which the manufacturer displays his taste by the variety of figures wrought with porcupine quills of different colours, and sometimes by beads when they can be obtained. The lower end of the shirt retains the natural shape of the fore legs and neck of the skin, with the addition of a slight fringe; the hair too is left on the tail and near the hoofs, part of which last is retained and split into a fringe.

The leggings are generally made of antelope skins, dressed without the hair, and with the legs, tail and neck hanging to them. Each legging is formed of a skin nearly entire, and reaches from the ankle to the upper part of the thigh, and the legs of the skin are tucked before and behind under a girdle round the waist. It fits closely to the leg, the tail being worn upwards, and the neck highly ornamented with fringe and porcupine quills, drags on the ground behind the heels. As the legs of the animal are tied round the girdle, the wide part of the skin is drawn so high as to conceal the parts usually kept from view, in which respect their dress is much more decent than that of any nation of Indians on the Missouri. The seams of the leggings down the sides, are also fringed and ornamented, and occasionally decorated with tufts of hair taken from enemies whom they have slain. In making all these dresses, their only thread is the sinew taken from the backs and loins of deer, elk, buffalo, or any other animal.

The moccasin is of the deer, elk, or buffalo skin, dressed without the hair, though in winter they use the buffalo skin with the hairy side inward, as do most of the Indians who inhabit the buffalo country. Like the Mandan moccasin, it is made with a single seam on the outer edge, and sewed up behind, a hole being left at the instep to admit the foot. It is variously ornamented with figures wrought with porcupine quills, and sometimes the young men most fond of dress cover it with the skin of a polecat, and trail at their heels the tail of the animal.

The dress of the women consists of the same articles as that of their husbands. The robe though smaller is worn in the same way: the moccasins are precisely similar. The shirt or chemise reaches half way down the leg, is in the same form, except that there is no shoulder-strap, the seam coming quite up to the shoulder; though for women who give suck both sides are open, almost down to the waist. It is also ornamented in the same way with the addition of little patches of red cloth, edged round with beads at the skirts. The chief ornament is over the breast, where there are curious figures made with the usual luxury of porcupine quills. Like the men they have a girdle round the waist, and when either sex wishes to disengage the arm, it is drawn up through the hole near the shoulder, and the lower part of the sleeve thrown behind the body.

Children alone wear beads round their necks; grown persons of both sexes prefer them suspended in little bunches from the ear, and sometimes intermixed with triangular pieces of the shell of the pearl oyster. Sometimes the men tie them in the same way to the hair of the forepart of the head, and increase the beauty of it by adding the wings and tails of birds, and particularly the feathers of the great eagle or calumet bird, of which they are extremely fond. The collars are formed either of sea shells procured from their relations to the southwest, or of the sweet-scented grass which grows in the neighbourhood, and which they twist or plait together, to the thickness of a man's finger, and then cover with porcupine quills of various colours. The first of these is worn indiscriminately by both sexes, the second principally confined to the men, while a string of elk's tusks is a collar almost peculiar to the women and children. Another collar worn by the men is a string of round bones like the joints of a fish's back, but the collar most preferred, because most honourable, is one of the claws of the brown bear. To kill one of these animals is as distinguished an achievement as to have put to death an enemy, and in fact with their weapons is a more dangerous trial of courage. These claws are suspended on a thong of dressed leather, and being ornamented with beads, are worn round the neck by the warriors with great pride. The men also frequently wear the skin of a fox, or a strip of otter skin round the head in the form of a bandeau.

In short, the dress of the Shoshonees is as convenient and decent as that of any Indians we have seen.

They have many more children than might have been expected, considering their precarious means of support and their wandering life. This inconvenience is however balanced by the wonderful facility with which their females undergo the operations of child-birth. In the most advanced state of pregnancy they continue their usual occupations, which are scarcely interrupted longer than the mere time of bringing the child into the world.

The old men are few in number, and do not appear to be treated with much tenderness or respect.

The tobacco used by the Shoshonees is not cultivated among them, but obtained from the Indians of the Rocky mountains, and from some of the bands of their own nation who live south of them: it is the same plant which is in use among the Minnetarees, Mandans, and Ricaras.

Their chief intercourse with other nations seems to consist in their association with other Snake Indians, and with the Flatheads when they go eastward to hunt buffalo, and in the occasional visits made by the Flatheads to the waters of the Columbia for the purpose of fishing. Their intercourse with the Spaniards is much more rare, and it furnishes them with a few articles, such as mules, and some bridles, and other ornaments for horses, which, as well as some of their kitchen utensils, are also furnished by the bands of Snake Indians from the Yellowstone. The pearl ornaments which they esteem so highly come from other bands, whom they represent as their friends and relations, living to the southwest beyond the barren plains on the other side of the mountains: these relations they say inhabit a good country, abounding with elk, deer, bear, and antelope, where horses and mules are much more abundant than they are here, or to use their own expression, as numerous as the grass of the plains.

The names of the Indians varies in the course of their life: originally given in childhood, from the mere necessity of distinguishing objects, or from some accidental resemblance to external objects, the young warrior is impatient to change it by some achievement of his own. Any important event, the stealing of horses, the scalping an enemy, or killing a brown bear, entitles him at once to a new name which he then selects for himself, and it is confirmed by the nation. Sometimes the two names subsist together: thus, the chief Cameahwait, which means, "one who never walks," has the war name of Tooettecone, or "black gun," which he acquired when he first signalised himself. As each new action gives a warrior a right to change his name, many of them have had several in the course of their lives. To give to a friend his own name is an act of high courtesy, and a pledge like that of pulling off the moccasin of sincerity and hospitality. The chief in this way gave his name to captain Clark when he first arrived, and he was afterwards known among the Shoshonees by the name of Cameahwait.

The diseases incident to this state of life may be supposed to be few, and chiefly the result of accidents. We were particularly anxious to ascertain whether they had any knowledge of the venereal disorder. After inquiring by means of the interpreter and his wife, we learnt that they sometimes suffered from it, and that they most usually die with it; nor could we discover what was their remedy. It is possible that this disease may have reached them in their circuitous communications with the whites through the intermediate Indians; but the situation of the Shoshonees is so insulated, that it is not probable that it could have reached them in that way, and the existence of such a disorder among the Rocky mountains [Indians] seems rather a proof of its being aboriginal.

Chapter 17

DOWN THE KOOSKOOSKEE RIVER

TUESDAY, AUGUST 27TH, 1805 We were now occupied in determining our route and procuring horses from the Indians. The old guide who had been sent on by captain Clark, now confirmed, by means of our interpreter, what he had already asserted, of a road up Berry creek which would lead to Indian establishments on another branch of the Columbia: his reports however were contradicted by all the Shoshonees. This representation we ascribed to a wish on their part to keep us with them during the winter, as well for the protection we might afford against their enemies, as for the purpose of consuming our merchandise amongst them; and as the old man promised to conduct us himself, that route seemed to be the most eligible. We were able to procure some horses, though not enough for all our purposes. This traffic, and our inquiries and councils with the Indians, consumed the remainder of the day.

AUGUST 28TH

[*End of separate account of Capt. Lewis's party*]

The purchase of horses was resumed, and our stock raised to twenty-two. Having now crossed more than once the country which separates the head waters of the Missouri from those of the Columbia, we can designate the easiest and most expeditious route for a portage: it is as follows:

From the forks of the [Jefferson] river north 60° west, five miles to the point of a hill on the right: then south 80° west, ten miles to a spot where the creek is ten miles [yards] wide, and the highlands approach within two hundred yards; southwest five miles to a narrow part of the bottom; then turning south 70° west, two miles to a creek on the right: thence south 80° west, three miles to a rocky point opposite to a thicket of pines on the left: from that place west, three miles to the gap where is the fountain of the Missouri: on leaving this fountain south 80° west, six miles across the dividing ridge, to a run from the right passing several small streams north 80° west, four miles over hilly ground to the east fork of Lewis's river, which is here forty yards wide.

AUGUST 29TH *Thursday.* Captain Clark joined us this morning, and we continued our bargains for horses. The late misfortunes of the Shoshonees make the price higher than common, so that one horse cost a pistol, one hundred balls, some powder and a knife; another was changed for a musket, and in this way we obtained twenty-nine. The horses themselves are young and vigorous, but they are very poor, and most of them have sore backs in consequence of the roughness of the Shoshonee saddle. We are therefore afraid of loading them too heavily and are anxious to obtain one at least for each man, to carry the baggage, or the man himself, or in the last resource to serve as food; but with all our exertions we could not provide all our men with horses. We have, however, been fortunate in obtaining for the last three days a sufficient supply of flesh, our hunters having killed two or three deer every day.

AUGUST 30TH *Friday.* The weather was fine, and having now made all our purchases, we loaded our horses, and prepared to start. The greater part of the band who had delayed their journey on our account, were also ready to depart. We then took our leave of the Shoshonees, who set out on their visit to the Missouri at the same time that we accompanied by the old guide, his four sons, and another Indian, began the descent of the river, along the same road which captain Clark had previously pursued. After riding twelve miles we encamped on the south bank of the river, and as the hunters had brought in three deer early in the morning we did not feel the want of provisions.

Saturday. At sunrise we resumed our journey, and halted for three hours on Salmon creek to let the horses graze. We then proceeded to the stream called Berry creek eighteen miles from the camp of last night: as we passed along, the valleys and prairies were on fire in several places, in order to collect the bands of the Shoshonees and the Flatheads, for their journey to the Missouri. The weather was warm and sultry, but the only inconvenience which we apprehend is a dearth of food, of which we had to-day an abundance, having procured a deer, a goose, one duck, and a prairie fowl. On reaching Tower creek we left the former track of captain Clark, and began to explore the new route, which is our last hope of getting out of the mountains. For four miles the road, which is tolerably plain, led us along Berry creek to some old Indian lodges where we encamped for the night; the next day, *Sunday, September 1st, 1805*, we followed the same road which here left the creek and turned to the northwest across the hills. During all day we were riding over these hills, from which are many drains and small streams running into the river to the left, and at the distance of eighteen miles, came to a large creek called Fish creek emptying into the Columbia which is about six miles from us. It had rained in the course of the day, and commenced raining again towards evening. We therefore determined not to leave the low grounds to-night, and after going up Fish creek four miles formed our encampment. The country over which we passed is well watered, but poor and rugged or stony, except the bottoms of Fish creek, and even these are narrow. Two men were sent to purchase fish of the Indians at the mouth of the creek, and with the dried fish which they obtained, and a deer and a few salmon killed by the party, we were still well supplied. Two bear also were wounded but we could procure neither of them.

AUGUST 31ST

Monday. This morning all the Indians left us, except the old guide, who now conducted us up Fish creek: at one mile and a half we passed a branch of the river coming in through a low ground covered with pine on the left, and two and a half miles further is a second branch from the right; after continuing our route along the hills covered with pine, and a low ground of the same growth, we arrived at the distance of three and a half miles at the forks of the creek. The road which we were following now turned up the east side of these forks, and as our guide informed us led to the Missouri. We were therefore left without any track; but as no time was to be lost we began to cut our road up the west branch of the creek. This we effected with much difficulty; the thickets of trees and brush through which we were obliged to cut our way required great labour; the road itself was over the steep and rocky sides of the hills where the horses could not move without danger of slipping down, while their feet were bruised by the rocks and stumps of trees. Accustomed as these animals were to this kind of life they suffered severely, several of them fell to some distance down the sides of the hills, some turned over with the baggage, one was crippled, and two gave out exhausted with fatigue. After crossing the creek several times we at last made five miles, with great fatigue and labour, and encamped on the left side of the creek in a small stony low ground. It was not, however, till after dark that

SEPTEMBER 2D

the whole party was collected, and then, as it rained, and we killed nothing, we passed an uncomfortable night. The party had been too busily occupied with the horses to make any hunting excursion, and though as we came along Fish creek we saw many beaver dams we saw none of the animals themselves.

SEPTEMBER 3D In the morning the horses were very stiff and weary. We sent back two men for the load of the horse which had been crippled yesterday, and which we had been forced to leave two miles behind. On their return we set out at eight o'clock, and proceeded up the creek, making a passage through the brush and timber along its borders. The country is generally supplied with pine, and in the low grounds is a great abundance of fir trees, and under bushes. The mountains are high and rugged, and those to the east of us, covered with snow. With all our precautions the horses were very much injured in passing over the ridges and steep points of the hills, and to add to the difficulty, at the distance of eleven miles, the high mountains closed the creek, so that we were obliged to leave the creek to the right, and cross the mountain abruptly. The ascent was here so steep, that several of the horses slipped and hurt themselves, but at last we succeeded in crossing the mountain, and encamped on a small branch of Fish creek. We had now made fourteen miles in a direction nearly north from the river; but this distance, though short, was very fatiguing, and rendered still more disagreeable by the rain which began at three o'clock. At dusk it commenced snowing, and continued till the ground was covered to the depth of two inches, when it changed into a sleet. We here met with a serious misfortune the last of our thermometers being broken by accident. After making a scanty supper on a little corn and a few pheasants killed in the course of the day, we laid down to sleep, and next morning, *Wednesday 4th*, found every thing frozen, and the ground covered with snow. We were obliged to wait some time in order to thaw the covers of the baggage, after which we began our journey at eight o'clock. We crossed a high mountain forming the dividing ridge between the waters of the creek we had been ascending, and those running to the north and west. We had not gone more than six miles over the snow, when we reached the head of a stream from the right, which directed its course more to the westward. We descended the steep sides of the hills along its border, and at the distance of three miles found a small branch coming in from the eastward. We saw several of the argalia [bighorns], but they were too shy to be killed, and we therefore made a dinner from a deer shot by one of the hunters. Then we pursued the course of the stream for three miles, till it emptied itself into a river from the east. In the wide valley at their junction, we discovered a large encampment of Indians: when we had reached them and alighted from our horses, we were received with great cordiality. A council was immediately assembled, white robes were thrown over our shoulders, and the pipe of peace introduced. After this ceremony, as it was too late to go any further, we encamped, and continued smoking and conversing with the chiefs till a late hour.

SEPTEMBER 5TH The next morning we assembled the chiefs and warriors, and informed them who we were, and the purpose for which we visited their country. All this was however conveyed to them through so many different languages, that it was not comprehended without difficulty. We therefore proceeded to the more intelligible language of presents, and made four chiefs by giving a medal and a small quantity of tobacco to each. We received in turn from the principal chief, a present consisting of the skins of a braro, an otter, and two antelopes, and were treated by the women to some dried roots and berries. We then began to traffic for horses, and succeeded in exchanging seven, purchasing eleven, for which we gave a few articles of merchandise.

This encampment consists of thirty-three tents, in which were about four hundred souls, among whom eighty were men. They are called Ootlashoots, and represent themselves as one band of a nation called Tushepaws, a numerous people of four hundred and fifty tents, residing on the heads of the Missouri and Columbia rivers, and some of them lower down the latter river. In person these Indians are stout, and their complexion lighter than that common among Indians. The hair of the men is worn in queues of otter skin, falling in front over the shoulders. A shirt of dressed skin covers the body to the knee, and on this is worn occasionally a robe. To these were added leggings and moccasins. The women suffer their hair to fall in disorder over the face and shoulders, and their chief article of covering is a long shirt of skin, reaching down to the ankles, and tied round the waist. In other respects, as also in the few ornaments which they possess, their appearance is similar to that of the Shoshonees.

There is however a difference between the language of these people which is still farther increased by the very extraordinary pronunciation of the Ootlashoots. Their words have all a remarkably guttural sound, and there is nothing which seems to represent the tone of their speaking more exactly than the clucking of a fowl, or the noise of a parrot. This peculiarity renders their voices scarcely audible, except at a short distance, and when many of them are talking, forms a strange confusion of sounds. The common conversation we overheard, consisted of low guttural sounds occasionally broken by a loud word or two, after which it would relapse and scarcely be distinguished. They seem kind and friendly and willingly shared with us berries and roots, which formed their only stock of provisions. Their only wealth is their horses, which are very fine, and so numerous that this party had with them at least five hundred.

Friday. We continued this morning with the Ootlashoots, from whom we purchased two more horses, and procured a vocabulary of their language. The Ootlashoots set off about two o'clock to join the different bands who were collecting at the three forks of the Missouri. We ourselves proceeded at the same time, and taking a direction N. 30 W. crossed within the distance of one mile and a half, a small river from the right, and a creek coming in from the north. This river is the main stream, and when it reaches the end of the valley, where the mountains close in upon it, is joined by the river on which we encamped last evening, as well as by the creek just mentioned. To the river thus formed we gave the name of captain Clark, he being the first white man who had ever visited its waters. At the end of five miles on this course we had crossed the valley, and reached the top of a mountain covered with pine; this we descended along the steep sides and ravines for a mile and a half, when we came to a spot on the river, where the Ootlashoots had encamped a few days before. We then followed the course of the river, SEPTEMBER 6TH which is from twenty-five to thirty yards wide, shallow, stony, and the low grounds on its borders narrow. Within the distance of three and a half miles, we crossed it several times, and after passing a run on each side, encamped on its right bank, after making ten miles during the afternoon. The horses were turned out to graze, but those we had lately bought were secured and watched, lest they should escape, or be stolen by their former owners. Our stock of flour was now exhausted, and we had but little corn, and as our hunters had killed nothing except two pheasants, our supper consisted chiefly of berries.

SEPTEMBER 7TH *Saturday*. The greater part of the day the weather was dark and rainy: we continued through the narrow low grounds along the river, till at the distance of six miles we came to a large creek from the left, after which the bottoms widen. Four miles lower is another creek on the same side, and the valley now extends from one to three miles, the mountains on the left being high and bald, with snow on the summits, while the country to the right is open and hilly. Four miles beyond this is a creek running from the snow-top'd mountains, and several runs on both sides of the river. Two miles from this last is another creek on the left. The afternoon was now far advanced, but not being able to find a fit place to encamp we continued six miles further till after dark, when we halted for the night. The river here is still shallow and stony, but is increased to the width of fifty yards. The valley through which we passed is of a poor soil, and its fertility injured by the quantity of stone scattered over it. We met two horses which had strayed from the Indians and were now quite wild. No fish was to be seen in the river, but we obtained a very agreeable supply of two deer, two cranes, and two pheasants.

SEPTEMBER 8TH *Sunday*. We set out early: the snow-top'd hills on the left approach the river near our camp, but we soon reached a valley four or five miles wide, through which we followed the course of the river in a direction due north. We passed three creeks on the right, and several runs emptying themselves into the opposite side of the river. At the distance of eleven miles the river turned more towards the west: we pursued it for twelve miles, and encamped near a large creek coming in from the right, which, from its being divided into four different channels, we called Scattering creek. The valley continues to be a poor stony land, with scarcely any timber, except some pine trees along the waters and partially scattered on the hills to the right, which, as well as those on the left, have snow on them. The plant which forces itself most on our attention is a species of prickly pear very common on this part of the river: it grows in clusters, in an oval form about the size of a pigeon's egg, and its thorns are so strong and bearded, that when it penetrates our feet it brings away the pear itself. We saw two mares and a colt, which, like the horses seen yesterday, seemed to have lost themselves and become wild. Our game to-day consisted of two deer, an elk, and a prairie fowl.

SEPTEMBER 9TH *Monday*. We resumed our journey through the valley, and leaving the road on our right crossed the Scattering creek, and halted at the distance of twelve miles on a small run from the east, where we breakfasted on the remains of yesterday's hunt: we here took a meridian altitude, which gave the

268

latitude of 46° 41′ 38.9″: we then continued, and at the distance of four miles passed over to the left bank of the river, where we found a large road through the valley. At this place is a handsome stream of very clear water, a hundred yards wide with low banks, and a bed formed entirely of gravel: it has every appearance of being navigable, but as it contains no salmon, we presume there must be some fall below which obstructs their passage. Our guide could not inform us where this river discharged its waters; he said that as far as he knew its course it ran along the mountains to the north, and that not far from our present position it was joined by another stream nearly as large as itself, which rises in the mountains to the east near the Missouri, and flows through an extensive valley or open prairie. Through this prairie is the great Indian road to the waters of the Missouri; and so direct is the route, that in four days' journey from this place we might reach the Missouri about thirty miles above what we called the Gates of the Rocky mountains, or the spot where the valley of that river widens into an extensive plain on entering the chain of mountains.

At ten miles from our camp is a small creek falling in from the eastward, five miles below which we halted at a large stream which empties itself on the west side of the river. It is a fine bold creek of clear water about twenty yards wide, and we called it *Traveller's-rest* creek; for as our guide told us that we should here leave the river, we determined to remain for the purpose of making celestial observations and collecting some food, as the country through which we are to pass has no game for a great distance.

The valley of the river through which we have been passing is generally a prairie from five to six miles in width, and with a cold gravelly white soil. The timber which it possesses is almost exclusively pine, chiefly of the long-leafed kind, with some spruce, and a species of fir resembling the Scotch fir: near the water courses are also seen a few narrow-leafed cottonwood trees, and the only underbrush is the redwood, honeysuckle, and rosebushes. Our game was four deer, three geese, four ducks, and three prairie fowls: one of the hunters brought in a red-headed woodpecker of the large kind common in the United States, but the first of the kind we have seen since leaving the Illinois.

Tuesday. The morning being fair all the hunters were sent out, and the rest of the party employed in repairing their clothes: two of them were sent to the junction of the river from the east, along which the Indians go to the Missouri: it is about seven miles below Traveller's-rest creek; the country at the forks is seven or eight miles wide, level and open, but with little timber: its course is to the north, and we incline to believe that this is the river which the Minnetarees had described to us as running from south to north along the west side of the Rocky mountains, not far from the sources of Medicine river: there is moreover reason to suppose, that after going as far northward as the head-waters of that river it turns to the westward and joins the Tacootchetessee.

Towards evening one of the hunters returned with three Indians, whom he had met in his excursion up Traveller's-rest creek: as soon as they saw him they prepared to attack him with arrows, but he quieted them by laying down his gun and advancing towards them, and soon persuaded them to come to the camp. Our Shoshonee guide could not speak the lan-

SEPTEMBER 10TH

guage of these people, but by the universal language of signs and gesticulations, which is perfectly intelligible among the Indians, he found that these were three Tushepaw Flatheads in pursuit of two men, supposed to be Shoshonees, who had stolen twenty-three of their horses: we gave them some boiled venison and a few presents; such as a fishhook, a steel to strike fire, and a little powder; but they seemed better pleased with a piece of ribbon which we tied in the hair of each of them. They were however in such haste, lest their horses should be carried off, that two of them set off after sunset in quest of the robbers: the third however was persuaded to remain with us and conduct us to his relations: these he said were numerous, and resided on the Columbia in the plain below the mountains. From that place he added, the river was navigable to the ocean; that some of his relations had been there last fall and seen an old white man who resided there by himself, and who gave them some handkerchiefs like those we have. The distance from this place is five sleeps or days' journey. When our hunters had all joined us we found our provisions consisted of four deer, a beaver, and three grouse. The observation of to-day gave 46° 48′ 28″ as the latitude of Traveller's-rest creek.

SEPTEMBER 11TH *Wednesday*. Two of our horses having strayed away we were detained all the morning before they were caught. In the meantime our Tushepaw Indian became impatient of the delay, and set out to return home alone. As usual we had despatched four of our best hunters ahead, and as we hoped with their aid and our present stock of provisions to subsist on the route, we proceeded at three o'clock up the right side of the creek, and encamped under some old Indian huts at the distance of seven miles. The road was plain and good: the valley is however narrower than that which we left and bordered by high and rugged hills to the right, while the mountains on the left were covered with snow. The day was fair and warm, the wind from the northwest.

SEPTEMBER 12TH *Thursday*. There was a white frost this morning. We proceeded at seven o'clock and soon passed a stream falling in on the right, near which was an old Indian camp with a bath or sweating-house covered with earth. At two miles distance we ascended a high, and thence continued through a hilly and thickly timbered country for nine miles, when we came to the forks of the creek, where the road branches up each fork. We followed the western route, and finding that the creek made a considerable bend at the distance of four miles, crossed a high mountain in order to avoid the circuit. The road had been very bad during the first part of the day, but the passage of the mountain, which was eight miles across, was very painful to the horses, as we were obliged to go over steep stony sides of hills and along the hollows and ravines, rendered more disagreeable by the fallen timber, chiefly pine, spruce pine and fir. We at length reached the creek, having made twenty-three miles of a route so difficult that some of the party did not join us before ten o'clock. We found the account of the scantiness of game but too true, as we were not able to procure any thing during the whole of yesterday, and to-day we killed only a single pheasant. Along the road we observed many of the pine trees peeled off, which is done by the Indians to procure the inner bark for food in the spring.

Friday. Two of the horses strayed away during the night, and one of them being captain Lewis's, he remained with four men to search for them while we proceeded up the creek: at the distance of two miles we came to several springs issuing from large rocks of a course hard grit, and nearly boiling hot. These seem to be much frequented as there are several paths made by elk, deer and other animals, and near one of the springs a hole or Indian bath, and roads leading in different directions. These embarrassed our guide, who mistaking the road took us three miles out of the proper course over an exceedingly bad route. We then fell into the right road, and proceeded on very well, when having made five miles we stopped to refresh the horses. Captain Lewis here joined us, but not having been able to find his horse, two men were sent back to continue the search. We then proceeded along the same kind of country which we passed yesterday, and after crossing a mountain and leaving the sources of the Traveller's-rest creek on the left, reached after five miles riding a small creek which also came in from the left hand, passing through open glades, some of which were half a mile wide. The road which had been as usual rugged and stony, became firm, plain and level after quitting the head of Traveller's-rest. We followed the course of this new creek for two miles and encamped at a spot where the mountains close on each side. Other mountains covered with snow are in view to the southeast and southwest. We were somewhat more fortunate to-day in killing a deer and several pheasants which were of the common species, except that the tail was black.

SEPTEMBER 13TH

Saturday. The day was very cloudy with rain and hail in the valleys, while on the top of the mountains some snow fell. We proceeded early, and continuing along the right side of Glade creek crossed a high mountain, and at the distance of six miles reached the place where it is joined by another branch of equal size from the right. Near the forks the Tushepaws have had an encampment which is but recently abandoned, for the grass is entirely destroyed by horses, and two fish weirs across the creek are still remaining; no fish were however to be seen. We here passed over to the left side of the creek and began the ascent of a very high and steep mountain nine miles across. On reaching the other side we found a large branch from the left, which seems to rise in the snowy mountains to the south and southeast. We continued along the creek two miles further, when night coming on we encamped opposite a small island at the mouth of a branch on the right side of the river. The mountains which we crossed to-day were much more difficult than those of yesterday; the last was particularly fatiguing, being steep and stony, broken by fallen timber, and thickly overgrown by pine, spruce, fir, hackmatack and tamarack. Although we had made only seventeen miles we were all very weary. The whole stock of animal food was now exhausted, and we therefore killed a colt, on which we made a hearty supper. From this incident we called the last creek we had passed from the south Colt-killed creek. The river itself is eighty yards wide, with a swift current, and a stony channel. Its Indian name is Kooskooskee.

SEPTEMBER 14TH

Sunday. At an early hour we proceeded along the right side of the Kooskooskee over steep rocky points of land, till at the distance of four miles we reached an old Indian fishing place: the road here turned to the right of the

SEPTEMBER 15TH

271

water, and began to ascend a mountain: but the fire and wind had prostrated or dried almost all the timber on the south side, and the ascents were so steep that we were forced to wind in every direction round the high knobs which constantly impeded our progress. Several of the horses lost their foothold and slipped: one of them which was loaded with a desk and small trunk, rolled over and over for forty yards, till his fall was stopped by a tree. The desk was broken; but the poor animal escaped without much injury. After clambering in this way for four miles, we came to a high snowy part of the mountain where was a spring of water, at which we halted two hours to refresh our horses.

On leaving the spring the road continued as bad as it was below, and the timber more abundant. At four miles we reached the top of the mountain, and foreseeing no chance of meeting with water, we encamped on the northern side of the mountain, near an old bank of snow, three feet deep. Some of this we melted, and supped on the remains of the colt killed yesterday. Our only game to-day was two pheasants, and the horses on which we calculated as a last resource begin to fail us, for two of them were so poor, and worn out with fatigue, that we were obliged to leave them behind. All around us are high rugged mountains, among which is a lofty range from southeast to northwest, whose tops are without timber, and in some places covered with snow. The night was cloudy and very cold, and three hours before daybreak, *Monday 16th*, it began to snow, and continued all day, so that by evening it was six or eight inches deep.

This covered the track so completely, that we were obliged constantly to halt and examine, lest we should lose the route. In many places we had nothing to guide us except the branches of the trees which, being low, have been rubbed by the burdens of the Indian horses. The road was, like that of yesterday, along steep hill sides, obstructed with fallen timber, and a growth of eight different species of pine, so thickly strewed that the snow falls from them as we pass, and keeps us continually wet to the skin, and so cold, that we are anxious lest our feet should be frozen, as we have only thin moccasins to defend them.

At noon we halted to let the horses feed on some long grass on the south side of the mountains, and endeavoured by making fires to keep ourselves warm. As soon as the horses were refreshed, captain Clark went ahead with one man, and at the distance of six miles reached a stream from the right, and prepared fires by the time of our arrival at dusk. We here encamped in a piece of low ground, thickly timbered, but scarcely large enough to permit us to lie level. We had now made thirteen miles. We were all very wet, cold, and hungry: but although before setting out this morning, we had seen four deer, yet we could not procure any of them, and were obliged to kill a second colt for our supper.

SEPTEMBER 17TH *Tuesday*. Our horses became so much scattered during the night, that we were detained till one o'clock before they were all collected. We then continued our route over high rough knobs, and several drains and springs, and along a ridge of country separating the waters of two small rivers. The road was still difficult, and several of the horses fell and injured themselves very much, so that we were unable to advance more than ten miles to a small stream, on which we encamped.

We had killed a few pheasants, but these being insufficient for our subsistence, we killed another of the colts. This want of provisions, and the extreme fatigue to which we were subjected, and the dreary prospects before us, began to dispirit the men. It was therefore agreed that captain Clark should go on ahead with six hunters, and endeavour to kill something for the support of the party.

He therefore set out *Wednesday 18th*, early in the morning in hopes of finding a level country from which he might send back some game. His route lay S. 85° W. along the same high dividing ridge, and the road was still very bad; but he moved on rapidly, and at the distance of twenty miles was rejoiced on discovering far off an extensive plain towards the west and southwest, bounded by a high mountain. He halted an hour to let the horses eat a little grass on the hill sides, and then went on twelve and a half miles till he reached a bold creek, running to the left, on which he encamped. To this stream he gave the very appropriate name of Hungry creek; for having procured no game, they had nothing to eat.

In the meantime we were detained till after eight o'clock by the loss of one of our horses which had strayed away and could not be found. We then proceeded, but having soon finished the remainder of the colt killed yesterday, felt the want of provisions, which was more sensible from our meeting with no water, till towards nightfall we found some in a ravine among the hills. By pushing on our horses almost to their utmost strength, we made eighteen miles.

We then melted some snow, and supped on a little portable soup, a few canisters of which, with about twenty weight of bear's oil, are our only remaining means of subsistence. Our guns are scarcely of any service, for there is no living creature in these mountains, except a few small pheasants, a small species of gray squirrel, and a blue bird of the vulture kind about the size of a turtle dove or jay, and even these are difficult to shoot.

Thursday. Captain Clark proceeded up the creek, along which the road was more steep and stony than any he had yet passed. At six miles distance he reached a small plain, in which he fortunately found a horse, on which he breakfasted, and hung the rest on a tree for the party in the rear. Two miles beyond this he left the creek, and crossed three high mountains, rendered almost impassable from the steepness of the ascent and the quantity of fallen timber. After clambering over these ridges and mountains, and passing the heads of some branches of Hungry creek, he came to a large creek running westward. This he followed for four miles, then turned to the right down the mountain, till he came to a small creek to the left. Here he halted, having made twenty-two miles on his course, south eighty degrees west, though the winding route over the mountains almost doubled the distance. On descending the last mountain, the heat became much more sensible after the extreme cold he had experienced for several days past. Besides the breakfast in the morning, two pheasants were their only food during the day, and the only kinds of birds they saw were the blue jay, a small white-headed hawk, a larger hawk, crows, and ravens.

SEPTEMBER 19TH

We followed soon after sunrise. At six miles the ridge terminated and we had before us the cheering prospect of the large plain to the southwest. On leaving the ridge we again ascended and went down several mountains, and six miles further came to Hungry creek where it was fifteen yards wide, and received the waters of a branch from the north. We went up it on a course nearly due west, and at three miles crossed a second branch flowing from the same quarter. The country is thickly covered with pine timber, of which we have enumerated eight distinct species. Three miles beyond this last branch of Hungry creek we encamped, after a fatiguing route of eighteen miles. The road along the creek is a narrow rocky path near the edges of very high precipices, from which a fall seems almost inevitable destruction. One of our horses slipped and rolling over with his load down the hill side, which was nearly perpendicular and strewed with large irregular rocks, nearly a hundred yards, and did not stop till he fell into the creek: we all expected he was killed, but to our astonishment, on taking off his load, he rose, and seemed but little injured, and in twenty minutes proceeded with his load. Having no other provision we took some portable soup, our only refreshment during the day. This abstinence, joined with fatigue, has a visible effect on our health. The men are growing weak and losing their flesh very fast: several are afflicted with the dysentery, and eruptions of the skin are very common.

SEPTEMBER 20TH *Friday.* Captain Clark went on through a country as rugged as usual, till on passing a low mountain he came at the distance of four miles to the forks of a large creek. Down this he kept on a course south 60° west for two miles, then turning to the right, continued over a dividing ridge where were the heads of several little streams, and at twelve miles distance descended the last of the rocky mountains and reached the level country. A beautiful open plain partially supplied with pine now presented itself. He continued for five miles when he discovered three Indian boys, who, on observing the party, ran off and hid themselves in the grass. Captain Clark immediately alighted, and giving his horse and gun to one of the men went after the boys. He soon relieved their apprehensions and sent them forward to the village about a mile off with presents of small pieces of ribbon.

Soon after the boys had reached home, a man came out to meet the party, with great caution, but he conducted them to a large tent in the village, and all the inhabitants gathered round to view with a mixture of fear and pleasure these wonderful strangers. The conductor now informed captain Clark by signs, that the spacious tent was the residence of the great chief, who had set out three days ago with all the warriors to attack some of their enemies towards the southwest; that he would not return before fifteen or eighteen days, and that in the meantime there were only a few men left to guard the women and children. They now set before them a small piece of buffalo meat, some dried salmon, berries, and several kinds of roots. Among these last is one which is round and much like an onion in appearance and sweet to the taste: it is called quamash, and is eaten either in its natural state, or boiled into a kind of soup or made into a cake, which is then called pasheco. After the long abstinence this was a sumptuous treat; we returned the kindness of the people by a few small presents, and then went on in company with one of the chiefs to a second village in the same plain, at the distance of two miles. Here the party was treated with great kindness and passed the night. The hunters were sent out, but though they saw some tracks of deer were not able to procure any thing.

INDIAN UTENSILS AND WEAPONS (Bodmer)

We were detained till ten o'clock before we could collect our scattered horses; we then proceeded for two miles, when to our great joy we found the horse which captain Clark had killed, and a note apprising us of his intention of going to the plains towards the southwest, and collect provisions by the time we reached him. At one o'clock we halted on a small stream, and made a hearty meal of horse flesh. On examination it now appeared that one of the horses was missing, and the man in whose charge he had been, was directed to return and search for him. He came back in about two hours without having been able to find the horse; but as the load was too valuable to be lost, two of the best woodsmen were directed to continue the search while we proceeded. Our general course was south 25° west through a thick forest of large pine, which has fallen in many places, and very much obstructs the road. After making about fifteen miles we encamped on a ridge where we could find but little grass and no water. We succeeded, however, in procuring a little from a distance, and supped on the remainder of the horse.

On descending the heights of the mountains the soil becomes gradually more fertile, and the land through which we passed this evening, is of an excellent quality. It has a dark gray soil, though very broken, and with large masses of gray freestone above the ground in many places. Among the vegetable productions we distinguished the alder, honeysuckle, and huckleberry, common in the United States, and a species of honeysuckle, known only westward of the Rocky mountains, which rises to the height of about four feet, and bears a white berry. There is also a plant resembling the chokecherry, which grows in thick clumps eight or ten feet high, and bears a black berry with a single stone of a sweetish taste. The arbor vitae, too, is very common, and grows to a great size, being from two to six feet in diameter.

SEPTEMBER 21ST

Saturday. The free use of food, to which he had not been accustomed, made captain Clark very sick both yesterday evening and during the whole of to-day. He therefore sent out all the hunters and remained himself at the village, as well on account of his sickness as for the purpose of avoiding suspicion and collecting information from the Indians as to the route.

The two villages consist of about thirty double tents, and the inhabitants call themselves Chopunnish or Pierced-nose [Nez-Percé]. The chief drew a chart of the river, and explained, that a greater chief than himself, who governed this village and was called the Twisted-hair, was now fishing at the distance of half a day's ride down the river: his chart made the Kooskooskee fork a little below his camp, a second fork below, still further on a large branch flowed in on each side, below which the river passed the mountains: here was a great fall of water, near which lived white people, from whom were procured the white beads and brass ornaments worn by the women.

A chief of another band made a visit this morning, and smoked with captain Clark. The hunters returned without having been able to kill any thing; captain Clark purchased as much dried salmon, roots and berries as he could, with the few articles he chanced to have in his pockets, and having sent them by one of the men and a hired Indian back to captain Lewis, he went on towards the camp of the Twisted-hair. It was four o'clock before he set out, and the night soon came on; but having met an Indian coming from the river, they engaged him by a present of a neck-cloth, to guide them to the Twisted-hair's camp. For twelve miles they proceeded through the plain before they reached the river hills, which are very high and steep. The whole valley from these hills to the Rocky mountain is a beautiful level country, with a rich soil covered with grass: there is however, but little timber, and the ground is badly watered: the plain is so much lower than the surrounding hills, or so much sheltered by them, that the weather is quite warm, while the cold of the mountains was extreme. From the top of the river hills they proceeded down for three miles till they reached the water side, between eleven and twelve o'clock at night: here we found a small camp of five squaws and three children, the chief himself being encamped, with two others, on a small island in the river: the guide called to him and he soon came over. Captain Clark gave him a medal, and they smoked together till one o'clock.

We could not set out till eleven o'clock, because being obliged in the evening to loosen our horses to enable them to find subsistence, it is always difficult to collect them in the morning. At that hour we continued along the ridge on which we had slept, and at a mile and a half reached a large creek running to our left, just above its junction with one of its branches. We proceeded down the low grounds of this creek, which are level, wide, and heavily timbered, but turned to the right at the distance of two and a half miles, and began to pass the broken and hilly country; but the thick timber had fallen in so many places that we could scarcely make our way. After going five miles we passed the creek on which captain Clark had encamped during the night of the *19th*, and continued five miles further over the same kind of road, till we came to the forks of a large creek. We crossed the northern branch of this stream, and proceeded down it on the west side for a mile: here we found a small plain where there was tolerable grass for the horses, and therefore remained during the night, having made fifteen miles on a course S. 30° W.

The arbor vitae increases in size and quantity as we advance: some of the trees we passed to-day being capable of forming periogues at least forty-five feet in length. We were so fortunate also as to kill a few pheasants and a prairie wolf, which, with the remainder of the horse, supplied us with one meal, the last of our provisions, our food for the morrow being wholly dependent on the chance of our guns.

SEPTEMBER 22D *Sunday*. Captain Clark passed over to the island with the Twisted-hair, who seemed to be cheerful and sincere in his conduct. The river at this place is about one hundred and sixty yards wide, but interrupted by shoals, and the low grounds on its borders are narrow. The hunters brought in three deer; after which captain Clark left his party, and accompanied by the Twisted-hair and his son, rode back to the village, where he arrived about sunset: they then walked up together to the second village, where we had just arrived. We had intended to set out early, but one of the men having neglected to hobble his horse he strayed away, and we were obliged to wait till nearly twelve o'clock. We then proceeded on a western course for two and a half miles, when we met the hunters sent by captain Clark from the village, seven and a half miles distant, with provisions. This supply was most seasonable, as we had tasted nothing since last night, and the fish, and roots, and berries, in addition to a crow which we killed on the route, completely satisfied our hunger. After this refreshment we proceeded in much better spirits, and at a few miles were overtaken by the two men who had been sent back after a horse on the *20th*. They were perfectly exhausted with the fatigue of walking and the want of food; but as we had two spare horses they were mounted and brought on to the village.

They had set out about three o'clock in the afternoon of the *20th* with one horse between them: after crossing the mountain they came to the place where we had eaten the horse. Here they encamped, and having no food made a fire and roasted the head of the horse, which even our appetites had spared, and supped on the ears, skin, lips, &c. of the animal. The next morning, *21st*, they found the track of the horse, and pursuing it recovered the saddle-bags, and at length about eleven o'clock, the horse himself. Being now both mounted, they set out to return and slept at a small stream: during the day they had nothing at all except two pheasants, which were so torn to pieces by the shot, that the head and legs were the only parts fit for food. In this situation they found the next morning, *22d*, that during the night their horses had run away from them or been stolen by the Indians. They searched for them until nine o'clock, when seeing that they could not recover them and fearful of starving if they remained where they were, they set out on foot to join us, carrying the saddle-bags alternately. They walked as fast as they could during the day, till they reached us in a deplorable state of weakness and inanition.

As we approached the village, most of the women, though apprised of our being expected, fled with their children into the neighbouring woods. The men, however, received us without any apprehension, and gave us a plentiful supply of provisions. The plains were now crowded with Indians, who came to see the persons of the whites, and the strange things they brought with them: but as our guide was perfectly a stranger to their language we could converse by signs only. Our inquiries were chiefly directed to the situation of the country, the courses of the rivers, and the Indian villages, of all which we received information from several of the Indians, and as their accounts varied but little from each other, we were induced to place confidence in them. Among others, the Twisted-hair drew a chart of the river on a white elk skin. According to this, the Kooskooskee forks a few miles from this place; two days towards the south is another and larger fork on which the Shoshonee or Snake Indians fish: five days' journey further is a large river from the northwest into which Clark's river empties itself: from the mouth of that river to the falls is five days' journey further: on all the forks as well as on the main river great numbers of Indians reside, and at the falls are establishments of whites. This was the story of the Twisted-hair.

Monday. The chiefs and warriors were all assembled this morning, and we explained to them where we came from, the objects of our visiting them, and our pacific intentions towards all the Indians. This being conveyed by signs, might not have been perfectly comprehended, but appeared to give perfect satisfaction. We now gave a medal to two of the chiefs, a shirt in addition to the medal already received by the Twisted-hair, and delivered a flag and a

SEPTEMBER 23D

handkerchief for the grand chief on his return. To these were added a knife, a handkerchief and a small piece of tobacco for each chief. The inhabitants did not give us any provisions gratuitously. We therefore purchased a quantity of fish, berries (chiefly red haws) and roots; and in the afternoon went on to the second village. The Twisted-hair introduced us into his own tent, which consisted however of nothing more than pine bushes and bark, and gave us some dried salmon boiled. We continued our purchases, and obtained as much provision as our horses could carry in their present weak condition as far as the river. The men exchanged a few old canisters for dressed elk skins, of which they made shirts: great crowds of the natives are round us all night, but we have not yet missed any thing except a knife and a few other articles stolen yesterday from a shot pouch. At dark we had a hard wind from the southwest accompanied with rain which lasted half an hour, but in the morning, *Tuesday, 24th*, the weather was fair. We sent back Colter in search of the horses lost in the mountains, and having collected the rest set out at ten o'clock along the same route already passed by captain Clark towards the river.

All round the village the women are busily employed in gathering and dressing the pasheco root, of which large quantities are heaped up in piles over the plain. We now felt severely the consequence of eating heartily after our late privations: captain Lewis and two of the men were taken very ill last evening, and to-day he could scarcely sit on his horse, while others were obliged to be put on horseback, and some from extreme weakness and pain, were forced to lie down along side of the road for some time. At sunset we reached the island where the hunters had been left on the 22d. They had been unsuccessful, having killed only two deer since that time, and two of them are very sick. A little below this island is a larger one on which we encamped, and administered Rush's pills to the sick.

SEPTEMBER 25TH *Wednesday.* The weather was very hot, and oppressive to the party, most of whom are now complaining of sickness. Our situation indeed, rendered it necessary to husband our remaining strength, and it was determined to proceed down the river in canoes. Captain Clark therefore set out with the Twisted-hair and two young men, in quest of timber for canoes. As he went down the river he crossed at the distance of a mile a creek from the right, which from the rocks that obstructed its passage, he called Rockdam river. The hills along the river are high and steep: the low grounds are narrow, and the navigation of the river embarrassed by two rapids. At the distance of three miles further he reached two nearly equal forks of the river, one of which flowed in from the north. Here he rested for an hour, and cooked a few salmon which one of the Indians caught with a gig. Here too, he was joined by two canoes of Indians from below: they were long, steady, and loaded with the furniture and provisions of two families. He now crossed the south fork, and returned to the camp on the south side, through a narrow pine bottom the greater part of the way, in which was found much fine timber for canoes. One of the Indian boats with two men, set out at the same time, and such was their dexterity in managing the pole, that they reached camp within fifteen minutes after him, although they had to drag the canoe over three rapids. He found captain Lewis, and several of the men still very sick; and distributed to such as were in need of it, salts and tartar emetic.

Thursday. Having resolved to go down to some spot calculated for building canoes, we set out early this morning and proceeded five miles, and encamped on low ground on the south, opposite the forks of the river. But so weak were the men that several were taken sick in coming down; the weather being oppressively hot. Two chiefs and their families followed us, and encamped with a great number of horses near us: and soon after our arrival we were joined by two Indians, who came down the north fork on a raft. We purchased some fresh salmon, and having distributed axes, and portioned off the labour of the party, began, *Friday 27th*, at an early hour, the preparations for making five canoes. But few of the men, however, were able to work, and of these several were soon taken ill, as the day proved very hot. The hunters too, returned without any game, and seriously indisposed, so that nearly the whole party was now ill. We procured some fresh salmon; and Colter, who now returned with one of the horses, brought half a deer, which was very nourishing to the invalids: several Indians from a camp below, came up to see us.

SEPTEMBER 26TH

Saturday. The men continue ill, though some of those first attacked are recovering. Their general complaint is a heaviness at the stomach, and a lax, which is rendered more painful by the heat of the weather, and the diet of fish and roots, to which they are confined, as no game is to be procured. A number of Indians collect about us in the course of the day to gaze at the strange appearance of every thing belonging to us.

SEPTEMBER 28TH

Sunday. The morning was cool, the wind from the southwest; but in the afternoon the heat returned. The men continue ill; but all those who are able to work are occupied at the canoes. The spirits of the party were much recruited by three deer brought in by the hunters; and the next day, *Monday 30th*, the sick began to recruit their strength, the morning being fair and pleasant. The Indians pass in great numbers up and down the river, and we observe large quantities of small duck going down this morning.

SEPTEMBER 29TH

Tuesday, October 1st, 1805

The morning was cool, the wind easterly, but the latter part of the day was warm. We were visited by several Indians from the tribes below, and others from the main south fork. To two of the most distinguished men we made presents of a ring and brooch, and to five others a piece of ribbon, a little tobacco, and the fifth part of a neckcloth. We now dried our clothes and other articles, and selected some articles such as the Indians admire, in order to purchase some provisions, as we have nothing left except a little dried fish, which operates as a complete purgative.

Wednesday. The day is very warm. Two men were sent to the village with a quantity of these articles to purchase food. We are now reduced to roots, which produce violent pains in the stomach. Our work continued as usual, and many of the party are convalescent. The hunters returned in the afternoon with nothing but a small prairie-wolf, so that our provisions being exhausted, we killed one of the horses to eat, and provide soup for the sick.

OCTOBER 2D

OCTOBER 3D *Thursday.* The fine cool morning and easterly wind had an agreeable effect upon the party, most of whom are now able to work. The Indians from below left us, and we were visited by others from different quarters.

OCTOBER 4TH *Friday.* Again we had a cool east wind from the mountains. The men were now much better, and captain Lewis himself so far recovered as to walk about a little. Three Indians arrived to-day from the Great river to the south. The two men also returned from the village with roots and fish, and as the flesh of the horse killed yesterday was exhausted, we were confined to that diet, though unwholesome as well as unpleasant. The afternoon was warm.

OCTOBER 5TH *Saturday.* The wind easterly, and the weather cool. The canoes being nearly finished it became necessary to dispose of our horses. They were therefore collected to the number of thirty-eight, and being branded and marked were delivered to three Indians, the two brothers and the son of a chief, who promises to accompany us down the river. To each of these men we gave a knife and some small articles, and they agreed to take good care of the horses till our return. The hunters with all their diligence are unable to kill any thing, the hills being high and rugged, and the woods too dry to hunt deer, which is the only game in the country. We therefore continue to eat dried fish and roots, which are purchased from the squaws, by means of small presents, but chiefly white beads, of which they are extravagantly fond. Some of these roots seem to possess very active properties, for after supping on them this evening, we were swelled to such a degree as to be scarcely able to breathe for several hours. Towards night we launched two canoes which proved to be very good.

OCTOBER 6TH *Sunday.* This morning is again cool, and the wind easterly. The general course of the winds seems to resemble that which we observed on the east side of the mountain. While on the head waters of the Missouri, we had every morning a cool wind from the west. At this place a cool breeze springs up during the latter part of the night, or near daybreak, and continues till seven or eight o'clock, when it subsides, and the latter part of the day is warm. Captain Lewis is not so well as he was, and captain Clark was also taken ill. We had all our saddles buried in a cache near the river, about half a mile below, and deposited at the same time a canister of powder, and a bag of balls. The time which could be spared from our labours on the canoes, was devoted to some astronomical observations. The latitude of our camp as deduced from the mean of two observations is 46° 34′ 56.3″ north.

OCTOBER 7TH *Monday.* This morning all the canoes were put in the water and loaded, the oars fixed, and every preparation made for setting out, but when we were all ready, the two chiefs who had promised to accompany us, were not to be found, and at the same time we missed a pipe tomahawk. We therefore proceeded without them. Below the forks this river is called the Kooskooskee, and is a clear rapid stream, with a number of shoals and difficult places. For some miles the hills are steep, the low grounds narrow, but then succeeds an open country with a few trees scattered along the river. At the distance of nine miles is a small creek on the left. We passed in the course of the day ten rapids, in descending which, one of the canoes struck a rock, and sprung a leak: we however continued for nineteen miles, and encamped on the left side of the river, opposite to the mouth of a small run. Here the canoe was unloaded and repaired, and two lead canisters of powder deposited; several camps of Indians were on the sides of the river, but we had little intercourse with any of them.

Tuesday. We set out at nine o'clock. At eight and a half miles we passed an island: four and a half miles lower a second island, opposite a small creek on the left side of the river. Five miles lower is another island on the left: a mile and a half below which is a fourth. At a short distance from this is a large creek from the right, to which we gave the name of Colter's creek, from Colter one of the men. We had left this creek about a mile and a half, and were passing the last of fifteen rapids which we had been fortunate enough to escape, when one of the canoes struck, and a hole being made in her side, she immediately filled and sunk. The men, several of whom could not swim, clung to the boat till one of our canoes could be unloaded, and with the assistance of an Indian boat, they were all brought to shore. All the goods were so much wet, that we were obliged to halt for the night, and spread them out to dry. While all this was exhibited, it was necessary to place two sentinels over the merchandise, for we found that the Indians, though kind and disposed to give us every aid during our distress, could not resist the temptation of pilfering some of the small articles. We passed during our route of twenty miles to-day, several encampments of Indians on the islands, and near the rapids, which places are chosen as most convenient for taking salmon. At one of these camps we found our two chiefs, who after promising to descend the river with us, had left us; they however willingly came on board after we had gone through the ceremony of smoking.

OCTOBER 8TH

Wednesday. The morning was as usual, cool; but as the weather both yesterday and to-day was cloudy, our merchandise dried but slowly. The boat, though much injured, was repaired by ten o'clock so as to be perfectly fit for service; but we were obliged to remain during the day till the articles were sufficiently dry to be reloaded: the interval we employed in purchasing fish for the voyage and conversing with the Indians. In the afternoon we were surprised at hearing that our old Shoshonee guide and his son had left us, and been seen running up the river several miles above. As he had never given any notice of his intention, nor had even received his pay for guiding us, we could not imagine the cause of his desertion, nor did he ever return to explain his conduct. We requested the chief to send a horseman after him to request that he would return and receive what we owed him. From this however he dissuaded us, and said very frankly, that his nation, the Chopunnish, would take from the old man any presents that he might have on passing their camp.

OCTOBER 9TH

The Indians came about our camp at night, and were very gay and good-humoured with the men. Among other exhibitions was that of a squaw who appeared to be crazy: she sang in a wild incoherent manner, and would offer to the spectators all the little articles she possessed, scarifying herself in a horrid manner if any one refused her present: she seemed to be an object of pity among the Indians, who suffered her to do as she pleased without interruption.

OCTOBER 10TH *Thursday.* A fine morning. We loaded the canoes and set off at seven o'clock. At the distance of two and a half miles we had passed three islands, the last of which is opposite to a small stream on the right. Within the following three and a half miles is another island and a creek on the left, with wide low grounds, containing willow and cottonwood trees, on which were three tents of Indians. Two miles lower is the head of a large island, and six and a half miles further we halted at an encampment of eight lodges on the left, in order to view a rapid before us: we had already passed eight, and some of them difficult; but this was worse than any of them, being a very hazardous ripple strewed with rocks: we here purchased roots and dined with the Indians. Among them was a man from the falls, who says that he saw white people at that place, and is very desirous of going down with us; an offer which however we declined. Just above this camp we had passed a tent, near which was an Indian bathing himself in a small pond or hole of water, warmed by throwing in hot stones.

After finishing our meal we descended the rapid with no injury, except to one of our boats which ran against a rock, but in the course of an hour was brought off with only a small split in her side. This ripple, from its appearance and difficulty, we named the Rugged rapid. We went on over five other rapids of a less dangerous kind, and at the distance of five miles reached a large fork of the river from the south; and after coming twenty miles, halted below the junction on the right side of the river.

Our arrival soon attracted the attention of the Indians, who flocked in all directions to see us. In the evening the Indian from the falls, whom we had seen at the Rugged rapid, joined us with his son in a small canoe, and insisted on accompanying us to the falls. Being again reduced to fish and roots we made an experiment to vary our food by purchasing a few dogs, and after having been accustomed to horse-flesh, felt no disrelish to this new dish. The Chopunnish have great numbers of dogs which they employ for domestic purposes, but never eat; and our using the flesh of that animal soon brought us into ridicule as dog-eaters.

The country at the junction of the two rivers is an open plain on all sides, broken towards the left by a distant ridge of highland, thinly covered with timber: this is the only body of timber which the country possesses; for at the forks there is not a tree to be seen, and during almost the whole descent of sixty miles down the Kooskooskee from its forks there are very few. This southern branch is in fact the main stream of Lewis's river on which we encamped when among the Shoshonees. The Indians inform us that it is navigable for sixty miles; that not far from its mouth it receives a branch from the south; and a second and larger branch, two days' march up, and nearly parallel to the first Chopunnish villages, we met near the mountains. This branch is called Pawnashte, and is the residence of a chief, who, according to their expression, has more horses than he can count. The river has many rapids, near which are situated many fishing camps; there being ten establishments of this before reaching the first southern branch; one on that stream, five between that and the Pawnashte; one on that river, and two above it; besides many other Indians who reside high up on the more distant waters of this river. All these Indians belong to the Chopunnish nation, and live in tents of an oblong form, covered with flat roofs.

At its mouth Lewis's river is about two hundred and fifty yards

Map locating Indian tribes, from a page of Captain Clark's field book.

wide, and its water is of a greenish blue colour. The Kooskooskee, whose waters are clear as crystal, one hundred and fifty yards in width, and after the union the river enlarges to the space of three hundred yards: at the point of the union is an Indian cabin, and in Lewis's river a small island.

The Chopunnish or Pierced-nose nation, who reside on the Kooskooskee and Lewis's rivers, are in person stout, portly, well-looking men: the women are small, with good features, and generally handsome, though the complexion of both sexes is darker than that of the Tushepaws. In dress they resemble that nation, being fond of displaying their ornaments. The buffalo or elk-skin robe decorated with beads, sea-shells, chiefly mother-of-pearl, attached to an otter-skin collar and hung in the hair, which falls in front in two queues; feathers, paints of different kinds, principally white, green, and light blue, all of which they find in their own country: these are the chief ornaments they use. In the winter they wear a short shirt of dressed skins, long painted leggings and moccasins, and a plait of twisted grass round the neck.

The dress of the women is more simple, consisting of a long shirt of argalia or ibex skin, reaching down to the ankles without a girdle: to this are tied little pieces of brass and shells and other small articles; but the head is not at all ornamented. The dress of the female is indeed more modest, and more studiously so than any we have observed, though the other sex is careless of the indelicacy of exposure.

The Chopunnish have very few amusements, for their life is painful and laborious; and all their exertions are necessary to earn even their precarious subsistence. During the summer and autumn they are busily occupied in fishing for salmon, and collecting their winter store of roots. In the winter they hunt the deer on snow shoes over the plains, and towards spring cross the mountains to the Missouri for the purpose of trafficking for buffalo robes. The inconveniences of that comfortless life are increased by frequent encounters with their enemies from the west, who drive them over the mountains with the loss of their horses, and sometimes the lives of many of the nation. Though originally the same people, their dialect varies very perceptibly from that of the Tushepaws: their treatment to us differed much from the kind and disinterested services of the Shoshonees: they are indeed selfish and avaricious; they part very reluctantly with every article of food or clothing; and while they expect a recompense for every service however small, do not concern themselves about reciprocating any presents we may give them.

They are generally healthy—the only disorders which we have had occasion to remark being of a scrofulous kind, and for these, as well as for the amusement of those who are in good health, hot and cold bathing is very commonly used.

The soil of these prairies is of a light yellow clay intermixed with small smooth grass: it is barren, and produces little more than a bearded grass about three inches high, and a prickly pear, of which we now found three species: the first is of the broad-leafed kind, common to the Missouri. The second has the leaf of a globular form, and is also frequent on the upper part of the Missouri, particularly after it enters the Rocky mountains. The third is peculiar to this country, and is much more inconvenient than the other two: it consists of small thick leaves of a circular form, which grow from the margin of each other as in the broad-leafed pear of the Missouri: these leaves are armed with a greater number of thorns, which are stronger, and appear to be barbed; and as the leaf itself is very slightly attached to the stem, as soon as one thorn touches the moccasin it adheres and brings with it the leaf, which is accompanied by a reinforcement of thorns.

Chapter 18
DOWN THE SNAKE AND COLUMBIA RIVERS

FRIDAY, OCTOBER 11TH, 1805   This morning the wind was from the east, and the weather cloudy. We set out early, and at the distance of a mile and a half reached a point of rocks in a bend of the river towards the left, near to which was an old Indian house, and a meadow on the opposite bank. Here the hills came down towards the water, and formed by the rocks, which have fallen from their sides, a rapid over which we dragged the canoes. We passed, a mile and a half further, two Indian lodges in a bend towards the right, and at six miles from our camp of last evening reached the mouth of a brook on the left. Just above this stream we stopped for breakfast at a large encampment of Indians on the same side; we soon began to trade with them for a stock of provisions, and were so fortunate as to purchase seven dogs and all the fish they would spare.

While this traffic was going on, we observed a vapour bath or sweating house in a different form from that used on the frontiers of the United States, or in the Rocky mountains. It was a hollow square of six or eight feet deep, formed in the river bank by damming up with mud the other three sides, and covering the whole completely except an aperture about two feet wide at the top. The bathers descend by this hole, taking with them a number of heated stones, and jugs of water; and after being seated round the room, throw the water on the stones till the steam becomes of a temperature sufficiently high for their purposes. The baths of the Indians in the Rocky mountains is of different sizes, the most common being made of mud and sticks like an oven, but the mode of raising the steam is exactly the same. Among both these nations it is very uncommon for a man to bathe alone, he is generally accompanied by one or sometimes several of his acquaintances; indeed it is so essentially a social amusement, that to decline going in to bathe when invited by a friend is one of the highest indignities which can be offered to him. The Indians on the frontiers generally use a bath which will accommodate only one person, and is formed of a wickered work of willows about four feet high, arched at the top, and covered with skins. In this the patient sits till by means of the heated stones and water he has perspired sufficiently. Almost universally these baths are in the neighbourhood of running water, into which the Indians plunge immediately on coming out of the vapour bath, and sometimes return again, and subject themselves to a second perspiration. This practice is, however, less frequent among our neighbouring nations than those to the westward. This bath is employed either for pleasure or for health, and is used indiscriminately for rheumatism, venereal, or in short for all kinds of diseases.

On leaving this encampment we passed two more rapids, and some swift water, and at the distance of four and a half miles reached one which was much more difficult to pass. Three miles beyond this rapid, are three huts of Indians on the right, where we stopped and obtained in exchange for a few trifles some pasheco roots, five dogs and a small quantity of dried fish. We made our dinner of part of each of these articles, and then proceeded on without any obstruction, till after making twelve and a half miles we came to a stony island on the right side of the river, opposite to which is a rapid, and a second at its lower point. About three and a half miles beyond the island is a small brook which empties itself into a bend on the right, where we encamped at two Indian huts, which are now inhabited. Here we met two Indians belonging to a nation who reside at the mouth of this river. We had made thirty-one miles to-day, although the weather was warm, and we found the current obstructed by nine different rapids, more or less difficult to pass.

All these rapids are fishing places of great resort in the season, and as we passed we observed near them slabs and pieces of split timber raised from the ground, and some entire houses which are vacant at present, but will be occupied as soon as the Indians return from the plains on both sides of the river, where our chief informs us they are now hunting the antelope. Near each of these houses is a small collection of graves, the burial places of those who frequent these establishments. The dead are wrapped up in robes of skins, and deposited in graves, which are covered over with earth and marked or secured by little pickets or pieces of wood, stuck promiscuously over and around it. The country on both sides, after mounting a steep ascent of about two hundred feet, becomes an open, level and fertile plain, which is, however, as well as the borders of the river itself, perfectly destitute of any kind of timber; and the chief growth which we observed consisted of a few low blackberries. We killed some geese and ducks. The wind in the after part of the day changed to the southwest and became high, but in the morning, *Saturday 12th*, it shifted to the east, and we had a fair cool morning.

After purchasing all the provisions these Indians would spare, which amounted to only three dogs and a few fish, we proceeded. We soon reached a small island, and in the course of three miles passed three other islands nearly opposite to each other, and a bad rapid on the left in the neighbourhood of them. Within the following seven miles we passed a small rapid, and an island on the left, another stony island and a rapid on the right, just below which a brook comes in on the same side, and came to a bend towards the right opposite to a small island. From this place we saw some Indians on the hills, but they were too far off for us to have any intercourse, and showed no disposition to approach us. After going on two miles to a bend towards the left, we found the plains, which till now had formed rugged cliffs over the river, leaving small and narrow bottoms, become much lower on both sides, and the river itself widens to the space of four hundred yards, and continues for the same width, the country rising by a gentle ascent towards the high plains. At two and a half miles is a small creek on the left opposite to an island. For the three following miles, the country is low and open on both sides, after which it gradually rises till we reached a bend of the river towards the right, three and a half miles further, in the course of which we passed a rapid and an island. The wind now changed to the southwest, and became violent. We passed an island at the distance of four miles, another one mile beyond it, where the water was swift and shallow, and two miles further, a rapid at the upper point of a small stony island. We went along this island by the mouth of a brook on the right, and encamped on the same side opposite to a small island close under the left shore.

Our day's journey had been thirty miles, and we might have gone still further, but as the evening was coming on we halted at the head of a rapid, which the Indians represented as dangerous to pass, for the purpose of examining it before we set out in the morning. The country has much the same appearance as that we passed yesterday, consisting of open plains, which when they approach the water are faced with a dark-coloured rugged stone. The river is as usual much obstructed by islands and rapids, some of which are difficult to pass. Neither the plains nor the borders of the river possess any timber, except a few hackberry bushes and willows, and as there is not much driftwood, fuel is very scarce.

Sunday. The morning was windy and dark, and the rain which began before daylight, continued till near twelve o'clock. Having viewed very accurately the whole of this rapid we set out, the Indians going on before us to pilot the canoes. We found it, as had been reported, a very dangerous rapid, about two miles in length, and strewed with rocks in every direction, so as to require great dexterity to avoid running against them. We however passed through the channel, which is towards the left, and about the centre of the rapid, without meeting with any accident. Two miles below it we had another bad rapid, a mile beyond which is a large creek in a bend to the left. This we called Kimooenim creek.

OCTOBER 13TH

On leaving it the river soon became crowded with rough black rocks, till at the distance of a mile it forms a rapid which continues for four miles, and during the latter part of it for a mile and a half, the whole river is compressed into a narrow channel, not more than twenty-five yards wide. The water happened to be low as we passed, but during the high waters, the navigation must be very difficult. Immediately at the end of this rapid, is a large stream in a bend to the right, which we called Drewyer's river, after George Drewyer one of the party. A little below the mouth of this river is a large fishing establishment, where there are the scaffolds and timbers of several houses piled up against each other, and the meadow adjoining contains a number of holes, which seem to have been used as places of deposits for fish for a great length of time. There were no entire houses standing, and we saw only two Indians who had visited the narrows, but we were overtaken by two others, who accompanied us on horseback down the river, informing us that they meant to proceed by land down to the great river. Nine and a half miles below Drewyer's river, we passed another rapid, and three and a half miles farther reached some high cliffs in a bend to the left. Here after passing the timbers of a house, which were preserved on forks, we encamped on the right side, near a collection of graves, such as we had seen above. The country was still an open plain without timber, and our day's journey had no variety, except the fishing houses which are scattered near the situations convenient for fishing, but are now empty. Our two Indian companions spent the night with us.

Monday. The wind was high from the southwest during the evening, and this morning it changed to the west, and the weather became very cold until about twelve o'clock, when it shifted to the southwest, and continued in that quarter during the rest of the day. We set out early, and after passing some swift water, reached at two and a half miles a rock of a very singular appearance. It was situated on a point to the left, at some distance from the ascending country, very high and large, and resembling in its shape the hull of a ship. At five miles we passed a rapid; at eight another rapid, and a small island on the right, and at ten and a half a small island on the right. We halted a mile and a half below for the purpose of examining a much larger and more dangerous rapid than those we had yet passed. It is three miles in length, and very difficult to navigate. We had scarcely set out, when three

OCTOBER 14TH

of the canoes stuck fast in endeavouring to avoid the rocks in the channel; soon after in passing two small rocky islands, one of the canoes struck a rock, but was prevented from upsetting, and fortunately we all arrived safe at the lower end of the rapid. Here we dined, and then proceeded, and soon reached another rapid on both sides of the river, which was divided by an island.

As we were descending it one of the boats was driven crosswise against a rock in the middle of the current. The crew attempted to get her off, but the waves dashed over her, and she soon filled; they got out on the rock and held her above water with great exertion, till another canoe was unloaded and sent to her relief; but they could not prevent a great deal of her baggage from floating down the stream. As soon as she was lightened, she was hurried down the channel leaving the crew on the rock. They were brought off by the rest of the party, and the canoe itself, and nearly all that had been washed overboard was recovered. The chief loss was the bedding of two of the men, a tomahawk, and some small articles. But all the rest were wet, and though by drying we were able to save the powder, all the loose packages of which were in this boat, yet we lost all the roots and other provisions, which are spoilt by the water. In order to diminish the loss as far as was in our power, we halted for the night on an island, and exposed every thing to dry.

On landing we found some split timber for houses which the Indians had very securely covered with stone, and also a place where they had deposited their fish. We have hitherto abstained scrupulously from taking any thing belonging to the Indians; but on this occasion we were compelled to depart from this rule; and as there was no other timber to be found in any direction for firewood, and no owner appeared from whom it could be purchased, we used a part of these split planks, bearing in mind our obligation to repay the proprietor whenever we should discover him. The only game which we observed were geese and ducks, of the latter we killed some, and a few of the blue-winged teal. Our journey was fifteen miles in length.

OCTOBER 15TH *Tuesday.* The morning was fair, and being obliged to remain for the purpose of drying the baggage, we sent out the hunters to the plains, but they returned at ten o'clock, without having seen even the tracks of any large game, but brought in three geese and two ducks. The plains are waving, and as we walked in them, we could plainly discover a range of mountains bearing southeast and northwest, becoming higher as they advanced towards the north, the nearest point bearing south about sixty miles from us. Our stores being sufficiently dry to be reloaded, and as we shall be obliged to stop for the purpose of making some celestial observations at the mouth of the river, which cannot be at a great distance, we concluded to embark and complete the drying at that place: we therefore set out at two o'clock.

For the first four miles we passed three islands, at the lower points of which were the same number of rapids, besides a fourth at a distance from them. During the next ten miles we passed eight islands and three more rapids, and reached a point of rocks on the left side. The islands were of various sizes, but were all composed of round stone and sand: the rapids were in many places difficult and dangerous to pass. About this place the country becomes lower than usual, the ground over the river not being higher than ninety or a hundred feet, and extending back into a waving plain. Soon after leaving this point of rocks, we entered a narrow channel formed by the projecting cliffs of the bank, which rise nearly perpendicular from the water. The river is not however rapid, but gentle and smooth during its confinement, which lasts for three miles, when it falls, or rather widens into a kind of basin nearly round, and without any perceptible current.

After passing through this basin, we were joined by the three Indians who had piloted us through the rapids since we left the forks, and who in company with our two chiefs had gone before us. They had now halted here to warn us of a dangerous rapid, which begins at the lower point of the basin. As the day was too far spent to descend it, we determined to examine before we attempted it, and therefore landed near an island at the head of the rapid, and studied particularly all its narrow and difficult parts. The spot where we landed was an old fishing establishment, of which there yet remained the timbers of a house carefully raised on scaffolds to protect them against the spring tide. Not being able to procure any other fuel, and the night being cold, we were again obliged to use the property of the Indians, who still remain in the plains hunting the antelope. Our progress was only twenty miles in consequence of the difficulty of passing the rapids. Our game consisted of two teal.

Wednesday. Having examined the rapids, which we found more difficult than the report of the Indians had induced us to believe, we set out early, and putting our Indian guide in front, our smallest canoe next, and the rest in succession, began the descent: the passage proved to be very disagreeable; as there is a continuation of shoals extending from bank to bank for the distance of three miles, during which the channel is narrow and crooked, and obstructed by large rocks in every direction, so as to require great dexterity to avoid being dashed on them. We got through the rapids with no injury to any of the boats except the hindmost, which ran on a rock; but by the assistance of the other boats, and of the Indians who were very alert, she escaped, though the baggage she contained was wet. Within three miles after leaving the rapid we passed three small islands, on one of which were the parts of a house put on scaffolds as usual, and soon after came to a rapid at the lower extremity of three small islands; and a second at the distance of a mile and a half below them; reaching six miles below the great rapid a point of rocks at a rapid opposite to the upper point of a small island on the left. Three miles further is another rapid; and two miles beyond this a very bad rapid, or rather a fall of the river: this, on examination, proved so difficult to pass, that we thought it imprudent to attempt, and therefore unloaded the canoes and made a portage of three quarters of a mile. The rapid, which is of about the same extent, is much broken by rocks and shoals, and has a small island in it on the right side.

After crossing by land we halted for dinner, and whilst we were eating were visited by five Indians, who came up the river on foot in great haste: we received them kindly, smoked with them, and gave them a piece of tobacco to smoke with their tribe: on receiving the present they set out to return, and continued running as fast as they could while they remained in sight. Their curiosity had been excited by the accounts of our two chiefs, who had gone on in order to apprise the tribes of our approach and of our

OCTOBER 16TH

Captain Clark's sketch-map of the junction of Lewis's River with the Columbia.

friendly dispositions towards them. After dinner we reloaded the canoes and proceeded: we soon passed a rapid opposite to the upper point of a sandy island on the left, which has a smaller island near it. At three miles is a gravelly bar in the river: four miles beyond this the Kimooenim empties itself into the Columbia, and at its mouth has an island just below a small rapid.

We halted above the point of junction on the Kimooenim to confer with the Indians, who had collected in great numbers to receive us. On landing we were met by our two chiefs, to whose good offices we were indebted for this reception, and also the two Indians who had passed us a few days since on horseback; one of whom appeared to be a man of influence, and harangued the Indians on our arrival. After smoking with the Indians, we formed a camp at the point where the two rivers unite, near to which we found some driftwood, and were supplied by our two old chiefs with the stalks of willows and some small bushes for fuel.

We had scarcely fixed the camp and got the fires prepared, when a chief came from the Indian camp about a quarter of a mile up the Columbia, at the head of nearly two hundred men: they formed a regular procession, keeping time to the noise, rather the music of their drums, which they accompanied with their voices. As they advanced they formed a semicircle round us, and continued singing for some time: we then smoked with them all, and communicated, as well as we could by signs, our friendly intentions towards all nations, and our joy at finding ourselves surrounded by our children: we then proceeded to distribute presents to them, giving the principal chief a large medal, a shirt and handkerchief; to the second chief, a medal of a smaller size, and to a third chief who came down from some of the upper villages, a small medal and a handkerchief. This ceremony being concluded they left us; but in the course of the afternoon several of them returned and remained with us till a late hour. After they had dispersed we proceeded to purchase provisions, and were enabled to collect seven dogs, to which some of the Indians added small presents of fish, and one of them gave us twenty pounds of fat dried horseflesh.

Thursday. The day being fair we were occupied in making the necessary observations for determining our longitude, and obtained a meridian altitude, from which it appeared that we were in latitude 46° 15′ 13.9″. We also measured the two rivers by angles, and found that at the junction the Columbia is nine hundred and sixty yards wide, and Lewis's river five hundred and seventy-five; but soon after they unite, the former widens to the space of from one to three miles, including the islands. From the point of junction the country is a continued plain, which is low near the water, from which it rises gradually, and the only elevation to be seen is a range of high country running from the northeast towards the southwest, where it joins a range of mountains from the southwest, and is on the opposite side about two miles from the Columbia. There is through this plain no tree and scarcely any shrub, except a few willow bushes; and even of smaller plants there is not much more than the prickly pear, which is in great abundance, and is even more thorny and troublesome than any we have yet seen. During this time the principal chief came down with several of his warriors and smoked with us: we were also visited by several men and women, who offered dogs and fish for sale, but as the fish was out of season, and at present abundant in the river, we contented ourselves with purchasing all the dogs we could obtain.

The nation among which we now are call themselves Sokulks; and with them are united a few of another nation, who reside on a western branch, emptying itself into the Columbia a few miles above the mouth of the latter river, and whose name is Chimnapum. The language of both these nations, of each of which we obtained a vocabulary, differs but little from

OCTOBER 17TH

each other, or from that of the Chopunnish who inhabit the Kooskooskee and Lewis's river. In their dress and general appearance also they resemble much those nations; the men wearing a robe of deer or antelope skin, under which a few of them have a short leathern shirt. The most striking difference between them is among the females, the Sokulk women being more inclined to corpulency than any we have yet seen: their stature is low, their faces broad, and their heads flattened in such a manner that the forehead is in a straight line from the nose to the crown of the head: their eyes are of a dirty sable, their hair too is coarse and black, and braided as above without ornament of any kind: instead of wearing, as do the Chopunnish, long leathern shirts, highly decorated with beads and shells, the Sokulk females have no other covering but a truss or piece of leather tied round the hips and then drawn tight between the legs. The ornaments usually worn by both sexes are large blue or white beads, either pendent from their ears, or round the necks, wrists, and arms: they have likewise bracelets of brass, copper, and horn, and some trinkets of shells, fish bones, and curious feathers.

The houses of the Sokulks are made of large mats of rushes, and are generally of a square or oblong form, varying in length from fifteen to sixty feet, and supported in the inside by poles or forks about six feet high: the top is covered with mats, leaving a space of twelve or fifteen inches the whole length of the house, for the purpose of admitting the light and suffering the smoke to pass through: the roof is nearly flat, which seems to indicate that rains are not common in this open country, and the house is not divided into apartments, the fire being in the middle of the large room, and immediately under the hole in the roof: the rooms are ornamented with their nets, gigs, and other fishing tackle, as well as the bow for each inhabitant, and a large quiver of arrows, which are headed with flint stones.

The Sokulks seem to be of a mild and peaceable disposition, and live in a state of comparative happiness. The men like those on the Kimooenim, are said to content themselves with a single wife, with whom we observe the husband shares the labours of procuring subsistence much more than is usual among savages. What may be considered as an unequivocal proof of their good disposition, is the great respect which was shown to old age. Among other marks of it, we observed in one of the houses an old woman perfectly blind, and who we were informed had lived more than a hundred winters. In this state of decrepitude, she occupied the best position in the house, seemed to be treated with great kindness, and whatever she said was listened to with much attention. They are by no means intrusive, and as their fisheries supply them with a competent, if not an abundant subsistence, although they receive thankfully whatever we choose to give, they do not importune us by begging. The fish is, indeed, their chief food, except the roots, and the casual supplies of the antelope, which to those who have only bows and arrows, must be very scanty. This diet may be the direct or the remote cause of the chief disorder which prevails among them, as well as among the Flatheads, on the Kooskooskee and Lewis's river. With all these Indians a bad soreness of the eyes is a very common disorder, which is suffered to ripen by neglect, till many are deprived of one of their eyes, and some have totally lost the use of both. This dreadful calamity may reasonably, we think, be imputed to the constant reflection of the sun on the waters where they are constantly fishing in the spring, summer and fall, and during the rest of the year on the snows of a country which affords no object to relieve the sight.

Among the Sokulks too, and indeed among all the tribes whose chief subsistence is fish, we have observed that bad teeth are very general: some have the teeth, particularly those of the upper jaw, worn down to the gums, and many of both sexes, and even of middle age, have lost them almost entirely. This decay of the teeth is a circumstance very unusual among the Indians, either of the mountains or the plains, and seems peculiar to the inhabitants of the Columbia. We cannot avoid regarding as one principal cause of it, the manner in which they eat their food. The roots are swallowed as they are dug from the ground, frequently nearly covered with a gritty sand: so little idea have they that this is offensive, that all the roots they offer us for sale are in the same condition. A second and a principal cause may be their great use of the dried salmon, the bad effects of which are most probably increased by their mode of cooking it, which is simply to warm, and then swallow the rind, scales and flesh without any preparation. The Sokulks possess but few horses, the greater part of their labours being performed in canoes. Their amusements are similar to those of the Missouri Indians.

In the course of the day captain Clark, in a small canoe with two men, ascended the Columbia. At the distance of five miles he passed an island in the middle of the river, at the head of which is a small and not a dangerous rapid. On the left bank of the river opposite to this river is a fishing place, consisting of three mat houses. Here were great quantities of salmon drying on scaffolds: and indeed from the mouth of the river upwards he saw immense numbers of dead salmon strewed along the shore or floating on the surface of the water, which is so clear that the salmon may be seen swimming in the water at the depth of fifteen or twenty feet. The Indians who had collected on the banks to view him, now joined him in eighteen canoes, and accompanied him up the river. A mile above the rapids he came to the lower point of an island where the course of the river, which had been from its mouth north 83° west, now became due west. He proceeded in that direction, when observing three houses of mats at a short distance he landed to visit them.

On entering one of the houses he found it crowded with men, women and children, who immediately provided a mat for him to sit on, and one of the party undertook to prepare something to eat. He began by bringing in a piece of pine wood that had drifted down the river, which he split into small pieces, with a wedge made of the elks' horn, by means of a mallet of stone curiously carved. The pieces were then laid on the fire, and several round stones placed upon them: one of the squaws now brought a bucket of water, in which was a large salmon about half dried, and as the stones became heated, they were put into the bucket till the salmon was sufficiently boiled for use. It was then taken out, put on a platter of rushes neatly made, and laid before captain Clark, and another was boiled for each of his men. During these preparations he smoked with those about him who would accept of tobacco, but very few were desirous of smoking, a custom which is not general among them, and chiefly used as a matter of form in great ceremonies.

After eating the fish, which was of an excellent flavour, captain Clark set out, and at the distance of four miles from the last island, came to the lower point of another near the left shore, where he halted at two large mat houses. Here as at the three houses below, the inhabitants were occupied in splitting and drying salmon. The multitudes of this fish are almost inconceivable. The water is so clear that they can readily be seen at the depth of fifteen or twenty feet, but at this season they float in such quantities down the stream, and are drifted ashore, that the Indians have only to collect, split and dry them on the scaffolds. Where they procure the timber of which these scaffolds are composed he could not learn, but as there are nothing but willow bushes to be seen for a great distance from the place, it rendered very probable, what the Indians assured him by signs, that they often used dried fish as fuel for the common occasions of cooking.

From this island they showed him the entrance of a western branch of the Columbia, called the *Tapteal*, which as far as could be seen bears nearly west, and empties itself about eight miles above into the Columbia; the general course of which is northwest: towards the southwest a range of highland runs parallel to the river, at the distance of two miles on the left, while on the right side the country is low and covered with the prickly pear, and a weed or plant two or three feet high resembling whins. To the eastward is a range of mountains about fifty or sixty miles distant, which bear north and south; but neither in the low grounds, nor in the highlands is any timber to be seen.

The evening coming on, he determined not to proceed further than the island, and therefore returned to camp, accompanied by three canoes, which contained twenty Indians. In the course of his excursion he shot several grouse and ducks, and received some presents of fish, for which he gave in return small pieces of ribbon. He also killed a prairie cock [sage-grouse], an animal of the pheasant kind, but about the size of a small turkey. It measured from the beak to the end of the toe two feet six inches and three-quarters, from the extremity of the wings three feet six inches, and the feathers of the tail were thirteen inches long. This bird we have seen nowhere except on this river. Its chief food is the grasshopper, and the seed of the wild plant which is peculiar to this river and the upper parts of the Missouri.

The men availed themselves of this day's rest to mend their clothes, dressing skins, and putting their arms in complete order, an object always of primary concern, but particularly at a moment when we are surrounded by so many strangers.

OCTOBER 18TH *Friday.* We were visited this morning by several canoes of Indians, who joined those who were already with us, and soon opened a numerous council. We informed them as we had done all the other Indian nations of our friendship for them, and of our desire to promote peace among all our red children in this country. This was conveyed by signs through the means of our two chiefs, and seemed to be perfectly understood. We then made a second chief, and gave to all the chiefs a string of wampum, in remembrance of what we had said. Whilst the conference was going on four men came in a canoe from a large encampment on an island about eight miles below, but after staying a few minutes returned without saying a word to us. We now procured from the principal chief and one of the Cuimnapum nation a sketch of the Columbia, and the tribes of his nation living along its banks and those of the Tapteet. They drew it with a piece of coal on a robe, and as we afterwards transferred to paper, it exhibited a valuable specimen of Indian delineation.

Having completed the purposes of our stay, we now began to lay in our stores, and fish being out of season, purchased forty dogs, for which we gave small articles, such as bells, thimbles, knitting-needles, brass wire, and a few beads, an exchange with which they all seemed perfectly satisfied. These dogs, with six prairie cocks killed this morning, formed a plentiful supply for the present. We here left our guide and the two young men who had accompanied him, two of the three not being willing to go any further, and the third could be of no use as he was not acquainted with the river below. We therefore took no Indians but our two chiefs, and resumed our journey in the presence of many of the Sokulks, who came to witness our departure. The morning was cool and fair, and the wind from the southeast.

Soon after proceeding, we passed the island in the mouth of Lewis river, and at eight miles reached a larger island, which extends three miles in length. On going down by this island there is another on the right, which commences about the middle of it, and continues for three and a half miles. While they continue parallel to each other, they occasion a rapid near the lower extremity of the first island, opposite to which on the second island are nine lodges built of mats, and intended for the accommodation of the fishermen, of whom we saw great numbers, and vast quantities of dried fish on their scaffolds.

On reaching the lower point of the island, we landed to examine a bad rapid, and then undertook the passage which is very difficult, as the channel lies between two small islands, with two others still smaller near the left side of the river. Here are two Indian houses, the inhabitants of which were as usual drying fish. We passed the rapid without injury, and fourteen and a half miles from the mouth of Lewis's river, came to an island near the right shore, on which were two other houses of Indians, pursuing the customary occupation. One mile and a half beyond this place, is a mouth of a small brook under a high hill on the left. It seems to run during its whole course through the high country, which at this place begins, and rising to the height of two hundred feet forms cliffs of rugged black rocks which project a considerable distance into the river. At this place too we observed a mountain to the S. W. [Mount St. Helens] the form of which is conical, and its top covered with snow. We followed the river as it entered these highlands, and at the distance of two miles reached three islands, one on each side of the river, and a third in the middle, on which were two houses, where the Indians were drying fish opposite a small rapid. Near these a fourth island begins, close to the right shore, where were nine lodges of Indians, all employed with their fish. As we passed they called to us to land, but as night was coming on, and there was no appearance of wood in the neighbourhood, we went on about a mile further, till observing a log that had drifted down the river, we landed near it on the left side, and formed our camp under a high hill, after having made twenty miles to-day.

Directly opposite to us are five houses of Indians, who were drying fish on the same island where we had passed the nine lodges, and on the other side of the river we saw a number of horses feeding. Soon after landing, we were informed by our chiefs that the large camp of nine houses, belonged to the first chief of all the tribes in this quarter, and that he had called to request us to land and pass the night with him as he had plenty of wood for us. This intelligence would have been very acceptable if it had been explained sooner, for we were obliged to use dried willows for fuel to cook with, not being able to burn the drift-log which had tempted us to land. We now sent the two chiefs along the left side of the river to invite the great chief down to spend the night with us. He came at a late hour, accompanied by twenty men, bringing a basket of mashed berries which he left as a present for us, and formed a camp at a short distance from us.

OCTOBER 19TH   The next morning the great chief with two of his inferior chiefs, and a third belonging to a band on the river below, made us a visit at a very early hour. The first of these is called *Yelleppit*, a handsome well proportioned man, about five feet eight inches high, and thirty-five years of age, with a bold and dignified countenance; the rest were not distinguished in their appearance. We smoked with them, and after making a speech gave a medal, a handkerchief, and a string of wampum to Yelleppit, and a string of wampum only to the inferior chiefs. He requested us to remain till the middle of the day, in order that all his nation might come and see us, but we excused ourselves by telling him that on our return we would spend two or three days with him. This conference detained us till nine o'clock, by which time great numbers of the Indians had come down to visit us. On leaving them, we went on for eight miles, when we came to an island near the left shore which continued six miles in length. At the lower extremity of it is a small island on which are five houses, at present vacant, though the scaffolds of fish are as usual abundant. A short distance below, are two more islands, one of them near the middle of the river. On this there were seven houses; but as soon as the Indians, who were drying fish, saw us, they fled to their houses, and not one of them appeared till we had passed, when they came out in greater numbers than is usual for houses of that size, which induced us to think that the inhabitants of the five lodges had been alarmed at our approach and taken refuge with them. We were very desirous of landing in order to relieve their apprehensions, but as there was a bad rapid along the island, all our care was necessary to prevent injury to the canoes. At the foot of this rapid is a rock, on the left shore, which is fourteen miles from our camp of last night, and resembles a hat in its shape.

Four miles beyond this island we came to a rapid, from the appearance of which it was judged prudent to examine it. After landing for that purpose on the left side, we began to enter the channel which is close under the opposite shore. It is a very dangerous rapid, strewed with high rocks and rocky islands, and in many places obstructed by shoals, over which the canoes were to be hauled, so that we were more than two hours in passing through the rapids, which extend for the same number of miles. The rapid has several small islands, and banks of muscleshells are spread along the river in several places.

In order to lighten the boats, captain Clark, with the two chiefs, the interpreter, and his wife, had walked across the low grounds on the left to the foot of the rapids. On the way, captain Clark ascended a cliff about two hundred feet above the water, from which he saw that the country on both sides of the river immediately from its cliffs, was low, and spreads itself into a level plain, extending for a great distance on all sides. To the west at the distance of about one hundred and fifty miles, is a very high mountain covered with snow, and from its direction and appearance, he supposed to be the mount St. Helens, laid down by Vancouver, as visible from the mouth of the Columbia: there is also another mountain [Mount Hood] of a conical form, whose top is covered with snow, in a southwest direction.

As captain Clark arrived at the lower end of the rapid before any, except one of the small canoes, he sat down on a rock to wait for them, and seeing a crane fly across the river, shot it, and it fell near him. Several Indians had been before this passing on the opposite side towards the rapids, and some few who had been nearly in front of him, being either alarmed at his appearance or the report of the gun, fled to their houses. Captain Clark was afraid that these people had not yet heard that white men were coming, and therefore, in order to allay their uneasiness before the whole party should arrive, he got into the small canoe with three men and rowed over towards the houses, and while crossing, shot a duck, which fell into the water. As he approached, no person was to be seen except three men in the plains, and they too fled as he came near the shore. He landed before five houses close to each other, but no one appeared, and the doors, which were of mat, were closed. He went towards one of them with a pipe in his hand, and pushing aside the mat entered the lodge, where he found thirty-two persons, chiefly men and women, with a few children, all in the greatest consternation; some hanging down their heads, others crying and wringing their hands. He went up to them all and shook hands with them in the most friendly manner; but their apprehensions, which had for a moment subsided, revived on his taking out a burning-glass, as there was no roof to the house, and lighting his pipe: he then offered it to several of the men, and distributed among the women and children some small trinkets which he carried about with him, and gradually restored some tranquillity among them. He then left this house, and directing each of the men to go into a house, went himself to a second: here he found the inhabitants more terrified than those he had first seen; but he succeeded in pacifying them, and then visited the other houses, where the men had been equally successful.

After leaving the houses he went out to sit on a rock, and beckoned to some of the men to come and smoke with him; but none of them ventured to join him till the canoes arrived with the two chiefs, who immediately explained our pacific intentions towards them. Soon after the interpreter's wife landed, and her presence dissipated all doubts of our being well-disposed, since in this country, no woman ever accompanies a war party: they therefore all came out and seemed perfectly reconciled; nor could we indeed blame them for their terrors, which were perfectly natural. They told the two chiefs that they knew we were not men, for they had seen us fall from the clouds: in fact, unperceived by them, captain Clark had shot the white crane, which they had seen fall just before he appeared to their eyes: the duck which he had killed also fell close by him, and as there were a few clouds flying over at the moment, they connected the fall of the birds and his sudden appearance, and believed that he had himself dropped from the clouds; the noise of the rifle, which they had never heard before, being considered merely as the sound to announce so extraordinary an event. This belief was strengthened, when on entering the room he brought down fire from the heavens by means of his burning-glass: we soon convinced them satisfactorily that we were only mortals, and after one of our chiefs had explained our history and objects, we all smoked together in great harmony.

These people do not speak precisely the same language as the Indians above, but understand them in conversation. In a short time we were joined by many of the inhabitants from below, several of them on horseback, and all pleased to see us, and to exchange their fish and berries for a few trinkets.

We remained here to dine, and then proceeded. At half a mile the hilly country on the right side of the river ceased: at eleven miles we found a small rapid, and a mile further came to a small island on the left, where there are some willows. Since we had left the five lodges, we passed twenty more, dispersed along the river at different parts of the valley on the right; but as they were now apprised of our coming they showed no signs of alarm. On leaving the island we passed three miles further along a country which is low on both sides of the river, and encamped under some willow trees on the left, having made thirty-six miles to-day.

Immediately opposite to us is an island close to the left shore, and another in the middle of the river, on which are twenty-four houses of Indians, all engaged in drying fish. We had scarcely landed before about a hundred of them came over in their boats to visit us, bringing with them a present of some wood, which was very acceptable: we received them in as kind a manner as we could—smoked with all of them, and gave the principal chief a string of wampum; but the highest satisfaction they enjoyed was the music of two of our violins, with which they seemed much delighted: they remained all night at our fires.

This tribe is a branch of the nation called Pishquitpaws, and can raise about three hundred and fifty men. In dress they resemble the Indians near the forks of the Columbia, except that their robes are smaller and do not reach lower than the waist; indeed, three-fourths of them have scarcely any robes at all. The dress of the females is equally scanty; for they wear only a small piece of a robe which covers their shoulders and neck, and reaches down the back to the waist, where it is attached by a piece of leather tied tight round the body: their breasts, which are thus exposed to view, are large, ill-shaped, and are suffered to hang down very low: their cheek-bones high, their heads flattened, and their persons in general adorned with scarcely any ornaments. Both sexes are employed in curing fish, of which they have great quantities on their scaffolds.

OCTOBER 20TH *Sunday.* The morning was cool, the wind from the southwest. Our appearance had excited the curiosity of the neighbourhood so much, that before we set out about two hundred Indians had collected to see us, and as we were desirous of conciliating their friendship, we remained to smoke and confer with them till breakfast. We then took our repast, which consisted wholly of dog-flesh, and proceeded. We passed three vacant houses near our camp, and at six miles reached the head of a rapid, on descending which we soon came to another, very difficult and dangerous. It is formed by a chain of large black rocks, stretching from the right side of the river, and with several small islands on the left, nearly choking the channel of the river. To this place we gave the name of the Pelican rapid, from seeing a number of pelicans and black cormorants about it. Just below it is a small island near the right shore, where are four houses of Indians, all busy in drying fish. At sixteen miles from our camp we reached a bend to the left

IOWA WARRIOR (King)

opposite to a large island, and at one o'clock halted for dinner on the lower point of an island on the right side of the channel. Close to this was a larger island on the same side, and on the left bank of the river a small one, a little below.

We landed near some Indian huts, and counted on this cluster of three islands, seventeen of their houses filled with inhabitants, resembling in every respect those higher up the river; like the inhabitants, they were busy in preparing fish. We purchased of them some dried fish, which were not good, and a few berries, on which we dined, and then walked to the head of the island for the purpose of examining a vault, which we had marked in coming along.

This place, in which the dead are deposited, is a building about sixty feet long and twelve feet wide, and is formed by placing in the ground poles or forks six feet high, across which a long pole is extended the whole length of the structure. Against this ridge-pole are placed broad boards, and pieces of canoes, in a slanting direction, so as to form a shed. It stands east and west, and neither of the extremities are closed. On entering the western end we observed a number of bodies wrapped carefully in leather robes, and arranged in rows on boards, which were then covered with a mat. This was the part destined for those who had recently died: a little farther on, the bones half decayed were scattered about, and in the centre of the building was a large pile of them heaped promiscuously on each other. At the eastern extremity was a mat, on which twenty-one skulls were placed in a circular form, the mode of interment being first to wrap the body in robes, and as it decays the bones are thrown into the heap, and the sculls placed together. From the different boards and pieces of canoes which form the vault, were suspended on the inside fishing-nets, baskets, wooden-bowls, robes, skins, trenchers, and trinkets of various kinds, obviously intended as offerings of affection to deceased relatives. On the outside of the vault were the skeletons of several horses, and great quantities of bones in the neighbourhood, which induced us to believe that these animals were most probably sacrificed at the funeral rites of their masters.

Having dined we proceeded past a small island, where were four huts of Indians, and at the lower extremity a bad rapid. Half a mile beyond this, and at the distance of twenty-four from our camp, we came to the commencement of the highlands on the right, which are the first we have seen on that side since near the Muscleshell rapids, leaving a valley forty miles in extent. Eight miles lower we passed a large island in the middle of the river, below which are eleven small islands, five on the right, the same number on the left and one in the middle of the stream. A brook falls in on the right side, and a small rivulet empties itself behind one of the islands. The country on the right consists of high and rugged hills; the left is a low plain with no timber on either side, except a few small willow-bushes along the banks; though a few miles after leaving these islands the country on the left rises to the same height with that opposite to it, and becomes an undulating plain. Two miles after passing a small rapid we reached a point of highland in a bend towards the right, and encamped for the evening, after a journey of forty-two miles. The river has been about a quarter of a mile in width, with a current much more uniform than it was during the last two days. We killed two speckled gulls, and several ducks of a delicious flavour.

Chapter 19

DOWN THE COLUMBIA TO THE GREAT RAPIDS

MONDAY, OCTOBER 21ST, 1805   The morning was cool, and the wind from the southwest. At five and a half miles we passed a small island, and one mile and a half further, another in the middle of the river, which has some rapid water near its head, and opposite to its lower extremity are eight cabins of Indians on the right side. We landed near them to breakfast; but such is the scarcity of wood, that last evening we had not been able to collect any thing except dry willows, and of these not more than barely sufficient to cook our supper, and this morning we could not find enough even to prepare breakfast. The Indians received us with great kindness, and examined every thing they saw with much attention. In their appearance and employments,

Map from Captain Clark's field book indicating the course and the camping-place of October 21, 1805.

as well as in their language, they do not differ from those higher up the river. The dress too is nearly the same; that of the men consisting of nothing but a short robe of deer or goat skin; while the women wear only a piece of dressed skin, falling from the neck so as to cover the front of the body as low as the waist; a bandage tied round the body and passing between the legs; and over this a short robe of deer and antelope skin is occasionally thrown. Here we saw two blankets of scarlet, and one of blue cloth, and also a sailor's round jacket; but we obtained only a few pounded roots, and some fish, for which we of course paid them. Among other things we observed some acorns, the fruit of the white oak. These they use as food either raw or roasted, and on enquiry informed us that they were procured from the Indians who live near the great falls. This place they designate by a name very commonly applied to it by the Indians, and highly expressive, the word *Timm*, which they pronounce so as to make it perfectly represent the sound of a distant cataract.

After breakfast we resumed our journey, and in the course of three miles passed a rapid where large rocks were strewed across the river, and at the head of which on the right shore were two huts of Indians. We stopped here for the purpose of examining it, as we always do whenever any danger is to be apprehended, and send round by land all those who cannot swim. Five miles further is another rapid, formed by large rocks projecting from each side, above which were five huts of Indians on the right side, occupied like those we had already seen, in drying fish. One mile below this is the lower point of an island close to the right side, opposite to which on that shore, are two Indian huts.

On the left side of the river at this place, are immense piles of rocks, which seem to have slipped from the cliffs under which they lie; they continue till spreading still farther into the river, at the distance of a mile from the island, they occasion a very dangerous rapid; a little below which on the right side are five huts. For many miles the river is now narrow and obstructed with very large rocks thrown into its channel; the hills continue high and covered, as is very rarely the case, with a few low pine trees on their tops. Between three and four miles below the last rapid occurs a second, which is also difficult, and three miles below it is a small river, which seems to rise in the open plains to the southeast, and falls in on the left. It is forty yards wide at its mouth; but discharges only a small quantity of water at present: we gave it the name of Lepage's river from Lepage one of our company. Near this little river and immediately below it, we had to encounter a new rapid. The river is crowded in every direction, with large rocks and small rocky islands; the passage crooked and difficult, and for two miles we were obliged to wind with great care along the narrow channels and between the huge rocks. At the end of this rapid are four huts of Indians on the right, and two miles below five more huts on the same side. Here we landed and passed the night, after making thirty-three miles.

The inhabitants of these huts explained to us that they were the relations of those who live at the great falls. They appear to be of the same nation with those we have seen above, whom, indeed, they resemble in every thing except that their language, although the same, has some words different. They have all pierced noses, and the men when in full dress wear a long tapering piece of shell or bead put through the nose. These people did not, however, receive us with the same cordiality to which we have been accustomed. They are poor; but we were able to purchase from them some wood to make a fire for supper, of which they have but little, and which they say they bring from the great falls. The hills in this neighbourhood are high and rugged, and a few scattered trees, either small pine or scrubby white oak, are occasionally seen on them. From the last rapids we also observed the conical mountain towards the southwest, which the Indians say is not far to the left of the great falls. From its vicinity to that place we called it the Timm or Falls mountain. The country through which we passed is furnished with several fine springs, which rise either high up the sides of the hills or else in the river meadows, and discharge themselves into the Columbia.

We could not help remarking that almost universally the fishing establishments of the Indians, both on the Columbia and the waters of Lewis's river, are on the right bank. On enquiry we were led to believe that the reason may be found in their fear of the Snake Indians; between whom and themselves, considering the warlike temper of that people, and the peaceful habits of the river tribes, it is very natural that the latter should be anxious to interpose so good a barrier. These Indians are described as residing on a great river to the south, and always at war with the people of this neighbourhood. One of our chiefs pointed out to-day a spot on the left where, not many years ago, a great battle was fought, in which numbers of both nations were killed.

We were agreeably surprised this evening by a present of some very good beer, made out of the remains of the bread, composed of the Pashecoquamash, part of the stores we had laid in at the head of the Kooskooskee, and which by frequent exposure becomes sour and moulded.

OCTOBER 22D *Tuesday.* The morning was fair and calm. We left our camp at nine o'clock, and after going on for six miles came to the head of an island, and a very bad rapid, where the rocks are scattered nearly across the river. Just above this and on the right side are six huts of Indians. At the distance of two miles below, are five more huts; the inhabitants of which are all engaged in drying fish, and some of them in their canoes killing fish with gigs; opposite to this establishment is a small island in a bend towards the right, on which there were such quantities of fish that we counted twenty stacks of dried and pounded salmon. This small island is at the upper point of one much larger, the sides of which are high uneven rocks, jutting over the water: here there is a bad rapid. The island continues for four miles, and at the middle of it is a large river, which appears to come from the southeast, and empties itself on the left.

We landed just above its mouth in order to examine it, and soon found the route intercepted by a deep, narrow channel, running into the Columbia above the large entrance, so as to form a dry and rich island about 400 yards wide and eight hundred long. Here as along the grounds of the river, the natives had been digging large quantities of roots, as the soil was turned up in many places. We reached the river about a quarter of a mile above its mouth, at a place where a large body of water is compressed within a channel of about two hundred yards in width, where it foams over rocks, many of which are above the surface of the water. These narrows are the end of a rapid which extends two miles back, where the river is closely confined between two high hills, below which it is divided by numbers of large rocks and small islands, covered with a low growth of timber. This river, which is called by the Indians Towahnahiooks, is two hundred yards wide at its mouth, has a very rapid current, and contributes about one fourth as much water as the Columbia possesses before the junction. Immediately at the entrance are three sand islands, and near it the head of an island which runs parallel to the large rocky island.

We now returned to our boats, and passing the mouth of the Towahnahiooks went between the islands. At the distance of two miles we reached the lower end of this rocky island, where were eight huts of Indians. Here too, we saw some large logs of wood, which were most probably rafted down the Towahnahiooks; and a mile below, on the right bank, were sixteen lodges of Indians, with whom we stopped to smoke. Then at the distance of about a mile passed six more huts on the same side, nearly opposite the lower extremity of the island, which has its upper end in the mouth of the Towahnahiooks. Two miles below we came to seventeen huts on the right side of the river, situated at the commencement of the pitch which includes the great falls. Here we halted, and immediately on landing walked down, accompanied by an old Indian from the huts, in order to examine the falls, and ascertain on which side we could make a portage most easily.

We soon discovered that the nearest route was on the right side, and therefore dropped down to the head of the rapid, unloaded the canoes and took all the baggage over by land to the foot of the rapid. The distance is twelve hundred yards. On setting out we crossed a solid rock, about one third of the whole distance; then reached a space of two hundred yards wide, which forms a hollow, where the loose sand from the low grounds has been driven by the winds, and is steep and loose, and therefore disagreeable to pass; the rest of the route is over firm and solid ground. The labour of crossing would have been very inconvenient, if the Indians had not assisted us in carrying some of the heavy articles on their horses; but for this service they repaid themselves so adroitly, that on reaching the foot of the ravine we formed a camp in a position which might secure us from the pilfering of the natives, which we apprehend much more than we do their hostilities.

Near our camp are five large huts of Indians engaged in drying fish and preparing it for the market. The manner of doing this, is by first opening the fish and exposing it to the sun on their scaffolds. When it is sufficiently dried it is pounded fine between two stones till it is pulverised, and is then placed in a basket about two feet long and one in diameter, neatly made of grass and rushes, and lined with the skin of a salmon stretched and dried for the purpose. Here they are pressed down as hard as possible, and the top covered with skins of fish which are secured by cords through the holes of the basket. These baskets are then placed in some dry situation, the corded part upwards, seven being usually placed as close as they can be put together, and five on the top of them. The whole is then wrapped up in mats, and made fast by cords, over which mats are again thrown. Twelve of these baskets, each of which contains from ninety to a hundred pounds, form a stack, which is now left exposed till it is sent to market; the fish thus preserved are kept sound and sweet for several years, and great quantities of it, they inform us, are sent to the Indians who live below the falls, whence it finds its way to the whites who visit the mouth of the Columbia. We observe both near the lodges and on the rocks in the river, great numbers of stacks of these pounded fish.

Besides fish, these people supplied us with filberts and berries, and we purchased a dog for supper; but it was with much difficulty that we were able to buy wood enough to cook it. In the course of the day we were visited by many Indians, from whom we learnt that the principal chiefs of the bands, residing in this neighbourhood, are now hunting in the mountains towards the southwest. On that side of the river none of the Indians have any permanent habitations, and on enquiry we were confirmed in our belief that it was for fear of attacks from the Snake Indians with whom they are at war. This nation they represent as very numerous, and residing in a great number of villages on the Towahnahiooks, where they live principally on salmon. That river they add is not obstructed by rapids above its mouth, but there becomes large and reaches to a considerable distance: the first villages of the Snake Indians on that river being twelve days' journey on a course about southeast from this place.

OCTOBER 23D *Wednesday.* Having ascertained from the Indians, and by actual examination, the best mode of bringing down the canoes, it was found necessary, as the river was divided into several narrow channels, by rocks and islands, to follow the route adopted by the Indians themselves. This operation captain Clark began this morning, and after crossing to the other side of the river, hauled the canoes over a point of land, so as to avoid a perpendicular fall of twenty feet. At the distance of four hundred and fifty-seven yards we reached the water, and embarked at a place where a long rocky island compresses the channel of the river within the space of a hundred and fifty yards, so as to form nearly a semicircle. On leaving this rocky island the channel is somewhat wider, but a second and much larger island of hard black rock, still divides it from the main stream, while on the left shore it is closely bordered by perpendicular rocks. Having descended in this way for a mile, we reached a pitch of the river, which being divided by two large rocks, descends with great rapidity down a fall eight feet in height: as the boats could not be navigated down this steep descent, we were obliged to land and let them down as slowly as possible by strong ropes of elk skin, which we had prepared for the purpose. They all passed in safety except one, which being loosed by the breaking of the ropes, was driven down, but was recovered by the Indians below. With this rapid ends the first pitch of the great falls, which is not great in point of height, and remarkable only for the singular manner in which the rocks have divided its channel. From the marks every where perceivable at the falls, it is obvious that in high floods, which must be in the spring, the water below the falls rises nearly to a level with that above them. Of this rise, which is occasioned by some obstructions which we do not as yet know, the salmon must avail themselves to pass up the river in such multitudes, that that fish is almost the only one caught in great abundance above the falls; but below that place, we observe the salmon trout, and the heads of a species of trout smaller than the salmon trout, which is in great quantities, and which they are now burying to be used as their winter food. A hole of any size being dug, the sides and bottom are lined with straw, over which skins are laid: on these the fish, after being well dried, is laid, covered with other skins, and the hole closed with a layer of earth twelve or fifteen inches deep.

About three o'clock we reached the lower camp, but our joy at having accomplished this object was somewhat diminished, by the persecution of a new acquaintance. On reaching the upper point of the portage, we found that the Indians had been encamped there not long since, and had left behind them multitudes of fleas. These sagacious animals were so pleased to exchange the straw and fish skins, in which they had been living, for some better residence, that we were soon covered with them, and during the portage the men were obliged to strip to the skin, in order to brush them from their bodies. They were not, however, so easily dislodged from our clothes, and accompanied us in great numbers to our camp.

We saw no game except a sea otter, which was shot in the narrow channel as we came down, but we could not get it. Having therefore scarcely any provisions, we purchased eight small fat dogs, a food to which we are now compelled to have recourse, for the Indians are very unwilling to sell us any of their good fish, which they reserve for the market below. Fortunately, however, the habit of using this animal has completely overcome the repugnance which we felt at first, and the dog, if not a favourite dish, is always an acceptable one. The meridian altitude of to-day gives $45° \, 42' \, 57\frac{3}{10}''$ north, as the latitude of our camp.

On the beach near the Indian huts, we observed two canoes of a different shape and size from any which we had hitherto seen: one of these we got in exchange for our smallest canoe, giving a hatchet and a few trinkets to the owner, who said he had purchased it from a white man below the falls, by giving him a horse. These canoes are very beautifully made; they are wide in the middle and tapering towards each end, with curious figures carved on the bow. They are thin, but being strengthened by cross bars, about an inch in diameter, which are tied with strong pieces of bark through holes in the sides, are able to bear very heavy burdens, and seem calculated to live in the roughest water.

A great number of Indians both from above and below the falls visited us to-day, and towards evening we were informed by one of the chiefs who had accompanied us, that he had overheard that the Indians below intended to attack us as we went down the river: being at all times ready for any attempt of that sort, we were not under greater apprehensions than usual at this intelligence: we, therefore, only reexamined our arms and increased the ammunition to one hundred rounds. Our chiefs, who had not the same motives of confidence, were by no means so much at their ease, and when at night they saw the Indians leave us earlier than usual, their suspicions of an intended attack were confirmed, and they were very much alarmed.

The next morning, *Thursday*, the Indians approached us with apparent caution, and behaved with more than usual reserve. Our two chiefs, by whom these circumstances were not unobserved, now told us that they wished to return home; that they could be no longer of any service to us, and they could not understand the language of the people below the falls; that those people formed a different nation from their own; that the two people had been at war with each other, and as the Indians had expressed a resolu-

OCTOBER 24TH

tion to attack us, they would certainly kill them. We endeavoured to quiet their fears, and requested them to stay two nights longer, in which time we would see the Indians below, and make a peace between the two nations.

They replied that they were anxious to return and see their horses; we however insisted on their remaining with us, not only in hopes of bringing about an accommodation between them and their enemies, but because they might be able to detect any hostile designs against us, and also assist us in passing the next falls, which are not far off, and represented as very difficult: they at length, agreed to stay with us two nights longer.

About nine o'clock we proceeded, and on leaving our camp near the lower fall, found the river about four hundred yards wide, with a current more rapid than usual, though with no perceptible descent. At the distance of two and a half miles, the river widened into a large bend or basin on the right, at the beginning of which are three huts of Indians. At the extremity of this basin stands a high black rock, which, rising perpendicularly from the right shore, seems to run wholly across the river; so totally indeed does it appear to stop the passage, that we could not see where the water escaped, except that the current appeared to be drawn with more than usual velocity to the left of the rock, where was a great roaring. We landed at the huts of the Indians, who went with us to the top of this rock, from which we saw all the difficulties of the channel. We were no longer at a loss to account for the rising of the river at the falls, for this tremendous rock stretches across the river, to meet the high hills of the left shore, leaving a channel of only forty-five yards wide, through which the whole body of the Columbia must press its way. The water thus forced into so narrow a channel, is thrown into whirls, and swells and boils in every part with the wildest agitation. But the alternative of carrying the boats over this high rock was almost impossible in our present situation, and as the chief danger seemed to be not from any rocks in the channel, but from the great waves and whirlpools, we resolved to try the passage in our boats, in hopes of being able by dexterous steering to escape. This we attempted, and with great care were able to get through, to the astonishment of all the Indians of the huts we had just passed, who now collected to see us from the top of the rock. The channel continues thus confined within a space of about half a mile, when the rock ceased. We passed a single Indian hut at the foot of it, where the river again enlarges itself to the width of two hundred yards, and at the distance of a mile and a half stopped to view a very bad rapid; this is formed by two rocky islands which divide the channel, the lower and larger of which is in the middle of the river. The appearance of this place was so unpromising, that we unloaded all the most valuable articles, such as guns, ammunition, our papers, &c. and sent them by land with all the men that could not swim to the extremity of the rapids. We then descended with the canoes two at a time, and though the canoes took in some water, we all went through safely; after which we made two miles, and stopped in a deep bend of the river towards the right, and encamped a little above a large village of twenty-one houses. Here we landed, and as it was late before all the canoes joined us, we were obliged to remain here this evening, the difficulties of the navigation having permitted us to make only six miles.

This village is situated at the extremity of a deep bend towards the right, and immediately above a ledge of high rocks, twenty feet above the marks of the highest flood, but broken in several places, so as to form channels which are at present dry, extending nearly across the river; this forms the second fall, or the place most probably which the Indians indicate by the word *Timm*. While the canoes were coming on, captain Clark walked with two men down to examine these channels. On these rocks the Indians are accustomed to dry fish, and as the season for that purpose is now over, the poles which they use are tied up very securely in bundles, and placed on the scaffolds. The stock of fish dried and pounded were so abundant that he counted one hundred and seven of them making more than ten thousand pounds of that provision. After examining the narrows as well as the lateness of the hour would permit, he returned to the village through a rocky open country, infested with polecats.

This village, the residence of a tribe called the Echeloots, consists of twenty-one houses, scattered promiscuously over an elevated situation, near a mound about thirty feet above the common level, which has some remains of houses on it, and bears every appearance of being artificial. The houses, which are the first wooden buildings we have seen since leaving the Illinois country, are nearly equal in size, and exhibit a very singular appearance. A large hole, twenty feet wide and thirty in length, is dug to the depth of six feet. The sides are then lined with split pieces of timber, rising just above the surface of the ground, which are smoothed to the same width by burning, or shaved with small iron axes. These timbers are secured in their erect position by a pole, stretched along the side of the building near the eaves, and supported on a strong post fixed at each corner. The timbers at the gable ends rise gradually higher, the middle pieces being the broadest. At the top of these is a sort of semicircle, made to receive a ridge-pole, the whole length of the house, propped by an additional post in the middle, and forming the top of the roof. From this ridge-pole to the eaves of the house, are placed a number of small poles or rafters, secured at each end by fibres of the cedar. On these poles, which are connected by small transverse bars of wood, is laid a covering of the white cedar, or arbor vitae, kept on by the strands of the cedar fibres: but a small distance along the whole length of the ridge-pole is left uncovered for the purpose of light, and permitting the smoke to pass through. The roof thus formed has a descent about equal to that common amongst us, and near the eaves is perforated with a number of small holes, made most probably to discharge their arrows in case of an attack. The only entrance is by a small door at the gable end, cut out of the middle piece of timber, twenty-nine and a half inches high, and fourteen inches broad, and reaching only eighteen inches above the earth. Before this hole is hung a mat, and on pushing it aside and crawling through, the descent is by a small wooden ladder, made in the form of those used amongst us. One half of the inside is used as a place of deposit for their dried fish, of which there are large quantities stored away, and with a few baskets of berries form the only family provisions; the other half adjoining the door, remains for the accommodation of the family. On each side are arranged near the walls, small beds of mats placed on little scaffolds or bedsteads, raised from eighteen inches to three feet from the ground, and in the middle of the vacant space is the fire, or sometimes two or three fires, when, as is indeed usually the case, the house contains three families.

The inhabitants received us with great kindness—invited us to their houses, and in the evening, after our camp had been formed, came in great numbers to see us: accompanying them was a principal chief, and several of the warriors of the nation below the great narrows. We made use of this opportunity to attempt a reconciliation between them and our two chiefs, and to put an end to the war which had disturbed the two nations. By representing to the chiefs the evils which the war inflicted on them, and the wants and privations to which it subjects them, they soon became disposed to conciliate with each other, and we had some reason to be satisfied with the sincerity of the mutual professions that the war should no longer continue, and that in future they would live in peace with each other. On concluding this negotiation we proceeded to invest the chief with the insignia of command, a medal and some small articles of clothing; after which the violin was produced, and our men danced to the great delight of the Indians, who remained with us till a late hour.

OCTOBER 25TH *Friday.* We walked down with several of the Indians to view the part of the narrows which they represented as most dangerous: we found it very difficult, but, as with our large canoes the portage was impracticable, we concluded on carrying our most valuable articles by land, and then hazarding the passage. We therefore returned to the village, and after sending some of the party with our best stores to make a portage, and fixed others on the rock to assist with ropes the canoes that might meet with any difficulty, we began the descent, in the presence of great numbers of Indians who had collected to witness this exploit. The channel for three miles is worn through a hard rough black rock from fifty to one hundred yards wide, in which the water swells and boils in a tremendous manner. The three first canoes escaped very well; the fourth, however, had nearly filled with water; the fifth passed through with only a small quantity of water over her. At half a mile we had got through the worst part, and having reloaded our canoes went on very well for two and a half miles, except that one of the boats was nearly lost by running against a rock. At the end of this channel of three miles, in which the Indians inform us they catch as many salmon as they wish, we reached a deep basin or bend of the river towards the right, near the entrance of which are two rocks. We crossed the basin, which has a quiet and gentle current, and at the distance of a mile from its commencement, and a little below where the river resumes its channel, reached a rock which divides it.

    At this place we met our old chiefs, who, when we began the portage, had walked down to a village below to smoke a pipe of friendship on the renewal of peace. Just after our meeting we saw a chief of the village above, with a party who had been out hunting, and were then crossing the river with their horses on their way home. We landed to smoke with this chief, whom we found a bold looking man of a pleasing appearance, about fifty years of age, and dressed in a war jacket, a cap, leggings and moccasins: we presented him with a medal and other small articles, and he gave us some meat, of which he had been able to procure but little; for on his route he had met with a war party of Indians from the Towahnahiooks, between whom there was a battle. We here smoked a parting pipe with our two faithful friends, the chiefs, who had accompanied us from the heads of the river, and who now had each bought a horse, intending to go home by land.

On leaving this rock the river is gentle, but strewed with a great number of rocks for a few miles, when it becomes a beautiful still stream about half a mile wide. At five miles from the large bend we came to the mouth of a creek twenty yards wide, heading in the range of mountains which run S. S. W. and S. W. for a long distance, and discharging a considerable quantity of water: it is called by the Indians Quenett. We halted below it under a high point of rocks on the left; and as it was necessary to make some celestial observations, we formed a camp on the top of these rocks. This situation is perfectly well calculated for defence in case the Indians should incline to attack us, for the rocks form a sort of natural fortification with the aid of the river and creek, and is convenient to hunt along the foot of the mountains to the west and southwest, where there are several species of timber which form fine coverts for game. From this rock, the pinnacle of the round mountain covered with snow, which we had seen a short distance below the forks of the Columbia, and which we had called the Falls or Timm mountain, is south 43° west, and about thirty-seven miles distant. The face of the country on both sides of the river above and below the falls is steep, rugged, and rocky, with a very small proportion of herbage, and no timber, except a few bushes: the hills, however, to the west, have some scattered pine, white oak and other kinds of trees. All the timber used by the people at the upper falls is rafted down the Towahnahiooks; and those who live at the head of the narrows we have just passed, bring their wood in the same way from this creek to the lower part of the narrows, from which it is carried three miles by land to their habitations.

Both above and below, as well as in the narrows, we saw a great number of sea-otter or seals, and this evening one deer was killed, and great signs of that animal seen near the camp. In the creek we shot a goose, and saw much appearance of beaver, and one of the party also saw a fish, which he took to be a drum-fish. Among the willows we found several snares, set by the natives for the purpose of catching wolves.

OCTOBER 26TH

Saturday. The morning was fine: we sent six men to hunt and to collect resin to pitch the canoes, which, by being frequently hauled over rocks, have become very leaky. The canoes were also brought out to dry, and on examination it was found that many of the articles had become spoiled by being repeatedly wet. We were occupied with the observations necessary to determine our longitude, and with conferences among the Indians, many of whom came on horseback to the opposite shore in the forepart of the day, and showed some anxiety to cross over to us: we did not however think it proper to send for them, but towards evening two chiefs with fifteen men came over in a small canoe: they proved to be the two principal chiefs of the tribes at and above the falls, who had been absent on a hunting excursion as we passed their residence: each of them on their arrival made us a present of deer's flesh, and small white cakes made of roots. Being anxious to ingratiate ourselves in their favour so as to ensure a friendly reception on our return, we treated them with all the kindness we could show: we acknowledged the chiefs, gave a medal of the small size, a red silk handkerchief, an arm-band, a knife, and a piece of paint to each chief, and small presents to several of the party, and half a deer: these attentions were not lost on the Indians, who appeared very well pleased with them. At night a fire was made in the middle of our camp, and as the Indians sat round it our men danced to the music of the violin, which so delighted them that several resolved to remain with us all night: the rest crossed the river. All the tribes in this neighbourhood are at war with the Snake Indians, whom they all describe as living on the Towahnahiooks, and whose nearest town is said to be four days' march from this place, and in a direction nearly southwest: there has lately been a battle between these tribes, but we could not ascertain the loss on either side.

The water rose to-day eight inches, a rise which we could only ascribe to the circumstance of the wind's having been up the river for the last twenty-four hours, since the influence of the tide cannot be sensible here on account of the falls below. The hunters returned in the evening; they had seen the tracks of elk and bear in the mountains, and killed five deer, four very large gray squirrels, and a grouse: they inform us that the country off the river is broken, stony, and thinly timbered with pine and white oak; besides these delicacies one of the men killed with a gig a salmon trout, which, being fried in some bear's oil, which had been given to us by the chief whom we had met this morning below the narrows, furnished a dish of a very delightful flavour. A number of white cranes were also seen flying in different directions, but at such a height that we could not procure any of them.

The fleas, with whom we had contracted an intimacy at the falls, are so unwilling to leave us, that the men are obliged to throw off all their clothes, in order to relieve themselves from their persecution.

OCTOBER 27TH *Sunday.* The wind was high from the westward during last night and this morning, but the weather being fair we continued our celestial observations. The two chiefs who remained with us, were joined by seven Indians, who came in a canoe from below. To these men we were very particular in our attentions; we smoked and eat with them; but some of them who were tempted by the sight of our goods exposed to dry, wished to take liberties with them; to which we were under the necessity of putting an immediate check; this restraint displeased them so much, that they returned down the river in a very ill humour. The two chiefs however remained with us till the evening, when they crossed the river to their party.

Before they went we procured from them a vocabulary of the Echeloot, their native language, and on comparison were surprised at its difference from that of the Eneeshur tongue. In fact although the Echeloots, who live at the great narrows, are not more than six miles from the Eneeshurs or residents at and above the great falls, the two people are separated by a broad distinction of language. The Eneeshurs are understood by all the tribes residing on the Columbia, above the falls; but at that place they meet with the unintelligible language of the Echeloots, which then descends the river to a considerable distance. Yet the variation may possibly be rather a deep shade of dialect than a radical difference, since among both many words are the same, and the identity cannot be accounted for by supposing that their neighbourhood has interwoven them into their daily conversations, because the same words are equally familiar among all the Flathead bands which we have passed. To all these tribes too the strange clucking or guttural noise which first struck us is common. They also flatten the heads of the children in nearly the same manner, but we now begin to observe that the heads of the males, as well as of the other sex, are subjected to this operation, whereas among the mountains the custom has confined it almost to the females. The hunters brought home four deer, one grouse, and a squirrel.

Monday. The morning was again cool and windy. Having dried our goods, we were about setting out, when three canoes came from above to visit us, and at the same time two others from below arrived for the same purpose. Among these last was an Indian who wore his hair in a queue, and had on a round hat and a sailor's jacket, which he said he had obtained from the people below the great rapids, who bought them from the whites. This interview detained us till nine o'clock, when we proceeded down the river, which is now bordered with cliffs of loose dark coloured rocks about ninety feet high, with a thin covering of pine and other small trees. At the distance of four miles we reached a small village of eight houses under some high rocks on the right, with a small creek on the opposite side of the river. OCTOBER 28TH

We landed and found the houses similar to those we had seen at the great narrows: on entering one of them we saw a British musket, a cutlass, and several brass teakettles, of which they seemed to be very fond. There were figures of men, birds, and different animals, which were cut and painted on the boards which form the sides of the room, and though the workmanship of these uncouth figures was very rough, they were as highly esteemed by the Indians as the finest frescoes of more civilised people. This tribe is called the Chilluckittequaw, and their language although somewhat different from that of the Echeloots, has many of the same words, and is sufficiently intelligible to the neighbouring Indians. We procured from them a vocabulary, and then after buying five small dogs, some dried berries, and a white bread or cake made of roots, we left them. The wind however rose so high, that we were obliged after going one mile to land on the left side opposite to a rocky island, and pass the day there. We formed our camp in a niche above a point of high rocks, and as it was the only safe harbour we could find, submitted to the inconvenience of lying on the sand, exposed to the wind and rain during all the evening. The high wind, which obliged us to consult the safety of our boats by not venturing further, did not at all prevent the Indians from navigating the river.

We had not been long on shore, before a canoe with a man, his wife and two children, came from below through the high waves with a few roots to sell; and soon after we were visited by many Indians from the village above, with whom we smoked and conversed. The canoes used by these people are like those already described, built of white cedar or pine, very light, wide in the middle, and tapering towards the ends, the bow being raised and ornamented with carvings of the heads of animals. As the canoe is the vehicle of transportation, the Indians have acquired great dexterity in the management of it, and guide it safely over the highest waves. They have among their utensils bowls and baskets very neatly made of small bark and grass, in which they boil their provisions. The only game seen to-day were two deer, of which only one was killed, the other was wounded but escaped.

Tuesday. The morning was still cloudy, and the wind from the west, but as it had abated its violence, we set out at daylight. At the distance of four miles we passed a creek on the right, one mile below which is a village of OCTOBER 29TH seven houses on the same side. This is the residence of the principal chief of the Chilluckittequaw nation, whom we now found to be the same between whom and our two chiefs we had made a peace at the Echeloot village. He received us very kindly, and set before us pounded fish, filberts, nuts, the berries of the Sacacommis, and white bread made of roots. We gave in return a bracelet of ribbon to each of the women of the house, with which they were very much pleased. The chief had several articles, such as scarlet and blue cloth, a sword, a jacket and hat, which must have been procured from the whites, and on one side of the room were two wide split boards placed together, so as to make space for a rude figure of a man cut and painted on them. On pointing to this and asking them what it meant, he said something, of which all we understood was "good," and then stepped to the image and brought out his bow and quiver, which, with some other warlike instruments, were kept behind it.

The chief then directed his wife to hand him his medicine-bag, from which he brought out fourteen fore-fingers, which he told us had once belonged to the same number of his enemies, whom he had killed in fighting with the nations to the southeast, to which place he pointed, alluding no doubt to the Snake Indians, the common enemy of the nations on the Columbia. This bag is about two feet in length, containing roots, pounded dirt, &c. which the Indians only know how to appreciate. It is suspended in the middle of the lodge, and it is supposed to be a species of sacrilege to be touched by any but the owner. It is an object of religious fear, and it is from its sanctity the safest place to deposit their medals and their more valuable articles. The Indians have likewise small bags which they preserve in their great medicine-bag, from whence they are taken and worn around their waists and necks as amulets against any real or imaginary evils. This was the first time we had ever known the Indians to carry from the field any other trophy except the scalp. They were shown with great exultation, and after an harangue which we were left to presume was in praise of his exploits, the fingers were carefully replaced among the valuable contents of the red medicine-bag.

This village being part of the same nation with the village we passed above, the language of the two is the same, and their houses of similar form and materials, and calculated to contain about thirty souls. The inhabitants were unusually hospitable and good-humoured, so that we gave to the place the name of the Friendly village.

We breakfasted here, and after purchasing twelve dogs, four sacks of fish, and a few dried berries, proceeded on our journey. The hills as we passed are high with steep and rocky sides, and some pine and white oak, and an undergrowth of shrubs scattered over them. Four miles below this village is a small river on the right side; immediately below is a village of Chilluckittequaws, consisting of eleven houses. Here we landed and smoked a pipe with the inhabitants, who were very cheerful and friendly. They as well as the people of the last village inform us, that this river comes a considerable distance from the N. N. E., that it has a great number of falls, which prevent the salmon from passing up, and that there are ten nations residing on it who subsist on berries, or such game as they can procure with their bows and arrows. At its mouth the river is sixty yards wide, and has a deep and very rapid channel. From the number of falls of which the Indians spoke, we gave it the name of Cataract river. We purchased four dogs, and then proceeded.

The country as we advance is more rocky and broken, and the pine and low white oak on the hills increase in great quantity. Three miles below Cataract river we passed three large rocks in the river; that in the middle is large and longer than the rest, and from the circumstance of its having several square vaults on it, obtained the name of Sepulchre island. A short distance below are two huts of Indians on the right: the river now widens, and in three miles we came to two more houses on the right; one mile beyond which is a rocky island in a bend of the river towards the left. Within the next six miles we passed fourteen huts of Indians, scattered on the right bank, and then reached the entrance of a river on the left, which we called Labieshe's river, after Labieshe one of our party. Just above this river is a low ground more thickly timbered than usual, and in front are four huts of Indians on the bank, which are the first we have seen on that side of the Columbia. The exception may be occasioned by this spot's being more than usually protected from the approach of their enemies, by the creek, and the thick wood behind.

We again embarked, and at the distance of a mile passed the mouth of a rapid creek on the right eighteen yards wide: in this creek the Indians whom we left take their fish, and from the number of canoes which were in it, we called it Canoe creek. Opposite to this creek is a large sandbar, which continues for four miles along the left side of the river. Just below this a beautiful cascade falls in on the left over a precipice of rock one hundred feet in height. One mile further are four Indian huts in the low ground on the left: and two miles beyond this a point of land on the right, where the mountains become high on both sides, and possess more timber and greater varieties of it than hitherto, and those on the left are covered with snow. One mile from this point we halted for the night at three Indian huts on the right, having made thirty-two miles.

On our first arrival they seemed surprised, but not alarmed at our appearance, and we soon became intimate by means of smoking and our favourite entertainment for the Indians, the violin. They gave us fruit, some roots, and root-bread, and we purchased from them three dogs. The houses of these people are similar to those of the Indians above, and their language the same: their dress also, consisting of robes or skins of wolves, deer, elk, and wild-cat, is made nearly after the same model: their hair is worn in plaits down each shoulder, and round their neck is put a strip of some skin with the tail of the animal hanging down over the breast: like the Indians above they are fond of otter skins, and give a great price for them. We here saw the skin of a mountain sheep [goat], which they say live among the rocks in the mountains: the skin was covered with white hair, the wool long, thick, and coarse, with long coarse hair on the top of the neck, and the back resembling somewhat the bristles of a goat. Immediately behind the village is a pond, in which were great numbers of small swan.

Wednesday. A moderate rain fell during all last night, but the morning was cool, and after taking a scanty breakfast of deer, we proceeded. The river is now about three-quarters of a mile wide, with a current so gentle, that it does not exceed one mile and a half an hour; but its course is obstructed by

OCTOBER 30TH

the projection of large rocks, which seemed to have fallen promiscuously from the mountains into the bed of the river. On the left side four different streams of water empty themselves in cascades from the hills: what is, however, most singular is, that there are stumps of pine trees scattered to some distance in the river, which has the appearance of being dammed below and forced to encroach on the shore: these obstructions continue till at the distance of twelve miles, when we came to the mouth of a river on the right, where we landed: we found it sixty yards wide, and its banks possess two kinds of timber which we had not hitherto seen: one is a very large species of ash; the other resembling in its bark the beech; but the tree itself, as also the leaves, are smaller. We called this stream Crusatte's river, after Crusatte, one of our men: opposite to its mouth the Columbia widens to the distance of a mile, with a large sandbar, and large stones and rocks scattered through the channel. We here saw several of the large buzzards, which are of the size of the largest eagle, with the under part of their wings white: we also shot a deer and three ducks; on part of which we dined, and then continued down the Columbia.

Above Crusatte's river the low grounds are about three quarters of a mile wide, rising gradually to the hills, and with a rich soil covered with grass, fern, and other small undergrowth; but below, the country rises with a steep ascent, and soon the mountains approach to the river with steep rugged sides, covered with a very thick growth of pine, cedar, cottonwood, and oak. The river is still strewed with large rocks. Two and a half miles below Crusatte's river is a large creek on the right, with a small island in the mouth. Just below this creek we passed along the right side of three small islands on the right bank of the river, with a larger island on the opposite side, and landed on an island very near the right shore at the head of the great shoot, and opposite two smaller islands at the fall or shoot itself. Just above the island on which we were encamped is a small village of eight large houses in a bend on the right, where the country, from having been very mountainous, becomes low for a short distance. We had made fifteen miles to-day, during all which time we were kept constantly wet with the rain; but as we were able to get on this island some of the ash which we saw for the first time to-day, and which makes a tolerable fire, we were as comfortable as the moistness of the evening would permit.

As soon as we landed, captain Lewis went with five men to the village, which is situated near the river, with ponds in the low grounds behind: the greater part of the inhabitants were absent collecting roots down the river: the few, however, who were at home, treated him very kindly, and gave him berries, nuts, and fish; and in the house were a gun and several articles which must have been procured from the whites; but not being able to procure any information, he returned to the island. Captain Clark had in the meantime gone down to examine the shoot, and to discover the best route for a portage. He followed an Indian path, which, at the distance of a mile, led to a village on an elevated situation, the houses of which had been large, but built in a different form from any we had yet seen, but which had been lately abandoned, the greater part of the boards being put into a pond near the village: this was most probably for the purpose of drowning the fleas, which were in immense quantities near the houses. After going about three miles the night obliged him to return to camp.

Thursday. He resumed his search in the morning, through the rain. At the extremity of the basin, in which is situated the island where we are encamped, several rocks and rocky islands are interspersed through the bed of the river. The rocks on each side have fallen down from the mountains; that on the left being high, and on the right the hill itself, which is lower, slipping into the river; so that the current is here compressed within a space of one hundred and fifty yards. Within this narrow limit it runs for the distance of four hundred yards with great rapidity, swelling over the rocks with a fall of about twenty feet: it then widens to two hundred paces, and the current for a short distance becomes gentle; but at the distance of a mile and a half, and opposite to the old village mentioned yesterday, it is obstructed by a very bad rapid, where the waves are unusually high, the river being confined between large rocks, many of which are at the surface of the water. Captain Clark proceeded along the same path he had taken before, which led him through a thick wood and along a hill side, till two and a half miles below the shoots, he struck the river at the place whence the Indians make their portage to the head of the shoot: he here sent Crusatte, the principal waterman, up the stream, to examine if it were practicable to bring the canoes down the water. In the meantime, he, with Joseph Fields, continued his route down the river, along which the rapids seem to stretch as far as he could see. At half a mile below the end of the portage, he came to a house, the only remnant of a town, which, from its appearance, must have been of great antiquity. The house was uninhabited, and being old and decayed, he felt no disposition to encounter the fleas, which abound in every situation of that kind, and therefore did not enter.

OCTOBER 31ST

About half a mile below this house, in a very thick part of the woods, is an ancient burial place: it consists of eight vaults made of pine or cedar boards closely connected, about eight feet square and six in height; the top secured, covered with wide boards sloping a little, so as to convey off the rain: the direction of all of them is east and west, the door being on the eastern side, and partially stopped with wide boards decorated with rude pictures of men and other animals. On entering we found in some of them four dead bodies, carefully wrapped in skins, tied with cords of grass and bark, lying on a mat in a direction east and west: the other vaults contained only bones, which were in some of them piled to the height of four feet: on the tops of the vaults, and on poles attached to them, hung brass kettles and frying-pans with holes in their bottoms, baskets, bowls, sea-shells, skins, pieces of cloth, hair, bags of trinkets and small bones, the offerings of friendship or affection, which have been saved by a pious veneration from the ferocity of war, or the more dangerous temptations of individual gain: the whole of the walls as well as the door were decorated with strange figures cut and painted on them; and besides these were several wooden images of men, some of them so old and decayed as to have almost lost their shape, which were all placed against the sides of the vaults. These images, as well as those in the houses we have lately seen, do not appear to be at all the objects of adoration: in this place they were most probably intended as resemblances of those whose decease they indicate; and when we observe them in houses, they occupy the most conspicuous part; but are treated more like ornaments than objects of worship. Near the vaults which are standing, are the remains of others on the ground completely rotted and covered with moss; and as they are formed of the most durable pine and cedar timber, there is every appearance, that for a very long series of years this retired spot has been the depository for the Indians near this place.

After examining this place captain Clark went on, and found the river as before strewed with large rocks, against which the water ran with great rapidity. Just below the vaults the mountain, which is but low on the right side, leaves the river, and is succeeded by an open stony level, which extends down the river, while on the left the mountain is still high and rugged. At two miles distance he came to a village of four houses, which were now vacant and the doors barred up: on looking in he saw the usual quantity of utensils still remaining, from which he concluded that the inhabitants were at no great distance collecting roots or hunting, in order to lay in their supply of food for the winter: he left them and went on three miles to a difficult rocky rapid, which was the last in view. Here, on the right, are the remains of a large and ancient village, which could be plainly traced by the holes for the houses and the deposits for fish: after he had examined these rapids and the neighbouring country he returned to camp by the same route: the only game he had obtained was a sandhill crane.

In the meantime we had been occupied in preparations for making the portage, and in conference with the Indians, who came down from the village to visit us. Towards evening two canoes arrived from the village at the mouth of Cataract river, loaded with fish and bears' grease for the market below: as soon as they landed they unloaded the canoes, turned them upside down on the beach, and encamped under a shelving rock near our camp.

We had an opportunity of seeing to-day the hardihood of the Indians of the neighbouring village: one of the men shot a goose, which fell into the river, and was floating rapidly towards the great shoot, when an Indian observing it plunged in after it: the whole mass of the waters of the Columbia, just preparing to descend its narrow channel, carried the animal down with great rapidity: the Indian followed it fearlessly to within one hundred and fifty feet of the rocks, where he would inevitably have been dashed to pieces; but seizing his prey he turned round and swam ashore with great composure. We very willingly relinquished our right to the bird in favour of the Indian who had thus saved it at the imminent hazard of his life: he immediately set to work, and picked off about half the feathers, and then without opening it ran a stick through it and carried it off to roast.

Friday, November 1st, 1805

The morning was cool and the wind high from the northeast. The Indians who arrived last night, took their empty canoes on their shoulders and carried them below the great shoot, where they put them in the water and brought them down the rapid, till at the distance of two and a half miles they stopped to take in their loading, which they had been afraid to trust in the last rapid, and had therefore carried by land from the head of the shoot.

After their example we carried our small canoe, and all the baggage across the slippery rocks, to the foot of the shoot. The four large canoes were next brought down, by slipping them along poles, placed from one

Sketch-map by Captain Clark to show the Great Rapids of the Columbia.

rock to another, and in some places by using partially streams which escaped along side of the river. We were not, however, able to bring them across without three of them receiving injuries, which obliged us to stop at the end of the shoot to repair them. At this shoot we saw great numbers of sea-otters; but they are so shy that it is difficult to reach them with the musket: one of them that was wounded to-day sunk and was lost. Having by this portage avoided the rapid and shoot of four hundred yards in length, we reembarked, passed at a mile and a half the bad rapid opposite to the old village on the right, and making our way through the rocks, saw the house just below the end of the portage; the eight vaults near it; and at the distance of four miles from the head of the shoot, reached a high rock, which forms the upper part of an island near the left shore. Between this island and the right shore we proceeded, leaving at the distance of a mile and a half, the village of four houses on our right, and a mile and a half lower came to the head of a rapid near the village on the right. Here we halted for the night, having made only seven miles from the head of the shoot. During the whole of the passage the river is very much obstructed by rocks. The island, which is about three miles long, reaches to the rapid which its lower extremity contributes to form. The meridian altitude of to-day gave us the latitude of 45° 44′ 3″ north.

As we passed the village of four houses, we found that the inhabitants had returned, and stopped to visit them. The houses are similar to those already described, but larger, from thirty-five to fifty feet long, and thirty feet wide, being sunk in the ground about six feet, and raised the same height above. Their beds are raised about four feet and a half above the floor, and the ascent is by a new painted ladder, with which every family is provided, and under them are stored their dried fish, while the space between the part of the bed on which they lie and the wall of the house is occupied by the nuts, roots, berries, and other provisions, which are spread on mats. The fireplace is about eight feet long, and six feet wide, sunk a foot below the floor, secured by a frame, with mats placed around for the family to sit on. In all of the houses are images of men of different shapes, and placed as ornaments in the parts of the house where they are most seen. They gave us nuts, berries, and some dried fish to eat, and we purchased, among other articles, a hat made after their own taste, such as they wear, without a brim. They ask high prices for all that they sell, observing that the whites below, pay dearly for all which they carry there.

We cannot learn precisely the nature of the trade carried on by the Indians with the inhabitants below. But as their knowledge of the whites seems to be very imperfect, and the only articles which they carry to market, such as pounded fish, bear-grass and roots, cannot be an object of much foreign traffic, their intercourse appears to be an intermediate trade with the natives near the mouth of the Columbia: from them these people obtain in exchange for their fish, roots and bear-grass, blue and white beads, copper tea-kettles, brass arm-bands, some scarlet and blue robes, and a few articles of old European clothing. But their great object is to obtain beads, an article which holds the first place in their ideas of relative value, and to procure which they will sacrifice their last article of clothing or the last mouthful of food. Independently of their fondness for them as an ornament, these beads are the medium of trade, by which they obtain from the Indians still higher up the river, robes, skins, chappelel bread, bear-grass, &c. Those Indians in turn, employ them to procure from the Indians in the Rocky mountains, bear-grass, pachico, roots, robes, &c.

These Indians are rather below the common size, with high cheekbones, their noses pierced, and in full dress, ornamented with a tapering piece of white shell or wampum about two inches long. Their eyes are exceedingly sore and weak, many of them have only a single eye, and some perfectly blind. Their teeth prematurely decayed, and in frequent instances, altogether worn away. Their general health, however, seems to be good, the only disorder we have remarked, being tumours in different parts of the body. The women are small and homely in their appearance, their legs and thighs much swelled, and their knees remarkably large; deformities, which are no doubt owing to the manner in which they set on their hams. They go nearly naked, having only a piece of leather tied round the breast, falling thence, nearly as low as the waist; a small robe about three feet square, and a piece of leather, which ill supplies the place of a cover, tied between their legs. Their hair is suffered to hang loose in every direction; and in their persons, as well as in their cookery, they are filthy to a most disgusting degree. We here observe that the women universally have their heads flattened, and in many of the villages, we have lately seen the female children undergo the operation.

Chapter 20

FROM TIDE-WATER TO THE PACIFIC OCEAN

SATURDAY, NOVEMBER 2D, 1805   We now examined the rapid below more particularly, and the danger appearing to be too great for the loaded canoes, all those who could not swim were sent with the baggage by land. The canoes then passed safely, and were reloaded; at the foot of the rapid we took a meridian altitude of 59° 45′ 45″. Just as we were setting out seven squaws arrived across the portage loaded with dried fish and bear-grass, neatly packed in bundles, and soon after four Indians came down the rapid in a large canoe. After breakfasting we left our camp at one o'clock, passed the upper point of an island which is separated from the right shore by a narrow channel, through which in high tides the water passes. But at present it contains no running water, and a creek which falls into it from the mountains on the right, is in the same dry condition, though it has the marks of discharging immense torrents at some seasons. The island thus made is three miles in length and about one in width; its situation is high and open, the land rich, and at this time covered with grass and a great number of strawberry vines, from which we gave it the name of Strawberry island. In several places we observed that the Indians had been digging for roots, and indeed the whole island bears every appearance of having been at some period in a state of cultivation. On the left side of the river the low ground is narrow and open: the rapid which we have just passed is the last of all the descents of the Columbia.

At this place the first tide-water commences, and the river in consequence widened immediately below the rapid. As we descended, we reached at the distance of one mile from the rapid a creek under a bluff on the left, at three miles is the lower point of Strawberry island. To this immediately succeed three small islands covered with wood; in the meadow to the right, and at some distance from the hills, stands a high perpendicular rock, about eight hundred feet high, and four hundred yards round the base; this we called the Beacon rock. Just below is an Indian village of nine houses, situated between two small creeks.

At this village the river widens to nearly a mile in extent, the low grounds too become wider, and they as well as the mountains on each side are covered with pine, spruce-pine, cottonwood, a species of ash, and some alder. After being so long accustomed to the dreary nakedness of the country above, the change is as grateful to the eye, as it is useful in supplying us with fuel. Four miles from the village is a point of land on the right, where the hills become lower, but are still thickly timbered. The river is now about two miles wide, the current smooth and gentle, and the effect of the tide has been sensible since leaving the rapid. Six miles lower is a rock rising from the middle of the river to the height of one hundred feet, and about eighty yards at its base. We continued six miles further, and halted for the night under a high projecting rock on the left side of the river opposite the point of a large meadow.

The mountains, which from the great shoot to this place are high, rugged, and thickly covered with timber chiefly of the pine species, here leave the river on each side; the river becomes two and a half miles in width, and the low grounds are extensive and well supplied with wood. The Indians whom we left at the portage passed us, on their way down the river, and seven others who were descending in a canoe for the purpose of trading below, encamped with us. We had made from the foot of the great shoot twenty-nine miles to-day. The ebb-tide rose at our camp about nine inches, the flood must rise much higher. We saw great numbers of water-fowl, such as swan, geese, ducks of various kinds, gulls, plover, and the white and grey brant, of which last we killed eighteen.

Sunday. We were detained until ten o'clock by a fog so thick that a man could not be discerned at the distance of fifty steps. As soon as it cleared off we set out in company with our new Indian acquaintances, who came from a village near the great falls. The low grounds along the river are covered so thickly with rushes, vines, and other small growth, that they are almost impassable. At the distance of three miles we reached the mouth of a river on the left, which seemed to lose its waters in a sandbar opposite; the stream itself being only a few inches in depth. But on attempting to wade across, we discovered that the bed was a very bad quicksand, too deep to be passed on foot. We went up a mile and a half to examine this river, and found it to be at this distance a very considerable stream one hundred and twenty yards wide at its narrowest part, with several small islands. Its character resembles very much that of the river Platte. It drives its quicksand over the low grounds with great impetuosity, and such is the quantity of coarse sand which it discharges, that the accumulation has formed a large sandbar or island, three miles long, and a mile and a half wide, which divides the waters of the Quicksand river into two channels. This sand island compresses the Columbia within a space of half a mile, and throws its whole current against the right shore. Opposite to this river, which we call Quicksand river, is a large creek to which we gave the name of Seal river. The first appears to pass through the low country, at the foot of the high range of mountains towards the southeast, while the second as well as all the large creeks on the right side of the Columbia, rise in the same ridge of mountains N. N. E. from this place. The mountain, which we have supposed to be the Mount Hood of Vancouver, bears S. 85° E. about forty-seven miles from the mouth of the Quicksand river.

NOVEMBER 3D

After dinner we proceeded, and at the distance of three miles reached the lower mouth of Quicksand river. On the opposite side a large creek falls in near the head of an island, which extends for three miles and a half down the river; it is a mile and a half in width, rocky at the upper end, has some timber round its borders, but in the middle is open and has several ponds. Half a mile lower is another island in the middle of the river, to which from its appearance we gave the name of Diamond island. Here we met fifteen Indians ascending the river in two canoes, but the only information we could procure from them was, that they had seen three vessels, which we presume to be European, at the mouth of the Columbia. We went along its right side for three miles, and encamped opposite to it, after making to-day thirteen miles.

A canoe soon after arrived from the village at the foot of the last rapid, with an Indian and his family, consisting of a wife, three children, and a woman who had been taken prisoner from the Snake Indians, living on a river from the south, which we afterwards found to be the Multnomah. Sacajawea was immediately introduced to her, in hopes that being a Snake Indian also, they might understand each other, but their language was not sufficiently intelligible to permit them to converse together. The Indian had a gun with a brass barrel and cock, which he appeared to value very highly.

Below Quicksand river the country is low, rich and thickly wooded on each side of the river: the islands have less timber, but are furnished with a number of ponds near which are vast quantities of fowls, such as swan, geese, brants, cranes, storks, white gulls, cormorants and plover. The river is wide, and contains a great number of sea otters.

In the evening the hunters brought in game for a sumptuous supper, which we shared with the Indians, both parties of whom spent the night with us.

NOVEMBER 4TH *Monday.* The weather was cloudy and cool, and the wind from the west. During the night, the tide rose eighteen inches near our camp. We set out about eight o'clock, and at the distance of three miles came to the lower end of Diamond island. It is six miles long, nearly three in width, and like the other islands, thinly covered with timber, and has a number of ponds or small lakes scattered over its surface. Besides the animals already mentioned we shot a deer on it this morning. Near the end of Diamond island are two others, separated by a narrow channel filled at high tides only, which continue on the right for the distance of three miles, and like the adjacent low grounds, are thickly covered with pine. Just below the last, we landed on the left bank of the river, at a village of twenty-five houses; all of these were thatched with straw, and built of bark, except one which was about fifty feet long, built of boards in the form of those higher up the river, from which it differed however, in being completely above ground, and covered with broad split boards; this village contains about two hundred men of the Skilloot nation, who seem well provided with canoes, of which there were at least fifty-two, and some of them very large, drawn up in front of the village. On landing we found the Indian from above, who had left us this morning, and who now invited us into a lodge of which he appeared to own a part. Here he treated us with a root, round in shape, and about the size of a small Irish potato, which they call wappatoo, it is the common arrowhead or sagittifolia, so much cultivated by the Chinese, and when roasted in the embers till it becomes soft, has an agreeable taste, and is a very good substitute for bread. After purchasing some more of this root, we resumed our journey, and at seven miles distance came to the head of a large island near the left. On the right shore is a fine open prairie for about a mile, back of which the country rises, and is supplied with timber, such as white oak, pine of different kinds, wild crab, and several species of undergrowth, while along the borders of the river, there are only a few cottonwood and ash trees. In this prairie were also signs of deer and elk.

When we landed for dinner, a number of Indians from the last village, came down for the purpose, as we supposed, of paying us a friendly visit, as they had put on their favourite dresses. In addition to their usual covering they had scarlet and blue blankets, sailors' jackets and trowsers, shirts and hats. They had all of them either war axes, spears and bow arrows, or muskets and pistols, with tin powder flasks. We smoked with them and endeavoured to show them every attention, but we soon found them very assuming and disagreeable companions. While we were eating they stole the pipe with which they were smoking, and the great coat of one of the men. We immediately searched them all, and discovered the coat stuffed under the root of a tree near where they were sitting; but the pipe we could not recover. Finding us determined not to suffer any imposition, and discontented with them, they showed their displeasure in the only way which they dared, by returning in an ill humour to their village.

We then proceeded and soon met two canoes with twelve men of the same Skilloot nation, who were on their way from below. The larger of the canoes was ornamented with the figure of a bear in the bow, and a man in the stern, both nearly as large as life, both made of painted wood, and very neatly fixed to the boat. In the same canoe were two Indians finely dressed and with round hats. This circumstance induced us to give the name of Image canoe to the large island, the lower end of which we now passed at the distance of nine miles from its head. We had seen two smaller islands to the right, and three more near its lower extremity. The Indians in the canoe here made signs that there was a village behind those islands, and indeed we presumed there was a channel on that side of the river, for one of the canoes passed in that direction between the small islands, but we were anxious to press forward, and therefore did not stop to examine more minutely. The river was now about a mile and a half in width, with a gentle current, the bottoms extensive and low, but not subject to be overflowed. Three miles below the Image canoe island we came to four large houses on the left side, at which place we had a full view of the mountain which we first saw on the *19th of October*, from the Muscleshell rapid, and which we now find to be the mount St. Helen of Vancouver. It bears north 25° east, about ninety miles distant; it rises in the form of a sugar-loaf to a very great height, and is covered with snow. A mile lower we passed a single house on the left, and another on the right. The Indians had now learnt so much of us, that their curiosity was without any mixture of fear, and their visits became very frequent and troublesome. We therefore continued on till after night, in hopes of getting rid of them; but after passing a village on each side, which on account of the lateness of the hour we saw indistinctly, we found there was no escaping from their importunities. We therefore landed at the distance of seven miles below Image canoe island, and encamped near a single house on the right, having made during the day twenty-nine miles.

The Skilloots whom we passed to-day, speak a language somewhat different from that of the Echeloots or Chilluckittequaws near the long narrows. Their dress is similar, except that the Skilloots possess more articles procured from the white traders; and there is further difference between them, inasmuch as the Skilloots, both males and females, have the head flattened. Their principal food is fish, and wappatoo roots, and some elk and deer, in killing which with their arrows, they seem very expert, for during the short time we remained at the village three deer were brought in. We also observed there a tame brairo.

As soon as we landed we were visited by two canoes loaded with Indians, from whom we purchased a few roots. The grounds along the river continue low and rich, and among the shrubs which cover them is a large quantity of vines resembling the raspberry. On the right the low grounds are terminated at the distance of five miles by a range of high hills covered with tall timber, and running southeast and northwest. The game as usual very abundant, and among other birds we observe some white geese with a part of their wings black.

NOVEMBER 5TH *Tuesday.* Our choice of a camp had been very unfortunate; for on a sand island opposite to us were immense numbers of geese, swan-ducks, and other wild fowl, who, during the whole night, serenaded us with a confusion of noises which completely prevented our sleeping. During the latter part of the night it rained, and we therefore willingly left our encampment at an early hour. We passed at three miles a small prairie, where the river is only three quarters of a mile in width, and soon after two houses on the left, half a mile distant from each other; from one of which three men came in a canoe merely to look at us, and having done so returned home. At eight miles we came to the lower point of an island, separated from the right side by a narrow channel, on which, a short distance above the end of the island, is situated a large village: it is built more compactly than the generality of the Indian villages, and the front has fourteen houses, which are ranged for a quarter of a mile along the channel. As soon as we were discovered seven canoes came out to see us, and after some traffic, during which they seemed well-disposed and orderly, accompanied us a short distance below. The river here again widens to the space of a mile and a half. As we descended we soon observed, behind a sharp point of rocks, a channel a quarter of a mile wide, which we suppose must be the one taken by the canoes yesterday on leaving Image-canoe island. A mile below the channel are some low cliffs of rocks, near which is a large island on the right side, and two small islands a little further on. Here we met two canoes ascending the river. At this place the shore on the right becomes bold and rocky, and the bank is bordered by a range of high hills covered with a thick growth of pine: on the other side is an extensive low island, separated from the left side by a narrow channel.

Here we stopped to dine, and found the island open, with an abundant growth of grass, and a number of ponds well supplied with fowls; and at the lower extremity are the remains of an old village. We procured a swan, several ducks, and a brant, and saw some deer on the island. Besides this island, the lower extremity of which is seventeen miles from the channel just mentioned, we passed two or three smaller ones in the same distance. Here the hills on the right retire from the river, leaving a high plain, between which, on the left bank, a range of high hills running southeast and covered with pine, forms a bold and rocky shore. At the distance of six miles, however, these hills again return and close the river on both sides.

We proceeded on, and at four miles reached a creek on the right, about twenty yards in width, immediately below which is an old village. Three miles further, and at the distance of thirty-two miles from our camp of last night, we halted under a point of highland, with thick pine trees on the left bank of the river. Before landing we met two canoes, the largest of which had at the bow the image of a bear, and that of a man on the stern: there were twenty-six Indians on board, but they all proceeded upwards, and we were left, for the first time since we reached the waters of the Columbia, without any of the natives with us during the night. Besides the game already mentioned, we killed a grouse much larger than the common size, and observed along the shore a number of striped snakes.

The river is here deep, and about a mile and a half in width. Here too the ridge of low mountains running northwest and southeast, cross the river, and form the western boundary of the plain through which we have just passed. This great plain or valley begins above the mouth of Quicksand river, and is about sixty miles wide in a straight line, while on the right and left it extends to a great distance: it is a fertile and delightful country, shaded by thick groves of tall timber, watered by small ponds, and running on both sides of the river. The soil is rich, and capable of any species of culture; but in the present condition of the Indians, its chief production is the wappatoo root, which grows spontaneously and exclusively in this region. Sheltered as it is on both sides, the temperature is much milder than that of the surrounding country; for even at this season of the year we observe very little appearance of frost. During its whole extent it is inhabited by numerous tribes of Indians, who either reside in it permanently, or visit its waters in quest of fish and wappatoo roots: we gave it the name of the Columbia valley.

Wednesday. The morning was cool, wet, and rainy. We proceeded at an early hour between the high hills on both sides of the river, till at the distance of four miles we came to two tents of Indians in a small plain on the left, where the hills on the right recede a few miles from the river, and a long narrow island stretches along the right shore. Behind this island is the mouth of a large river a hundred and fifty yards wide, and called by the Indians, Coweliske. We halted for dinner on the island, but the red wood and green briars are so interwoven with the pine, alder, ash, a species of beech, and other trees, that the woods form a thicket, which our hunters could not penetrate. Below the mouth of the Coweliske a very remarkable knob rises from the water's edge to the height of eighty feet, being two hundred paces round the base; and as it is in a low part of the island, and some distance from the high grounds, the appearance of it is very singular.

NOVEMBER 6TH

On setting out after dinner we overtook two canoes going down to trade: one of the Indians, who spoke a few words of English, mentioned, that the principal person who traded with them was a Mr. Haley, and he showed a bow of iron and several other things which he said Mr. Haley had given him. Nine miles below that river is a creek on the same; and between them three smaller islands; one on the left shore, the other about the middle of the river; and a third near the lower end of the long narrow island, and opposite a high cliff of black rocks on the left, sixteen miles from our camp. Here we were overtaken by the Indians from the two tents we passed in the morning, from whom we now purchased wappatoo roots, salmon, trout, and two beaver skins, for which last we gave five small fishhooks. At these cliffs the mountains, which had continued high and rugged on the left, retired from the river, and as the hills on the other side had left the water at the Coweliske, a beautiful extensive plain now presented itself before us: for a few miles we passed along side of an island a mile in width and three miles long, below which is a smaller island, where the high rugged hills, thickly covered with timber, border the right bank of the river, and terminate the low grounds: these were supplied with common rushes, grass, and nettles; in the moister parts with bullrushes and flags, and along the water's edge some willows. Here also were two ancient villages, now abandoned by their inhabitants, of whom no vestige remains, except two small dogs almost starved, and a prodigious quantity of fleas. After crossing the plain and making five miles, we proceeded through the hills for eight miles. The river is about a mile in width, and the hills so steep that we could not for several miles find a place sufficiently level to suffer us to sleep in a level position: at length, by removing the large stones, we cleared a place fit for our purpose above the reach of the tide, and after a journey of twenty-nine miles slept among the smaller stones under a mountain to the right. The weather was rainy during the whole day; we therefore made large fires to dry our bedding and to kill the fleas, who have accumulated upon us at every old village we have passed.

NOVEMBER 7TH   *Thursday.* The morning was rainy and the fog so thick that we could not see across the river. We observed however, opposite to our camp, the upper point of an island, between which and the steep hills on the right we proceeded for five miles. Three miles lower is the beginning of an island separated from the right shore by a narrow channel; down this we proceeded under the direction of some Indians whom we had just met going up the river, and who returned in order to show us their village. It consists of four houses only, situated on this channel behind several marshy islands formed by two small creeks. On our arrival they gave us some fish, and we afterwards purchased wappatoo roots, fish, three dogs, and two otter skins, for which we gave fishhooks chiefly, that being an article of which they are very fond.

These people seem to be of a different nation from those we have just passed: they are low in stature, ill shaped, and all have their heads flattened. They call themselves Wahkiacum, and their language differs from that of the tribes above, with whom they trade for wappatoo roots. The houses too are built in a different style, being raised entirely above ground, with the eaves about five feet high, and the door at the corner. Near the end opposite to this door is a single fireplace, round which are the beds, raised four feet from the floor of earth; over the fire are hung the fresh fish, and when dried they are stowed away with the wappatoo roots under the beds. The dress of the men is like that of the people above, but the women are clad in a peculiar manner, the robe not reaching lower than the hip, and the body being covered in cold weather by a sort of corset of fur, curiously plaited, and reaching from the arms to the hip; added to this is a sort of petticoat, or rather tissue of white cedar bark, bruised or broken into small strands, and woven into a girdle by several cords of the same material. Being tied round the middle, these strands hang down as low as the knee in front, and to midleg behind, and are of sufficient thickness to answer the purpose of concealment whilst the female stands in an erect position, but in any other attitude is but a very ineffectual defence. Sometimes the tissue is strings of silk grass, twisted and knotted at the end.

After remaining with them about an hour, we proceeded down the channel with an Indian dressed in a sailor's jacket for our pilot, and on reaching the main channel were visited by some Indians who have a temporary residence on a marshy island in the middle of the river, where is a great abundance of water fowl. Here the mountainous country again approaches the river on the left, and a higher mountain is distinguished towards the southwest. At a distance of twenty miles from our camp we halted at a village of Wahkiacums, consisting of seven ill-looking houses, built in the same form with those above, and situated at the foot of the high hills on the

The mouth of the Columbia, where the expedition reached the Pacific Ocean and camped during November 1805, prior to the establishment of Fort Clatsop.

right, behind two small marshy islands. We merely stopped to purchase some food and two beaver skins, and then proceeded. Opposite to these islands the hills on the left retire, and the river widens into a kind of bay crowded with low islands, subject to be overflowed occasionally by the tide.

We had not gone far from this village when the fog cleared off, and we enjoyed the delightful prospect of the ocean; that ocean, the object of all our labours, the reward of all our anxieties. This cheering view exhilarated the spirits of all the party, who were still more delighted on hearing the distant roar of the breakers. We went on with great cheerfulness under the high mountainous country which continued along the right bank; the shore was however so bold and rocky, that we could not, until after going fourteen miles from the last village, find any spot fit for an encampment. At that distance, having made during the day thirty-four miles, we spread our mats on the ground, and passed the night in the rain. Here we were joined by our small canoe, which had been separated from us during the fog this morning. Two Indians from the last village also accompanied us to the camp, but, having detected them in stealing a knife, they were sent off.

NOVEMBER 8TH *Friday*. It rained this morning; and having changed the clothing which had been wet during yesterday's rain, we did not set out till nine o'clock. Immediately opposite our camp is a rock at the distance of a mile in the river, about twenty feet in diameter and fifty in height, and towards the southwest some high mountains, one of which is covered with snow at the top. We proceeded past several low islands in the bay or bend of the river to the left, which is here five or six miles wide. We were here overtaken by three Indians in a canoe who had salmon to sell. On the right side we passed an old village, and then, at the distance of three miles, entered an inlet or niche about six miles across, and making a deep bend of nearly five miles into the hills on the right shore, where it receives the waters of several creeks. We coasted along this inlet, which, from its little depth, we called Shallow bay, and at the bottom of it halted to dine near the remains of an old village, from which, however, we kept at a cautious distance, as it was occupied by great numbers of fleas. At this place we observed a number of fowl, among which we killed a goose and two ducks, exactly resembling in appearance and flavour the canvassback duck of the Susquehannah. After dinner the three Indians left us, and we then took advantage of the returning tide, to go on about three miles to a point on the right, eight miles distant from our camp; but here the waves ran so high, and dashed about our canoes so much, that several of the men became seasick. It was therefore judged imprudent to go on in the present state of the weather, and we landed at the point. The situation was extremely uncomfortable; the high hills jutted in so closely that there was not room for us to lie level, nor to secure our baggage free from the tide; and the water of the river is too salt to be used; but the waves increasing every moment so much, that we could not move from the spot with safety: we therefore fixed ourselves on the beach left by the ebb-tide, and having raised the baggage on poles, passed a disagreeable night, the rain during the day having wet us completely, as indeed we have been for some days past.

Saturday. Fortunately for us, the tide did not rise as high as our camp during the night; but being accompanied by high winds from the south, the canoes, which we could not place beyond its reach, were filled with water, and were saved with much difficulty: our position was very uncomfortable, but as it was impossible to move from it, we waited for a change of weather. It rained, however, during the whole day, and at two o'clock in the afternoon, the flood tide set in, accompanied by a high wind from the south, which, about four o'clock, shifted to the southwest, and blew almost a gale directly from the sea. The immense waves now broke over the place where we were encamped, and the large trees, some of them five or six feet thick, which had lodged at the point, were drifted over our camp, and the utmost vigilance of every man could scarcely save our canoes from being crushed to pieces. We remained in the water and drenched with rain during the rest of the day; our only food being some dried fish, and some rain-water which we caught. Yet, though wet and cold, and some of them sick from using the salt-water, the men are cheerful, and full of anxiety to see more of the ocean. The rain continued all night.

Sunday. The following morning, the wind, however, lulled, and the waves not being so high, we loaded our canoes and proceeded. The mountains on the right are high, covered with timber, chiefly pine, and descend in a bold and rocky shore to the water. We went through a deep niche and several inlets on the right, while on the opposite side is a large bay, above which the hills are close on the river. At the distance of ten miles the wind rose from the northwest and the waves became so high that we were forced to return for two miles to a place where we could with safety unload. Here we landed at the mouth of a small run, and having placed our baggage on a pile of drifted logs waited until low water. The river then appeared more calm: we therefore started, but after going a mile found the waves too high for our canoes and were obliged to put to shore. We unloaded the canoes, and having placed the baggage on a rock above the reach of the tide, encamped on some drift logs which formed the only place where we could lie, the hills rising steep over our heads to the height of five hundred feet. All our baggage as well as ourselves were thoroughly wet with the rain, which did not cease during the day; it continued violently during the night, in the course of which the tide reached the logs on which we lay, and set them afloat.

Monday. The wind was still high from the southwest, and drove the waves against the shore with great fury: the rain too fell in torrents, and not only drenched us to the skin, but loosened the stones on the hill sides, which then came rolling down upon us. In this comfortless situation we remained all day wet, cold, with nothing but dried fish to satisfy our hunger; the canoes in one place at the mercy of the waves; the baggage in another, and all the men scattered on floating logs, or sheltering themselves in the crevices of the rocks and hill sides. A hunter was despatched in hopes of finding some fresh meat, but the hills were so steep, and covered with undergrowth and fallen timber, that he could not penetrate them, and he was forced to return. About twelve o'clock we were visited by five Indians in a canoe: they came from above this place on the opposite side of the river, and their language much resembles that of the Wahkiacum: they called themselves

Cathlamahs. In person they are small, ill made, and badly clothed; though one of them had on a sailor's round jacket and pantaloons, which, as he explained by signs, he had received from the whites below the point: we purchased from them thirteen red char, a fish which we found very excellent. After some time they went on board the boat, and crossed the river, which is here five miles wide, through a very heavy sea.

NOVEMBER 12TH *Tuesday*. About three o'clock a tremendous gale of wind arose, accompanied with lightning, thunder, and hail: at six it became light for a short time, but a violent rain soon began and lasted during the day. During this storm one of our boats, secured by being sunk with great quantities of stone, got loose, but drifting against a rock, was recovered without having received much injury. Our situation became now much more dangerous, for the waves were driven with fury against the rocks and trees, which till now had afforded us refuge: we therefore took advantage of a low tide, and moved about half a mile round a point to a small brook, which we had not observed till now on account of the thick bushes and driftwood which concealed its mouth. Here we were more safe; but still cold and wet, our clothes and bedding rotten as well as wet, our baggage at a distance, and the canoes, our only means of escape from this place, at the mercy of the waves: we were, however, fortunate enough to enjoy good health, and even had the luxury of getting some fresh salmon and three salmon trout in the brook. Three of the men attempted to go round a point in our small Indian canoe, but the high waves rendered her quite unmanageable; these boats requiring the seamanship of the natives themselves to make them live in so rough a sea.

NOVEMBER 13TH *Wednesday*. During the night we had short intervals of fair weather, but it began to rain in the morning, and continued through the day. In order to obtain a view of the country below, captain Clark followed up the course of the brook, and with much fatigue, and after walking three miles, ascended the first spur of the mountains. The whole lower country was covered with almost impenetrable thickets of small pine, with which is mixed a species of plant resembling arrowwood, twelve or fifteen feet high, with a thorny stem, almost interwoven with each other, and scattered among the fern and fallen timber: there is also a red berry, somewhat like the solomon's seal, which is called by the natives, solme, and used as an article of diet. This thick growth rendered travelling almost impossible, and it was rendered more fatiguing by the steepness of the mountain, which was so great as to oblige him to draw himself up by means of the bushes. The timber on the hills is chiefly of a large tall species of pine, many of them eight or ten feet in diameter at the stump, and rising sometimes more than one hundred feet in height. The hail which fell two nights since is still to be seen on the mountains: there was no game, and no traces of any, except some old signs of elk: the cloudy weather prevented his seeing to any distance, and he therefore returned to camp, and sent three men in the Indian canoe to try if they could double the point and find some safer harbour for our canoes. At every flood-tide the seas break in great swells against the rocks, and drift the trees among our establishment, so as to render it very insecure. We were confined as usual to dried fish, which is our last resource.

Thursday. It rained without intermission during last night and to-day: the wind too is very high, and one of our canoes much injured by being dashed against rocks. Five Indians from below came to us in a canoe, and three of them having landed, informed us that they had seen the men sent down yesterday. At this moment one of them arrived, and informed us that these Indians had stolen his gig and basket: we therefore ordered the two women who remained in the canoe, to restore them; but this they refused, till we threatened to shoot, when they gave back the articles, and we then ordered them to leave us. They were of the Wahkiacum nation. The man now informed us that they had gone round the point as far as the high sea would suffer them in the canoe, and then landed, and that in the night he had separated from his companions, who had gone further down: that at no great distance from where we are is a beautiful sand beach and a good harbour. Captain Lewis concluded to examine more minutely the lower part of the bay, and taking one of the large canoes was landed at the point, whence he proceeded by land with four men, and the canoe returned nearly filled with water.

NOVEMBER 14TH

Friday. It continued raining all night, but in the morning the weather became calm and fair: we therefore began to prepare for setting out, but before we were ready a high wind sprang up from the southeast, and obliged us to remain. The sun shone until one o'clock, and we were thus enabled to dry our bedding and examine our baggage. The rain, which has continued for the last ten days without an interval of more than two hours, has completely wet all our merchandise, and spoiled some of our fish, destroyed the robes, and rotted nearly one half of our few remaining articles of clothing, particularly the leather dresses. About three o'clock the wind fell, and we instantly loaded the canoes, and left the miserable spot to which we have been confined the last six days. On turning the point we came to the sand beach, through which runs a small stream from the hills; at the mouth of which is an ancient village of thirty-six houses, which has at present no inhabitants except fleas.

NOVEMBER 15TH

    Here we met Shannon, who had been sent back to meet us by captain Lewis. The day Shannon left us in the canoe, he and Willard proceeded on till they met a party of twenty Indians, who never having heard of us, did not know where they came from: they however behaved with so much civility, and seemed so anxious that the men should go with them towards the sea, that their suspicions were excited, and they declined going on: the Indians, however, would not leave them, and the men being confirmed in their suspicions, and fearful if they went into the woods to sleep they would be cut to pieces in the night, thought it best to pass the night in the midst of the Indians; they therefore made a fire, and after talking with them to a late hour, laid down with their rifles under their heads. As they awoke this morning they found that the Indians had stolen and concealed their guns; having demanded them in vain, Shannon seized a club, and was about assaulting one of the Indians whom he suspected as a thief, when another Indian began to load a fowling piece, with an intention of shooting him. He therefore stopped and explained by signs, that if they did not give up the guns, a large party would come down the river before the sun rose to such a height, and put every one of them to death. Fortunately, captain Lewis and his party appeared at this time, and the terrified Indians immediately brought the guns, and five of them came on with Shannon. To these men we declared, that if ever any of their nation stole any thing from us he should be instantly shot. They reside to the north of this place, and speak a language different from that of the people higher up the river.

It was now apparent that the sea was at all times too rough for us to proceed further down the bay by water; we therefore landed, and having chosen the best spot we could select, made our camp of boards from the old village. We were now situated comfortably, and being visited by four Wahkiacums with wappatoo roots, were enabled to make an agreeable addition to our food.

NOVEMBER 16TH *Saturday.* The morning was clear and beautiful. We therefore, put out all our baggage to dry, and sent several of the party to hunt. Our camp is in full view of the ocean, on the bay laid down by Vancouver, which we distinguish by the name of Haley's bay, from a trader who visits the Indians here, and is a great favourite among them. The meridian altitude of this day gave $46° 19' 11 \frac{7}{10}''$ as the latitude of our camp. The wind was strong from the southwest, and the waves very high, yet the Indians were passing up and down the bay in canoes, and several of them encamped near us. We smoked with them, but after our recent experience of their thievish disposition, treated them with caution. Though so much exposed to the bad weather, none of the party have suffered, except one, who has a violent cold, in consequence of sleeping for several nights in wet leather. The hunters brought in two deer, a crane, some geese and ducks, and several brant, three of which were white, except a black part of the wing, and much larger than the grey brant, which is itself a size beyond the duck.

NOVEMBER 17TH *Sunday.* A fair cool morning and easterly wind. The tide rises at this place eight feet six inches in height, and rolls over the beach in great waves.

About one o'clock captain Lewis returned, after having coasted down Haley's bay to cape Disappointment, and some distance to the north along the sea coast. He was followed by several Chinnooks, among whom were the principal chief and his family. They made us a present of a boiled root, very much like the common liquorice in taste and size, and called culwhamo; in return we gave double the value of their present, and now learnt the danger of accepting any thing from them, since no return, even if ten times the value of their gift, can satisfy them. We were chiefly occupied in hunting, and were able to procure three deer, four brant and two ducks, and also saw some signs of elk.

Captain Clark now prepared for an excursion down the bay, and accordingly started, *Monday 18th* at daylight, accompanied by eleven men. He proceeded along the beach one mile to a point of rocks about forty feet high, where the hills retire, leaving a wide beach, and a number of ponds covered with water-fowl, between which and the mountain is a narrow bottom of alder and small balsam trees. Seven miles from the rocks is the entrance of a creek, or rather drain from the ponds and hills, where is a cabin of Chinnooks. The cabin contained some children, and four women, one of whom was in a most miserable state, covered with ulcers, proceeding as we imagine, from the veneral disease, with which several of the Chinnooks we have seen appear to be afflicted. We were taken across in a canoe by two squaws, to each of whom we gave a fishhook, and then coasting along the bay, passed at two miles the low bluff of a small hill, below which are the ruins of some old huts, and close to it the remains of a whale. The country is low, open and marshy; interspersed with some high pine and a thick undergrowth. Five miles from the creek, we came to a stream forty yards wide at low water, which we called Chinnook river. The hills up this river and towards the bay are not high, but very thickly covered with large pine of several species: in many places pine trees, three or four feet in thickness, are seen growing on the bodies of large trees, which though fallen and covered with moss, were in part sound.

    Here we dined on some brant and plover, killed as we came along, and after crossing in a boat lying in the sand near some old houses, proceeded along a bluff of yellow clay and soft stone to a little bay or harbour, into which a drain from some ponds empties: at this harbour the land is low, but as we went on it rose to hills of eighty or ninety feet above the water. At the distance of one mile is a second bay, and a mile beyond it, a small rocky island in a deep bend, which seems to afford a very good harbour, and where the natives inform us European vessels anchor for the purpose of trading. We went on round another bay, in which is a second small island of rocks, and crossed a small stream, which rises in a pond near the sea coast, and after running through a low isthmus empties into the bay. This narrow low ground, about two or three hundred yards wide, separates from the main hills a kind of peninsula, the extremity of which is two miles from the anchoring place; and this spot, which was called cape Disappointment, is an elevated, circular knob, rising with a steep ascent one hundred and fifty or one hundred and sixty feet above the water, formed like the whole shore of the bay, as well as of the seacoast, and covered with thick timber on the inner side, but open and grassy in the exposure next the sea.

    From this cape a high point of land bears south 20° west, about twenty-five miles distant. In the range between these two eminences, is the opposite point of the bay, a very low ground, which has been variously called cape Rond by Lapeyrouse, and point Adams by Vancouver. The water for a great distance off the mouth of the river, appears very shallow, and within the mouth nearest to point Adams, is a large sandbar, almost covered at high tide. We could not ascertain the direction of the deepest channel, for the waves break with tremendous force the whole distance across the bay, but the Indians point nearer to the opposite side as the best passage. After remaining for some time on this elevation, we descended across the low isthmus, and reached the ocean at the foot of a high hill, about a mile in circumference, and projecting into the sea. We crossed this hill, which is open and has a growth of high coarse grass, and encamped on the north side of it, having made nineteen miles. Besides the pounded fish and brant, we had for supper a flounder, which we picked up on the beach.

Tuesday. In the night it began to rain, and continued till eleven o'clock. Two hunters were sent on to kill something for breakfast, and the rest of the party after drying their blankets soon followed. At three miles we overtook the hunters, and breakfasted on a small deer, which they had been fortunate enough to kill. This, like all those we have seen on this coast, are much

NOVEMBER 19TH

darker than our common deer. Their bodies too, are deeper, their legs shorter, and their eyes larger. The branches of the horns are similar, but the upper part of the tail is black, from the root to the end, and they do not leap, but jump like a sheep frightened.

We then continued over rugged hills and steep hollows, near the sea, on a course about north 20° west, in a direct line from the cape, till at the distance of five miles, we reached a point of high land, below which a sandy beach extends, in a direction north 10° west, to another high point about twenty miles distant. This eminence we distinguished by the name of point Lewis. It is there that the highlands, which at the commencement of the sandy beach, recede towards Chinnook river, again approach the ocean. The intermediate country is low, with many small ponds, crowded with birds, and watered by the Chinnook, on the borders of which resides the nation of the same name. We went four miles along the sandy beach to a small pine tree, on which captain Clark marked his name, with the year and day, and then returned to the foot of the hills, passing on the shore a sturgeon ten feet long, and several joints of the back bone of a whale, both which seem to have been thrown ashore and foundered. After dining on the remains of the small deer, we crossed in a southeastern direction to the bay, where we arrived at the distance of two miles, then continued along the bay, crossed Chinnook river, and encamped on its upper side, in a sandy bottom.

NOVEMBER 20TH *Wednesday.* It rained in the course of the night. A hunter despatched early to kill some food, returned with eight ducks, on which we breakfasted, and then followed the course of the bay to the creek or outlet of the ponds. It was now high tide, the stream three hundred yards wide, and no person in the cabin to take us across. We therefore made a small raft, on which one of the men passed and brought a canoe to carry us over. As we went along the beach we were overtaken by several Indians, who gave us dried sturgeon and wappatoo roots, and soon met several parties of Chinnooks returning from the camp. When we arrived there we found many Chinnooks, and two of them being chiefs, we went through the ceremony of giving to each a medal, and to the most distinguished a flag. Their names were Comcommoly and Chillahlawil. One of the Indians had a robe made of two sea-otter skins, the fur of which was the most beautiful we had ever seen; the owner resisted every temptation to part with it, but at length could not resist the offer of a belt of blue beads which Chaboneau's wife wore round her waist. During our absence the camp had been visited by many Indians, and the men who had been employed in hunting killed several deer, and a variety of wild fowls.

NOVEMBER 21ST *Thursday.* The morning was cloudy, and from noon till night it rained. The wind too was high from the southeast, and the sea so rough that the water reached our camp. Most of the Chinnooks returned home, but we were visited in the course of the day by people of different bands in the neighbourhood, among whom are the Chiltz, a nation residing on the seacoast near point Lewis, and the Clatsops, who live immediately opposite on the south side of the Columbia. A chief from the grand rapid also came to see us, and we gave him a medal. To each of our visitors we made a present of a small piece of ribbon, and purchased some cranberries and some articles of their manufacture, such as mats, and household furniture, for all which we paid high prices. After we had been relieved from these Indians, we were surprised at a visit of a different kind; an old woman who is the wife of a Chinnook chief, came with six young women, her daughters and nieces, and having deliberately encamped near us, proceeded to cultivate an intimacy between our men and her fair wards.

Chapter 21
ESTABLISHMENT OF FORT CLATSOP

FRIDAY, NOVEMBER 22D, 1805   It rained during the whole night, and about daylight a tremendous gale of wind rose from the S. S. E. and continued during the whole day with great violence. The sea runs so high that the water comes into our camp, which the rain prevents us from leaving. We purchased from the old squaw for armbands and rings, a few wappatoo roots, on which we subsisted. They are nearly equal in flavour to the Irish potato, and afford a very good substitute for bread. The bad weather has driven several Indians to our camp, but they are still under the terrors of the threat which we made on first seeing them, and now behave with the greatest decency.

NOVEMBER 23D   *Saturday.* The rain continued through the night, but the morning was calm and cloudy. The hunters were sent out and killed three deer, four brant, and three ducks. Towards evening seven Clatsops came over in a canoe with two skins of the sea-otter. To this article they attach an extravagant value, and their demands for it were so high that we were fearful of reducing our small stock of merchandise, on which we must depend for subsistence as we return, to venture on purchasing. To ascertain however their ideas as to the value of different objects, we offered for one of the skins a watch, a handkerchief, an American dollar, and a bunch of red beads; but neither the curious mechanism of the watch, nor even the red beads could tempt him; he refused the offer, but asked for tiacomoshack or chief beads, the most common sort of coarse blue-coloured beads, the article beyond all price in their estimation. Of these blue beads we have but few, and therefore reserve them for more necessitous circumstances.

NOVEMBER 24TH   *Sunday.* The morning being fair, we dried our wet articles and sent out the hunters, but they returned with only a single brant. In the evening a chief and several men of the Chinnooks came to see us; we smoked with them, and bought a sea-otter skin for some blue beads. Having now examined the coast, it becomes necessary to decide on the spot for our wintering quarters. The people of the country subsist chiefly on dried fish and roots, but of these there does not seem to be a sufficient quantity for our support, even were we able to purchase, and the extravagant prices as well as our small store of merchandise forbid us to depend on that resource. We must therefore rely for subsistence on our arms, and be guided in the choice of our residence by the abundance of game which any particular spot may offer. The Indians say that the deer is most numerous at some distance above on the river, but that the country on the opposite side of the bay is better supplied with elk, an animal much larger and more easily killed than deer, with a skin better fitted for clothing, and the meat of which is more nutritive during the winter, when they are both poor. The climate too is obviously much milder here than above the first range of mountains, for the Indians are thinly clad, and say they have little snow, indeed since our arrival the weather has been very warm, and sometimes disagreeably so, and dressed as we are altogether in leather, the cold would be very unpleasant if not injurious. The neighbourhood of the sea is moreover recommended by the facility of supplying ourselves with salt, and the hope of meeting some of the trading vessels, who are expected in about three months, and from whom we may procure a fresh supply of trinkets for our route homewards. These considerations induced us to determine on visiting the opposite side of the bay, and if there was an appearance of much game to establish ourselves there during the winter.

Next day, however, the wind was too high to suffer us to cross the river, but as it blew generally from the east southeast, the coast on the north was in some degree sheltered by the highlands. We therefore set out, and keeping near the shore, halted for dinner in the shallow bay, and after dark, reached a spot near a rock, at some distance in the river, and close to our former camp of the 7th inst. On leaving our camp, seven Clatsops accompanied us in a canoe, but after going a few miles crossed the bay through immense high waves, leaving us in admiration, at the dexterity with which they threw aside each wave as it threatened to come over their canoe. The evening was cloudy, and in the morning it rained. NOVEMBER 25TH

Tuesday. We set out with the wind from east northeast, and a short distance above the rock, near our camp, began to cross the river. We passed between some low, marshy islands, which we called the Seal islands, and reached the south side of the Columbia at a bottom three miles below a point, to which we gave the name of point Samuel. After going along the shore for five miles, we entered a channel two hundred yards in width, which separates from the main land a large, but low island. On this channel, and at the foot of some highlands, is a village where we landed. It consists of nine large wooden houses, inhabited by a tribe called Cathlamahs, who seem to differ neither in dress, language, nor manners, from the Chinnooks and Wahkiacums: like whom they live chiefly on fish and wappatoo roots. We found, however, as we hoped, some elk meat: after dining on some fresh fish and roots, which we purchased from them at an immoderate price, we coasted along a deep bend of the river towards the south, and at night encamped under a high hill; all the way from the village the land is high, and has a thick growth of pine balsam, and other timber; but as it was still raining very hard, it was with difficulty we procured wood enough to make fires. Soon after we landed, three Indians from the Cathlamah village came down with wappatoo roots, some of which we purchased with fish-hooks. NOVEMBER 26TH

Wednesday. At daylight the next morning, eleven more came down with provisions, skins and mats for sale, but the prices were too high for our reduced finances, and we bought nothing. As we were preparing to set out we missed an axe, which was found under the robe of one of the Indians, and they were all prohibited in consequence from following us. We went on in the rain, which had continued through the night, and passing between a number of islands came to a small river, called by the Indians Kekemahke. We afterwards came to a very remarkable knob of land, projecting about a mile and a half towards Shallow bay, and about four miles round, while the neck of land which connects it to the main shore is not more than fifty yards wide. We went round this projection, which we named point William; but the waves then became so high that we could not venture any farther, and we therefore landed on a beautiful shore of pebbles of various colours, and encamped near an old Indian hut on the isthmus. In drawing our canoes in shore, we had the misfortune to make a split two feet long in one of them. This isthmus opposed a formidable barrier to the sea, for we now found that NOVEMBER 27TH

337

the water below is salt, while that above is fresh and well tasted. It rained hard during the whole day; it continued all night, and in the morning began more violently, attended with a high wind from the southwest.

It was now impossible to proceed on so rough a sea. We therefore sent several men to hunt, and the rest of us remained during the day, in a situation the most cheerless and uncomfortable. On this little neck of land we are exposed with a miserable covering, which does not deserve the name of a shelter to the violence of the winds; all our bedding and stores, as well as our bodies are completely wet, our clothes rotting with constant exposure, and no food except the dried fish brought from the falls, to which we are again reduced. The hunters all returned hungry, and drenched with rain, having seen neither deer nor elk, and the swan and brant too shy to be approached. At noon the wind shifted to the northwest, and blew with such tremendous fury that many trees were blown down near us. This gale lasted with short intervals during the whole night; but towards morning the wind lulled, though the rain continued, and the waves were still high.

NOVEMBER 29TH *Friday*. Captain Lewis took the Indian canoe, which is better calculated for rough weather, and with five men went down to a small bay below us, where we expect to find elk. Three other men set out at the same time to hunt in different directions, and the rest remained round the smoke of our fires drying leather, in order to make some new clothes. The night brought only a continuation of rain and hail, with short intervals of fair weather, till in the morning it cleared up about nine o'clock, and the sun shone for several hours.

Other hunters were now sent out, and we passed the remainder of the day in drying our merchandise so long exposed. Several of the men complain of disorders in their bowels, which can be ascribed only to their diet of pounded fish mixed with salt-water: and they are therefore directed to use for that purpose, the fresh water above the point. The hunters had seen three elk, but could not obtain any of them: they however brought in three hawks and a few black ducks, of a species common in the United States, living in large flocks, and feeding on grass: they are distinguished by a sharp white beak, toes separated, and by having no craw. Besides these wild fowls, there are in this neighbourhood a large kind of buzzard with white wings, the grey and the bald eagle, the large red-tailed hawk, the blue magpie, and great numbers of ravens and crows. We observe, however, few small birds, the one which has most attracted our attention being a small brown bird, which seems to frequent logs and the roots of trees. Of other animals there is a great abundance. We see great quantities of snakes, lizards, worms, and spiders, as well as small bugs, flies, and insects of different kinds. The vegetable productions are also numerous. The hills along the coast are high and steep, and the general covering is a growth of lofty pines of different species, some of which rise more than two hundred feet, and are ten or twelve feet in diameter near the root. Besides these trees we observe on the point a species of ash, the alder, the laurel, one species of the wild crab, and several kinds of underbrush, among which the rosebushes are conspicuous.

Left, ASSINIBOIN; right, YANKTONAI INDIAN (Bodmer)

Sunday, December 1st, 1805

Again we had a cloudy day, and the wind so high from the east, that having ventured in a boat with a view to hunt at some distance, we were obliged to return. We resumed our occupation of dressing leather and mending our old clothes, in which we passed the day. The hunters came in with a report of their having seen two herds of elk, but they could kill nothing, and we therefore again fed upon dried fish. At sunset it began to rain violently, and continued all night, and the next day.

Monday. This disagreeable food, pounded fish, has occasioned so much sickness among the men that it is now absolutely necessary to vary it. Three hunters therefore set out, and three more were sent up the Kekemahke creek in search of fish or birds. Towards evening one of them returned: he had observed great appearances of elk, and even seen two herds of them; but it rained so hard that he could with difficulty get a shot: he had, however, at last killed one, at the distance of six miles from the camp, and a canoe was now sent to bring it. The party from Kekemahke creek were less successful: they had seen no fish, and all the birds, in consequence probably of being much hunted by the Indians, were too shy to be approached. DECEMBER 2D

Tuesday. The wind was from the east, and the morning fair; but, as if a whole day of fine weather was not permitted, towards night it began to rain. Even this transient glimpse of sunshine revived the spirits of the party, who were still more pleased, when the elk killed yesterday was brought into camp. This was the first elk we had killed on the west side of the Rocky mountains, and condemned as we have been to the dried fish, forms a most nourishing food. After eating the marrow of the shank-bones, the squaw chopped them fine, and by boiling, extracted a pint of grease, superior to the tallow itself of the animal. A canoe of eight Indians, who were carrying down wappatoo roots to trade with the Clatsops, stopped at our camp: we bought a few roots for small fish-hooks, and they then left us: but accustomed as we are to the sight, we could not but view with admiration the wonderful dexterity with which they guide their canoes over the most boisterous seas; for though the waves were so high, that before they had gone half a mile the canoe was several times out of sight, they proceeded with the greatest calmness and security. Two of the hunters who set out yesterday had lost their way, and did not return till this evening: they had seen in their ramble great signs of elk, and had killed six elk, which they had butchered and left at a great distance. DECEMBER 3D

Wednesday. A party was sent in the morning, to carry the elk to a bay, some distance below, to which place, if the weather permitted, we would all remove our camp this evening; but the rain which had continued during the night lasted all next day, and was accompanied by so high a wind from the southeast and south, that we dared not risk our canoes on the water. It was high water at eleven o'clock, when the spring-tide rose two feet higher than the common flood-tides. We passed the day around our fires, and as we are so situated that the smoke will not immediately leave the camp, we are very DECEMBER 4TH much incommoded, and our eyes injured by it. No news has yet been received from captain Lewis, and we begin to have much uneasiness for his safety.

DECEMBER 5TH *Thursday.* It rained during the whole night, and this morning the rain and high wind compelled us to remain at our camp. Besides the inconvenience of being thus stopped on our route, we now found that all our stores and bedding are again wet with rain. The high water was at twelve o'clock, and rose two inches beyond that of yesterday. In the afternoon we were rejoiced at the return of captain Lewis, who came in a canoe with three of his men, the other two being left to guard six elk and five deer which they had killed. He had examined the coast, and found a river a short distance below, on which we might encamp during the winter, with a sufficiency of elk for our subsistence within reach. This information was very satisfactory, and we decided on going thither as soon as we could move from the point; but all night and the following day, it rained, and the wind blew hard from the southwest, so that the sea was still too rough for us to proceed. The high-tide of to-day rose thirteen inches higher than it did yesterday, and obliged us to move our camp to a high situation. Here we remained waiting for better weather, till about dark the wind shifted to the north, and the sky was clear. We had now some prospect of being able to leave our situation, and indeed although some rain fell in the course of the night, the next morning was fair.

DECEMBER 7TH *Saturday.* We therefore loaded our canoes, and proceeded. But the tide was against us, and the waves very high, so that we were obliged to proceed slowly and cautiously. We at length turned a point, and found ourselves in a deep bay; here we landed for breakfast, and were joined by the party sent out three days ago to look for the six elk. In seeking for the elk they had missed their way for a day and a half, and when they reached the place, found the elk so much spoiled that they brought the skins only of four of them. After breakfast we coasted round the bay, which is about four miles across, and receives, besides several small creeks, two rivers called by the Indians, the one Kilhowanakel, the other Netul. We called it Meriwether's bay, from the christian name of captain Lewis, who was no doubt the first white man who surveyed it. As we went along the wind was high from the northeast, and in the middle of the day it rained for two hours, and then cleared off. On reaching the south side of the bay, we ascended the Netul for three miles to the first point of highland on its western bank, and formed our camp in a thick grove of lofty pines, about two hundred yards from the water, and thirty feet above the level of the high tides.

DECEMBER 8TH *Sunday.* This seemed the most eligible spot for our winter establishment. In order therefore to find a place for making salt, and to examine the country further, captain Clark set out with five men, and pursuing a course south, 60° west, over a dividing ridge, through thick pine timber, much of which had fallen, passed the heads of two small brooks. In the neighbourhood of these the land was swampy and overflowed, and we waded knee-deep till we came to an open ridgy prairie, covered with the plant known on our frontier by the name of Sacacommis. Here is a creek about sixty yards wide, and running towards point Adams; they passed it on a small raft. At this place

Sketch-map showing the location of Fort Clatsop and the trail to the Indian Village

they discovered a large herd of elk, and after pursuing them for three miles over bad swamps and small ponds, we killed one of them. The agility with which the elk crossed the swamps and bogs, seems almost incredible; as we followed their track, the ground for a whole acre would shake at our tread, and sometimes we sunk to our hips without finding any bottom. Over the surface of these bogs is a species of moss, among which are great numbers of cranberries, and occasionally there rise from the swamp steep and small knobs of earth, thickly covered with pine and laurel. On one of these we halted at night, but it was scarcely large enough to suffer us to lie clear of the water, and had very little dry wood. We succeeded however in collecting enough to make a fire, and having stretched the elk skin to keep off the rain, which still continued, slept till morning when we rose, perfectly wet with rain during the night.

Three men were then sent in pursuit of the elk, while with the other three, captain Clark proceeded westward towards the sea. He passed over three swamps, and then arrived at a creek, which was too deep to ford, and there was no wood to make a raft. He therefore proceeded down it for a short distance, till he found that he was between the forks of a creek. One branch of which he had passed yesterday, turns round towards the southwest to meet another of equal size from the south, and together they form a small river, about seventy yards wide. He returned to the place where he had left the raft, and having crossed proceeded down about a mile, when he met three Indians. They were loaded with fresh salmon which they had taken with a gig, and were now returning to their village on the seacoast, where they invited him to accompany them. He agreed, and they brought out a canoe hid along the banks of the creek. In this they passed over the branch which he had just crossed on a raft, and then carried the canoe a quarter of a mile to the other fork, which they crossed and continued down to the mouth of the

DECEMBER 9TH

341

river. At this place it makes a great bend, where the river is seventy yards wide; just above, or to the south of which is the village.

We crossed over, and found that it consisted of three houses, inhabited by twelve families of Clatsops. They were on the south exposure of a hill, and sunk about four feet deep into the ground; the walls, roof, and gable-ends being formed of split pine boards; the descent through a small door down a ladder. There are two fires in the middle of the room, and the beds disposed round the walls two or three feet from the fall [floor], so as to leave room under them for their bags, baskets and household articles. The floor itself is covered with mats. Captain Clark was received with much attention. As soon as he entered, clean mats were spread, and fish, berries and roots set before him on small neat platters of rushes. After he had eaten, the men of the other houses came and smoked with him. They all appeared much neater in their persons and diet than Indians generally are, and frequently wash their hands and faces, a ceremony by no means frequent elsewhere. While he was conversing with them, a flock of brant lighted on the water, and he with a small rifle shot one of them at a great distance. They immediately jumped in, and brought it on shore, very much astonished at the shot, which contributed to make them increase their attention. Towards evening it began to rain and blow very violently from the southwest; and captain Clark therefore, determined to remain during the night. When they thought his appetite had returned, an old woman presented him in a bowl, made of light coloured horn, a kind of syrup, pleasant to the taste, and made from a species of berry common in this country, about the size of a cherry, and called by the Indians shelwel: of these berries a bread is also prepared, which being boiled with roots forms a soup, which was served in neat wooden trenchers: this, with some cockles, was his repast.

The men of the village now collected, and began to gamble. The most common game, was one in which one of the company was banker, and played against all the rest. He had a piece of bone, about the size of a large bean, and having agreed with any individual as to the value of the stake, would pass the bone from one hand to the other, with great dexterity, singing at the same time, to divert the attention of his adversary; and then holding it in his hands, his antagonist was challenged to guess in which of them the bone was, and lost or won as he pointed to the right or wrong hand. To this game of hazard they abandoned themselves with great ardour; sometimes every thing they possess is sacrificed to it, and this evening several of the Indians lost all the beads which they had with them. This lasted for three hours, when captain Clark appearing disposed to sleep, the man who had been most attentive, and whose name was Cuskalah, spread two new mats near the fire, and ordering his wife to retire to her own bed, the rest of the company dispersed at the same time. Captain Clark then lay down, but the violence with which the fleas attacked him, did not leave his rest unbroken, and he rose early.

DECEMBER 10TH *Tuesday.* The morning was cloudy, with some rain: he walked out on the seashore, and observed the Indians walking up and down the creek and examining the shore: he was at a loss to understand their object, till one of them came to him and explained that they were in search of fish which had been thrown on shore and left by the tide, adding in English, "sturgeon is very good." There is indeed, every reason to suppose, that these Clatsops depend for their subsistence during the winter, chiefly on the fish thus casually thrown on the coast. After amusing himself for some time on the beach, he returned towards the village, and shot on his way two brant. As he came near the village, one of the Indians asked him to shoot a duck about thirty steps distant: he did so, and having accidentally shot off its head, the bird was brought to the village by the Indians, all of whom came round in astonishment: they examined the duck, the musket, and the very small bullet, which were a hundred to the pound, and then exclaimed, "Clouch musquet, wake, commatax musquet" (a good musket, do not understand this kind of

Captain Clark's plan of Fort Clatsop and vicinity. As can be seen in his sketch of the fort on the next page, the stockade was 50 ft. square. Of the seven rooms, five apparently had their own fireplaces and one had an outside chimney. The gates closing off the 20 x 48 ft. parade ground opened to the south.

musket). They now placed before him their best roots, fish, and syrup, after which he attempted to purchase a sea-otter skin with some red beads which he happened to have about him; but they declined trading, as they valued none except blue or white beads: he therefore bought nothing but a little berry bread and a few roots in exchange for fish-hooks, and then set out to return by the same route on which he came. He was accompanied by Cuskalah and his brother as far as the third creek, and then proceeded to the camp through a heavy rain. The whole party had been occupied during his absence in cutting down trees to make huts, and in hunting.

DECEMBER 11TH *Wednesday.* The rain continued last night and the whole of this day. We were, however, all employed in putting up our winter cabins, which we are anxious to finish, as several of the men are beginning to suffer from the excessive dampness: four of them have very violent colds, one has a dysentery, a third has tumours on his legs, and two have been injured by dislocation and straining of their limbs.

DECEMBER 12TH *Thursday.* We continued to work in the rain at our houses. In the evening there arrived two canoes of Clatsops, among whom was a principal chief, called Comowool. We gave him a medal, and treated his companions with great attention; after which we began to bargain for a small sea-otter skin, some wappatoo roots, and another species of root called shanataque. We readily perceived that they were close dealers, stickled much for trifles, and never closed the bargain until they thought they had the advantage. The wappatoo is dear, as they themselves are obliged to give a high price for it to the Indians above. Blue beads are the articles most in request, the white occupy the next place in their estimation; but they do not value much those of any other colour. We succeeded at last in purchasing their whole cargo for a few fish-hooks and a small sack of Indian tobacco, which we had received from the Shoshonees.

DECEMBER 13TH The next morning, we treated them to a breakfast on elk meat, of which they seemed very fond, and having purchased from them two skins of the lucervia [loup-cervier, or lynx], and two robes made of the skin of an animal about the size of a cat, they left us. Two hunters returned with the pleasing intelligence of their having killed eighteen elk about six miles off. Our huts begin to rise, for though it rains all day we continue our labours, and are rejoiced to find that the beautiful balsam pine splits into excellent boards, more than two feet in width. In the evening three Indians came in a canoe with provisions and skins for sale, and spent the night with us.

Saturday. Again it rained all day, but by working constantly we finished the walls of our huts, and nearly completed a house for our provisions. The constant rains have completely spoiled our last supply of elk; but notwithstanding that scarcely a man has been dry for a great number of days, the sick are recovering. Four men were despatched to guard the elk which were killed yesterday, till a larger party joined them. DECEMBER 14TH

Sunday. Accordingly, captain Clark with sixteen men set out in three canoes, and having rowed for three miles up the river turned up a large creek from the right, and after going three miles further landed about the height of the tide water. The men were then despatched in small parties to bring in the elk, each man returning with a quarter of the animal. In bringing the third and last load, nearly half the men missed their way, and did not return till after night; five of them indeed were not able to find their way at all. It had been cloudy all day, and in the night began to rain, and as we had no cover were obliged to sit up the greater part of the night, for as soon as we lay down the rain would come under us, and compel us to rise. DECEMBER 15TH

It was indeed a most uncomfortable situation, but the five men who joined us in the morning had been more unlucky, for in addition to the rain which had poured down upon them all night, they had no fire, and drenched and cold as they were when they reached us, exhibited a most distressing sight. They had left their loads where they slept, and some men were sent after them, while others were despatched after two more elk in another bend of the creek, who after taking these last on board, proceeded to our camp. It rained and hailed during the day, and a high wind from the southeast not only threw down trees as we passed along, but made the river so rough that we proceeded with great risk. We now had the meat house covered, and all our game carefully hung up in small pieces.

Tuesday. It rained all night, and this morning there was a high wind, and hail as well as rain fell; and on the top of a mountain about ten miles to the southeast of us we observed some snow. The greater part of our stores is wet, and our leathern tent is so rotten that the slightest touch makes a rent in it, and it will now scarcely shelter a spot large enough for our beds. We were all busy in finishing the inside of the huts. The after part of the day was cool and fair. But this respite was of very short duration, for all night it continued raining and snowing alternately, and in the morning we had snow and hail till twelve o'clock, after which it changed to rain. The air now became cool and disagreeable, the wind high and unsettled, so that being thinly dressed in leather, we were able to do very little on the houses. DECEMBER 17TH

Thursday. The rain continued all night with short intervals, but the morning was fair and the wind from the southwest. Situated as we are, our only occupation is to work as diligently as we can on our houses, and to watch the changes of the weather, on which so much of our comfort depends. We availed ourselves of this glimpse of sunshine, to send across Meriwether's bay for the boards of an old Indian house; but before the party returned with them, the weather clouded, and we again had hail and rain during the rest of the day. Our only visitors were two Indians who spent a short time with us. DECEMBER 19TH

DECEMBER 20TH   *Friday.* A succession of rain and hail during the night. At ten o'clock it cleared off for a short time, but the rain soon recommenced; we now covered in four of our huts; three Indians came in a canoe with mats, roots, and the berries of the sacacommis. These people proceed with a dexterity and finesse in their bargains, which, if they have not learnt from their foreign visitors, it may show how nearly allied is the cunning of savages to the little arts of traffic. They begin by asking double or treble the value of what they have to sell, and lower their demand in proportion to the greater or less degree of ardour or knowledge of the purchaser, who with all his management is not able to procure the article for less than its real value, which the Indians perfectly understand. Our chief medium of trade consists of blue and white beads, files with which they sharpen their tools, fish-hooks, and tobacco: but of all these articles blue beads and tobacco are the most esteemed.

DECEMBER 21ST   *Saturday.* As usual it rained all night and continued without intermission during the day. One of our Indian visitors was detected in stealing a horn spoon, and turned out of the camp. We find that the plant called sacacommis forms an agreeable mixture with tobacco, and we therefore despatched two men to the open lands near the ocean, in order to collect some of it, while the rest continued their work.

DECEMBER 22D   *Sunday.* There was no interval in the rain last night and to-day; so that we cannot go on rapidly with our buildings. Some of the men are indeed quite sick, others have received bruises, and several complain of boils. We discover too, that part of our elk meat is spoiling in consequence of the warmth of the weather, though we have kept a constant smoke under it.

DECEMBER 23D   *Monday.* It continued raining the whole day, with no variation except occasional thunder and hail. Two canoes of Clatsops came to us with various articles for sale; we bought three mats and bags neatly made of flags and rushes, and also the skin of a panther seven feet long, including the tail. For all these we gave six small fish-hooks, a worn-out file, and some pounded fish which had become so soft and mouldy by exposure, that we could not use it: it is, however, highly prized by the Indians of this neighbourhood. Although a very portable and convenient food, the mode of curing seems known, or at least practised only by the Indians near the great falls, and coming from such a distance, has an additional value in the eyes of these people, who are anxious to possess some food less precarious than their ordinary subsistence.

Among these Clatsops was a second chief to whom we gave a medal, and sent some pounded fish to Cuscalah, who could not come to see us, on account of sickness. The next day, however, he came in a canoe with his young brother and two squaws. Having treated captain Clark so kindly at his village we were pleased to see him, and he gave us two mats and a parcel of roots. These we accepted, as it would have been offensive to decline the offer but afterwards two files were demanded in return for the presents, and not being able to spare those articles, we restored the mats and roots. Cuscalah was a little displeased: in the evening however he offered each of us one of the squaws, and even this being declined, Cuscalah as well as the

Captain Clark's own journal entry for the expedition's second Christmas in the wilderness.

whole party of Indians were highly offended: the females particularly seemed to be much incensed at our indifference about their favours. The whole stock of meat being now completely spoiled, our pounded fish became again our chief dependence. It had rained constantly all day, but we still continued working and at last moved into our huts.

Wednesday. We were awaked at daylight by a discharge of firearms, which was followed by a song from the men, as a compliment to us on the return

DECEMBER 25TH

of Christmas, which we have always been accustomed to observe as a day of rejoicing. After breakfast we divided our remaining stock of tobacco, which amounted to twelve carrots, into two parts; one of which we distributed among such of the party as made use of it, making a present of a handkerchief to the others. The remainder of the day was passed in good spirits, though there was nothing in our situation to excite much gaiety. The rain confined us to the house, and our only luxuries in honour of the season, were some poor elk, so much spoiled that we eat it through mere necessity, a few roots, and some spoiled pounded fish.

DECEMBER 26TH *Thursday.* The next day brought a continuation of rain, accompanied with thunder, and a high wind from the southeast. We were therefore still obliged to remain in our huts, and endeavoured to dry our wet articles before the fire. The fleas which annoyed us near the portage of the great falls, have taken such possession of our clothes, that we are obliged to have a regular search every day through our blankets as a necessary preliminary to sleeping at night. These animals indeed are so numerous, that they are almost a calamity to the Indians of this country. When they have once obtained the mastery of any house it is impossible to expel them, and the Indians have frequently different houses, to which they resort occasionally when the fleas have rendered their permanent residence intolerable; yet in spite of these precautions, every Indian is constantly attended by multitudes of them, and no one comes into our houses without leaving behind him swarms of these tormenting insects.

DECEMBER 27TH *Friday.* The rain did not cease last night, nor the greater part of the day. In the evening we were visited by Comowool, the chief, and four men of the Clatsop nation, who brought a very timely supply of roots and berries. Among these was one called culwhomo, resembling liquorice in size and taste, and which they roast like a potato; there was also the shanataque, a root of which they are very fond. It is of a black colour, sweet to the taste, and is prepared for eating in a kiln, as the Indians up the Columbia dry the pasheco. These as well as the shellwell berries, they value highly, but were perfectly satisfied with the return we made them, consisting of a small piece of sheepskin, to wear round the chief's head, a pair of earbobs for his son, a small piece of brass, and a little ribbon. In addition to our old enemies the fleas, we observed two mosquitoes, or insects so completely resembling them, that we can perceive no difference in their shape and appearance.

DECEMBER 28TH *Saturday.* Again it rained during the greater part of last night, and continued all day. Five men were sent out to hunt, and five others despatched to the seaside, each with a large kettle, in order to begin the manufacture of salt. The route to the seacoast is about seven miles in length, in a direction nearly west. Five miles of the distance is through thick wood varied with hills, ravines and swamps, though the land in general possesses a rich black mould. The remaining two miles is formed of open waving prairies of sand, with ridges running parallel to the river, and covered with green grass. The rest of the men were employed in making pickets and gates for our new fort. Although we had no sun, the weather was very warm.

DECEMBER 29TH *Sunday.* It rained the whole night, but ceased this morning, and but little rain fell in the course of the day; still the weather was cloudy and the wind high from the southeast. The Clatsop chief and his party left us, after begging for a great number of articles, which, as we could not spare them, we refused except a razor. We were employed all day in picketting the fort: in the evening a young Wahkiacum chief, with four men and two women, arrived with some dressed elk skin and wappatoo for sale. We purchased about a bushel and a half of those roots for some red beads, and small pieces of brass wire and old check. The chief too made us a present of half a bushel more, for which we gave him a medal, and a piece of ribbon, to tie round his hat. These roots are extremely grateful, since our meat has become spoiled, and we were desirous of purchasing the remainder; but the chief would not dispose of any more, as he was on his way to trade with the Clatsops. They remained with us however till the next day, when they were joined by four more of their countrymen, from the Wahkiacum village. These last began by offering us some roots; but as we had now learned that they always expect three or four times as much in return, as the real value of the articles, and are even dissatisfied with that, we declined such dangerous presents.

Towards evening the hunters brought in four elk, and after a long course of abstinence and miserable diet, we had a most sumptuous supper of elk's tongues and marrow. Besides this agreeable repast, the state of the weather had been quite exhilarating. It had rained during the night, but in the morning, though the high wind continued, we enjoyed the fairest and most pleasant weather since our arrival; the sun having shone at intervals, and there being only three showers in the course of the day. By sunset we had completed the fortification, and now announced to the Indians that every day at that hour the gates would be closed, and they must leave the fort and not enter it till sunrise. The Wahkiacums, who had remained with us, and who are very forward in their deportment, complied very reluctantly with this order; but being excluded from our houses, formed a camp near us.

DECEMBER 31ST *Tuesday.* As if it were impossible to have twenty-four hours of pleasant weather, the sky last evening clouded, and the rain began and continued through the day. In the morning there came down two canoes, one from the Wahkiacum village, the other contained three men and a squaw of the Skilloot nation. They brought wappatoo, and shanataque roots, dried fish, mats made of flags and rushes, dressed elk skins and tobacco; for which, particularly the skins, they asked a very extravagant price. We purchased some wappatoo, and a little tobacco, very much like that we had seen among the Shoshonees, put up in small neat bags made of rushes. These we obtained in exchange for a few articles, among which fish-hooks are the most esteemed. One of the Skilloots brought a gun which wanted some repair, and having put it in order, we received from him a present of about a peck of wappatoo; we then gave him a piece of sheep skin and blue cloth, to cover the lock, and he very thankfully offered a further present of roots. There is, in fact, an obvious superiority in these Skilloots over the Wahkiacums, who are intrusive, thievish, and impertinent. Our new regulations, however, and the appearance of the sentinel, have improved the behaviour of all our Indian visitors. They left the fort before sunset, even without being ordered.

Besides the fleas, we observe a number of insects in motion to-day. Snakes are yet to be seen; snails too, without covers, are common. On the rivers, and along the shores of Meriwether's bay, are many kinds of large water fowls, but at this period they are excessively wild. The early part of the night was fair.

Wednesday, January 1st, 1806

We were awaked at an early hour, by a discharge of a volley of small arms, to salute the new year. This is the only mode of doing honour to the day which our situation permits, for though we have reason to be gayer than we were at Christmas, our only dainties are the boiled elk and wappatoo, enlivened by draughts of pure water.

We were visited by a few Clatsops, who came by water, bringing roots and berries for sale. Among this nation we have observed a man about twenty-five years old, of a much lighter complexion than the Indians generally: his face was even freckled, and his hair long, and of a colour inclining to red. He was in habits and manners perfectly Indian; but, though he did not speak a word of English, he seemed to understand more than the others of his party; and, as we could obtain no account of his origin, we concluded that one of his parents, at least, must have been completely white. These Indians stayed with us during the night, and left the fort next morning, having disposed of their cargo for fishing-hooks and other trifling articles.

JANUARY 2D *Thursday*. The hunters brought in two elk, and we obtained from the traps an otter. This animal, as well as the beaver and the raccoon, are in plenty near the seacoast, and along the small creeks and rivers as high as the grand rapids, and in this country possess an extremely good fur.

The birds which most strike our attention are the large as well as the small or whistling swan, the sandhill crane, the large and small geese, cormorants, brown and white brant, duck and mallard, the canvass and several other species of ducks. There is also a small crow, the blue crested corvus, and the smaller corvus with a white breast, the little brown wren, a large brown sparrow, the bald eagle, and the beautiful buzzard [condor] of the Columbia. All these wild fowl continue with us, though they are not in such numbers as on our first arrival in this neighbourhood.

JANUARY 3D *Friday*. At eleven o'clock we were visited by our neighbour the Tia, or chief Comowool, who is also called Coone, and six Clatsops. Besides roots, and berries, they brought for sale three dogs and some fresh blubber. Having been so long accustomed to live on the flesh of dogs, the greater part of us have acquired a fondness for it, and our original aversion for it is overcome, by reflecting that while we subsisted on that food we were fatter, stronger, and in general enjoyed better health than at any period since leaving the buffalo country eastward of the mountains. The blubber, which is esteemed by the Indians an excellent food, has been obtained, they tell us, from their neighbours the Killamucks, a nation who live on the seacoast to the southeast, and near one of whose villages a whale had recently been thrown and foundered. Three of the hunters who had been despatched on the *28th*, returned about dark; they had been fifteen miles up the river to the east of us, which falls into Meriwether's bay, and had hunted a considerable distance to the east; but they had not been able to kill more than a single deer, and a few fowls, scarcely sufficient for their subsistence; an incident which teaches us the necessity of keeping out several parties of hunters, in order to procure a supply against any exigency.

Saturday. Comowool left us this morning with his party, highly pleased with a present of an old pair of satin breeches. The hunters were all sent in different directions, and we are now becoming more anxious for their success since our store of wappatoo is all exhausted. JANUARY 4TH

Sunday. Two of the five men who had been despatched to make salt returned. They had carefully examined the coast, but it was not till the fifth day after their departure that they discovered a convenient situation for their manufacture. At length they formed an establishment about fifteen miles southwest of the fort, near some scattered houses of the Clatsop and Killamuck nation, where they erected a comfortable camp, and had killed a stock of provisions. The Indians had treated them very kindly, and made them a present of the blubber of the whale, some of which the men brought home. It was white and not unlike the fat of pork, though of a coarser and more spongy texture, and on being cooked was found to be tender and palatable, and in flavour resembling the beaver. The men also brought with them a gallon of the salt, which was white, fine, and very good, but not so strong as the rock salt common to the western parts of the United States. It proves to be a most agreeable addition to our food, and as the saltmakers can manufacture three or four quarts a day, we have a prospect of a very plentiful supply. JANUARY 5TH

The appearance of the whale seemed to be a matter of importance to all the neighbouring Indians, and as we might be able to procure some of it for ourselves, or at least purchase blubber from the Indians, a small parcel of merchandise was prepared, and a party of the men held in readiness to set out in the morning. As soon as this resolution was known, Chaboneau and his wife requested that they might be permitted to accompany us. The poor woman stated very earnestly that she had travelled a great way with us to see the great water, yet she had never been down to the coast, and now that this monstrous fish was also to be seen, it seemed hard that she should not be permitted to see either the ocean or the whale. So reasonable a request could not be denied; they were therefore suffered to accompany captain Clark, who after an early breakfast set out with twelve men in two canoes.

Monday. He proceeded down the Netul into Meriwether bay, intending to go to the Clatsop town, and there procure a guide through the creeks, which there was reason to believe communicated not only with the bay, but with a small river running towards the sea, near where our saltmakers were encamped. Before however he could reach the Clatsop village, the high wind from the northwest compelled him to put into a small creek. He therefore resolved to attempt the passage without a guide, and proceeded up the creek three miles, to some high open land where he found a road. He therefore left the canoes, and followed the path over three deep marshes to a pond about JANUARY 6TH a mile long, and two hundred yards wide. He kept on the left of this pond, and at length came to the creek which he had crossed on a raft, when he had visited Cuscalah's village on the ninth of December. He proceeded down it, till he found a small canoe, fit to hold three persons, in which the whole party crossed the creek. Here they saw a herd of elk, and the men were divided into small parties, and hunted them till after dark, when they met again at the forks of the river. Three of the elk were wounded, but night prevented their taking more than one, which was brought to the camp, and cooked with some sticks of pine which had drifted down the creeks. The weather was beautiful, the sky clear, the moon shone brightly, a circumstance the more agreeable as this is the first fair evening we have enjoyed for two months.

Two swords, a bludgeon, and a paddle, sketched in Captain Lewis's diary.

Chapter 22
AT FORT CLATSOP

TUESDAY, JANUARY 7TH, 1806 There was a frost this morning. We rose early, and taking eight pounds of flesh, which were all the remains of the elk, proceeded up the south fork of the creek. At the distance of two miles we found a pine tree, which had been felled by one of our saltmakers, and on which we crossed the deepest part of the creek, and waded through the rest. We then went over an open ridgy prairie, three quarters of a mile, to the seabeach; after following which for three miles, we came to the mouth of a beautiful river, with a bold, rapid current, eighty-five yards wide, and three feet deep, in its shallowest crossings. On its northeast side are the remains of an old village of Clatsops, inhabited by only a single family, who appeared miserably poor and dirty. We gave a man two fish-hooks, to ferry the party over the river, which, from the tribe on its banks, we called Clatsop river. The creek, which we had passed on a tree, approaches this river within about an hundred yards, and by means of a portage, supplies a communication with the villages near Point Adams. After going on for two miles, we found the saltmakers encamped near four houses of Clatsops and Killamucks, who, though poor, dirty, and covered with fleas, seemed kind and well disposed.

We persuaded a young Indian, by a present of a file, and a promise of some other articles, to guide us to the spot where the whale lay. He led us for two and a half miles over the round slippery stones at the foot of a high hill projecting into the sea, and then suddenly stopping, and uttering the word "peshack" (or bad), explained by signs that we could no longer follow the coast, but must cross the mountain. This promised to be a most laborious undertaking, for the side is nearly perpendicular, and the top lost in clouds. He, however, followed an Indian path which wound along as much as possible, but still the ascent was so steep, that at one place we drew ourselves for about an hundred feet by means of bushes and roots. At length, after two hours' labour, we reached the top of the mountain, where we looked down with astonishment on the prodigious height of ten or twelve hundred feet, which we had ascended. Immediately below us, in the face of this precipice, is a stratum of white earth, used, as our guide informed us, as a paint by the neighbouring Indians. It obviously contains argile, and resembles the earth of which the French porcelain is made, though whether it contains silex or magnesia, or in what proportions, we could not observe. We were here met by fourteen Indians, loaded with oil and blubber, the spoils of the whale, which they were carrying in very heavy burdens, over this rough mountain. On leaving them, we proceeded over a bad road till night, when we encamped on a small run: we were all much fatigued, but the weather was pleasant, and, for the first time since our arrival here, an entire day has passed without rain.

JANUARY 8TH

Wednesday. In the morning we set out early and proceeded to the top of the mountain, the highest point of which is an open spot facing the ocean. It is situated about thirty miles southeast of cape Disappointment, and projects nearly two and a half miles into the sea. Here one of the most delightful views in nature presents itself. Immediately in front is the ocean, which breaks with fury on the coast, from the rocks of cape Disappointment as far as the eye can discern to the northwest, and against the highlands and irregular piles of rock which diversify the shore to the southeast. To this

Captain Lewis's meteorological record for January, 1806.

boisterous scene, the Columbia, with its tributary waters, widening into bays as it approaches the ocean, and studded on both sides with the Chinnook and Clatsop villages, forms a charming contrast; while immediately beneath our feet, are stretched the rich prairies, enlivened by three beautiful streams, which conduct the eye to small lakes at the foot of the hills. We stopped to enjoy the romantic view from this place, which we distinguished by the name of Clark's Point of View, and then followed our guide down the mountain. The descent was steep and dangerous: in many places the hill sides, which are formed principally of yellow clay, has been washed by the late rains, and is now slipping into the sea, in large masses of fifty and an hundred acres. In other parts, the path crosses the rugged perpendicular rocks which overhang the sea, into which a false step would have precipitated us. The mountains are covered with a very thick growth of timber, chiefly pine and fir; some of which, near Clark's Point of View, perfectly sound and solid, rise to the height of two hundred and ten feet, and are from eight to twelve in diameter. Intermixed is the white cedar, or arbor vitae, and a small quantity of black alder, two or three feet thick, and sixty or seventy in height.

At length we reached a single house, the remains of an old Killamuck village, situated among some rocks, in a bay immediately on the coast. We then continued for two miles along the sand beach; and after crossing a creek, eighty yards in width, near which are five cabins, reached the place where the waves had thrown the whale on shore. The animal had been placed between two Killamuck villages, and such had been their industry, that there now remained nothing more than the skeleton, which we found to be one hundred and five feet in length. Captain Clark then returned to the village of five huts, on the creek, to which he gave the name of Ecola, or Whale creek. The natives were all busied in boiling the blubber, in a large square trough of wood, by means of heated stones, and preserving the oil, thus extracted, in bladders and the entrails of the whale. The refuse of the blubber, which still contained a portion of oil, are hung up in large flitches, and when wanted for use, are warmed on a wooden spit before the fire, and eaten either alone, or dipped in oil, or with roots of the rush and shanataque. These Killamucks, though they had great quantities, parted with it reluctantly, and at such high prices, that our whole stock of merchandise was exhausted in the purchase of about three hundred pounds of blubber, and a few gallons of oil. With these we set out to return; and having crossed Ecola creek, encamped on its bank, where there was abundance of fine timber.

We were soon joined by the men of the village, with whom we smoked, and who gave us all the information they possessed, relative to their country. These Killamucks are part of a much larger nation of the same name, and they now reside chiefly in four villages, each at the entrance of a creek, all of which fall into a bay on the southwest coast; that at which we now are, being the most northern, and at the distance of about forty-five miles southeast of Point Adams. The rest of the nation are scattered along the coast, and on the banks of a river, which, as we found it in their delineations, we called Killamuck's river, emptying itself in the same direction. During the salmon season they catch great quantities of that fish, in the small creeks, and when they fail, their chief resource was the sturgeon and other fish stranded along the coast. The elk were very numerous in the mountains, but they could not procure many of them with their arrows; and their principal communication with strangers, was by means of the Killamuck river, up which they passed to the Shocatilcum (or Columbia) to trade for wappatoo roots. In their dress, appearance, and indeed every circumstance of life, they differ very little from the Chinnooks, Clatsops, and other nations in the neighbourhood. The chief variation we have observed is in the manner of burying the dead; the bodies being secured in an oblong box of plank, which is placed in an open canoe, lying on the ground, with a paddle, and other small articles of the deceased by his side.

Whilst smoking with the Indians, captain Clark was surprised about ten o'clock by a loud shrill outcry from the opposite village; on hearing which, all the Indians immediately started up to cross the creek, and the guide informed him that some one had been killed. On examination, one of the men was discovered to be absent, and a guard despatched, who met him crossing the creek in great haste. An Indian belonging to another band, and who happened to be with the Killamucks that evening, had treated him with much kindness, and walked arm in arm with him to a tent where our man found a Chinnook squaw, who was an old acquaintance. From the conversation and manner of the stranger, this woman discovered that his object was to murder the white man, for the sake of the few articles on his person, and when he rose, and pressed our man to go to another tent where they would find something better to eat, she held M'Neal by the blanket; not knowing her object, he freed himself from her, and was going on with his pretended friend, when she ran out and gave the shriek which brought the men of the village over, and the stranger ran off before M'Neal knew what had occasioned the alarm.

JANUARY 9TH *Thursday.* The morning was fine, the wind from the northeast; and having divided our stock of the blubber, we began at sunrise to retread our steps, in order to reach fort Clatsop, at the distance of thirty-five miles. We met several parties of Indians on their way to trade for blubber and oil with the Killamucks; (our route lay across the same mountains which we had already passed) we also overtook a party returning from the village, and could not but regard with astonishment the heavy loads which the women carry over these fatiguing and dangerous paths. As one of the women was descending a steep part of the mountain, her load slipped from her back, and she stood holding it by a strap with one hand, and with the other supporting herself by a bush: captain Clark being near her, undertook to replace the load, and found it almost as much as he could lift, and above one hundred pounds in weight. Loaded as they were, they kept pace with us, till we reached the saltmakers' tents, where we passed the night, while they continued their route.

JANUARY 10TH *Friday.* We proceeded across Clatsop river, to the place where we had left our canoes; and as the tide was coming in, immediately embarked for the fort, at which place we arrived about ten o'clock at night. During their absence, the men had been occupied in hunting and dressing skins, but in this they were not very successful, as the deer have become scarce, and are, indeed, seen chiefly near the prairies and open grounds, along the coast.

This morning, however, there came to the fort twelve Indians, in a large canoe. They are of the Cathlamah nation, our nearest neighbours above, on the south side of the river. The tia, or chief, whose name was Shahawacap, having been absent on a hunting excursion, as we passed his village, had never yet seen us, and we therefore showed him the honours of our country, as well as our reduced finances would permit. We invested him with a small medal, and received a present of Indian tobacco and a basket of wappatoo in return, for which we gave him a small piece of our tobacco, and thread for a fishing net. They had brought dried salmon, wappatoo, dogs, and mats made of rushes and flags: but we bought only some dogs and wappatoo. These Cathlamahs speak the same language as the Chinnooks and Clatsops, whom they also resemble in dress and manners.

Saturday. A party was sent out to bring in some elk killed yesterday, and several were despatched after our Indian canoe, which drifted away last night; but, though the whole neighbourhood was diligently searched, we were unable to find it. This is a serious loss, as she is much superior to our own canoes, and so light that four men can carry her readily without fatigue, though she will carry from ten to twelve hundred pounds, besides a crew of four. In the evening the Cathlamahs left us, on their way to barter their wappatoo with the Clatsops, for some blubber and oil, which these last have procured from the Killamucks, in exchange for beads and other articles. JANUARY 11TH

Sunday. Our meat is now becoming scarce; we, therefore, determined to jerk it, and issue it in small quantities, instead of dividing it among the four messes, and leaving to each the care of its own provisions; a plan by which much is lost, in consequence of the improvidence of the men. Two hunters had been despatched in the morning, and one of them, Drewyer, had before evening, killed seven elk. We should scarcely be able to subsist, were it not for the exertions of this most excellent hunter. The game is scarce, and nothing is now to be seen, except elk, which to almost all the men, are very difficult to be procured: but Drewyer, who is the offspring of a Canadian Frenchman, and an Indian woman, has passed his life in the woods, and unites, in a wonderful degree, the dexterous aim of the frontier huntsman, with the intuitive sagacity of the Indian, in pursuing the faintest tracks through the forest. All our men, however, have indeed, become so expert with the rifle, that we are never under apprehensions as to food, since, whenever there is game of any kind, we are almost certain of procuring it. JANUARY 12TH

Monday. Captain Lewis took all the men who could be spared, and brought in the seven elk, which they had found untouched by the wolves, of which there are a few in the neighbourhood. The last of the candles which we brought with us being exhausted, we now began to make others of elk tallow. JANUARY 13TH

From all that we have seen and learnt of the Chinnooks, we have been induced to estimate the nation at about twenty-eight houses, and four hundred souls. They reside chiefly along the banks of a river, to which we gave the same name; and which, running parallel to the seacoast, waters a low country with many stagnant ponds, and then empties itself into Haley's bay. The wild fowl of these ponds, and the elk and deer of the neighbourhood, furnish them with occasional luxuries; but their chief subsistence is derived from the salmon and other fish, which are caught in the small streams, by means of nets and gigs, or thrown on shore by the violence of the tide. To these are added some roots, such as the wild liquorice, which is the most common, the shanataque, and the wappatoo, brought down the river by the traders.

The men are low in stature, rather ugly, and ill made: their legs being small and crooked, their feet large, and their heads, like those of the women, flattened in a most disgusting manner. These deformities are in part concealed by robes made of sea-otter, deer, elk, beaver, or fox skins. They also employ in their dress, robes of the skin of a cat peculiar to this country, and of another animal of the same size, which is light and durable, and sold at a high price by the Indians, who bring it from above. In addition to these are worn blankets, wrappers of red, blue, or spotted cloth, and some old sailors' clothes, which were very highly prized. The greater part of the men have guns, powder, and ball.

The women have, in general, handsome faces, but are low and disproportioned, with small feet and large legs and thighs, occasioned, probably, by strands of beads, or various strings, drawn so tight above the ankles, as to prevent the circulation of the blood. Their dress, like that of the Wahkiacums, consists of a short robe, and a tissue of cedar bark. Their hair hangs loosely down the shoulders and back; and their ears, neck, and wrists are ornamented with blue beads. Another decoration which is very highly prized, consists of figures made by puncturing the arms or legs; and on the arm of one of the squaws, we observed the name of J. Bowman, executed in the same way.

In language, habits, and in almost every other particular, they resemble the Clatsops, Cathlamahs, and indeed all the people near the mouth of the Columbia. They, however, seem to be inferior to their neighbours in honesty as well as spirit. No ill treatment or indignity, on our part, seems to excite any feeling, except fear; nor, although better provided than their neighbours with arms, have they enterprise enough to use them advantageously against the animals of the forest, nor offensively against their neighbours; who owe their safety more to the timidity than the forbearance of the Chinnooks. We had heard instances of pilfering whilst we were amongst them, and therefore had a general order, excluding them from our encampment; so that whenever an Indian wished to visit us, he began by calling out "No Chinnook." It may be probable that this first impression left a prejudice against them, since when we were among the Clatsops, and other tribes at the mouth of the Columbia, the Indians had less opportunity of stealing, if they were so disposed.

JANUARY 14TH *Tuesday*, we were employed in jerking the meat of the elk, and searching for one of the canoes which had been carried off by the tide last night. Having found it, we now had three of them drawn up out of reach of the water, and the other secured by a strong cord, so as to be ready for any emergency.

After many inquiries and much observation, we are at length enabled to obtain a connected view of the nations, who reside along the coast, on both sides of the Columbia. To the south, our personal observation has not extended beyond the Killamucks; but we obtained from those who were acquainted with the seacoast, a list of the Indian tribes, in the order in which they succeed each other, to a considerable distance.

The first nation to the south are the Clatsops, who reside on the southern side of the bay, and along the seacoast, on both sides of Point Adams. They are represented as the remains of a much larger nation; but about four years ago, a disorder, to which till then they were strangers, but which seems, from their description, to have been the small-pox, destroyed four chiefs, and several hundreds of the nation. These are deposited in canoes, a few miles below us on the bay, and the survivors do not number more than fourteen houses, and about two hundred souls.

Next to them along the southeast coast, is a much larger nation, the Killamucks, who number fifty houses, and a thousand souls. Their first establishment are the four huts at the mouth of Ecola creek, thirty-five miles from Point Adams; and two miles below are a few more huts; but the principal town is situated twenty miles lower, at the entrance of a creek, called Nielee, into the bay, which we designate by the name of Killamucks bay. Into the same bay empties a second creek, five miles further, where is a Killamuck village, called Kilherhurst; at two miles a third creek, and a town called Kilherner; and at the same distance a town called *Chishuck*, at the mouth of Killamuck river. Towerquotton and *Chucktin*, are the names of two other towns, situated on creeks which empty into the bottom of the bay, the last of which is seventy miles from Point Adams. The Killamuck river is about one hundred yards wide, and very rapid; but having no perpendicular fall, is the great avenue for trade. There are two small villages of Killamucks settled above its mouth, and the whole trading part of the tribe ascend it, till by a short portage, they carry their canoes over to the Columbian valley, and descend the Multnomah to Wappatoo island. Here they purchase roots, which they carry down the Chockalilum or Columbia; and, after trafficking with the tribes on its banks for the various articles which they require, either return up the Columbia, or cross over through the country of the Clatsops. This trade, however, is obviously little more than a loose and irregular barter, on a very small scale; for the materials for commerce are so extremely scanty and precarious, that the stranding of a whale was an important commercial incident, which interested all the adjoining country. The Killamucks have little peculiar, either in character or manners, and resemble, in almost every particular, the Clatsops and Chinnooks.

Adjoining the Killamucks, and in a direction S. S. E. are the Lucktons, a small tribe inhabiting the seacoast. They speak the same language as the Killamucks, but do not belong to the same nation. The same observation applies to the Kahunkle nation, their immediate neighbours, who are supposed to consist of about four hundred souls, the Lickawis, a still more numerous nation, who have a large town of eight hundred souls; the Youkone nation, who live in very large houses, and number seven hundred souls; the Necketo nation, of the same number of persons; the Ulseah nation, a small town of one hundred and fifty souls; the Youitts, a tribe who live in a small town, containing not more than one hundred and fifty souls; the Shiastuckle nation, who have a large town of nine hundred souls; the Killawats nation of five hundred souls collected into one large town.

With this last nation ends the language of the Killamucks: and the coast, which then turns towards the southwest, is occupied by nations whose languages vary from that of the Killamucks, and from each other. Of these, the first in order are:

The Cookooooose, a large nation of one thousand five hundred souls, inhabiting the shore of the Pacific and the neighbouring mountains. We have seen several of this nation who were taken prisoners by the Clatsops and Killamucks. Their complexion was much fairer than that of the Indians near the mouth of the Columbia, and their heads were not flattened.

Next to these are the Shalalahs, of whom we know nothing, except their numbers, which are computed at twelve hundred souls. Then follow the Luckasos, of about the same number, and the Hannakalals, whom we estimate at six hundred souls.

This is the extent of the Indian information, and judging, as we can do, with considerable accuracy from the number of sleeps, or days journey, the distance which these tribes occupy along the coast, may be estimated at three hundred and sixty miles.

On the north of the Columbia, we have already seen the Chinnooks, of four hundred souls, along the shores of Haley's bay, and the low grounds on Chinnook river. Their nearest neighbours to the northeast are the Killaxthokle, a small nation on the coast, of not more than eight houses, and a hundred souls.

To these succeed the Chilts, who reside above Point Lewis, and who are estimated at seven hundred souls, and thirty-eight houses. Of this nation, we saw, transiently, a few among the Chinnooks, from whom they did not appear to differ. Beyond the Chilts we have seen none of the northwest Indians, and all that we learnt, consisted of an enumeration of their names and numbers.

The nations next to the Chilts, are: the Clamoitomish, of twelve houses, and two hundred and sixty souls; the Potoashees, of ten houses, and two hundred souls; the Pailsk, of ten houses, and two hundred souls; the Quinults, of sixty houses, and one thousand souls; the Chillates, of eight houses, and one hundred and fifty souls; the Calasthorte, of ten houses, and two hundred souls; the Quinnechant, consisting of two thousand souls.

A particular detail of the characters, manners, and habits of the tribes, must be left to some future adventurers, who may have more leisure and a better opportunity than we had to accomplish this object. Those who first visit the ground, can only be expected to furnish sketches rude and imperfect.

JANUARY 15TH *Wednesday.* Two hunting parties intended setting out this morning, but they were prevented by incessant rain, which confined us all to the fort.

The Chinnooks, Clatsops, and most of the adjoining nations dispose of the dead in canoes. For this purpose a scaffold is erected, by fixing perpendicularly in the ground four long pieces of split timber. These are placed two by two just wide enough apart to admit the canoe, and sufficiently long to support its two extremities. The boards are connected by a bar of wood run through them at the height of six feet, on which is placed a small canoe containing the body of the deceased, carefully wrapped in a robe of dressed skins, with a paddle, and some articles belonging to the deceased, by his side. Over this canoe is placed one of a larger size, reversed, with its gunwale resting on the crossbars, so as to cover the body completely. One or more large mats of rushes or flags are then rolled round the canoes, and the whole secured by cords usually made of the bark of the white cedar. On these crossbars are hung different articles of clothing, or culinary utensils. The method practised by the Killamucks differs somewhat from this; the body being deposited in an oblong box, of plank, which, with the paddle, and other articles, is placed in a canoe, resting on the ground.

With the religious opinions of these people we are but little acquainted, since we understand their language too imperfectly to converse on a subject so abstract; but it is obvious, from the different deposits which they place by their dead, that they believe in a future state of existence. [This fact is much too equivocal to warrant an inference so important. These deposits might have been intended for nothing more than the testimonials of surviving affection. Amongst those savages, where the language was better understood, it does not appear that the Indians intended any thing more by such sacrifices than to testify their reverence for the dead.— *Editor.*]

Thursday. To-day we finished curing our meat, and having now a plentiful supply of elk, and salt, and our houses dry and comfortable, we wait patiently for the moment of resuming our journey. JANUARY 16TH

The implements used in hunting, by the Clatsops, Chinnooks, and other neighbouring nations, are the gun, bow and arrow, deadfall, pits, snares, and spears or gigs. The guns are generally old American or British muskets repaired for this trade; and although there are some good pieces among them, they are constantly out of order, as the Indians have not been sufficiently accustomed to arms to understand the management of them. The powder is kept in small japanned tin flasks, in which the traders sell it; and when the ball or shot fails, they make use of gravel or pieces of metal from their pots, without being sensible of the injury done to their guns. These arms are reserved for hunting elk, and the few deer and bears in this neighbourhood; but as they have no rifles, they are not very successful hunters. The most common weapon is the bow and arrow, with which every man is provided, even though he carries a gun, and which is used in every kind of hunting. The bow is extremely neat, and being very thin and flat, possesses great elasticity. It is made of the heart of the white cedar, about two feet and a half in length, two inches wide at the centre, whence it tapers to the width of half an inch at the extremities; and the back is covered with the sinews of elk, fastened on by means of a glue made from the sturgeon. The string is formed of the same sinews. The arrow generally consists of two parts; the first is about twenty inches long, and formed of light white pine, with the feather at one end, and at the other a circular hole, which receives the second part, formed of some harder wood, and about five inches long, and secured in its place by means of sinews. The barb is either stone, or else of iron or copper, in which latter place, the angle is more obtuse than any we have seen. If, as sometimes happens, the arrow is formed of a single piece, the whole is of a more durable wood, but the form just described is preferred; because, as much of the game consists of wild fowl, on the ponds, it is desirable that they should be constructed so as to float, if they fall into the water. These arrows are kept in a quiver of elk or young bear skin, opening not at the ends, as the common quivers, but at the sides; which, for those who hunt in canoes, is much more convenient. These weapons are not, however, very powerful, for many of the elk we kill have been wounded with them; and, although the barb with the small end of the arrows remain, yet the flesh closes, and the animal suffers no permanent injury. The deadfalls and snares are used in taking the wolf, the raccoon, and the fox, of which there are, however, but few in this country. The spear or gig employed in pursuit of the sea-otter (which they call spuck), the common otter, and beaver, consists of two points of barbs, and is like those already described, as common among the Indians on the upper part of the Columbia. The pits are chiefly for the elk, and are therefore usually large and deep cubes of twelve or fourteen feet in depth, and are made by the side of some fallen tree lying across the path frequented by the elk. They are covered with slender boughs and moss, and the elk either sinks into it as he approaches the tree, or in leaping over the tree, falls into the pit on the other side.

JANUARY 17TH *Friday.* Comowool and seven other Clatsops spent the day with us. He made us a present of some roots and berries, and in return we gave him an awl and some thread, which he wanted for the purpose of making a net. We were not able to purchase any more of their provisions, the prices being too high for our exhausted stock of merchandise. One of the Indians was dressed in three very elegant skins of the sea-otter: for these we were very desirous of trafficking; but he refused every exchange except that of blue beads, of which he asked six fathom for each skin, and as we had only four fathom left, he would not accept for the remaining two, either a knife, or any quantity of beads of another sort.

In fishing, the Clatsops, Chinnooks and other nations near this place employ the common straight net, the scooping or dipping net with a long handle, the gig, and the hook and line. The first is of different lengths and depths, and used in taking salmon, char, and trout, in the deep inlets among the marshy grounds, and the mouths of deep creeks. The scooping net is used for small fish in the spring and summer season; and in both kinds the net is formed of silk grass, or the bark of white cedar. The gig is used at all seasons, and for all kinds of fish they can procure with it; so too is the hook and line, of which the line is made of the same material as the net, and the hook generally brought by the traders; though before the whites came, they made hooks out of two small pieces of bone, resembling the European hook, but with a much more acute angle, where the two pieces were joined.

JANUARY 18TH *Saturday.* We were all occupied in dressing skins, and preparing clothes for our journey homewards.

The houses in this neighbourhood are all large wooden buildings, varying in length from twenty to sixty feet, and from fourteen to twenty in width. They are constructed in the following manner. Two posts of split timber or more, agreeably to the number of partitions, are sunk in the ground, above which they rise to the height of fourteen or eighteen feet. They are hollowed at the top, so as to receive the ends of a round beam or pole, stretching from one to the other, and forming the upper point of the roof for the whole extent of the building. On each side of this range is placed another, which forms the eaves of the house, and is about five feet high; but as the building is often sunk to the depth of four or five feet, the eaves come very near the surface of the earth. Smaller pieces of timber are now extended by pairs, in the form of rafters, from the lower to the upper beam, where they are attached at both ends with cords of cedar bark. On these rafters two or three ranges of small poles are placed horizontally, and secured in the same way with strings of cedar bark. The sides are now made with a range of wide boards, sunk a small distance into the ground, with the upper ends projecting above the poles at the eaves, to which they are secured

362

by a beam passing outside, parallel with the eave-poles, and tied by cords of cedar bark passing through holes made in the boards at certain distances. The gable ends and partitions are formed in the same way, being fastened by beams on the outside, parallel to the rafters. The roof is then covered with a double range of thin boards, except an aperture of two or three feet in the centre, for the smoke to pass through. The entrance is by a small hole, cut out of the boards, and just large enough to admit the body.

The very largest houses only are divided by partitions, for though three or four families reside in the same room, there is quite space enough for all of them. In the centre of each room is a space six or eight feet square, sunk to the depth of twelve inches below the rest of the floor, and enclosed by four pieces of square timber. Here they make the fire, for which purpose pine bark is generally preferred. Around this fireplace, mats are spread, and serve as seats during the day, and very frequently as beds at night; there is however a more permanent bed made, by fixing, in two or sometimes three sides of the room, posts reaching from the roof down to the ground, and at the distance of four feet from the wall. From these posts to the wall itself, one or two ranges of boards are placed so as to form shelves, on which they either sleep, or where they stow away their various articles of merchandise. The uncured fish is hung in the smoke of their fires, as is also the flesh of the elk, when they are fortunate enough to procure any, which is but rarely.

Sunday. This morning we sent out two parties of hunters in different directions. Soon after we were visited by two Clatsop men and a woman, who brought several articles to trade: we purchased a small quantity of train oil for a pair of brass armbands, and succeeded in obtaining a sea-otter skin, for which we gave our only remaining four fathoms of blue beads, the same quantity of white ones, and a knife: we gave a fish-hook also in exchange for one of their hats. These are made of cedar bark and bear-grass, interwoven together in the form of an European hat, with a small brim of about two inches, and a high crown, widening upwards. They are light, ornamented with various colours and figures, and being nearly water-proof, are much more durable than either chip or straw hats. These hats form a small article of traffic with the whites, and the manufacture is one of the best exertions of Indian industry.

JANUARY 19TH

They are, however, very dexterous in making a variety of domestic utensils, among which are bowls, spoons, skewers, spits, and baskets. The bowl or trough is of different shapes, sometimes round, semicircular, in the form of a canoe, or cubic, and generally dug out of a single piece of wood, the larger vessels having holes in the sides by way of handle, and all executed with great neatness. In these vessels they boil their food, by throwing hot stones into the water, and extract oil from different animals in the same way. Spoons are not very abundant, nor is there any thing remarkable in their shape, except that they are large and the bowl broad. Meat is roasted on one end of a sharp skewer, placed erect before the fire, with the other fixed in the ground. The spit for fish is split at the top into two parts, between which the fish is placed, cut open, with its sides extended by means of small splinters. The usual plate is a small mat of rushes or flags, on which every thing is served. The instrument with which they dig up roots, is a strong stick, about three feet and a half long, sharpened and a little curved at the lower end, while the upper is inserted into a handle, standing transversely, and made of part of an elk or buck's horn.

But the most curious workmanship is that of the basket. It is formed of cedar bark and bear-grass, so closely interwoven, that it is water tight, without the aid of either gum or resin. The form is generally conic, or rather the segment of a cone, of which the smaller end is the bottom of the basket; and being made of all sizes, from that of the smallest cup to the capacity of five or six gallons, answer the double purpose of a covering for the head or to contain water. Some of them are highly ornamented with strands of bear-grass, woven into figures of various colours, which require great labour; yet they are made very expeditiously and sold for a trifle. It is for the construction of these baskets, that the bear-grass forms an article of considerable traffic. It grows only near the snowy region of the high mountains, and the blade, which is two feet long and about three-eighths of an inch wide, is smooth, strong and pliant; the young blades particularly, from their not being exposed to the sun and air, have an appearance of great neatness, and are generally preferred. Other bags and baskets, not water-proof, are made of cedar bark, silk-grass, rushes, flags, and common coarse sedge, for the use of families.

In the manufactures, as well as in the ordinary work of the house, the instrument most in use is a knife, or rather a dagger. The handle of it is small, and has a strong loop of twine for the thumb, to prevent its being wrested from the hand. On each side is a blade, double-edged and pointed; the longer from nine to ten inches, the shorter from four to five. This knife is carried about habitually in the hand, sometimes exposed, but mostly when in company with strangers, put under the robe.

JANUARY 20TH *Monday.* We were visited by three Clatsops, who came merely for the purpose of smoking and conversing with us. We have now only three days' provision, yet so accustomed have the men become to live sparingly, and fast occasionally, that such a circumstance excites no concern, as we all calculate on our dexterity as hunters.

The industry of the Indians is not confined to household utensils: the great proof of their skill is the construction of their canoes. In a country, indeed, where so much of the intercourse between different tribes is carried on by water, the ingenuity of the people would naturally direct itself to the improvement of canoes, which would gradually become, from a mere safe conveyance, an elegant ornament. We have accordingly seen, on the Columbia, canoes of many forms, beginning with the simple boats near the mountains, to those more highly decorated, because more useful nearer the mouth of the Columbia. Below the grand cataract there are four forms of canoes: the first and smallest is about fifteen feet long, and calculated for one or two persons: it is, indeed, by no means remarkable in its structure, and is chiefly employed by the Cathlamahs and Wahkiacums among the marshy islands. The second is from twenty to thirty-five feet long, about two and a half or three feet in the beam, and two feet in the hold. It is chiefly remarkable in having the bowsprit, which rises to some height above the bow, formed by tapering gradually from the sides into a sharp point. Canoes of this shape are common to all the nations below the grand rapids.

But the canoes most used by the Columbia Indians, from the Chil-

364

luckittequaws inclusive, to the ocean, are about thirty or thirty-five feet long. The bow, which looks more like the stern of our boats, is higher than the other end, and is ornamented with a sort of comb, an inch in thickness, cut out of the same log which forms the canoe, and extending nine or eleven inches from the bowsprit to the bottom of the boat. The stern is nearly rounded off, and gradually ascends to a point. This canoe is very light and convenient; for though it will contain ten or twelve persons, it may be carried with great ease by four.

Two common types of Columbia River canoes: the one at the left, 30–35 ft. long, carried up to a dozen persons; at right is the largest type, used in the tidewater area. Below are sketched two smaller canoes of the area; and a typical paddle, some 5 ft. in length.

The fourth and largest species of canoe we did not meet till we reached tide-water, near the grand rapids below, in which place they are found among all the nations, especially the Killamucks, and others residing on the seacoast. They are upwards of fifty feet long, and will carry from eight to ten thousand pounds weight, or from twenty to thirty persons. Like all the canoes we have mentioned, they are cut out of a single trunk of a tree, which is generally white cedar, though the fir is sometimes used. The sides are secured by cross-bars, or round sticks, two or three inches in thickness, which are inserted through holes made just below the gunwale, and made fast with cords. The upper edge of the gunwale itself is about five-eighths of an inch thick, and four or five in breadth, and folds outwards, so as to form a kind of rim, which prevents the water from beating into the boat. The bow and stern are about the same height, and each provided with a comb, reaching to the bottom of the boat. At each end, also, are pedestals, formed of the same solid piece, on which are placed strange grotesque figures of men or animals, rising sometimes to the height of five feet, and composed of small pieces of wood, firmly united, with great ingenuity, by inlaying and mortising, without a spike of any kind. The paddle is usually from four feet and a half to five feet in length; the handle being thick for one third of its length, when it widens, and is hollowed and thinned on each side of the centre, which forms a sort of rib. When they embark, one Indian sits in the stern, and steers with a paddle, the others kneel in pairs in the bottom of the canoe, and sitting on their heels, paddle over the gunwale next to them. In this way they ride with perfect safety the highest waves, and venture without the least concern in seas, where other boats or seamen could not live an instant. They sit quietly and paddle, with no other movement; except, when any large wave throws the boat on her side, and, to the eye of a spectator, she seems lost: the man to windward then steadies her by throwing his body towards the upper side, and sinking his paddle deep into the wave, appears to catch the water and force it under the boat, which the same stroke pushes on with great velocity. In the management of these canoes the women are equally expert with the men; for in the smaller boats, which contain four oarsmen, the helm is generally given to the female. As soon as they

365

land, the canoe is generally hauled on shore, unless she be very heavily laden; but at night the load is universally discharged, and the canoe brought on shore.

Our admiration of their skill in these curious constructions was increased by observing the very inadequate implements with which they are made. These Indians possess very few axes, and the only tool employed in their building, from felling of the tree to the delicate workmanship of the images, is a chisel made of an old file, about an inch or an inch and a half in width. Even of this tool they have not yet learnt the management, for the chisel is sometimes fixed in a large block of wood, and being held in the right hand, the block is pushed with the left without the aid of a mallet. But under all these disadvantages, these canoes, which one would suppose to be the work of years, are made in a few weeks. A canoe, however, is very highly prized: in traffic, it is an article of the greatest value, except a wife, which is of equal consideration; so that a lover generally gives a canoe to the father in exchange for his daughter.

Chapter 23

INDIANS OF THE VICINITY

TUESDAY, JANUARY 21ST, 1806   Two of the hunters came back with three elk, which form a timely addition to our stock of provisions. The Indian visitors left us at twelve o'clock.

The Killamucks, Clatsops, Chinnooks, and Cathlamahs, the four neighbouring nations with whom we have had most intercourse, preserve a general resemblance in person, dress, and manners. They are commonly of a diminutive stature, badly shaped, and their appearance by no means prepossessing. They have broad thick flat feet, thick ankles, and crooked legs: the last of which deformities is to be ascribed, in part, to the universal practice of squatting, or sitting on the calves of their legs and heels, and also to the tight bandages of beads and strings worn round the ankles, by the women, which prevent the circulation of the blood, and render the legs, of the females, particularly, ill shaped and swollen. The complexion is the usual copper coloured brown of the North American tribes, though the complexion is rather lighter than that of the Indians of the Missouri, and the frontier of the United States: the mouth is wide and the lips thick; the nose of a moderate size, fleshy, wide at the extremities, with large nostrils, and generally low between the eyes, though there are rare instances of high aquiline noses; the eyes are generally black, though we occasionally see them of a dark yellowish brown, with a black pupil.

But the most distinguishing part of their physiognomy, is the peculiar flatness and width of their forehead, a peculiarity which they owe to one of these customs by which nature is sacrificed to fantastic ideas of beauty. The custom, indeed, of flattening the head by artificial pressure during infancy, prevails among all the nations we have seen west of the Rocky mountains. To the east of that barrier, the fashion is so perfectly unknown, that there the western Indians, with the exception of the Alliatan or Snake nation, are designated by the common name of Flatheads. The singular usage, which nature could scarcely seem to suggest to remote nations, might perhaps incline us to believe in the common and not very ancient origin of all the western nations. Such an opinion might well accommodate itself with the fact, that while on the lower parts of the Columbia, both sexes are universally flatheads, the custom diminishes in receding eastward, from the common centre of the infection, till among the remoter tribes near the mountains, nature recovers her rights, and the wasted folly is confined to a few females. Such opinions, however, are corrected or weakened by considering that the flattening of the head is not, in fact, peculiar to that part of the continent, since it was among the first objects which struck the attention of Columbus.

But wherever it may have begun, the practice is now universal among these nations. Soon after the birth of her child, the mother, anxious to procure for her infant the recommendation of a broad forehead, places it in the compressing machine, where it is kept for ten or twelve months; though the females remain longer than the boys. The operation is so gradual, that it is not attended with pain; but the impression is deep and permanent. The heads of the children, when they are released from the bandage, are not more than two inches thick about the upper edge of the forehead, and still thinner above: nor with all its efforts can nature ever restore its shape; the heads of grown persons being often in a straight line from the nose to the top of the forehead.

The hair of both sexes is parted at the top of the head, and thence falls loosely behind the ears, over the back and shoulders. They use combs, of which they are very fond, and indeed, contrive without the aid of them, to keep their hair in very good order. The dress of the man consists in a small robe, reaching to the middle of the thigh, tied by a string across the breast, with its corners hanging loosely over their arms. These robes are, in general, composed of the skins of a small animal, which we have supposed to be the brown mungo. They have besides, those of the tiger-cat [lynx], deer, panther [cougar], bear, and elk, which last is principally used in war parties. Sometimes they have a blanket woven with the fingers, from the wool of their native sheep; occasionally a mat is thrown over them to keep off rain; but except this robe, they have no other article of clothing during winter or summer, so that every part of the body, but the back and shoulders, is exposed to view. They are very fond of the dress of the whites, whom they call pashisheooks or clothmen; and whenever they can procure any clothes, wear them in our manner: the only article, indeed, which we have not seen among them is the shoe.

The robe of the women is like that worn by the men, except that it does not reach below the waist. Those most esteemed are made of strips of sea-otter skin, which being twisted are interwoven with silk-grass, or the bark of the white cedar, in such a manner that the fur appears equally on both sides, so as to form a soft and warm covering. The skins of the raccoon or beaver are also employed in the same way, though on other occasions these skins are simply dressed in the hair, and worn without further preparation. The garment which covers the body from the waist as low as the knee before and the thigh behind, is the tissue already described, and is made either of the bruised bark of white cedar, the twisted cords of silk-grass, or of flags and rushes. Neither leggings nor moccasins are ever used, the mildness of the climate not requiring them as a security from the weather, and their being so much in the water rendering them an incumbrance. The only covering for the head is a hat made of bear-grass, and the bark of cedar, interwoven in a conic form, with a knob of the same shape at the top. It has no brim, but is held on the head by a string passing under the chin, and tied to a small rim inside of the hat. The colours are generally black and white only, and these are made into squares, triangles, and sometimes rude figures of canoes and seamen harpooning whales. This is all the usual dress of females; but if the weather be unusually severe, they add a vest formed of skins like the robe, tied behind, without any shoulder-straps to keep it up. As this vest covers the body from the armpits to the waist, it conceals the breasts, but on all other occasions they are suffered to remain loose and exposed, and present, in old women especially, a most disgusting appearance.

Sometimes, though not often, they mark their skins by puncturing and introducing some coloured matter: this ornament is chiefly confined to the women, who imprint on their legs and arms, circular or parallel dots. On the arm of one of the squaws we read the name of J. Bowman, apparently a trader who visits the mouth of the Columbia. The favourite decoration however of both sexes, are the common coarse blue or white beads, which are folded very tightly round their wrists and ankles, to the width of three or four inches, and worn in large loose rolls round the neck, or in the shape of

Captain Clark's sketches of the Clatsop head-flattening process and its consequences (on the same page with a note on the tides at Fort Clatsop).

earrings, or hanging from the nose, which last mode is peculiar to the men. There is also a species of wampum very much in use, which seems to be worn in its natural form without any preparation. Its shape is a cone somewhat curved, about the size of a raven's quill at the base, and tapering to a point, its whole length being from one to two and a half inches, and white, smooth, hard and thin. A small thread is passed through it, and the wampum is either suspended from the nose, or passed through the cartilage horizontally, and forms a ring, from which other ornaments hang. This wampum is employed in the same way as the beads, but is the favourite decoration for the noses of the men. The men also use collars made of bears' claws, the women and children those of elks' tusks, and both sexes are adorned with bracelets of copper, iron, or brass, in various forms.

Yet all these decorations are unavailing to conceal the deformities of nature and the extravagance of fashion; nor have we seen any more disgusting object than a Chinnook or Clatsop beauty in full attire. Their broad flat foreheads, their falling breasts, their ill shaped limbs, the awkwardness of their positions, and the filth which intrudes through their finery; all these render a Chinnook or Clatsop beauty in full attire, one of the most disgusting objects in nature. Fortunately this circumstance conspired with the low diet and laborious exercise of our men, to protect them from the persevering gallantry of the fair sex, whose kindness always exceeded the ordinary courtesies of hospitality. Among these people, as indeed among all Indians, the prostitution of unmarried women is so far from being considered criminal or improper, that the females themselves solicit the favours of the other sex, with the entire approbation of their friends and connections. The person is in fact often the only property of a young female, and is therefore the medium of trade, the return for presents, and the reward for services. In most cases, however, the female is so much at the disposal of her husband or parent, that she is farmed out for hire. The Chinnook woman, who brought her six female relations to our camp, had regular prices, proportioned to the beauty of each female; and among all the tribes, a man will lend his wife or daughter for a fish-hook or a strand of beads. To decline an offer of this sort is indeed to disparage the charms of the lady, and therefore gives such offence, that although we had occasionally to treat the Indians with rigour, nothing seemed to irritate both sexes more than our refusal to accept the favours of the females. On one occasion we were amused by a Clatsop, who having been cured of some disorder by our medical skill, brought his sister as a reward for our kindness. The young lady was quite anxious to join in this expression of her brother's gratitude, and mortified that we did not avail ourselves of it, she could not be prevailed on to leave the fort, but remained with Chaboneau's wife, in the next room to ours, for two or three days, declining all the solicitations of the men, till finding, at last, that we did not relent, she went away, regretting that her brother's obligations were unpaid.

The little intercourse which the men have had with these women is, however, sufficient to apprise us of the prevalence of the venereal disease, with which one or two of the party had been so much afflicted, as to render a salivation necessary. The infection in these cases was communicated by the Chinnook women. The others do not appear to be afflicted with it to any extent: indeed, notwithstanding this disorder is certainly known to the Indians on the Columbia, yet the number of infected persons is very inconsiderable. The existence of such a disorder is very easily detected, particularly in the men, in their open style of dress; yet in the whole route down the Columbia, we have not seen more than two or three cases of gonorrhoea, and about double that number of lues venerea. There does not seem to be any simples which are used as specifics in this disorder, nor is any complete cure ever effected. When once a patient is seized, the disorder ends with his life only;

though from the simplicity of their diet, and the use of certain vegetables, they support it for many years with but little inconvenience, and even enjoy tolerable health; yet their life is always abridged by decrepitude or premature old age. The Indians, who are mostly successful in treating this disorder, are the Chippeways. Their specifics are the root of the lobelia, and that of a species of sumac, common to the United States, the neighbourhood of the Rocky mountains, and to the countries westward, and which is readily distinguished by being the smallest of its kind, and by its winged rib, or common footstalk, supporting leaves oppositely pinnate. Decoctions of the roots are used very freely, without any limitation, and are said to soften the violence of the lues, and even to be sovereign in the cure of the gonorrhoea.

The Clatsops and other nations at the mouth of the Columbia, have visited us with great freedom, and we have endeavoured to cultivate their intimacy, as well for the purpose of acquiring information, as to leave behind us impressions favourable to our country. In their intercourse with us they are very loquacious and inquisitive. Having acquired much of their language, we are enabled with the assistance of gestures, to hold conversations with great ease. We find them inquisitive and loquacious, with understandings by no means deficient in acuteness, and with very retentive memories; and though fond of feasts, and generally cheerful, they are never gay. Every thing they see excites their attention and inquiries, but having been accustomed to see the whites, nothing appeared to give them more astonishment than the air-gun. To all our inquiries they answer with great intelligence, and the conversation rarely slackens, since there is a constant discussion of the events, and trade, and politics, in the little but active circle of Killamucks, Clatsops, Cathlamahs, Wahkiacums, and Chinnooks. Among themselves, the conversation generally turns on the subjects of trade, or smoking, or eating, or connection with females, before whom this last is spoken of with a familiarity which would be in the highest degree indecent, if custom had not rendered it inoffensive.

The treatment of women is often considered as the standard by which the moral qualities of savages are to be estimated. Our own observation, however, induced us to think that the importance of the female in savage life, has no necessary relation to the virtues of the men, but is regulated wholly by their capacity to be useful. The Indians whose treatment of the females is mildest, and who pay most deference to their opinions, are by no means the most distinguished for their virtues; nor is this deference attended by any increase of attachment, since they are equally willing with the most brutal husband, to prostitute their wives to strangers. On the other hand, the tribes among whom the women are very much debased, possess the loftiest sense of honour, the greatest liberality, and all the good qualities of which their situation demands the exercise. Where the women can aid in procuring subsistence for the tribe, they are treated with more equality, and their importance is proportioned to the share which they take in that labour; while in countries where subsistence is chiefly procured by the exertions of the men, the women are considered and treated as burdens. Thus, among the Clatsops and Chinnooks, who live upon fish and roots, which the women are equally expert with the men in procuring, the former have a rank and influence very rarely found among Indians. The females are permitted to speak freely before the men, to whom indeed they sometimes address themselves in a tone of authority. On many subjects their judgments and opinions are respected, and in matters of trade, their advice is generally asked and pursued. The labours of the family too, are shared almost equally. The men collect wood and make fires, assist in cleansing the fish, make the houses, canoes, and wooden utensils; and whenever strangers are to be entertained, or a great feast prepared, the meats are cooked and served up by the men. The peculiar province of the female is to collect roots, and to manufacture the various articles which are formed of rushes, flags, cedar-bark, and bear-grass; but the management of the canoes, and many of the occupations, which elsewhere devolves wholly on the female, are here common to both sexes.

The observation with regard to the importance of females, applies with equal force to the treatment of old men. Among tribes who subsist by hunting, the labours of the chase, and the wandering existence to which that occupation condemns them, necessarily throws the burden of procuring provisions on the active young men. As soon, therefore, as a man is unable to pursue the chase, he begins to withdraw something from the precarious supplies of the tribe. Still, however, his counsels may compensate his want of activity; but in the next stage of infirmity, when he can no longer travel from camp to camp, as the tribe roams about for subsistence, he is then found to be a heavy burden. In this situation they are abandoned among the Sioux, Assiniboins, and the hunting tribes on the Missouri. As they are setting out for some new excursion, where the old man is unable to follow, his children, or nearest relations, place before him a piece of meat and some water, and telling him that he has lived long enough, that it is now time for him to go home to his relations, who could take better care of him than his friends on earth, leave him, without remorse, to perish, when his little supply is exhausted. The same custom is said to prevail among the Minnetarees, Ahnahawas, and Ricaras, when they are attended by old men on their hunting excursions. Yet, in their villages, we saw no want of kindness to old men. On the contrary, probably because in villages, the means of more abundant subsistence renders such cruelty unnecessary, the old people appeared to be treated with attention, and some of their feasts, particularly the buffalo dances, were intended chiefly as a contribution for the old and infirm.

The dispositions of these people seem mild and inoffensive, and they have uniformly behaved to us with great friendship. They are addicted to begging and pilfering small articles, when it can be done without danger of detection, but do not rob wantonly, nor to any large amount; and some of them having purloined some of our meat, which the hunters had been obliged to leave in the woods, they voluntarily brought some dogs a few days after, by way of compensation. Our force and great superiority in the use of firearms, enable us always to command, and such is the friendly deportment of these people, that the men have been accustomed to treat them with the greatest confidence. It is therefore with difficulty that we can impress on our men a conviction of the necessity of being always on our guard, since we are perfectly acquainted with the treacherous character of Indians in general. We are always prepared for an attack, and uniformly exclude all large parties of Indians from the fort.

Their large houses usually contain several families, consisting of the parents, their sons and daughters-in-law, and grandchildren, among whom the provisions are common, and whose harmony is scarcely ever interrupted by disputes. Although polygamy is permitted by their customs, very few have more than a single wife, and she is brought immediately after the marriage into the husband's family, where she resides until increasing numbers oblige them to seek another house. In this state the old man is not considered as the head of the family, since the active duties, as well as the responsibility, fall on some of the younger members. As these families gradually expand into bands or tribes or nations, the paternal authority is represented by the chief of each association. This chieftain however is not hereditary; his ability to render service to his neighbours, and the popularity which follows it, is at once the foundation and the measure of his authority, the exercise of which does not extend beyond a reprimand for some improper action.

The harmony of their private life is indeed secured by their ignorance of spirituous liquors, the earliest and most dreadful present which civilisation has given to the other natives of the continent. Although they have had so much intercourse with whites, they do not appear to possess any knowledge of those dangerous luxuries; at least they have never inquired after them; which they probably would have done if once they had been introduced among them. Indeed we have not observed any liquor of an intoxicating quality used among these or any Indians west of the Rocky mountains, the universal beverage being pure water. They however sometimes almost intoxicate themselves by smoking tobacco of which they are excessively fond, and the pleasures of which they prolong as much as possible, by retaining vast quantities at a time, till after circulating through the lungs and stomach it issues in volumes from the mouth and nostrils.

But the natural vice of all these people is an attachment for games of hazard which they pursue with a strange and ruinous avidity. The games are of two kinds. In the first, one of the company assumes the office of banker, and plays against the rest. He takes a small stone, about the size of a bean, which he shifts from one hand to the other with great dexterity, repeating at the same time a song adapted to the game, and which serves to divert the attention of the company, till having agreed on the stake, he holds out his hands, and the antagonist wins or loses as he succeeds or fails at guessing in which hand the stone is. After the banker has lost his money, or whenever he is tired, the stone is transferred to another, who in turn challenges the rest of the company. The other game is something like the play of ninepins; two pins are placed on the floor, about the distance of a foot from each other, and a small hole made behind them. The players then go about ten feet from the hole, into which they try to roll a small piece resembling the men used at draughts; if they succeed in putting it into the hole, they win the stake; if the piece rolls between the pins, but does not go into the hole, nothing is won or lost; but the wager is wholly lost if the chequer rolls outside of the pins. Entire days are wasted at these games, which are often continued through the night round the blaze of their fires, till the last article of clothing or even the last blue bead is won from the desperate adventurer.

In traffic they are keen, acute and intelligent, and they employ in all their bargains a dexterity and finesse, which, if it be not learnt from their foreign visitors, may show how nearly the cunning of savages is allied to the little arts of more civilised trade. They begin by asking double or treble the value of their merchandise, and lower the demand in proportion to the ardour or experience in trade of the purchaser; and if he expresses any anxiety, the smallest article, perhaps a handful of roots, will furnish a whole morning's negotiation. Being naturally suspicious, they of course conceive that you are pursuing the same system. They, therefore, invariably refuse the first offer, however high, fearful that they or we have mistaken the value of the merchandise, and therefore cautiously wait to draw us on to larger offers. In this way, after rejecting the most extravagant prices, which we have offered merely for experiment, they have afterwards importuned us for a tenth part of what they had before refused. In this respect, they differ from almost all Indians, who will generally exchange in a thoughtless moment the most valuable article they possess, for any bauble which happens to please their fancy.

These habits of cunning, or prudence, have been formed or increased by their being engaged in a large part of the commerce of the Columbia; of that trade, however, the great emporium is the falls, where all the neighbouring nations assemble. The inhabitants of the Columbian plains, after having passed the winter near the mountains, come down as soon as the snow has left the valleys, and are occupied in collecting and drying roots, till about the month of May. They then crowd to the river, and fixing themselves on its north side, to avoid the incursions of the Snake Indians, continue fishing, till about the first of September, when the salmon are no longer fit for use. They then bury their fish and return to the plains, where they remain gathering quamash, till the snow obliges them to desist. They come back to the Columbia, and taking their store of fish, retire to the foot of the mountains, and along the creeks, which supply timber for houses, and pass the winter in hunting deer or elk, which, with the aid of their fish, enables them to subsist till in the spring they resume the circle of their employments. During their residence on the river, from May to September, or rather before they begin the regular fishery, they go down to the falls, carrying with them skins, mats, silk grass, rushes, and chappelell bread. They are here overtaken by the Chopunnish, and other tribes of the Rocky mountains, who descend the Kooskooskee and Lewis's river for the purpose of selling bear-grass, horses, quamash, and a few skins which they have obtained by hunting, or in exchange for horses, with the Tushepaws.

At the falls, they find the Chilluckittequaws, Eneeshurs, Echeloots, and Skilloots, which last serve as intermediate traders or carriers between the inhabitants above and below the falls. These tribes prepare pounded fish for the market, and the nations below bring wappatoo roots, the fish of the seacoast, berries, and a variety of trinkets and small articles which they have procured from the whites.

The trade then begins. The Chopunnish, and Indians of the Rocky mountains, exchange the articles which they have brought for wappatoo, pounded fish, and beads. The Indians of the plains being their own fishermen, take only wappatoo, horses, beads, and other articles, procured from Europeans. The Indians, however, from Lewis's river to the falls, consume as food or fuel all the fish which they take; so that the whole stock for exportation is prepared by the nations between the Towahnahiooks and the falls, and amounts, as nearly as we could estimate, to about thirty thousand weight, chiefly salmon, above the quantity which they use themselves, or barter with the more eastern Indians. This is now carried down the river by the Indians at the falls, and is consumed among the nations at the mouth of the Columbia, who in return give the fish of the seacoast, and the articles which they obtain from the whites. The neighbouring people catch large quantities of salmon and dry them, but they do not understand or practise the art of drying and pounding it in the manner used at the falls, and being very fond of it, are forced to purchase it at high prices. This article, indeed, and the wappatoo, form the principal subjects of trade with the people of our immediate vicinity. The traffic is wholly carried on by water; there are even no roads or paths through the country, except across the portages which connect the creeks.

But the circumstance which forms the soul of this trade, is the visit of the whites. They arrive generally about the month of April, and either remain until October, or return at that time; during which time, having no establishment on shore, they anchor on the north side of the bay, at the place already described, which is a spacious and commodious harbour, perfectly secure from all except the south and southeast winds; and as they leave it before winter, they do not suffer from these winds, which, during that season, are the most usual and the most violent. This situation is recommended by its neighbourhood to fresh water and wood, as well as to excellent timber for repairs. Here they are immediately visited by the tribes along the seacoast, by the Cathlamahs, and lastly by the Skilloots, that numerous and active people, who skirt the river between the marshy islands and the grand rapids, as well as the Coweliskee, and who carry down the fish prepared by their immediate neighbours the Chilluckittequaws, Eneeshurs, and Echeloots, residing from the grand rapids to the falls, as well as all the articles which they have procured in barter at the market in May. The accumulated trade of the Columbia now consists of dressed and undressed skins of elk, sea-otter, the common otter, beaver, common fox, spuck, and tiger cat. The articles of less importance, are a small quantity of dried or pounded salmon, the biscuits made of the chapelell roots, and some of the manufactures of the neighbourhood.

In return they receive guns (which are principally old British or American muskets), powder, ball and shot, copper and brass kettles, brass tea-kettles, and coffee-pots, blankets, from two to three points, coarse scarlet and blue cloth, plates and strips of sheet copper and brass, large brass wire, knives, tobacco, fish-hooks, buttons, and a considerable quantity of sailors' hats, trousers, coats and shirts. But as we have had occasion to remark more than once, the object of foreign trade which is the most desired, are the common cheap, blue or white beads, of about fifty or seventy to the pennyweight, which are strung on strands a fathom in length, and sold by the yard, or the length of both arms: of these blue beads, which are called tia commashuck, or chief beads, hold the first rank in their ideas of relative value: the most inferior kind, are esteemed beyond the finest wampum, and are temptations which can always seduce them to part with their most valuable effects. Indeed, if the example of civilised life did not completely vindicate their choice, we might wonder at their infatuated attachment to a bauble in itself so worthless. Yet these beads are, perhaps, quite as reasonable objects of research as the precious metals, since they are at once beautiful ornaments for the person, and the great circulating medium of trade with all the nations on the Columbia.

These strangers who visit the Columbia for the purpose of trade or hunting, must be either English or Americans. The Indians inform us that they speak the same language as we do, and indeed the few words which the Indians have learnt from the sailors, such as musket, powder, shot, knife, file, heave the lead, damned rascal, and other phrases of that description, evidently show that the visitors speak the English language. But as the greater part of them annually arrive in April, and either remain till autumn, or revisit them at that time, which we could not clearly understand, the trade cannot be direct from either England or the United States, since the ships could not return thither during the remainder of the year. When the Indians are asked where these traders go on leaving the Columbia, they always point to the southwest, whence we presume that they do not belong to any establishment at Nootka Sound. They do, however, mention a trader by the name of Moore, who sometimes touches at this place, and the last time he came, he had on board three cows; and when he left them, continued along the northwest coast, which renders it probable, that there may be a settlement of whites in that direction. The names and description of all these persons who visit them in the spring and autumn are remembered with great accuracy, and we took down, exactly as they were pronounced, the following list:

The favourite trader is Mr. Haley, who visits them in a vessel with three masts, and continues some time. The others are Youens, who comes also in a three masted vessel, and is a trader; Tallamon, in a three-masted vessel, but he is not a trader; Callalamet in a ship of the same size; he is a trader, and they say has a wooden leg;

Swipton	three-masted vessel,	trader
Moore	four- do.	do.
Mackey	three- do.	do.
Washington	three- do.	do.
Mesship	three- do.	do.
Davidson	three- do.	does not trade, but hunts elk
Jackson	three- do.	trader
Bolch	three- do.	do.

Skelley, also a trader, in a vessel with three masts, but he has been gone for some years. He had only one eye.

It might be difficult to adjust the balance of the advantages or the dangers of this trade to the nations of the Columbia, against the sale of their furs, and the acquisition of a few bad guns and household utensils.

The nations near the mouth of the Columbia enjoy great tranquillity; none of the tribes being engaged in war. Not long since, however, there was a war on the coast to the southwest, in which the Killamucks took several prisoners. These, as far as we could perceive, were treated very well, and though nominally slaves, yet were adopted into the families of their masters, and the young ones placed on the same footing with the children of the purchaser.

February and March, 1806

The month of February and the greater part of March were passed in the same manner. Every day, parties as large as we could spare them from our other occupations were sent out to hunt, and we were thus enabled to command some days' provision in advance. It consisted chiefly of deer and elk; the first is very lean, and the flesh by no means as good as that of the elk, which, though poor, is getting better: it is indeed our chief dependence. At this time of the year it is in much better order in the prairies near the point, where they feed on grass and rushes, considerable quantities of which are yet green, than in the woody country up the Netul. There, they subsist on huckleberry bushes and fern, but chiefly on evergreen, called shallun, resembling the laurel, which abounds through all the timbered lands, particularly along the broken sides of hills. Toward the latter end of the month [*February*], however, they left the prairies near Point Adams, and retired back to the hills; but fortunately, at the same time the sturgeon and anchovies began to appear, and afforded us a delightful variety of food. In the mean time, the party on the seacoast supplied us with salt: but though the kettles were kept boiling all day and night, the salt was made but slowly; nor was it till the middle of this month that we succeeded in procuring twenty gallons, of which twelve were put in kegs for our journey as far as the deposits on the Missouri.

The neighbouring tribes continued to visit us, for the purpose of trading, or merely to smoke with us. But on the *21st*, a Chinnook chief, whom we had never seen, came over with twenty-five of his men. His name was Tahcum, a man of about fifty years of age, with a larger figure and a better carriage than most of his nation. We received him with the usual ceremonies, gave the party something to eat, smoked most copiously with them all, and presented the chief with a small medal. They were all satisfied with their treatment; and though we were willing to show the chief every civility, could not dispense with our rule of not suffering so many strangers to sleep in the fort. They, therefore, left us at sunset. On the *24th*, Comowool, who is by far the most friendly and decent savage we have seen in this neighbourhood, came with a large party of Clatsops, bringing among other articles, sturgeon and a small fish, which has just begun, within a day or two past, to make their appearance in the Columbia.

From this time, as the elk became scarce and lean, we made use of these fish whenever we could catch them, or purchase them from the Indians. But as we were too poor to indulge very largely in these luxuries, the diet was by no means pleasant, and to the sick, especially, was unwholesome. On the *15th of March* we were visited by Delashilwilt, the Chinnook chief, and his wife, accompanied by the same six damsels, who in the autumn had encamped near us, on the other side of the bay, and whose favours had been so troublesome to several of the men. They formed a camp close to the fort, and began to renew their addresses very assiduously, but we warned the men of the dangers of intercourse with this frail society, and they cautiously abstained from connection with them.

During the greater part of this month, five or six of the men were sick; indeed, we have not had so many complaining since we left Wood river; the general complaint is a bad cold and fever, something in the nature of an influenza, which, joined with a few cases of venereal, and accidental injuries, complete our invalid corps. These disorders may chiefly be imputed to the nature of the climate.

VEGETABLE PRODUCE   The vegetable productions of the country, which furnish a large proportion of the food of the Indians, are the roots of a species of thistle, the fern, the rush, the liquorice, and a small cylindric root, resembling in flavour and consistency the sweet potato.

Chapter 24

BOTANY AND ZOOLOGY

1st. The thistle, called by the natives shanataque, is a plant which grows in a deep, rich, dry loam, with a considerable mixture of sand. The stem is simple, ascending, cylindric, and hispid, and rising to the height of three or four feet. The cauline leaf, which, as well as the stem of the last season is dead, is simple, crenate, and oblong; rather more obtuse at its apex than at its insertion, which is decurrent, and its position declining; whilst the margin is armed with prickles, and its disc is hairy. The flower too is dry and mutilated; but the pericarp seems much like that of the common thistle. The root-leaves, which still possess their verdure, and are about half grown, are of a pale green colour. The root, however, is the only part used. It is from nine to fifteen inches long, about the size of a man's thumb, perpendicular, fusiform, and with from two to four radicles. The rind is of a brown colour, and somewhat rough. When first taken from the earth, it is white, and nearly as crisp as a carrot, and in this state is sometimes eaten without any preparation. But after it is prepared by the same process used for the pasheco quamash, which is the most usual and the best method, it becomes black, and much improved in flavour. Its taste is exactly that of sugar, and it is indeed the sweetest vegetable employed by the Indians. After being baked in the kiln, it is either eaten simply or with train oil; sometimes pounded fine and mixed with cold water, until it is reduced to the consistence of sagamity, or Indian mush, which last method is the most agreeable to our palates.

2. Three species of fern grow in this neighbourhood, but the root of only one is eaten. It is very abundant in those parts of the open lands and prairies which have a deep, loose, rich, black loam, without any sand. There, it attains the height of four or five feet, and is a beautiful plant with a fine green colour in summer. The stem, which is smooth, cylindric, and slightly grooved on one side, rises erectly about half its height, when it divides into two branches, or rather long footstalks, which put forth in pairs from one side only, and near the edges of the groove, declining backwards from the grooved side. These footstalks are themselves grooved and cylindric, and as they gradually taper toward the extremities, put forth others of a smaller size, which are alternate, and have forty or fifty alternate, pinnate, horizontal, and sessile leaves: the leaves are multipartite for half the length of their footstalk, when they assume the tongue-like form altogether; being, moreover, revolute, with the upper disc smooth, and the lower resembling cotton: the top is annual, and therefore dead at present, but it produces no flower or fruit: the root itself is perennial and grows horizontally; sometimes a little diverging, or obliquely descending, and frequently dividing itself as it proceeds, and shooting up a number of stems. It lies about four inches under the surface of the earth, in a cylindrical form, with few or no radicles, and varies from the size of a goose quill to that of a man's finger. The bark is black, thin, brittle, and rather rough, and easily separates in flakes from the part which is eaten: the centre is divided into two parts by a strong, flat, and white ligament, like a piece of thin tape; on each side of which is a white substance, resembling, after the root is roasted, both in ap-

379

pearance and flavour, the dough of wheat. It has, however, a pungency which is disagreeable, but the natives eat it voraciously, and it seems to be very nutritious.

3. The [horsetail] rush is most commonly used by the Killamucks, and other Indians on the seacoast, along the sands of which it grows in greatest abundance. From each root a single stem rises erectly to the height of three or four feet, somewhat thicker than a large quill, hollow and jointed; about twenty or thirty long, lineal, stellate, or radiate and horizontal leaves surround the stem at each joint, about half an inch above which, its stem is sheathed like the sand rush. When green, it resembles that plant also in appearance, as well as in having a rough stem. It is not branching; nor does it bear, as far as we can discover, either flower or seed. At the bottom of this stem, which is annual, is a small, strong radicle, about an inch long, descending perpendicularly to the root, while just above the junction of the radicle with the stem, the latter is surrounded in the form of a wheel, with six or nine small radicles, descending obliquely: the root attached to this radicle is a perennial solid bulb, about an inch long, and of the thickness of a man's thumb, of an ovate form, depressed on one or two of its sides, and covered with a thin, smooth, black rind: the pulp is white, brittle, and easily masticated. It is commonly roasted, though sometimes eaten raw; but in both states is rather an insipid root.

4. The liquorice of this country does not differ from that common to the United States. It here delights in a deep, loose, sandy soil, and grows very large, and abundantly. It is prepared by roasting in the embers, and pounding it slightly with a small stick, in order to separate the strong ligament in the centre of the root, which is then thrown away, and the rest chewed and swallowed. In this way it has an agreeable flavour, not unlike that of the sweet potato. The root of the cattail, or cooper's flag, is eaten by the Indians. There is also, a species of small, dry, tuberous root, two inches in length, and about the thickness of the finger. They are eaten raw, are crisp, milky, and of an agreeable flavour.

5. Beside the small cylindric root mentioned above, is another of the same form and appearance, which is usually boiled and eaten with train oil. Its taste, however, is disagreeably bitter. But the most valuable of all the Indian roots, is:

6. The wappatoo, or the bulb of the common sagittafolia, or common arrowhead. It does not grow in this neighbourhood, but is in great abundance in the marshy grounds of that beautiful valley, which extends from near Quicksand river for seventy miles westward, and is a principal article of trade between the inhabitants of that valley and those of the seacoast.

The shrub rises to the height of four or five feet; the stem simple and much branched. The bark is of a reddish dark brown; the main stem somewhat rough, while that of the bough is smooth; the leaf is about one-tenth of an inch long, obtuse at the apex, and acute and angular at the insertion of the pedicle. The leaf is three fourths of an inch in length, and three eighths in width, smooth, and of a paler green than evergreens generally are. The fruit is a small deep purple berry, and of a pleasant flavour; the natives eat the berry when ripe, but seldom collect such quantities as to dry for winter use.

The native fruits and berries in use among the Indians, are what they call **FRUITS AND** the shallun; the solme; the cranberry; a berry like the black haw; the scarlet **BERRIES** berry, of the plant called sacacommis; a purple berry, like the huckleberry.

1. The shallun is an evergreen plant, abounding in this neighbourhood, and its leaves are the favourite food of the elk. It is a thick growth, cylindrically rising to the height of three, and sometimes five feet, and varying from the size of a goose quill, to that of a man's thumb. The stem is simple, branching, reclining, and partially fluxuose, with a bark which, on the elder part, is of a reddish brown colour, while the younger branches are red where exposed to the sun, and green elsewhere. The leaf is three fourths of an inch in length, and two and a half in breadth; of an oval form; the upper disc of a glossy deep green, the under of a pale green; the fruit is a deep purple berry, about the size of a common black cherry, oval, and rather bluntly pointed; the pericarp is divided into five acute angular points, and envelops a soft pulp, containing a great number of small brown seeds.

2. The solme is a small, pale, red berry, the production of a plant, resembling in size and shape that which produces the fruit, called in the United States, Solomon's seal-berry. The berry is attached to the stem in the same manner. It is of a globular form; containing a soft pulp, which envelops four seeds about the size of the seed of the common small grape. It grows amongst the woodland moss, and is, to all appearance, an annual plant.

3. The cranberry is of the low and viny kind, and grows in the marshes or bogs of this neighbourhood: it is precisely the same as the cranberry of the United States.

4. The fruit which, though rather larger, resembles the black haw, is a light brown berry, the fruit of a tree about the size, shape, and appearance in every respect, of that of the United States, called the wild crab-apple. The leaf is also precisely the same, as also the bark in texture and colour. The berries grow in clumps at the end of the small branches; each berry supported by a separate stem, and as many as from three to eighteen or twenty in a clump: the berry is ovate, with one of its extremities attached to a peduncle, where it is to a small degree concave, the wood of which is excessively hard. The natives make their wedges of this wood, in splitting their boards, their firewood, and in hollowing out their canoes; the wedge when driven into solid dry pine, receives not the slightest injury. Our party made use of it likewise for wedges and axe-handles. The fruit is exceedingly acid, and resembles the flavour of the wild crab. The pericarp of the berry contains a soft pulpy substance, divided into four cells, each containing a single seed; the outer coat of the pericarp, is a thin smooth though firm and tough pellicle.

5. The plant [bearberry], called sacacommis by the Canadian traders derives its name from this circumstance: that the clerks of the trading companies are generally very fond of smoking its leaves, which they carry about with them in a small bag. It grows generally in an open piny woodland country, or on its borders. We found this berry in the prairies bordering on the Rocky mountains, or in the more open woodlands. It is indiscriminately the growth of a very rich or a very poor soil, and is found in the same abundance in both. The natives on the western side of the Rocky mountains are very fond of this berry, although to us it was a very tasteless and insipid fruit: the shrub is an evergreen, and retains its verdure in the same perfection the whole season round. However inclement the climate, the root puts forth a great number of stems which separate near the surface of the ground, each stem from the size of a small quill to that of a man's finger: these are much branched, the branches forming an acute angle with the stem, and all more properly procumbent than creeping: although it sometimes puts forth radicles from the stems and branches, which strike obliquely into the ground: these radicles are by no means general or equable in their distances from each other, nor do they appear calculated to furnish nutriment to the plant: the bark is formed of several layers of a smooth, thin, brittle and reddish substance easily separated from the stem: the leaves with respect to their position are scattered, yet closely arranged, and particularly near the extremities of the twigs: the leaf is about three-fourths of an inch in length; oval, pointed and obtuse; of a deep green, slightly grooved; and the footstalk is of proportionable length: the berry is attached in an irregular manner to the small boughs among the leaves, and always supported by separate, small and short peduncles: the insertion produces a slight concavity in the berry, while its opposite side is slightly convex. The outer coat of the pericarp is a thin, firm, tough pellicle: the inner coat consists of a dry, mealy powder, of a yellowish white colour, enveloping from four to six large, light, brown seeds: the colour of the fruit is a fine scarlet: the natives eat these berries without any preparation: the fruit ripens in September, and remains on the bushes all winter unaffected by the frost: they are sometimes gathered and hung in the lodges in bags, where they are dried without further trouble.

6. The deep purple berry, like the huckleberry, terminates bluntly, and has a cap or cover at the end: the berries are attached separately to the sides of the boughs by a short stem, hanging underneath and they often grow very near each other, on the same bough: the berry separates very easily from the stem; the leaves adhere closely: the shrub rises to the height of six or eight feet, and sometimes grows on high lands, but more frequently on low marshy grounds: the shrub is an evergreen, and about ten inches in circumference, divides into many irregular branches, and seldom more than one stem springs from one root, although they associate very thickly: the bark is somewhat rough and of a reddish brown colour: the wood is very hard: the leaves are alternate and attached by a short footstalk to the horizontal sides of the boughs: the form is a long oval, rather more acute towards the apex than at the point of insertion: its margin slightly serrate, its sides collapsing, thick, firm, smooth and glossy: the under surface is of a pale or whitish green, and the upper of a fine deep green. This beautiful shrub retains its verdure throughout the year, and is more peculiarly beautiful in winter. The natives sometimes eat the berries without preparation: sometimes they dry them in the sun, and at others in their sweating kilns: they very frequently pound them, and bake them in large loaves, weighing from ten to fifteen pounds: the bread keeps very well for one season, and retains its juices better by this mode of preparation than any other: this bread when broken is stirred in cold water, until it acquires the consistency of soup, and then eaten.

The trees of a larger growth are very abundant; the whole neighbourhood of the coast is supplied with great quantities of excellent timber. The predominating growth is the fir, of which we have seen several species. There is one singular circumstance attending all the pine of this country, which is, that when consumed it yields not the slightest particle of ashes.

The *first* species grows to an immense size, and is very commonly twenty-seven feet in circumference six feet above the earth's surface: they rise to the height of two hundred and thirty feet, and one hundred and twenty of that height without a limb. We have often found them thirty-six feet in circumference. One of our party measured one, and found it to be forty-two feet in circumference, at a point beyond the reach of an ordinary man. This trunk for the distance of two hundred feet was destitute of limbs: this tree was perfectly sound, and at a moderate calculation, its size may be estimated at three hundred feet. The timber is [sound] throughout, and rives better than any other species; the bark scales off in flakes irregularly round, and of a reddish brown colour, particularly the younger growth: the trunk is simple, branching, and not very proliferous. The leaf is acerose, one tenth of an inch in width, and three fourths in length, firm, stiff, and acuminate. It is triangular, a little declining, thickly scattered on all sides of the bough, and springs from small triangular pedestals of soft, spongy, elastic bark at the junction of the boughs. The bud scales continue to encircle their respective twigs for several years. Captain Lewis has counted as many as the growth of four years beyond their scales; it yields but little resin, and we have never been able to discover the cone, although we have killed several.

The *second* [hemlock-spruce] is a much more common species, and constitutes at least one half of the timber in this neighbourhood. It seems to resemble the spruce, rising from one hundred and sixty to one hundred and eighty feet, and is from four to six in diameter, straight, round, and regularly tapering. The bark is thin, of a dark colour, much divided in small longitudinal interstices: the bark of the boughs and young trees is somewhat smooth, but not equal to the balsam fir: the wood is white, very soft, but difficult to rive: the trunk is a simple, branching, and diffuse stem, not so proliferous as the pines and firs usually are. It puts forth buds from the sides of the small boughs, as well as from their extremities: the stem terminates like the cedar, in a slender pointed top: the leaves are petiolate, the footstalks short, acerose, rather more than half a line in width, and very unequal in length; the greatest length seldom exceeds one inch, while other leaves intermixed on every part of the bough, do not exceed a quarter of an inch. The leaf has a small longitudinal channel on the upper disc, which is of a deep and glossy green, while the under disc is of a whitish green only: it yields but little resin. What is remarkable, the cane is not longer than the end of a man's thumb, it is soft, flexible, of an ovate form, and produced at the ends of the small twigs.

The *third* species resembles in all points, the Canadian balsam fir. It grows from two and a half to four feet in diameter, and rises to the height of eighty or an hundred feet. The stem is simple, branching, and proliferous: its leaves are sessile, acerose, one eighth of an inch in length, and one sixteenth in width, thickly scattered on the twigs, and adhere to the three under sides only; gibbous, a little declining, obtusely pointed, soft, and flexible. The upper disc is longitudinally marked with a slight channel, of a deep glossy-green; the under of a pale green and not glossy. This tree affords in considerable quantities, a fine deep aromatic balsam, resembling the balsam of Canada in taste and appearance. The small pistils filled, rise like a blister on the trunk and the branches. The bark that envelops these pistils, is soft and easily punctured: the general appearance of the bark is dark and smooth; but not so remarkable for that quality as the white pine of our country. The wood is white and soft.

The *fourth* species in size resembles the second. The stem is simple, branching, ascending, and proliferous; the bark is of a reddish dark brown, and thicker than that of the third species, divided by small longitudinal interstices, not so much magnified as in the second species. The relative position of the leaves resembles those of the balsam fir, excepting that they are only two thirds the width, and little more than half the length, and that the upper disc is not so green and glossy. The wood yields no balsam, and but little resin. The wood is white and tough although rather porous.

The *fifth* species [Douglas fir] in size resembles the second, and has a trunk simple, branching, and proliferous. The bark is of a thin dark brown, divided longitudinally by interstices, and scaling off in thin rolling flakes. It yields but little balsam: two-thirds of the diameter of the trunk in the centre, presents a reddish white; the remainder is white, porous, and tough: the twigs are much longer and more slender than in either of the other species; the leaves are acerose, one-twentieth of an inch in width, and one inch in length; sextile, inserted on all sides of the bough, straight, and obliquely pointing towards the extremities. The upper disc has a small longitudinal channel, and is of a deep green, and not so glossy as the balsam fir. The under disc is of a pale green.

We have seen a species of this fir on low marshy grounds, resembling in all points the foregoing, except that it branches more diffusively. This tree is generally thirty feet in height, and two in diameter. The diffusion of its branches may result from its open situation, as it seldom grows in the neighbourhood of another tree. The cone is two and a half inches in length, and three and three-quarters in its greatest circumference. It tapers regularly to a point, and is formed of the imbricated scales, of a bluntly rounded form. A thin leaf is inserted in the pith of the cone, which overlays the centre of, and extends half an inch beyond the point of each scale.

The *sixth* species [giant white pine] does not differ from what is usually denominated the white pine in Virginia. The unusual length of the cone seems to constitute the only difference. It is sometimes sixteen or eighteen inches in length, and is about four in circumference. It grows on the north side of the Columbia, near the ocean.

The *seventh* and last species [spruce] grows in low grounds, and in places frequently overflown by the tide, seldom rising higher than thirty-five feet, and not more than from two and a half to four in diameter: the stem is simple, branching and proliferous: the bark resembles that of the first species, but more rugged: the leaves are acerose, two-tenths of an inch in width, three-fourths in length, firm, stiff, and a little acuminated: they end in short pointed tendrils, gibbous, and thickly scattered on all sides of the branch, though they adhere to the three under sides only: those inserted on the under side incline sidewise, with upward points, presenting the leaf in the shape of a scythe: the others are pointing upwards, sextile and like those of the first species, grow from the small triangular pedestals, of a bark, spongy, soft and elastic. The under disc is of a deep glossy green, the other of a pale whitish green: the boughs retain the leaves of a six years' growth: the bud scales resemble those of the first species: the cone is of an ovate figure, three and a half inches in length, and three in circumference, thickest in the middle, and tapering and terminating in two obtuse points: it is composed of small, flexible scales, imbricated, and of a reddish brown colour. Each of these scales covers two small seeds, and is itself covered in the centre by a small, thin, inferior scale, acutely pointed: these scales proceed from the sides of the bough, as well as from its extremities. It was nowhere seen above the Wappatoo.

The stem of the black alder arrives to a great size. It is simple, branching, and diffuse: the bark is smooth, of a light colour, with white spreading spots, resembling those of the beech: the leaf, fructification, &c. resemble precisely those of the common alder of our country: the shrubs grow separately from different roots, and not in clusters, like those of the United States. The black alder does not cast its leaf until the first of December. It is sometimes found growing to the height of sixty or seventy feet, and is from two to four in diameter.

There is a tree [broad-leaf maple] common to the Columbia river, below the entrance of Cataract river, when divested of its foliage, much resembling the ash. The trunk is simple, branching, and diffuse: the leaf is petiolate, plain, divided by four deep lines, and resembling those of the palm, and considerably lobate: the lobes terminate in from three to five angular points, and their margins are indented with irregular and somewhat circular incisures: the petiolate is cylindrical, smooth, and seven inches long; the leaf itself eight inches in length, and twelve in breadth: this tree is frequently three feet in diameter, and rises from forty to fifty feet: the fruit is a winged seed, somewhat resembling that of the maple.

In the same part of the country there is also another growth [vine maple], resembling the white maple, though much smaller, and is seldom to be seen of more than six or seven inches in diameter. These trees grow in clusters, from fifteen to twenty feet in height, from the same bed of roots, spreading, and leaning outwards: the twigs are long and slender, the stem simple and branching, the bark, in colour, resembling the white maple, the leaf is petiolate, plain, scattered, nearly circular, with acute, angular incisures round the margin, of an inch in length, and from six to eight in number: the acute angular points so formed, are crenate, three inches in length and four in width; the petiole is cylindric, smooth, and an inch and a quarter in length, and the fruit is not known.

The undergrowth consists of honeysuckles, elder, seven bark or nine bark, huckleberry, a shrub like the quillwood, a plant like the mountain-holly, a green briar, the fern. SHRUBS

1. The honeysuckle common to the United States we found in this neighbourhood. We first discovered the honeysuckle on the waters of the Kooskooskee, near the Chopunnish nation; also below the grand rapids.

2. The elder which is also common to our country, was found in great abundance in the woodlands, on this side of the Rocky mountains. It

differs in the colour of its berry: this being of a pale sky blue, while that of the United States is of a deep purple.

3. The seven bark, or, as it is usually denominated, the nine bark of the United States, is also common to this country.

4. The huckleberry. There is a species of huckleberry, common to the highlands, from the commencement of the Columbian valley to the sea-coast, rising to the height of six or eight feet, branching and diffuse: the trunk is cylindrical, of a dark brown colour; the collateral branches are green, smooth, and square, and put forth a number of alternate branches of the same colour, and from the two horizontal sides only. The fruit is a small deep purple berry, held in much esteem by the natives: the leaf is of a pale green, and small, three-fourths of an inch in length, and three-eighths in width, oval, terminating more acutely at the apex than at the insertion of the footstalk: the base is nearly entire, and but slightly serrate: the footstalks are short; their relative position is alternate, two-ranked, and proceeding from the horizontal sides of the boughs only.

5. There are two species of shrubs, first seen at the grand rapids of the Columbia, and which have since been seen elsewhere; they grow in rich dry grounds, usually in the neighbourhood of some water course: the roots are creeping and cylindrical. The stem of the first species is from a foot to eighteen inches in height, and about as large as an ordinary goose quill: it is simple, unbranched, and erect: its leaves are cauline, compound and spreading: the leaflets are jointed, and oppositely pinnate, three pair, and terminating in one sextile, widest at the base, and tapering to an acuminate point: it is an inch and a quarter in its greatest width, and three inches and a quarter in length: each point of the margin is armed with a subulate thorn, and from thirteen to seventeen in number: are veined, glossy, carinated and wrinkled: their points obliquely tending towards the extremity of the common footstalk.

The stem of the second species is procumbent, about the size of that of the first species, jointed and unbranched: its leaves are cauline, compound, and oppositely pinnate: the rib is from fourteen to sixteen inches in length, cylindric and smooth: the leaflets are two inches and a half long, and one inch wide, and of the greatest width half an inch from the base: this they regularly surround, and from the same point tapering to an acute apex: this is usually terminated with a small subulate thorn: they are jointed and oppositely pinnate, consisting of six pair, and terminating in one: sessile, serrate, and ending in a small subulate spire, from twenty-five to twenty-seven in number: they are smooth, plain, and of a deep green, and all obliquely tending towards the extremity of the footstalk: they retain their green all winter.

The large-leafed thorn, has a leaf about two inches and a half long, which is petiolate, and conjugate: the leaflets are petiolate, acutely pointed, having their margins cut with unequal and irregular incisures: the shrub, which we had once mistaken for the large-leafed thorn, resembled the stem of that shrub, excepting the thorn: it bears a large three-headed leaf.

6. The briar is of the class Polyandria, and order Polygynia: the flowers are single: the peduncle long and cylindrical: the calyx is a perianth, of one leaf, five cleft, and acutely pointed: the perianth is proper, erect, inferior in both petals, and germen [ovary]; the corolla consists of five acute, pale scarlet petals, inserted in the receptacle with a short and narrow cleft: the corolla is smooth, moderately long, situated at the base of the germen, permanent, and in shape resembling a cup: the stamens and filaments are subulate, inserted into the receptacle, unequal and bent inwards, concealing the pystilium [pistils]; the anther is two-lobed and inflated, situated on the top of the filament of the pystilium: the germ is conical, imbricated, superior, sessile and short: the styles are short, compared with the stamen, capillary smooth and obtuse: they are distributed over the surface of the germ, and deciduous without any perceptible stamen.

7. The green-briar grows most abundantly in rich dry lands, in the vicinity of a water course, and is found in small quantities in piny lands at a distance from the water. In the former situation the stem is frequently of the size of a man's finger, and rises perpendicularly four or five feet: it then descends in an arch, becomes procumbent, or rests on some neighbouring plants: it is simple, unbranched, and cylindric: in the latter situation it grows much smaller, and usually procumbent: the stem is armed with sharped and forked briars: the leaf is petiolate, ternate and resembles in shape and appearance that of the purple raspberry, so common to the Atlantic states: the fruit is a berry resembling the blackberry in all points, and is eaten when ripe by the natives, which they hold in much esteem, although it is not dried for winter consumption. This shrub was first discovered at the entrance of Quicksand river: it grows so abundantly in the fertile valley of Columbia, and the islands, that the country is almost impenetrable: it retains its verdure late in summer.

8. Besides the fern already described, as furnishing a nutritious root, there are two other plants of the same species, which may be divided into the large and the small:

The large fern rises three or four feet: the stem is a common footstalk, proceeding immediately from the radix, somewhat flat, about the size of a man's arm, and covered with innumerable black coarse capillary radicles, issuing from every part of its surface: one of these roots will send forth from twenty to forty of these common footstalks, bending outwards from the common centre: the ribs are cylindric and marked longitudinally their whole length, with a groove on the upper side: on either side of this groove, and a little below its edge the leaflets are inserted: these are shortly petiolate for about two thirds the length of the middle rib, commencing from the bottom, and from thence to the extremity sessile: the rib is terminated by a single undivided lanceolate leaflet: these are from two to four inches in length, and have a small acute angular projection, and obliquely cut at the base: the upper surface is smooth, and of a deep green: the under surface of a pale green and covered with a brown protuberance of a woolly appearance, particularly near the central fibre: the leaflets are alternately pinnate, and in number, from one hundred and ten to one hundred and forty: they are shortest at the two extremities of the common footstalk, largest in the centre, gradually lengthening, and diminishing as they succeed each other.

The small fern rises likewise with a common footstalk from the radix, from four to eight in number: from four to eight inches long: the central rib is marked with a slight longitudinal groove throughout its whole length: the leaflets are oppositely pinnate, about one third of the length of the common footstalk, from the bottom, and thence alternately pinnate: the footstalk terminates in a simple undivided lanceolate leaflet: these are oblong, obtuse, convex, absolutely entire, and the upper disc is marked with a slight longitudinal groove: near the upper extremity these leaflets are decursively pinnate, as are all those of the large fern. Both of these species preserve green during the winter.

DOMESTIC ANIMALS

The quadrupeds of this country from the Rocky mountains to the Pacific ocean, may be conveniently divided into the domestic and the wild animals. The first embraces the horse and dog only.

1. The horse is confined principally to the nations inhabiting the great plains of Columbia, extending from latitude 40° to 50° N., and occupying the tract of territory lying between the Rocky mountains, and a range of mountains which pass the Columbia river about the great falls from longitude 16° to 121° W. The Shoshonees, the Chopunnish, Sokulks, Escheloots, Eneshures, and Chilluckittequaws, all enjoy the benefit of that docile, noble, and generous animal; and all of them, except the three last, possess immense numbers.

They appear to be of an excellent race, lofty, elegantly formed, active and durable: many of them appear like fine English coursers; some of them are pied with large spots of white irregularly scattered, and intermixed with a dark brown bay: the greater part, however, are of an uniform colour, marked with stars and white feet, and resemble in fleetness and bottom, as well as in form and colour, the best blooded horses of Virginia. The natives suffer them to run at large in the plains, the grass of which affords them their only winter subsistence; their masters taking no trouble to lay in a winter's store for them: notwithstanding, they will, unless much exercised, fatten on the dry grass afforded by the plains during the winter. The plains are rarely if ever moistened by rain, and the grass is consequently short and thin. The natives, excepting those of the Rocky mountains, appear to take no pains in selecting their male horses for breed; and indeed, those of that class appear much the most indifferent. Whether the horse was originally a native of this country or not, the soil and climate appear to be perfectly well adapted to the nature of this animal. Horses are said to be found wild in many parts of this extensive country. The several tribes of Shoshonees who reside towards Mexico, on the waters of the Mutlomah river, and particularly one of them, called Shaboboah, have also a great number of mules, which the Indians prize more highly than horses. An elegant horse may be purchased of the natives for a few beads or other paltry trinkets, which in the United States, would not cost more than one or two dollars. The abundance and cheapness of horses, will be extremely advantageous to those who may hereafter attempt the fur trade to the East Indies, by the way of Columbia river, and the Pacific ocean.

2. The dog is unusually small, about the size of an ordinary cur: he is usually parti-coloured, amongst which, the black, white, brown, and brindle are the colours most predominant: the head is long, the nose pointed, the eyes small, the ears erect and pointed, like those of the wolf: the hair is short and smooth, excepting on the tail, where it is long and straight, like that of the ordinary cur-dog. The natives never eat the flesh of this animal, and he appears to be in no other way servicable to them than in hunting elk.

The second division comprehends the brown, white, or grisly bear, the black bear; the deer, common red deer, the black-tailed fallow deer, the mule deer, the elk, the wolves, the large brown wolf, the small wolf of the plains, the large wolf of the plains, the tiger-cat, the foxes, the common red fox, the silver fox, the fisher or black fox, the large red fox of the plains, the kit-fox, or small fox of the plains, the antelope, the sheep, beaver, common otter, sea-otter, mink, seal, raccoon, squirrels, large grey squirrel, small grey squirrel, small brown squirrel, ground squirrel, braro, rat, mouse, mole, panther, hare, rabbit, polecat or skunk.

First, the brown, white or grisly bear, which seem to be of the same family, with an accidental variation of colour only, inhabit the timbered parts of the Rocky mountains. They are rarely found on the westerly side, and are more commonly below the Rocky mountains, in the plains, or on their borders, amidst copses of brush and underwood, and near the water courses. We are unable to learn that they inhabit at all in the woody country, bordering on the coast, as far in the interior as the range of mountains which pass the Columbia, between the great falls and the rapids of that river.

2. The black bear differs in no respect from those common to the United States. They chiefly inhabit timbered parts of the Rocky mountains, and likewise the borders of the great plains of the Columbia. They are sometimes found in the tract which lies between those plains and the Pacific ocean. One of our hunters saw one of this species, which was the only one we have discovered since our residence in fort Clatsop.

3. The deer are of three kinds: the common red deer, the black-tailed fallow deer, and the mule deer.

(1) The common red deer inhabit the Rocky mountains, in the neighbourhood of the Chopunnish, and about the Columbia, and down the river as low as where the tide water commences. They do not appear to differ essentially from those of the United States, being the same in shape, size, and appearance. The tail is however different, which is of an unusual length, far exceeding that of the common deer. Captain Lewis measured one, and found it to be seventeen inches long.

(2) The black-tailed fallow deer are peculiar to this coast, and are a distinct species, partaking equally of the qualities of the mule and the common deer. Their ears are longer, and their winter coat darker than those of the common deer. The receptacle of the eye more conspicuous, their legs shorter, their bodies thicker and larger. The tail is of the same length with that of the common deer, the hair on the under side white, and on its sides and top of a deep jetty black: the hams resemble in form and colour those of the mule, which it likewise resembles in its gait. The black-tailed deer never runs at full speed, but bounds with every foot from the ground, at the same time, like the mule deer. He sometimes inhabits the woodlands, but more often the prairies and open grounds. It may be generally said, that he is of a size larger than the common deer, and less than the mule deer. The flesh is seldom fat, and in flavour is far inferior to any other of the species.

(3) The mule deer inhabit both the seacoast and the plains of the Missouri, and likewise the borders of the Kooskooskee river, in the neighbourhood of the Rocky mountains. It is not known whether they exist in the interior of the great plains of the Columbia, or on the lower borders, near

the mountains which pass the river above the great falls. The properties of this animal have already been noticed.

4. The elk [wapiti] is of the same species with that which inhabits much the greatest part of North America. They are common to every part of this country, as well the timbered lands as the plains, but are much more abundant in the former than in the latter. In the month of March we discovered several which had not cast their horns, and others where the new horns had grown to the length of six inches. The latter were in much the best order, and from hence we draw the inference that the leanest elk retain their horns the longest.

5. The wolf is either the large brown wolf, or the wolf of the plains, of which last there are two kinds, the large and the small. The large brown wolf inhabits the woody countries on the borders of the Pacific, and the mountains which pass the Columbia river, between the great falls and rapids, and resembles in all points those of the United States. The large and small wolves of the plains, principally inhabit the open country and the woodlands on their borders. They resemble, both in appearance and habit, those of the Missouri plains. They are by no means abundant in the plains of the Columbia, as they meet there but very little game for their subsistence.

6. The tiger-cat [lynx] inhabits the borders of the plains, and the woody country in the neighbourhood of the Pacific. This animal is of a size larger than the wild cat of our country, and much the same in form, agility, and ferocity. The colour of the back, neck, and sides is of a reddish brown, irregularly variegated with small spots of dark brown: the tail is about two inches long, and nearly white, except the extremity, which is black. It terminates abruptly, as if it had been amputated: the belly is white, and beautifully variegated with small black spots: the legs are of the same colour with the sides, and the back legs are marked transversely with black stripes: the ears are black on the outer side, covered with fine, short hair, except at the upper point, which is furnished with a pencil of hair, fine, straight, and black, three-fourths of an inch in length. The hair of this animal is long and fine, far exceeding that of the wild cat of the United States, but inferior in that quality to that of the bear of the northwest. The skin of this animal is in great demand amongst the natives, for of this they form their robes, and it requires four to make up the complement.

7. Of the foxes we have seen several species.

The large red fox of the plains, and the kit-fox or small red fox of the plains, are the same which are found on the banks of the Missouri. They are found almost exclusively in the open plains, or on the tops of brush within the level country: the common red fox of the United States, inhabits the country bordering the coast, nor does this animal appear to have undergone any alteration.

The black fox [sic], or as it is termed in the neighbourhood of Detroit, the fisher, is found in the woody country bordering on the coast. How it should have acquired this appellation it is difficult to imagine, as it certainly does not prey upon fish. These animals are extremely strong and active, and admirably expert in climbing: this they perform with the greatest ease, and bound from tree to tree in pursuit of the squirrel or raccoon, their most usual food. Their colour is of a jetty black, excepting a small white spot upon the breast: the body is long, the legs short, and resembling those

MUSKWAKI (FOX) INDIAN (Bodmer)

of the ordinary turnspit dog. The tail is remarkably long, and not differing in other particulars from that of the ordinary fox.

The silver fox is an animal very rare, even in the country he inhabits. We have seen nothing but the skins of this animal, and those in the possession of the natives of the woody country below the Columbia falls, which makes us conjecture it to be an inhabitant of that country exclusively. From the skin it appeared to be of the size of the large red fox of the plains, resembling that animal in form, and particularly in the dimensions of the tail. The legs captain Lewis conjectured to be somewhat larger. It has a long deep lead coloured fur, for foil, intermixed with long hairs, either of a black or white colour at the lower part, and invariably white at the top, forming a most beautiful silver grey. Captain Lewis thought this the most beautiful of the whole species, excepting one which he discovered on the Missouri near the natural walls.

8. The antelope [pronghorn] inhabits the great plains of the Columbia, and resembles those found on the banks of the Missouri, and indeed in every part of the untimbered country, but they are by no means so abundant on this as on the other side of the Rocky mountains. The natives in this place make themselves robes of their skins, and preserve the hair entire. In the summer and autumn, when the salmon begin to decline, the majority of the natives leave the sides of the river, and reside in the open plains, to hunt the antelope, which they pursue on horseback, and shoot with their arrows.

9. The sheep [mountain goat] is found in many places, but mostly in the timbered parts of the Rocky mountains. They live in greater numbers on the chain of mountains forming the commencement of the woody country on the coast, and passing the Columbia between the falls and rapids. We have only seen the skins of these animals, which the natives dress with the wool, and the blankets which they manufacture from the wool. The animal from this evidence appears to be of the size of our common sheep, of a white colour: the wool is fine on many parts of the body, but in length not equal to that of our domestic sheep. On the back, and particularly on the top of the head, this is intermixed with a considerable proportion of long straight hairs. From the Indian account these animals have erect pointed horns: one of our engagées informed us that he had seen them in the black hills, and that the horns were lunated like those of our domestic sheep. We have nevertheless too many proofs to admit a doubt of their existing, and in considerable numbers on the mountains near the coast.

10. The beaver of this country is large and fat: the flesh is very palatable, and at our table was a real luxury. On the *7th of January*, 1806, our hunter found a beaver in his traps, of which he made a bait for taking others: this bait will entice the beaver to the trap, as far as he can smell it, and this may be fairly stated to be at the distance of a mile, as their sense of smelling is very acute. To prepare beaver bait, the castor or bark stone is first gently pressed from the bladder-like bag which contains it, into a vial of four ounces, with a large mouth: five or six of these stones are thus taken, to which must be added a nutmeg, a dozen or fifteen cloves, and thirty grains of cinnamon, finely pulverized and stirred together, and as much ardent spirits added to the composition as will reduce the whole to the consistency of mustard. All this must be carefully corked, as it soon loses its efficacy if exposed to open air. The scent becomes much stronger in four or five days after preparation, and, provided proper precaution is exercised, will preserve its efficacy for months. Any strong aromatic spices will answer; their sole virtue being to give variety and pungency to the scent of the bark stone.

The male beaver has six stones, two of which contain a substance much like finely pulverized bark, of a pale yellow colour, and in smell resembling tanners' ooze; these are called bark stones or castors. Two others, which like the bark stone resemble small bladders, contain pure strong oil, of a strong rank smell, and are called the oil stone, and the other two are the testicles. The bark stones are two inches in length: the others are somewhat smaller, of an oval form, and lie in a bunch together, between the skin and the root of the tail, with which they are closely connected, and seem to communicate. The female brings forth once in a year only, and has sometimes two and sometimes four at a birth, which usually happens in the latter end of May and the beginning of June: at this time she is said to drive the male from the lodge, who would otherwise destroy the young. They propagate like the fowl, by the gut, and the male has no other sexual distinction that we could discover.

11. The common otter has already been described, and this species does not differ from those inhabiting the other parts of America.

12. The sea-otter resides only on the seacoast, or in the neighbourhood of the salt water. When fully grown, he arrives to the size of a large mastiff dog. The ears and eyes, particularly the former, which are not an inch in length, are thick, pointed, fleshy, and covered with short hair: the tail is ten inches long, thick at the point of insertion and partially covered with a deep fur on the upper side: the legs are very short, and the feet, which have five toes each, are broad, large, and webbed: the legs are covered with fur, and the feet with short hair: the body of this animal is long, and of the same thickness throughout: from the extremity of the tail to the nose they measure five feet. The colour is a uniform dark brown, and, when in good order and season, perfectly black. This animal is unrivalled for the beauty, richness, and softness of his fur: the inner part of the fur, when opened, is lighter than the surface in its natural position: there are some black and shining hairs intermixed with the fur, which are rather longer, and add much to its beauty: the fur about the ears, nose and eyes, in some of this species, presents a lighter colour, sometimes a brown: their young are often seen of a cream-coloured white about the nose, eyes and forehead, and which are always much lighter than their other parts: their fur is however much inferior to that of the full grown otter.

13. The mink inhabits the woody country bordering on the coast, and does not differ in any point from those of the United States.

14. The seal are found on this coast in great numbers, and as far up the Columbia river as the Great Falls, and none have been discovered beyond them. The skins of such as captain Lewis examined, were covered with a short, coarse, stiff, and glossy hair, of a reddish brown colour. This animal, when in the water, appeared of a black colour, and sometimes spotted with white. We believe that there are several species of this animal to be found in this country, but we could not procure a sufficient number to make the examination: the skins were precisely of the same kind as our countrymen employ in the manufacture of trunks.

15. The raccoon inhabits woody countries bordering on the coast, in considerable numbers, and are caught by the natives with snares or pitfalls: they hold their skins in but little or no estimation, and very seldom make them into robes.

16. The squirrels we have seen, are:

The large grey squirrel. This animal appears to be an inhabitant of a narrow tract of country, well covered with whiteoak timber, and situated on the upper side of the mountains just below Columbia falls. This animal we have only found in those tracts which have been covered with timber; for in countries where pine is most abundant, he does not appear: he is much superior in size to the common grey squirrel, and resembles in form, colour and size, the fox squirrel of the Atlantic states: the tail exceeds the whole length of the body and the head: the eyes are dark, the whiskers long and black: the back, sides of the head and tail, and outward part of the legs, are all of a blue-coloured grey: the breast, belly, and inner part of the body, are all of a pure white: the hair is short, like that of the fox squirrel, though much finer, and intermixed with a portion of fur. The natives hold the skin of this animal in high estimation, which they use in forming their robes. He subsists on the acorn and filberts, which last grows in great abundance in the oak country.

The small grey squirrel is common to every part of the Rocky mountains where timber abounds. He differs from the dark brown squirrel in colour only. The back, sides, neck, head, tail and outer side of the legs, are of a brownish lead-coloured grey: the tail is slightly touched with a dark reddish colour, near the extremity of some of the hairs: the throat, breast, belly, and inner parts of the legs, are of the colour of a tanner's ooze, and have a narrow strip of black, commencing behind each shoulder, and entering longitudinally about three inches, between the colours of the sides and belly. Their habits are precisely those of the dark brown squirrel, and like them they are extremely nimble and active.

There is also a species of squirrel, evidently distinct, which we have denominated the burrowing squirrel. He inhabits these plains, and somewhat resembles those found on the Missouri: he measures one foot and five inches in length, of which the tail comprises two and a half inches only: the neck and legs are short; the ears are likewise short, obtusely pointed, and lie close to the head, and the aperture larger than will generally be found among burrowing animals. The eyes are of a moderate size, the pupil black, and the iris of a dark sooty brown: the whiskers are full, long, and black: the teeth, and, indeed, the whole contour, resemble those of the squirrel: each foot has five toes; the two inner ones of the fore feet are remarkably short, and are equipped with blunt nails: the remaining toes on the front feet are long, black, slightly curved, and sharply pointed: the hair of the tail is thickly inserted on the sides only, which gives it a flat appearance, and a long oval form: the tips of the hair forming the outer edges of the tail are white, the other extremity of a fox red: the under part of the tail resembles an iron grey; the upper is of a reddish brown: the lower part of the jaws, the under part of the neck, legs and feet, from the body and belly downwards, are of a light brick red: the nose and eyes are of a darker shade, of the same colour: the upper part of the head, neck and body, are of a curious brown grey, with a slight tinge of brick red: the longer hairs of these parts are of a reddish white colour, at their extremities, and falling together, give this animal a speckled appearance.

These animals form in large companies, like those on the Missouri, occupying with their burrows sometimes two hundred acres of land: the burrows are separate, and each possesses, perhaps, ten or twelve of these inhabitants. There is a little mound in front of the hole, formed of the earth thrown out of the burrow, and frequently there are three or four distinct holes, forming one burrow, with these entrances around the base of these little mounds. These mounds, sometimes about two feet in height and four in diameter, are occupied as watch-towers by the inhabitants of these little communities. The squirrels, one or more, are irregularly distributed on the tract they thus occupy, at the distance of ten, twenty, or sometimes from thirty to forty yards. When any one approaches, they make a shrill whistling sound, somewhat resembling tweet, tweet, tweet, the signal for their party to take the alarm, and to retire into their entrenchments. They feed on the roots of grass, &c.

The small brown squirrel is a beautiful little animal, about the size and form of the red squirrel of the eastern Atlantic states and western lakes. The tail is as long as the body and neck, and formed like that of the red squirrel: the eyes are black, the whiskers long and black but not abundant: the back, sides, head, neck, and outer part of the legs are of a reddish brown: the throat, breast, belly, and inner part of the legs are of a pale red: the tail is a mixture of black and fox-coloured red, in which the black predominates in the middle, and the other on the edges and extremity: the hair of the body is about half an inch long, and so fine and soft it has the appearance of fur: the hair of the tail is coarser and double in length. This animal subsists chiefly on the seeds of various species of pine and is always found in the pine country.

The ground squirrel [chipmunk] is found in every part of this country, as well in the prairies as in the woodlands, and is one of the few animals which we have seen in every part of our journey, and differs in no respect from those of the United States.

There is still another species [prairie-dog], denominated by captain Lewis the barking squirrel, found in the plains of the Missouri. This animal commonly weighs three pounds: the colour is a uniform bright brick red and grey, and the former predominates: the under side of the neck and belly are lighter than the other parts of the body: the legs are short, and the breast and shoulders wide: the head is stout and muscular, and terminates more bluntly, wider, and flatter than that of the common squirrel: the ears are short, and have the appearance of amputation: the jaw is furnished with a pouch to contain his food, but not so large as that of the common squirrel: the nose is armed with whiskers on each side, and a few long hairs are inserted on each jaw, and directly over the eyes: the eye is small and black: each foot has five toes, and the two outer ones are much shorter than those in the centre. The two inner toes of the fore-feet are long, sharp, and well adapted to digging and scratching. From the extremity of the nose to the end of the tail this animal measures one foot and five inches, of which the tail occupies four inches.

Notwithstanding the clumsiness of his form, he is remarkably active, and he burrows in the ground with great rapidity. These animals burrow and reside in their little subterraneous villages like the burrowing squirrel. To these apartments, although six or eight usually associate together, there is but one entrance. They are of great depth, and captain Lewis once pursued one to the depth of ten feet, and did not reach the end of the burrow. They occupy, in this manner, several hundred acres of ground, and when at rest their position is generally erect on their hinder feet and rump: they sit with much confidence, and bark at the intruder as he approaches, with a fretful and harmless intrepidity. The note resembles that of the little toy-dog: the yelps are in quick and angry succession, attended by rapid and convulsive motions, as if they were determined to sally forth in defence of their freehold. They feed on the grass of their village, the limits of which they never venture to exceed. As soon as the frost commences, they shut themselves up in their caverns, and continue until the spring opens. The flesh of this animal is not unpleasant to the taste.

17. Sewellel is a name given by the natives to a small animal found in the timbered country on this coast. It is more abundant in the neighbourhood of the great falls and rapids of the Columbia than on the coast which we inhabit.

The natives make great use of the skins of this animal in forming their robes, which they dress with the fur on, and attach them together with sinews of the elk or deer: the skin, when dressed, is from fourteen to eighteen inches long, and from seven to nine in width: the tail is always separated from the skin by the natives when making their robes. This animal mounts a tree and burrows in the ground precisely like a squirrel: the ears are short, thin, and pointed, and covered with a fine short hair, of a uniform reddish brown: the bottom or the base of the long hairs, which exceed the fur but little in length, as well as the fur itself, are of a dark colour next to the skin for two-thirds of the length of this animal: the fur and hair are very fine, short, thickly set, and silky: the ends of the fur and tip of the hair are of a reddish brown, and that colour predominates in the usual appearance of the animal. Captain Lewis offered considerable rewards to the Indians, but was never able to procure one of these animals alive.

18. The braro [blaireau, or badger], so called from the French engagées, appears to be an animal of the civet species, and much resembles the common badger. These animals inhabit the open plains of the Columbia, sometimes those of the Missouri, and are sometimes found in the woods: they burrow in hard grounds with surprising ease and dexterity, and will cover themselves in a very few moments: they have five long fixed nails on each foot; those on the fore feet are much the longest, and one of those on each hind foot is double, like that of the beaver: they weigh from fourteen to eighteen pounds: the body is long in proportion to its thickness: the fore legs are remarkably large, muscular, and are formed like those of the turnspit dog, and, as well as the hind legs, are short: these animals are broad across the shoulders and breast: the neck is short, the mouth wide, and furnished with sharp, straight teeth, both above and below, with four sharp, straight, pointed tusks, two in the upper, and two in the lower jaw: the eyes are black and small; whiskers are placed in four points on each side near the nose, and on the jaws near the opening of the mouth: the ears are short, wide, and oppressed, as if a part had been amputated: the tail is four inches in length, the hair of which is longest at the point of the junction with the

body, and growing shorter until it ends in an acute point: the hairs of the body are much shorter on the sides and rump than those on any other part, which gives the body an apparent flatness, particularly when the animal rests upon his belly: the hair is upwards of three inches in length, especially on the rump, where it extends so far towards the point of the tail, it conceals the shape of that part, and gives to the whole of the hinder parts of the body the appearance of a right angled triangle, of which the point of the tail forms an acute angle: the small quantity of coarse fur intermixed with the hair is of a reddish pale yellow.

19. The rat which inhabits the Rocky mountains, like those on the borders of the Missouri, in the neighbourhood of the mountains, has the distinguishing traits of possessing a tail covered with hair like the other parts of the body. These animals are probably of the same species with those of the Atlantic states, which have not this characteristic distinction: the ordinary house rat we found on the banks of the Missouri, as far up as the woody country extends, and the rat, such as has been described, captain Lewis found in the state of Georgia, and also in Madison's cave in Virginia.

20. The mouse which inhabits this country is precisely the same with those which inhabit the United States.

21. The mole. This animal differs in no respect from the species so common in the United States.

22. The panther [cougar] is found indifferently, either in the great plains of the Columbia, the western side of the Rocky mountains, or on the coast of the Pacific. He is the same animal so well known on the Atlantic coast, and most commonly found on the frontiers, or unsettled parts of our country. He is very seldom found, and when found, so wary, it is difficult to reach him with a musket.

23. The hare ["jack-rabbit"] on this side of the Rocky mountains inhabits the great plains of the Columbia. On the eastward of those mountains they inhabit the plains of the Missouri. They weigh from seven to eleven pounds: the eye is large and prominent, the pupil of a deep sea-green, occupying one-third of the diameter of the eye; the iris is of a bright yellowish and silver colour; the ears are placed far back, and very near each other, which the animal can, with surprising ease and quickness, dilate, and throw forward, or contract, and hold upon his back at pleasure: the head, neck, back, shoulders, thighs, and outer part of the legs and thighs are of a lead colour: the sides, as they approach the belly, become gradually more white: the belly, breast, and inner part of the legs and thighs are white, with a light shade of lead colour: the tail is round and bluntly pointed, covered with white, soft, fine fur, not quite so long as on the other parts of the body: the body is covered with a deep, fine, soft, close fur. The colours here described are those which the animal assumes from the middle of April to the middle of November; the rest of the year he is of a pure white, except the black and reddish brown of the ears, which never change. A few reddish brown spots are sometimes intermixed with the white, at this season (February 26, 1806) on their heads and the upper part of their necks and shoulders: the body of the animal is smaller and longer in proportion to its height than the rabbit: when he runs he conveys his tail straight behind, in the direction of his body: he appears to run and bound with surprising agility and ease: he is extremely fleet, and never burrows or takes shelter in the ground when pursued. His teeth are like those of the rabbit, as is also his upper lip, which is divided as high as the nose. His food is grass, herbs, and in winter he feeds much on the bark of several aromatic herbs, growing on the plains. Captain Lewis measured the leaps of this animal, and found them commonly from eighteen to twenty-one feet: they are generally found separate, and are never seen to associate in greater numbers than two or three.

24. The rabbit is the same with those of our own country, and are found indifferently, either on the prairies or the woodlands, and are not very abundant.

25. The polecat is also fund in every part of this country: they are very abundant on some parts of the Columbia, particularly in the neighbourhood of the Great falls and narrows of that river, where they live in the cliffs along the river, and feed on the offal of the Indian fishing shores. They are of the same species as those found in the other parts of North America.

The birds which we have seen between the Rocky mountains and the Pacific may be divided into two classes, the terrestrial and the aquatic. In the former class are to be arranged:

TERRESTRIAL BIRDS

1. The grouse or prairie hen. This is peculiarly the inhabitant of the great plains of the Columbia, and does not differ from those of the upper portion of the Missouri. The tail is pointed, the feathers in the centre, and much longer than those on the sides. This species differs essentially in the formation of the plumage from those of the Illinois, which have their tails composed of feathers of an equal length. In the winter season this bird is booted to the first joint of the toes; the toes are curiously bordered on their lower edges with narrow hard scales, which are placed very close to each other, and extend horizontally about one eighth of an inch on each side of the toes, adding much to the broadness of the feet, a security which bounteous nature has furnished them for passing over the snows with more ease, and what is very remarkable, in the summer season these scales drop from the feet. This bird has four toes on each foot, the colour is a mixture of dark brown, reddish and yellowish brown, with white confusedly mixed. In this assemblage of colours, the reddish brown prevails most on the upper parts of the body, wings, and tail, and the white underneath the belly, and the lower parts of the breast and tail. These birds associate in large flocks in autumn and winter, and even in summer are seen in companies of five or six. They feed on grass, insects, leaves of various shrubs in the plains, and on the seeds of several species of speth [spilt] and wild rye, which grow in richer soils. In winter their food consists of the buds of the willow and cottonwood, and native berries.

2. The cock of the plains [sage-grouse] is found on the plains of the Columbia in great abundance, from the entrance of the southeast fork of the Columbia to that of Clark's river. It is about two-thirds the size of our ordinary turkey. The beak is large, short, covered and convex, the upper exceeding the lower chop: the nostrils are large, and the back black. The colour is an uniform mixture of a dark brown, resembling the dove, and a reddish and yellowish brown, with some small black specks. In this mixture the dark brown prevails, and has a slight cast of the dove-colour: the wider side of the large feathers of the wings are of a dark brown only. The tail is com-

posed of nineteen feathers, and that inserted in the centre is the longest, the remaining nine on each side gradually diminish. The tail when folded comes to a very sharp point, and appears proportionably long, when compared with the other parts of the body. In the act of flying, the tail resembles that of the wild pigeon, although the motion of the wings is much like that of the pheasant and grouse. This bird has four toes on each foot, of which the hindmost is the shortest, and the leg is covered with feathers about half the distance between the knee and foot. When the wing is expanded there are wide openings between its feathers, the plumage being too narrow to fill up the vacancy: the wings are short in comparison with those of the grouse or pheasant. The habits of this bird resemble those of the grouse, excepting that his food is that of the leaf and buds of the pulpy-leafed thorn. Captain Lewis did not remember to have seen this bird but in the neighbourhood of that shrub, which they sometimes feed on, the prickly pear. The gizzard is large, and much less compressed and muscular than in most fowls, and perfectly resembles a maw. When this bird flies he utters a cackling sound, not unlike that of the dunghill fowl. The flesh of the cock of the plains is dark, and only tolerable in point of flavour, and is not so palatable either as that of the pheasant or grouse. The feathers about the head are pointed and stiff and short, fine and stiff about the ears; at the base of the beak several hairs are to be seen. This bird is invariably found in the plains.

3. The pheasant, of which we distinguish the large black and white pheasant, the small speckled pheasant, the small brown pheasant:

(*1*) The large black and white pheasant differs but little from those of the United States; the brown is rather brighter, and has a more reddish tint. This bird has eighteen feathers in the tail, of about six inches in length. He is also booted to the toes: the two tufts of long black feathers on each side of the neck, so common in the male of this species inhabiting the United States, are no less observable in this pheasant: the feathers on the body are of a dark brown, tipped with white and black, in which mixture the black predominates; the white are irregularly intermixed with those of the black and dark brown in every part, but in greater proportion about the neck, breast, and belly: this mixture makes this bird resemble much that kind of dunghill fowl, which the housewives of our country call Domminicker. On the breast of some of these species the white predominates: the tufts on the neck leave a space about two and a half inches long, and one inch in width, where no feathers grow, though concealed by the plumage connected with the higher and under parts of the neck; this space enables them to contract or dilate the feathers on the neck with more ease: the eye is dark, the beak is black, curved, somewhat pointed, and the upper exceeds the under chop: a narrow vermillion stripe runs above each eye, not protuberant but uneven, with a number of minute rounded dots. The bird feeds on wild fruits, particularly the berry of the sacacommis, and exclusively resides in that portion of the Rocky mountains watered by the Columbia.

(*2*) The small speckled pheasant resides in the same country with the foregoing, and differs only in size and colour. He is half the size of the black and white pheasant, associates in much larger flocks, and is very gentle: the black is more predominant, and the dark brown feathers less frequent in this than in the larger species: the mixture of white is more general on every part. This bird is smaller than our pheasant, and the body more round: the flesh of both these species is dark, and with our means of cooking, not well flavoured.

(3) The small brown pheasant [ruffed grouse] is an inhabitant of the same country, and is of the same size and shape of the speckled pheasant, which he likewise resembles in his habits. The stripe above the eye in this species is scarcely perceptible, and is, when closely examined, of a yellow or orange colour, instead of the vermillion of the other species: the colour is a uniform mixture of dark yellowish brown, with a slight aspersion of brownish white on the breast, belly, and feathers underneath the tail: the whole appearance has much the resemblance of the common quail: this bird is also booted to the toes: the flesh of this is preferable to the other two.

4. The buzzard [vulture] is, we believe, the largest bird of North America. One which was taken by our hunters was not in good condition, and yet the weight was twenty-five pounds. Between the extremity of the wings the bird measured nine feet and two inches: from the extremity of the beak to the toe, three feet nine and a half inches; from the hip to the toe, two feet; the circumference of the head was nine and three-quarter inches: that of the neck seven and a half inches; that of the body inclusive of two feet three inches: the diameter of the eye is four and a half tenths of an inch; the iris is of a pale scarlet red, and the pupil of a deep sea-green: the head and part of the neck are uncovered by feathers: the tail is composed of twelve feathers of equal length, each of the length of fourteen inches: the legs are uncovered and not entirely smooth: the toes are four in number, three forward, and that in the centre much the largest; the fourth is short, inserted near the inner of the three other toes, and rather projecting forward: the thigh is covered with feathers as low as the knee, the top or upper part of the toes are imbricated with broad scales, lying transversely: the nails are black, short, and bluntly pointed: the under side of the wing is covered with white down and feathers: a white stripe of about two inches in width marks the outer part of the wing, embracing the lower points of the plumage, covering the joints of the wing: the remainder is of a deep black: the skin of the beak and head to the joining of the neck, is of a pale orange colour; the other part, destitute of plumage, is of a light flesh colour. It is not known that this bird preys upon living animals: we have seen him feeding on the remains of the whale and other fish thrown upon the coast by the violence of the waves. This bird was not seen by any of the party until we had descended Columbia river, below the great falls, and he is believed to be of the vulture genus, although the bird lacks some of the characteristics, particularly the hair on the neck, and the plumage on the legs.

5. The robin is an inhabitant of the Rocky mountains: the beak is smooth, black, and convex; the upper chop exceeds the other in length, and a few small black hairs garnish the sides of its base: the eye is of a uniform deep sea-green colour: the legs, feet, and talons are white, of which the front one is of the same length of the leg, including the talon; these are slightly imbricated, curved, and sharply pointed: the crown, from the beak back to the neck, embracing more than half the circumference of the neck, the back, and tail, are all of a bluish dark brown: the two outer feathers of the tail are dashed with white near their tips, imperceptible when the tail is folded: a fine black forms the ground of their wings; two stripes of the same colour pass on either side of the head, from the base of the beak to the junction, and

embrace the eye to its upper edge: a third stripe of the same colour passes from the sides of the neck to the tips of the wings, across the croup, in the form of a gorget: the throat, neck, breast, and belly, are of a fine brick red, tinged with yellow; a narrow stripe of this colour commences just above the centre of each eye, and extends backwards to the neck till it comes in contact with the black stripe before mentioned, to which it seems to answer as a border: the feathers forming the first and second ranges of the coverts of the two joints of the wing next to the body, are beautifully tipped with this brick red, as is also each large feather of the wing, on the short side of its plumage. This beautiful little bird feeds on berries. The robin is an inhabitant exclusively of the woody country; we have never heard its note, which the coldness of the season may perhaps account for.

6. The crow and raven is exactly the same in appearance and note as that on the Atlantic, except that it is much smaller on the Columbia.

7. The hawks too of this coast do not differ from those of the United States. We here see the large brown hawk, the small or sparrow hawk, and one of an intermediate size, called in the United States, the hen hawk, which has a long tail and blue wings, and is extremely fierce, and rapid in its flight. The hawks, crows, and ravens are common to every part of this country, their nests being scattered in the high cliffs, along the whole course of the Columbia and its southeastern branches.

8. The large blackbird [grackle] is the same with those of our country, and is found every where in this country.

9. The large hooting owl we saw only on the Kooskooskee under the Rocky mountains. It is the same in form and size with the owl of the United States, though its colours, particularly the reddish brown, seem deeper and brighter.

10. The turtle-dove and the robin (except the Columbian robin already described) are the same as those of the United States, and are found in the plains as well as in the common broken country.

11. The magpie is most commonly found in the open country, and resemble those of the Missouri, already described.

12. The large woodpecker or laycock, the lark woodpecker, and the common small white woodpecker, with a red head, are the inhabitants exclusively of the timbered lands, and differ in no respect from birds of the same species in the United States.

13. The lark, which is found in the plains only, and is not unlike what is called in Virginia, the old field lark, is the same with those already described as seen on the Missouri.

14. The flycatcher is of two species:

The first [winter-wren] is of a small body, of a reddish brown colour: the tail and neck short, and the beak pointed: some fine black specks are intermingled with the reddish brown. This is of the same species with that which remains all winter in Virginia, where it is sometimes called the wren.

The second species has recently returned, and emigrates during the winter. The colours of this bird are, a yellowish brown, on the back, head, neck, wing and tail; the breast and belly are of a yellowish white; the tail is in the same proportion as that of the wren, but the bird itself is of a size smaller than the wren: the beak is straight, pointed, convex, rather large at the base, and the chops are of equal length. The first species is smaller, and in fact the smallest bird which captain Lewis had ever seen, excepting the humming bird. Both of this species are found exclusively in the woody country.

15. Corvus. The blue-crested, and the small white-breasted corvus, are both natives of the piny country, and are invariably found as well on the Rocky mountains as on this coast. They have already been described.

16. The snipe, &c. The common snipe of the marshes, and the common sand snipe, are of the same species as those so well known in the United States. They are by no means found in such abundance here as they are on the coast of the Atlantic.

17. The leathern winged bat, so familiar to the natives of the United States, is likewise found on this side of the Rocky mountains.

18. The white woodpecker, likewise frequents these regions, and reminds our party of their native country, by his approaches. The head of this bird is of a deep red colour, like that of the United States. We have conjectured that he has lately returned, as he does not abide in this country during the winter. The large woodpecker, and the lark woodpecker, are found in this country, and resemble those of the United States.

19. The black woodpecker is found in most parts of the Rocky mountains, as well as in the western and southwestern mountains. He is about the size of the lark woodpecker, or turtle-dove, although his wings are longer than the wings of either of those birds: the beak is one inch in length, black, curved at the base, and sharply pointed: the chops are the same in length; around the base of the beak, including the eye and a small part of the throat, there is a fine crimson red: the neck, as low down as the croup [breast] in front, is of an iron grey: the belly and breast present a curious mixture of white and blood-red, which has much the appearance of paint, where the red predominates: the top of the head, back, sides, and upper surface of the wings and tail, exhibit the appearance of a glossy green, in a certain exposure to the light: the under side of the wings and tail, is of a sooty black: the tail is equipped with ten feathers, sharply pointed, and those in the centre the longest, being about two and a half inches in length: the tongue is barbed and pointed, and of an elastic and cartilaginous substance: the eye is rather large, the pupil black, and the iris of a dark and yellowish brown: the bird in its actions when flying, resembles the small red-headed woodpecker common to the United States, and likewise in its notes: the pointed tail renders essential service when the bird is sitting and retaining his resting position against the perpendicular sides of a tree: the legs and feet are black, and covered with wide imbricated scales: he has four toes on each foot, two in the rear and two in front, the nails of which are much curved and pointed remarkably sharp: he feeds on bugs and a variety of insects.

20. The calumet [golden] eagle, sometimes inhabits this side of the Rocky mountains. This information captain Lewis derived from the natives, in whose possession he had seen their plumage. These are of the same species with those of the Missouri, and are the most beautiful of all the family of eagles in America. The colours are black and white, and beautifully variegated. The tail feathers, so highly prized by the natives, are composed of twelve broad feathers of unequal length, which are white, except within two inches of their extremities, where they immediately change to a jetty black: the wings have each a large circular white spot in the middle, which is only visible when they are extended: the body is variously marked with black and white: in form they resemble the bald eagle, but they are rather smaller, and fly with much more rapidity. This bird is feared by all his carnivorous competitors, who, on his approach, leave the carcase instantly, on which they had been feeding. The female breeds in the most inaccessible parts of the mountains, where she makes her summer residence, and descends to the plains only in the fall and winter seasons. The natives are at this season on the watch, and so highly is this plumage prized by the Mandans, the Minnetarees, and the Ricaras, that the tail feathers of two of these eagles will be purchased by the exchange of a good horse or gun, and such accoutrements. Amongst the great and little Osages, and those nations inhabiting the countries where the bird is more rarely seen, the price is even double of that above mentioned. With these feathers the natives decorate the stems of their sacred pipes or calumets, from whence the name of the calumet eagle is derived. The Ricaras have domesticated this bird in many instances, for the purpose of obtaining its plumage. The natives, on every part of the continent, who can procure the feathers, attach them to their own hair, and the manes and tails of their favourite horses, by way of ornament. They also decorate their war caps or bonnets with these feathers.

AQUATIC BIRDS As to the aquatic birds of this country, we have to repeat the remark, that, as we remained near the coast during the winter only, many birds, common both in the summer and autumn, might have retired from the cold, and been lost to our observation. We saw, however, the large blue, and brown heron; the fishing hawk; the blue-crested fisher; several species of gulls; the cormorant; two species of loons; brant of two kinds; geese; swan; and several species of ducks.

  1. The large blue and brown herons, or cranes, as they are usually termed in the United States, are found on the Columbia below tide-water. They differ in no respect from the same species of bird in the United States. The same may be observed of

  2. The fishing hawk, with the crown of the head white, and the back of a mealy white, and of

  3. The blue-crested or king-fisher, both of which are found every where on the Columbia and its tributary waters; though the fishing hawk is not abundant, particularly in the mountains.

  4. Of gulls, we have remarked four species on the coast and the river, all common to the United States.

  5. The cormorant is, properly speaking, a large black duck that feeds on fish. Captain Lewis could perceive no difference between this bird and those ducks which inhabit the Potomack and other rivers on the Atlantic coast. He never remembered to have seen those inhabiting the Atlantic states, so high up the river as they have been found in this quarter. We first discovered the cormorant on the Kooskooskee, at the entrance of Chopunnish river: they increased in numbers as we descended, and formed much the greatest portion of the water-fowl which we saw until we reached the Columbia at the entrance of the tides. They abound even here, but bear no proportion to the number of other water-fowl seen at this place.

6. The loon. There are two species of loons:

The speckled loon, found on every part of the rivers of this country. They are of the same size, colour and form, with those of the Atlantic coast.

The second species [grebe] we found at the falls of Columbia, and from thence downwards to the ocean. This bird is not more than half the size of the speckled loon; the neck is, in front, long, slender and white: the plumage on the body and back of the head and neck are of a dun or ash colour: the breast and belly are white, the beak like that of the speckled loon; and like them, it cannot fly, but flutters along on the surface of the water, or dives for security when pursued.

7. The brant are of three kinds; the white, the brown, and the pied.

(1) The white brant [snow-goose] are very common on the shores of the Pacific, particularly below the water, where they remain in vast numbers during the winter: they feed like the swan-geese, on the grass, roots, and seeds which grow in the marshes: this bird is about the size of the brown brant, or a third less than the common Canadian wild goose: the head is rather larger, the beak thicker than that of the wild goose, shorter, and of much the same form, being of a yellowish white colour, except the edges of the chops, which are frequently of a dark brown: the legs and feet are of the same form of the goose, and are of a pale flesh colour: the tail is composed of sixteen feathers of equal length as those of the geese and brown brant are, and bears about the same proportion in point of length: the eye is of a dark colour, and nothing remarkable in size: the wings are larger when compared with those of the geese, but not so much so as in the brown brant: the colour of the plumage is a pure uniform white, except the large feathers at the extremity of the wings, which are black: the large feathers at the first joint of the wing next to the body are white: the note of this bird differs essentially from that of the goose; it more resembles that of the brown brant, but is somewhat different; it is like the note of a young domestic goose, that has not perfectly attained its full sound: the flesh of this bird is exceedingly fine, preferable to either the goose or brown brant.

(2) The brown brant are much of the same colour, form, and size as the white, only that their wings are considerably longer and more pointed: the plumage of the upper part of the body, neck, head, and tail, are much the colour of the Canadian goose, but somewhat darker, in consequence of some dark feathers irregularly scattered throughout; they have not the same white on the neck and sides of the head as the goose, nor is the neck darker than the body: like the goose, they have some white feathers on the rump at the joining of the tail: the beak is dark, and the legs and feet also dark with a greenish cast: the breast and belly are of a lighter colour than the back, and is also irregularly intermixed with dark brown and black feathers, which give it a pied appearance: the flesh is darker and better than that of the goose: the habits of these birds resemble those of the geese, with this difference, that they do not remain in this climate in such numbers during the winter as the others, and that they set out earlier in the fall season on their return to the south, and arrive later in the spring than the goose. There is no difference between this bird and that called simply the brant, so common on the lakes, on the Ohio and Mississippi. The small goose of this country is rather less than the brant; its head and neck like the brant.

(3) The pied brant weigh about eight and a half pounds, differing

403

from the ordinary pied brant in their wings, which are neither so long nor so pointed: the base of the beak is for a little distance white, suddenly succeeded by a narrow line of dark brown: the remainder of the neck, head, back, wings and tail, all except the tips of the feathers, are of a bluish brown of the common wild goose: the breast and belly are white, with an irregular mixture of black feathers, which give those parts a pied appearance. From the legs back underneath the tail and around its junction with the body above, the feathers are white: the tail is composed of eighteen feathers, the longest in the centre, and measures six inches with the barrel of the quill: those on the sides of the tail are something shorter, and bend with the extremities inwards towards the centre of the tail: the extremities of these feathers are white: the beak is of a light flesh colour: the legs and feet, which do not differ in structure from those of the goose or brant of other species, are of an orange colour: the eye is small, the iris of a dark yellowish brown, and pupil black: the note is much that of the common pied brant, from which in fact, they are not to be distinguished at a distance, although they certainly are of a distinct species: the flesh is equally palatable with that of common pied brant. They do not remain here during the winter in such numbers as the bird above mentioned: this bird is here denominated the pied brant, on account of the near resemblance, and for want of another appellation.

8. The geese are either the large or small kind: the large goose resembles our ordinary wild or Canadian goose; the small is rather less than the brant, which it resembles in the head and neck, where it is larger in proportion than that of the goose: the beak is thicker and shorter; the note like that of a tame goose. In all other points it resembles the large goose, with which it associates so frequently, that it was some time before it was discovered to be of a distinct species.

9. The swan are of two kinds, the large and the small: The large swan is the same common to the Atlantic states; the small differs only from the large in size and in note: it is about one fourth less, and its note is entirely different. It cannot be justly imitated by the sound of letters; it begins with a kind of whistling sound, and terminates in a round full note, louder at the end: this note is as loud as that of the large species; whence it might be denominated the whistling swan: its habits, colour, and contour appear to be precisely those of the larger species. These birds were first found below the great narrows of the Columbia, near the Chilluckittequaw nation: they are very abundant in this neighbourhood, and remained with the party all winter, and in number they exceed those of the larger species in the proportion of five to one.

10. Of ducks, we enumerate many kinds: the duckinmallard; the canvass-back duck; the red-headed fishing duck, the black and white duck; the little brown duck; black duck; two species of divers, and blue-winged teal.

(1) The duckinmallard, or common large duck, resembles the domestic duck, are very abundant, and found in every part of the river below the mountains: they remain here all winter, but during this season do not continue much above tide-water.

(2) The canvass-back duck is a most beautiful fowl, and most delicious to the palate: it is found in considerable numbers in this neighbour-

hood. It is of the same species with those of the Delaware, Susquehannah and Potomack, where it is called the canvass-back duck, and in James' river it is known by the name of the shelled drake [sheldrake]. From this last mentioned river, it is said, however, that they have almost totally disappeared. To the epicure of those parts of the United States, where this game is in plenty, nothing need be said in praise of its exquisite flavour, and those on the banks of the Columbia are equally delicious. We saw nothing of them until after we had reached the marshy islands.

(3) The red-headed fishing duck is common to every part of the river, and was likewise found in the Rocky mountains, and was the only duck discovered in the waters of the Columbia within those mountains. They feed chiefly on crawfish, and are the same in every respect as those on the rivers and the mountains bordering on the Atlantic ocean.

(4) The black and white duck is small, and a size larger than the teal. The male is beautifully variegated with black and white: the white occupies the side of the head, breast and back, the tail, feathers of the wings, and two tufts of feathers which cover the upper part of the wings, when folded, and likewise the neck and head: the female is darker. This is believed to be the same species of duck common to the Atlantic coast, and called the butter-box: the beak is wide and short, and, as well as the legs, of a dark colour, and the flesh extremely well flavoured. In form it resembles the duckinmallard, although not more than half the size of that bird. It generally resorts to the grassy marshes, and feeds on grass seeds, as well as roots.

(5) The black duck [coot] is about the size of the blue-winged teal; the colour of a dusky black; the breast and belly somewhat lighter, and of a dusky brown: the legs stand longitudinally with the body, and the bird when on shore, stands very erect: the legs and feet are of a dark brown: it has four toes on each foot, and a short one at the heel: the long toes are in front, unconnected with the web: the webs are attached to each side of the several joints of the toe, and divided by several sinews [sinus] at each joint, the web assuming in the intermediate part an elliptical form: the beak is about two inches long, straight, fluted on the sides, and tapering to a sharp point: the upper chop is the longest, and bears on its base, at its junction with the head, a little conic protuberance of a cartilaginous substance, being of a reddish brown at the point: the beak is of an ivory colour; the eye dark. These ducks usually associate in large flocks, are very noisy, and have a sharp shrill whistle: they are fat and agreeably flavoured; feed principally on moss and vegetable productions of the water: they are not exclusively confined to the water at all seasons, captain Lewis has noticed them on many parts of the rivers Ohio and Mississippi.

(6) The divers [grebes] are the same with those of the United States. The smaller species have some white feathers about the rump, with no perceptible tail, and are very acute and quick in their motion: the body is of a reddish brown; the beak sharp, and somewhat curved, like that of the pheasant: the toes are not connected, but webbed, like those of the black duck. The larger species are about the size of the teal, and can fly a short distance, which the smaller but seldom attempt: they have a short tail; their colour is also a uniform brick reddish-brown: the beak is straight and pointed: the feet are of the same form with the other species: the legs re-

markably thin and flat, one edge being in front. The food of both species is fish and flesh: their flesh is unfit for use.

(7) The blue-winged teal is an excellent duck, and in all respects the same as those of the United States.

One of our hunters killed a [scaup] duck which appeared to be a male. It was of a size less than the duckinmallard; the head, the neck as low as the croup, the back, tail, and covert of the wings were all of a deep fine black, with a slight mixture of purple about the head and neck: the belly and breast are white: some long feathers which lie underneath the wings, and cover the thighs, were of a pale dove colour, with fine black specks: the large feathers of the wings are of a dove colour: the legs are dark; the feet are composed of four toes, of which three are in front connected by a web: the fourth is short and flat, and placed high on the heel behind the leg: the tail is composed of fourteen short pointed feathers: the beak of this duck is remarkably wide, and two inches in length: the upper chop exceeds the under one, both in length and width, insomuch, that when the beak is closed, the under chop is entirely concealed by the upper: the tongue indenture on the margin of the chops, is like those of the mallard: the nostrils are large, longitudinal, and connected: a narrow strip of white garnishes the base of the upper chop: this is succeeded by a pale sky-blue colour, occupying about an inch; which again is succeeded by a transverse stripe of white, and the extremity is a fine black: the eye is moderately large, the pupil black, and of a fine orange colour: the feathers on the crown of the head are longer than those on the upper part of the neck and other parts of the head, which give it the appearance of being crested.

FISH The fish, which we have had an opportunity of seeing, are, the whale, porpoise, skate, flounder, salmon, red char, two species of salmon trout, mountain, or speckled trout, bottlenose, anchovy, and sturgeon.

1. The whale is sometimes pursued, harpooned and taken by the Indians, although it is much more frequently killed by running foul of the rocks in violent storms, and thrown on shore by the action of the wind and tide. In either case, the Indians preserve and eat the blubber and oil; the bone they carefully extract and expose to sale.

2. The porpoise is common on this coast, and as far up the river as the water is brackish. The Indians sometimes gig them, and always eat their flesh when they can procure it.

3. The skate is also common in the salt water: we saw several of them which had perished, and were thrown on shore by the tide.

4. The flounder is also well known here, and we have often seen them left on the beach after the departure of the tide. The Indians eat this fish, and think it very fine. These several species of fish are the same with those on the Atlantic coast.

5. The common salmon and red char are the inhabitants of both the sea and rivers. The former are usually the largest, and weigh from five to fifteen pounds: they extend themselves into all the rivers and little creeks on this side of the continent, and to them the natives are much indebted for their subsistence: the body of the fish is from two and an half to three feet long, and proportionably broad: it is covered with imbricated scales, of a moderate size, and gills: the eye is large, and the iris of a silvery colour: the

406

pupil is black, the rostrum or nose extends beyond the under jaw, and both jaws are armed with a single series of long teeth, which are subulate and inflected near the extremities of the jaws, where they are also more closely arranged: they have some sharp teeth of smaller size, and some sharp points placed on the tongue, which is thick and fleshy: the fins of the back are two; the first is placed nearer the head than the ventral fins, and has several rays: the second is placed far back, near the tail, and has no rays. The flesh of this fish is, when in order, of a deep flesh-coloured red, and every shade from that to an orange yellow: when very meagre it is almost white: the roes of this fish are in high estimation among the natives, who dry them in the sun, and preserve them for a great length of time: they are of the size of a small pea, nearly transparent, and of a reddish yellow cast; they resemble very much, at a little distance, our common garden currants, but are more yellow. Both the fins and belly of this fish are sometimes red, particularly the male. The red char are rather broader, in proportion to their length, than the common salmon: the scales are also imbricated, but rather larger; the rostrum exceeds the under jaw more, and the teeth are neither so large or so numerous as those of the salmon: some of them are almost entirely red on the belly and sides; others are much more white than the salmon, and none of them are variegated with the dark spots which mark the body of the other: their flesh, roes, and every other particular, with regard to the form, are those of the salmon.

6. Of the salmon trout, we observe two species, differing only in colour; they are seldom more than two feet in length, and narrow in proportion to their length, much more so than the salmon or red char. The jaws [of the silver salmon] are nearly of the same length, and are furnished with a single series of small subulate straight teeth, not so long nor as large as those of the salmon. The mouth is wide, and the tongue is also furnished with some teeth: the fins are placed much like those of the salmon. At the great falls we found this fish of a silvery white colour on the belly and sides, and a bluish light brown on the back and head. The second species [salmon trout] is of a dark colour on its back, and its sides and belly are yellow, with transverse stripes of dark brown; sometimes a little red is intermixed with these colours on the belly and sides towards the head. The eye, flesh, and roe, are like those described of the salmon: the white species found below the falls, were in excellent order, when the salmon were entirely out of season and not fit for use. They associate with the red char, in little rivulets and creeks: the Indians say that the salmon begin to run early in May. The white salmon trout is about two feet and eight inches long, and weighs ten pounds: the eye is moderately large, the pupil black, with a small admixture of yellow, and iris of a silvery white, and a little turbid near its border with a yellowish brown. The fins are small in proportion to the fish; are bony but not pointed, except the tail and back fins, which are pointed a little: the prime back fin and ventral ones contain each ten rays, those of the gills thirteen, that of the tail twelve, and the small fin placed near and above the tail has no bony rays, but is a tough flexible substance, covered with smooth skin. It is thicker in proportion to its width than the salmon: the tongue is thick and firm, beset on each border with small subulate teeth, in a single series: the teeth and the mouth are as before described. Neither this fish nor the salmon are caught with the hook, nor do we know on what they feed.

7. The mountain or speckled trout are found in the waters of the Columbia within the mountains: they are the same with those found in the upper part of the Missouri, but are not so abundant in the Columbia as on that river. We never saw this fish below the mountains, but from the transparency and coldness of the Kooskooskee, we should not doubt of its existence in that stream as low as its junction with the southeast branch of the Columbia.

8. The bottlenose is the same with that before mentioned on the Missouri, and is found exclusively within the mountains.

9. The anchovy, which the natives call olthen, is so delicate a fish that it soon becomes tainted, unless pickled or smoked: the natives run a small stick through the gills and hang it up to dry in the smoke of their lodges, or kindle small fires under it for the purpose of drying: it needs no previous preparation of gutting, and will be cured in twenty-four hours: the natives do not appear to be very scrupulous about eating them when a little foetid.

MOLLUSKS, ETC. Of shell fish we observe the clam, periwinkle, common mussel, the cockle, and a species with a circular flat shell.

The clams [mussels] of this coast are very small; the shell consists of two valves, which open with hinges: the shell is smooth, thin, of an oval form like that of the common mussel, and of sky-blue colour. It is about one and a half inches in length and hangs in clusters to the moss of the rocks: the natives sometimes eat them.

The periwinkles, both of the river and the ocean, are similar to those found in the same situation on the Atlantic coast.

The common mussels of the river are also the same with those on the rivers of the Atlantic coast. The cockle is small, and resembles much that of the Atlantic.

There is also an animal that inhabits a shell perfectly circular, about three inches in diameter, thin and entire on the margin, convex and smooth on the upper side, plain on the under part, and covered with a number of minute capillary fibres, by means of which it attaches itself to the sides of the rocks: the shell is thin, and consists of one valve; a small circular aperture is formed in the centre of the under shell: the animal is soft and boneless.

The pellucid substance and fuci. The pellucid jelly-like substance, called the sea-nettle, is found in great abundance along the strand, where it has been thrown up by the waves and tide.

There are two species of the fuci thrown up in that manner: The first species at one extremity consists of a large vesicle or hollow vessel, which will contain from one to two gallons: it is of a conic form, the base of which forms the extreme end, and is convex and globular, bearing at its centre some short, broad, and angular fibres: the substance is about the consistence of the rind of a citron melon, and three-fourths of an inch thick: the rind is smooth from the small extremity of the cone; a long hollow cylindric and regular tapering tube extends to twenty or thirty feet, and is then terminated with a number of branches, which are flat, half an inch in width, rough, particularly on the edges, where they are furnished with a number of little ovate vesicles or bags of the size of a pigeon's egg: this plant seems to be calculated to float at each extremity, while the little end of the tube, from whence the branches proceed, lie deepest in the water. The other species seen on the coast towards the Killamucks, resembles a large pumpkin; it is solid, and its specific gravity is greater than the water, though sometimes thrown out by the waves: it is of a yellowish brown colour; the rind smooth, and its consistence is harder than that of the pumpkin; but easily cut with a knife: there are some dark brown fibres, rather harder than any other part, which pass longitudinally through the pulp or fleshy substance which forms the interior of this marine production.

The reptiles of this country are the rattlesnake, the gartersnake, lizard, and snail.

REPTILES

The gartersnake appears to belong to the same family with the common gartersnakes of the Atlantic coast, and like that snake they inherit no poisonous qualities: they have one hundred and sixty scuta on the abdomen, and seventy on the tail: those on the abdomen near the head and jaws as high as the eye, are of a bluish white, which, as it recedes from the head, becomes of a dark brown: the field of the back and sides black: a narrow stripe of a light yellow runs along the centre of the back; on each side of this stripe there is a range of small transverse, oblong spots, of a pale brick red, diminishing as they recede from the head, and disappear at the commencement of the tail: the pupil of the eye is black, with a narrow ring of white bordering on its edge; the remainder of the iris is of a dark yellowish brown.

The horned lizard, called, and for what reason we never could learn, the prairie buffalo, is a native of these plains, as well as those on the Missouri: they are of the same size, and much the same in appearance as the black lizard: the belly is however broader, the tail shorter, and the action much slower: the colour is generally brown intermixed with yellowish brown spots: the animal is covered with minute scales, interspersed with small horny points, like blunt prickles on the upper surface of the body: the belly and throat resemble those of the frog, and are of a light yellowish brown: the edge of the belly is likewise beset with small horny projections, imparting to those edges a serrate appearance: the eye is small and dark: above and behind the eyes there are several projections of that bone, and their extremities also being armed with a firm black substance, resemble the appearance of horns sprouting from the head: these animals are found in greatest numbers in the sandy open plains, and appear in the greatest abundance after a shower of rain: they are sometimes found basking in the sunshine, but conceal themselves in little holes of the earth in much the greatest proportion of the time: this may account for their appearance in such numbers after the rain, as their holes may thus be rendered untenantable.

Chapter 25
HOMEWARD BOUND

Many reasons had determined us to remain at fort Clatsop till the first of April. Besides the want of fuel in the Columbian plains, and the impracticability of passing the mountains before the beginning of June, we were anxious to see some of the foreign traders, from whom, by means of our ample letters of credit, we might have recruited our exhausted stores of merchandise. About the middle of March however, we become seriously alarmed for the want of food: the elk, our chief dependence, had at length deserted their usual haunts in our neighbourhood, and retreated to the mountains. We were too poor to purchase other food from the Indians, so that we were sometimes reduced, notwithstanding all the exertions of our hunters, to a single day's provision in advance. The men too, whom the constant rains and confinement had rendered unhealthy, might we hoped be benefitted by leaving the coast, and resuming the exercise of travelling. We therefore determined to leave fort Clatsop, ascend the river slowly, consume the month of March in the woody country, where we hope to find subsistence, and in this way reach the plains about the first of April, before which time it will be impossible to attempt crossing them: for this purpose we began our preparations.

During the winter we had been very industrious in dressing skins, so that we now had a sufficient quantity of clothing, besides between three and four hundred pair of moccasins. But the whole stock of goods on which we are to depend, either for the purchase of horses or of food, during the long tour of nearly four thousand miles, is so much diminished, that it might all be tied in two handkerchiefs. We have in fact nothing but six blue robes, one of scarlet, a coat and hat of the United States artillery uniform, five robes made of our large flag, and a few old clothes trimmed with ribbon. We therefore feel that our chief dependence must be on our guns, which fortunately for us are all in good order, as we had taken the precaution of bringing a number of extra locks, and one of our men proved to be an excellent artist in that way. The powder had been secured in leaden canisters, and though on many occasions they had been under water, it remained perfectly dry, and we now found ourselves in possession of one hundred and forty pounds of powder, and twice that quantity of lead, a stock quite sufficient for the route homewards.

After much trafficking, we at last succeeded in purchasing a canoe for a uniform coat and half a carrot of tobacco, and took a canoe from the Clatsops, as a reprisal for some elk which some of them had stolen from us in the winter. We were now ready to leave fort Clatsop, but the rain prevented us for several days from caulking the canoes, and we were forced to wait for calm weather, before we could attempt to pass point William. In the meantime we were visited by many of our neighbours, for the purpose of taking leave of us. The Clatsop Commowool has been the most kind and hospitable of all the Indians in this quarter: we therefore gave him a certificate of the kindness and attention which we had received from him, and added a more substantial proof of our gratitude, the gift of all our houses and furniture. To the Chinnook chief Delashelwilt, we gave a certificate of the same kind: we also circulated among the natives several papers, one of which we also posted up in the fort, to the following effect:

410

"The object of this last, is, that through the medium of some civilised person, who may see the same, it may be made known to the world, that the party consisting of the persons whose names are hereunto annexed, and who were sent out by the government of the United States to explore the interior of the continent of North America, did penetrate the same by the way of the Missouri and Columbia rivers, to the discharge of the latter into the Pacific ocean, where they arrived on the 14th day of November 1805, and departed the 23d day of March, 1806, on their return to the United States, by the same route by which they had come out."

On the back of some of these papers, we sketched the connection of the upper branches of the Missouri and Columbia rivers, with our route, and the track which we intended to follow on our return. This memorandum was all that we deemed it necessary to make; for there seemed but little chance that any detailed report to our government, which we might leave in the hands of the savages, to be delivered to foreign traders, would ever reach the United States. To leave any of our men here, in hopes of their procuring a passage home in some transient vessel, would too much weaken our party, which we must necessarily divide during our route; besides that, we will most probably be there ourselves sooner than any trader, who, after spending the next summer here, might go on some circuitous voyage.

The rains and wind still confined us to the fort; but at last our provisions dwindled down to a single day's stock, and it became absolutely necessary to remove: we therefore sent a few hunters ahead, and stopped the boats as well as we could with mud.

Sunday. The next morning the canoes were loaded, and at one o'clock in the afternoon we took a final leave of fort Clatsop. The wind was still high, but the alternative of remaining without provisions was so unpleasant, that we hoped to be able to double point William. We had scarcely left the fort when we met Delashelwilt, and a party of twenty Chinnooks, who understanding that we had been trying to procure a canoe, had brought one for sale. Being, however, already supplied, we left them, and after getting out of Meriwether's bay, began to coast along the south side of the river: we doubled point William without any injury, and at six o'clock reached, at the distance of sixteen miles from fort Clatsop, the mouth of a small creek, where we found our hunters. They had been fortunate enough to kill two elk, but at such a distance that we could not send for them before the next morning, *Monday, March 24th,* when they were brought in for breakfast. We then proceeded. The country is covered with a thick growth of timber: the water however is shallow to the distance of four miles from shore; and although there is a channel deep enough for canoes on the south side, yet as the tide was low, we found some difficulty in passing along. At one o'clock we reached the Cathlamah village, where we halted for about two hours, and purchased some wappatoo and a dog for the invalids. This village we have already described, as situated opposite to the Seal islands: on one of these the Indians have placed their dead in canoes, raised on scaffolds, above the reach of the tide. These people seem to be more fond of carving in wood than their neighbours, and have various specimens of their taste about the houses. The broad pieces supporting the roof and the board through which

MARCH 23D

doors are cut, are the objects on which they chiefly display their ingenuity, and are ornamented with curious figures, sometimes representing persons in a sitting posture supporting a burden.

On resuming our route among the Seal islands, we mistook our way, which an Indian observing, he pursued us and put us into the right channel. He soon, however, embarrassed us, by claiming the canoe we had taken from the Clatsops, and which he declared was his property: we had found it among the Clatsops, and seized it as a reprisal for a theft committed by that nation; but being unwilling to do an act of injustice to this Indian, and having no time to discuss the question of right, we compromised with him for an elk skin, with which he returned perfectly satisfied. We continued our route along the shore, and after making fifteen miles encamped at an old village of nine houses, opposite to the lower village of the Wahkiacums. Here we were overtaken by two Chinnooks, who came to us after dark, and spent the night at our camp. We found plenty of wood for fires, which were quite necessary, as the weather had become cold.

MARCH 25TH *Tuesday.* This morning proved so disagreeably cold that we did not set out before seven o'clock, when having breakfasted, we continued along the southern side of the river. The wind, however, as well as a strong current was against us, so that we proceeded slowly. On landing for dinner at noon, we were joined by some Clatsops, who had been on a trading voyage to the Skilloots, and were now on their return loaded with dried anchovies, wappatoo, and sturgeon. After dinner we crossed the river to a large island, along the side of which we continued about a mile till we reached a single house, occupied by three men, two women, and the same number of boys, all of the Cathlamah nation. They were engaged in fishing or trolling for sturgeon, of which they had caught about a dozen, but they asked so much for them that we were afraid to purchase. One of the men purchased the skin of a sea-otter, in exchange for a dressed elk skin and a handkerchief. Near adjoining this house was another party of Cathlamahs, who had been up the river on a fishing excursion, and been successful in procuring a large supply, which they were not disposed to sell.

We proceeded on to the head of the island, and then crossed to the north side of the river. Here the coast formed a continued swamp for several miles back, so that it was late in the evening before we were able to reach a spot fit for our camp. At length we discovered the entrance of a small creek, opposite to the place where we were encamped on the sixth of November, and though the ground was low and moist, yet as the spot was sheltered from the wind, we resolved to pass the night there: we had now made fifteen miles. Here we found another party of ten Cathlamahs, who had established a temporary residence here for the purpose of fishing sturgeon and taking seal, in both of which they had been successful. They gave us some of the flesh of the seal, which was a valuable addition to the lean elk. The low grounds which we passed are supplied with cottonwood, and the tree [broad-leaf maple] resembling the ash, except in its leaf, with red willow, broad-leafed willow, seven bark [Douglas hardhack], gooseberry, green briar, and the large-leafed thorn.

The wind was very high towards evening, and continued to blow so violent in the morning, *March 26th*, that we could not set out before eight o'clock. In the meantime finding that one of our neighbours, the Cathlamahs, by name Wallale, was a person of distinction, we gave him a medal of a small size, with which he was invested with the usual ceremonies. He appeared highly gratified, and requited us with a large sturgeon. The wind having abated, we proceeded to an old village, where we halted for dinner, having met on the way Sahawacap the principal chief of all the Cathlamahs, who was on his return from a trading voyage up the river, with wappatoo and fish, some of which he gave us, and we purchased a little more. At dinner we were overtaken by two Wahkiacums, who have been following us for twenty-four hours, with two dogs, for which they are importuning us to give them some tobacco; but as we have very little of that article left, they were obliged to go off disappointed. We received at the same time an agreeable supply of three eagles and a large goose, brought in by the hunters. After dinner we passed along the north shore opposite to a high fine bottom and dry prairie, at the upper end of which, near a grove of white-oak trees, is an island which we called Fanny's island. There were some deer and elk at a distance in the prairie, but as we could not stay to hunt, we continued till late in the evening, when we encamped on the next island above Fanny's. According to the estimate we made in descending the river, which we begin, however, to think was short, our journey of to-day was eighteen miles. Some Indians came to us, but we were occupied in procuring wood, which we found it difficult to obtain in sufficient quantity for our purposes, and they therefore did not remain long.

Thursday. We set out early, and were soon joined by some Skilloots, with fish and roots for sale. At ten o'clock we stopped to breakfast at two houses of the same nation, where we found our hunters, who had not returned to camp last night, but had killed nothing. The inhabitants seemed very kind and hospitable. They gave almost the whole party as much as they could eat of dried anchovies, wappatoo, sturgeon, quamash, and a small white tuberous root, two inches long and as thick as a man's finger, which, when eaten raw, is crisp, milky, and of an agreeable flavour. The Indians also urged us to remain with them all day, and hunt elk and deer, which they said were abundant in the neighbourhood; but as the weather would not permit us to dry and pitch our canoes, we declined their offer and proceeded.

MARCH 27TH

At the distance of two miles we passed the entrance of Coweliskee river. This stream discharges itself on the north side of the Columbia, about three miles above a remarkably high rocky knoll, the south side of which it washes in passing, and which is separated from the northern hills by a wide bottom of several miles in extent. The Coweliskee is one hundred and fifty yards wide, deep and navigable, as the Indians assert, for a considerable distance, and most probably waters the country west and north of the range of mountains which cross the Columbia between the great falls and rapids. On the lower side of this river, a few miles from its entrance into the Columbia, is the principal village of the Skilloots, a numerous people, differing, however, neither in language, dress, nor manners, from the Clatsops, Chinnooks, and other nations at the mouth of the Columbia. With the Chinnooks they have lately been at war, and though hostilities have ceased, yet they have not resumed their usual intercourse, so that the Skilloots do not go as far as the sea, nor do the Chinnooks come higher up than the Seal islands, the trade between them being carried on by the Clatsops, Cathlamahs, and Wahkiacums, their mutual friends. On this same river, above the Skilloots, resides the nation called Hullooetell, of whom we learnt nothing, except that the nation was numerous. Late in the evening we halted at the beginning of the bottom land, below Deer island, after having made twenty miles. Along the low grounds on the river were the cottonwood, sweet-willow, the oak, ash, the broad-leafed ash [maple], and the growth resembling the beech; while the hills are occupied almost exclusively by different species of fir, and the black alder is common to the hills as well as the low grounds. During the day we passed a number of fishing camps, on both sides of the river, and were constantly attended by small parties of the Skilloots, who behaved in the most orderly manner, and from whom we purchased as much fish and roots as we wanted on very moderate terms. The night continued as the day had been, cold, wet, and disagreeable.

MARCH 28TH *Friday*. We left our camp at an early hour, and by nine o'clock reached an old Indian village on the left side of Deer island. Here we found a party of our men whom we had sent on yesterday to hunt, and who now returned after killing seven deer, in the course of the morning, out of upwards of a hundred which they had seen. They were the common fallow deer with long tails, and though very poor are better than the black-tailed fallow deer of the coast, from which they differ materially. Soon after our arrival the weather became fair, and we therefore immediately hauled the boats on shore, and having dried them by means of large fires, put on the pitch. We also took this opportunity of drying our baggage; and as some of the hunters had not yet returned, it was deemed advisable to pass the night at our present camp. This island, which has received from the Indians the appropriate name of Elalah, or Deer island, is surrounded on the water side by an abundant growth of cottonwood, ash, and willow, while the interior consists chiefly of prairies interspersed with ponds. These afford refuge to great numbers of geese, ducks, large swan, sandhill cranes, a few canvass-backed ducks, and particularly the duckinmallard, the most abundant of all. There are also great numbers of snakes resembling our gartersnakes in appearance, and like them not poisonous. Our hunters brought in three deer, a goose, some ducks, an eagle, and a tiger-cat, but such is the extreme voracity of the vultures, that they had devoured in the space of a few hours, four of the deer killed this morning; and one of our men declared, that they had besides dragged a large buck about thirty yards, skinned it, and broke the backbone. We were visited during the day by a large canoe with ten Indians of the Quathlapotle nation, who reside about seventeen miles above us. We had advanced only five miles to-day.

MARCH 29TH *Saturday*. At an early hour we proceeded along the side of Deer island, and halted for breakfast at the upper end of it, which is properly the commencement of the great Columbian valley. We were here joined by three men of the Towahnahiook nation, with whom we proceeded, till at the distance of fourteen miles from our camp of last evening we reached a large inlet or arm of the river, about three hundred yards wide, up which they went to their villages. A short distance above this inlet a considerable river empties itself from the north side of the Columbia. Its name is Chawahnahiooks. It is about one hundred and fifty yards wide, and at present discharges a large body of water, though the Indians assure us that at a short distance above its mouth, the navigation is obstructed by falls and rapids. Three miles beyond the inlet is an island near the north shore of the river, behind the lower end of which is a village of Quathlapotles, where we landed, about three o'clock. The village consists of fourteen large wooden houses. The people themselves received us very kindly, and voluntarily spread before us wappatoo and anchovies, but as soon as we had finished enjoying this hospitality, if it deserves that name, they began to ask us for presents. They were, however, perfectly satisfied with the small articles which we distributed according to custom, and equally pleased with our purchasing some wappatoo, twelve dogs and two sea-otter skins. We also gave to the chief a small medal, which he, however, soon transferred to his wife. After remaining some time we embarked, and coasting along this island, which after the nation we called Quathlapotle island, encamped for this night in a small prairie on the north side of the Columbia, having made by estimate nineteen miles. The river is rising fast.

In the course of the day we saw great numbers of geese, ducks, and large and small swans, which last are very abundant in the ponds where the wappatoo grows, as they feed much on that root. We also observed the crested king-fisher, and the large and small blackbird: and this evening heard, without seeing, the large hooting owl. The frogs, which we have not found in the wet marshes near the entrance of the Columbia, are now croaking in the swamps and marshes with precisely the same note common in the United States. The gartersnakes appear in vast quantities, and are scattered through the prairies in large bundles of forty or fifty entwined round each other: among the moss on the rocks we observed a species of small wild onions growing so closely together as to form a perfect turf, and equal in flavour to the chives of our gardens, which they resemble in appearance.

Sunday. Soon after our departure we were met by three Clanaminamuns, one of whom we recognised as our companion yesterday. He pressed us very much to visit his countrymen on the inlet, but we had no time to make the circuit, and parted. We had not proceeded far before a party of Claxtars, and Cathlacumups, passed us in two canoes, on their way down the river; and soon after we were met by several other canoes, filled with persons of different tribes on each side of the river. We passed, also, several fishing camps, on Wappatoo island, and then halted for breakfast on the north side of the river, near our camp of the *4th of November*. Here we were visited by several canoes from two villages on Wappatoo island; the first, about two miles above us, is called Clahnaquah, the other a mile above them, has the name of Multnomah. After higgling much in the manner of those on the seacoast, these Indians gave us a sturgeon with some wappatoo and pashequaw in exchange for small fishhooks. As we proceeded we were joined by other Indians, and on coming opposite to the Clahnaquah village, we were shown another village about two miles from the river on the northeast side, and behind a pond running parallel with it. Here they said the tribe called Shotos resided. About four o'clock the Indians all left us. Their chief object in accompanying us appeared to be to gratify curiosity; but though they behaved in the most friendly manner, most of them were prepared with their

MARCH 30TH

instruments of war. About sunset we reached a beautiful prairie, opposite the middle of what we had called Image-canoe island, and having made twenty-three miles, encamped for the night. In the prairie is a large pond or lake, and an open grove of oak borders the back part. There are many deer and elk in the neighbourhood, but they are very shy, and the annual fern which is now abundant and dry, makes such a rustling as the hunters pass through it, that they could not come within reach of the game, and we obtained nothing but a single duck.

MARCH 31ST *Monday.* We set out very early, and at eight o'clock landed on the north side of the river and breakfasted. Directly opposite is a large wooden house, belonging to the Shahala nation, the inhabitants of which came over to see us. We had observed in descending the river last year, that there were at the same place, twenty-four other houses built of wood and covered with straw, all of which are now destroyed: on inquiry the Indians informed us, that their relations whom we saw last fall, usually visit them at that season for the purpose of hunting deer and elk, and collecting wappatoo, but that they had lately returned to their permanent residence at the Rapids, we presume in order to prepare for the salmon season, as that fish will soon begin to run. At ten o'clock we resumed our route along the north side of the river, and having passed Diamond island, and Whitebrant island, halted for the night at the lower point of a handsome prairie. Our camp which is twenty-five miles from that of last night, is situated opposite to the upper entrance of Quicksand river: a little below a stream from the north empties itself into the Columbia, near the head of Whitebrant island. It is about eighty yards wide, and at present discharges a large body of very clear water, which near the Columbia overflows its low banks, and forms several large ponds. The natives inform us that this river is of no great extent, and rises in the mountains near us, and that at a mile from its mouth it is divided into two nearly equal branches, both of which are incapable of being navigated, on account of their numerous falls and rapids. Not being able to learn any Indian name, we called it Seal river, from the abundance of those animals near its mouth. At the same place we saw a summer duck, or a wood duck, as it is sometimes called; it is the same with those of the United States, and the first we had seen since entering the Rocky mountains last summer.

The hunters, who had been obliged to halt below Seal river on account of the waves being too high for their small canoe, returned after dark with the unwelcome news that game was scarce in that quarter.

Tuesday, April 1st, 1806

Three Indians had followed us yesterday, and encamped near us last night. On putting to them a variety of questions relative to their country, they assured us that Quicksand river, which we had hitherto deemed so considerable, extends no further than the southwest side of mount Hood, which is south 85° east, forty miles distant from this place; that it is moreover navigable for a very short distance only, in consequence of falls and rapids, and that no nation inhabits its borders. Several other persons affirmed that it rose near mount Hood, and sergeant Pryor, who was sent for the purpose of

416

examining it, convinced us of the truth of their statement. He had found the river three hundred yards wide, though the channel was not more than fifty yards, and about six feet deep. The current was rapid, the water turbid, the bed of the river is formed entirely of quicksand, and the banks low and at present overflowed. He passed several islands, and at three and a half miles distance a creek from the south, fifty yards wide; his farthest course was six miles from the mouth of the river, but there it seemed to bend to the east, and he heard the noise of waterfalls. If Quicksand river then does not go beyond mount Hood, it must leave the valley a few miles from its entrance, and run nearly parallel with the Columbia. There must therefore be some other large river, which we have not yet seen, to water the extensive country between the mountains of the coast and Quicksand river: but the Indians could give us no satisfactory information of any such stream.

Whilst we were making these inquiries, a number of canoes came to us, and among the rest a number of families were descending the river. They told us that they lived at the Great rapids, but that a great scarcity of provisions there, had induced them to come down in hopes of finding subsistence in this fertile valley. All those who lived at the rapids, as well as the nations above them, were in much distress for want of food, having consumed their winter store of dried fish, and not expecting the return of the salmon before the next full moon, which will happen on the second of May: this intelligence was disagreeable and embarrassing. From the falls to the Chopunnish nation, the plains afford no deer, elk, or antelope, on which we can rely for subsistence. The horses are very poor at this season, and the dogs must be in the same condition if their food the fish have failed, so that we had calculated entirely on purchasing fish. On the other hand it is obviously inexpedient to wait for the return of the salmon, since in that case we might not reach the Missouri before the ice would prevent our navigating it. We might besides hazard the loss of our horses, for the Chopunnish, with whom we left them, intend crossing the mountains as early as possible, which is about the beginning of May, and they would take our horses with them, or suffer them to disperse, in either of which cases the passage of the mountains will be almost impracticable. We therefore, after much deliberation, decided to remain here till we collect meat enough to last us till we reach the Chopunnish nation, to obtain canoes from the natives as we ascend, either in exchange for our periogues, or by purchasing them with skins and merchandise. These canoes may in turn be exchanged for horses with the natives of the plains, till we obtain enough to travel altogether by land. On reaching the southeast branch of the Columbia, four or five men shall be sent on to the Chopunnish to have our horses in readiness, and thus we shall have a stock of horses sufficient to transport our baggage and to supply us with provisions, for we now perceive that they will form our only certain resource for food.

The hunters returned from the opposite side of the river with some deer and elk, which were abundant there, as were also the tracks of the black bear; while on the north side we could kill nothing.

In the course of our dealings to-day we purchased a canoe from an Indian, for which we gave six fathom of wampum beads. He seemed perfectly satisfied and went away, but returned soon after, cancelled the bargain, and giving back the wampum requested that we would restore him the canoe. To this we consented, as we knew this method of trading to be very common and deemed perfectly fair.

APRIL 2D *Wednesday.* Being now determined to collect as much meat as possible, two parties, consisting of nine men, were sent over the river to hunt, three were ordered to range the country on this side, while all the rest were employed in cutting and scaffolding the meat which we had already. About eight o'clock several canoes arrived to visit us, and among the rest were two young men, who were pointed out as Cushooks. On inquiry, they said that their nation resided at the falls of a large river, which empties itself into the south side of the Columbia, a few miles below us, and they drew a map of the country, with a coal on a mat. In order to verify this information, captain Clark persuaded one of the young men, by a present of a burning-glass, to accompany him to the river, in search of which he immediately set out with a canoe and seven of our men. After his departure other canoes arrived from above, bringing families of women and children, who confirmed the accounts of a scarcity of provisions. One of these families, consisting of ten or twelve persons, encamped near us, and behaved perfectly well. The hunters on this side of the river, returned with the skins of only two deer, the animals being too poor for use.

APRIL 3D *Thursday.* A considerable number of Indians crowded us to-day, many of whom came from the upper part of the river. These poor wretches confirm the reports of scarcity among the nations above; which, indeed, their appearance sufficiently prove, for they seem almost starved, and greedily pick the bones and refuse meat thrown away by us.

In the evening captain Clark returned from his excursion. On setting out yesterday at half past eleven o'clock, he directed his course along the south side of the river, where, at the distance of eight miles, he passed a village of the Nechecolee tribe, belonging to the Eloot nation. The village itself is small, and being situated behind Diamond island, was concealed from our view as we passed both times along the northern shore. He continued till three o'clock, when he landed at the single house already mentioned, as the only remains of a village of twenty-four straw huts. Along the shore were great numbers of small canoes for gathering wappatoo, which were left by the Shahalas, who visit the place annually. The present inhabitants of the house are part of the Neerchokioo tribe of the same nation. On entering one of the apartments of the house, captain Clark offered several articles to the Indians, in exchange for wappatoo, but they appeared sullen and ill-humoured, and refused to give him any. He therefore sat down by the fire, opposite to the men, and taking a port-fire match from his pocket, threw a small piece of it into the flame, at the same time took his pocket compass, and by means of a magnet, which happened to be in his inkhorn, made the needle turn round very briskly. The match now took fire, and burned violently, on which, the Indians terrified at this strange exhibition, immediately brought a quantity of wappatoo, and laid it at his feet, begging him to put out the bad fire: while an old woman continued to speak with great vehemence, as if praying and imploring protection. Having received the roots, captain Clark put up the compass, and as the match went out of itself, tranquillity was restored, though the women and children still took refuge in their beds, and behind the men. He now paid them for what he had used, and after lighting his pipe, and smoking with them, he continued down the river.

He now found what we had called Image-canoe island, to consist of three islands, the one in the middle concealing the opening between the other two in such a way, as to present to us on the opposite side of the river, the appearance of a single island. At the lower point of the third, and thirteen miles below the last village, he entered the mouth of a large river which was concealed by three small islands in its mouth, from those who descend or go up the Columbia. This river, which the Indians call Multnomah, from a nation of the same name, residing near it on Wappatoo island, enters the Columbia, one hundred and forty miles from the mouth of the latter river, of which it may justly be considered as forming one fourth, though it had now fallen eighteen inches below its greatest annual height. From its entrance mount Regnier [Rainier] bears nearly north, mount St. Helen's north, with a very high humped mountain a little to the east of it, which seems to lie in the same chain with the conic-pointed mountains before mentioned. Mount Hood bore due east, and captain Clark now discovered to the southeast, a mountain which we had not yet seen, and to which he gave the name of mount Jefferson. Like mount St. Helen's its figure is a regular cone covered with snow, and is probably of equal height with that mountain, though being more distant, so large a portion of it does not appear above the range of mountains which lie between these and this point.

Soon after entering the Multnomah he was met by an old Indian descending the river alone in a canoe. After some conversation with him, the pilot informed captain Clark, that this old man belonged to the Clackamos nation, who reside on a river forty miles up the Multnomah. The current of this latter river, is as gentle as that of the Columbia, its surface is smooth and even, and it appears to possess water enough for the largest ship, since, on sounding with a line of five fathoms, he could find no bottom for at least one-third of the width of the stream. At the distance of seven miles, he passed a sluice or opening, on the right, eighty yards wide, and which separates Wappatoo island from the continent, by emptying itself into the inlet below. Three miles further up, he reached a large wooden house, on the east side, where he intended to sleep, but on entering the rooms he found such swarms of fleas that he preferred lying on the ground in the neighbourhood. The guide informed him that this house is the temporary residence of the Nemalquinner tribe of the Cushook nation, who reside just below the falls of the Multnomah, but come down here occasionally to collect wappatoo: it was thirty feet long, and forty deep; built of broad boards, covered with the bark of white cedar; the floor on a level with the surface of the earth, and the arrangement of the interior like those near the seacoast. The inhabitants had left their canoes, mats, bladders, train-oil, baskets, bowls, and trenchers, lying about the house at the mercy of every visitor; a proof, indeed, of the mutual respect for the property of each other, though we have had very conclusive evidence that the property of white men is not deemed equally sacred. The guide informed him further, that a small distance above were two bayous, on which were a number of small houses belonging to the Cushooks, but that the inhabitants had all gone up to the falls of the Multnomah, for the purpose of fishing.

Early the next morning captain Clark proceeded up the river, which during the night, had fallen about five inches. At the distance of two miles he came to the centre of a bend under the highlands on the right side, from which its course, as could be discerned, was to the east of southeast. At this place the Multnomah is five hundred yards wide, and for half that distance across, the cord of five fathoms would not reach the bottom. It appears to be washing away its banks, and has more sandbars and willow points than the Columbia. Its regular gentle current, the depth and smoothness, and uniformity with which it rolls its vast body of water, prove that its supplies are at once distant and regular; nor, judging from its appearance and courses, is it rash to believe that the Multnomah and its tributary streams water the vast extent of country between the western mountains and those of the seacoast, as far perhaps as the waters of the gulf of California. About eleven o'clock he reached the house of the Neerchokioo, which he now found to contain eight families; but they were all so much alarmed at his presence, notwithstanding his visit yesterday, that he remained a very few minutes only. Soon after setting out, he met five canoes filled with the same number of families, belonging to the Shahala nation. They were descending the river in search of subsistence, and seemed very desirous of coming alongside of the boat; but as there were twenty-one men on board, and the guide said that all these Shahalas, as well as their relations at the house which we had just left, were mischievous bad men, they were not suffered to approach. At three o'clock he halted for an hour at the Nechecolee house, where his guide resided.

This large building is two hundred and twenty-six feet in front, entirely above ground, and may be considered as a single house, because the whole is under one roof; otherwise it would seem more like a range of buildings, as it is divided into seven distinct apartments, each thirty feet square, by means of broad boards set on end from the floor to the roof. The apartments are separated from each other by a passage or alley four feet wide, extending through the whole depth of the house, and the only entrance is from this alley, through a small hole about twenty-two inches wide, and not more than three feet high. The roof is formed of rafters and round poles laid on them longitudinally. The whole is covered with a double row of the bark of the white cedar, extending from the top eighteen inches over the eaves, and secured as well as smoothed by splinters of dried fir, inserted through it at regular distances. In this manner the roof is made light, strong, and durable. Near this house are the remains of several other large buildings, sunk in the ground and constructed like those we had seen at the great narrows of the Columbia, belonging to the Eloots, with whom these people claim an affinity. In manners and dress these Nechecolees differ but little from the Quathlapotles and others of this neighbourhood; but their language is the same used by the Eloots, and though it has some words in common with the dialects spoken here, yet the whole air of the language is obviously different. The men too are larger, and both sexes better formed than among the nations below; and the females are distinguished by wearing larger and longer robes, which are generally of deer skin dressed in the hair, than the neighbouring women. In the house were several old people of both sexes, who were treated with much respect, and still seemed healthy, though most of them were perfectly blind. On inquiring the cause of the decline of their vil-

420

lage, an old man, the father of the guide, and a person of some distinction, brought forward a woman very much marked with the small-pox, and said, that when a girl she was very near dying with the disorder which had left those marks, and that all the inhabitants of the houses now in ruins had fallen victims to the same disease. From the apparent age of the woman, connected with her size at the time of her illness, captain Clark judged that the sickness must have been about thirty years ago, the period about which we have supposed that the small-pox prevailed on the seacoast.

He then entered into a long conversation with regard to all the adjacent country and its inhabitants, which the old man explained with great intelligence, and then drew with his finger in the dust a sketch of the Multnomah, and Wappatoo island. This captain Clark copied and preserved. He now purchased five dogs, and taking leave of the Nechecolee village, returned to camp.

Chapter 26

UP THE COLUMBIA TO THE DALLES

FRIDAY, APRIL 4, 1806 The hunters were still out in every direction. Those from the opposite side of the river returned with the flesh of a bear and some venison, but the flesh of six deer and an elk which they had killed was so meagre and unfit for use, that they had left it in the woods. Two other deer were brought in, but as the game seemed poor, we despatched a large party to some low grounds on the south, six miles above us, to hunt there until our arrival. As usual many of the Indians came to our camp, some descending the rivers with their families, and others from below with no object except to gratify their curiosity.

The visit of captain Clark to the Multnomahs, now enabled us to combine all that we had seen or learnt of the neighbouring countries and nations. Of these the most important spot is Wappatoo island, a large extent of country lying between the Multnomah, and an arm of the Columbia, which we have called Wappatoo inlet, and separated from the main land by a sluice eighty yards wide, which at the distance of seven miles up the Multnomah connects that river with the inlet. The island thus formed is about twenty miles long, and varies in breadth from five to ten miles: the land is high and extremely fertile, and on most parts is supplied with a heavy growth of cottonwood, ash, the large-leafed ash, and sweet-willow, the black alder, common to the coast, having now disappeared.

But the chief wealth of this island consists of the numerous ponds in the interior, abounding with the common arrowhead (sagittaria sagittifolia) to the root of which is attached a bulb growing beneath it in the mud. This bulb, to which the Indians give the name of wappatoo, is the great article of food, and almost the staple article of commerce on the Columbia. It is never out of season; so that at all times of the year, the valley is frequented by the neighbouring Indians who come to gather it. It is collected chiefly by the women, who employ for the purpose canoes from ten to fourteen feet in length, about two feet wide, and nine inches deep, and tapering from the middle, where they are about twenty inches wide. They are sufficient to contain a single person and several bushels of roots, yet so very light that a woman can carry them with ease; she takes one of these canoes into a pond where the water is as high as the breast, and by means of her toes, separates from the root this bulb, which on being freed from the mud rises immediately to the surface of the water, and is thrown into the canoe. In this manner these patient females remain in the water for several hours even in the depth of winter. This plant is found through the whole extent of the valley in which we now are, but does not grow on the Columbia farther eastward.

This valley is bounded westward by the mountainous country bordering the coast, from which it extends eastward thirty miles in a direct line, till it is closed by the range of mountains crossing the Columbia above the great falls. Its length from north to south we are unable to determine, but we believe that the valley must extend to a great distance: it is in fact the only desirable situation for a settlement on the western side of the Rocky mountains, and being naturally fertile, would, if properly cultivated, afford subsistence for forty or fifty thousand souls. The highlands are generally of a dark rich loam, not much injured by stones, and though waving, by no means too steep for cultivation, and a few miles from the river they widen at least on the north side, into rich extensive prairies. The timber on them is abundant, and consists almost exclusively of the several species of fir already described, and some of which grow to a great height. We measured a fallen tree of that species, and found that including the stump of about six feet, it was three hundred and eighteen feet in length, though its diameter was only three feet. The dogwood is also abundant on the uplands: it differs from that of the United States in having a much smoother bark, and in being much larger, the trunk attaining a diameter of nearly two feet. There is some white cedar of a large size, but no pine of any kind. In the bottom lands are the cotton wood, ash, large-leafed ash, and sweet willow. Interspersed with these are the pashequaw, shanataque, and compound fern, of which the natives use the roots, the red flowering currant abounds on the upland, while along the river bottoms grow luxuriantly the watercress, strawberry, cinquefoil, narrowdock, sandrush, and the flowering pea, which is not yet in bloom.

There is also a species of the bear's-claw now blooming, but the large-leafed thorn has disappeared, nor do we see any longer the huckleberry, the shallun, nor any of the other evergreen shrubs which bear berries, except the species, the leaf of which has a prickly margin.

Among the animals, we observe the martin, small geese, the small speckled woodpecker, with a white back, the blue-crested corvus, ravens, crows, eagles, vultures, and hawks. The mellow bug, long-legged spider, as well as the butterfly and blowingfly, and tick, have already made their appearance, but none of all these are distinguished from animals of the same sort in the United States. The mosquitoes too have resumed their visits, but are not yet troublesome.

The nations who inhabit this fertile neighbourhood are very numerous. The Wappatoo inlet extends three hundred yards wide, for ten or twelve miles to the south, as far as the hills near which it receives the waters of a small creek whose sources are not far from those of the Killamuck river. On that creek resides the Clackstar nation, a numerous people of twelve hundred souls, who subsist on fish and wappatoo, and who trade by means of the Killamuck river, with the nation of that name on the seacoast. Lower down the inlet, towards the Columbia, is the tribe called Cathlacumup. On the sluice which connects the inlet with the Multnomah, are the tribes, Cathlanahquiah, and Cathlacomatup: and on Wappatoo island, the tribes of Clannahminamun, and Clahnaquah. Immediately opposite, near the Towahnahiooks, are the Quathlapotles, and higher up on the side of the Columbia, the Shotos. All these tribes, as well as the Cathlahaws, who live somewhat lower on the river, and have an old village on Deer island, may be considered as parts of the great Multnomah nation, which has its principal residence on Wappatoo island, near the mouth of the large river to which they give their name. Forty miles above its junction with the Columbia, it receives the waters of the Clackamos, a river which may be traced through a woody and fertile country to its sources in mount Jefferson, almost to the foot of which it is navigable for canoes. A nation of the same name resides in eleven villages along its borders: they live chiefly on fish and roots, which abound in the Clackamos and along its banks, though they sometimes descend to the Columbia to gather wappatoo, where they cannot be distinguished by dress or manners, or language from the tribes of Multnomahs. Two days' journey from the Columbia, or about twenty miles beyond the entrance of the Clackamos, are the falls of the Multnomah. At this place are the permanent residences of the Cushooks and Chahcowahs, two tribes who are attracted to that place by the fish, and by the convenience of trading across the mountains and down Killamuck river, with the nation of Killamucks, from whom they procure train oil. These falls were occasioned by the passage of a high range of mountains; beyond which the country stretches into a vast level plain, wholly destitute of timber. As far as the Indians, with whom we conversed, had ever penetrated that country, it was inhabited by a nation called Calahpoewah, a very numerous people whose villages, nearly forty in number, are scattered along each side of the Multnomah, which furnish them with their chief subsistence, fish, and the roots along its banks.

All the tribes in the neighbourhood of Wappatoo island, we have considered as Multnomahs; not because they are in any degree subordinate to that nation; but they all seem to regard the Multnomahs as the most powerful. There is no distinguished chief, except the one at the head of the Multnomahs; and they are moreover linked by a similarity of dress and manners, and houses and language, which much more than the feeble restraints of Indian government contribute to make one people. These circumstances also separate them from nations lower down the river. The Clatsops, Chinnooks, Wahkiacums and Cathlamahs understand each other perfectly; their language varies, however, in some respects from that of the Skilloots; but on reaching the Multnomah Indians, we found, that although many words were the same, and a great number differed only in the mode of accenting them, from those employed by the Indians near the mouth of the Columbia, yet there was a very sensible variation of language.

The natives of the valley are larger and rather better shaped than those of the seacoast: their appearance too is generally healthy, but they are afflicted with the common disease of the Columbia, soreness of the eyes. To whatever this disorder may be imputed it is a great national calamity: at all ages their eyes are sore and weak, and the loss of one eye is by no means uncommon, while in grown persons total blindness is frequent, and almost universal in old age. The dress of the men has nothing different from that used below, but are chiefly remarked by a passion for large brass buttons, which they fix on a sailor's jacket, when they are so fortunate as to obtain one, without regard to any arrangement. The women also wear the short robe already described; but their hair is most commonly braided into two tresses falling over each ear in front of the body, and instead of the tissue of bark, they employ a piece of leather in the shape of a pocket handkerchief tied round the loins. This last is the only and ineffectual defence when the warmth of the weather induces them to throw aside the robe.

The houses are in general on a level with the ground, though some are sunk to the depth of two or three feet into the ground, and like those near the coast adorned or disfigured by carvings or paintings on the posts, doors and beds: they do not possess any peculiar weapon except a kind of broad sword made of iron, from three to four feet long, the blade about four inches wide, very thin and sharp at all its edges, as well as at the point. They have also bludgeons of wood in the same form; and both kinds generally hang at the head of their beds. These are formidable weapons.

Like the natives of the seacoast, they are also very fond of cold, hot, and vapour baths, which are used at all seasons, and for the purpose of

424

health as well as pleasure. They, however, add a species of bath peculiar to themselves, by washing the whole body with urine every morning.

The mode of burying the dead in canoes, is no longer practised by the natives here. The place of deposit is a vault formed of boards, slanting like the roof of a house from a pole supported by two forks. Under this vault the dead are placed horizontally on boards, on the surface of the earth, and carefully covered with mats. Many bodies are here laid on each other, to the height of three or four corpses, and different articles, which were most esteemed by the dead, are placed by their side; their canoes themselves being sometimes broken to strengthen the vault.

The trade of all these inhabitants is in anchovies, sturgeon, but chiefly in wappatoo, to obtain which, the inhabitants both above and below them on the river, come at all seasons, and supply in turn, beads, cloth, and various other articles procured from the Europeans.

Saturday. We dried our meat as well as the cloudy weather would permit. In the course of his chase yesterday, one of our men who killed the bear, found a nest of another with three cubs in it. He returned to-day in hopes of finding her, but he brought only the cubs, without being able to see the dam, and on this occasion, Drewyer, our most experienced huntsman, assured us that he had never known a single instance where a female bear, who had once been disturbed by a hunter and obliged to leave her young, returned to them again. The young bears were sold for wappatoo to some of the many Indians who visited us in parties during the day, and behaved very well. APRIL 5TH

Having made our preparations of dried meat, we set out next morning, *Sunday 6th*, by nine o'clock, and continued along the north side of the river for a few miles, and then crossed to the river to look for the hunters, who had been sent forward the day before yesterday. We found them at the upper end of the bottom with some Indians, for we are never freed from the visits of the natives. They had killed three elk, and wounded two others so badly, that it was still possible to get them. We therefore landed, and having prepared scaffolds and secured the five elk, we encamped for the night.

The following morning, the weather having been fair and pleasant, had dried a sufficient quantity of meat to serve us as far as the Chopunnish, with occasional supplies, if we can procure them, of dogs, roots, and horses. In the course of the day several parties of Shahalas, from a village eight miles above us, came to visit us, and behaved themselves very properly, except that we were obliged to turn one of them from the camp for stealing a piece of lead. Every thing was now ready for our departure, but in the morning, *Tuesday 8th*, the wind blew with great violence, and we were obliged to unload our boats, which were soon after filled with water. The same cause prevented our setting out to-day; we therefore despatched several hunters round the neighbourhood, but in the evening they came back with nothing but a duck. They had, however, seen some of the black-tailed, jumping, or fallow deer, like those about fort Clatsop, which are scarce near this place, where the common long-tailed fallow deer are most abundant. They had also observed two black bears, the only kind that we have discovered in this quarter. A party of six Indians encamped at some distance, and late at night the sentinel stopped one of the men, an old man who was creeping into camp APRIL 7TH in order to pilfer: he contented himself with frightening the Indian, and then giving him a few stripes with a switch, turned the fellow out, and he soon afterwards left the place with all his party.

APRIL 9TH *Wednesday.* The wind having moderated, we reloaded the canoes, and set out by seven o'clock. We stopped to take up two hunters who had left us yesterday, but were unsuccessful in the chase, and then proceeded to the Wahclellah village, situated on the north side of the river, about a mile below Beacon rock. During the whole of the route from our camp, we passed along under high, steep, and rocky sides of the mountains, which now close on each side of the river, forming stupendous precipices, covered with the fir and white cedar. Down these heights frequently descend the most beautiful cascades, one of which, a large creek, throws itself over a perpendicular rock three hundred feet above the water, while other smaller streams precipitate themselves from a still greater elevation, and evaporating in a mist, again collect and form a second cascade before they reach the bottom of the rocks. We stopped to breakfast at this village. We here found the tomahawk which had been stolen from us on the fourth of last November: they assured us they had bought it of the Indians below; but as the latter had already informed us that the Wahclellahs had such an article, which they had stolen, we made no difficulty about retaking our property.

This village appears to be the wintering station of the Wahclellahs and Clahclellahs, two tribes of the Shahala nation. The greater part of the first tribe have lately removed to the falls of the Multnomah, and the second have established themselves a few miles higher up the Columbia, opposite the lower point of Brant island, where they take salmon, that being the commencement of the rapids. They are now in the act of removing, and carrying off with them, not only the furniture and effects, but the bark and most of the boards of their houses. In this way nine have been lately removed. There are still fourteen standing, and in the rear of the village are the traces of ten or twelve others of more ancient date. These houses are either sunk in the ground or on a level with the surface, and are generally built of boards and covered with cedar bark. In the single houses there is generally a division near the door, which is in the end; or in case the house be double, opens on the narrow passage between the two. Like those we had seen below at the Neerchokioo tribe, the women wear longer and larger robes than their neighbours the Multnomahs, and suspend various ornaments from the cartilage of the nose: the hair is, however, worn in the same sort of braid, falling over each ear, and the truss is universal from the Wappatoo island to Lewis's river. The men also form their hair into two queues by means of otter skin thongs, which fall over the ears so as to give that extraordinary width to the face which is here considered so ornamental. These people seemed very unfriendly, and our numbers alone seemed to secure us from ill treatment.

While we were at breakfast the grand chief of the Chilluckittequaws arrived, with two inferior chiefs, and several men and women of his nation. They were returning home, after trading in the Columbian valley, and were loaded with wappatoo and dried anchovies, which, with some beads, they had obtained in exchange for chappelell, bear-grass and other small articles. As these people had been very kind to us as we descended the river, we endeavoured to repay them by every attention in our power. After purchasing, with much difficulty, a few dogs and some wappatoo from the Wahclellahs, we left them at two o'clock, and passing under the Beacon rock, reached in two hours the Clahclellah village.

This Beacon rock, which we now observed more accurately than as we descended, stands on the north side of the river, insulated from the hills. The northern side has a partial growth of fir or pine. To the south it rises in an unbroken precipice to the height of seven hundred feet, where it terminates in a sharp point, and may be seen at the distance of twenty miles below. This rock may be considered as the commencement of tide-water, though the influence of the tide is perceptible here in autumn only, at which time the water is low. What the precise difference at those seasons is, we cannot determine; but on examining a rock which we lately passed, and comparing its appearance now with that which we observed last November, we judge the flood of this spring to be twelve feet above the height of the river at that time. From Beacon rock as low as the marshy islands, the general width of the river is from one to two miles, though in many places it is still greater.

On landing at the Clahclellahs we found them busy in erecting their huts, which seem to be of a temporary kind only, so that most probably they do not remain longer than the salmon season. Like their countrymen, whom we had just left, these people were sulky and ill-humoured, and so much on the alert to pilfer, that we were obliged to keep them at a distance from our baggage. As our large canoes could not ascend the rapids on the north side, we passed to the opposite shore, and entered the narrow channel which separates it from Brant island. The weather was very cold and rainy, and the wind so high, that we were afraid to attempt the rapids this evening, and therefore, finding a safe harbour, we encamped for the night. The wood in this neighbourhood has lately been on fire, and the firs have discharged considerable quantities of pitch, which we collected for some of our boats. We saw to-day some turkey-buzzards, which are the first we have observed on this side of the Rocky mountains.

Thursday. Early in the morning we dropped down the channel to the lower end of Brant island, and then drew our boats up the rapid. At the distance of a quarter of a mile we crossed over to a village of Clahclellahs, consisting of six houses, on the opposite side. The river is here about four hundred yards wide, and the current so rapid, that although we employed five oars for each canoe, we were borne down a considerable distance. While we were at breakfast, one of the Indians offered us two sheep-skins for sale, one, which was the skin of a full grown sheep [mountain goat], was as large as that of a common deer: the second was smaller, and the skin of the head, with the horns remaining, was made into a cap, and highly prized as an ornament by the owner. He however sold the cap to us for a knife, and the rest of the skin for those of two elk; but as they observed our anxiety to purchase the other skin, they would not accept the same price for it, and as we hoped to procure more in the neighbourhood, we did not offer a greater. The horns of the animal were black, smooth, and erect, and they rise from the middle of the forehead, a little above the eyes, in a cylindrical form, to the height of four inches, where they are pointed. The Clahclellahs informed us that the

APRIL 10TH

sheep are very abundant on the heights, and among the cliffs of the adjacent mountains; and that these two had been lately killed out of a herd of thirty-six, at no great distance from the village.

We were soon joined by our hunters with three black-tailed fallow deer, and having purchased a few white salmon, proceeded on our route. The south side of the river is impassable, and the rapidity of the current as well as the large rocks along the shore, render the navigation of even the north side extremely difficult. During the greater part of the day it was necessary to draw them along the shore, and as we have only a single tow-rope that is strong enough, we are obliged to bring them one after the other. In this tedious and laborious manner, we at length reached the portage on the north side, and carried our baggage to the top of a hill, about two hundred paces distant, where we encamped for the night. The canoes were drawn on shore and secured, but one of them having got loose, drifted down to the last village, the inhabitants of which brought her back to us; an instance of honesty which we rewarded with a present of two knives.

It rained all night and the next morning, *Friday, 11th*, so that the tents, and skins which covered the baggage, were wet. We therefore determined to take the canoes first over the portage, in hopes that by the afternoon the rain would cease, and we might carry our baggage across without injury. This was immediately begun by almost the whole party, who in the course of the day dragged four of the canoes to the head of the rapids, with great difficulty and labour. A guard, consisting of one sick man and three who had been lamed by accidents, remained with captain Lewis to guard the baggage. This precaution was absolutely necessary to protect it from the Wahclellahs, whom we discovered to be great thieves, notwithstanding their apparent honesty in restoring our boat: indeed, so arrogant and intrusive have they become, that nothing but our numbers, we are convinced, saves us from attack. They crowded about us while we were taking up the boats, and one of them had the insolence to throw stones down the bank at two of our men.

We now found it necessary to depart from our mild and pacific course of conduct. On returning to the head of the portage, many of them met our men, and seemed very ill disposed. Shields had stopped to purchase a dog, and being separated from the rest of the party, two Indians pushed him out of the road, and attempted to take the dog from him. He had no weapon but a long knife, with which he immediately attacked them both, hoping to put them to death before they had time to draw their arrows, but as soon as they saw his design, they fled into the woods. Soon afterwards we were told by an Indian who spoke Clatsop, which we had ourselves learnt during the winter, that the Wahclellahs had carried off captain Lewis's dog to their village below. Three men well armed were instantly despatched in pursuit of them, with orders to fire if there was the slightest resistance or hesitation. At the distance of two miles, they came within sight of the thieves, who finding themselves pursued, left the dog and made off. We now ordered all the Indians out of our camp, and explained to them, that whoever stole any of our baggage, or insulted our men, should be instantly shot; a resolution which we were determined to enforce, as it was now our only means of safety.

We were visited during the day by a chief of the Clahclellahs, who seemed mortified at the behaviour of the Indians, and told us that the persons at the head of their outrages were two very bad men, who belonged to the Wahclellah tribe, but that the nation did not by any means wish to displease us. This chief seemed very well disposed, and we had every reason to believe was much respected by the neighbouring Indians. We therefore gave him a small medal, and showed him all the attentions in our power, with which he appeared very much gratified, and we trust his interposition may prevent the necessity of our resorting to force against his countrymen.

Many Indians from the villages above, passed us in the course of the day, on their return from trading with the natives of the valley, and among others, we recognised an Eloot, who with ten or twelve of his nation were on their way home to the long narrows of the Columbia. These people do not, as we are compelled to do, drag their canoes up the rapids, but leave them at the head, as they descend, and carrying their goods across the portage, hire or borrow others from the people below. When the trade is over they return to the foot of the rapids, where they leave these boats and resume their own at the head of the portage. The labour of carrying the goods across is equally shared by the men and women, and we were struck by the contrast between the decent conduct of all the natives from above, and the profligacy and ill manners of the Wahclellahs. About three quarters of a mile below our camp is a burial ground, which seems common to the Wahclellahs, Clahclellahs, and Yehhuhs. It consists of eight sepulchres on the north bank of the river.

Saturday. The rain continued all night and this morning. Captain Lewis now took with him all the men fit for duty, and began to drag the remaining periogues over the rapids. This has become much more difficult than when we passed in the autumn; at that time there were in the whole distance of seven miles only three difficult points; but the water is now very considerably higher, and during all that distance the ascent is exceedingly laborious and dangerous, nor would it be practicable to descend, except by letting down the empty boats by means of ropes. The route over this part, from the head to the foot of the portage, is about three miles: the canoes which had been already dragged up were very much injured, by being driven against the rocks, which no precautions could prevent. This morning as we were drawing the fifth canoe round a projecting rock, against which the current sets with great violence, she unfortunately offered too much of her side to the stream. It then drove her with such force, that with all the exertions of the party we were unable to hold her, and were forced to let go the cord, and see her drift down the stream, and be irrecoverably lost. We then began to carry our effects across the portage, but as all those who had short rifles took them in order to repel any attack from the Indians, it was not until five o'clock in the afternoon that the last of the party reached the head of the rapids, accompanied by our new friend the Wahclellah chief. The afternoon being so far advanced, and the weather rainy and cold, we determined to halt for the night, though very desirous of going on, for during the three last days we have not advanced more than seven miles.

APRIL 12TH

The portage is two thousand eight hundred yards, along a narrow road, at all times rough, and now rendered slippery by the rain. About half way is an old village which the Clahclellah chief informs us is the occasional residence of his tribe. These houses are uncommonly large, one of them measured one hundred and sixty by forty feet, and the frames are constructed in the usual manner, except that it is double so as to appear like one house within another. The floors are on a level with the ground, and the roofs have been taken down and sunk in a pond behind the village. We find that our conduct yesterday has made the Indians much more respectful; they do not crowd about us in such numbers, and behave with much more propriety. Among those who visited us were about twenty of the Yehhuhs, a tribe of Shahalas, whom we had found on the north side of river, immediately above the rapids, but who had now emigrated to the opposite shore, where they generally take salmon. Like their relations, the Wahclellahs, they have taken their houses with them, so that only one is now standing where the old village was. We observe generally, that the houses which have the floor on a level with the earth, are smaller, and have more the appearance of being temporary than those which are sunk in the ground, whence we presume that the former are the dwellings during spring and summer, while the latter are reserved for the autumn and winter. Most of the houses are built of boards and covered with bark, though some of the more inferior kind are constructed wholly of cedar bark, kept smooth and flat by small splinters fixed crosswise through the bark, at the distance of twelve or fourteen inches apart. There is but little difference in appearance between these Yehhuhs, Wahclellahs, Clahclellahs, and Neerchokioos, who compose the Shahala nation. On comparing the vocabulary of the Wahclellahs with that of the Chinnooks, we found that the names for numbers were precisely the same, though the other parts of the language were essentially different. The women of all these tribes braid their hair, pierce the nose, and some of them have lines of dots reaching from the ankle as high as the middle of the leg. These Yehhuhs behaved with great propriety, and condemned the treatment we had received from the Wahclellahs. We purchased from one of them the skin of a sheep killed near this place, for which we gave in exchange the skins of a deer and an elk. These animals, he tells us, usually frequent the rocky parts of the mountains, where they are found in great numbers. The bighorn is also an inhabitant of these mountains, and the natives have several robes made of their skins. The mountains near this place are high, steep, and strewed with rocks, which are principally black. Several species of fir, white pine, and white cedar, forms their covering, while near the river we see the cottonwood, sweet-willow, a species of maple, the broad-leafed ash, the purple haw, a small species of cherry, the purple currant, gooseberry, red-willow, the vining and whiteberry honeysuckle, the huckleberry, sacacommis, two kinds of mountain holly, and the common ash.

APRIL 13TH *Sunday.* The loss of our periogue yesterday obliges us to distribute our loading between the two canoes, and the two remaining periogues. This being done, we proceeded along the north side of the river, but soon finding that the increased loading rendered our vessels difficult to manage, if not dangerous in case of high wind, the two periogues only continued on their route, while captain Lewis with the canoes crossed over to the Yehhuh village, with a view of purchasing one or two more canoes. The village now consisted of eleven houses, crowded with inhabitants, and about sixty fighting men. They were very well disposed, and we found no difficulty in procuring

OTO WARRIOR (King)

two small canoes, in exchange for two robes and four elk skins. We also purchased with deer skins, three dogs, an animal which has now become a favourite food, for it is found to be a strong healthy diet, preferable to lean deer or elk, and much superior to horseflesh in any state. With these he proceeded along the south side of the river, and joined us in the evening. We had gone along the north shore as high as Cruzatte's river, to which place we had sent some hunters the day before yesterday, and where we were detained by the high winds. The hunters however did not join us, and we therefore, as soon as the wind had abated, proceeded on for six miles, where we halted for captain Lewis, and in the meantime went out to hunt. We procured two black-tailed fallow deer, which seem to be the only kind inhabiting these mountains. Believing that the hunters were still below us, we despatched a small canoe back for them, and in the morning, *April 14th*, they all joined us with four more deer. After breakfast we resumed our journey, and though the wind was high during the day, yet by keeping along the northern shore, we were able to proceed without danger. At one o'clock we halted for dinner at a large village situated in a narrow bottom, just above the entrance of Canoe creek. The houses are detached from each other, so as to occupy an extent of several miles, though only twenty in number. Those which are inhabited are on the surface of the earth, and built in the same shape as those near the rapids; but there were others at present evacuated, which are completely under ground. They are sunk about eight feet deep, and covered with strong timbers, and several feet of earth in a conical form. On descending by means of a ladder through a hole at the top, which answers the double purpose of a door and a chimney, we found that the house consisted of a single room, nearly circular and about sixteen feet in diameter.

The inhabitants, who call themselves Weocksockwillacum, differ but little from those near the rapids, the chief distinction in dress, being a few leggings and moccasins, which we find here like those worn by the Chopunnish. These people have ten or twelve very good horses, which are the first we have seen since leaving this neighbourhood last autumn. The country below is, indeed, of such a nature, as to prevent the use of this animal, except in the Columbian valley, and there they would [not] be of great service, for the inhabitants reside chiefly on the river side, and the country is too thickly wooded to suffer them to hunt game on horseback. Most of these, they inform us, have been taken in a warlike excursion, which was lately made against the Towahnahiooks, a part of the Snake nation living in the upper part of the Multnomah, to the southeast of this place. Their language is the same with that of the Chilluckittequaws. They seemed inclined to be very civil, and gave us in exchange, some roots, chapelell, filberts, dried berries, and five dogs.

After dinner we proceeded, and passing at the distance of six miles, the high cliffs on the left, encamped at the mouth of a small run on the same side. A little above us is a village, consisting of about one hundred fighting men of a tribe called Smackshops, many of whom passed the evening with us: They do not differ in any respect from the inhabitants of the village below.

APRIL 15TH In hopes of purchasing horses we did not set out the next morning, *Tuesday*, till after breakfast, and in the meantime exposed our merchandise, and made them various offers; but as they declined bartering, we left them and soon reached the Sepulchre rock, where we halted a few minutes. The rock itself stands near the middle of the river, and contains about two acres of ground above high water. On this surface are scattered thirteen vaults, constructed like those below the Rapids, and some of them more than half filled with dead bodies. After satisfying our curiosity with these venerable remains, we returned to the northern shore, and proceeded to a village at the distance of four miles: on landing, we found that the inhabitants belonged to the same nation we had just left, and as they also had horses, we made a second attempt to purchase a few of them: but with all our dexterity in exhibiting our wares, we could not induce them to sell, as we had none of the only articles which they seemed desirous of procuring, a sort of war hatchet, called by the northwest traders an eye-dog. We therefore purchased two dogs, and taking leave of these Weocksockwillacums, proceeded to another of their villages, just below the entrance of Cataract river. Here too, we tried in vain to purchase some horses, nor did we meet with more success at the two villages of Chilluckittequaws, a few miles farther up the river. At three in the afternoon, we came to the mouth of Quinett creek, which we ascended a short distance and encamped for the night, at the spot we had called Rock fort. Here we were soon visited by some of the people from the great narrows and falls: and on our expressing a wish to purchase horses, they agreed to meet us to-morrow on the north side of the river, where we would open a traffic. They then returned to their villages to collect the horses.

APRIL 16TH *Wednesday.* In the morning, captain Clark crossed with nine men, and a large part of the merchandise, in order to purchase twelve horses to transport our baggage, and some pounded fish, as a reserve during the passage of the Rocky mountains. The rest of the men were employed in hunting and preparing saddles.

From the rapids [Cascades] to this place, and indeed as far as the commencement of the narrows [Dalles], the Columbia is from half a mile to three quarters in width, and possesses scarcely any current: its bed consists principally of rock, except at the entrance of Labiche river, which takes its rise in mount Hood, from which, like Quicksand river, it brings down vast quantities of sand. During the whole course of the Columbia from the Rapids to the Chilluckittequaws are the trunks of many large pine trees standing erect in water, which is thirty feet deep at present, and never less than ten. These trees could never have grown in their present state, for they are all very much doated [doted, decayed], and none of them vegetate; so that the only reasonable account which can be given of this phenomenon, is, that at some period, which the appearance of the trees induces us to fix within twenty years, the rocks from the hill sides have obstructed the narrow pass at the rapids, and caused the river to spread through the woods. The mountains which border as far as the Sepulchre rock, are high and broken, and its romantic views occasionally enlivened by beautiful cascades rushing from the heights, and forming a deep contrast with the firs, cedars and pines, which darken their sides. From the Sepulchre rock, where the low country begins, the long-leafed pine is the almost exclusive growth of timber; but our present camp is the last spot where a single tree is to be seen on the wide plains, which are now spread before us to the foot of the Rocky mountains. It is, however, covered with a rich verdure of grass and herbs, some inches in height, which forms a delightful and exhilarating prospect, after being confined to the mountains and thick forests on the seacoast. The climate too, though only on the border of the plains, is here very different from that we have lately experienced. The air is drier and more pure, and the ground itself is as free from moisture as if there had been no rain for the last ten days. Around this place are many esculent plants used by the Indians: among which is a currant, now in bloom, with a yellow blossom like that of the yellow currant of the Missouri, from which however it differs specifically. There is also a species of hyacinth growing in the plains, which presents at this time a pretty flower of a pale blue colour, and the bulb of which is boiled or baked, or dried in the sun, and eaten by the Indians. This bulb, of the present year, is white, flat in shape and not quite solid, and it overlays and presses closely that of the last year, which, though much thinner and withered, is equally wide, and sends forth from its sides a number of small radicles.

Our hunters obtained one of the long-tailed deer with the young horns, about two inches, and a large black or dark brown pheasant, such as we had seen on the upper part of the Missouri. They also brought in a large grey squirrel, and two others resembling it in shape, but smaller than the common grey squirrel of the United States, and of a pied grey and yellowish brown colour. In addition to this game, they had seen some antelopes, and the tracks of several black bear, but no appearance of elk. They had seen no birds, but found three eggs of the parti-coloured corvus [magpie]. Though the salmon has not yet appeared, we have seen less scarcity than we apprehended from the reports we had heard below. At the rapids, the natives subsist chiefly on a few white salmon-trout, which they take at this time, and considerable quantities of a small indifferent mullet of an inferior quality. Beyond that place we see none except dried fish of the last season, nor is the sturgeon caught by any of the natives above the Columbia, their whole stores consisting of roots, and fish either dried or pounded.

Captain Clark had, in the meantime, been endeavouring to purchase horses, without success, but they promised to trade with him if he would go up to the Skilloot village, above the long narrows. He therefore sent over to us for more merchandise, and then accompanied them in the evening to that place, where he passed the night.

Thursday. The next day he sent to inform us that he was still unable to purchase any horses, but intended going as far as the Eneeshur village to-day, whence he would return to meet us to-morrow at the Skilloot village. In the evening the principal chief of the Chilluckittequaws came to see us, accompanied by twelve of his nation, and hearing that we wanted horses, he promised to meet us at the narrows with some for sale.

APRIL 17TH

Chapter 27

FROM THE DALLES TO WALLA WALLA RIVER

FRIDAY, APRIL 18TH, 1806   We set out this morning after an early breakfast, and crossing the river, continued along the north side for four miles, to the foot of the first rapid. Here it was necessary to unload and make a portage of seven paces over a rock, round which we then drew the empty boats by means of a cord, and the assistance of setting poles. We then reloaded, and at the distance of five miles, reached the basin at the foot of the long narrows. After unloading and arranging the camp, we went up to the Skilloot village, where we found captain Clark. He had not been able to procure more than four horses, for which he was obliged to give double the price of those formerly purchased from the Shoshonees and the first tribe of Flatheads. These, however, we hoped might be sufficient with the aid of the small canoes to convey our baggage as far as the villages near the Muscleshell rapid, where horses are cheaper and more abundant, and where we may probably exchange the canoes for as many horses as we want. The Skilloots, indeed, have a number of horses, but they are unwilling to part with them, though at last we laid out three parcels of merchandise, for each of which they promised to bring us a horse in the morning. The long narrows have a much more formidable appearance than when we passed them in the autumn, so that it would, in fact, be impossible either to descend or go up them in any kind of boat. As we had therefore no further use for the two periogues, we cut them up for fuel.

APRIL 19TH   *Saturday.* Early in the morning, all the party began to carry the merchandise over the portage. This we accomplished with the aid of our four horses, by three o'clock in the afternoon, when we formed our camp a little above the Skilloot village. Since we left them in the autumn they have removed their village a few hundred yards lower down the river, and have exchanged the cellars in which we then found them, for more pleasant dwellings on the surface of the ground. These are formed by sticks, and covered with mats and straw, and so large, that each is the residence of several families. They are also much better clad than any of the natives below, or than they were themselves last autumn; the dress of the men consists generally of leggings, moccasins, and large robes, and many of them wear shirts in the same form used by the Chopunnish and Shoshonees, highly ornamented, as well as the leggings and moccasins, with porcupine quills. Their modesty is protected by the skin of a fox or some other animal, drawn under a girdle and hanging in front like a narrow apron. The dress of the women differs but little from that worn near the rapids; and both sexes wear the hair over the forehead as low as the eyebrows, with large locks cut square at the ears, and the rest hanging in two queues in front of the body. The robes are made principally of the skins of deer, elk, bighorn, some wolf and buffalo, while the children use the skins of the large grey squirrel. The buffalo is procured from the nations higher up the river, who occasionally visit the Missouri; indeed, the greater proportion of their apparel is brought by the nations to the northwest, who come to trade for pounded fish, copper, and beads. Their chief fuel is straw, southern-wood, and small willows. The bear-grass, the bark of the cedar, and the silk-grass are employed in various articles of manufacture.

The whole village was filled with rejoicing to-day, at having caught a single salmon, which was considered as the harbinger of vast quantities in four or five days. In order to hasten their arrival the Indians according to custom, dressed fish and cut it into small pieces, one of which was given to each child in the village. In the good humour excited by this occurrence, they parted, though reluctantly, with four other horses, for which we gave them two kettles, reserving only a single small one for a mess of eight men. Unluckily, however, we lost one of the horses by the negligence of the person to whose charge he was committed. The rest were therefore hobbled and tied; but as the nations here do not understand gelding, all the horses but one were stallions, and this being the season when they are most vicious, we had great difficulty in managing them, and were obliged to keep watch over them all night. In the afternoon captain Clark set out with four men for the Eneeshur village at the grand falls, in order to make further attempts to procure horses.

Sunday. As it was obviously our interest to preserve the good will of these people, we passed over several small thefts which they have committed, but this morning we learnt that six tomahawks and a knife had been stolen during the night. We addressed ourselves to the chief, who seemed angry with his people and made a harangue to them, but we did not recover the articles, and soon after, two of our spoons were missing. We therefore ordered them all from our camp, threatening to beat severely any one detected in purloining. This harshness irritated them so much that they left us in an ill-humour, and we therefore kept on our guard against any insult. Besides this knavery, the faithlessness of the people is intolerable, frequently after receiving goods in exchange for a horse, they return in a few hours and insist on revoking the bargain, or receiving some additional value. We discovered too, that the horse which was missing yesterday, had been gambled away by the fellow from whom we had purchased him, to a man of a different nation, who had carried him off. Besides these, we bought two more horses, two dogs, and some chapelell, and also exchanged a couple of elk skins for a gun belonging to the chief. This was all we could obtain, for though they had a great abundance of dried fish, they would not sell it, except at a price too exorbitant for our finances.

APRIL 20TH

We now found that no more horses could be procured, and therefore prepared for setting out to-morrow. One of the canoes, for which the Indians would give us very little, was cut up for fuel, two others, together with some elk skins and pieces of old iron, we bartered for beads, and the remaining two small canoes were despatched early next morning, *Monday, 21st*, with all the baggage which could not be carried on horseback. We had intended setting out at the same time, but one of our horses broke loose during the night, and we were under the necessity of sending several men in search of him.

In the meantime, the Indians, who were always on the alert, stole a tomahawk, which we could not recover, though several of them were searched. Another fellow was detected in carrying off a piece of iron, and kicked out of camp: captain Lewis then, addressing the Indians, declared that he was not afraid to fight them; for if he chose, he might easily put them to death, and burn their village; that he did not wish to treat them ill if they did not steal; and that although if he knew who had the tomahawks he would take away the horses of the thieves, yet he would rather lose the property altogether than take the horse of an innocent man. The chiefs were present at this harangue, hung their heads and made no reply. At ten o'clock the men returned with the horse, and soon after, an Indian who had promised to go with us as far as the Chopunnish, came with two horses, one of which he politely offered to carry our baggage. We therefore loaded nine horses, and giving the tenth to Bratton, who was still too sick to walk, about ten o'clock left the village of these disagreeable people.

At one o'clock we arrived at the village of the Eneeshurs, where we found captain Clark, who had been completely unsuccessful in his attempts to purchase horses, the Eneeshurs being quite as unfriendly as the Skilloots. Fortunately, however, the fellow who had sold a horse, and afterwards lost him at gambling, belonged to this village, and we insisted on taking the kettle and knife which had been given to him for the horse, if he did not replace it by one of equal value. He preferred the latter, and brought us a very good horse. Being here joined by the canoes and baggage across the portage, we halted half a mile above the town, and took dinner on some dogs, after which we proceeded on about four miles and encamped at a village of Eneeshurs, consisting of nine mat huts, a little below the mouth of the Towahnahiooks. We obtained from these people a couple of dogs and a small quantity of fuel, for which we were obliged to give a higher price than usual. We also bought a horse with a back so much injured, that he can scarcely be of much service to us, but the price was some trifling articles, which in the United States would cost about a dollar and a quarter. The dress, the manners, and the language of the Eneeshurs differ in no respect from those of the Skilloots. Like them too, these Eneeshurs are inhospitable and parsimonious, faithless to their engagements, and in the midst of poverty and filth, retain a degree of pride and arrogance which render our numbers our only protection against insult, pillage, and even murder. We are, however, assured by our Chopunnish guide, who appears to be a very sincere, honest Indian, that the nations above will treat us with much more hospitality.

APRIL 22D *Tuesday.* Two of our horses broke loose in the night and straggled to some distance, so that we were not able to retake them and begin our march before seven o'clock. We had just reached the top of a hill near the village, when the load of one of the horses turned, and the animal taking fright at a robe which still adhered to him, ran furiously towards the village: just as he came there the robe fell, and an Indian hid it in his hut. Two men went back after the horse which they soon took, but the robe was still missing, and the Indians denied having seen it. These repeated acts of knavery now exhausted our patience, and captain Lewis therefore set out for the village, determined to make them deliver up the robe, or to burn the village to the ground. This disagreeable alternative was rendered unnecessary, for on his way he met one of our men, who had found the robe in an Indian hut hid behind some baggage.

We resumed our route, and soon after halted at a hill, from the top of which we enjoyed a commanding view of the range of mountains in which mount Hood stands, and which continue south as far as the eye can reach, with their tops covered with snow. Mount Hood itself bears south 30° west, and the snowy summit of mount Jefferson south 10° west. Towards the south and at no great distance we discern some woody country, and opposite this point of view is the mouth of the Towahnahiooks. This river receives, at the distance of eighteen or twenty miles, a branch from the right, which takes its rise in mount Hood, while the main stream comes in a course from the southeast, and at ten or fifteen miles is joined by a second branch from mount Jefferson. From this place we proceeded with our baggage in the centre, escorted both before and behind by those of the men who were without the care of horses, and having crossed a plain eight miles in extent, reached a village of Eneeshurs, consisting of six houses. Here we bought some dogs on which we dined near the village, and having purchased another horse, went up the river four miles further, to another Eneeshur village of seven mat houses. Our guide now informed us that the next village was at such a distance that we should not reach it this evening, and as we should be able to procure both dogs and wood at this place, we determined to encamp. We here purchased a horse, and engaged for a second in exchange for one of our canoes, but as they were on the opposite side of the river, and the wind very high, they were not able to cross before sunset, at which time the Indian had returned home to the next village above. This evening, as well as at dinner-time, we were obliged to buy wood to cook our meat, for there is no timber in the country, and all the fuel is brought from a great distance. We obtained as much as answered our purposes on moderate terms, but as we are too poor to afford more than a single fire, and lie without any shelter, we find the nights disagreeably cold, though the weather is warm during the daytime.

Wednesday. The next morning two of the horses strayed away in consequence of neglecting to tie them as had been directed. One of them was recovered, but as we had a long ride to make before reaching the next village, we could wait no longer than eleven o'clock for the other. Not being found at that time we set out, and after marching for twelve miles over the sands of a narrow rocky bottom on the north side of the river, came to a village near the Rock rapid, at the mouth of a large creek, which we had not observed in descending. It consisted of twelve temporary huts of mat, inhabited by a tribe called Wahhowpum, who speak a language very similar to that of the Chopunnish, whom they resemble also in dress, both sexes being clad in robes and shirts as well as leggings and moccasins. These people seemed much pleased to see us, and readily gave us four dogs and some chapelell and wood in exchange for small articles, such as pewter-buttons, strips of tin, iron, and brass, and some twisted wire, which we had previously prepared for our journey across the plains. These people, as well as some more living in five huts a little below them, were waiting the return of the salmon. We also found a Chopunnish returning home with his family and a dozen young horses, some of which he wanted us to hire, but this we declined, as in that case we should be obliged to maintain him and his family on the route. After arranging the camp we assembled all the warriors, and having smoked with them, the violins were produced, and some of the men danced. This civility was returned by the Indians in a style of dancing such as we had not yet seen. The spectators formed a circle round the dancers, who with their robes drawn tightly round the shoulders, and divided into parties of five or six men, perform by crossing in a line from one side of the circle to the other. All the parties, performers as well as spectators, sang,

APRIL 23D

and after proceeding in this way for some time, the spectators join, and the whole concludes by a promiscuous dance and song. Having finished, the natives retired at our request, after promising to barter horses with us in the morning. The river is by no means so difficult of passage nor obstructed by so many rapids as it was in the autumn, the water being now sufficiently high to cover the rocks in the bed.

APRIL 24TH *Thursday.* In the morning we began early to look for our horses, but they were not collected before one o'clock. In the meantime we prepared saddles for three new horses which we purchased from the Wahhowpums, and agreed to hire three more from the Chopunnish Indian who was to accompany us with his family. The natives also had promised to take our canoes in exchange for horses; but when they found that we were resolved on travelling by land, they refused giving us any thing, in hopes that we would be forced to leave them. Disgusted at this conduct, we determined rather to cut them to pieces than suffer these people to enjoy them, and actually began to split them, on which they gave us several strands of beads for each canoe. We had now a sufficient number of horses to carry our baggage, and therefore proceeded wholly by land. At two o'clock we set out, and passing between the hills and the northern shore of the river, had a difficult and fatiguing march over a road alternately sandy and rocky. At the distance of four miles, we came to four huts of the Metcowwee tribe, two miles further the same number of huts, and after making twelve miles from our last night's camp, halted at a larger village of five huts of Metcowwees.

As we came along many of the natives passed and repassed without making any advances to converse, though they behaved with distant respect. We observed in our route no animals except the killdeer, the brown lizard, and a moonax, which the people had domesticated as a favourite. Most of the men complain of a soreness in their feet and legs, occasioned by walking on rough stones and deep sands, after being accustomed for some months past to a soft soil. We therefore determined to remain here this evening, and for this purpose bought three dogs and some chapelell, which we cooked with dry grass and willow boughs. The want of wood is a serious inconvenience, on account of the coolness of the nights, particularly when the wind sets from mount Hood, or in any western direction: those winds being much colder than the winds from the Rocky mountains. There are no dews in the plains, and from the appearance, we presume, that no rain has fallen for several weeks.

By nine o'clock the following morning, *Friday 25th*, we collected our horses and proceeded eleven miles to a large village of fifty-one mat houses, where we purchased some wood and a few dogs, on which we made our dinner. The village contained about seven hundred persons of a tribe called Pishquitpah, whose residence on the river is only during the spring and summer, the autumn and winter being passed in hunting through the plains, and along the borders of the mountains. The greater part of them were at a distance from the river as we descended, and never having seen white men before, they flocked round us in great numbers; but although they were exceedingly curious they treated us with great respect, and were very urgent that we should spend the night with them. Two principal chiefs were pointed out by our Chopunnish companion, and acknowledged by the tribe, and we therefore invested each of them with a small medal. We were also very desirous of purchasing more horses; but as our principal stock of merchandise consists of a dirk, a sword, and a few old clothes, the Indians could not be induced to traffic with us. The Pishquitpahs are generally of a good stature and proportion, and as the heads of neither males nor females are so much flattened as those lower down the river, their features are rather pleasant. The hair is braided in the manner practised by their western neighbours; but the generality of the men are dressed in a large robe, under which is a shirt reaching to the knees, where it is met by long leggings, and the feet covered with moccasins: others, however, wear only the truss and robe. As they unite the occupations of hunting and fishing life, both sexes ride very dexterously, their caparison being a saddle or pad of dressed skin, stuffed with goats' hair, and from which wooden stirrups are suspended; and a hair rope tied at both ends to the under jaw of the animal. The horses, however, though good, suffer much, as do in fact all Indian horses, from sore backs.

Finding them not disposed to barter with us, we left the Pishquitpahs at four o'clock, accompanied by eighteen or twenty of their young men on horseback. At the distance of four miles, we passed, without halting, five houses belonging to the Wollawollahs; and five miles further, observing as many willows as would answer the purpose of making fires, availed ourselves of the circumstance, by encamping near them. The country through which we passed bore the same appearance as that of yesterday. The hills on both sides of the river are about two hundred and fifty feet high, generally abrupt and craggy, and in many places presenting a perpendicular face of black, hard, and solid rock. From the top of these hills, the country extends itself in level plains to a very great distance, and though not as fertile as the land near the falls, produces an abundant supply of low grass, which is an excellent food for horses. This grass must indeed be unusually nutritious, for even at this season of the year, after wintering on the dry grass of the plains, and being used with greater severity than is usual among the whites, many of these horses are perfectly fat, nor have we, indeed, seen a single one who was poor. In the course of the day we killed several rattlesnakes, like those of the United States, and saw many of the common as well as the horned-lizard. We also killed six ducks, one of which proved to be of a different species [shoveler duck] from any we had yet seen, being distinguished by yellow legs, and feet webbed like those of the duckinmallard. The Pishquitpahs passed the night with us, and at their request, the violin was played, and some of the men amused themselves with dancing. At the same time we succeeded in obtaining two horses at nearly the same prices which had already been refused in the village.

Saturday. In the morning we set out early. At the distance of three miles, the river hills become low, and retiring to a great distance, leave a low, level, extensive plain, which on the other side of the river, had begun thirteen miles lower. As we were crossing this plain, we were overtaken by several families travelling up the river with a number of horses, and although their company was inconvenient, for the weather was warm, the roads dusty, and their horses crowded in and broke our line of march, yet we were unwilling to displease the Indians by any act of severity. The plain possesses much grass

APRIL 26TH

and a variety of herbaceous plants and shrubs; but after going twelve miles, we were fortunate enough to find a few willows, which enabled us to cook a dinner of jerked elk, and the remainder of the dogs purchased yesterday. We then went on sixteen miles further, and six miles above our camp of the nineteenth of October, encamped in the rain, about a mile below three houses of Wollawollahs. Soon after we halted, an Indian boy took a piece of bone, which he substituted for a fish-hook, and caught several chub, nine inches long.

APRIL 27TH *Sunday.* We were detained till nine o'clock, before a horse, which broke loose in the night, could be recovered. We then passed, near our camp, a small river, called Youmalolam, proceeded through a continuation, till at the distance of fifteen miles, the abrupt and rocky hills three hundred feet high, return to the river. These we ascended, and then crossed a higher plain for nine miles, when we again came to the water side. We had been induced to make this long march because we had but little provisions, and hoped to find a Wollawollah village, which our guide had told us we should reach when next we met the river. There was, however, no village to be seen, and as both the men and horses were fatigued, we halted, and collecting some dry stalks of weeds and the stems of a plant resembling southern wood, cooked a small quantity of jerked meat for dinner. Soon after we were joined by seven Wollawollahs, among whom we recognised a chief by the name of Yellept, who had visited us on the nineteenth of October, when we gave him a medal with the promise of a larger one on our return. He appeared very much pleased at seeing us again, and invited us to remain at his village three or four days, during which he would supply us with the only food they had, and furnish us with horses for our journey. After the cold, inhospitable treatment we have lately received, this kind offer was peculiarly acceptable, and after a hasty meal, we accompanied him to his village, six miles above, situated on the edge of the low country, and about twelve miles below the mouth of Lewis's river.

Immediately on our arrival, Yellept, who proved to be a man of much influence, not only in his own, but in the neighbouring nations, collected the inhabitants, and after having made an harangue, the purport of which was to induce the nations to treat us hospitably, set them an example, by bringing himself an armful of wood, and a platter containing three roasted mullets. They immediately assented to one part, at least of the recommendation, by furnishing us with an abundance of the only sort of fuel they employ, the stems of shrubs growing in the plains. We then purchased four dogs, on which we supped heartily, having been on short allowance for two days past. When we were disposed to sleep, the Indians retired immediately on our request, and indeed, uniformly conducted themselves with great propriety. These people live on roots, which are very abundant in the plains, and catch a few salmon-trout; but at present they seem to subsist chiefly on a species of mullet, weighing from one to three pounds. They now informed us that opposite to the village, there was a route which led to the mouth of the Kooskooskee, on the south side of Lewis's river, that the road itself was good, and passed over a level country, well supplied with water and grass, and that we should meet with plenty of deer and antelope. We knew that a road in that direction would shorten the distance at least eighty miles, and as the report of our guide was confirmed by Yellept and other Indians, we did not hesitate to adopt that course; they added, however, that there were no houses or permanent residence of Indians on the road, and it was therefore deemed prudent not to trust wholly to our guns, but to lay in a stock of provisions.

Monday. In the morning, therefore, we purchased ten dogs. While this trade was carrying on by our men, Yellept brought a fine white horse, and presented him to captain Clark, expressing at the same time, a wish to have a kettle; but on being informed that we had already disposed of the last kettle we could spare, he said he would be content with any present we should make in return. Captain Clark therefore gave his sword, for which the chief had before expressed a desire, adding one hundred balls, some powder, and other small articles, with which he appeared perfectly satisfied. We were now anxious to depart, and requested Yellept to lend us canoes for the purpose of crossing the river. But he would not listen to any proposal of leaving the village. He wished us to remain two or three days; but would not let us go to-day, for he had already sent to invite his neighbours, the Chimnapoos, to come down this evening and join his people in a dance for our amusement. We urged, in vain, that by setting out sooner, we would the earlier return with the articles they desired; for a day, he observed, would make but little difference. We at length mentioned, that as there was no wind, it was now the best time to cross the river, and would merely take the horses over, and return to sleep at their village. To this he assented, and we then crossed with our horses, and having hobbled them, returned to their camp.

APRIL 28TH

Fortunately there was among these Wollawollahs, a prisoner belonging to a tribe of Shoshonee or Snake Indians, residing to the south of the Multnomah, and visiting occasionally the heads of the Wollawollah creek. Our Shoshonee woman, Sacajawea, though she belonged to a tribe near the Missouri, spoke the same language as this prisoner, and by their means we were able to explain ourselves to the Indians, and answer all their inquiries with respect to ourselves and the object of our journey. Our conversation inspired them with much confidence, and they soon brought several sick persons, for whom they requested our assistance. We splintered the broken arm of one, gave some relief to another, whose knee was contracted by rheumatism, and administered what we thought beneficial for ulcers and eruptions of the skin, on various parts of the body, which are very common disorders among them. But our most valuable medicine was eye-water, which we distributed, and which, indeed, they required very much: the complaint of the eyes, occasioned by living on the water, and increased by the fine sand of the plains, being now universal.

A little before sunset, the Chimnapoos, amounting to one hundred men, and a few women, came to the village, and joining the Wollawollahs, who were about the same number of men, formed themselves in a circle round our camp, and waited very patiently till our men were disposed to dance, which they did for about an hour, to the tune of the violin. They then requested to see the Indians dance. With this they readily complied, and the whole assemblage, amounting, with the women and children of the village, to several hundred, stood up, and sang and danced at the same time. The exercise was not, indeed, very violent nor very graceful, for the greater part of them were formed into a solid column, round a kind of hollow square, stood on the same place, and merely jumped up at intervals, to keep time to the music. Some, however, of the more active warriors, entered the square, and danced round it sidewise, and some of our men joined in the dance, to the great satisfaction of the Indians. The dance continued till ten o'clock.

APRIL 29TH *Tuesday.* The next morning Yellept supplied us with two canoes in which we crossed with all our baggage by eleven o'clock, but the horses having strayed to some distance, we could not collect them in time to reach any fit place to encamp if we began our journey, as night would overtake us before we came to water. We therefore thought it advisable to encamp about a mile from the Columbia, on the mouth of the Wollawollah river. This is a handsome stream, about fifty yards wide, and four and a half feet in depth: its waters, which are clear, roll over a bed composed principally of gravel, intermixed with some sand and mud, and though the banks are low they do not seem to be overflowed. It empties into the Columbia, about twelve or fifteen miles from the entrance of Lewis's [Snake] river, and just above a range of high hills crossing the Columbia. Its sources, like those of the Towahnahiooks, Lapage, Youmalolam, and Wollawollah, come, as the Indians inform us, from the north side of a range of mountains which we see to the east and southeast, and which, commencing to the south of mount Hood, stretch in a northeastern direction to the neighbourhood of a southern branch of Lewis's river, at some distance from the Rocky mountains. Two principal branches however of the Towahnahiooks take their rise in mount Jefferson and mount Hood, which in fact appear to separate the waters of the Multnomah and Columbia. They are now about sixty-five or seventy miles from this place, and although covered with snow, do not seem high. To the south of these mountains the Indian prisoner says there is a river, running towards the northwest, as large as the Columbia at this place, which is nearly a mile. This account may be exaggerated, but it serves to show that the Multnomah must be a very large river, and that with the assistance of a southeastern branch of Lewis's river, passing round the eastern extremity of that chain of mountains in which mounts Hood and Jefferson are so conspicuous, waters the vast tract of country to the south, till its remote sources approach those of the Missouri and Rio del Norde.

Near our camp is a fish-weir, formed of two curtains of small willow switches, matted together with withes of the same plant, and extending across the river in two parallel lines, six feet asunder. These are supported by several parcels of poles, in the manner already described, as in use among the Shoshonees, and are either rolled up or let down at pleasure for a few feet, so as either to suffer the fish to pass or detain them. A seine of fifteen or eighteen feet in length is then dragged down the river by two persons, and the bottom drawn up against the curtain of willows. They also employ a smaller seine like a scooping net, one side of which is confined to a semicircular bow five feet long, and half the size of a man's arm, and the other side is held by a strong rope, which being tied at both ends to the bow, forms the chord to the semicircle. This is used by one person, but the only fish which they can take at this time is a mullet of from four to five pounds in weight, and this is the chief subsistence of a village of twelve houses of Wollawollahs, a little below us on this river, as well as of others on the opposite side of the Columbia.

In the course of the day we gave small medals to two inferior chiefs, each of whom made us a present of a fine horse. We were in a poor condition to make an adequate acknowledgment for this kindness, but gave several articles, among which was a pistol, with some hundred rounds of ammunition. We have indeed been treated by these people with an unusual degree of kindness and civility. They seem to have been successful in their hunting during the last winter, for all of them, but particularly the women, are much better clad than when we saw them last; both sexes among the Wollawollahs, as well as the Chimnapoos, being provided with good robes, moccasins, long shirts, and leggings. Their ornaments are similar to those used below, the hair cut in the forehead, and queues falling over the shoulders in front of the body: some have some small plaits at the earlocks, and others tie a bundle of the docked foretop in front of the forehead.

They were anxious that we should repeat our dance of last evening, but as it rained a little and the wind was high, we found the weather too cold for such amusement.

APRIL 30TH

Wednesday. Although we had hobbled and secured our new purchases, we found some difficulty in collecting all our horses. In the meantime we purchased several dogs, and two horses, besides exchanging one of our least valuable horses for a very good one belonging to the Chopunnish who is accompanying us with his family. The daughter of this man is now about the age of puberty, and being incommoded by the disorder incident to that age, she is not permitted to associate with the family, but sleeps at a distance from her father's camp, and on the route always follows at some distance alone. This delicacy or affection is common to many nations of Indians, among whom a girl in that state is separated from her family, and forbidden to use any article of the household or kitchen furniture, or to engage in any occupation. We have now twenty-three horses, many of whom are young and excellent animals, but the greater part of them are afflicted with sore backs. The Indians in general are cruel masters; they ride very hard, and as the saddles are so badly constructed that it is almost impossible to avoid wounding the back, yet they continue to ride when the poor creatures are scarified in a dreadful manner.

At eleven o'clock we left these honest, worthy people, accompanied by our guide and the Chopunnish family, and directed our course north 30° east, across an open level sandy plain, unbroken except by large banks of pure sand, which have drifted in many parts of the plain to the height of fifteen or twenty feet. The rest of the plain is poor in point of soil, but throughout is generally short grass interspersed with aromatic shrubs, and a number of plants, the roots of which supply the chief sustenance of the natives. Among these we observe a root something like the sweet potato. At the distance of fourteen miles we reached a branch of Wollawollah river, rising in the same range of mountains, and empties itself six miles above the mouth of the latter. It is a bold deep stream, about ten yards wide, and seems to be navigable for canoes. The hills of this creek are generally abrupt and rocky, but the narrow bottom is very fertile, and both possess twenty times as much timber as the Columbia itself; indeed, we now find, for the first time since leaving Rockfort, an abundance of firewood. The growth consists of cottonwood, birch, the crimson haw, red and sweet willow, chokecherry, yellow currants, gooseberry, the honeysuckle with a white berry, rosebushes, sevenbark, sumac, together with some corn-grass and rushes. The advantage of a comfortable fire induced us, as the night was come, to halt at this place. We were soon supplied by Drewyer with a beaver and an otter, of which we took only a part of the beaver, and gave the rest to the Indians. The otter is a favourite food, though much inferior, at least in our estimation, to the dog, which they will not eat. The horse too is seldom eaten, and never except when absolute necessity compels them to eat it, as the only alternative to prevent their dying of hunger. This fastidiousness does not, however, seem to proceed so much from any dislike to the food, as from attachment to the animal itself, for many of them eat very heartily of the horse-beef which we give them.

Thursday, May 1st, 1806

At an early hour in the morning we collected our horses, and after breakfast set out about seven o'clock, and followed the road up the creek. The low grounds and plains presented the same appearance as that of yesterday, except that the latter were less sandy. At the distance of nine miles, the Chopunnish Indian, who was in front, pointed out an old unbeaten road to the left, which he informed us was our shortest route. Before venturing, however, to quit our present road, which was level, and not only led us in the proper direction, but was well supplied with wood and water, we halted to let our horses graze till the arrival of our other guide, who happened to be at some distance behind. On coming up he seemed much displeased with the other Indian, and declared that the road we were pursuing was the proper one; that if we decided on taking the left road, it would be necessary to remain till to-morrow morning, and then make an entire day's march before we could reach either water or wood. To this the Chopunnish assented, but declared that he himself meant to pursue that route, and we therefore gave him some powder and lead which he requested.

Four hunters whom we had sent out in the morning, joined us while we halted, and brought us a beaver for dinner. We then took our leave of the Chopunnish at one o'clock, and pursued our route up the creek, through a country similar to that we had passed in the morning. But at the distance of three miles, the hills on the north side became lower, and the bottoms of the creek widened into a pleasant country, two or three miles in extent. The timber too, is now more abundant, and our guide tells us that we shall not want either wood or game from this place as far as the Kooskooskee. We have already seen a number of deer, of which we killed one, and observed great quantities of the curlew, as well as some cranes, ducks, prairie larks, and several species of sparrow, common to the prairies. There is, in fact, very little difference in the general face of the country here from that of the plains on the Missouri, except that the latter are enlivened by vast herds of buffalo, elk and other animals, which give it an additional interest. Over these wide bottoms we continued on a course north, 75° east, till, at the distance of seventeen miles from where we dined, and twenty-six from our last encampment, we halted for the night.

We had scarcely encamped, when three young men came up from

the Wollawollah village, with a steel trap, which had been left behind inadvertently, and which they had come a whole day's journey in order to restore. This act of integrity was the more pleasing, because, though very rare among Indians, it corresponds perfectly with the general behaviour of the Wollawollahs, among whom we had lost carelessly several knives, which were always returned as soon as found. We may, indeed, justly affirm, that of all the Indians whom we have met since leaving the United States, the Wollawollahs were the most hospitable, honest and sincere.

Chapter 28

FROM THE WALLA WALLA TO COMMEARP CREEK

FRIDAY, MAY 2D, 1806 We despatched two hunters ahead; but the horse we had yesterday purchased from the Chopunnish, although closely hobbled, contrived to break loose in the night, and went back to rejoin his companions. He was however overtaken and brought to us about one o'clock, and we then set forward. For three miles we followed a hilly road on the north side of the creek, opposite to a wide bottom, where a branch falls in from the southwest mountains, which, though covered with snow, are about twenty-five miles distant, and do not appear high. We then entered an extensive level bottom, with about fifty acres of land well covered with pine near the creek, and the long-leafed pine occasionally on the sides of the hills along its banks. After crossing the creek at the distance of seven miles from our camp, we repassed it seven miles further, near the junction of one of its branches from the northeast. The main stream here bears to the south, towards the mountains where it rises, and its bottoms then become narrow, as the hills are higher. We followed the course of this northeast branch in a direction N. 45° E. for eight and three quarter miles, when having made nineteen miles, we halted in a little bottom on the north side. The creek is here about four yards wide, and as far as we can perceive, it comes from the east, but the road here turns from it into the high open plain. The soil of the country seems to improve as we advance, and this afternoon we see, in the bottoms, an abundance of quamash now in bloom. We killed nothing but a duck, though we saw two deer at a distance, as well as many sandhill crows, curlews, and other birds common to the prairies, and there is much sign of both beaver and otter, along the creeks. The three young Wollawollahs continued with us. During the day we observed them eating the inner part of the young succulent stem of a plant very common in the rich lands on the Mississippi, Ohio and its branches. It is a large coarse plant, with a ternate leaf, the leaflets of which are three-lobed, and covered with a woolly pubescence, while the flower and fructification resemble that of the parsnip. On tasting this plant, we found it agreeable, and eat heartily of it without any inconvenience.

MAY 3D *Saturday.* We set out at an early hour, and crossed the high plains, which we found more fertile and less sandy than below; yet, though the grass is taller, there are very few aromatic shrubs. After pursuing a course N. 25° E. for twelve miles, we reached the Kinnooenim. This creek rises in the southwest mountains, and though only twelve yards wide, discharges a considerable body of water into Lewis's river, a few miles above the narrows. Its bed is pebbled, its banks low, and the hills near its sides high and rugged; but in its narrow bottoms are found some cottonwood, willow, and the underbrush, which grows equally on the east branch of the Wollawollah. After dining at the Kinnooenim, we resumed our journey over the high plains, in the direction of N. 45° E. and reached, at the distance of three miles, a small branch of that creek about five yards wide. The lands in its neighbourhood are composed of a dark rich loam; its hill sides, like those of the Kinnooenim, are high, its bottoms narrow, and possess but little timber. It increased however in quantity as we advanced along the north side of the creek for eleven miles.

At that distance we were agreeably surprised by the appearance of Weahkoonut, or the Indian whom we had called the Bighorn, from the circumstance of his wearing a horn of that animal, suspended from his left arm. He had gone down with us last year along Lewis's river, and was highly serviceable in preparing the minds of the natives for our reception. He is, moreover, the first chief of a large band of Chopunnish; and hearing that we were on our return, he had come with ten of his warriors to meet us. He now turned back with us, and we continued up the bottoms of the creek for two miles, till the road began to leave the creek, and cross the hill to the plains. We therefore encamped for the night in a grove of cottonwood, after we had made a disagreeable journey of twenty-eight miles. During the greater part of the day the air was keen and cold, and it alternately rained, hailed and snowed; but, though the wind blew with great violence, it was fortunately from the southwest, and on our backs. We had consumed at dinner the last of our dried meat, and nearly all that was left of the dogs; so that we supped very scantily on the remainder, and had nothing for to-morrow. Weahkoonut, however, assured us that there was a house on the river at no great distance, where we might supply ourselves with provisions. We now missed our guide and the Wollawollahs, who left us abruptly this morning, and never returned.

Sunday. After a disagreeable night, we collected our horses at an early hour and proceeded with a continuation of the same weather. We are now nearer to the southwest mountains, which appear to become lower as they advance towards the northeast. We followed the road over the plains, north 60° east, for four miles to a ravine, where was the source of a small creek, down the hilly and rocky sides of which we proceeded for eight miles to its entrance into Lewis's river, about seven miles and a half above the mouth of the Kooskooskee. Near this place we found the house of which Weahkoonut had mentioned, and where we now halted for breakfast. It contained six families, but so miserably poor that all we could obtain from them were two lean dogs and a few large cakes of half cured bread, made of a root resembling the sweet potato, of all which we contrived to form a kind of soup. The soil of the plain is good, but it has no timber. The range of southwest mountains is about fifteen miles above us, but continues to lower, and is still covered with snow to its base. After giving a passage to Lewis's river, near their northeastern extremity, they terminate in a high level plain between that river and the Kooskooskee. The salmon not having yet called them to the rivers, the greater part of the Chopunnish are now dispersed in villages through this plain, for the purpose of collecting quamash and cows, which here grow in great abundance, the soil being extremely fertile, and in many places covered with the long-leafed pine, the larch, and balsam-fir, which contribute to render it less thirsty than the open unsheltered plains.

MAY 4TH

After our repast we continued our route along the west side of the river, where as well as on the opposite shore, the high hills approach it closely, till at the distance of three miles we halted opposite to two houses: the inhabitants consisted of five families of Chopunnish, among whom were Tetoh, or Sky, the younger of the two chiefs who accompanied us in the autumn to the great falls of the Columbia, and also our old pilot who had conducted us down the river to the Columbia. They both advised us to cross here, and ascend the Kooskooskee on the northeast side, this being the shortest and best route to the forks of that river, where we should find the Twistedhair, in whose charge we left our horses, and to which place they promised to show us the way. We did not hesitate to accept this offer, and therefore crossed with the assistance of three canoes; but as the night was coming on, we purchased a little wood and some roots of cows, and encamped, though we had made only fifteen miles to-day. The evening proved cold and disagreeable, and the natives crowded round our fire in such numbers that we could scarcely cook or even keep ourselves warm.

At these houses of Chopunnish we observed a small hut with a single fire, which we are informed is appropriated for women who are undergoing the operation of the menses; there they are obliged to retreat; the men are not permitted to approach within a certain distance of them, and when any thing is to be conveyed to those deserted females, the person throws it to them forty or fifty paces off, and then retires. It is singular, indeed, that amongst the nations of the wilderness, there should be found customs and rites so nearly resembling those of the Jews. It is scarcely necessary to allude more particularly to the uncleanness of Jewish females and the rites of purification.

MAY 5TH *Monday.* We collected our horses, and at seven o'clock set forward alone; for Weahkoonut, whose people resided above on the west side of Lewis's river, continued his route homeward when we crossed to the huts. Our road was across the plains for four and a half miles, to the entrance of the Kooskooskee. We then proceeded up that river, and at five miles reached a large mat house, but could not procure any provisions from the inhabitants, but on reaching another three miles beyond, we were surprised at the liberality of an Indian, who gave captain Clark a very elegant grey mare, for which, all he requested was a vial of eye-water.

Last autumn, while we were encamped at the mouth of the Chopunnish river, a man who complained of a pain in his knee and thigh, was brought to us in hopes of receiving relief. The man was to appearance recovered from his disorder, though he had not walked for some time. But that we might not disappoint them, captain Clark, with much ceremony, washed and rubbed his sore limb, and gave him some volatile liniment to continue the operation, which either caused, or rather did not prevent his recovery. The man gratefully circulated our praises, and our fame as physicians was increased by the efficacy of some eye-water which we gave them at the same time. We are by no means displeased at this new resource for obtaining subsistence, as they will give us no provisions without merchandise, and our stock is now very much reduced: we cautiously abstain from giving them any but harmless medicines, and as we cannot possibly do harm, our prescriptions, though unsanctioned by the faculty, may be useful, and are entitled to some remuneration.

Four miles beyond this house we came to another large one, containing ten families, where we halted, and made our dinner on two dogs and a small quantity of roots, which we did not procure without much difficulty. Whilst we were eating, an Indian standing by, and looking with great derision at our eating dogs, threw a poor half-starved puppy almost into captain Lewis's plate, laughing heartily at the humour of it. Captain Lewis took up the animal and flung it with great force into the fellow's face, and seizing his tomahawk, threatened to cut him down if he dared to repeat such insolence.

He immediately withdrew, apparently much mortified, and we continued our repast of dog very quietly. Here we met our old Chopunnish guide, with his family, and soon afterwards one of our horses, which had been separated from the rest in the charge of the Twistedhair, and been in this neighbourhood for several weeks, was caught and restored to us.

After dinner we proceeded to the entrance of Colter's creek, at the distance of four miles, and having made twenty and a half miles, encamped on the lower side of it. Colter's creek rises not far from the Rocky mountains, and passing in the greater part of its course through a country well supplied with pine, discharges a large body of water. It is about twenty-five yards wide, with a pebbled bed and low banks. At a little distance from us are two Chopunnish houses, one of which contains eight families, and the other, which is by much the largest we have ever seen, inhabited by at least thirty. It is rather a kind of shed, built like all the other huts, of straw and mats in the form of the roof of a house, one hundred and fifty-six feet long, and about fifteen wide, closed at the ends, and having a number of doors on each side. The vast interior is without partitions, but the fire of each family is kindled in a row along the middle of the building, and about ten feet apart.

This village is the residence of one of the principal chiefs of the nation, who is called Neeshnepahkeook, or *Cutnose*, from the circumstance of having his nose cut from the stroke of a lance in battle with the Snake Indians. We gave him a small medal, but though he is a great chief, his influence among his own people does not seem to be considerable, and his countenance possesses very little intelligence. We arrived very hungry and weary, but could not purchase any provisions, except a small quantity of the roots and bread of the cows. They had, however, heard of our medical skill, and made many applications for assistance, but we refused to do any thing unless they gave us either dogs or horses to eat. We had soon nearly fifty patients. A chief brought his wife with an abscess on her back, and promised to furnish us with a horse to-morrow if we would relieve her. Captain Clark, therefore, opened the abscess, introduced a tent, and dressed it with basilicon. We prepared also, and distributed some doses of the flour of sulphur and cream of tartar, with directions for its use. For these we obtained several dogs, but too poor for use, and we therefore postponed our medical operations till the morning. In the meantime a number of Indians, beside the residents of the village, gathered about us or encamped in the woody bottom of the creek.

In the evening, we learnt by means of a Snake Indian, who happens to be at this place, that one of the old men has been endeavouring to excite prejudices against us, by observing that he thought we were bad men, and came here, most probably, for the purpose of killing them. In order to remove such impressions, we made a speech, in which, by means of the Snake Indian, we told them our country and all the purposes of our visit. While we were engaged in this occupation, we were joined by Weahkoonut, who assisted us in effacing all unfavourable impressions from the minds of the Indians.

MAY 6TH

Tuesday. The following morning our practice became more valuable. The woman declared that she had slept better than at any time since her illness. She was therefore dressed a second time, and her husband, according to promise, brought us a horse, which we immediately killed. Besides this woman, we had crowds of other applicants, chiefly afflicted with sore eyes, and after administering to them for several hours, found ourselves once more in possession of a plentiful meal, for the inhabitants began to be more accommodating, and one of them even gave us a horse for our remedies to his daughter, a little girl, who was afflicted with the rheumatism. We moreover, exchanged one of our horses with Weahkoonut, by the addition of a small flag, which procured us an excellent sorrel horse.

We here found three men, of a nation called Skeetsomish, who reside at the falls of a large river, emptying itself into the north side of the Columbia. This river takes its rise from a large lake in the mountains, at no great distance from the falls where these natives live. We shall designate this river, hereafter, by the name of Clark's river, as we do not know its Indian appellation, and we are the first whites who have ever visited its principal branches; for the Great Lake river mentioned by Mr. Fidler, if at all connected with Clark's river, must be a very inconsiderable branch. To this river, moreover, which we have hitherto called Clark's river, which rises in the southwest mountains, we restored the name of Towahnahiooks, the name by which it is known to the Eneeshurs. In dress and appearance these Skeetsomish were not to be distinguished from the Chopunnish, but their language is entirely different, a circumstance which we did not learn till their departure, when it was too late to procure from them a vocabulary.

About two o'clock we collected our horses and set out, accompanied by Weahkoonut, with ten or twelve men, and a man who said he was the brother of the Twistedhair. At four miles we came to a single house of three families, but we could not procure provisions of any kind; and five miles further we halted for the night near another house, built like the rest, of sticks, mats and dried hay, and containing six families. It was now so difficult to procure any thing to eat that our chief dependence was on the horse which we received yesterday for medicine; but to our great disappointment, he broke the rope by which he was confined, made his escape, and left us supperless in the rain.

MAY 7TH *Wednesday.* The next morning, Weahkoonut and his party left us, and we proceeded up the river with the brother of the Twistedhair as a guide. The Kooskooskee is now rising fast, the water is clear and cold, and as all the rocks and shoals are now covered, the navigation is safe, notwithstanding the rapidity of the current. The timber begins about the neighbourhood of Colter's creek, and consists chiefly of long-leafed pine. After going four miles, we reached a house of six families, below the entrance of a small creek, where our guide advised us to cross the river, as the route was better, and the game more abundant near the mouth of the Chopunnish. We therefore unloaded, and by means of a single canoe, passed to the south side in about four hours, during which time we dined. An Indian of one of the houses now brought two canisters of powder, which his dog had discovered under ground in a bottom some miles above. We immediately knew them to be the same we had buried last autumn, and as he had kept them safely, and had honesty enough to return them, we rewarded him inadequately, but as well as we could, with a steel for striking fire. We set out at three o'clock, and pursued a difficult and stony road for two miles, when we left the river and ascended the hills on the right, which begin to resemble mountains.

But when we reached the heights, we saw before us a beautiful level country, partially ornamented with the long-leafed pine, and supplied with an excellent pasture of thick grass, and a variety of herbaceous plants, the abundant productions of a dark rich soil. In many parts of the plain, the earth is thrown up into little mounds, by some animal [the pocket-gopher], whose habits most resemble those of the salamander; but although these tracks are scattered over all the plains from the Mississippi to the Pacific, we have never yet been able to obtain a sight of the animal itself.

As we entered the plain Neeshnepahkee, the Cutnose, overtook us, and after accompanying us a few miles, turned to the right to visit some of his people, who were now gathering roots in the plain. Having crossed the plain a little to the south of east, we descended a long steep hill, at the distance of five miles, to a creek six yards wide, which empties itself into the Kooskooskee. We ascended this little stream for a mile, and encamped at an Indian establishment of six houses, which seem to have been recently evacuated. Here we were joined by Neeshnepahkee, and the Shoshonee who had interpreted for us on the fifth.

From the plain we observed that the spurs of the Rocky mountains are still perfectly covered with snow, which the Indians inform us is so deep that we shall not be able to pass before the next full moon, that is, the first of June: though others place the time for crossing at a still greater distance. To us, who are desirous of reaching the plains of the Missouri, if for no other reason, for the purpose of enjoying a good meal, this intelligence was by no means welcome, and gave no relish to the remainder of the horse killed at Colter's creek, which formed our supper, part of which had already been our dinner. Observing, however, some deer, and a great appearance of more, we determined to make an attempt to get some of them.

Thursday. Therefore, after a cold night's rest, most of the hunters set out at daylight. By eleven o'clock they all returned, with four deer, and a duck of an uncommon kind, which, with the remains of our horse, formed a stock of provisions such as we had not lately possessed. Without our facilities of procuring subsistence with guns, the natives of this country must often suffer very severely. During last winter they were so much distressed for food, that they were obliged to boil and eat the moss growing on the pine trees. At the same period they cut down nearly all the long-leafed pines, which we observed on the ground, for the purpose of collecting its seed, which resemble in size and shape that of the large sunflower, and when roasted or boiled, is nutritious and not disagreeable to the taste. At the present season they peel this pine tree, and eat the inner and succulent bark. In the creek near us, they also procure trout by means of a falling trap, constructed on the same plan with those common to the United States. We gave Neeshnepahkee and his people some of our game and horse-beef, besides the entrails of the deer, and four fawns which we found inside of two of them. They did not eat any of it perfectly raw, but the entrails had very little cooking, and the fawns were boiled whole, and the hide, hair, and entrails all consumed. The Shoshonee was offended at not having as much venison as he wished, and refused to interpret; but as we took no notice of him, he became very officious in the course of a few hours, and made many efforts to reinstate himself in our favour. The mother [brother] of the Twistedhair, and Neeshnepahkee-

MAY 8TH

ook now drew a sketch, which we preserved, of all the waters west of the Rocky mountains. They make the main southern branch of Lewis's river, much more extensive than the other, and place a great number of Shoshonee villages on its western side.

Between three and four o'clock in the afternoon we set out, in company with Neeshnepahkeeook and other Indians, the brother of the Twistedhair having left us. Our route was up a high steep hill to a level plain, with little wood, through which we passed in a direction parallel to the river, for four miles, when we met the Twistedhair and six of his people. To this chief we had confided our horses and a part of our saddles, last autumn, and we therefore formed very unfavourable conjectures on finding that he received us with great coldness. Shortly after he began to speak in a very loud, angry manner, and was answered by Neeshnepahkeeook. We now discovered that a violent quarrel had arisen between these chiefs, on the subject, as we afterwards understood, of our horses. But as we could not learn the cause, and were desirous of terminating the dispute, we interposed, and told them we should go on to the first water and encamp. We therefore set out, followed by all the Indians, and having reached, at two miles distance, a small stream, running to the right, we encamped with the two chiefs and their little bands, forming separate camps, at a distance from each other. They all appeared to be in an ill humour, and as we had already heard reports that the Indians had discovered and carried off our saddles, and that the horses were very much scattered, we began to be uneasy, lest there should be too much foundation for the report. We were therefore anxious to reconcile the two chiefs as soon as possible, and desired the Shoshonee to interpret for us, while we attempted a mediation: but he peremptorily refused to speak a word: he observed that it was a quarrel between the two chiefs, and he had therefore no right to interfere; nor could all our representations, that by merely repeating what we said, he could not possibly be considered as meddling between the chiefs, induce him to take any part in it.

Soon afterwards Drewyer returned from hunting, and was sent to invite the Twistedhair to come and smoke with us. He accepted the invitation, and as we were smoking the pipe over our fire, he informed us, that according to his promise, on leaving us at the falls of the Columbia, he had collected our horses and taken charge of them, as soon as he had reached home. But about this time Neeshnepahkeeooks and Tunnachemootoolt (the Brokenarm) who, as we passed, had been on a war-party against the Shoshonees on the south branch of Lewis's river, returned, and becoming jealous of him, because the horses had been confided to his care, were constantly quarrelling with him. At length, being an old man, and unwilling to live in perpetual dispute with the two chiefs, he had given up the care of the horses, which had consequently become very much scattered. The greater part of them were, however, still in this neighbourhood; some in the forks between the Chopunnish and Kooskooskee, and three or four at the village of the Brokenarm, about half a day's march higher up the river. He added, that on the rise of the river in the spring, the earth had fallen from the door of the cache and exposed the saddles, some of which had probably been lost; but as soon as he was acquainted with the situation of them, he had them buried in another deposit, where they now are. He now promised that if we would stay to-morrow at his house, a few miles from this place, he would collect such of the horses as were in the neighbourhood, and send his young men for those in the forks over the Kooskooskee. He moreover advised us to visit the Brokenarm, who was a chief of great eminence, and that he would himself guide us to his dwelling. We told him that we meant to follow his advice in every respect; that we had confided our horses to his charge, and expected that he would deliver them to us, on which we should willingly pay him the two guns and ammunition, as we had promised. With this he seemed very much pleased, and declared that he would use every exertion to restore our horses. We now sent for the Cutnose, and after smoking for some time, took occasion to express to the two chiefs, our regret at seeing a misunderstanding between them. Neeshnepahkeeook told us that the Twistedhair was a bad old man, and wore two faces; for instead of taking care of our horses, he had suffered his young men to hunt with them, so that they had been very much injured, and that it was for this reason that the Brokenarm and himself had forbidden him to use them. The Twistedhair made no reply to this speech, after which we told Neeshnepahkeeook of our arrangement for to-morrow. He appeared very well satisfied, and said that he would himself go with us to the Brokenarm, who expected that we would see him, and who had "two bad horses for us," an expression by which was meant that he intended making us a present of two valuable horses. That chief, he also informed us, had been apprised of our want of provisions, and sent four young men to meet us with a supply; but having taken a different road, they had missed us. After this interview we retired to rest at a late hour.

Friday. In the morning, after sending out several hunters, we proceeded through a level rich country, similar to that of yesterday, for six miles, when we reached the house of the Twistedhair, situated near some larch trees, and a few bushes of balsam fir. It was built in the usual form, of sticks, mats, and dried hay, and although it contained no more than two fires and twelve persons, was provided with the customary appendage of a small hut, to which females in certain situations were to retreat. As soon as we halted at this place, we went with the Twistedhair to the spot where he had buried our saddles, and two other young Indians were despatched after the horses. Our hunters joined us with nothing but a few pheasants, the only deer which they killed being lost in the river. We therefore dined on soup, made of the roots of cows, which we purchased of the Indians. Late in the afternoon, the Twistedhair returned with about half the saddles we had left in the autumn, and some powder and lead which was buried at the same place. Soon after, the Indians brought us twenty-one of our horses, the greater part of whom were in excellent order, though some had not yet recovered from hard usage, and three had sore backs. We were however very glad to procure them in any condition. Several Indians came down from the village of Tunnachemootoolt, and passed the night with us. The Cutnose and Twistedhair seem now perfectly reconciled, for they both slept in the house of the latter. The man who had imposed himself upon us as a brother of the Twistedhair, also came and renewed his advances, but we now found that he was an impertinent proud fellow, of no respectability in the nation, and we therefore felt no inclination to cultivate his intimacy. Our camp was in an open plain, and soon became very uncomfortable, for the wind was high and cold, and the rain and hail which began about seven o'clock, changed in about two hours

MAY 9TH

to a heavy fall of snow, which continued till after six o'clock the next morning, when it ceased, after covering the ground eight inches deep, and leaving the air keen and cold.

MAY 10TH *Saturday.* We soon collected our horses, and after a scanty breakfast of roots, set out on a course S. 35° E. across the plains, the soil of which being covered with snow, we could only judge from observing that near the ravines, where it had melted, the mud was deep, black, and well supplied with quamash. The road was very slippery, and the snow stuck to the horses' feet and made them slip down very frequently. After going about sixteen miles, we came to the hills of Commearp creek, which are six hundred feet in height, but the tops of which only are covered with snow, the lower parts as well as the bottoms of the creek having had nothing but rain while it snowed in the high plains. On descending these hills to the creek, we reached about four o'clock, the house of Tunnachemootoolt, where was displayed the flag which we had given him, raised on a staff: under this we were received with due form, and then conducted a short distance to a good spot for an encampment, on Commearp creek.

We soon collected the men of consideration, and after smoking, explained how destitute we were of provisions. The chief spoke to the people, who immediately brought about two bushels of dried quamash roots, some cakes of the roots of cows, and a dried salmon trout: we thanked them for this supply, but observed that, not being accustomed to live on roots alone, we feared that such diet might make our men sick, and therefore proposed to exchange one of our good horses, which was rather poor, for one that was fatter, and which we might kill. The hospitality of the chief was offended at the idea of an exchange; he observed that his people had an abundance of young horses, and that if we were disposed to use that food, we might have as many as we wanted. Accordingly, they soon gave us two fat young horses, without asking any thing in return, an act of liberal hospitality much greater than any we have witnessed since crossing the Rocky mountains, if it be not in fact the only really hospitable treatment we have received in this part of the world. We killed one of the horses, and then telling the natives that we were fatigued and hungry, and that as soon as we were refreshed, we would communicate freely with them, began to prepare our repast.

During this time, a principal chief, called Hohastillpilp, came from his village about six miles distant, with a party of fifty men, for the purpose of visiting us. We invited him into our circle, and he alighted and smoked with us, while his retinue, who had five elegant horses, continued mounted at a short distance. While this was going on, the chief had a large leathern tent spread for us, and desired that we would make that our home whilst we remained at his village. We removed there, and having made a fire, and cooked a supper of horse-beef and roots, collected all the distinguished men present, and spent the evening in explaining who we were, the objects of our journey, and giving answers to their inquiries. To each of the chiefs, Tunnachemootoolt, and Hohastillpilp, we gave a small medal, explaining their use and importance, as honorary distinctions both among the whites and red men. Our men are delighted at once more having made a hearty meal. They have generally been in the habit of crowding the houses of the Indians, and endeavouring to purchase provisions on the best terms they could; for the inhospitality of the country was such, that in the extreme of hunger they were often obliged to treat the natives with but little ceremony, but this the Twistedhair had told us was disagreeable. Finding that these people are so kind and liberal, we ordered our men to treat them with great respect and not to throng round their fires, so that they now agree perfectly well together. After our council, the Indians felt no disposition to retire, and our tent was crowded with them all night.

Sunday. The next morning we arose early and breakfasted again on horseflesh. This village of Tunnachemootoolt, is in fact only a single house, one hundred and fifty feet long, built after the Chopunnish fashion, with sticks, straw, and dried grass. It contains twenty-four fires, about double that number of families, and might perhaps muster one hundred fighting men. The usual outhouse, or retiring hut for females, is not omitted. Their chief subsistence is roots, and the noise made by the women in pounding them, gives the hearer the idea of a nail factory. Yet, notwithstanding so many families are crowded together, the Chopunnish are much more cleanly in their persons and habitations, than any people we have met since we left the Ottoes on the river Platte.

MAY 11TH

In the course of the morning, a chief named Yoompahkatim, a stout good looking man, of about forty years of age, who had lost his left eye, arrived from his village on the south side of Lewis's river. We gave him a small medal, and finding that there were now present the principal chiefs of the Chopunnish nation, Tunnachemootoolt (the Brokenarm) Neeshnepahkeeook, Yoompahkatim, and Hohastilpilp, whose rank is in the order they are mentioned, we thought this a favourable moment to explain to them the intentions of our government. We therefore collected the chiefs and warriors, and having drawn a map of the relative situation of our country, on a mat, with a piece of coal, detailed the nature and power of the American nation, its desire to preserve harmony between all its red brethren, and its intention of establishing trading houses for their relief and support. It was not without difficulty, nor till after nearly half the day was spent, that we were able to convey all this information to the Chopunnish, much of which might have been lost or distorted, in its circuitous route through a variety of languages; for in the first place, we spoke in English to one of our men, who translated it into French to Chaboneau; he interpreted it to his wife in the Minnetaree language, and she then put it into Shoshonee, and the young Shoshonee prisoner explained it to the Chopunnish in their own dialect. At last we succeeded in communicating the impression they wished, and then adjourned the council; after which we amused them by showing the wonders of the compass, the spy-glass, the magnet, the watch and air-gun, each of which attracted its share of admiration. They said that after we had left the Minnetarees last autumn, three young Chopunnish had gone over to that nation, who had mentioned our visit and the extraordinary articles we had with us, but they placed no confidence in it until now. Among other persons present, was a youth, son of the Chopunnish chief, of much consideration, killed not long since by the Minnetarees of Fort de Prairie. As soon as the council was over, he brought a very fine mare with a colt, and begged us to accept them as a proof that he meant to pursue our advice, for he had opened his ears to our councils, which had made his heart glad.

We now resumed our medical labours, and had a number of patients afflicted with scrofula, rheumatism and sore eyes, to all which we administered very cheerfully as far as our skill and supplies of medicine would permit. We also visited a chief who has for three years past so completely lost the use of his limbs, that he lies like a perfect corpse in whatever position he is placed, yet he eats heartily, digests his food very well, has a regular pulse, and retains his flesh; in short, were he not somewhat pale from lying so long out of the sun, he might be mistaken for a man in perfect health. This disease does not seem to be common; indeed, we have seen only three cases of it among the Chopunnish, who alone are afflicted with it. The scrofulous disorders we may readily conjecture to originate in the long confinement to vegetable diet; which may perhaps also increase the soreness of the eyes; but this strange disorder baffles at once our curiosity and our skill.

MAY 12TH *Monday.* Our assistance was again demanded early the next morning by a crowd of Indians, to whom we gave eye-water. Shortly after, the chiefs and warriors held a council among themselves, to decide on the answer to our speech; and the result was, as we were informed, that they confided in what we had told them, and resolved to follow our advice. This resolution once made the principal chief, Tunnachemootoolt, took a quantity of flour of the roots of cows, and going round to all the kettles and baskets, in which his people were cooking, thickened the soup into a kind of mush. He then began a harangue, making known the result of the deliberations among the chiefs, and after exhorting them to unanimity, concluded by an invitation to all who agreed to the proceedings of the council, to come and eat, while those who would not abide by the decision of the chiefs were requested to show their dissent by not partaking in the feast. During this animated harangue, the women, who were probably uneasy at the prospect of forming this new connection with strangers, tore their hair, and wrung their hands with the greatest appearance of distress. But the concluding appeal of the orator effectually stopped the mouths of every malcontent, and the proceedings were ratified, and the mush devoured with the most zealous unanimity.

The chiefs and warriors then came in a body to visit us, as we were seated near our tent, and at their instance, two young men, one of whom was the son of Tunnachemootoolt, and the other the youth whose father had been killed by the Pahkees, presented to each of us a fine horse. We caused the chiefs to be seated, and gave every one of them a flag, a pound of powder, and fifty balls, and a present of the same kind to the young men from whom we had received the horses. They then invited us into the tent, and told us that they now wished to answer what we had told them yesterday; but that many of their people were at that moment waiting in great pain for our medical assistance. It was therefore agreed that captain Clark, who is the favourite physician, should visit the sick, while captain Lewis would hold the council; which was accordingly opened by an old man, the father of Hohas-stilpilp.

He began by declaring that the nation had listened with attention to our advice, and had only one heart and one tongue in declaring their determination to follow it. They knew well the advantages of peace, for they valued the lives of their young men too much to expose them to the dangers of war; and their desire to live quietly with their neighbours, had induced them last summer to send three warriors with a pipe to the Shoshonees, in the plains of Columbia, south of Lewis's river. These ministers of peace had been killed by the Shoshonees, against whom the nation immediately took up arms. They had met them last winter, and killed forty-two men, with the loss of only three of their own party; so that having revenged their deceased brethren, they would no longer make war on the Shoshonees, but receive them as friends. As to going with us to the plains of the Missouri, they would be very willing to do so, for though the Blackfoot Indians and the Pahkees had shed much of their blood, they still wished to live in peace with them. But we had not yet seen either of these nations, and it would therefore be unsafe for them to venture, till they were assured of not being attacked by them. Still, however, some of their young men would accompany us across the mountains, and if they could effect a peace with their enemies, the whole nation would go over to the Missouri in the course of next summer. On our proposal that one of the chiefs should go with us to the country of the whites, they had not yet decided, but would let us know before we left them. But that, at all events, the whites might calculate on their attachment and their best services, for though poor, their hearts were good. The snow was, however, still so deep on the mountains, that we should perish in attempting the passage, but if we waited till after the next full moon, the snows would have sufficiently melted to enable our horses to subsist on the grass.

As soon as this speech was concluded, captain Lewis replied at some length: with this they appeared highly gratified, and after smoking the pipe, made us a present of another fat horse for food. We, in turn, gave the Brokenarm a vial of eye-water, with directions to wash the eyes of all who should apply for it; and as we promised to fill it again when it was exhausted, he seemed very much pleased with our liberality. To the Twistedhair, who had last night collected six more horses, we gave a gun, an hundred balls, and two pounds of powder, and told him he should have the same quantity when we received the remainder of our horses. In the course of the day three more of them were brought in, and a fresh exchange of small presents put the Indians in excellent humour. On our expressing a wish to cross the river, and form a camp, in order to hunt and fish till the snows had melted, they recommended a position a few miles distant, and promised to furnish us to-morrow with a canoe to cross. We invited the Twistedhair to settle near our camp, for he has several young sons, one of whom we hope to engage as a guide, and he promised to do so. Having now settled all their affairs, the Indians divided themselves into two parties, and began to play the game of hiding a bone, already described, as common to all the natives of this country, which they continued playing for beads and other ornaments.

Chapter 29

ENCAMPED ON THE UPPER KOOSKOOSKEE

TUESDAY, MAY 13TH, 1806 Our medical visits occupied us till a late hour, after which we collected our horses and proceeded for two miles in a southeastern direction, crossing a branch from the right, at the distance of a mile. We then turned nearly north, and crossing an extensive open bottom, about a mile and a half wide, reached the bank of the Kooskooskee. Here we expected the canoe which they had promised; but although a man had been despatched with it at the appointed time, he did not arrive before sunset. We therefore encamped, with a number of Indians who had followed us from the village.

MAY 14TH *Wednesday.* In the morning, after sending out some hunters, transported the baggage by means of the canoe, and then drove our horses into the river, over which they swam without accident, although it is one hundred and fifty yards wide, and the current very rapid. We then descended the river about half a mile, and formed our camp on the spot which the Indians had recommended. It was about forty paces from the river, and formerly an Indian habitation; but nothing remained at present but a circle thirty yards in diameter, sunk in the ground about four feet, with a wall round it of nearly three and a half feet in height. In this place we deposited our baggage, and round its edges formed our tents of sticks and grass. This situation is in many respects advantageous. It is an extensive level bottom, thinly covered with long-leafed pine, with a rich soil, affording excellent pasture, and supplied, as well as the high and broken hills on the east and northeast, with the best game in the neighbourhood; while its vicinity to the river makes it convenient for the salmon, which are now expected daily. As soon as we had encamped, Tunnachemootoolt and Hohastilpilp, with about twelve of their nation, came to the opposite side and began to sing, this being the usual token of friendship on similar occasions. We sent the canoe for them, and the two chiefs came over with several of the party, among whom were the two young men who had given us the two horses in behalf of the nation. After smoking some time, Hohastilpilp presented to captain Lewis an elegant gray gelding, which he had brought for the purpose, and was perfectly satisfied at receiving in return a handkerchief, two hundred balls, and four pounds of powder.

The hunters killed some pheasants, two squirrels, and a male and a female bear, the first of which was large and fat, and of a bay colour; the second meagre, grisly, and of smaller size. They were of the species common to the upper part of the Missouri, and might well be termed the variegated bear, for they are found occasionally of a black grisly brown or red colour. There is every reason to believe them to be of precisely the same species. Those of different colours are killed together, as in the case of these two, and as we found the white and bay associated together on the Missouri; and some nearly white were seen in this neighbourhood by the hunters. Indeed, it is not common to find any two bears of the same colour, and if the difference in colour were to constitute a distinction of species, the number would increase to almost twenty. Soon after they killed a female bear with two cubs. The mother was black, with a considerable intermixture of white hairs and a white spot on the breast. One of the cubs was jet black, and the other of a light reddish brown, or bay colour. The poil [hair] of these variegated bears is much finer, longer, and more abundant than that of the common black bear: but the most striking difference between them is, that the former are larger, have longer tusks, and longer as well as blunter talons; that they prey more on other animals; that they lie neither so long nor so closely in winter quarters, and never climb a tree, however closely pressed by the hunters. This variegated bear, though specifically the same with those we met on the Missouri, are by no means so ferocious, probably, because of the scarcity of game, and the habit of living on roots may have weaned them from the practices of attacking and devouring animals. Still, however, they are not so passive as the common black bear, which are also to be found here; for they have already fought with our hunters, though with less fury than those on the other side of the mountain.

A large part of the meat we gave to the Indians, to whom it was a real luxury, as they scarcely taste flesh once in a month. They immediately prepared a large fire of dried wood, on which were thrown a number of smooth stones from the river. As soon as the fire went down, and the stones were heated, they were laid next to each other, in a level position, and covered with a quantity of branches of pine, on which were placed flitches of the bear, and thus placing the boughs and flesh alternately for several courses, leaving a thick layer of pine on the top. On this heap was then poured a small quantity of water, and the whole covered with earth to the depth of four inches. After remaining in this state about three hours, the meat was taken off, and was really more tender than that which we had boiled or roasted, though the strong flavour of the pine, rendered it disagreeable to our palates. This repast gave them much satisfaction, for though they sometimes kill the black bear, yet they attack very reluctantly the furious variegated bear, and only when they can pursue him on horseback, through the plains, and shoot him with arrows.

The stone-horses we found so troublesome that we have endeavoured to exchange them for either mares or geldings; but although we offered two for one, they were unwilling to barter. It was therefore determined to castrate them; and being desirous of ascertaining the best method of performing this operation, two were gelded in the usual manner, while one of the natives tried the experiment in the Indian way, without tying the string of the stone (which he assured us was much the better plan) and carefully scraping the string clean and separating it from the adjoining veins before cutting it. All the horses recovered; but we afterwards found that those on which the Indian mode had been tried, although they bled more profusely at first, neither swell nor appear to suffer as much as the others, and recovered sooner, so that we are fully persuaded that the Indian method is preferable to our own.

MAY 15TH

As we shall now be compelled to pass some time in this neighbourhood, a number of hunters were sent in different directions, and the rest were employed in completing the camp. From this labour we, however, exempted five of the men, two of whom are afflicted with colic, and the others complain of violent pains in the head, all which are occasioned, we presume, by the diet of roots, to which they have recently been confined. We secured the baggage with a shelter of grass, and made a kind of bower of the under part of an old sail, the leathern tent being now too rotten for use, while the men formed very comfortable huts in the shape of the awning of a wagon, by means of willow poles and grass. Tunnachemootoolt and his young men left us this morning on their way home; and soon after we were visited by a party of fourteen Indians on horseback, armed with bows and arrows going on a hunting excursion. The chief game is the deer, and whenever the ground will permit, the favourite hunt is on horseback; but in the woodlands, where this is impracticable, they make use of a decoy. This consists of the skin of the head and upper part of the neck of a deer, kept in its natural shape by a frame of small sticks on the inside. As soon as the hunter perceives a deer he conceals himself, and with his hand moves the decoy so as to represent a real deer in the act of feeding, which is done so naturally that the game is seduced within reach of their arrows. We also exercised our horses by driving them together, so as to accustom them to each other, and incline them the less to separate.

MAY 16TH *Friday.* The next morning, an Indian returned with one of them, which had strayed away in the night to a considerable distance, an instance of integrity and kindness by no means singular among the Chopunnish. Hohastilpilp, with the rest of the natives left us to-day. The hunters who have as yet come in, brought nothing, except a few pheasants, so that we still place our chief reliance on the mush made of roots (among these the cows and the quamash are the principal) with which we use a small onion, which grows in great abundance, and which corrects any bad effects they may have on the stomach. The cows and quamash, particularly, incline to produce flatulency, to obviate which we employ a kind of fennel, called by the Shoshonees, year-hah, resembling aniseed in flavour, and a very agreeable food.

In the course of the day two other hunters brought in a deer. The game they said was scarce; but they had wounded three bear as white as sheep. The last hunters who had left us yesterday, also came in to-night, with information, that at the distance of five or six miles, they attempted to cross Collins's creek, on the other side, where game is most abundant, but that they could not ford it with their horses, on account of its depth, and the rapidity of the current.

MAY 17TH *Saturday.* It rained during the greater part of the night, and our flimsy covering being insufficient for our protection, we lay in the water most of the time. What was more unlucky, our chronometer became wet, and, in consequence, somewhat rusty, but by care we hope to restore it. The rain continued nearly the whole day, while on the high plains the snow is falling, and already two or three inches in depth. The bad weather confined us to the camp and kept the Indians from us, so that for the first time since we left the narrows of the Columbia, a day has passed without our being visited by any of the natives.

The country along the Rocky mountains for several hundred miles in length and about fifty wide, is a high level plain; in all its parts extremely fertile, and in many places covered with a growth of tall long-leafed pine. This plain is chiefly interrupted near the streams of water, where the hills are steep and lofty; but the soil is good, being unincumbered by much stone, and possesses more timber than the level country. Under shelter of these hills, the bottom lands skirt the margin of the rivers, and though narrow and confined, are still fertile and rarely inundated. Nearly the whole of this wide spread tract is covered with a profusion of grass and plants, which are at this time as high as the knee. Among these are a variety of esculent plants and roots, acquired without much difficulty, and yielding not only a nutritious, but a very agreeable food. The air is pure and dry, the climate quite as mild, if not milder, than the same parallels of latitude in the Atlantic states, and must be equally healthy, for all the disorders which we have witnessed, may fairly be imputed more to the nature of the diet than to any intemperance of climate. This general observation is of course to be qualified, since in the same tract of country, the degrees of the combination of heat and cold obey the influence of situation. Thus the rains of the low grounds near our camp, are snows in the high plains, and while the sun shines with intense heat in the confined bottoms, the plains enjoy a much colder air, and the vegetation is retarded at least fifteen days, while at the foot of the mountains the snows are still many feet in depth; so that within twenty miles of our camp we observe the rigours of winter cold, the cool air of spring, and the oppressive heat of midsummer. Even on the plains, however, where the snow has fallen, it seems to do but little injury to the grass and other plants, which, though apparently tender and susceptible, are still blooming, at the height of nearly eighteen inches through the snow. In short, this district affords many advantages to settlers, and if properly cultivated, would yield every object necessary for the subsistence and comfort of civilized man.

The Chopunnish themselves are in general stout, well formed, and active; they have high, and many of them aquiline noses, and the general appearance of the face is cheerful and agreeable, though without any indication of gaiety and mirth. Like most of the Indians they extract their beards; but the women only pluck the hair from the rest of the body. That of the men is very often suffered to grow, nor does there appear to be any natural deficiency in that respect; for we observe several men, who, if they had adopted the practice of shaving, would have been as well supplied as ourselves. The dress of both sexes resembles that of the Shoshonees, and consists of a long shirt reaching to the thigh, leggings as high as the waist, moccasins and robes, all of which are formed of skins.

Their ornaments are beads, shells, and pieces of brass attached to different parts of the dress, or tied round the arms, neck, wrists, and over the shoulders: to these are added pearls and beads, suspended from the ears, and a single shell of wampum through the nose. The head-dress of the men is a bandeau of fox or otter skin, either with or without the fur, and sometimes an ornament is tied to a plait of hair, falling from the crown of the head: that of the women is a cap without rim, formed of bear grass and cedar bark; while the hair itself, of both sexes, falls in two rows down the front of the body. Collars of bears' claws are also common. But the personal ornament most esteemed is a sort of breastplate, formed of a strip of otter skin, six inches wide, cut out of the whole length of the back of the animal, including the head; this being dressed with the hair on, a hole is made at the upper end, through which the head of the wearer is placed, and the skin hangs in front with the tail reaching below the knee, and ornamented with pieces of pearl, red cloth, and wampum; or, in short, any other fanciful decoration. Tippets also are occasionally worn. That of Hohastilpilp was formed of human scalps, and adorned with the thumbs and fingers of several men slain by him in battle.

The Chopunnish are among the most amiable men we have seen. Their character is placid and gentle, rarely moved into passion, yet not often enlivened by gaiety. Their amusements consist in running races, shooting with arrows at a target, and they partake of the great and prevailing vice of gambling. They are, however, by no means so much attached to baubles as the generality of Indians, but are anxious to obtain articles of utility, such as knives, tomahawks, kettles, blankets, and awls for moccasins. They have also suffered so much from the superiority of their enemies, that they are equally desirous of procuring arms and ammunition, which they are gradually acquiring, for the band of Tunnachemootoolt have already six guns, which they acquired from the Minnetarees.

The Chopunnish bury their dead in sepulchres, formed of boards, constructed like the roof of a house. The body is rolled in skins and laid one over another, separated by a board only, both above and below. We have sometimes seen their dead buried in wooden boxes, and rolled in skins in the manner above mentioned. They sacrifice their horses, canoes, and every other species of property to their dead; the bones of many horses are seen lying round their sepulchres.

Among the reptiles common to this country are the two species of innocent snakes already described, and the rattlesnake, which last is of the same species as that of the Missouri, and though abundant here, is the only poisonous snake we have seen between the Pacific and the Missouri. Besides these there are the common black lizard and horned lizard. Of frogs there are several kinds, such as the small green tree frog, the small frog common in the United States, which sings in the spring of the year, a species of frog frequenting the water, much larger than the bull-frog, and in shape between the delicate length of the bull-frog, and the shorter and less graceful form of the toad like; the last of which, however, its body is covered with little pustules, or lumps: we have never heard it make a noise of any kind. Neither the toad bull-frog; the moccasin-snake, nor the copperhead-snake are to be found here. Captain Lewis killed a snake near the camp three feet and eleven inches in length, and much the colour of the rattlesnake. There was no poisonous tooth to be found. It had two hundred and eighteen scuta on the abdomen, and fifty-nine squama or half-formed scuta on the tail. The eye was of a moderate size: the iris of a dark yellowish brown, and the pupil black. There was nothing remarkable in the form of the head, which was not so wide across the jaws as that of the poisonous class of snakes usually are.

There is a species of lizard, which we have called the horned lizard, about the size and much resembling in figure the ordinary black lizard. The belly is, notwithstanding, broader, the tail shorter, and the action much slower than the ordinary lizard. It crawls like the toad, is of a brown colour, and interspersed with yellowish brown spots; it is covered with minute shells [scales], interspersed with little horny projections like prickles on the upper part of the body. The belly and throat resemble the frogs, and are of a light yellowish brown. The edge of the belly is regularly beset with these horny projections, which give to those edges a serrate figure; the eye is small and of a dark colour. Above and behind the eyes are several projections of the bone, which being armed at the extremities with a firm black substance, having the appearance of horns sprouting from the head, has induced us to

INTERIOR OF A MANDAN HUT (Bodmer)

call it the horned lizard. These animals are found in great abundance in the sandy parts of the plains, and after a shower of rain are seen basking in the sun. For the greatest part of the time they are concealed in holes. They are found in great numbers on the banks of the Missouri, and in the plains through which we have passed above the Wollawollahs.

Most of the insects common to the United States are seen in this country: such as the butterfly, the common housefly, the blowingfly, the horsefly, except one species of it, the gold-coloured earfly, the place of which is supplied by a fly of a brown colour, which attaches itself to the same part of the horse, and is equally troublesome. There are likewise nearly all the varieties of beetles known in the Atlantic states, except the large cow beetle, and the black beetle, commonly called the tumblebug. Neither the hornet, the wasp, nor the yellowjacket inhabit this part of the country, but there is an insect resembling the last of these, though much larger, which is very numerous, particularly in the Rocky mountains and on the waters of the Columbia; the body and abdomen are yellow, with transverse circles of black, the head black, and the wings, which are four in number, of a dark brown colour: their nests are built in the ground, and resemble that of the hornet, with an outer covering to the comb. These insects are fierce, and sting very severely, so that we found them very troublesome in frightening our horses as we passed the mountains. The silkworm is also found here, as well as the humble-bee, though the honey-bee is not.

MAY 18TH

Twelve hunters set out this morning after the bear, which are now our chief dependence; but as they are now ferocious, the hunters henceforward never go except in pairs. Soon after they left us, a party of Chopunnish erected a hut on the opposite side of the river in order to watch the salmon, which is expected to arrive every day. For this purpose they have constructed with sticks, a kind of wharf, projecting about ten feet into the river, and three feet above its surface, on the extremity of which one of the fishermen exercised himself with a scooping net, similar to that used in our country; but after several hours labour he was still unsuccessful. In the course of the morning three Indians called at our camp and told us that they had been hunting near the place where we met the Chopunnish last autumn, and which is called by them the quamash grounds, but after roaming about for several days had killed nothing. We gave them a small piece of meat, which they said they would keep for their small children, which they said were very hungry, and then, after smoking, took leave of us. Some of our hunters returned almost equally unsuccessful. They had gone over the whole country between Collins's creek and the Kooskooskee, to their junction, at the distance of ten miles, without seeing either a deer or bear, and at last brought in a single hawk and a salmon dropped by an eagle. This last was not in itself considerable, but gave us hopes of soon seeing that fish in the river, an event which we ardently desire, for though the rapid rise of the river denotes a great decrease of snow on the mountains, yet we shall not be able to leave our camp for some time.

MAY 19TH

Monday. After a cold rainy night, during a greater part of which we lay in the water, the weather became fair, and we then sent some men to a village above us, on the opposite side, to purchase some roots. They carried with them for this purpose a small collection of awls, knitting pins, and armbands, with which they obtained several bushels of the root of cows, and some bread of the same material. They were followed too by a train of invalids from the village, who came to ask for our assistance. The men were generally afflicted with sore eyes, but the women had besides this a variety of other disorders, chiefly rheumatic, a violent pain and weakness in the loins, which is a common complaint among the females, and one of them seemed much dejected, and as we thought, from the account of her disease, hysterical. We gave her thirty drops of laudanum, and after administering eye-water and rubbing the rheumatic patients with volatile liniment, and giving cathartics to others, they all thought themselves much relieved, and returned highly satisfied to the village. We were fortunate enough to retake one of the horses on which we crossed the Rocky mountains in the autumn, and which had become almost wild since that time.

MAY 20TH *Tuesday.* Again it rained during the night, and the greater part of this day. Our hunters were out in different directions, but though they saw a bear and a deer or two, they only killed one of the latter, which proved to be of the mule-deer species. The next day, *Wednesday 21st,* finding the rain still continue we left our ragged sail tent, and formed a hut with willow poles and grass. The rest of the men were occupied in building a canoe for present use, as the Indians promise to give us a horse for it when we leave them. We received nothing from our hunters except a single sandhill crane, which are very abundant in this neighbourhood, and consumed at dinner the last morsel of meat which we have. As there now seems but little probability of our procuring a stock of dried meat, and the fish is as yet an uncertain resource, we made a division of all our stock of merchandise, so as to enable the men to purchase a store of roots and bread for the mountains. We might ourselves collect those roots, but as there are several species of hemlock growing among the cows, and difficult to be distinguished from that plant, we are afraid to suffer the men to collect them, lest the party might be poisoned by mistaking them. On parcelling out the stores, the stock of each man was found to consist of only one awl and one knitting-pin, half an ounce of vermillion, two needles, a few skeins of thread, and about a yard of ribbon—a slender means of bartering for our subsistence; but the men have been now so much accustomed to privations, that neither the want of meat, nor the scanty funds of the party, excite the least anxiety among them.

MAY 22D *Thursday.* We availed ourselves of the fair weather to dry our baggage and store of roots, and being still without meat, killed one of our colts, intending to reserve the other three for the mountains. In the afternoon we were amused by a large party of Indians, on the opposite side of the river, hunting on horseback. After riding at full speed down the steep hills, they at last drove the deer into the river, where we shot it, and two Indians immediately pursued it on a raft, and took it. Several hunters, who had gone to a considerable distance near the mountains, returned with five deer. They had purchased also two red salmon trout, which the Indians say remain in this river during the greater part of the winter, but are not good at this season, as it in fact appeared, for they were very meagre. The salmon, we understand, are now arrived at no great distance, in Lewis's river, but some days will yet elapse before they come up to this place. This, as well as the scarcity of game, made us wish to remove lower down; but on examination we found that there was no place in that direction calculated for a camp, and therefore resolved to remain in our present position. Some uneasiness has been excited by a report, that two nights ago a party of Shoshonees had surrounded a Chopunnish house, on the south side of Lewis's river, but the inhabitants having discovered their intentions, had escaped without injury.

Friday. The hunters were sent out to make a last effort to procure provisions, but after examining the whole country between Collins's creek and the Kooskooskee, they found nothing except a few pheasants of the dark brown kind. In the meantime we were visited by four Indians who had come from a village on Lewis's river, at the distance of two days' ride, who came for the purpose of procuring a little eye-water: the extent of our medical fame is not a little troublesome, but we rejoice at any circumstance which enables us to relieve these poor creatures, and therefore willingly washed their eyes, after which they returned home. MAY 23D

Saturday. This proved the warmest day we have had since our arrival here. Some of our men visited the village of the Brokenarm, and exchanged some awls, which they had made of the links of a small chain belonging to one of their steel traps, for a plentiful supply of roots. MAY 24TH
    Besides administering medical relief to the Indians, we are obliged to devote much of our time to the care of our own invalids. The child of Sacajawea is very unwell; and with one of the men we have ventured an experiment of a very robust nature. He has been for some time sick, but has now recovered his flesh, eats heartily and digests well, but has so great a weakness in the loins that he cannot walk nor even sit upright without extreme pain. After we had in vain exhausted the resources of our art, one of the hunters mentioned that he had known persons in similar situations restored by violent sweats, and at the request of the patient, we permitted the remedy to be applied. For this purpose, a hole about four feet deep and three in diameter was dug in the earth, and heated well by a large fire in the bottom of it. The fire was then taken out, and an arch formed over the hole by means of willow poles, and covered with several blankets, so as to make a perfect awning. The patient being stripped naked, was seated under this on a bench, with a piece of board for his feet, and with a jug of water sprinkled the bottom and sides of the hole, so as to keep up as hot a steam as he could bear. After remaining twenty minutes in this situation, he was taken out, immediately plunged twice in cold water, and brought back to the hole, where he resumed the vapour bath. During all this time he drank copiously a strong infusion of horse-mint, which was used as a substitute for the seneca root, which our informant said he had seen employed on these occasions, but of which there is none in this country. At the end of three quarters of an hour, he was again withdrawn from the hole, carefully wrapped, and suffered to cool gradually. This operation was performed yesterday, and this morning he walked about, and is nearly free from pain. About eleven o'clock a canoe arrived with three Indians, one of whom was the poor creature who had lost the use of his limbs, and for whose recovery the natives seem very anxious, as he is a chief of considerable rank among them. His situation is beyond

the reach of our skill. He complains of no pain in any peculiar limb, and we therefore think his disorder cannot be rheumatic, as his limbs would have been more diminished if his disease had been a paralytic affection. We had already ascribed it to his diet of roots, and had recommended his living on fish and flesh, and using the cold bath every morning, with a dose of cream of tartar, or flowers of sulphur, every third day. These prescriptions seem to have been of little avail, but as he thinks himself somewhat better for them, we concealed our ignorance by giving him a few drops of laudanum and a little portable soup, with a promise of sweating him, as we had done our own man.

MAY 25TH On attempting it however, in the morning, we found that he was too weak to sit up or be supported in the hole: we therefore told the Indians that we knew of no other remedy except frequent perspirations in their own sweathouses, accompanied by drinking large quantities of the decoction of horsemint, which we pointed out to them. Three hunters set out to hunt towards the Quamash flats if they could pass Collins's creek. Others crossed the river for the same purpose, and one of the men was sent to a village on the opposite side, about eight miles above us. Nearly all the inhabitants were either hunting, digging roots, or fishing in Lewis's river, from which they had brought several fine salmon. In the course of the day, some of our hunters wounded a female bear with two cubs, one of which was white and the other perfectly black.

The Indians who accompanied the sick chief are so anxious for his safety that they remained with us all night, and in the morning, when we gave him some cream of tartar, and portable soup, with directions how to treat him, they still lingered about us in hopes we might do something effectual, though we desired them to take him home.

The hunters sent out yesterday returned with Hohastilpilp, and a number of inferior chiefs and warriors. They had passed Commearp creek at the distance of one and a half miles, and a larger creek three miles beyond; they then went on till they were stopped by a large creek ten miles above our camp, and finding it too deep and rapid to pass, they returned home. On their way, they stopped at a village four miles up the second creek, which we have never visited, and where they purchased bread and roots on very moderate terms; an article of intelligence very pleasing at the present moment, when our stock of meat is again exhausted. We have however still agreeable prospects, for the river is rising fast, as the snows visibly diminish, and we saw a salmon in the river to-day. We also completed our canoe.

MAY 27TH *Tuesday.* The horse which the Indians gave us some time ago, had gone astray; but in our present dearth of provisions we searched for him and killed him. Observing that we were in want of food, Hohastilpilp informed us that most of the horses which we saw running at large belonged to him or his people, and requested that whenever we wished any meat we would make use of them without restraint. We have, indeed, on more than one occasion, had to admire the generosity of this Indian, whose conduct presents a model of what is due to strangers in distress. A party was sent to the village discovered yesterday, and returned with a large supply of bread and roots. Sergeant Ordway and two men were also despatched to Lewis's river, about half a day's ride to the south, where we expect to obtain salmon, which are said to be very abundant at that place. The three men who had attempted to go to the Quamash flats, returned with five deer; but although they had proceeded some distance up Collins's creek, it continued too deep for them to cross. The Indians who accompanied the chief, were so anxious to have the operation of sweating him performed under our inspection, that we determined to gratify them by making a second attempt. The hole was therefore enlarged, and the father of the chief, a very good looking old man, went in with him, and held him in a proper position. This strong evidence of feeling is directly opposite to the received opinions of the insensibility of savages, nor are we less struck by the kindness and attention paid to the sick man by those who are unconnected with him, which are the more surprising, as the long illness of three years might be supposed to exhaust their sympathy. We could not produce as complete a perspiration as we desired, and after he was taken out, he complained of suffering considerable pain, which we relieved with a few drops of laudanum, and he then rested well.

Wednesday. The next morning he was able to use his arms, and feels better than he has done for many months, and sat up during the greater part of the day. MAY 28TH

We sent to the village of Tunnachemootoolt for bread and roots, and a party of hunters set out to hunt up a creek, about eight miles above us. In the evening, another party, who had been so fortunate as to find a ford across Collins's creek, returned from the Quamash flats with eight deer, of which they saw great numbers, though there were but few bears. Having now a tolerable stock of meat, we were occupied during the following day, *Thursday*, in various engagements in the camp.

The Indian chief is still rapidly recovering, and for the first time during the last twelve months, had strength enough to wash his face. We had intended to repeat the sweating to-day, but as the weather was cloudy, with occasional rain, we declined it. This operation, though violent, seems highly efficacious; for our own man, on whom the experiment was first made, is recovering his strength very fast, and the restoration of the chief is wonderful. He continued to improve, and on the following day, after a very violent sweating, was able to move one of his legs and thighs, and some of his toes; the fingers and arms being almost entirely restored to their former strength. Parties were sent out as usual to hunt and trade with the Indians. Among others, two of the men who had not yet exchanged their stock of merchandise for roots, crossed the river for that purpose, in our boat. But as they reached the opposite shore, the violence of the current drove the boat broadside against some trees, and she immediately filled and went to the bottom. With difficulty one of the men was saved, but the boat itself, with three blankets, a blanket-coat, and their small pittance of merchandise, were irrevocably lost.

Saturday. Two men visited the Indian village, where they purchased a dressed bear skin, of a uniform pale reddish brown colour, which the Indians called yackah in contradistinction to hohhost, or the white bear. This remark induced us to inquire more particularly into their opinions as to the several species of bears; and we therefore produced all the skins of that ani- MAY 31ST mal which we had killed at this place, and also one very nearly white, which we had purchased. The natives immediately classed the white, the deep and the pale grizzly red, the grizzly dark brown, in short, all those with the extremities of the hair of a white or frosty colour, without regard to the colour of the ground of the poil, under the name of hohhost. They assured us, that they were all of the same species with the white bear; that they associated together, had longer nails than the others, and never climbed trees. On the other hand, the black skins, those which were black, with a number of entire white hairs intermixed, or with a white breast, the uniform bay, the brown, and light reddish brown, were ranged under the class yackah, and were said to resemble each other in being smaller, and having shorter nails than the white bear, in climbing trees, and being so little vicious that they could be pursued with safety.

This distinction of the Indians seems to be well founded, and we are inclined to believe, first, that the white or grizzly bear of this neighbourhood form a distinct species, which moreover is the same with those of the same colour on the upper part of the Missouri, where the other species are not found; second, that the black and reddish brown, &c. is a second species, equally distinct from the white bear of this country, as from the black bear of the Atlantic and Pacific oceans, which two last seem to form only one species. The common black bear are indeed unknown in this country; for the bear of which we are speaking, though in most respects similar, differs from it in having much finer, thicker, and longer hair, with a greater proportion of fur mixed with it, and also in having a variety of colours, while the common black bear has no intermixture or change of colour, but is of a uniform black.

In the course of the day the natives brought us another of our original stock of horses, of which we have now recovered all except two, and those, we are informed, were taken back by our Shoshonee guide, when he returned home. They amount to sixty-five, and most of them fine strong active horses, in excellent order.

Sunday, June 1st, 1806

Two of our men who had been up the river to trade with the Indians, returned quite unsuccessful. Nearly opposite to the village, their horse fell with his load, down a steep cliff, into the river, across which he swam. An Indian on the opposite side, drove him back to them, but in crossing most of the articles were lost, and the paint melted. Understanding their intentions, the Indians attempted to come over to them, but having no canoe, were obliged to use a raft, which struck on a rock, upset, and the whole store of roots and bread were destroyed. This failure completely exhausted our stock of merchandise; but the remembrance of what we suffered from cold and hunger during the passage of the Rocky mountains, makes us anxious to increase our means of subsistence and comfort when we again encounter the same inconvenience. We therefore created a new fund, by cutting off the buttons from our clothes, preparing some eye-water, and basilicon, to which were added some vials, and small tin boxes, in which we had once kept phosphorus.

Monday. With this cargo two men set out in the morning to trade, and brought home three bushels of roots and some bread, which, in our situation, was as important as the return of an East India ship. In the meantime, several hunters went across Collins's creek to hunt on the Quamash grounds, and the Indians informed us that there were great quantities of moose to the southeast of the east branch of Lewis's river, which they call the Tommanamah. We had lately heard that some Indians who reside at some distance, on the south side of the Kooskooskee, are in possession of two tomahawks, one of which was left at our camp at Musquitoe creek, the other had been stolen while we were encamped at the Chopunnish last autumn. This last we were anxious to obtain, in order to give to the relations of our unfortunate companion, sergeant Floyd, to whom it once belonged. We therefore sent Drewyer yesterday with Neeshnepahkeeook and Hohastilpilp, the two chiefs, to demand it. On their arrival, it seemed that the present owner, who had purchased it from the thief, was himself at the point of death; so that his relations were unwilling to give it up, as they meant to bury it in the grave with the deceased. But the influence of Neeshnepahkeeook at length succeeded; and they consented to surrender the tomahawk on receiving two strands of beads and a handkerchief, from Drewyer, and from each of the chiefs a horse, to be killed at the funeral of the deceased, according to the custom of the country.

Soon after their return, sergeant Ordway and his party, for whose safety we had now become extremely anxious, came home from Lewis's river, with some roots of cows and seventeen salmon. The distance, however, from which they were brought, was so great, that most of them were nearly spoiled; but such as continued sound, were extremely delicious, the flesh being of a fine rose colour, with a small mixture of yellow, and so fat that they were cooked very well without the addition of any oil or grease.

When they set out on the *27th* they had hoped to reach the salmon fishery in the course of that day, but the route by which the guides led them was so circuitous, that they rode seventy miles before they reached their place of destination, in the evening of the *29th*. After going for twenty miles up the Commearp creek, through an open plain, broken only by the hills and timber along the creek, they then entered a high, irregular, mountainous country, the soil of which was fertile, and well supplied with pine. Without stopping to hunt, although they saw great quantities of deer, and some of the bighorn, they hastened for thirty miles across this district to the Tommanamah, or east branch of Lewis's river; and not finding any salmon, descended that stream for twenty miles, to the fishery at a short distance below its junction with the south branch. Both these forks appear to come from or enter a mountainous country. The Tommanamah itself, they said, was about one hundred and fifty yards wide; its banks, for the most part, formed of solid perpendicular rocks, rising to a great height, and as they passed along some of its hills, they found that the snow had not yet disappeared, and the grass was just springing up. During its whole course it presented one continued rapid, till at the fishery itself, where the river widens to the space of two hundred yards, the rapid is nearly as considerable as at the great rapids of the Columbia. Here the Indians have erected a large house of split timber, one hundred and fifty feet long, and thirty-five wide, with a flat roof; and at this season is much resorted to by the men, while the women are employed in collecting roots. After remaining a day, and purchasing some fish, they returned home.

JUNE 3D *Tuesday.* Finding that the salmon has not yet appeared along the shores, as the Indians assured us they would in a few days, and that all the salmon which they themselves use, are obtained from Lewis's river, we begin to lose our hopes of subsisting on them. We are too poor, and at too great a distance from Lewis's river, to purchase fish at that place, and it is not probable that the river will fall sufficiently to take them before we leave this place. Our Indian friends sent an express to-day over the mountains to Traveller's-rest, in order to procure intelligence from the Ootlashoots, a band of Flatheads who have wintered on the east side of the mountains, and the same band which we first met on that river. As the route was deemed practicable for this express, we also proposed setting out, but the Indians dissuaded us from attempting it, as many of the creeks, they said, were still too deep to be forded; the roads very deep and slippery, and no grass as yet for our horses; but in twelve or fourteen days we shall no longer meet with the some obstacles: we therefore determined to set out in a few days for the Quamash flats, in order to lay in a store of provisions, so as to cross the mountains about the middle of the month.

For the two following days we continued hunting in our own neighbourhood, and by means of our own exertions, and trading with the Indians for trifling articles, succeeded in procuring as much bread and roots, besides other food, as will enable us to subsist during the passage of the mountains. The old chief in the meantime gradually recovered the use of his limbs, and our own man was nearly restored to his former health. The Indians who had been with us, now returned, and invited us to their village on the following day, *Friday, June 6th*, to give us their final answer to a number of proposals which we had made to them.

Neeshnepahkeeook then informed us, that they could not accompany us, as we wished, to the Missouri; but that in the latter end of the summer they meant to cross the mountain and spend the winter to the eastward. We had also requested some of their young men to go with us, so as to effect a reconciliation between them and the Pahkees, in case we should meet these last. He answered, that some of their young men would go with us, but they were not selected for that purpose, nor could they be until a general meeting of the whole nation, who were to meet in the plain on Lewis's river, at the head of Commearp. This meeting would take place in ten or twelve days, and if we set out before that time, the young men should follow us. We therefore depend but little on their assistance as guides, but hope to engage for that purpose, some of the Ootlashoots near Traveller's-rest creek. Soon after this communication, which was followed by a present of dried quamash, we were visited by Hohastilpilp and several others, among whom were the two young chiefs who had given us horses some time ago.

Chapter 30
AGAIN IN THE BITTER-ROOT MOUNTAINS

SATURDAY, JUNE 7TH, 1806 The two young chiefs returned after breakfast to their village on Commearp creek, accompanied by several of our men, who were sent to purchase ropes and bags for packing, in exchange for some parts of an old seine, bullets, old files, and pieces of iron. In the evening they returned with a few strings but no bags. Hohastilpilp crossed the river in the course of the day, and brought with him a horse, which he gave one of our men who had previously made him a present of a pair of Canadian shoes or shoepacks. We were all occupied in preparing packs and saddles for our journey; and as we intend to visit the Quamash flats on the tenth, in order to lay in a store of provisions for the journey over the mountains, we do not suffer the men to disturb the game in that neighbourhood.

JUNE 8TH

Sunday. The Cutnose visited us this morning with ten or twelve warriors: among these were two belonging to a band of Chopunnish, which we had not yet seen, who call themselves Willetpos, and reside on the south side of Lewis's river. One of them gave a good horse, which he rode, in exchange for one of ours, which was unable to cross the mountain, on receiving a tomahawk in addition. We were also fortunate in exchanging two other horses of inferior value for others much better, without giving any thing else to the purchaser. After these important purchases, several foot races were run between our men and the Indians: the latter, who are very active, and fond of these races, proved themselves very expert, and one of them was as fleet as our swiftest runners. After the races were over, the men divided themselves into two parties and played prison base, an exercise which we are desirous of encouraging, before we begin the passage over the mountains, as several of them are becoming lazy from inaction. At night these games were concluded by a dance.

One of the Indians informed us that we could not pass the mountains before the next full moon, or about the first of July; because, if we attempted it before that time, the horses would be forced to travel without food three days on the top of the mountains. This intelligence was disagreeable, as it excited a doubt as to the most proper time for passing the mountains; but having no time to lose, we are determined to risk the hazards, and start as soon as the Indians generally consider it practicable, which is about the middle of this month.

JUNE 9TH

Monday. Our success yesterday encouraged us to attempt to exchange some more of our horses, whose backs were unsound, but we could dispose of one only. Hohastilpilp, who visited us yesterday, left us with several Indians, for the plains near Lewis's river, where the whole nation are about to assemble. The Brokenarm too, with all his people, stopped on their way to the general rendezvous, at the same place. The Cutnose, or Neeshnepahkeeook, borrowed a horse, and rode down a few miles after some young eagles. He soon returned with two of the grey kind, nearly grown, which he meant to raise for the sake of the feathers. The young chief, who some time since made us a present of two horses, came with a party of his people, and passed the night with us.

The river, which is about one hundred and fifty yards wide, has been discharging vast bodies of water, but notwithstanding its depth, the water has been nearly transparent, and its temperature quite as cold as our best springs. For several days, however, the river has been falling, and is now six feet lower than it has been, a strong proof that the great body of snow has left the mountains. It is, indeed, nearly at the same height as when we arrived here; a circumstance which the Indians consider as indicating the time when the mountains may be crossed. We shall wait, however, a few days, because the roads must still be wet and slippery, and the grass on the mountains will be improved in a short time. The men are in high spirits at the prospect of setting out, and amused themselves during the afternoon with different games.

JUNE 10TH *Tuesday*. After collecting our horses, which took much time, we set out at eleven o'clock for the Quamash flats. Our stock is now very abundant, each man being well mounted, with a small load on a second horse, and several supernumerary ones, in case of accident or want of food. We ascended the river hills, which are very high, and three miles in extent; our course being north 22° east, and then turned to north 15° west, for two miles till we reached Collins's creek. It is deep and difficult to cross, but we passed without any injury, except wetting some of our provisions, and then proceeded due north for five miles to the eastern edge of the Quamash flats, near where we first met the Chopunnish in the autumn. We encamped on the bank of a small stream, in a point of woods, bordering the extensive level and beautiful prairie which is intersected by several rivulets, and as the quamash is now in blossom, presents a perfect resemblance of lakes of clear water.

    A party of Chopunnish, who had overtaken us a few miles above, halted for the night with us, and mentioned that they too had come down to hunt in the flats, though we fear they expect that we will provide for them during their stay.

    The country through which we passed is generally free from stone, extremely fertile, and supplied with timber, consisting of several species of fir, long-leafed pine and larch. The undergrowth is chokecherry, near the water courses, and scattered through the country, black alder, a large species of red root now in bloom, a plant resembling the pawpaw in its leaf, and bearing a berry with five valves of a deep purple colour. There were also two species of sumac, the purple haw, seven bark, serviceberry, gooseberry, the honeysuckle, bearing a white berry, and a species of dwarf pine, ten or twelve feet high, which might be confounded with the young pine of the long-leafed species, except that the former bears a cone of a globular form, with small scales, and that its leaves are in fascicles of two resembling in length and appearance the common pitch pine. We also observed two species of wild rose, both quinquepetalous, both of a damask red colour, and similar in the stem; but one of them is as large as the common red rose of our gardens; its leaf too is somewhat larger than that of the other species of wild rose, and the apex, as we saw them last year, were more than three times the size of the common wild rose.

    We saw many sandhill cranes, and some ducks in the marshes near our camp, and a greater number of burrowing squirrels, some of which we killed, and found them as tender and well flavoured as our grey squirrels.

JUNE 11TH *Wednesday*. All our hunters set out by daylight; but on their return to dinner, had killed nothing except a black bear and two deer. Five of the Indians also began to hunt, but they were quite unsuccessful, and in the afternoon returned to their village. Finding that the game had become shy and scarce, the hunters set out after dinner with orders to stay out during the night, and hunt at a greater distance from the camp, in ground less frequented. But the next day they returned with nothing except two deer. They were therefore again sent out, and about noon the following day, seven of them came in with eight deer out of a number, as well as a bear, which they had wounded, but could not take. In the meantime we had sent two men forward about eight miles to a prairie on this side of Collins's creek, with orders to hunt till our arrival. Two other hunters returned towards night, but they had killed only one deer, which they had hung up in the morning, and it had been devoured by the buzzards. An Indian who had spent the last evening with us, exchanged a horse for one of ours, which being sick, we gave a small axe and a knife in addition. He seemed very much pleased, and set out immediately to his village, lest we should change our minds and give up the bargain, which is perfectly allowable in Indian traffic. The hunters resumed the chase in the morning, but the game is now so scarce that they killed only one deer. We therefore cut up and dried all the meat we had collected, packed up all our baggage, and hobbled our horses to be in readiness to set out.

Sunday. But in the morning they had straggled to such a distance that we could not collect them without great difficulty, and as it rained very hard, we waited till it should abate. It soon, however, showed every appearance of a settled rain, and we therefore set out at ten o'clock. We crossed the prairie at the distance of eight miles, where we had sent our hunters, and found two deer which they had hung up for us. Two and a half miles farther, we overtook the two men at Collins's creek. They had killed a third deer, and had seen one large and another white bear. After dining we proceeded up the creek about half a mile, then crossing through a high broken country for about ten miles, reached an eastern branch of the same creek, near which we encamped in the bottom, after a ride of twenty-two miles. The rains during the day made the roads very slippery, and joined to the quantity of fallen timber, rendered our progress slow and laborious to the horses, many of which fell through without suffering any injury. The country through which we passed has a thick growth of long-leafed pine, with some pitch-pine, larch, white-pine, white cedar or arbor vitae of large size, and a variety of firs. The undergrowth consists chiefly of reed root, from six to ten feet in height, with the other species already enumerated. The soil is in general good, and has somewhat of a red cast, like those near the southwest mountain in Virginia. We saw in the course of our ride the speckled woodpecker, the logcock or large woodpecker, the bee-martin, and found the nest of a humming bird, which had just began to lay its eggs.

JUNE 15TH

Monday. We readily collected our horses, and having taken breakfast, proceeded at six o'clock up the creek, through handsome meadows of fine grass, and a great abundance of quamash. At the distance of two miles we crossed the creek, and ascended a ridge in a direction towards the northeast. Fallen timber still obstructed our way so much, that it was eleven o'clock before we had made seven miles, to a small branch of Hungry creek. In the hollows

JUNE 16TH

and on the north side of the hills large quantities of snow still remain, in some places to the depth of two or three feet. Vegetation too is proportionally retarded, the dog-tooth violet being just in bloom, and the honeysuckle, huckleberry, and a small species of white maple, beginning to put forth their leaves. These appearances in a part of the country comparatively low, are ill omens of the practicability of passing the mountains. But being determined to proceed, we halted merely to take a hasty meal, while the horses were grazing, and then resumed our march. The route was through thick woods and over high hills, intersected by deep ravines and obstructed by fallen timber. We found much difficulty also in following the road, the greater part of it being now covered with snow, which lies in great masses eight or ten feet deep, and would be impassable were it not so firm as to bear our horses. Early in the evening we reached Hungry creek, at the place where captain Clark had left a horse for us as we passed in September, and finding a small glade with some grass, though not enough for our horses, we thought it better to halt for the night, lest by going further we should find nothing for the horses to eat. Hungry creek is small at this place, but is deep, and discharges a torrent of water, perfectly transparent, and cold as ice. During the fifteen miles of our route to-day, the principal timber was the pitch-pine, white-pine, larch, and fir. The long-leafed pine extends but a small distance on this side of Collins's creek, and the white-cedar does not reach beyond the branch of Hungry creek on which we dined. In the early part of the day we saw the columbine, the bluebell, and the yellow flowering pea in bloom. There is also in these mountains a great quantity of angelica, stronger to the taste, and more highly scented than that common in the United States. The smell is very pleasant, and the natives, after drying and cutting them into small pieces, wear them in strings around their necks.

JUNE 17TH *Tuesday.* We find lately that the air is pleasant in the course of the day, but notwithstanding the shortness of the night, becomes very cold before morning. At an early hour we collected our horses, and proceeded down the creek, which we crossed twice with much difficulty and danger, in consequence of its depth and rapidity. We avoided two other crossings of the same kind, by crossing over a steep and rocky hill. At the distance of seven miles, the road begins the ascent of the main ridges which divide the waters of the Chopunnish and Kooskooskee rivers. We followed it up a mountain for about three miles, when we found ourselves enveloped in snow, from twelve to fifteen feet in depth, even on the south side of the mountain, with the fullest exposure to the sun. The winter now presented itself in all its rigours, the air was keen and cold, no vestige of vegetation was to be seen, and our hands and feet were benumbed.

We halted at the sight of this new difficulty. We already knew, that to wait till the snows of the mountains had dissolved, so as to enable us to distinguish the road, would defeat our design of returning to the United States this season. We now found also that as the snow bore our horses very well, travelling was infinitely easier than it was last fall, when the rocks and fallen timber had so much obstructed our march. But it would require five days to reach the fish-weirs at the mouth of Colt creek, even if we were able to follow the proper ridges of the mountains; and the danger of missing our direction is exceedingly great, while every track is covered with snow. During these five days too we have no chance of finding either grass or underwood for our horses, the snow being so deep. To proceed, therefore, under such circumstances, would be to hazard our being bewildered in the mountains, to insure the loss of our horses, and should we even be so fortunate as to escape with our lives, we might be obliged to abandon all our papers and collections. It was therefore decided not to venture any further; to deposit here all the baggage and provisions, for which we had no immediate use, and reserving only subsistence for a few days, return while our horses were yet strong, to some spot where we might live by hunting, till a guide could be procured to conduct us across the mountains. Our baggage was placed on scaffolds and carefully covered, as were also the instruments and papers, which we thought it safer to leave than to risk them over the roads and creeks by which we came.

Having completed this operation, we set out at one o'clock, and treading back our steps, reached Hungry creek, which we ascended for two miles, and finding some scanty grass, we encamped. The rain fell during the greater part of the evening, and as this was the first time that we have ever been compelled to make any retrograde movement, we feared that it might depress the spirits of the men; but though somewhat dejected at the circumstance, the obvious necessity precluded all repining. During the night our horses straggled in search of food to a considerable distance among the thick timber on the hill sides, nor could we collect them till nine o'clock the next morning.

Wednesday. Two of them were however still missing, and we therefore directed two of the party to remain and hunt for them. At the same time, we despatched Drewyer and Shannon to the Chopunnish, in the plains beyond the Kooskooskee, in order to hasten the arrival of the Indians who had promised to accompany us; or at any rate, to procure a guide to conduct us to Traveller's-rest. For this purpose they took a rifle, as a reward to any one who would engage to conduct us, with directions to increase the reward, if necessary, by an offer of two other guns, to be given immediately, and ten horses, at the falls of the Missouri.

JUNE 18TH

We then resumed our route. In crossing Hungry creek, one of the horses fell, and rolling over with the rider, was driven for a considerable distance among the rocks; but he fortunately escaped without losing his gun or suffering any injury. Another of the men was cut very badly, in a vein in the inner side of the leg, and we had great difficulty in stopping the blood. About one o'clock we halted for dinner at the glade, on a branch of Hungry creek, where we had dined on the *16th*. Observing much track of deer, we left two men at this place to hunt, and then proceeded to Collins's creek, where we encamped in a pleasant situation, at the upper end of the meadows two miles above our encampment of the *15th* inst. The hunters were immediately sent out, but they returned without having killed any thing, though they saw some few tracks of deer, very great appearance of bear, and what is of more importance, a number of what they thought were salmon-trout, in the creek. We therefore hope, by means of these fish and other game to subsist at this place without returning to the Quamash flats, which we are unwilling to do, since there are in these meadows great abundance of good food for our horses.

JUNE 19TH *Thursday.* The hunters renewed the chase at a very early hour, but they brought only a single fish at noon. The fishermen were more unsuccessful, for they caught no fish, and broke their two Indian gigs. We, however, mended them with a sharp piece of iron, and towards evening they took a single fish, but instead of finding it the salmon of this spring's arrival, which would of course have been fine, it proved to be a salmon-trout of the red kind, which remain all winter in the upper parts of the rivers and creeks, and are generally poor at this season. In the afternoon, the two men who were left behind, in search of the horses, returned without being able to find them, and the other two hunters arrived from Hungry creek with a couple of deer. Several large morels were brought in to-day, and eaten, as we were now obliged to use them without either salt, pepper or grease, and seemed a very tasteless insipid food. Our stock of salt is now wholly exhausted, except two quarts, which we left on the mountain. The mosquitoes have become very troublesome since we arrived here, particularly in the evening.

JUNE 20TH *Friday.* The scantiness of our subsistence was now such that we were determined to make one effort to ascertain if it be possible to remain here. The hunters therefore set out very early. On their return in the evening, they brought one deer, and a brown bear of the species called by the Chopunnish yahhar, the talons of which were remarkably short, broad at the base, and sharply pointed. It was in bad order, and the flesh of bear in this situation is much inferior to lean venison or elk. We also caught seven trout. But the hunters now reported that game was so scarce, and so difficult to be approached, in consequence of thick underbrush and fallen timber, that with their utmost exertions, they could not procure us subsistence for more than one or two days longer. We determined, therefore, to set out in the morning for the Quamash flats, where we should hear sooner from the Chopunnish on the subject of our guide, and also renew our stock of food, which is now nearly exhausted.

Determined, as we now are, to reach the United States, if possible, this winter, it would be destructive to wait till the snows have melted from the road. The snows have formed a hard coarse bed without crust, on which the horses walk safely without slipping; the chief difficulty, therefore, is to find the road. In this we may be assisted by the circumstance, that, although, generally ten feet in depth, the snow has been thrown off by the thick and spreading branches of the trees, and from round the trunk: the warmth of the trunk itself, acquired by the reflection of the sun, or communicated by natural heat of the earth, which is never frozen under these masses, has dissolved the snow so much, that immediately at the roots, its depth is not more than one or two feet. We therefore hope, that the marks of the baggage rubbing against the trees, may still be perceived, and we have decided, in case the guide cannot be procured, that one of us will take three or four of our most expert woodsmen, and with several of our best horses, and an ample supply of provisions, go on two days' journey in advance, and, endeavour to trace the route by the marks of the Indian baggage on the trees, which they would then mark more distinctly, with a tomahawk. When they should have reached two days' journey beyond Hungry creek, two of the men were to be sent back, to apprise the rest of their success, and if necessary, cause them to delay there, lest, by advancing too soon, they should be forced to halt where no food could be obtained for the horses. If the trace of the baggage is too indistinct, the whole party is to return to Hungry creek, and we will then attempt the passage by ascending the main southwest branch of Lewis's river through the country of the Shoshonees, over to Madison or Gallatin rivers. On that route, the Chopunnish inform us, there is a passage not obstructed by snow at this period of the year. That there is such a passage, we learnt from the Shoshonees, whom we first met on the east fork of Lewis's river; but they also represented it as much more difficult than that by which we came, being obstructed by high steep rugged mountains, followed by an extensive plain, without either wood or game. We are, indeed, inclined to prefer the account of the Shoshonees, because they would have certainly recommended that route had it been better than the one we have taken; and because there is a war between the Chopunnish and the Shoshonees, who live on that route, the former are less able to give accurate information of the state of the country. This route too, is so circuitous, that it would require a month to perform it, and we therefore consider it as the extreme resource.

Saturday. In hopes of soon procuring a guide to lead us over a more practicable route, we collected our horses at an early hour in the morning, and proceeded towards the flats. The mortification of being obliged to tread back our steps, rendered still more tedious a route always so obstructed by brush and fallen timber, that it could not be passed without difficulty and even danger to our horses. One of these poor creatures wounded himself so badly in jumping over fallen logs that he was rendered unfit for use, and sickness has deprived us of the service of a second. At the pass of Collins's creek we met two Indians, who returned with us about half a mile, to the spot where we had formerly slept in September, and where we now halted to dine and let our horses graze. These Indians had four supernumerary horses, and were on their way to cross the mountains. They had seen Drewyer and Shannon, who they said would not return for two days. We pressed them to remain with us till that time, in order to conduct us over the mountains, to which they consented, and deposited their stores of roots and bread in the bushes at a little distance. After dinner we left three men to hunt till our return, and then proceeded; but we had not gone further than two miles when the Indians halted in a small prairie, where they promised to remain at least two nights, if we did not overtake them sooner. We left them, and about seven in the evening found ourselves at the old encampment on the flats; and were glad to find that four of our hunters had killed a deer for supper.

JUNE 21ST

Sunday. At daylight all the hunters set out, and having chased through the whole country, were much more successful than we even hoped, for they brought in eight deer and three bear. Hearing too that the salmon was now abundant in the Kooskooskee, we despatched a man to our old encampment above Collins's creek, for the purpose of purchasing some with a few beads, which were found accidentally in one of our waistcoat pockets. He did not return in the evening, nor had we heard from Drewyer and Shannon, who we begin to fear have had much difficulty in engaging a guide, and we were equally apprehensive that the two Indians might set out to-morrow for the mountains.

JUNE 22D

477

JUNE 23D *Monday.* Early in the morning, therefore, we despatched two hunters to prevail on them, if possible, to remain a day or two longer, and if they persisted in going on, they were to accompany them with the three men at Collins's creek, and mark the route, as far as Traveller's rest, where they were to remain till we joined them by pursuing the same road.

Our fears for the safety of Drewyer, Shannon, and Whitehouse, were fortunately relieved by their return in the afternoon. The former brought three Indians, who promised to go with us to the falls of the Missouri, for the compensation of two guns. One of them is the brother of the Cutnose, and the other two had each given us a horse, at the house of the Brokenarm, and as they are men of good character, and respected in the nation, we have the best prospect of being well served. We therefore secured our horses near the camp, and at an early hour next morning, set out on a second attempt to cross the mountains. On reaching Collins's creek, we found only one of our men, who informed us that a short time before he arrived there yesterday, the two Indians, tired of waiting, had set out, and the other four of our men had accompanied them as they were directed. After halting, we went on to Fish creek, the branch of Hungry creek, where we had slept on the nineteenth instant. Here we overtook two of the party who had gone on with the Indians, and had now been fortunate enough to persuade them to wait for us. During their stay at Collins's creek, they had killed a single deer only, and of this they had been very liberal to the Indians, whom they were prevailing upon to remain, so that they were without provisions, and two of them had set out for another branch of Hungry creek, where we shall meet them to-morrow.

In the evening the Indians, in order as they said to bring fair weather for our journey, set fire to the woods. As these consist chiefly of tall fir trees, with very numerous dried branches, the blaze was almost instantaneous, and as the flame mounted to the tops of the highest trees, resembled a splendid display of fire-works.

JUNE 25TH *Wednesday.* In the morning, one of our guides complained of being sick, a symptom by no means pleasant, for sickness is generally with an Indian the pretext for abandoning an enterprise which he dislikes. He promised, however, to overtake us, and we therefore left him with his two companions, and set out at an early hour. At eleven o'clock we halted for dinner at the branch of Hungry creek, where we found our two men, who had killed nothing. Here too we were joined, rather unexpectedly by our guides, who now appeared disposed to be faithful to their engagements. The Indian was indeed really sick, and having no other covering except a pair of moccasins and an elk skin dressed without the hair, we supplied him with a buffalo robe. In the evening we arrived at Hungry creek, and halted for the night about a mile and a half below our encampment of the sixteenth.

JUNE 26TH *Thursday.* Having collected our horses, and taken breakfast, we set out at six o'clock, and pursuing our former route, at length began to ascend, for the second time, the ridge of mountains. Near the snowy region we killed two of the small black pheasants, and one of the speckled pheasant. These birds generally inhabit the higher parts of the mountains, where they feed on the leaves of pines and firs; but both of them seem solitary and silent birds, for we have never heard either of them make a noise in any situation, and the Indians inform us that they do not in flying drum or produce a whirring sound with their wings. On reaching the top of the mountain, we found our deposit perfectly untouched. The snow in the neighbourhood has melted nearly four feet since the seventeenth. By measuring it accurately, and comparing it by a mark which we then made, the general depth we discover to have been ten feet ten inches, though in some places still greater; but at this time it is about seven feet.

It required two hours to arrange our baggage and to prepare a hasty meal, after which the guides urged us to set off, as we had a long ride to make before reaching a spot where there was grass for our horses. We mounted, and following their steps, sometimes crossed abruptly steep hills, and then wound along their sides, near tremendous precipices, where, had our horses slipped, we should have been lost irrecoverably. Our route lay on the ridgy mountains which separate the waters of the Kooskooskee and Chopunnish, and above the heads of all the streams, so that we met no running water. The whole country was completely covered with snow, except that occasionally we saw a few square feet of earth at the roots of some trees, round which the snow had dissolved. We passed our camp of September 18, and late in the evening reached the deserted spot, and encamped near a good spring of water. It was on the steep side of a mountain, with no wood and a fair southern aspect, from which the snow seems to have melted for about ten days, and given place to an abundant growth of young grass, resembling the green sward. There is also another species of grass, not unlike a flag, with a broad succulent leaf which is confined to the upper parts of the highest mountains. It is a favourite food of the horses, but at present is either covered with snow, or just making its appearance. There is a third plant peculiar to the same regions, and is a species of whortleberry. There are also large quantities of a species of bear-grass, which, though it grows luxuriantly over all these mountains, and preserves its verdure during the whole winter, is never eaten by horses.

In the night there came to the camp a Chopunnish, who had pursued us with a view of accompanying us to the falls of the Missouri. We now learnt that the two young Indians whom we had met on the twenty-first, and detained several days, were going merely on a party of pleasure to the Ootlashoots, or as they call them, Shallees, a band of Tushepahs, who live on Clark's river, near Traveller's-rest.

Friday. Early the next morning, we resumed our route over the heights and steep hills of the same great ridge. At eight miles distance we reached an eminence where the Indians have raised a conic mound of stone, six or eight feet high, on which is fixed a pole made of pine, about fifteen feet. Here we halted and smoked for some time at the request of the Indians, who told us, that in passing the mountains with their families, some men are usually sent on foot from this place to fish at the entrance of Colt creek, whence they rejoin the main party at the Quamash glade on the head of the Kooskooskee. From this elevated spot we have a commanding view of the surrounding mountains, which so completely enclose us, that although we have once passed them, we almost despair of ever escaping from them without the assistance of the Indians. The marks on the trees, which had been our chief

JUNE 27TH

dependence, are much fewer and more difficult to be distinguished than we had supposed; but our guides traverse this trackless region with a kind of instinctive sagacity; they never hesitate, they are never embarrassed; yet so undeviating is their step, that wherever the snow has disappeared, for even a hundred paces, we find the summer road. With their aid the snow is scarcely a disadvantage, for although we are often obliged to slip down, yet the fallen timber and the rocks, which are now covered, were much more troublesome when we passed in the autumn. The travelling road is indeed comparatively pleasant, as well as more rapid, the snow being hard and coarse, without a crust, and perfectly hard enough to prevent the horses sinking more than two or three inches. After the sun has been on it for some hours it becomes softer than early in the morning, yet they are almost always able to get a sure foothold.

After some time we resumed our route, and at the distance of three miles descended a steep mountain, then crossing two branches of the Chopunnish river, just above their forks, began to mount a second ridge. Along this we proceeded for some time, and then, at the distance of seven miles, reached our camp of the sixteenth of September. Near this place we crossed three small branches of the Chopunnish, and then ascended a second dividing ridge, along which we continued for nine miles, when the ridge became somewhat lower, and we halted for the night on a position similar to that of our encampment last evening.

We had now travelled twenty-eight miles without taking the loads from our horses or giving them any thing to eat, and as the snow where we halted has not much dissolved, there was still but little grass. Among the vegetation we observed great quantities of the white lily, with reflected petals, which are now in bloom, and in the same forwardness as they were in the plains on the tenth of May. As for ourselves, the whole stock of meat being gone, we distributed to each mess a pint of bear's oil, which, with boiled roots, made an agreeable dish. We saw several black-tailed or mule-deer, but could not get a shot at them, and were informed that there is an abundance of elk in the valley, near the fishery, on the Kooskooskee. The Indians also assert that on the mountains to our right are large numbers of what they call white buffalo or mountain sheep.

Our horses strayed to some distance to look for food, and in the morning, when they were brought up, exhibited rather a gaunt appearance. The Indians, however, promised that we should reach some good grass at noon, and we therefore set out after an early breakfast. Our route lay along the dividing ridge, and across a very deep hollow, till at the distance of six miles we passed our camp of the fifteenth of September. A mile and a half further we passed the road from the right, immediately on the dividing ridge, leading by the fishery. We went on as we had done during the former part of the route over deep snows, when having made thirteen miles we reached the side of a mountain, just above the fishery, which having no timber, and a southern exposure, the snow had disappeared, leaving an abundance of fine grass. Our horses were very hungry as well as fatigued, and as there was no other spot within our reach this evening, where we could find any food for them, we determined to encamp, though it was not yet midday. But as there was no water in the neighbourhood, we melted snow for cooking.

Sunday. Early in the morning we continued along the ridge which we have been following for several days, till at the end of five miles it terminated; and now bidding adieu to the snows in which we have been imprisoned, we descended to the main branch of the Kooskooskee. On reaching the water side, we found a deer which had been left for us by two hunters who had been despatched at an early hour to the warm springs, and which proved a very seasonable addition to our food; for having neither meat nor oil, we were reduced to a diet of roots, without salt or any other addition. At this place, about a mile and a half from the spot where Quamash creek falls in from the northeast, the Kooskooskee is about thirty yards wide, and runs with great velocity over a bed, which, like those of all the mountain streams, is composed of pebbles. We forded the river, and ascended for two miles the steep acclivities of a mountain, and at its summit found coming in from the right the old road which we had passed on our route last autumn. It was now much plainer and more beaten, which the Indians told us was owing to the frequent visits of the Ootlashoots, from the valley of Clark's river to the fishery; though there was no appearance of their having been here this spring. Twelve miles from our camp we halted to graze our horses on the Quamash flats, on the creek of the same name. This is a handsome plain of fifty acres in extent, covered with an abundance of quamash, and seems to form a principal stage or encampment for the Indians in passing the mountains. We saw here several young pheasants, and killed one of the small black kind, which is the first we have observed below the region of snow. In the neighbourhood were also seen the tracks of two barefoot Indians, which our companions supposed to be Ootlashoots, who had fled in distress from the Pahkees. Here we discovered that two of the horses were missing. We therefore sent two men in quest of them, and then went on seven miles further to the warm springs, where we arrived early in the afternoon. The two hunters who had been sent forward in the morning had collected no game, nor were several others, who went out after our arrival, more successful. We therefore had a prospect of continuing our usual diet of roots, when late in the afternoon the men returned with the stray horses and a deer for supper.

JUNE 29TH

These warm springs are situated at the foot of a hill, on the north side of Traveller's-rest creek, which is ten yards wide at this place. They issue from the bottoms, and through the interstices of a grey freestone rock, which rises in irregular masses round their lower side. The principal spring, which the Indians have formed into a bath by stopping the run with stone and pebbles, is about the same temperature as the warmest bath used at the hot springs in Virginia. On trying, captain Lewis could with difficulty remain in it nineteen minutes, and then was affected with a profuse perspiration. The two other springs are much hotter, the temperature being equal to that of the warmest of the hot springs in Virginia. Our men as well as the Indians amused themselves with going into the bath; the latter, according to their universal custom, going first into the hot bath, where they remain as long as they can bear the heat, then plunging into the creek, which is now of an icy coldness, and repeating this operation several times, but always ending with the warm bath.

Chapter 31
CAPTAIN LEWIS SEEKS A SHORT-CUT

MONDAY, JUNE 30TH, 1806 We despatched some hunters ahead, and were about setting out, when a deer came to lick at the springs; we killed it, and being now provided with meat for dinner, proceeded along the north side of the creek, sometimes in the bottoms, and over the steep sides of the ridge, till at the distance of thirteen miles, we halted at the entrance of a small stream where we had stopped on the *12th of September*. Here we observed a road to the right, which the Indians inform us leads to a fine extensive valley on Clark's river, where the Shallees or Ootlashoots occasionally reside. After permitting our horses to graze, we went on along a road much better than any we have seen since entering the mountains, so that before sunset we made nineteen miles, and reached our old encampment on the south side of the creek near its entrance into Clark's river. In the course of the day we killed six deer, of which there are great numbers, as well as big-horn and elk, in this neighbourhood. We also obtained a small grey squirrel like that on the coast of the Pacific, except that its belly was white. Among the plants was a kind of lady's slipper, or moccasin flower, resembling that common in the United States, but with a white corolla, marked with longitudinal veins of a pale red colour on the inner side.

Tuesday, July 1st, 1806

We had now made one hundred and fifty-six miles from the Quamash flats, to the mouth of Traveller's-rest creek. This being the point where we proposed to separate, it was resolved to remain a day or two in order to refresh ourselves, and the horses, which have borne the journey extremely well, and are still in fine order, but require some little rest. We had hoped to meet here some of the Ootlashoots, but no tracks of them can be discovered. Our Indian companions express much anxiety lest they should have been cut off by the Pahkees during the winter, and mention the tracks of the two barefooted persons as a proof how much the fugitives must have been distressed.

We now formed the following plan of operations. Captain Lewis with nine men, are to pursue the most direct route to the falls of the Missouri, where three of his party are to be left to prepare carriages for transporting the baggage and canoes across the portage. With the remaining six he will ascend Maria's river, to explore the country and ascertain whether any branch of it reaches as far north as the latitude of fifty degrees, after which he will descend that river to its mouth. The rest of the men will accompany captain Clark to the head of Jefferson river, which sergeant Ordway and a party of nine men will descend with the canoes and other articles deposited there. Captain Clark's party, which will then be reduced to ten, will proceed to the Yellowstone at its nearest approach to the three forks of the Missouri. There he will build canoes, and go down that river with seven of his party, and wait at its mouth till the rest of the party join him. Sergeant Pryor, with two others, will then take the horses by land to the Mandans. From that nation he is to go to the British posts on the Assiniboin with a letter to Mr. Henry, to procure his endeavours to prevail on some of the Sioux chiefs to accompany him to the city of Washington.

Having made these arrangements, this and the following day were employed in hunting and repairing our arms. We were successful in procuring a number of fine large deer, the flesh of which was exposed to dry. Among other animals in this neighbourhood, are the dove, black woodpecker, lark woodpecker, logcock, prairie lark, sandhill crane, prairie hen, with the short and pointed tail; the robin, a species of brown plover, a few curlews, small blackbirds [cowbirds], ravens, hawks, and a variety of sparrows, as well as the bee martin, and several species of corvus. The mosquitoes too have been excessively troublesome since our arrival here. The Indians assert also, that there are great numbers of the white buffalo or mountain sheep, on the snowy heights of the mountains, west of Clark's river. They generally inhabit the rocky and most inaccessible parts of the mountains, but as they are not fleet, are easily killed by the hunters.

The plants which most abound in this valley are the wild rose, the honeysuckle, with a white berry, the sevenbark, serviceberry, the elder, aspen and alder, the chokecherry, and both the narrow and broad-leafed willow. The principal timber consists of long-leafed pine, which grows as well in the river bottoms as on the hills; the firs and larch are confined to the higher parts of the hills, while on the river itself, is a growth of cottonwood, with a wider leaf than that of the upper part of the Missouri, though narrower than that which grows lower down that river. There are also two species of clover in this valley; one with a very narrow small leaf, and a pale red flower; the other with a white flower, and nearly as luxuriant in its growth as our red clover.

The Indians who had accompanied us, intended leaving us in order to seek their friends, the Ootlashoots; but we prevailed on them to accompany captain Lewis a part of his route, so as to show him the shortest road to the Missouri, and in the meantime amused them with conversation and running races, both on foot and with horses, in both of which they proved themselves hardy, athletic and active. To the chief, captain Lewis gave a small medal and a gun, as a reward for having guided us across the mountains; in return, the customary civility of exchanging names passed between them, by which the former acquired the title of Yomekollick, or white bearskin unfolded. The Chopunnish who had overtaken us on the 26th, made us a present of an excellent horse, for the good advice we gave him, and as a proof of his attachment to the whites, as well as of his desire to be at peace with the Pahkees.

Thursday. The next morning, all our preparations being completed, we saddled our horses, and the two parties who had been so long companions, now separated with an anxious hope of soon meeting, after each had accomplished the purpose of his destination.

JULY 3D

The nine men and five Indians who accompanied captain Lewis, proceeded in a direction due north, down the west side of Clark's river. Half a mile from the camp we forded Traveller's-rest creek, and two and a half miles further, passed a western branch of the river; a mile beyond this, was a small creek on the eastern side, and a mile lower down, the entrance of the eastern branch of the river. This stream is from ninety to one hundred and twenty yards wide, and its water, which is discharged through two channels, is more turbid than that of the main river. The latter is one hundred and fifty yards in width, and waters an extensive level plain and prairie, which on its lower parts are ornamented with long-leafed pine, and cottonwood, while the tops of the hills are covered with pine, larch, and fir. We proceeded two miles further to a place where the Indians advised us to cross, but having no boats, and timber being scarce, four hours were spent in collecting timber to make three small rafts; on which, with some difficulty and danger, we passed the river. We then drove our horses into the water and they swam to the opposite shore, but the Indians crossed on horseback, drawing at the same time their baggage alongside of them in small basins of deer skins. The whole party being now reassembled, we continued for three miles, and encamped about sunset at a small creek. The Indians now showed us a road at no great distance, which they said would lead up the eastern branch of Clark's river, and another river called Cokalahishkit, or the *river of the road to buffalo*, thence to Medicine river and the falls of the Missouri. They added, that not far from the dividing ridge of the waters of Clark's river and the Missouri, the roads forked, and though both led to the falls, the left hand route was the best. The route was so well beaten that we could no longer mistake it, and having now shown us the way, they were anxious to go on in quest of their friends, the Shahlees, besides which, they feared, by venturing further with us, to encounter the Pahkees, for we had this afternoon seen a fresh track of a horse, which they supposed to be a Shahlee scout. We could not insist on their remaining longer with us; but as they had so kindly conducted us across the mountains, we were desirous of giving them a supply of provisions, and therefore distributed to them half of three deer, and the hunters were ordered to go out early in the morning, in hopes of adding to the stock.

The horses suffer so dreadfully from the mosquitoes, that we are obliged to kindle large fires and place the poor animals in the midst of the smoke. Fortunately, however, it became cold after dark, and the mosquitoes disappeared.

JULY 4TH *Friday*. The hunters accordingly set out, but returned unsuccessful about eleven o'clock. In the meantime we were joined by a young man of the Palloatpallah tribe, who had set out a few days after us, and had followed us alone across the mountains, the same who had attempted to pass the mountains in June, while we were on the Kooskooskee, but was obliged to return. We now smoked a farewell pipe with our estimable companions, who expressed every emotion of regret at parting with us, which they felt the more, because they did not conceal their fears of our being cut off by the Pahkees. We also gave them a shirt, a handkerchief, and a small quantity of ammunition. The meat which they received from us was dried and left at this place as a store during the homeward journey. This circumstance confirms our belief, that there is no route along Clark's river to the Columbian plains, so near or so good as that by which we came; for, although these people mean to go for several days' journey down that river, to look for the Shahlees, yet they intend returning home by the same pass of the mountain through which they conducted us. This route is also used by all the nations whom we know west of the mountains who are in the habit of visiting the plains of the Missouri; while on the other side all the war paths of the Pahkees, which fall into this valley of Clark's river, concentre at Traveller's-rest, beyond which these people have never ventured to the west.

Having taken leave of the Indians, we mounted our horses, and proceeded up the eastern branch of Clark's river through the level plain in which we were encamped. At the distance of five miles we had crossed a small creek fifteen yards wide, and now entered the mountains. The river is here closely confined within the hills for two miles, when the bottom widens into an extensive prairie, and the river is one hundred and ten yards in width. We went three miles further, over a high plain succeeded by a low and level prairie, to the entrance of the Cokalahishkit. This river empties itself from the northeast, is deep, rapid, and about sixty yards wide, with banks, which though not high, are sufficiently bold to prevent the water from overflowing. The eastern branch of Clark's river is ninety yards wide above the junction, but below it spreads to one hundred. The waters of both are turbid, though the Cokalahishkit is the clearer of the two; the beds of both are composed of sand and gravel, but neither of them is navigable on account of the rapids and shoals which obstruct their currents. Before the junction of these streams, the country had been bare of trees, but as we turned up the north branch of the Cokalahishkit, we found a woody country, though the hills were high and the low grounds narrow and poor. At the distance of eight miles in a due east course, we encamped in a bottom, where there was an abundance of excellent grass. The evening proved fine and pleasant, and we were no longer annoyed by mosquitoes. Our only game were two squirrels, one of the kind common to the Rocky mountains, the second a ground squirrel of a species we had not seen before. Near the place where we crossed Clark's river, we saw at a distance, some wild horses, which are said, indeed, to be very numerous on this river as well as on the heads of the Yellowstone.

Saturday. Early in the morning we proceeded on for three and a half miles, in a direction north 75° east, then inclining to the south, crossed an extensive, beautiful, and well watered valley, nearly twelve miles in length, at the extremity of which we halted for dinner. Here we obtained a great quantity of quamash, and shot an antelope from a gang of females, who at this season herd together, apart from the bucks. After dinner we followed the course of the river eastwardly for six miles, to the mouth of a creek thirty-five yards wide, which we called Werner's creek. It comes in from the north, and waters a high extensive prairie, the hills near which are low, and supplied with the long-leafed pine, larch, and some fir. The road then led north 22° west, for four miles, soon after which it again turned north 73° east, for two and a half miles, over a handsome plain, watered by Werner's creek, to the river, which we followed on its eastern direction, through a high prairie, rendered very unequal by a vast number of little hillocks and sinkholes, and at three miles distance encamped near the entrance of a large creek, twenty yards wide, to which we gave the name of Seaman's creek. We had seen no Indians, although near the camp were the concealed fires of a war party, who had passed about two months ago.

JULY 5TH

Sunday. At sunrise we continued our course eastward along the river. At seven miles distance we passed the north fork of the Cokalahishkit, a deep and rapid stream, forty-five yards in width, and like the main branch itself somewhat turbid, though the other streams of this country are clear. Seven miles further the river enters the mountains, and here end those extensive

JULY 6TH

prairies on this side, though they widen in their course towards the southeast, and form an Indian route to Dearborn's river, and thence to the Missouri. From the multitude of knobs irregularly scattered through them, captain Lewis called this country the Prairie of the Knobs. They abound in game, as we saw goats, deer, great numbers of the burrowing squirrels, some curlews, bee martins, woodpeckers, plover, robins, doves, ravens, hawks, ducks, a variety of sparrows, and yesterday observed swans on Werner's creek. Among the plants we observed the southern wood, and two other species of shrubs, of which we preserved specimens.

On entering the high grounds we followed the course of the river through the narrow bottoms, thickly timbered with pine and cottonwood intermixed, and variegated with the boisrouge [redwood], which is now in bloom, the common small blue flag and pepper-grass; and at the distance of three and a half miles, reached the two forks of the river mentioned by the Indians. They are nearly equal in width, and the road itself here forks and follows each of them. We followed that which led us in a direction north 75° east, over a steep high hill, thence along a wide bottom to a thickly wooded side of a hill, where the low grounds are narrow, till we reached a large creek, eight miles from the forks and twenty-five from our last encampment. Here we halted for the night. In the course of the day the track of the Indians, whom we supposed to be the Pahkees, continued to grow fresher, and we passed a number of old lodges and encampments.

JULY 7TH *Monday.* At seven o'clock the next morning, we proceeded through a beautiful plain on the north side of the river, which seems here to abound in beaver. The low grounds possess much timber, and the hills are covered chiefly with pitch pine, that of the long-leafed kind having disappeared since we left the Prairie of the Knobs. At the distance of twelve miles we left the river or rather the creek, and having for four miles crossed, in a direction north 15° east, two ridges, again struck to the right, which we followed through a narrow bottom, covered with low willows and grass, and abundantly supplied with both deer and beaver. After seven miles we reached the foot of a ridge, which we ascended in a direction north 45° east, through a low gap of easy ascent from the westward, and on descending it were delighted at discovering that this was the dividing ridge between the waters of the Columbia and those of the Missouri. From this gap the Fort mountain is about twenty miles in a northeastern direction. We now wound through the hills and hollows of the mountains, passing several rivulets, which run to the right, and at the distance of nine miles from the gap encamped, after making thirty-two miles. We procured some beaver, and this morning saw some signs and tracks of buffalo, from which it seems those animals do sometimes penetrate to a short distance within the mountains.

JULY 8TH *Tuesday.* At three miles from our camp we reached a stream, issuing from the mountains to the southwest, though it only contains water for a width of thirty feet, yet its bed is more than three times that width, and from the appearance of the roots and trees in the neighbouring bottom, must sometimes run with great violence; we called it Dearborn's river. Half a mile further we observed from a height the Shishequaw mountain, a high insulated mountain of a conic form, standing several miles in advance of the eastern range of the Rocky mountains, and now about eight miles from us, and immediately on our road, which was in a northwest direction. But as our object was to strike Medicine river, and hunt down to its mouth in order to procure skins for the food and gear necessary for the three men who are to be left at the falls, none of whom are hunters, we determined to leave the road, and therefore proceeded due north, through an open plain, till we reached Shishequaw creek, a stream about twenty yards wide, with a considerable quantity of timber in its low grounds. Here we halted and dined, and now felt, by the luxury of our food, that we were approaching once more the plains of the Missouri, so rich in game. We saw a great number of deer, goats, wolves, and some barking squirrels, and for the first time caught a distant prospect of two buffalo. After dinner we followed the Shishequaw for six and a half miles, to its entrance into Medicine river, and along the banks of this river for eight miles, when we encamped on a large island. The bottoms continued low, level, and extensive; the plains too are level; but the soil of neither is fertile, as it consists of a light coloured earth, intermixed with a large proportion of gravel; the grass in both is generally about nine inches high. Captain Lewis here shot a large and remarkably white wolf. We had now made twenty-eight miles.

Wednesday. We set out early the next morning, but the air soon became very cold, and it began to rain. We halted for a few minutes in some old Indian lodges, but finding that the rain continued we proceeded on, though we were all wet to the skin, and halted for dinner at the distance of eight miles. The rain, however, continued, and we determined to go no further. The river is about eighty yards wide, with banks which, though low, are seldom overflowed; the bed is composed of loose gravel and pebbles, the water clear and rapid, but not so much as to impede the navigation. The bottoms are handsome, wide, and level, and supplied with a considerable quantity of narrow-leafed cottonwood. During our short ride we killed two deer and a buffalo, and saw a number of wolves and antelopes. JULY 9TH

Thursday. The next morning early we set out and continued through a country similar to that of yesterday, with bottoms of wide-leafed cottonwood occasionally along the borders, though for the most part the low grounds are without timber. In the plains are great quantities of two species of prickly pear, now in bloom. Gooseberries of the common red kind are in abundance and just beginning to ripen, but there are no currants. The river has now widened to an hundred yards; is deep, crowded with islands, and in many parts rapid. At the distance of seventeen miles, the timber disappears totally from the river bottoms. About this part of the river, the wind, which had blown on our backs, and constantly put the elk on their guard, shifted round, and we then shot three of them, and a brown bear. Captain Lewis halted to skin them, while two of the men took the pack-horses forward to seek for an encampment. It was nine o'clock before he overtook them, at the distance of seven miles in the first grove of cottonwood. They had been pursued as they came along by a very large bear, on which they were afraid to fire, lest their horses being unaccustomed to the gun, might take fright and throw them. This circumstance reminds us of the ferocity of these animals, when we were last near this place, and admonishes us to be very cautious. JULY 10TH

We saw vast numbers of buffalo below us, which kept a dreadful bellowing during the night. With all our exertions we were unable to advance more than twenty-four miles, owing to the mire, through which we are obliged to travel, in consequence of the rain.

JULY 11TH *Friday.* The next morning, however, was fair, and enlivened by great numbers of birds, who sang delightfully in the clusters of cottonwood. The hunters were sent down Medicine river to hunt elk, while captain Lewis crossed the high plain, in a direction 75° east, to the Whitebear island, a distance of eight miles, where the hunters joined him. They had seen elk; but in this neighbourhood the buffalo are in such numbers, that on a moderate computation, there could not have been fewer than ten thousand within a circuit of two miles. At this season, they are bellowing in every direction, so as to form an almost continued roar, which at first alarmed our horses, who being from the west of the mountains, are unused to the noise and appearance of these animals. Among the smaller game are the brown thrush, pigeons, doves, and a beautiful bird called a buffalo-pecker [cowbird].

Immediately on our arrival we began to hunt, and by three in the afternoon had collected a stock of food and hides enough for our purpose. We then made two canoes, one in the form of a basin, like those used by the Mandans, the other consisting of two skins, in a form of our own invention. They were completed the next morning, but the wind continued so high that it was not till towards night that we could cross the river in them, and make our horses swim. In the meantime, nearly the whole day was consumed in search after our horses, which had disappeared last night, and seven of which were not recovered at dark, while Drewyer was still in quest of them. The river is somewhat higher than it was last summer, the present season being much more moist than the preceding one, as may be seen in the greater luxuriance of the grass.

JULY 13TH *Sunday.* We formed our camp this morning at our old station, near the head of the Whitebear islands, and immediately went to work in making gear. On opening the cache, we found the bear skins entirely destroyed by the water, which, in a flood of the river, had penetrated to them. All the specimens of plants were unfortunately lost; the chart of the Missouri, however, still remained unhurt, and several articles contained in trunks and boxes had suffered but little injury; but a vial of laudanum had lost its stopper, and ran into a drawer of medicines, which it spoiled beyond recovery. The mosquitoes have been so troublesome that it was impossible even to write without the assistance of a mosquito bier. The buffalo are leaving us fast on their way to the southeast.

JULY 14TH *Monday.* We continued making preparations for transporting our articles, and as the old deposit was too damp, we secured the trunks on a high scaffold, covered with skins, among the thick brush on a large island: a precaution against any visit from the Indians, should they arrive before the main party arrives here. The carriage wheels were in good order, and the iron frame of the boat had not suffered materially. The buffalo have now nearly disappeared, leaving behind them a number of large wolves who are now prowling about us.

Tuesday. To our great joy Drewyer returned to-day from a long search after the horses; for we had concluded, from his long stay, that he had probably met with a bear, and with his usual intrepidity attacked the animal, in which case, if by any accident he should be separated from his horse, his death would be almost inevitable. Under this impression, we resolved to set out to-morrow in quest of him, when his return relieved us from our apprehensions. He had searched for two days before he discovered that the horses had crossed Dearborn's river, near a spot where was an Indian encampment, which seemed to have been abandoned about the time the horses were stolen, and which was so closely concealed that no trace of a horse could be seen within the distance of a quarter of a mile. He crossed the river and pursued the track of these Indians westward, till his horse became so much fatigued that he despaired of overtaking them, and then returned. These Indians we suppose to be a party of Tushepaws, who have ventured out of the mountains to hunt buffalo. During the day we were engaged in drying meat and dressing skins.

JULY 15TH

At night M'Neal, who had been sent in the morning to examine the cache at the lower end of the portage, returned; but had been prevented from reaching that place by a singular adventure. Just as he arrived near Willow run, he approached a thicket of brush, in which was a white bear, which he did not discover till he was within ten feet of him: his horse started, and wheeling suddenly round, threw M'Neal almost immediately under the bear, who started up instantly, and finding the bear raising himself on his hind feet to attack him, struck him on the head with the butt end of his musket; the blow was so violent that it broke the breech of the musket and knocked the bear to the ground, and before he recovered, M'Neal seeing a willow tree close by, sprang up, and there remained while the bear closely guarded the foot of the tree until late in the afternoon. He then went off, and M'Neal being released came down, and having found his horse, which had strayed off to the distance of two miles, returned to camp. These animals are, indeed, of a most extraordinary ferocity, and it is matter of wonder, that in all our encounters we have had the good fortune to escape. We are now troubled with another enemy, not quite so dangerous, though even more disagreeable: these are the mosquitoes, who now infest us in such myriads, that we frequently get them into our throats when breathing, and the dog even howls with the torture they occasion.

Having now accomplished the object of our stay, captain Lewis determined to leave sergeant Gass with two men and four horses to assist the party who are expected to carry our effects over the portage, whilst he, with Drewyer, and the two Fields, with six horses, proceeded to the sources of Maria's river. Accordingly, early in the morning, captain Lewis descended in a skin canoe to the lower side of Medicine river, where the horses had previously been sent, and then rode with his party to the fall of forty-seven feet, where he halted for two hours to dine, and took a sketch of the fall. In the afternoon they proceeded to the great falls, near which they slept under a shelving rock, with a happy exemption from mosquitoes. These falls have lost much of their grandeur since we saw them, the river being much lower now than at that time, though they still form a most sublime spectacle. As we came along, we met several white bear, but they did not venture to attack us.

JULY 16TH

489

There were but few buffalo, however, the large having principally passed the river, directed their course downwards. There are, as usual, great numbers of goats and antelopes dispersed through the plains, and large flocks of geese, which raise their young about the entrance of Medicine river. We observe here also the cuckoo, or as it is sometimes called, the raincraw, a bird which is not known either within or west of the Rocky mountains.

JULY 17TH *Thursday.* After taking a second draught of the falls, captain Lewis directed his course N. 10° W. with an intention of striking Maria's river at the point to which he had ascended it in 1805. The country is here spread into wide and level plains, swelling like the ocean, in which the view is uninterrupted by a single tree or shrub, and is diversified only by the moving herds of buffalo. The soil consists of a light-coloured earth, intermixed with a large proportion of coarse gravel without sand, and is by no means so fertile as either the plains of the Columbia, or those lower down the Missouri. When dry it cracks, and is hard and thirsty while in its wet state: it is as soft and slimy as soap. The grass is naturally short, and at this time is still more so from the recent passage of the buffalo.

    Among the birds which we met was the parti-coloured plover [avocet], with the head and neck of a brick red, a bird which frequents the little ponds scattered over the plains. After travelling twenty miles we reached Tansy river, and as we could not go as far as Maria's river this evening, and perhaps not find either wood or water before we arrived there, we determined to encamp. As we approached the river, we saw the fresh track of a bleeding buffalo, a circumstance by no means pleasant, as it indicated the Indians had been hunting, and were not far from us. The tribes who principally frequent this country, are the Minnetarees of Fort de Prairie, and the Blackfoot Indians, both of whom are vicious and profligate rovers, and we have therefore every thing to fear, not only from their stealing our horses, but even our arms and baggage, if they are sufficiently strong. In order therefore to avoid, if possible, an interview with them, we hurried across the river to a thick wood, and having turned out the horses to graze, Drewyer went in quest of the buffalo to kill it, and ascertain whether the wound was given by the Indians, while the rest reconnoitred the whole country. In about three hours they all returned without having seen the buffalo or any Indians in the plains. We then dined, and two of the party resumed their search, but could see no signs of Indians, and we therefore slept in safety. Tansy river is here about fifty yards wide, though its water occupies only thirty-five feet, and is not more than three in depth. It most probably rises within the first range of the Rocky mountains, and its general course is from east to west, and as far as we are able to trace it through wide bottoms, well supplied with both the long and broad-leafed cottonwood. The hills on its banks, are from one hundred to one hundred and fifty feet in height, and possess bluffs of earth, like the lower part of the Missouri: the bed is formed of small gravel and mud; the water turbid, and of a whitish tint; the banks low, but never overflowed; in short, except in depth and velocity, it is a perfect miniature of the Missouri.

Friday. A little before sunrise we continued on a course N. 25° W. for six miles, when we reached the top of a high plain, which divides the waters of Maria and Tansy rivers, and a mile further reached a creek of the former, about twenty-five yards wide, though with no water except in occasional pools in the bed. Down this creek we proceeded for twelve miles through thick groves of timber on its banks, passing such immense quantities of buffalo, that the whole seemed to be a single herd. Accompanying them were great numbers of wolves, besides which we saw some antelopes and hares. After dinner we left the creek which we called Buffalo creek, and crossing the plain for six miles, came to Maria's river and encamped in a grove of cottonwood, on its western side, keeping watch through the night lest we should be surprised by the Indians.

JULY 18TH

Saturday. Captain Lewis was now convinced that he was above the point to which he had formerly ascended, and fearing that some branch might come in on the north, between that point and our present position, he early in the morning despatched two hunters, who descended the river in a direction north 80° east, till they came to our former position, at the distance of six miles, without seeing any stream except Buffalo creek. Having completed an observation of the sun's meridian altitude, captain Lewis proceeded along the north side of Maria's river. The bottoms are in general about half a mile wide, and possess considerable quantities of cottonwood timber, and an underbrush, consisting of honeysuckle, rose bushes, narrow-leafed willow, and the plant called by the engagées, buffalo grease. The plains are level and beautiful, but the soil is thin and overrun with prickly pears. It consists of a sort of white or whitish-blue clay, which after being trodden, when wet, by the buffalo, stands up in sharp hard points, which are as painful to the horses as the great quantity of small gravel, which is every where scattered over the ground, is in other parts of the plains. The bluffs of the river are high, steep, and irregular, and composed of a sort of earth which easily dissolves and slips into the water, though with occasional strata of freestone near the tops. The bluffs of the Missouri above Maria's river, differ from these, in consisting of a firm red or yellow clay, which does not yield to water, and a large proportion of rock. The buffalo are not so abundant as they were yesterday; but there are still antelopes, wolves, geese, pigeons, doves, hawks, ravens, crows, larks, and sparrows, though the curlew has disappeared.

JULY 19TH

At the distance of eight miles a large creek falls in on the south side, and seven miles beyond it, another thirty yards wide, which seem to issue from three mountains, stretching from east to west, in a direction north 10° west from its mouth, and which, from their loose, irregular, and rugged appearance, we called the Broken mountains. That in the centre terminates in a conic spire, for which reason we called it the Tower mountain. After making twenty miles we halted for the night.

Sunday. The next morning we continued our route up the river, through a country resembling that which we passed yesterday, except that the plains are more broken, and the appearances of mineral salts, common to the Missouri plains, are more abundant than usual; these are discerned in all the pools, which indeed at present contain the only water to be found through-

JULY 20TH

491

out the plains, and are so strongly impregnated as to be unfit for any use, except that of the buffalo, who seem to prefer it to even the water of the river. The low grounds are well timbered, and contain also silk-grass, sandrush, wild liquorice, and sunflowers, the barb of which are now in bloom. Besides the geese, ducks, and other birds common to the country, we have seen fewer buffalo to-day than yesterday though elk, wolves, and antelopes continue in equal numbers. There is also much appearance of beaver, though none of otter. At the distance of six miles we passed a creek from the south; eighteen miles further one from the north; four miles beyond which we encamped. The river is here one hundred and twenty yards wide, and its water is but little diminished as we ascend. Its general course is very straight. From the apparent descent of the country to the north and above the Broken mountains, it seems probable that the south branch of the Saskashawan receives some of its waters from these plains, and that one of its streams must, in descending from the Rocky mountains, pass not far from Maria's river, to the northeast of the Broken mountains. We slept in peace, without being annoyed by the mosquitoes, whom we have not seen since we left the Whitebear islands.

Chapter 32
CAPTAIN LEWIS COMPLETES HIS SEPARATE EXPLORATION

MONDAY, JULY 21ST, 1806   At sunrise we proceeded along the northern side of the river for a short distance, when finding the ravines too steep, we crossed to the south; but after continuing for three miles, returned to the north and took our course through the plains, at some distance from the river. After making fifteen miles, we came to the forks of the river, the largest branch of which bears south 75° west to the mountains, while the course of the other is north 40° west. We halted for dinner, and believing, on examination, that the northern branch came from the mountains, and would probably lead us to the most northern extent of Maria's river, we proceeded along, though at a distance over the plains, till we struck it eight miles from the junction. The river is about thirty yards wide, the water clear, but shallow, rapid, and unfit for navigation. It is closely confined between cliffs of freestone, and the adjacent country broken and poor. We crossed to the south side, and proceeded for five miles, till we encamped under a cliff, where not seeing any timber, we made a fire of buffalo dung, and passed the night.

Tuesday. The next day we went on; but as the ground was now steep and unequal, and the horses' feet very sore, we were obliged to proceed slowly. The river is still confirmed by freestone cliffs, till at the distance of seven miles the country opens, is less covered with gravel, and has some bottoms, though destitute of timber or underbrush. The river here makes a considerable bend to the northwest, so that we crossed the plains for eleven miles when we again crossed the river. Here we halted for dinner, and having no wood, made a fire of the dung of buffalo, with which we cooked the last of our meat, except a piece of spoiled buffalo. Our course then lay across a level beautiful plain, with wide bottoms near the bank of the river. The banks are about three or four feet high, but are not overflowed. After crossing for ten miles a bend of the river towards the south, we saw, for the first time during the day, a clump of cottonwood trees in an extensive bottom, and halted there for the night.

JULY 22D

    This place is about ten miles below the foot of the Rocky mountains; and being now able to trace distinctly that the point at which the river issued from those mountains, was to the south of west, we concluded that we had reached its most northern point, and as we have ceased to hope that any branches of Maria's river extend as far north as the fiftieth degree of latitude, we deem it useless to proceed further, and rely chiefly on Milk and Whiteearth rivers for the desired boundary. We therefore determined to remain here two days, for the purpose of making the necessary observations, and resting our horses.

Wednesday. The next morning, Drewyer was sent to examine the bearings of the river, till its entrance into the mountains, which he found to be at the distance of ten miles, and in a direction south 50° west; he had seen also the remains of a camp of eleven leathern lodges, recently abandoned, which induced us to suppose that the Minnetarees of Fort de Prairie are somewhere in this neighbourhood; a suspicion which was confirmed by the return of the hunters, who had seen no game of any kind. As these Indians have probably followed the buffalo towards the main branch of Maria's river, we shall not strike it above the north branch.

JULY 23D

The course of the mountains still continues from southeast to northwest; in which last direction from us, the front range appears to terminate abruptly at the distance of thirty-five miles. Those which are to the southwest, and more distinctly in view, are of an irregular form, composed chiefly of clay, with a very small mixture of rock, without timber, and although low are yet partially covered with snow to their bases. The river itself has nearly double the volume of water which it possessed when we first saw it below, a circumstance to be ascribed, no doubt, to the great evaporation and absorption of the water in its passage through these open plains. The rock in this neighbourhood is of a white colour, and a fine grit, and lies in horizontal strata in the bluffs of the river. We attempted to take some fish, but could procure only a single trout. We had, therefore, nothing to eat, except the grease which we pressed from our tainted meat, and formed a mush of cows, reserving one meal more of the same kind for to-morrow. We have seen near this place a number of the whistling squirrel, common in the country watered by the Columbia, but which we observed here for the first time in the plains of the Missouri. The cottonwood too, of this place, is similar to that of the Columbia. Our observations this evening were prevented by clouds.

JULY 24TH *Thursday.* The weather was clear for a short time in the morning, but the sky soon clouded over, and it rained during the rest of the day. We were therefore obliged to remain one day longer for the purpose of completing our observations. Our situation now became unpleasant from the rain, the coldness of the air, and the total absence of all game; for the hunters could find nothing of a large kind, and we were obliged to subsist on a few pigeons and a kettle of mush made of the remainder of our bread of cows. This supplied us with one more meal in the morning, when finding that the cold and rainy weather would still detain us here, two of the men were despatched to hunt. They returned in the evening with a fine buck, on which we fared sumptuously. In their excursion they had gone as far as the main branch of Maria's river, at the distance of ten miles, through an open extensive valley, in which were scattered a great number of lodges lately evacuated.

JULY 26TH *Saturday.* The next morning the weather was still cloudy, so that no observation could be made, and what added to our disappointment, captain Lewis's chronometer stopped yesterday from some unknown cause, though when set in motion again it went as usual. We now despaired of taking the longitude of this place; and as our staying any longer might endanger our return to the United States during the present season, we, therefore, waited till nine o'clock, in hopes of a change of weather; but seeing no prospect of that kind, we mounted our horses, and leaving with reluctance our position, which we now named Camp Disappointment, directed our course across the open plains, in a direction nearly southeast. At twelve miles distance we reached a branch of Maria's river, about sixty-five yards wide, which we crossed, and continued along its southern side for two miles, where it is joined by another branch, nearly equal in size from the southwest, and far more clear than the north branch, which is turbid, though the beds of both are composed of pebbles. We now decided on pursuing this river to its junction with the fork of Maria's river, which we had ascended, and then cross

BLACKFOOT INDIAN (Bodmer)

the country obliquely to Tansy river, and descend that stream to its confluence with Maria's river. We, therefore, crossed and descended the river, and at one mile below the junction, halted to let the horses graze in a fertile bottom, in which were some Indian lodges, that appear to have been inhabited during the last winter. We here discern more timber than the country in general possesses; for besides an undergrowth of rose, honeysuckle, and redberry bushes, and a small quantity of willow timber, the three species of cottonwood, the narrow-leafed, the broad-leafed, and the species known to the Columbia, though here seen for the first time on the Missouri, are all united at this place. Game too, appears in greater abundance. We saw a few antelopes and wolves, and killed a buck, besides which we saw also two of the small burrowing foxes of the plains, about the size of the common domestic cat, and of a reddish brown colour, except the tail, which is black.

At the distance of three miles, we ascended the hills close to the river side, while Drewyer pursued the valley of the river on the opposite side. But scarcely had captain Lewis reached the high plain, when he saw about a mile on his left, a collection of about thirty horses. He immediately halted, and by the aid of his spy-glass discovered that one half of the horses were saddled, and that on the eminence above the horses, several Indians were looking down towards the river, probably at Drewyer. This was a most unwelcome sight. Their probable numbers rendered any contest with them of doubtful issue; to attempt to escape would only invite pursuit, and our horses were so bad that we must certainly be overtaken; besides which, Drewyer could not yet be aware that the Indians were near, and if we ran he would most probably be sacrificed. We therefore determined to make the best of our situation, and advance towards them in a friendly manner. The flag which we had brought in case of any such accident was therefore displayed, and we continued slowly our march towards them. Their whole attention was so engaged by Drewyer, that they did not immediately discover us. As soon as they did see us, they appeared to be much alarmed and ran about in confusion, and some of them came down the hill and drove their horses within gunshot of the eminence, to which they then returned, as if to wait our arrival. When we came within a quarter of a mile, one of the Indians mounted and rode at full speed to receive us; but when within a hundred paces of us, he halted, and captain Lewis who had alighted to receive him, held out his hand, and beckoned to him to approach, he only looked at us for some time, and then, without saying a word, returned to his companions with as much haste as he had advanced. The whole party now descended the hill and rode towards us. As yet we saw only eight, but presumed that there must be more behind us, as there were several horses saddled. We however advanced, and captain Lewis now told his two men that he believed these were the Minnetarees of Fort de Prairie, who, from their infamous character, would in all probability attempt to rob them; but being determined to die, rather than lose his papers and instruments, he intended to resist to the last extremity, and advised them to do the same, and to be on the alert should there be any disposition to attack us. When the two parties came within a hundred yards of each other, all the Indians, except one, halted; captain Lewis therefore ordered his two men to halt while he advanced, and after shaking hands with the Indian, went on and did the same with the others in the rear, while the Indian himself shook hands with the two men. They all now came up, and after alighting, the Indians asked to smoke with us. Captain Lewis, who was very anxious for Drewyer's safety, told them that the man who had gone down the river had the pipe, and requested that as they had seen him one of them would accompany R. Fields to bring him back. To this they assented, and Fields went with a young man in search of Drewyer.

Captain Lewis now asked them by signs if they were the Minnetarees of the north, and was sorry to learn by their answer that his suspicion was too true. He then inquired if there was any chief among them. They pointed out three; but though he did not believe them, yet it was thought best to please them, and he therefore gave to one a flag, to another a medal, and to a third a handkerchief. They appeared to be well satisfied with these presents, and now recovered from the agitation into which our first interview had thrown them, for they were really more alarmed than ourselves at the meeting. In our turn, however, we became equally satisfied on finding that they were not joined by any more of their companions, for we consider ourselves quite a match for eight Indians, particularly as these have but two guns, the rest being armed with only eye-dogs and bows and arrows. As it was growing late captain Lewis proposed that they should encamp together near the river; for he was glad to see them and had a great deal to say to them. They assented; and being soon joined by Drewyer, we proceeded towards the river, and after descending a very steep bluff, two hundred and fifty feet high, encamped in a small bottom.

Here the Indians formed a large semicircular tent of dressed buffalo skins, in which the two parties assembled, and by the means of Drewyer, the evening was spent in conversation with the Indians. They informed us that they were a part of a large band which at present lay encamped on the main branch of Maria's river, near the foot of the Rocky mountains, and at the distance of a day and a half's journey from this place. Another large band were hunting buffalo near the Broken mountains, from which they would proceed in a few days to the north of Maria's river. With the first of these there was a white man. They added, that from this place to the establishment on the Saskashawan, at which they trade, is only six days' easy march; that is, such a day's journey as can be made with their women and children, so that we computed the distance at one hundred and fifty miles. There they carry the skins of wolves and some beavers, and exchange them for guns, ammunition, blankets, spirituous liquors, and the other articles of Indian traffic. Captain Lewis in turn informed them that he had come from a great distance up the large river which runs towards the rising sun; that he had been as far as the great lake where the sun sets; that he had seen many nations, the greater part of whom were at war with each other, but by his mediation were restored to peace; and all had been invited to come and trade with him west of the mountains; he was now on his way home, but had left his companions at the falls, and come in search of the Minnetarees, in hopes of inducing them to live at peace with their neighbours, and to visit the trading houses which would be formed at the entrance of Maria's river. They said that they were anxious of being at peace with the Tushepaws, but those people had lately killed a number of their relations, as they proved by showing several of the party who had their hair cut as a sign of mourning. They were equally willing, they added, to come down and trade with us. Captain Lewis therefore proposed that they should send some of their young men to invite all their band to meet us at the mouth of Maria's river, and the rest of the party to go with us to that place, where he hoped to find his men, offering them ten horses and some tobacco in case they would accompany us. To this they made no reply. Finding them very fond of the pipe, captain Lewis, who was desirous of keeping a constant watch during the night, smoked with them until a late hour, and as soon as they were all asleep, he woke R. Fields, and ordering him to rouse us all in case any Indian left the camp, as they would probably attempt to steal our horses, he lay down by the side of Drewyer in the tent with all the Indians, while the Fields were stretched near the fire at the mouth of it.

Captain Lewis shoots an Indian for just cause (from Sergeant Gass's journal).

Sunday. At sunrise the Indians got up and crowded round the fire near which J. Fields, who was then on watch, had carelessly left his rifle, near the head of his brother, who was still asleep. One of the Indians slipped behind him, and unperceived, took his brother's and his own rifle, while at the same time, two others seized those of Drewyer and captain Lewis. As soon as Fields turned round, he saw the Indian running off with the rifles, and instantly calling his brother, they pursued him for fifty or sixty yards, and just as they overtook him, in the scuffle for the rifles, R. Fields stabbed him through the heart with his knife; the Indian ran about fifteen steps and fell dead. They now ran back with their rifles to the camp. The moment the fellow touched his gun, Drewyer, who was awake, jumped up and wrested her from him. The noise awoke captain Lewis, who instantly started from the ground and reached to seize his gun, but finding her gone, drew a pistol from his belt and turning about saw the Indian running off with her. He followed him and ordered him to lay her down, which he was doing just as the Fields came up, and were taking aim to shoot him, when captain Lewis ordered them not to fire, as the Indian did not appear to intend any mischief. He dropped the gun and was going slowly off as Drewyer came out and asked permission to kill him, but this captain Lewis forbid as he had not yet attempted to shoot us. But finding that the Indians were now endeavouring to drive off all the horses, he ordered three of them to follow the main party who were chasing the horses up the river, and fire instantly upon the

JULY 27TH

thieves; while he, without taking time to run for his shot-pouch, pursued the fellow who had stolen his gun and another Indian, who were driving away the horses on the left of the camp. He pressed them so closely that they left twelve of their horses, but continued to drive off one of our own. At the distance of three hundred paces they entered a steep niche in the river bluffs, when captain Lewis, being too much out of breath to pursue them any further, called out, as he did several times before, that unless they gave up the horse he would shoot them. As he raised his gun one of the Indians jumped behind a rock and spoke to the other, who stopped at the distance of thirty paces, as captain Lewis shot him in the belly. He fell on his knees and right elbow, but raising himself a little, fired, and then crawled behind a rock. The shot had nearly been fatal, for captain Lewis, who was bareheaded, felt the wind of the ball very distinctly. Not having his shot-pouch, he could not reload his rifle, and having only a single load also for his pistol, he thought it most prudent not to attack the Indians, and therefore retired slowly to the camp. He was met by Drewyer, who hearing the report of the guns, had come to his assistance, leaving the Fields to pursue the Indians. Captain Lewis ordered him to call out to them to desist from the pursuit, as we could take the horses of the Indians in place of our own, but they were at too great a distance to hear him. He therefore returned to the camp, and whilst he was saddling the horses, the Fields returned with four of our own, having followed the Indians until two of them swam the river, two others ascended the hills, so that the horses became dispersed.

We, however, were rather gainers by this contest, for we took four of the Indian horses, and lost only one of our own. Besides which, we found in the camp four shields, two bows with quivers, and one of the guns which we took with us, and also the flag which we had presented to them, but left the medal round the neck of the dead man, in order that they might be informed who we were. The rest of their baggage, except some buffalo meat, we left; and as there was no time to be lost, we mounted our horses, and after ascending the river hills, took our course through the beautiful level plains, in a direction a little to the south of east. We had no doubt but that we should be immediately pursued by a much larger party, and that as soon as intelligence was given to the band near the Broken mountains, they would hasten to the mouth of Maria's river to intercept us. We hope, however, to be there before them, so as to form a junction with our friends. We therefore pushed our horses as fast as we possibly could; and fortunately for us, the Indian horses were very good, the plains perfectly level, and without many stones or prickly pears, and in fine order for travelling after the late rains. At eight miles from our camp we passed a stream forty yards wide, to which, from the occurrence of the morning, we gave the name of Battle river. At three o'clock we reached Rose river, five miles above where we had formerly passed it, and having now come by estimate sixty-three miles, halted for an hour and a half to refresh our horses; then pursued our journey seventeen miles further, when, as the night came on, we killed a buffalo, and again stopped for two hours. The sky was now overclouded, but as the moon gave light enough to show us the route, we continued along through immense herds of buffalo for twenty miles, and then almost exhausted with fatigue, halted at two in the morning to rest ourselves and the horses.

Monday. At daylight we awoke sore and scarcely able to stand; but as our own lives as well as those of our companions depended on our pressing forward, we mounted our horses and set out. The men were desirous of crossing the Missouri, at the Grog spring, where Rose river approaches so near the river, and passing down the southwest side of it, and thus avoid the country at the junction of the two rivers, through which the enemy would most probably pursue us. But as this circuitous route would consume the whole day, and the Indians might in the meantime attack the canoes at the point, captain Lewis told his party it was now their duty to risk their lives for their friends and companions; that he would proceed immediately to the point, to give the alarm to the canoes, and if they had not yet arrived, he would raft the Missouri, and after hiding the baggage, ascend the river on foot through the woods till he met them. He told them also that it was his determination, in case they were attacked in crossing the plains, to tie the bridles of the horses and stand together till they had either routed their enemies, or sold their lives as dearly as possible.

JULY 28TH

To this they all assented, and we therefore continued our route to the eastward, till at the distance of twelve miles we came near the Missouri, when we heard a noise which seemed like the report of a gun. We therefore quickened our pace for eight miles further, and about five miles from the Grog spring, now heard distinctly the noise of several rifles, from the river. We hurried to the bank, and saw with exquisite satisfaction our friends coming down the river. They landed to greet us, and after turning our horses loose, we embarked with our baggage, and went down to the spot where we had made a deposit. This, after reconnoitering the adjacent country, we opened; but unfortunately the cache had caved in, and most of the articles were injured. We took whatever was still worth preserving, and immediately proceeded to the point, where we found our deposits in good order.

By a singular good fortune we were here joined by sergeant Gass and Willard from the falls, who had been ordered to bring the horses here to assist in collecting meat for the voyage, as it had been calculated that the canoes would reach this place much sooner than captain Lewis's party. After a very heavy shower of rain and hail, attended with violent thunder and lightning, we left the point, and giving a final discharge to our horses, went over to the island where we had left our red periogue, which however we found so much decayed that we had no means of repairing her: we, therefore, took all the iron work out of her, and proceeded down the river fifteen miles, and encamped near some cottonwood trees, one of which was of the narrow-leafed species, and the first of that species we had remarked as we ascended the river.

Sergeant Ordway's party, which had left the mouth of Madison river on the *13th*, had descended in safety to the Whitebear islands, where he arrived on the *19th*, and after collecting the baggage, left the falls on the *27th* in the white periogue, and five canoes, while sergeant Gass and Willard set out at the same time by land with the horses, and thus fortunately met together.

Tuesday. A violent storm of rain and hail came on last night, and as we had no means of making a shelter, we lay in the rain, and during the whole day

JULY 29TH

499

continued so exposed. The two small canoes were sent ahead in order to hunt elk and buffalo, which are in immense quantities, so as to provide shelter as well as food for the party. We then proceeded very rapidly with the aid of a strong current, and after passing at one o'clock the Natural walls, encamped late in the evening at our former encampment of the *29th of May, 1805*. The river is now as high as it has been during the present season, and every little rivulet discharges torrents of water, which bring down such quantities of mud and sand, that we can scarcely drink the water of the Missouri. The buffalo continue to be very numerous, but the elk are few. The bighorns, however, are in great numbers along the steep cliffs of the river, and being now in fine order, their flesh is extremely tender, delicate, and well flavoured, and resembles in colour and flavour our mutton, though it is not so strong. The brown curlew has disappeared, and has probably gone to some other climate after rearing its young in these plains.

JULY 30TH *Wednesday*. The rain still prevented us from stopping to dry our baggage, and we therefore proceeded with a strong current, which joined to our oars, enabled us to advance at the rate of seven miles an hour. We went on shore several times for the purpose of hunting, and procured several bighorns, two buffalo, a beaver, an elk, and a female brown bear, whose talons were six and a quarter inches in length. In the evening we encamped on an island two miles above Goodrich's island, and early in the morning continued our route in the rain, passing, during the greater part of the day, through high pine hills, succeeded by low grounds abounding in timber and game. The buffalo are scarce; but we procured fifteen elk, fourteen deer, two bighorns, and a beaver. The elk are in fine order, particularly the males, who now herd together in small parties. Their horns have reached their full growth, but ill retain the velvet or skin which covers them. Through the bottoms are scattered a number of lodges, some of which seem to have been built last winter, and were probably occupied by the Minnetarees of Fort de Prairie. The river is still rising, and more muddy than we have ever seen it.

Friday, August 1st, 1806

Late last night we took shelter from the rain in some old Indian lodges, about eight miles below the entrance of North-mountain creek, and then set out at an early hour. We passed the Muscleshell river at eleven o'clock, and fifteen miles further landed at some Indian lodges, where we determined to pass the night, for the rain still continued, and we feared that the skins of the bighorn would spoil by being constantly wet. Having made fires, therefore, and exposed them to dry, we proceeded to hunt. The next day was fair and warm, and we availed ourselves of this occasion to dry all our baggage in the sun. Such is the immediate effect of fair weather, that since last evening the river has fallen eighteen inches. Two men were sent forward in a canoe to hunt; and now, having reloaded our canoes, we resolved to go on as fast as possible, and accordingly set out at an early hour, and without stopping as usual to cook a dinner, encamped in the evening two miles above our camp of *May 12, 1805*. We were here joined by the two hunters, who had killed twenty-nine deer since they left us. These animals are in great abundance in the river bottoms, and very gentle. We passed also a great number of elk, wolves, some bear, beaver, geese, a few ducks, the parti-coloured corvus, a calumet eagle, some bald eagles, and red-headed woodpeckers, but very few buffalo.

Monday. By four o'clock next morning we were again in motion. At eleven we passed the Bigdry river, which has now a bold, even, but shallow current, sixty yards in width, and halted for a few minutes at the mouth of Milk river. This stream is at present full of water, resembling in colour that of the Missouri, and as it possesses quite as much water as Maria's river, we have no doubt that it extends to a considerable distance towards the north. We here killed a very large rattlesnake. Soon after we passed several herds of buffalo and elk, and encamped at night, two miles below the gulf, on the northeast side of the river. For the first time this season we were saluted with the cry of the whippoorwill, or goatsucker of the Missouri.

AUGUST 4TH

Tuesday. We waited until noon in hopes of being overtaken by two of the men, who had gone ahead in a canoe to hunt two days ago, but who were at a distance from the river, as we passed them. As they did not arrive by that time, we concluded that they had passed us in the night, and therefore proceeded until late, when we encamped about ten miles below Littledry river. We again saw great numbers of buffalo, elk, deer, antelope, and wolves; also eagles, and other birds, among which were geese and a solitary pelican, neither of whom can fly at present, as they are now shedding the feathers of their wings. We also saw several bear, one of them the largest, except one, we had ever seen, for he measured nine feet from the nose to the extremity of the tail.

AUGUST 5TH

During the night a violent storm came on from the northeast with such torrents of rain that we had scarcely time to unload the canoes before they filled with water. Having no shelter, we ourselves were completely wet to the skin, and the wind and cold air made our situation very unpleasant. We left it early, *Wednesday, 6th;* but after we had passed Porcupine river, were, by the high wind, obliged to lie by until four o'clock, when the wind abating we continued, and at night encamped five miles below our camp of the *1st of May, 1805.* Here we were again drenched by the rain, which lasted all the next morning; but being resolved, if possible, to reach the Yellowstone, a distance of eighty-three miles, in the course of the day, we set out early, and being favoured by the rapid current and good oarsmen, proceeded with great speed.

In passing Martha's river, we observed that its mouth is at present a quarter of a mile lower than it was last year. Here we find for the first time the appearance of coal-burnt hills and pumicestone, which seem always to accompany each other. At this place also are the first elms and dwarf cedars in the bluffs of the river. The ash first makes its appearance in one solitary tree at the Ash rapid, but is seen occasionally scattered through the low grounds at the Elk rapid, and thence downwards, though it is generally small. The whole country on the northeast side, between Martha and Milk rivers, is a beautiful level plain, with a soil much more fertile than that higher up the river. The buffalo, elk, and other animals still continue numerous; as are also the bear, who lie in wait at the crossing places, where they seize elk and the weaker cattle, and then stay by the carcase in order to keep off the wolves, till the whole is devoured. At four o'clock we reached the mouth of Yellowstone, where we found a note from captain Clark, informing us of his intention of waiting for us a few miles below. We therefore left a memorandum for our two huntsmen, whom we now supposed must be behind us, and then pursued our course till night came on, and not being able to overtake captain Clark, we encamped.

AUGUST 8TH *Friday.* In the morning we set out in hopes of overtaking captain Clark; but after descending to nearly the entrance of White-earth river without being able to see him, we were at a loss what to conjecture. In this situation we landed, and began to caulk and repair the canoes, as well as prepare some skins for clothing, for since we left the Rocky mountains we have had no leisure to make clothes, so that the greater part of the men are almost naked. In these occupations we passed this and the following day, without any interruption except from the mosquitoes, which are very troublesome, and then having completed the repairs of the canoes, we embarked, *Sunday, 10th*, at five in the afternoon; but the wind and rain prevented us going further than near the entrance of White-earth river.

AUGUST 11TH *Monday.* The next day, being anxious to reach the Burnt hills by noon, in order to ascertain the latitude, we went forward with great rapidity; but by the time we reached that place, it was twenty minutes too late to take the meridian altitude.

Having lost the observation, captain Lewis observed on the opposite side of the river, a herd of elk on a thick sandbar of willows, and landed with Cruzatte to hunt them. Each of them fired and shot an elk. They then reloaded and took different routes in pursuit of the game, when just as captain Lewis was taking aim at an elk, a ball struck him in the left thigh, about an inch below the joint of the hip, and missing the bone, went through the left thigh and grazed the right to the depth of the ball. It instantly occurred to him that Cruzatte must have shot him by mistake for an elk, as he was dressed in brown leather, and Cruzatte had not a very good eye-sight. He therefore called out that he was shot, and looked towards the place from which the ball came; but seeing nothing, he called on Cruzatte by name several times, but received no answer. He now thought that as Cruzatte was out of hearing, and the shot did not seem to come from more than forty paces distance, it must have been fired by an Indian; and not knowing how many might be concealed in the bushes, he made towards the periogue, calling out to Cruzatte to retreat as there were Indians in the willows. As soon as he reached the periogue, he ordered the men to arms, and mentioning that he was wounded, though he hoped not mortally by the Indians, bade them follow him to relieve Cruzatte. They instantly followed for an hundred paces, when his wound became so painful, and his thigh stiffened in such a manner, that he could go no further. He therefore ordered the men to proceed, and if overpowered by numbers, retreat towards the boats, keeping up a fire; then limping back to the periogue, he prepared himself with his rifle, a pistol, and the air-gun, to sell his life dearly in case the men should be overcome. In this state of anxiety and suspense he remained for about twenty minutes, when the party returned with Cruzatte, and reported that no Indians could be seen in the neighbourhood. Cruzatte was now much alarmed and declared that he had shot an elk after captain Lewis left him, but disclaimed every idea of having intentionally wounded his officer. There was no doubt but that he was the person who gave the wound, yet as it seemed to be perfectly accidental, and Cruzatte had always conducted himself with propriety, no further notice was taken of it. The wound was now dressed, and patent lint put into the holes; but though it bled considerably, yet as the ball had touched neither a bone nor an artery, we hope that it may not prove fatal. As it was, however, impossible for him to make the observation of the latitude of the Burnt hills, which is chiefly desirable, as being the most northern parts of the Missouri, he declined remaining till to-morrow, and proceeded on till evening. Captain Lewis could not now be removed without great pain, as he had a high fever.

He therefore remained on board during the night, and early the next morning, proceeded with as much expedition as possible, and soon afterwards we put ashore to visit a camp, which we found to be that of Dickson and Hancock, the two Illinois traders, who told us that they had seen captain Clark yesterday. As we stopped with them, we were overtaken by our two hunters, Colter and Collins, who had been missing since the third, and whose absence excited much uneasiness. They informed us, that after following us the first day, they concluded that we must be behind, and waited for us during several days, when they were convinced of their mistake, and had then come on as rapidly as they could. We made some presents to the two traders, and then proceeded till at one o'clock we joined our friends and companions under captain Clark. AUGUST 12TH

Rivers and trails in the area where the expedition re-crossed the Continental Divide (the top of this sketch-map is toward the south).

Chapter 33
CAPTAIN CLARK EXPLORES THE YELLOWSTONE

THURSDAY, JULY 3D, 1806   On taking leave of captain Lewis and the Indians, the other division, consisting of captain Clark with fifteen men and fifty horses, set out through the valley of Clark's river, along the western side of which they rode in a southern direction. The valley is from ten to fifteen miles in width, tolerably level, and partially covered with the long-leafed and the pitch pine, with some cottonwood, birch, and sweet willow on the borders of the streams. Among the herbage are two species of clover, one the white clover common to the western parts of the United States, the other much smaller both in its leaf and blossom than either the red or white clover, and particularly relished by the horses. After crossing eight different streams of water, four of which were small, we halted at the distance of eighteen miles on the upper side of a large creek, where we let our horses graze, and after dinner resumed our journey in the same direction we had pursued during the morning, till at the distance of eighteen miles further, we encamped on the north side of a large creek. The valley became more beautiful as we proceeded, and was diversified by a number of small open plains, abounding with grass, and a variety of sweet-scented plants, and watered by ten streams which rush from the western mountains with considerable velocity. The mountains themselves are covered with snow about one-fifth from the top, and some snow is still to be seen on the high points and in the hollows of the mountains to the eastward. In the course of our ride we saw a great number of deer, a single bear, and some of the burrowing squirrels common about the Quamash flats. The mosquitoes too were very troublesome.

JULY 4TH

Friday. Early in the morning three hunters were sent out, and the rest of the party having collected the horses and breakfasted, we proceeded at seven o'clock up the valley, which is now contracted to the width of from eight to ten miles, with a good proportion of pitch pine, though its low lands, as well as the bottoms of the creeks, are strewed with large stones. We crossed five creeks of different sizes, but of great depth, and so rapid, that in passing the last, several of the horses were driven down the stream and some of our baggage wet. Near this river we saw the tracks of two Indians, whom we supposed to be Shoshonees. Having made sixteen miles, we halted at an early hour for the purpose of doing honour to the birth-day of our country's independence. The festival was not very splendid, for it consisted of a mush made of cows and a saddle of venison, nor had we any thing to tempt us to prolong it. We therefore went on till at the distance of a mile we came to a very large creek, which, like all those in the valley, had an immense rapidity of descent; and we therefore proceeded up for some distance, in order to select the most convenient spot for fording. Even there, however, such was the violence of the current, that although the water was not higher than the bellies of the horses, the resistance they made in passing, caused the stream to rise over their backs and loads. After passing the creek we inclined to the left, and soon after struck the road which we had descended last year, near the spot where we dined on the *7th of September.* Along this road we continued on the west side of Clark's river, till at the distance of thirteen miles, during which we passed three more deep large creeks, we reached its western branch, where we encamped, and having sent out two hunters, des-

505

patched some men to examine the best ford across the river. The game of today consisted of four deer; though we also saw a herd of ibex, or bighorn.

JULY 5TH *Saturday.* By daylight the next morning we again examined the fords, and having discovered what we conceived to be the best, began the passage at a place where the river is divided by small islands into six different channels. We, however, crossed them all without any damage, except wetting some of our provisions and merchandise; and at the distance of a mile came to the eastern branch, up which we proceeded about a mile, till we came into the old road we had descended in the autumn. It soon led us across the river, which we found had fallen to the same depth at which we found it last autumn, and along its eastern bank to the foot of the mountain nearly opposite Flower creek. Here we halted to let our horses graze, near a spot where there was still a fire burning and the tracks of two horses, which we presumed to be Shoshonees; and having dried all our provisions, proceeded at about four o'clock, across the mountain into the valley where we had first seen the Flatheads.

We then crossed the river, which we now perceived took its rise from a high peaked mountain at about twenty miles to the northeast of the valley, and then passed up it for two miles, and encamped after a ride of twenty miles during the day. As soon as we halted several men were despatched in different directions to examine the road, and from their report, concluded that the best path would be one about three miles up the creek. This is the road travelled by the Ootlashoots, and will certainly shorten our route two days at least, besides being much better, as we had been informed by the Indians, than by that we came last fall.

JULY 6TH *Sunday.* The night was very cold, succeeded by frost in the morning; and as the horses were much scattered, we were not able to set out before nine o'clock. We then went along the creek for three miles, and leaving to the right the path by which we came last fall, pursued the road taken by the Ootlashoots, up a gentle ascent to the dividing mountain which separates the waters of the middle fork of Clark's river, from those of Wisdom and Lewis's rivers. On reaching the other side, we came to Glade creek, down which we proceeded, crossing it frequently into the glades on each side, where the timber is small, and in many places destroyed by fire; where are great quantities of quamash now in bloom. Throughout the glades are great numbers of holes made by the whistling or burrowing squirrel; and we killed a hare of the large mountain species. Along these roads there are also appearances of old buffalo paths, and some old heads of buffaloes; and as these animals have wonderful sagacity in the choice of their routes, the coincidence of a buffalo with an Indian road, was the strongest assurance that it was the best.

In the afternoon we passed along the hill-side, north of the creek, till, in the course of six miles, we entered an extensive level plain. Here the tracks of the Indians scattered so much that we could no longer pursue it, but Sacajawea recognised the plain immediately. She had travelled it often during her childhood, and informed us that it was the great resort of the Shoshonees, who came for the purpose of gathering quamash and cows, and of taking beaver, with which the plain abounded, and that Glade creek was a branch of Wisdom river, and that on reaching the higher part of the plain, we should see a gap in the mountains, on the course to our canoes, and from that gap a high point of mountain covered with snow. At the distance of a mile we crossed a large creek from the right, rising, as well as Fish creek, in a snowy mountain, over which there is a gap. Soon after, on ascending a rising ground, the country spreads itself into a beautiful plain, extending north and south about fifteen miles wide and thirty in length, and surrounded on all sides by high points of mountains covered with snow, among which was the gap pointed out by the squaw, bearing S. 56° E. We had not gone two miles from the last creek when we were overtaken by a violent storm of wind, accompanied with hard rain, which lasted an hour and a half. Having no shelter, we formed a solid column to protect ourselves from the gust, and then went on five miles to a small creek, where finding some small timber, we encamped for the night, and dried ourselves. We here observed some fresh signs of Indians, who had been gathering quamash. Our distance was twenty-six miles.

[*Account of Capt. Clark's party*]

Monday. In the morning our horses were so much scattered, that although we sent out hunters in every direction, to range the country for six or eight miles, nine of them could not be recovered. They were the most valuable of all our horses, and so much attached to some of their companions, that it was difficult to separate them in the day-time. We therefore presumed that they must have been stolen by some roving Indians, and accordingly left a party of five men to continue the pursuit, while the rest went on to the spot where the canoes had been deposited. Accordingly we set out at ten o'clock, and pursued a course S. 56° E. across the valley which we found to be watered by four large creeks, with extensive low and miry bottoms; and then reached Wisdom river, along the northeast side of which we continued, till at the distance of sixteen miles we came to the three branches. Near that place we stopped for dinner at a hot spring situated in the open plain. The bed of the spring is about fifteen yards in circumference, and composed of loose, hard, gritty stones, through which the water boils in great quantities. It is slightly impregnated with sulphur, and so hot that a piece of meat about the size of three fingers, was completely done in twenty-five minutes. After dinner we proceeded across the eastern branch, and along the north side of the middle branch for nine miles, when we reached the gap in the mountains, and took our last leave of this extensive valley, which we called the Hotspring valley. It is indeed a beautiful country; though enclosed by mountains covered with snow, the soil is exceedingly fertile and well supplied with esculent plants; while its numerous creeks furnish immense quantities of beaver. Another valley less extensive and more rugged opened itself to our view as we passed through the gap; but as we had made twenty-five miles, and the night was advancing, we halted near some handsome springs, which fall into Willard's creek.

JULY 7TH

Tuesday. After a cold night, during which our horses separated and could not be collected till eight o'clock in the morning, we crossed the valley along the southwest side of Willard's creek for twelve miles, when it entered the mountains, and then turning S. 20° E. came to the Shoshonee cove, after riding seven miles; whence we proceeded down the west branch of Jefferson

JULY 8TH

river, and at the distance of nine miles, reached its forks, where we had deposited our merchandise in the month of August. Most of the men were in the habit of chewing tobacco; and such was their eagerness to procure it after so long a privation, that they scarcely took the saddles from their horses before they ran to the cave, and were delighted at being able to resume this fascinating indulgence. This was one of the severest privations which we have encountered. Some of the men, whose tomahawks were so constructed as to answer the purposes of pipes, broke the handles of these instruments, and after cutting them into small fragments, chewed them; the wood having, by frequent smoking, become strongly impregnated with the taste of that plant. We found every thing safe, though some of the goods were a little damp, and one of the canoes had a hole. The ride of this day was twenty-seven miles in length, and through a country diversified by low marshy grounds, and high, open, and stony plains, terminated by high mountains, on the tops and along the northern sides of which the snow still remained. Over the whole were scattered great quantities of hyssop and the different species of shrubs, common to the plains of the Missouri.

We had now crossed the whole distance from Traveller's-rest creek to the head of Jefferson's river, which seems to form the best and shortest route over the mountains, during almost the whole distance of one hundred and sixty-four miles. It is, in fact, a very excellent road, and by cutting a few trees, might be rendered a good route for wagons, with the exception of about four miles over one of the mountains, which would require some levelling.

JULY 9TH *Wednesday.* We were all occupied in raising and repairing the canoes, and making the necessary preparations for resuming our journey to-morrow. The day proved cold and windy, so that the canoes were soon dried. We were here overtaken by sergeant Ordway and his party, who had discovered our horses near the head of the creek on which we encamped, and although they were very much scattered, and endeavoured to escape as fast as they could, he brought them back. The squaw found to-day a plant which grows in the moist lands, the root of which is eaten by the Indians. The stem and leaf, as well as the root of this plant, resemble the common carrot, in form, size and taste, though the colour is of somewhat a paler yellow. The night continued very cold.

JULY 10TH *Thursday.* In the morning a white frost covered the ground; the grass was frozen, and the ice three quarters of an inch thick in a basin of water. The boats were now loaded, and captain Clark divided his men into two bands, one to descend the river with the baggage, while he, with the other, proceeded on horseback to the Rochejaune [Yellowstone river].

After breakfast the two parties set out, those on shore skirting the eastern side of Jefferson river, through Service valley, and over the Rattlesnake mountain, into a beautiful and extensive country, known among the Indians by the name of Hahnahappapchah, or Beaverhead valley, from the number of those animals to be found in it, and also from a point of land resembling the head of a beaver. It extends from the Rattlesnake mountain as low as Frazier's creek, and is about fifty miles in length, in a direct line, while its width varies from ten to fifteen miles, being watered in its whole course by the Jefferson and six different creeks. The valley is open and fertile, and besides the innumerable quantities of beaver and otter, with which its creeks are supplied, the bushes of the low grounds are a favourite resort for deer, while on the higher parts of the valley are seen scattered groups of antelopes, and still further, on the steep sides of the mountains, we observed many of the bighorn, which take refuge there from the wolves and bears. At the distance of fifteen miles the two parties stopped to dine, when captain Clark finding that the river became wider and deeper, and that the canoes could advance more rapidly than the horses, determined to go himself by water, leaving sergeant Pryor with six men, to bring on the horses. In this way they resumed their journey after dinner, and encamped on the eastern side of the river, opposite the head of the Three-thousand-mile island. The beaver were basking in great numbers along the shore; they saw also some young wild geese and ducks. The mosquitoes were very troublesome during the day, but after sunset the weather became cool and they disappeared.

[*Account of Capt. Clark's party*]

Friday. The next morning captain Clark sent four men ahead to hunt, and after an early breakfast proceeded down a very narrow channel, which was rendered more difficult by a high southwest wind, which blew from the high snowy mountains in that quarter, and met them in the face at every bend of the river, which was now become very crooked. At noon they passed the high point of land on the left, to which Beaverhead valley owes its name, and at six o'clock reached Philanthropy river, which was at present very low. The wind now shifted to the northeast, and though high, was much warmer than before. At seven o'clock they reached their encampment at the entrance of Wisdom river on the sixth of August. They found the river very high, but falling. Here too, they overtook the hunters, who had killed a buck and some young geese. Besides these they had seen a great number of geese and sandhill cranes, and some deer. The beaver too were in great quantities along the banks of the rivers, and through the night were flapping their tails in the water round the boats.

JULY 11TH

Saturday. Having found the canoe which had been left here as they ascended, they employed themselves, till eight o'clock in drawing out the nails and making paddles of the sides of it. Then leaving one of their canoes here, they set out after breakfast. Immediately below the forks the current became stronger than above, and the course of the river straighter, as far as Panther creek, after which it became much more crooked. A high wind now arose from the snowy mountains to the northwest, so that it was with much difficulty and some danger they reached, at three o'clock, the entrance of Fields's creek. After dining at that place, they pursued their course and stopped for the night below their encampment of the *31st of July* last. Beaver, young geese, and deer continued to be their game, and they saw some old signs of buffalo. The mosquitoes also were still very troublesome.

JULY 12TH

Sunday. Early in the morning they set out, and at noon reached the entrance of Madison river, where sergeant Pryor had arrived with the horses about an hour before. The horses were then driven across Madison and Gallatin rivers, and the whole party halted to dine and unload the canoes below the mouth of the latter. Here the two parties separated; sergeant Ordway with

JULY 13TH

509

nine men set out in six canoes to descend the river, while captain Clark with the remaining ten, and the wife and child of Chaboneau, were to proceed by land, with fifty horses, to Yellowstone river. They set out at five in the afternoon from the forks of the Missouri, in a direction nearly eastward; but as many of the horses had sore feet, they were obliged to move slowly, and after going four miles, halted for the night on the bank of Gallatin's river.

This is a beautiful stream, and though the current is rapid and obstructed by islands near its mouth, is navigable for canoes. On its lower side the land rises gradually to the foot of a mountain, running almost parallel to it; but the country below it and Madison's river is a level plain, covered at present with low grass, the soil being poor, and injured by stones and strata of hard white rock along the hill sides. Throughout the whole, game was very abundant. They procured deer in the low grounds; beaver and otter were seen in Gallatin's river, and elk, wolves, eagles, hawks, crows, and geese, were seen at different parts of the route. The plain was intersected by several great roads, leading to a gap in the mountain, about twenty miles distant, in a direction E. N. E. but the Indian woman, who was acquainted with the country, recommended a gap more to the southward.

JULY 14TH *Monday.* This course captain Clark determined to pursue; and therefore at an early hour in the morning, crossed Gallatin's river in a direction south 78° east, and passing over a level plain, reached the Jefferson at the distance of six miles. That river is here divided into many channels, which spread themselves for several miles through the low grounds, and are dammed up by the beaver in such a manner, that after attempting in vain to reach the opposite side, they were obliged to turn short about to the right, till with some difficulty they reached a low but firm island, extending nearly in the course they desired to follow. The squaw now assured captain Clark that the large road from Medicine river to the gap we were seeking, crossed the upper part of this plain. He therefore proceeded four miles up the plain and reached the main channel of the river, which is still navigable for canoes, though much divided and dammed up by multitudes of beaver. Having forded the river, they passed through a little skirt of cottonwood timber to a low open plain, where they dined. They saw elk, deer, and antelopes, and in every direction the roads made by the buffalo; as well as some old signs of them. The squaw informed them, that but a few years ago these animals were numerous, not only here but even to the sources of Jefferson's river; but of late they have disappeared, for the Shoshonees being fearful of going west of the mountains, have hunted this country with more activity, and of course driven the buffalo from their usual haunts. After dinner they continued inclining to the south of east, through an open level plain, till at the distance of twelve miles they reached the three forks of Gallatin's river. On crossing the southerly branch, they fell into the buffalo road, described by the squaw, which led them up the middle branch for two miles; this branch is provided with immense quantities of beaver, but is sufficiently navigable for small canoes, by unlading at the worst dams. After crossing, they went on a mile further, and encamped at the beginning of the gap in the mountain, which here forms a kind of semicircle, through which the three branches of the river pass. Several roads come in from the right and left, all tending to the gap. A little snow still remains on a naked mountain to the eastward, but in every other direction the mountains are covered with great quantities. [Account of Capt. Clark's party]

Tuesday. After an early breakfast they pursued the buffalo road over a low gap in the mountain to the heads of the eastern fork of Gallatin's river, near which they had encamped last evening, and at the distance of six miles reached the top of the dividing ridge, which separates the waters of the Missouri and the Yellowstone; and on descending the ridge, they struck one of the streams of the latter river. They followed its course through an open country, with high mountains on each side, partially covered with pine, and watered by several streams, crowded as usual with beaver dams. Nine miles from the top of the ridge they reached the Yellowstone itself, about a mile and a half below where it issues from the Rocky mountains. JULY 15TH

It now appeared that the communication between the two rivers was short and easy. From the head of the Missouri at its three forks to this place is a distance of forty-eight miles, the greater part of which is through a level plain; indeed, from the forks of the eastern branch of Gallatin's river, which is there navigable for small canoes, to this part of the Yellowstone, the distance is no more than eighteen miles, with an excellent road over a high, dry country, with hills of inconsiderable height and no difficulty in passing. They halted three hours to rest their horses, and then pursued the buffalo road along the bank of the river.

Although just leaving a high snowy mountain, the Yellowstone is already a bold, rapid, and deep stream, one hundred and twenty yards in width. The bottoms of the river are narrow within the mountains, but widen to the extent of nearly two miles in the valley below, where they are occasionally overflowed, and the soil gives nourishment to cottonwood, rose bushes, honeysuckle, rushes, common coarse grass, a species of rye, and such productions of moist lands. On each side these low grounds are bounded by dry plains of coarse gravel and sand, stretching back to the foot of the mountains, and supplied with a very short grass. The mountains on the east side of the river are rough and rocky, and still retain great quantities of snow, and two other high snowy mountains may be distinguished, one bearing north fifteen or twenty miles, the other nearly east. They have no covering except a few scattered pine, nor indeed was any timber fit for even a small canoe to be seen. At the distance of nine miles from the mountain, a river discharges itself into the Yellowstone, from the northwest, under a high rocky cliff. It rises from the snowy mountains in that direction; is about thirty-five yards wide; has a bold, deep current; is skirted by some cottonwood and willow trees, and like the Yellowstone itself, seems to abound in beaver. They gave it the name of Shields's river, after one of the party. Immediately below is a very good buffalo road, which obviously leads from its head through a gap in the mountain, over to the waters of the Missouri. They passed Shields's river, and at three miles further, after crossing a high rocky hill, encamped in a low bottom, near the entrance of a small creek. As they came through the mountains they had seen two black bear and a number of antelopes, as well as several herds of elk, of between two and three hundred in number, but they were able to kill only a single elk.

JULY 16TH *Wednesday.* The next morning, therefore, a hunter was despatched ahead, while the party collected the straggling horses. They then proceeded down the river, which is very straight, and has several islands covered with cottonwood and willow; but they could not procure a single tree large enough for a canoe, and being unwilling to trust altogether to skin canoes, captain Clark preferred going on until they found some timber. The feet of the horses were now nearly worn to the quick, particularly the hind feet, so that they were obliged to make a sort of moccasin of green buffalo skin, which relieved them very much in crossing the plains. After passing a bold creek from the south, of twenty yards in width, they halted for dinner on an island, then went on till at night they encamped near the entrance of another small stream, having made twenty-six miles during the day. They saw some bear and great numbers of antelopes and elks; but the soreness of their horses' feet rendered it difficult to chase them. One of the men caught a fish which they had not seen before; it was eight inches long, and resembled a trout in form, but its mouth was like that of the sturgeon, and it had a red streak passing on each side from the gills to the tail. In the plains were but few plants except the silk-grass, the wild indigo, and the sunflower, which are now all in bloom. The high grounds on the river are faced with a deep freestone rock, of a hard, sharp grit, which may also be seen in perpendicular strata throughout the plain.

JULY 17TH *Thursday.* It rained during the night, and as the party had no covering but a buffalo skin, they rose drenched with water; and pursuing their journey at an early hour, over the point of a ridge, and through an open low bottom, reached at the distance of six and a half miles, a part of the river, where two large creeks enter immediately opposite to each other; one from the northwest, the other from the south of southwest. These captain Clark called

Sketch-map of a stretch on the Yellowstone River, from Captain Clark's journal.

512

Rivers-across. Ten miles and a half further they halted for dinner below the entrance of a large creek on the northeast side, about thirty yards in width, which they named Otter river. Nearly opposite to this is another, to which they gave the name of Beaver river. The waters of both are of a milky colour, and the banks well supplied with small timber. The river is now becoming more divided by islands, and a number of small creeks fall in on both sides. The largest of these is about seven miles from the Beaver river, and enters on the right: they called it Bratton's river, from one of the men. The highlands too approach the river more nearly than before, but although their sides are partially supplied with pine and cedar, the growth is still too small for canoes. The buffalo is beginning to be more abundant, and to-day, for the first time on this river, they saw a pelican; but deer and elk are now more scarce than before. In one of the low bottoms of the river was an Indian fort, which seems to have been built during the last summer. It was built in the form of a circle, about fifty feet in diameter, five feet high, and formed of logs, lapping over each other, and covered on the outside with bark set up on end. The entrance also was guarded by a work on each side of it, facing the river. These entrenchments, the squaw informs us, are frequently made by the Minnetarees and other Indians at war with the Shoshonees, when pursued by their enemies on horseback. After making thirty-three miles, they encamped near a point of woods in the narrow bottom of the river.

[Account of Capt. Clark's party]

Friday. Before setting out they killed two buffalo, which ventured near the camp, and then pursued their route over the ridges of the highlands, so as to avoid the bends of the river, which now washes the feet of the hills. The face of the country is rough and stony, and covered with immense quantities of the prickly pear. The river is nearly two hundred yards wide, rapid as usual, and with a bed of coarse gravel and round stones. The same materials are the basis of the soil in the high bottoms, with a mixture of dark brown earth. The river hills are about two hundred feet high, and still faced with a dark freestone rock; and the country back of them broken into open waving plains. Pine is the only growth of importance; but among the smaller plants were distinguished the purple, yellow, and black currants, which are now ripe, and of an excellent flavour.

JULY 18TH

About eleven o'clock a smoke was descried to the S. S. E. towards the termination of the Rocky mountains, intended most probably, as a signal by the Crow Indians, who have mistaken us for their enemies, or as friends to trade with them. They could not however stop to ascertain the truth of this conjecture, but rode on, and after passing another old Indian fort, similar to that seen yesterday, halted for the night on a small island, twenty-six miles from their camp of last evening.

One of the hunters in attempting to mount his horse, after shooting a deer, fell on a small piece of timber, which ran nearly two inches into the muscular part of his thigh. The wound was very painful; and were it not for their great anxiety to reach the United States this season, the party would have remained till he was cured: but the time was too precious to wait. The gentlest and strongest horse was therefore selected, and a sort of litter formed in such a manner as to enable the sick man to lie nearly at full length. They then proceeded gently, and at the distance of two miles passed a river entering from the southeast side, about forty yards wide, and called by the Indians Itchkeppearja, or Rose river, a name which it deserves, as well from its beauty as from the roses which we saw budding on its borders. Soon after they passed another Indian fort on an island, and after making nine miles, halted to let the horses graze, and sent out a hunter to look for timber to make a canoe, and procure, if possible, some wild ginger to make a poultice for Gibson's thigh, which was now exceedingly painful, in consequence of his constrained position. He returned, however, without being able to find either; but brought back two bucks, and had had a contest with two white bears who had chased him; but being on horseback he escaped, after wounding both of them. There are great quantities of currants in the plains, but almost every blade of grass for many miles have been destroyed by immense swarms of grasshoppers, who appear to be ascending the river. After taking some refreshment they proceeded, and found that the hills became lower on both sides; those on the right overhanging the river in cliffs of a darkish yellow earth, and the bottoms widening to several miles in extent. The timber too, although chiefly cottonwood, is coming large.

They had not gone far when Gibson's wound became so violently painful that he could no longer remain on horseback. He was therefore left with two men under the shade of a tree, while captain Clark went on to seek for timber. At the distance of eighteen miles from his camp of last night he halted near a thick grove of trees, some of which were large enough for small canoes, and then searched all the adjacent country till evening, when Gibson was brought on to the camp. The game of to-day consisted of six deer, seven elk, and an antelope. The smoke which had been seen on the *17th*, was again distinguished this afternoon, and one of the party reported that he had observed an Indian on the highlands on the opposite side of the river.

JULY 20TH *Sunday*. The next morning at daylight, two good judges of timber were sent down the river in quest of lumber, but returned without being able to find any trees larger than those near the camp, nor could they procure any for axe-handles except chokecherry. Captain Clark determined therefore to make two canoes, which being lashed together, might be sufficient to convey the party down the river, while a few men might lead the horses to the Mandan nation. Three axes were now sharpened with a file, and some of the men proceeded to cut down two of the largest trees, on which they worked till night. The rest of the party were occupied in dressing skins for clothes, or in hunting, in which they were so fortunate as to procure a deer, two buffalo and an elk. The horses being much fatigued, they were turned out to rest for a few days; but in the morning, twenty-four of them were missing. Three hunters were sent in different directions to look for them; but all returned unsuccessful, and it now seemed probable that the Indians who had made the smoke a few days since, had stolen the horses. In the meantime the men worked so diligently on the canoes that one of them was nearly completed. Late in the evening, a very black cloud accompanied with thunder and lightning rose from the southeast, and rendered the weather extremely warm and disagreeable. The wind too was very high, but shifted towards morning to the northeast, and became moderately cool.

Tuesday. Three men were now despatched in quest of the horses, but they came back without being able to discover even a track, the plains being so hard and dry that the foot makes no impression. This confirms the suspicion of their being stolen by the Indians, who would probably take them across the plains, to avoid being pursued by their traces; besides, the improbability of their voluntarily leaving rushes and grass of the river bottoms to go on the plains, where they could find nothing but a short dry grass. Four men were again sent out with orders to encircle the camp for a great distance round, but they too returned with no better success than those who had preceded them.

JULY 22D

[*Account of Capt. Clark's party*]

Wednesday. The search was resumed in the morning, and a piece of a robe, and a moccasin, were discovered not far from the camp. The moccasin was worn out in the sole, and yet wet, and had every appearance of having been left but a few hours before. This sign was conclusive that the Indians had taken our horses, and were still prowling about for the remainder, who fortunately escaped last night, by being in a small prairie, surrounded by thick timber. At length Labiche, who is one of the best trackers, returned from a very wide circuit, and informed captain Clark that he had traced the tracks of the horses, which were bending their course rather down the river towards the open plains, and from the track, going very rapidly. All hopes of recovering them were now abandoned. The Indians are not the only plunderers who surround the camp, for last night the wolves or dogs stole the greater part of the dried meat from the scaffold. The wolves, which constantly attend the buffalo, are here in great numbers, for this seems to be the commencement of the buffalo country. Besides them, are seen antelopes, pigeons, doves, hawks, ravens, crows, larks, sparrows, eagles, bank-martins, &c. &c., great numbers of geese too, which raise their young on this river, have passed the camp. The country itself consists of beautiful level plains, but the soil is thin and stony, and both plains and low grounds are covered with great quantities of prickly pear.

JULY 23D

  At noon the two canoes were finished. They are twenty-eight feet long, sixteen or eighteen inches deep, and from sixteen to twenty-four inches wide, and being lashed together, every thing was prepared for setting out to-morrow; Gibson having now recovered. Sergeant Pryor was now directed with Shannon and Windsor, to take our horses to the Mandans, and if he found that Mr. Henry was on the Assiniboin river, to go thither and deliver him a letter, the object of which was to prevail on the most distinguished chiefs of the Sioux to accompany him to Washington.

Chapter 34

DOWN THE YELLOWSTONE; REUNION OF THE PARTIES

THURSDAY, JULY 24TH, 1806 The canoes were loaded, and sergeant Pryor and his party set out with orders to proceed down to the entrance of the Bighorn river, which was supposed to be at no great distance, and where they should be taken in the boats across the Yellowstone. At eight o'clock captain Clark embarked in the little flotilla, and proceeded on very steadily down the river, which continues to be about two hundred yards wide, and contains a number of islands, some of which are supplied with a small growth of timber. At the distance of a mile from the camp, the river passes under a high bluff for about twenty-three miles, when the bottoms widen on both sides. At the distance of twenty-nine miles, a river falls in from the south. This was the river supposed to be the Bighorn; but afterwards, when the Bighorn was found, the name of Clark's fork was given to this stream. It is a bold river, one hundred and fifty yards wide at the entrance, but a short distance above, is contracted to a hundred yards. The water is of a light muddy colour, and much colder than that of the Yellowstone, and its general course is south and east of the Rocky mountains. There is a small island situated immediately at the entrance; and this or the adjoining main land would form a very good position for a fort. The country most frequented by the beaver begins here, and that which lies between this river and the Yellowstone is, perhaps, the best district for the hunters of that animal. About a mile before reaching this river, there is a ripple in the Yellowstone, on passing which the canoes took in some water. The party therefore landed to bail the boats, and then proceeded six miles further to a large island, where they halted for the purpose of waiting for sergeant Pryor.

It is a beautiful spot with a rich soil, covered with wild rye, and a species of grass like the blue-grass, and some of another kind, which the Indians wear in plaits round the neck, on account of a strong scent resembling that of the vanilla. There is also a thin growth of cottonwood scattered over the island. In the centre is a large Indian lodge which seems to have been built during the last summer. It is in the form of a cone, sixty feet in diameter at the base, composed of twenty poles, each forty-five feet long, and two and a half in circumference, and the whole structure covered with bushes. The interior was curiously ornamented. On the tops of the poles were feathers of eagles, and circular pieces of wood, with sticks across them in the form of a girdle: from the centre was suspended a stuffed buffalo skin: on the side fronting the door was hung a cedar bush: on one side of the lodge a buffalo's head; on the other several pieces of wood stuck in the ground. From its whole appearance, it was more like a lodge for holding councils, than an ordinary dwelling house.

Sergeant Pryor not having yet arrived, they went on about fifteen and a half miles further to a small creek on the right, to which they gave the name of Horse creek, and just below it overtook sergeant Pryor with the horses. He had found it almost impossible, with two men, to drive on the remaining horses, for as soon as they discovered a herd of buffalo the loose horses, having been trained by the Indians to hunt, immediately set off in pursuit of them, and surrounded the buffalo herd with almost as much skill as their riders could have done. At last he was obliged to send one horseman forward, and drive all the buffalo from the route. The horses were here driven across, and sergeant Pryor again proceeded with an additional man to his party. The river is now much more deep and navigable, and the current more regular than above Clark's fork, and although much divided by well-wooded islands, when collected, the stream is between two and three hundred feet in width. Along its banks are some beaver, and an immense number of deer, elk, and buffalo. Towards night they passed a creek from the southeast, thirty-five yards wide, which they called Pryor's creek; half a mile below which they encamped, after making sixty-nine and a half miles during the day.

[Account of Capt. Clark's party]

Friday. At sunrise the next morning they resumed their voyage, and passed a number of islands and small streams, and occasionally high bluffs, composed of a yellow gritty stone. A storm of rain and high southwest wind soon overtook them, and obliged them to land and form a sort of log hut, covered with deer skins. As soon as it ceased they proceeded, and about four o'clock, after having made forty-nine miles, captain Clark landed to examine a very remarkable rock situated in an extensive bottom on the right, about two hundred and fifty paces from the shore. It is nearly four hundred paces in circumference, two hundred feet high, and accessible only from the northeast, the other sides being a perpendicular cliff of a light coloured gritty rock. The soil of the top is five or six feet deep, of a good quality, and covered with short grass. The Indians have carved the figures of animals and other objects on the sides of the rock, and on the top are raised two piles of stones.

JULY 25TH

From this height the eye ranged over a large extent of variegated country: On the southwest the Rocky mountains covered with snow; a low mountain, about forty miles distant, bearing south 15° east, and in a direction north 55° west; and at the distance of thirty-five miles, the southern extremity of what are called the Littlewolf mountains. The low grounds of the river extend nearly six miles to the southward, when they rise into plains reaching to the mountains, and watered with a large creek, while at some distance below a range of highland, covered with pine, stretches on both sides of the river, in a direction north and south. The north side of the river, for some distance, is surrounded by jutting romantic cliffs; these are succeeded by rugged hills, beyond which the plains are again open and extensive; and the whole country is enlivened by herds of buffalo, elk and wolves.

After enjoying the prospect from this rock, to which captain Clark gave the name of Pompey's pillar, he descended, and continued his course. At the distance of six or seven miles, he stopped to get two bighorns, which were shot from the boat; and while on shore, saw in the face of the cliff on the left, about twenty feet above the water, the fragment of a rib of a fish, three feet long, and nearly three inches round, incrusted in the rock itself, and though neither decayed nor petrified is very rotten. After making fifty-eight miles they reached the entrance of a stream on the right, about twenty-two yards wide, and which discharges a great quantity of muddy water. Here they encamped rather earlier than usual, on account of a heavy squall, accompanied with some rain.

Saturday. Early next morning they proceeded. The river is now much divided by stony islands and bars; but the current, though swift, is regular, and there are many handsome islands covered with cottonwood. On the left shore the bottoms are very extensive; the right bank is formed of high cliffs

JULY 26TH

of a whitish gritty stone; and beyond these, the country on both sides is diversified with waving plains, covered with pine. At the distance of ten miles is a large creek on the right, about forty yards in width, but containing very little water; and in the course of the day, two smaller streams on the left, and a fourth on the right. At length, after coming sixty-two miles, they landed at the entrance of the Bighorn river; but finding the point between the two composed of soft mud and sand, and liable to be overflowed, they ascended the Bighorn for half a mile, then crossed and formed a camp on its lower side. Captain Clark then walked up the river.

At the distance of seven miles, a creek, twenty yards wide, which from the colour of the water he called Muddy creek, falls in on the northeast, and a few miles further, the river bends to the east of south. The bottoms of the river are extensive, and supplied chiefly with cottonwood trees, variegated with great quantities of rosebushes. The current is regular and rapid; and like the Missouri, constantly changes so as to wash away the banks on one side, leaving sandbars on the other. Its bed contains much less of the large gravel than that of the Yellowstone, and its water is more muddy, and of a brownish colour, while the Yellowstone has a lighter tint. At the junction, the two rivers are nearly equal in breadth, extending from two hundred to two hundred and twenty yards, but the Yellowstone contains much more water, being ten or twelve feet deep, while the depth of the Bighorn varies from five to seven feet. This is the river which had been described by the Indians as rising in the Rocky mountains, near the Yellowstone, and the sources of the river Platte, and then finds its way through the Côte Noir, and the eastern range of the Rocky mountains. In its long course it receives two large rivers, one from the north and the other from the south, and being unobstructed by falls, is navigable in canoes for a great distance, through a fine rich open country, supplied with a great quantity of timber, and inhabited by beaver, and by numerous species of animals, among which are those from which it derives the name of Bighorn. There are no permanent settlements near it; but the whole country which it waters, is occasionally visited by roving bands of hunters from the Crow tribe, the Paunch, a band of Crows, and the Castahana, a small band of Snake Indians.

JULY 27TH *Sunday.* They again set out very early, and on leaving the Bighorn, took a last look at the Rocky mountains, which had been constantly in view from the first of May. The river now widens to the extent of from four to six hundred yards; is much divided by islands and sandbars; its banks generally low and falling in, and resembles the Missouri in many particulars; but its islands are more numerous, its waters less muddy, and the current more rapid. The water too is of a yellowish-white, and the round stones, which form the bars above the Bighorn, have given place to gravel. On the left side the river runs under cliffs of light, soft, gritty stone, varying in height from seventy to an hundred feet, behind which are level and extensive plains. On the right side of the river are low extensive bottoms, bordered with cottonwood, various species of willow, rosebushes, grape-vines, the redberry or buffalo-grease bushes, and a species of sumac; to these succeed high grounds, supplied with pine, and still further on are level plains. Throughout the country are vast quantities of buffalo, which, as this is the running season, keep a continued bellowing. Large herds of elk also are lying in every point, and are so gentle that they may be approached within twenty paces without being alarmed. Several beaver were seen in the course of the day; indeed, there is a greater appearance of those animals than there was above the Bighorn. Deer, however, are by no means abundant, and the antelopes, as well as the bighorns, are scarce.

[*Account of Capt. Clark's party*]

Fifteen miles from the Bighorn river they passed a large dry creek on the left, to which they gave the name of Elk creek, and halted for breakfast about three miles further, at the entrance of Windsor's river, a stream from the left, which though fifty yards wide, contains scarcely any water. Forty-eight miles from the Bighorn is a large bed of a stream sixty yards wide, but with very little water. They called it Labiche's river. Several other smaller streams, or rather beds of creeks, were passed in the course of the day, and after coming eighty and a half miles, they encamped on a large island.

Monday. At daylight the next morning they proceeded down the smooth gentle current, passing by a number of islands and several creeks, which are now dry. These are, indeed, more like torrents, and like the dry brooks of the Missouri, merely serve to carry off the vast quantities of water which fall in the plains, and bring them also a great deal of mud, which contributes to the muddiness of the Yellowstone. The most distinguished of these are at the distance of six miles, a creek of eighty yards in width, from the northwest, and called by the Indians, Littlewolf river: twenty-nine miles lower another on the left, seventy yards in width, which they call Table creek, from several mounds in the plains to the northwest, the tops of which resemble a table. Four miles further a stream of more importance enters behind an island from the south. It is about one hundred yards in width, with a bold current of muddy water, and is probably the river called by the Indians the Little Bighorn; and another stream on the right, twenty-five yards wide, the Indian name of which is Mashaskap. Nearly opposite to this creek they encamped after making seventy-three miles. The river during part of the route is confined by cliffs, which on the right are of a soft, yellowish, gritty rock, while those on the left are harder, and of a lighter colour. In some of these cliffs were several stratas of coal of different thickness and heights above the water; but like that of the Missouri, is of an inferior quality.

JULY 28TH

Tuesday. During the night there was a storm of thunder and lightning, with some rain, a high northeast wind, which continued during the morning, and prevented the party from making more than forty-one miles. The country resembles that passed yesterday; the dry beds of rivers continue, and large quantities of coal are seen in the sides of the cliffs. The river itself is now between five hundred yards and half a mile in width, and has more sand and bars of gravel than above. The beaver are in great numbers; and in the course of the day some catfish and a soft-shelled turtle were procured. In the evening they encamped on the left, opposite to the entrance of a stream, called by the Indians Lazeka, or Tongue river. This stream rises in the Côte Noir, and is formed of two branches, one having its sources with the heads of the Chayenne, the other with one of the branches of the Bighorn. It has a very wide bed, and a channel of water a hundred and fifty yards wide, but the water is of a light brown colour, very muddy, and nearly milk-warm. It

JULY 29TH

519

is shallow, and its rapid current throws out great quantities of mud and some coarse gravel. Near the mouth is a large proportion of timber, but the warmth of the water would seem to indicate that the country through which it passed was open and without shade.

JULY 30TH *Wednesday.* They set out at an early hour, and after passing, at the distance of twelve miles, the bed of a river one hundred yards wide, but nearly dry at present, reached two miles below it a succession of bad shoals, interspersed with a hard, dark brown, gritty rock, extending for six miles, the last of which stretches nearly across the river, and has a descent of about three feet. At this place they were obliged to let the canoes down with the hand, for fear of their splitting on a concealed rock; though when the shoals are known a large canoe could with safety pass through the worst of them. This is the most difficult part of the whole Yellowstone river, and was called the Buffalo shoals, from the circumstance of one of those animals being found in them. The neighbouring cliffs on the right are about one hundred feet high; on the left the country is low, but gradually rises, and at some distance from the shore present the first appearance of burnt hills which have been seen on the Yellowstone. Below the Buffalo shoals the river is contracted to the width of three or four hundred yards, the islands less numerous, and a few scattering trees only are seen either on its banks or on the highlands: twenty miles from those shoals is a rapid, caused by a number of rocks strewed over the river; but though the waves are high, there is a very good channel on the left, which renders the passage secure. There was a bear standing on one of these rocks, which occasioned the name of the Bear rapid. As they were descending this rapid a violent storm from the northwest obliged them to take refuge in an old Indian lodge near the mouth of a river on the left, which has lately been very high, has widened to the distance of a quarter of a mile, but though its present channel is eighty-eight yards wide, there is not more water in it than would easily pass through a hole of an inch in diameter. It was called York's dry river.

As soon as the rain and wind had abated, they resumed their journey, and at seven miles encamped under a spreading cottonwood tree on the left side, after making forty-eight miles. A mile and a half above on the opposite side is a river containing one hundred yards width of water, though the bed itself is much wider. The water is very muddy, and like its banks of a dark brown colour. Its current throws out great quantities of red stones; and this circumstance, with the appearance of the distant hills, induced captain Clark to call it the Redstone, which he afterwards found to be the meaning of its Indian name, Wahasah.

JULY 31ST *Thursday.* During the whole night the buffalo were prowling about the camp, and excited much alarm, lest in crossing the river they should tread on the boats and split them to pieces. They set out as usual, and at the distance of two miles passed a rapid of no great danger, which they called Wolf rapid, from seeing a wolf in them. At this place commences a range of highlands. These highlands have no timber, and are composed of earth of different colours, without much rock, but supplied throughout with great quantities of coal, or carbonated wood. After passing these hills the country again opens into extensive plains, like those passed yesterday, and the river is diversified with islands, and partially supplied with water by a great number of wide, but nearly dry brooks. Thus eighteen miles below the camp is a shallow, muddy stream on the left, one hundred yards wide, and supposed to be that known among the Indians by the name of Saasha, or Littlewolf river: five miles below on the right side is another river, forty yards wide, and four feet in depth, which, from the steep coal banks on each side, they called Oaktaroup, or Coal river; and at eighteen miles further a third stream of sixty yards in width, to which they gave the name of Gibson's river. Having made sixty-six miles, they halted for the night, and just as they landed, saw the largest white bear that any of the party had ever before seen, devouring a dead buffalo on a sandbar. They fired two balls into him, and he then swam to the main land and walked along the shore. Captain Clark pursued him, and lodged two more balls in his body; but though he bled profusely he made his escape, as night prevented them from following him.

[*Account of Capt. Clark's party*]

Friday, August 1st, 1806

The next day a high wind from ahead made the water rough, and retarded their progress, and as it rained during the whole day, their situation in the open boats was very disagreeable. The country bears in every respect the same appearance as that of yesterday, though there is some ash timber in the bottom, and low pine and cedar on the sides of the hills. The current of the river is less rapid, has more soft mud, and is more obstructed by sandbars, and the rain has given an unusual quantity of water to the brooks. The buffalo now appear in vast numbers. A herd happened to be on their way across the river. Such was the multitude of these animals, that although the river, including an island, over which they passed was a mile in length, the herd stretched as thick as they could swim, completely from one side to the other, and the party was obliged to stop for an hour. They consoled themselves for the delay by killing four of the herd, and then proceeded till at the distance of forty-five miles on an island, below which two other herds of buffalo, as numerous as the first, soon after crossed the river.

Saturday. The river is now about a mile wide, less rapid, and more divided by islands and bars of sand and mud than hitherto: the low grounds too are more extensive, and contain a greater quantity of cottonwood, ash, and willow trees. On the northwest is a low, level plain; on the southeast some rugged hills, on which we saw, without being able to approach, some of the bighorns. The buffalo and elk, as well as the pursuers of both, the wolves, are in great numbers. On each side of the river are several dry brooks; but the only stream of any size is that they called Ibex river, on the right, about thirty yards wide, and sixteen miles from the camp. The bear which gave so much trouble on the head of the Missouri, are equally fierce in this quarter. This morning one of them, which was on a sandbar as the boat passed, raised himself on his hind feet, and after looking at the party, plunged in and swam towards them. He was received with three balls in the body; he then turned round and made for the shore. Towards evening another entered the water to swim across. Captain Clark ordered the boat towards the shore, and just as the bear landed, shot the animal in the head. It proved to be the largest

AUGUST 2D

female they had ever seen, and so old that its tusks were worn quite smooth. The boats escaped with difficulty between two herds of buffalo, which were crossing the river, and would probably have again detained the party. Among the elk of this neighbourhood are an unusual number of males, while higher up the river the numerous herds consist of females chiefly. After making eighty-four miles, they encamped among some ash and elm trees on the right. They, however, rather passed the night than slept there, for the mosquitoes were so troublesome, that scarcely any of the party could close their eyes during the greater part of the time.

AUGUST 3D *Sunday.* They therefore set out early in the morning to avoid the persecution of those insects. At the distance of two miles they passed Fields's creek, a stream thirty-five yards wide, which enters on the right, immediately above a high bluff, which is rapidly sinking into the river. Here captain Clark went ashore in pursuit of some bighorns, but the mosquitoes were so numerous, that he was unable to shoot with certainty. He therefore returned to the canoes: and soon after observing a ram of the same animals, sent one of the hunters, who shot it, and it was preserved entire as a specimen. About two o'clock they reached, eight miles below Fields's creek, the junction of the Yellowstone with the Missouri, and formed a camp on the point where they had encamped on the *26th of April, 1805.* The canoes were now unloaded, and the baggage exposed to dry, as many of the articles were wet, and some of them spoiled.

The Rochejaune, or Yellowstone river, according to Indian information, has its remote sources in the Rocky mountains, near the peaks of the Rio del Norde, on the confines of New Mexico, to which country there is a good road during the whole distance along the banks of the Yellowstone. Its western waters are probably connected with those of Lewis's river, while the eastern branches approach the heads of Clark's river, the Bighorn, and the Platte; so that it waters the middle portion of the Rocky mountains for several hundred miles from northwest to southeast. During its whole course from the point at which captain Clark reached it to the Missouri, a distance which he computed at eight hundred and thirty-seven miles, this river is large and navigable for periogues, and even batteaux, there being none of the moving sandbars which impede the navigation of the Missouri, and only a single ledge of rocks, which, however, is not difficult to pass. Even its tributary waters, the Bighorn, Clark's fork, and Tongue river, may be ascended in boats for a considerable distance. The banks of the river are low, but bold, and nowhere subject to be overflowed, except for a short distance below the mountains. The predominating colour of the river is a yellowish-brown; that of the Missouri, which possesses more mud, is of a deep drab colour; the bed of the former being chiefly composed of loose pebble; which, however, diminish in size in descending the river, till after passing the Lazeka, the pebble cease as the river widens, and the mud and sand continue to form the greater part of the bottom. Over these the water flows with a velocity constantly and almost equally decreasing in proportion to its distance from the mountains. From the mountains to Clark's fork, the current may be estimated at four and a half miles per hour; thence as low as the Bighorn, at three and a half miles; between that and the Lazeka at three miles; and from that river to the Wolf rapid, at two and three quarter miles; from which to its entrance, the general rapidity is two miles per hour. The appearance and character of the country present nearly similar varieties of fertile, rich, open lands. Above Clark's fork, it consists of high waving plains bordered by stony hills, partially supplied with pine; the middle portion, as low as the Buffalo shoals, contains less timber, and the number diminishes still lower, where the river widens, and the country spreads itself into extensive plains.

[Account of Capt. Clark's party]

Like all the branches of the Missouri which penetrate the Rocky mountains, the Yellowstone and its streams, within that district of country beyond Clark's fork, abound in beaver and otter; a circumstance which strongly recommends the entrance of the latter river as a judicious position for the purposes of trade. To an establishment at that place, the Shoshonees, both within and westward of the Rocky mountains, would willingly resort, as they would be farther from the reach of the Blackfoot Indians, and the Minnetarees of Fort de Prairie, than they could be in trading with any factories on the Missouri. The same motive of personal safety, would most probably induce many of the tribes on the Columbia and Lewis's river to prefer this place to the entrance of Maria's river, at least for some years; and as the Crow and Paunch Indians, the Castahanahs, and the Indians residing south of Clark's fork, would also be induced to visit it, the mouth of that river might be considered as one of the most important establishments for the western fur trade. This too may be the more easily effected, as the adjacent country possesses a sufficiency of timber for the purpose, an advantage which is not found on any spot between Clark's fork and the Rocky mountains.

Monday. The camp became absolutely uninhabitable, in consequence of the multitude of mosquitoes; the men could not work in preparing skins for clothing, nor hunt in the timbered low grounds; in short, there was no mode of escape, except by going on the sandbars in the river; where, if the wind should blow, the insects do not venture; but when there is no wind, and particularly at night, when the men have no covering except their worn-out blankets, the pain they suffer is scarcely to be endured. There was also a want of meat, for the buffalo were not to be found; and though the elk are very abundant, yet their fat and flesh is more difficult to dry in the sun, and is also much more easily spoiled than the meat or fat of either deer or buffalo. Captain Clark therefore determined to go on to some spot which should be free from mosquitoes, and furnish more game. After having written a note to captain Lewis, to inform him of his intention, and stuck it on a pole, at the confluence of the two rivers, he loaded the canoes at five in the afternoon, and proceeded down the river to the second point and encamped on a sandbar; but here the mosquitoes seemed to be even more numerous than above. The face of the Indian child is considerably puffed up and swollen with the bites of these animals, nor could the men procure scarcely any sleep during the night, and they continued to harass them the next morning as they proceeded.

AUGUST 4TH

Tuesday. On one occasion captain Clark went on shore and ascended a hill after one of the bighorns; but the mosquitoes were in such multitudes that he could not keep them from the barrel of his rifle long enough to take aim.

AUGUST 5TH

523

About ten o'clock, however, a light breeze sprung up from the northwest, and dispersed them in some degree. Captain Clark then landed on a sandbar, intending to wait for captain Lewis, and went out to hunt. But not finding any buffalo, he again proceeded in the afternoon, and having killed a large white bear, encamped under a high bluff exposed to a light breeze from the southwest, which blew away the mosquitoes. About eleven o'clock, however, the wind became very high and a storm of rain came on, which lasted for two hours, accompanied with sharp lightning and loud peals of thunder.

AUGUST 6TH *Wednesday.* They therefore rose, very wet, and proceeded to a sandbar below the entrance of Whiteearth river. Just above this place, the Indians had, apparently within seven or eight days past, been digging a root which they employ in making a kind of soup. Having fixed their tents, the men were employed in dressing skins and hunting. They shot a number of deer; but only two of them were fat, owing probably to the great quantities of mosquitoes who annoy them whilst feeding. The next day, after some severe rain, they proceeded at eleven o'clock, through intervals of rain and high wind till six in the evening, when they encamped on a sandbar. Here they had a very violent wind, for two hours, which left the air clear and cold, so that the mosquitoes completely disappeared.

AUGUST 8TH *Friday.* On the following morning, sergeant Pryor, accompanied by Shannon, Hall, and Windsor, arrived, but without the horses. They reported that on the second day after they left captain Clark, they halted to let the horses graze near the bed of a large creek, which contained no running water; but soon after a shower of rain fell, and the creek swelled so suddenly, that several horses which had straggled across the dry bed of the creek, were obliged to swim back. They now determined to form their camp; but the next morning were astonished at not being able to find a single one of their horses. They immediately examined the neighbourhood, and soon finding the track of the Indians who had stolen the horses, pursued them for five miles, where the fugitives divided into two parties. They now followed the largest party five miles further, till they lost all hopes of overtaking the Indians, and returned to the camp; and packing the baggage on their backs, pursued a northeast course towards the Yellowstone. On the following night a wolf bit sergeant Pryor through the hand as he lay asleep, and made an attempt to seize Windsor, when Shannon discovered and shot him. They passed over a broken open country, and having reached the Yellowstone near Pompey's pillar, they determined to descend the river, and for this purpose made two skin canoes, such as they had seen among the Mandans and Ricaras. They are made in the following manner:—Two sticks of an inch and a quarter in diameter are tied together so as to form a round hoop, which serves for the brim, while a second hoop, for the bottom of the boat, is made in the same way, and both secured by sticks of the same size from the sides of the hoops, fastened by thongs at the edges of the hoops and at the interstices of the sticks: over this frame the skin is drawn closely and tied with thongs, so as to form a perfect basin, seven feet and three inches in diameter, sixteen inches deep, and with sixteen ribs or cross-sticks, and capable of carrying six or eight men with their loads. Being unacquainted with the river, they thought it most prudent to divide their guns and ammunition, so that in case of accident all might not be lost, and therefore built two canoes. In these frail vessels they embarked, and were surprised at the perfect security in which they passed through the most difficult shoals and rapids of the river, without ever taking in water, even during the highest winds.

In passing the confluence of the Yellowstone and Missouri, he took down the note from the pole, supposing that captain Lewis had passed; and now learning where the party was, pressed on in the skin canoes to join them. The day was spent in hunting, so as to procure a number of skins to trade with the Mandans; for having now neither horses nor merchandise, our only resort in order to obtain corn and beans, is a stock of skins, which those Indians very much admire.

Saturday. A heavy dew fell this morning. Captain Clark now proceeded slowly down the river, hunting through the low grounds in the neighbourhood after the deer and elk, till late in the afternoon he encamped on the southeast side. Here they remained during the next day, *Sunday, 10th*, attempting to dry the meat, while the hunters were all abroad; but they could obtain nothing except an antelope and one black-tailed deer; those animals being very scarce on this part of the river. In the low grounds of the river captain Clark found to-day a species of cherry which he had never seen before, and which seems peculiar to this small district of country, though even there it is not very abundant.

The men also dug up quantities of a large and very insipid root, called by the Indians hankee, and by the engagées, the white apple. It is used by them in a dry and pounded state, so as to mix with their soup; but our men boiled it and eat it with meat. In descending the river yesterday, the squaw brought in a large well-flavoured gooseberry, of a rich crimson colour; and a deep purple berry of a species of currant, common on this river as low as the Mandans, and called by the engagées, the Indian currant.

Monday. The next morning captain Clark set out early, and landed on a sandbar about ten o'clock for the purpose of taking breakfast and drying the meat. At noon they proceeded on about two miles, when they observed a canoe near the shore. They immediately landed, and were equally surprised and pleased at discovering two men by the names of Dickson and Hancock, who had come from the Illinois on a hunting excursion up the Yellowstone. They had left the Illinois in the summer of 1804, and had spent the last winter with the Tetons, in company with a Mr. Ceautoin, who had come there as a trader, but whom they had robbed, or rather they had taken all his merchandise and given him a few robes in exchange. These men had met the boat which we had despatched from fort Mandan, on board of which they were told there was a Ricara chief on his way to Washington; and also another party of Yankton chiefs, accompanying Mr. Durion on a visit of the same kind. We were sorry to learn that the Mandans and Minnetarees were at war with the Ricaras, and had killed two of them. The Assiniboins too, are at war with the Mandans. They have, in consequence, prohibited the Northwestern company from trading to the Missouri, and even killed two of their traders near the Mouse river, and are now lying in wait for Mr. M'Kenzie of the Northwestern company, who had been for a long time

[*Account of Capt. Clark's party*]

AUGUST 9TH

AUGUST 11TH

among the Minnetarees. These appearances are rather unfavourable to the project of carrying some of the chiefs to the United States; but we still hope, that by effecting a peace between the Mandans, Minnetarees, and Ricaras, the views of our government may be accomplished.

After leaving these trappers, captain Clark went on and encamped nearly opposite the entrance of Goatpen creek, where the party were again assailed by their old enemies, the mosquitoes.

Chapter 35
DOWN THE MISSOURI TO WHITE RIVER

TUESDAY, AUGUST 12TH, 1806 The party continued slowly to descend the river. One of the skin canoes was by accident pierced with a small hole, and they halted for the purpose of mending it with a piece of elk skin, and also to wait for two of the party who were behind. Whilst there, they were overjoyed at seeing captain Lewis's boats heave in sight about noon. But this feeling was changed into alarm on seeing the boats reach the shore without captain Lewis, who they then learnt had been wounded the day before, and was then lying in the periogue. After giving to his wound all the attention in our power, we remained here some time, during which we were overtaken by our two men, accompanied by Dickson and Hancock, who wished to go with us as far as the Mandans. The whole party being now happily reunited, we left the two skin canoes, and all embarked together, about 3 o'clock, in the boats. The wind was however very high from the southwest, accompanied with rain, so that we did not go far before we halted for the night on a sandbar. Captain Lewis's wound was now sore and somewhat painful.

Wednesday. The next day they set out by sunrise, and having a very strong breeze from the northwest, proceeded on rapidly. At eight o'clock we passed the mouth of the Little Missouri. Some Indians were seen at a distance below in a skin canoe, and were probably some of the Minnetarees on their return from a hunting excursion, as we passed one of their camps on the southwest side, where they had left a canoe. Two other Indians were seen far off on one of the hills, and we shall therefore soon meet with our old acquaintances the Mandans. At sunset we arrived at the entrance of Miry river, and encamped on the northeast side, having come by the assistance of the wind and our oars, a distance of eighty-six miles. The air was cool, and the mosquitoes ceased to trouble us as they had done.

AUGUST 13TH

Thursday. We again set out at sunrise, and at length approached the grand village of the Minnetarees, where the natives had collected to view us as we passed. We fired the blunderbuss several times by way of salute, and soon after landed at the bank near the village of the Mahahas, or Shoe Indians, and were received by a crowd of people, who came to welcome our return. Among these were the principal chief of the Mahahas, and the chief of the Little Minnetaree village, both of whom expressed great pleasure at seeing us again; but the latter wept most bitterly. On inquiry, it appeared that his tears were excited because the sight of us reminded him of his son, who had been lately killed by the Blackfoot Indians.

AUGUST 14TH

After remaining there a few minutes, we crossed to the Mandan village of the Blackcat, where all the inhabitants seemed very much pleased at seeing us. We immediately sent Chaboneau with an invitation for the Minnetarees to visit us, and despatched Drewyer to the lower village of the Mandans to bring Jesseaume as an interpreter. Captain Clark, in the meantime, walked up to the village of the Blackcat, and smoked and eat with the chief. This village has been rebuilt since our departure, and was now much smaller; a quarrel having arisen among the Indians, in consequence of which a number of families had removed to the opposite side of the river. On the arrival of Jesseaume, captain Clark addressed the chiefs. We spoke to them now, he said, in the same language we had done before; and repeated his invitation to accompany him to the United States, to hear in person the counsels of their great father, who can at all times protect those who open their ears to his counsels, and punish his enemies. The Blackcat [Poscopsahe] in reply, declared that he wished to visit the United States, and see his great father, but was afraid of the Sioux, who had killed several of the Mandans since our departure, and who were now on the river below, and would intercept him if he attempted to go. Captain Clark endeavoured to quiet his apprehensions by assuring him that he would not suffer the Sioux to injure one of our red children who should accompany us, and that they should return loaded with presents, and protected at the expense of the United States.

The council was then broken up, after which we crossed and formed our camp on the other side of the river, where we should be sheltered from the rain. Soon after the chief of the Mahahas informed us, that if we would send to his village, we should have some corn. Three men were therefore despatched, and soon after returned loaded with as much as they could carry; and were soon followed by the chief and his wife, to whom we presented a few needles and other articles fit for women.

In a short time the Borgne (the great chief of all the Minnetarees) came down, attended by several other chiefs, to whom, after smoking a pipe, captain Clark now made a harangue, renewing his assurances of friendship and the invitation to go with us to Washington. He was answered by the Borgne, who began by declaring that he much desired to visit his great father, but that the Sioux would certainly kill any of the Mandans who should attempt to go down the river. They were bad people, and would not listen to any advice. When he saw us last, we had told him that we had made peace with all the nations below, yet the Sioux had since killed eight of his tribe, and stolen a number of their horses. The Ricaras too had stolen their horses, and in the contest his people had killed two of the Ricaras. Yet in spite of these dispositions he had always had his ears open to our counsels, and had actually made a peace with the Chayennes and the Indians of the Rocky mountains. He concluded by saying, that however disposed they were to visit the United States, the fear of the Sioux would prevent them from going with us. The council was then finished, and soon afterwards an invitation was received from the Blackcat, who, on captain Clark's arrival at his village, presented him with a dozen bushels of corn, which he said was a large proportion of what his people owned; and after smoking a pipe, declared that his people were too apprehensive of the Sioux to venture with us.

Captain Clark then spoke to the chiefs and warriors of the village. He told them of his anxiety that some of them should see their great father, and hear his good words and receive his gifts, and requested them to fix on some confidential chief who might accompany us. To this they made the same objections as before, till at length a young man offered to go, and the warriors all assented to it. But the character of this man was known to be bad, and one of the party with captain Clark informed him that at the moment he had in his possession a knife which he had stolen. Captain Clark therefore told the chief of this theft, and ordered the knife to be given up. This was done with a poor apology for having it in his possession, and captain Clark then reproached the chiefs for wishing to send such a fellow to see and hear so distinguished a person as their great father. They all hung down their heads for some time, till the Blackcat apologised by saying, that the danger was such that they were afraid of sending any of their chiefs, as they considered his loss almost inevitable. Captain Clark remained some time with them, smoking and relating various particulars of his journey, and then left them to visit the second chief of the Mandans (or the Blackcrow) [Kagohami, or Little Raven], who had expressed some disposition to accompany us. He seemed well inclined to the journey, but was unwilling to decide till he had called a council of his people, which he intended to do in the afternoon. On returning to the camp, he found the chief of the Mahahas, and also the chief of the Little Minnetaree village, who brought a present of corn on their mules, of which they possess several, and which they procure from the Crow Indians, who either buy or steal them on the frontiers of the Spanish settlements. A great number of the Indians visited us for the purpose of renewing their acquaintance, or of exchanging robes or other articles for the skins brought by the men.

In the evening we were applied to by one of our men, Colter, who was desirous of joining the two trappers who had accompanied us, and who now proposed an expedition up the river, in which they were to find traps and give him a share of the profits. The offer was a very advantageous one, and as he had always performed his duty, and his services might be dispensed with, we agreed that he might go, provided none of the rest would ask or expect a similar indulgence. To this they cheerfully answered, that they wished Colter every success, and would not apply for liberty to separate before we reached St. Louis. We, therefore, supplied him, as did his comrades also, with powder and lead, and a variety of articles which might be useful to him, and he left us the next day. The example of this man shows how easily men may be weaned from the habits of a civilised life to the ruder, but scarcely less fascinating manners of the woods. This hunter has been now absent for many years from the frontiers, and might naturally be presumed to have some anxiety, or some curiosity at least to return to his friends and his country; yet just at the moment when he is approaching the frontiers, he is tempted by a hunting scheme, to give up those delightful prospects, and go back without the least reluctance to the solitude of the woods.

In the evening Chaboneau, who had been mingling with the Indians, and had learned what had taken place during our absence, informed us, that as soon as we had left the Minnetarees, they sent out a war party against the Shoshonees, whom they attacked and routed, though in the engagement they lost two men, one of whom was the son of the chief of the Little Minnetaree village. Another war party had gone against the Ricaras, two of whom they killed. A misunderstanding too had taken place between the Mandans and Minnetarees, in consequence of a dispute about a woman, which had nearly occasioned a war; but at length a pipe was presented by the Minnetarees, and a reconciliation took place.

Saturday. The Mandans had offered to give us corn, and on sending this morning, we found a greater quantity collected for our use than all our canoes would contain. We therefore thanked the chief and took only six loads. At ten o'clock the chiefs of the different villages came down to smoke with us. We therefore took this opportunity of endeavouring to engage the Borgne in our interests by a present of the swivel, which is no longer serv-

AUGUST 16TH

iceable, as it cannot be discharged from our largest perogue. It was now loaded, and the chiefs being formed into a circle round it, captain Clark addressed them with great ceremony. He said that he had listened with much attention to what had yesterday been declared by the Borgne, whom he believed to be sincere, and then reproached them with their disregard of our counsels, and their wars on the Shoshonees and Ricaras. Littlecherry, the old Minnetaree chief, answered that they had long stayed at home and listened to our advice, but at last went to war against the Sioux because their horses had been stolen, and their companions killed; and that in an expedition against those people, they had met the Ricaras, who were on their way to strike them, and a battle ensued. But in future he said they would attend to our words and live at peace. The Borgne added, that his ears too would always be open to the words of his good father, and shut against bad counsel. Captain Clark then presented to the Borgne the swivel, which he told him had announced the words of his great father to all the nations we had seen, and which, whenever it was fired, should recall those which we had delivered to him. The gun was then discharged, and the Borgne had it conveyed in great pomp to his village. The council was then adjourned.

In the afternoon captain Clark walked up to the village of the Littlecrow, taking a flag, which he intended to present to him, but was surprised on being told by him, that he had given over all intention of accompanying us, and refused the flag. He found that this was occasioned by a jealousy between him and the principal chief, Bigwhite [Sheheke]; on the interference, however, of Jesseaume, the two chiefs were reconciled, and it was agreed that the Bigwhite himself should accompany us with his wife and son.

AUGUST 17TH *Sunday.* The principal chiefs of the Minnetarees came down to bid us farewell, as none of them could be prevailed on to go with us. This circumstance induced our interpreter, Chaboneau, with his wife and child, to remain here, as he could be no longer useful; and notwithstanding our offers of taking him with us to the United States, he said that he had there no acquaintance, and no chance of making a livelihood, and preferred remaining among the Indians. This man has been very serviceable to us, and his wife particularly useful among the Shoshonees. Indeed, she has borne with a patience truly admirable, the fatigues of so long a route, incumbered with the charge of an infant, who is even now only nineteen months old. We therefore paid him his wages, amounting to five hundred dollars and thirty-three cents, including the price of a horse and a lodge purchased of him; and soon afterwards dropped down to the village of the Bigwhite, attended on shore by all the Indian chiefs who went to take leave of him.

We found him surrounded by his friends, who sat in a circle smoking, while the women were crying. He immediately sent his wife and son, with their baggage, on board, accompanied by the interpreter and his wife, and two children; and then after distributing among his friends some powder and ball, which we had given to him, and smoking a pipe with us, went with us to the river side. The whole village crowded about us, and many of the people wept aloud at the departure of the chief. As captain Clark was shaking hands with the principal chiefs of all the villages, they requested that he would sit with them one moment longer. Being willing to gratify them, he stopped and ordered a pipe, after smoking which, they informed

HUNTING THE BISON (Bodmer)

him that when they first saw us, they did not believe all that we then told them; but having now seen that our words were all true, they would carefully remember them, and follow our advice; that he might tell their great father that the young men should remain at home and not make war on any people except in defence of themselves. They requested him to tell the Ricaras to come and visit them without fear, as they meant that nation no harm, but were desirous of peace with them. On the Sioux, however, they had no dependence, and must kill them whenever they made war parties against their country.

Captain Clark, in reply, informed them that we had never insisted on their not defending themselves, but requested only that they would not strike those whom we had taken by the hand; that we would apprise the Ricaras of their friendly intentions, and that, although we had not seen those of the Sioux with whom they were at war, we should relate their conduct to their great father, who would take measures for producing a general peace among all his red children. The Borgne now requested that we would take good care of this chief, who would report whatever their great father should say; and the council being then broken up, we took leave with a salute from a gun, and then proceeded.

On reaching fort Mandan, we found a few pickets standing on the river side, but all the houses except one, had been burnt by an accidental fire. At the distance of eighteen miles we reached the old Ricara village, where we encamped on the southwest side, the wind being too violent, and the waves too high to permit us to go any further. The same cause prevented us from setting out before eight o'clock the next day.

Monday. Soon after we embarked, an Indian came running down to the beach, who appeared very anxious to speak to us. We went ashore, and found it was the brother of the Bigwhite, who was encamped at no great distance, and hearing of our departure, came to take leave of the chief. The Bigwhite gave him a pair of leggings, and they separated in a most affectionate manner; and we then continued though the wind and waves were still high. The Indian chief seems quite satisfied with his treatment, and during the whole of his time was employed in pointing out the ancient monuments of the Mandans, or in relating their traditions. At length, after making forty miles, we encamped on the northeast side, opposite an old Mandan village, and below the mouth of Chesshetah river. AUGUST 18TH

Tuesday. The wind was so violent that we were not able to proceed until four in the afternoon, during which time the hunters killed four elk and twelve deer. We then went on for ten miles, and came to on a sandbar. The rain and wind continued through the night, and during the whole of the next day, the waves were so high, that one man was constantly occupied in bailing the boats. We passed at noon, Cannonball river; and at three in the afternoon, the entrance of the river Wardepon, the boundary of the country claimed by the Sioux; and after coming eighty-one miles, passed the night on a sandbar. The plains are beginning to change their appearance, the grass becoming of a yellow colour. We have seen great numbers of wolves to-day, and some buffalo and elk, though these are by no means so abundant as on the Yellowstone. AUGUST 19TH

Since we passed in 1804, a very obvious change has taken place in the current and appearance of the Missouri. In places where at that time there were sandbars, the current of the river now passes, and the former channel of the river is in turn a bank of sand. Sandbars then naked, are covered with willows several feet high: the entrance of some of the creeks and rivers changed in consequence of the quantity of mud thrown into them; and in some of the bottoms are layers of mud eight inches in depth.

AUGUST 21ST *Thursday.* We rose after a night of broken rest, owing to the mosquitoes, and having put our arms in order, so as to be prepared for an attack, continued our course. We soon met three traders, two of whom had wintered with us among the Mandans in 1804, and who were now on their way there. They had exhausted all their powder and lead; we therefore supplied them with both. They informed us that seven hundred Sioux had passed the Ricara towns on their way to make war against the Mandans and Minnetarees, leaving their women and children encamped near the Big-bend of the Missouri, and that the Ricaras all remained at home, without taking any part in the war. They also told us that the Pawnee, or Ricara chief, who went to the United States in the spring of 1805, died on his return near Sioux river.

We then left them, and soon afterwards arrived opposite to the upper Ricara villages. We saluted them with the discharge of four guns, which they answered in the same manner; and on our landing we were met by the greater part of the inhabitants of each village, and also by a band of Chayennes, who were encamped on a hill in the neighbourhood.

As soon as captain Clark stepped on shore, he was greeted by the two chiefs to whom we had given medals on our last visit, and as they, as well as the rest, appeared much rejoiced at our return, and desirous of hearing from the Mandans, he sat down on the bank, while the Ricaras and Chayennes formed a circle round him; and after smoking, he informed them, as he had already done the Minnetarees, of the various tribes we had visited, and our anxiety to promote peace among our red brethren. He then expressed his regret at their having attacked the Mandans, who had listened to our counsels, and had sent on a chief to smoke with them, and to assure them that they might now hunt in the plains, and visit the Mandan villages in safety, and concluded by inviting some of the chiefs to accompany us to Washington. The man whom we had acknowledged as the principal chief when we ascended, now presented another, who he said was a greater chief than himself, and to him, therefore, he had surrendered the flag and medal with which we had honoured him. This chief, who was absent at our last visit, is a man of thirty-five years of age, a stout, well-looking man, and called by the Indians, Grayeyes.

He now made a very animated reply. He declared that the Ricaras were willing to follow the counsels we had given them, but a few of their bad young men would not live in peace, but had joined the Sioux, and thus embroiled them with the Mandans. These young men had, however, been driven out of the villages, and as the Ricaras were now separated from the Sioux, who were a bad people, and the cause of all their misfortunes, they now desired to be at peace with the Mandans, and would receive them with kindness and friendship. Several of the chiefs he said were desirous of visiting their great father, but as the chief who went to the United States last summer had not returned, and they had some fears for his safety, on account of the Sioux, they did not wish to leave home until they heard of him. With regard to himself, he would continue with his nation, to see that they followed our advice.

The sun being now very hot, the chief of the Chayennes invited us to his lodge, which was at no great distance from the river. We followed him, and found a very large lodge, made of twenty buffalo skins, surrounded by eighteen or twenty lodges, nearly equal in size. The rest of the nation are expected to-morrow, and will make the number of one hundred and thirty or fifty lodges, containing from three hundred and fifty to four hundred men, at which the men of the nation may be computed. These Chayennes are a fine looking people, of a large stature, straight limbs, high cheek-bones and noses, and of a complexion similar to that of the Ricaras. Their ears are cut at the lower part, but few wear ornaments in them, the hair is generally cut over the eyebrows and small ornaments fall down the cheeks, the remainder being either twisted with horse or buffalo hair, and divided over each shoulder, or else flowing loosely behind. Their decorations consist chiefly of blue beads, shells, red paint, brass rings, bears' claws, and strips of otter skins, of which last they, as well as the Ricaras, are very fond. The women are coarse in their features, with wide mouths, and ugly. Their dress consists of a habit falling to the midleg, and made of two equal pieces of leather, sewed from the bottom with arm holes, with a flap hanging nearly half way down the body, both before and behind. These are burnt in various figures by means of a hot stick, and adorned with beads, shells, and elks' tusks, which all Indians admire. The other ornaments are blue beads in the ears, but the hair is plain and flows down the back. The summer dress of the men is a simple buffalo robe, a cloth round the waist, moccasins, and occasionally leggings. Living remote from the whites, they are shy and cautious, but are peaceably disposed, and profess to make war against no people except the Sioux, with whom they have been engaged in contests immemorially. In their excursions they are accompanied by their dogs and horses, which they possess in great numbers, the former serving to carry almost all their light baggage.

After smoking for some time, captain Clark gave a small medal to the Chayenne chief, and explained at the same time the meaning of it. He seemed alarmed at this present, and sent for a robe and a quantity of buffalo meat, which he gave to captain Clark, and requested him to take back the medal, for he knew that all white people were medicine, and he was afraid of the medal, or of any thing else which the white people gave to the Indians. Captain Clark then repeated his intention in giving the medal, which was the medicine his great father had directed him to deliver to all chiefs who listened to his word and followed his counsels; and that as he had done so, the medal was given as a proof that we believed him sincere. He now appeared satisfied and received the medal, in return for which he gave double the quantity of buffalo meat he had offered before. He seemed now quite reconciled to the whites, and requested that some traders might be sent among the Chayennes, who lived he said, in a country full of beaver, but did not understand well how to catch them, and were discouraged from it by having no sale for them when caught. Captain Clark promised that they should be soon supplied with goods, and taught the best mode of catching beaver.

The Bigwhite, chief of the Mandans, now addressed them at some length, explaining the pacific intentions of his nation; and the Chayenne observed that both the Ricaras and Mandans seemed to be in fault; but at the end of the council the Mandan chief was treated with great civility, and the greatest harmony prevailed among them. The great chief, however, informed us, that none of the Ricaras could be prevailed on to go with us till the return of the other chief, and that the Chayennes were a wild people, and afraid to go. He invited captain Clark to his house, and gave him two carrots of tobacco, two beaver skins, and a trencher of boiled corn and beans. It is the custom of all the nations on the Missouri, to offer to every white man food and refreshment when he first enters their tents.

Captain Clark returned to the boats, where he found the chief of the lower village, who had cut off part of his hair, and disfigured himself in such a manner that we did not recognise him at first, until he explained that he was in mourning for his nephew, who had been killed by the Sioux. He proceeded with us to the village on the island, where we were met by all the inhabitants. The second chief, on seeing the Mandan, began to speak to him in a loud and threatening tone, till captain Clark declared that the Mandans had listened to our counsels, and that if any injury was done to the chief, we should defend him against every nation. He then invited the Mandan to his lodge, and after a very ceremonious smoking, assured captain Clark that the Mandan was as safe as at home, for the Ricaras had opened their ears to our counsels, as well as the Mandans. This was repeated by the great chief, and the Mandan and Ricara chiefs now smoked and conversed in great apparent harmony; after which we returned to the boats. The whole distance to-day was twenty-nine miles.

AUGUST 22D *Friday.* It rained all night, so that we all rose this morning quite wet, and were about proceeding, when captain Clark was requested to visit the chiefs. They now made several speeches, in which they said that they were unwilling to go with us, until the return of their countryman; and that, although they disliked the Sioux as the origin of all their troubles, yet as they had more horses than they wanted, and were in want of guns and powder, they would be obliged to trade once more with them for those articles, after which they would break off all connection with them. He now returned to the boats, and after taking leave of the people, who seemed to regret our departure, and firing a salute of two guns, proceeded seventeen miles, and encamped below Grouse island. We made only seventeen miles to-day, for we were obliged to land near Wetarhoo river to dry our baggage, besides which the sandbars are now unusually numerous as the river widens below the Ricara villages. Captain Lewis is now so far recovered that he was able to walk a little to-day for the first time. While here we had occasion to notice that the Mandans as well as the Minnetarees and Ricaras keep their horses in the same lodges with themselves.

AUGUST 23D *Saturday.* We set out early, but the wind was so high, that soon after passing the Sahwacanah, we were obliged to go on shore, and remain till three o'clock, when a heavy shower of rain fell and the wind lulled. We then continued our route, and after a day's journey of forty miles encamped. Whilst on shore we killed three deer and as many elk. Along the river are great quantities of grapes and chokecherries, and also a species of currant which we have never seen before: it is black, with a leaf much larger than that of the other currants, and inferior in flavour to all of them.

Sunday. We set out at sunrise, and at eight o'clock passed Lahoocat's island, opposite to the lower point of which we landed to examine a stratum of stone, near the top of a bluff of remarkably black clay. It is soft, white, and contains a very fine grit; and on being dried in the sun will crumble to pieces. The wind soon after became so high that we were obliged to land for several hours, but proceeded at five o'clock. After making forty-three miles, we encamped at the gorge of the Lookout bend of the Missouri. The Sioux have lately passed in this quarter, and there is now very little game, and that so wild, that we were unable to shoot any thing. Five of the hunters were therefore sent ahead before daylight next morning to hunt in the Pawnee island, and we followed them soon after.

AUGUST 24TH

Monday. At eight o'clock we reached the entrance of the Chayenne, where we remained till noon, in order to take a meridian observation. At three o'clock we passed the old Pawnee village, near which we had met the Tetons in 1804, and encamped in a large bottom on the northeast side, a little below the mouth of Notimber creek. Just above our camp the Ricaras had formerly a large village on each side of the river, and there are still seen the remains of five villages on the southwest side, below the Chayenne, and one also on Lahoocat's island; but these have all been destroyed by the Sioux. The weather was clear and calm, but by means of our oars we made forty-eight miles. Our hunters procured nothing except a few deer.

AUGUST 25TH

The skirt of timber in the bend above the Chayenne is inconsiderable, and scattered from four to sixteen miles on the southwest side of the river, and the thickest part is from the distance of from ten to six miles of the Chayenne. A narrow bottom of small cottonwood trees is also on the northeast point, at the distance of four miles above the river. A few large trees, and a small undergrowth of willows on the lower side bottom on the Missouri half a mile, and extend a quarter of a mile up the Chayenne: there is a bottom of cotton timber in the part above the Chayenne. The Chayenne discharges but a little water at its mouth, which resembles that of the Missouri.

Tuesday. After a heavy dew we set out, and at nine o'clock reached the entrance of Teton river, below which were a raft and a skin canoe, which induced us to suspect that the Tetons were in the neighbourhood. The arms were therefore put in perfect order, and every thing prepared to revenge the slightest insult from those people, to whom it is necessary to show an example of salutary rigour. We, however, went on without seeing any of them, although we were obliged to land near Smoke creek for two hours, to stop a leak in the periogue. Here we saw great quantities of plums and grapes, but not yet ripe. At five o'clock we passed Louisville's fort, on Cedar island, twelve miles below which we encamped, having been able to row sixty miles, with the wind ahead during the greater part of the day.

AUGUST 26TH

The Big White (Sheheke), a subordinate Mandan chief whom the explorers took back east with them (from a crayon portrait by St. Memin).

AUGUST 27TH *Wednesday.* Before sunrise we set out with a stiff eastern breeze in our faces, and at the distance of a few miles landed on a sandbar near Tylor's river, and sent out the hunters, as this was the most favourable spot to recruit our stock of meat, which was now completely exhausted. But after a hunt of three hours, they reported that no game was to be found in the bottoms, the grass having been laid flat by the immense number of buffaloes which had recently passed over it; and that they saw only a few buffalo bulls, which they did not kill, as they were quite unfit for use. Near this place we observed, however, the first signs of the wild turkey; and not long after landed in the Bigbend, and killed a fine fat elk, on which we feasted.

Towards night we heard the bellowing of the buffalo bulls, on the lower island of the Bigbend. We pursued this agreeable sound, and after killing some of the cows, encamped on the island, forty-five miles from the camp of last night.

Thursday. We proceeded at an early hour, having previously despatched some hunters ahead, with orders to join us at our old camp a little above Corvus creek, where we intended remaining one day, in order to procure the skins and skeletons of some animals, such as the mule-deer, the antelope, the barking squirrel, and the magpie, which we were desirous of carrying to the United States, and which we had seen in great abundance. After rowing thirty-two miles we landed at twelve, and formed a camp in a high bottom, thinly timbered and covered with grass, and not crowded with mosquitoes. Soon after we arrived the squaws and several of the men went to the bushes near the river, and brought great quantities of large well flavoured plums of three different species.

AUGUST 28TH

The hunters returned in the afternoon, without being able to procure any of the game we wished, except the barking squirrel, though they killed four common deer, and had seen large herds of buffalo, of which they brought in two.

Friday. They resumed their hunt in the morning, and the rest of the party were employed in dressing skins, except two, who were sent to the village of the barking squirrels, but could not see one of them out of their holes. At ten o'clock the skins were dressed, and we proceeded; and soon passed the entrance of White river, the water of which is at this time nearly the colour of milk. The day was spent in hunting along the river, so that we did not advance more than twenty miles; but with all our efforts we were unable to kill either a mule-deer or an antelope, though we procured the common deer, a porcupine, and some buffalo. These last animals are now so numerous that from an eminence we discovered more than we had ever seen before, at one time; and if it be not impossible to calculate the moving multitude, which darkened the whole plains, we are convinced that twenty thousand would be no exaggerated number. With regard to game in general, we observe that the greatest quantity of wild animals are usually found in the country lying between two nations at war.

AUGUST 29TH

Saturday. We set out at the usual hour, but after going some distance were obliged to stop for two hours, in order to wait for one of the hunters. During this time we made an excursion to a large orchard of delicious plums, where we were so fortunate as to kill two buck elks. We then proceeded down the river, and were about landing at a place where we had agreed to meet all the hunters, when several persons appeared on the high hills to the northeast, whom, by the help of the spy-glass, we distinguished to be Indians. We landed on the southwest side of the river, and immediately after saw, on a height opposite to us, about twenty persons, one of whom, from his blanket great-coat, and a handkerchief round his head, we supposed to be a Frenchman. At the same time, eighty or ninety more Indians, armed with guns and bows and arrows, came out of a wood some distance below them, and fired a salute, which we returned. From their hostile appearance, we were appre-

AUGUST 30TH

hensive that they might be Tetons; but as from the country through which they were roving, it was possible that they were Yanktons, Pawnees, or Mahas, and therefore less suspicious, we did not know in what way to receive them.

In order, however, to ascertain who they were, without risk to the party, captain Clark crossed, with three persons who could speak different Indian languages, to a sandbar near the opposite side, in hopes of conversing with them. Eight young men soon met him on the sandbar, but none of them could understand either the Pawnee or Maha interpreter. They were then addressed in the Sioux language, and answered that they were Tetons, of the band headed by the Black-buffalo, Tahtackasabah. This was the same who had attempted to stop us in 1804; and being now less anxious about offending so mischievous a tribe, captain Clark told them that they had been deaf to our counsels, had ill treated us two years ago, and had abused all the whites who had since visited them. He believed them, he added, to be bad people and they must therefore return to their companions, for if they crossed over to our camp we would put them to death. They asked for some corn, which captain Clark refused; they then requested permission to come and visit our camp, but he ordered them back to their own people. He then returned, and all the arms were prepared in case of an attack; but when the Indians reached their comrades, and had informed their chiefs of our intention, they all set out on their way to their own camp; but some of them halted on a rising ground, and abused us very copiously, threatening to kill us if we came across. We took no notice of this for some time, till the return of three of our hunters, whom we were afraid the Indians might have met; but as soon as they joined us, we embarked; and to see what the Indians would attempt, steered near the side of their river. At this the party on the hill seemed agitated, some set out for their camp, others walked about, and one man walked towards the boats and invited us to land. As he came near, we recognised him to be the same who had accompanied us for two days in 1804, and who is considered as the friend of the whites. Unwilling, however, to have any interview with these people, we declined his invitation; upon which he returned to the hill, and struck the earth three times with his gun, a great oath among the Indians, who consider swearing by the earth as one of the most sacred forms of imprecation.

At the distance of six miles we stopped on a bleak sandbar; where, however, we thought ourselves safe from attack during the night, and also free from mosquitoes. We had now made only twenty-two miles; but in the course of the day had procured a mule-deer, which we much desired. About eleven in the evening the wind shifted to the northwest, and it began to rain, accompanied with hard claps of thunder and lightning; after which the wind changed to southwest, and blew with such violence that we were obliged to hold the canoes for fear of their being driven from the sandbar; the cables of two of them however broke, and two others were blown quite across the river, nor was it till two o'clock that the whole party was reassembled, waiting in the rain for daylight.

SUNDAY, AUGUST 31ST, 1806   We examined our arms, and proceeded with the wind in our favour. For some time we saw several Indians on the hills, but soon lost sight of them. In passing the dome, and the first village of barking squirrels, we stopped and killed two fox squirrels, an animal which we have not seen on the river higher than this place. At night we encamped on the northeast side, after a journey of seventy miles. We had seen no game, as usual, on the river; but in the evening the mosquitoes soon discovered us.

Chapter 36
THE EXPEDITION RETURNS IN SAFETY TO ST. LOUIS

Monday, September 1st, 1806

We set out early, but were shortly compelled to put to shore, for half an hour, till a thick fog disappeared. At nine o'clock we passed the entrance of the Quicurre, which presents the same appearance as when we ascended, the water rapid and of a milky-white colour. Two miles below several Indians ran down to the bank, and beckoned to us to land; but as they appeared to be Tetons, and of a war party, we paid no attention to them, except to inquire to what tribe they belonged; but as the Sioux interpreter did not understand much of the language, they probably mistook his question. As one of our canoes was behind, we were afraid of an attack on the men, and therefore landed on an open commanding situation, out of the view of the Indians, in order to wait for them.

We had not been in this position fifteen minutes, when we heard several guns, which we immediately concluded were fired at the three hunters; and being now determined to protect them against any number of Indians, captain Clark with fifteen men ran up the river, whilst captain Lewis hobbled up the bank, and formed the rest of the party in such a manner as would best enable them to protect the boats. On turning a point of the river, captain Clark was agreeably surprised at seeing the Indians remaining in the place where we left them, and our canoe at the distance of a mile. He now went on a sandbar, and when the Indians crossed, gave them his hand, and was informed that they had been amusing themselves with shooting at an old keg, which we had thrown into the river, and was floating down. We now found them to be part of a band of eighty lodges of Yanktons, on Plum creek, and therefore invited them down to the camp, and after smoking several pipes, told them that we had mistaken them for Tetons, and had intended putting every one of them to death, if they had fired at our canoe; but finding them Yanktons, who were good men, we were glad to take them by the hand as faithful children, who had opened their ears to our counsels. They saluted the Mandan with great cordiality, and one of them declared that their ears had indeed been opened, and that they had followed our advice since we gave a medal to their great chief, and should continue to do so. We now tied a piece of ribbon to the hair of each Indian, and gave them some corn. We made a present of a pair of leggings to the principal chief, and then took our leave, being previously overtaken by our canoe.

At two o'clock we landed to hunt on Bonhomme island, but obtained a single elk only. The bottom on the northeast side is very rich, and so thickly overgrown with pea-vines and grass, interwoven with grape-vines, that some of the party who attempted to hunt there, were obliged to leave it

539

and ascend the plain, where they found the grass nearly as high as their heads. These plains are much richer below than above the Quicurre, and the whole country is now very beautiful. After making fifty-two miles against a head wind, we stopped for the night on a sandbar, opposite to the Calumet bluff, where we had encamped on the first of September, 1804, and where our flag-staff was still standing. We suffered very much from the mosquitoes, till the wind became so high as to blow them all away.

SEPTEMBER 2D   *Tuesday.* At eight o'clock we passed the river Jacques, but soon after were compelled to land, in consequence of the high wind from the northeast, and remain till sunset: after which we went on to a sandbar twenty-two miles from our camp of last evening. Whilst we were on shore we killed three buffaloes, and four prairie fowls, which are the first we have seen in descending. Two turkeys were also killed, and were very much admired by the Indians, who had never seen that animal before. The plains continue level and fertile, and in the low grounds there is much white oak, and some white ash in the ravines and high bottoms, with lyn and slippery elm occasionally. During the night the wind shifted to the southwest and blew the sand over us in such a manner, that our situation was very unpleasant. It lulled, however, towards daylight, and we then proceeded.

SEPTEMBER 3D   *Wednesday.* At eleven o'clock we passed the Redstone. The river is now crowded with sandbars, which are very differently situated now from what they were when we ascended. But notwithstanding these and the head wind, we made sixty miles before night, when we saw two boats and several men on shore. We landed, and found a Mr. James Airs, a partner of a house at Prairie de Chien, who had come from Mackinau by the way of Prairie de Chien and St. Louis with a license to trade among the Sioux for one year. He had brought two canoes loaded with merchandise, but lost many of his most useful articles in a squall some time since. After so long an interval, the sight of any one who could give us information of our country, was peculiarly delightful, and much of the night was spent in making inquiries into what had occurred during our absence. We found Mr. Airs a very friendly and liberal gentleman, and when we proposed to him to purchase a small quantity of tobacco, to be paid for in St. Louis, he very readily furnished every man of the party with as much as he could use during the rest of the voyage, and insisted on our accepting a barrel of flour. This last we found very agreeable, although we have still a little flour which we had deposited at the mouth of Maria's river. We could give in return only about six bushels of corn, which was all that we could spare.

SEPTEMBER 4TH   *Thursday.* The next morning we left Mr. Airs about eight o'clock, and after passing the Big Sioux river, stopped at noon near Floyd's bluff. On ascending the hill we found that the grave of Floyd had been opened, and was now half uncovered. We filled it up, and then continued down to our old camp near the Maha village, where all our baggage, which had been wet by the rain of last night, was exposed to dry. There is no game on the river except wild geese and pelicans. Near Floyd's grave are some flourishing black walnut trees, which are the first we have seen on our return.

At night we heard the report of several guns in a direction towards the Maha village, and supposed it to be the signal of the arrival of some trader. But not meeting him when we set out, the next morning, *Friday*, we concluded that the firing was merely to announce the return of the Mahas to the village, this being the season at which they return home from buffalo hunting, to take care of their corn, beans and pumpkins. The river is now more crooked, the current more rapid, and crowded with snags and sawyers, and the bottoms on both sides well supplied with timber. At three o'clock we passed the Bluestone bluff, where the river leaves the highlands and meanders through a low rich bottom, and at night encamped, after making seventy-three miles.

Saturday. The wind continued ahead, but the mosquitoes were so tormenting that to remain was more unpleasant than even to advance, however slowly, and we therefore proceeded. Near the Little Sioux river we met a trading boat belonging to Mr. Augustus Chateau, of St. Louis, with several men, on their way to trade with the Yanktons at the river Jacques. We obtained from them a gallon of whiskey, and gave each of the party a dram, which is the first spirituous liquor any of them have tasted since the fourth of July, 1805. After remaining with them for some time we went on to a sandbar, thirty miles from our last encampment, where we passed the night in expectation of being joined by two of the hunters. But as they did not come on, we set out next morning, *Sunday*, leaving a canoe with five men, to wait for them, but had not gone more than eight miles, when we overtook them; we therefore fired a gun, which was a signal for the men behind, which, as the distance in a direct line was about a mile, they readily heard and soon joined us. A little above the Soldier's river we stopped to dine on elk, of which we killed three, and at night, after making forty-four miles, encamped on a sandbar, where we hoped in vain to escape from the mosquitoes.

SEPTEMBER 6TH

Monday. We therefore set out early the next morning and stopped for a short time at the Council bluffs, to examine the situation of the place, and were confirmed in our belief that it would be a very eligible spot for a trading establishment. Being anxious to reach the Platte, we plied our oars so well, that by night we had made seventy-eight miles, and landed at our old encampment at White-catfish camp, twelve miles above that river. We had here occasion to remark the wonderful evaporation from the Missouri, which does not appear to contain more water, nor is its channel wider than at the distance of one thousand miles nearer its source, although within that space it receives about twenty rivers, some of them of considerable width, and a great number of creeks. This evaporation seems, in fact, to be greater now than when we ascended the river, for we are obliged to replenish the inkstand every day with fresh ink, nine-tenths of which must escape by evaporation.

SEPTEMBER 8TH

Tuesday. By eight o'clock we passed the river Platte, which is lower than it was, and its waters almost clear, though the channel is turbulent as usual. The sandbars which obstructed the Missouri are, however, washed away, and nothing is to be seen except a few remains of the bar. Below the Platte, the current of the Missouri becomes evidently more rapid, and the obstruc-

SEPTEMBER 9TH

541

tions from fallen timber increased. The river bottoms are extensive, rich, and covered with tall, large timber, which is still more abundant in the hollows of the ravines, where may be seen, oak, ash, elm, interspersed with some walnut and hickory. The mosquitoes also, though still numerous, seem to lose some of their vigour. As we advance so rapidly, the change of climate is very perceptible, the air is more sultry than we have experienced for a long time before, and the nights so warm that a thin blanket is now sufficient, although a few days ago two were not burdensome. Late in the afternoon we encamped opposite to the Baldpated prairie, after a journey of seventy-three miles.

SEPTEMBER 10TH   *Wednesday.* We again set out early and the wind being moderate, though still ahead, we came sixty-five miles to a sandbar, a short distance above the grand Nemaha. In the course of the day we met a trader, with three men, on his way to the Pawnee Loups or Wolf Pawnees, on the Platte. Soon after another boat passed us with seven men from St. Louis, bound to the Mahas. With both of these trading parties we had some conversation, but our anxiety to go on would not suffer us to remain long with them. The Indians, and particularly the squaws and children are weary of the long journey, and we are not less desirous of seeing our country and friends. We saw on the shore, deer, raccoons, and turkeys.

SEPTEMBER 11TH   *Thursday.* A high wind from the northwest detained us till after sunrise, when we proceeded slowly; for as the river is rapid and narrow, as well as more crowded with sandbars and timber than above, much caution is necessary in avoiding these obstacles, particularly in the present low state of the water. The Nemaha seems less wide than when we saw it before, and Wolf river has scarcely any water. In the afternoon we halted above the Nadowa to hunt, and killed two deer, after which we went on to a small island, forty miles from our last night's encampment. Here we were no longer annoyed by mosquitoes, which do not seem to frequent this part of the river; and after having been persecuted with these insects during the whole route from the falls, it is a most agreeable exemption. Their noise was very agreeably changed for that of the common wolves, which were howling in different directions, and the prairie wolves, whose barking resembles precisely that of the common cur dog.

SEPTEMBER 12TH   *Friday.* After a thick fog and a heavy dew we set out by sunrise, and at the distance of seven miles met two periogues, one of them bound to the Platte, for the purpose of trading with the Pawnees, the other on a trapping expedition to the neighbourhood of the Mahas. Soon after we met the trading party under Mr. M'Clellan; and with them was Mr. Gravelines, the interpreter, whom we had sent with a Ricara chief to the United States. The chief had unfortunately died at Washington, and Gravelines was now on his way to the Ricaras, with a speech from the president, and the presents which had been made to the chief. He had also directions to instruct the Ricaras in agriculture. He was accompanied on this mission by old Mr. Durion, our former Sioux interpreter, whose object was to procure by his influence, a safe passage for the Ricara presents through the bands of Sioux, and also to engage some of the Sioux chiefs, not exceeding six, to visit Washington.

Both of them were instructed to inquire particularly after the fate of our party, no intelligence having been received from us during a long time. We authorised Mr. Durion to invite ten or twelve Sioux chiefs to accompany him, particularly the Yanktons, whom we had found well disposed towards our country. The afternoon being wet, we determined to remain with Mr. M'Clellan during the night; and therefore, after sending on five hunters ahead, spent the evening in inquiries after occurrences in the United States during our absence; and by eight o'clock next morning overtook the hunters; but they had killed nothing.

Saturday. The wind being now too high to proceed safely through timber stuck in every part of the channel, we landed, and sent the small canoes ahead to hunt. Towards evening we overtook them, and encamped, not being able to advance more than eighteen miles. The weather was very warm, and the rushes in the bottoms so high and thick that we could scarcely hunt, but were fortunate enough to obtain four deer and a turkey, which, with the hooting owl, the common buzzard, crow, and hawk, were the only game we saw. Among the timber is the cottonwood, sycamore, ash, mulberry, papaw, walnut, hickory, prickly ash, several species of elm, intermixed with great quantities of grape-vines, and three kinds of peas.   SEPTEMBER 13TH

Sunday. We resumed our journey, and this being a part of the river to which the Kanzas resort, in order to rob the boats of traders, we held ourselves in readiness to fire upon any Indians who should offer us the slightest indignity, as we no longer needed their friendship, and found that a tone of firmness and decision is the best possible method of making proper impression on these freebooters. We, however, did not encounter any of them; but just below the old Kanzas village met three trading boats from St. Louis, on their way to the Yanktons and Mahas. After leaving them we saw a number of deer, of which we killed five, and encamped on an island, fifty-three miles from our encampment of last evening.   SEPTEMBER 14TH

Monday. A strong breeze ahead prevented us from advancing more than forty-nine miles to the neighbourhood of Haycabin creek. The river Kanzas is very low at this time. About a mile below it we landed to view the situation of a high hill, which has many advantages for a trading house or fort; while on the shore we gathered great quantities of papaws, and shot an elk. The low grounds are now delightful, and the whole country exhibits a rich appearance; but the weather is oppressively warm, and descending as rapidly as we do from a cool open country, between the latitude of 46 and 49°, in which we have been for nearly two years, to the wooded plains in 38 and 39°, the heat would be almost insufferable were it not for the constant winds from the south and southeast.   SEPTEMBER 15TH

Tuesday. We set out at an early hour, but the weather soon became so warm that the men rowed but little. In the course of the day we met two trading parties, on their way to the Pawnees and Mahas, and after making fifty-two miles, remained on an island till next morning, *Wednesday,* when we passed in safety the island of the Little Osage village. This place is considered by the navigators of the Missouri, as the most dangerous part of it, the   SEPTEMBER 16TH whole water being compressed, for two miles, within a narrow channel, crowded with timber, into which the violence of the current is constantly washing the banks. At the distance of thirty miles we met a captain M'Clellan, lately of the United States army, with whom we encamped. He informed us that the general opinion in the United States was that we were lost; the last accounts which had been heard of us being from the Mandan villages. Captain M'Clellan is on his way to attempt a new trade with the Indians. His plan is to establish himself on the Platte, and after trading with the Pawnees and Ottoes, prevail on some of their chiefs to accompany him to Santa Fee, where he hopes to obtain permission to exchange his merchandise for gold and silver, which is there in abundance. If this be granted, he can transport his goods on mules and horses from the Platte to some part of Louisiana, convenient to the Spanish settlements, where he may be met by the traders from New Mexico.

SEPTEMBER 18TH *Thursday.* We parted with captain M'Clellan, and within a few miles passed the Grand river, below which we overtook the hunters, who had been sent forward yesterday afternoon. They had not been able to kill any thing, nor did we see any game except one bear and three turkeys, so that our whole stock of provisions is one biscuit for each person; but as there is an abundance of papaws, the men are perfectly contented. The current of the river is more gentle than it was when we ascended, the water being lower though still rapid in places where it is confined. We continued to pass through a very fine country, for fifty-two miles, when we encamped nearly opposite to Mine river.

SEPTEMBER 19TH *Friday.* We worked our oars all day, without taking time to hunt, or even landing, except once to gather papaws; and at eight o'clock reached the entrance of the Osage river, a distance of seventy-two miles. Several of the party have been for a day or two attacked with a soreness in the eyes; the eye-ball being very much swelled and the lid appearing as if burnt by the sun, and extremely painful, particularly when exposed to the light. Three of the men are so much affected by it, as to be unable to row. We therefore turned one of the boats adrift, and distributed the men among the other canoes, when we set out a little before daybreak.

SEPTEMBER 20TH *Saturday.* The Osage is at this time low, and discharges but a very small quantity of water. Near the mouth of Gasconade, where we arrived at noon, we met five Frenchmen on their way to the Great Osage village. As we moved along rapidly, we saw on the banks some cows feeding, and the whole party almost involuntarily raised a shout of joy at seeing this image of civilisation and domestic life.

Soon after we reached the little French village of Lacharette, which we saluted with a discharge of four guns, and three hearty cheers. We then landed, and were received with kindness by the inhabitants, as well as some traders from Canada, who were going to traffic with the Osages and Ottoes. They were all equally surprised and pleased at our arrival, for they had long since abandoned all hopes of ever seeing us return.

These Canadians have boats prepared for the navigation of the Missouri, which seem better calculated for the purpose than those in any other form. They are in the shape of batteaux, about thirty feet long, and eight wide; the bow and stern pointed, the bottom flat, and carrying six oars only, and their chief advantage is their width and flatness, which saves them from the danger of rolling sands.

Having come sixty-eight miles, and the weather threatening to be bad, we remained at La Charette till the next morning, *Sunday*, when we proceeded, and as several settlements have been made during our absence, were refreshed with the sight of men and cattle along the banks. We also passed twelve canoes of Kickapoo Indians, going on a hunting excursion. At length, after coming forty-eight miles, we saluted, with heartfelt satisfaction, the village of St. Charles, and on landing were treated with the greatest hospitality and kindness by all the inhabitants of that place. Their civility detained us till ten o'clock the next morning.

Monday. The rain having ceased, we set out for Coldwater creek, about three miles from the mouth of the Missouri, where we found a cantonment of troops of the United States, with whom we passed the day, and then, *Tuesday, 23d*, descended to the Mississippi, and round to St. Louis, where we arrived at twelve o'clock, and having fired a salute went on shore and received the heartiest and most hospitable welcome from the whole village.

SEPTEMBER 22D

The expedition's return, as reported in "The Columbian Centinel," Boston, on November 5, 1806.

ACKNOWLEDGMENTS

For their constant cooperation in providing research material used in preparing this edition, the publishers express their gratitude to Gerald D. McDonald, Chief of the American History Division of the New York Public Library, and to his staff. The material included the following books:

Patrick Gass's *Journal of the Voyages and Travels of a Corps of Discovery* ... (Pittsburgh, 1807)

Prince Maximilian of Wied-Neuwied's *Travels in the Interior of North America* ... (3 volumes, London, 1843)

Elliott Coues' *History of the Expedition* ... (a revised version of the Biddle edition in 4 volumes, Harper, 1893)

Olin D. Wheeler's *The Trail of Lewis and Clark* (2 volumes, Putnam, 1904)

Reuben Gold Thwaites' *The Original Journals of the Lewis and Clark Expedition* (8 volumes, Dodd, Mead, 1904–1905)

Publications of the State Historical Society of Wisconsin

Carl Bodmer's water-colors were made while he was accompanying Prince Maximilian of Wied-Neuwied on an epochal tour of North America in 1833–1834, and engravings of them first appeared in the "Atlas" volume of Maximilian's account. Several of our Bodmer reproductions are made from specimens kindly loaned by Harry Shaw Newman of The Old Print Shop, Inc., New York. The others, together with the paintings by George Bird King (made *ca.* 1837), are from *The Indian Journals* of Lewis Henry Morgan, by arrangement with the publisher, The University of Michigan Press, Ann Arbor.

The original William Clark map is in the Coe Collection of Western Americana at Yale University Library, New Haven, which has granted permission for our facsimile.

The Peale portraits (*ca.* 1807) of Meriwether Lewis and William Clark in Volume One appear by courtesy of Independence Hall, Philadelphia; those of Lewis and Clark in Volume Two by courtesy of the Missouri Historical Society, St. Louis (the Lewis is from an engraving by Strickland of a water-color by Charles de St.-Memin; the head of Clark was painted *ca.* 1820 by Chester Harding, but the figure is attributed to a local scenery painter). St.-Memin's crayon portrait of She-He-Ke ("Big White") is in the collection of the American Philosophical Society, Philadelphia.

We also gratefully acknowledge the assistance of Frederick J. Dockstader, Director of the Museum of the American Indian (Heye Foundation), New York, and that of Robert M. Metzdorf at the Yale University Library.

This edition of
THE LEWIS AND CLARK JOURNALS
has been made to the typographic plan of
Eugene Ettenberg.

The two volumes have been designed in the form of an explorer's journal, and the text has been set in the MONTICELLO *type. Though of recent design, Monticello is based on the first successful American typeface. The parent face, cast by* Archibald Binny *at Philadelphia in* 1789, *was the most popular native typeface of* Jefferson's *time.*